american business
an introduction   third edition

american

business
an introduction   third edition

FERDINAND F. MAUSER

Wayne State University and Keio University

DAVID J. SCHWARTZ

Georgia State University

HARCOURT BRACE JOVANOVICH, INC.

New York   Chicago   San Francisco   Atlanta

American Business: An Introduction, Third Edition
© 1966, 1970, 1974 by Harcourt Brace Jovanovich, Inc.

Parts of this book appeared in somewhat different form in
Introduction to American Business by Ferdinand F. Mauser and David J. Schwartz,
American Book Company, 1956.

Photo credits appear on page 810.

ISBN: 0-15-502273-3

Library of Congress Catalog Card Number: 73-20127

Printed in the United States of America

preface

A textbook for the introductory business course should, in our opinion, be written and organized with the beginning student in mind. It should present a full and lucid amount of the fundamentals of American business operations, while at the same time relate business to the community and to society as a whole. Moreover, a business textbook should live up to the standards set by American business itself: It should be interesting, challenging, and lively, giving students a sense of the excitement that business generates.

Our aim in first writing *AMERICAN BUSINESS: An Introduction* was to provide such a textbook; that aim continued to guide us as we revised the book.

In preparing this revision we kept one broad fundamental question in mind: How could we make this instructional program—the textbook and supplementary materials—simpler and easier to comprehend, more relevant to the real world, and more meaningful and useful for the beginning student of business?

In the Third Edition, we have reduced the number of chapters. No subject treated in previous editions has been neglected or eliminated, but several have been combined in response to the comments of users. Long- and short-term financing have been combined in a single chapter. Part 6 (Management of the Marketing Function) is now four chapters instead of five.

Chapters 27 and 28 of the Second Edition have been revised and combined as Chapter 3. This was done to accommodate the greater emphasis placed on the societal aspects of business in the introductory course and to introduce the topic early so it could be woven into later chapters. The societal aspects of business are now included in the discussions of computers, multinational corporations, conglomerates, marketing, and factors to consider in choosing a business location.

Some chapters have been completely revamped. The business location chapter ties space logistics to ecology. International trade has been conceptually expanded and is now international business rather than trade. Considerable emphasis has been given to multinational corporations and trade expansion policies that relate to our balance of payments and dollar value erosion problems.

Since the last edition appeared, vast changes have occurred in business and in the environment in which it is conducted. All data, figures, and tables are the most recent available. In addition, new federal legislation affecting business is introduced in the pertinent sections.

New to this edition are the Special Readings. Each reading briefly summarizes a book related to the subject matter of the text. It is hoped that this feature will encourage outside reading by students.

The end-of-chapter materials have been significantly strengthened. The popular business chronicle has been completely reworked. In this edition, we use a hypothetical real estate company called Kingmaker Estates, Inc. A survey of students clearly revealed that they preferred a service company that concerned itself not only with the developmental stages of business but with matters involving society and its inhabitants. All students are interested in real estate, for home buying or rental is likely to be part of every young person's future. Selective replacements were made in the Contemporary Issues feature to reflect changes in major socioeconomic issues. The historical sketches feature, now called People and Their Ideas, includes several new personalities, such as Estée Lauder and Ralph Nader.

We do not expect, of course, that instructors will be able to use all the end-of-chapter materials provided. Experimentation will quickly reveal which materials are most suitable for a given class. To engage student interest and achieve a change of pace, instructors may want to switch from one type of material to another as the course progresses.

In addition to the numerous student aids built into the text, we have again provided two separate workbooks, each of which parallels the organization of the book:

The *Manual of Student Assignments*, revised for the Third Edition, offers a variety of highly realistic exercises designed to teach the student to duplicate the decision-making processes he will use on entering the business world.

The *Student Guide*, revised for the Third Edition, provides intensive, step-by-step coverage of the main points in the textbook. It is based on the techniques of programmed instruction and is intended for the student's self-study.

In preparing this revision we turned to experienced classroom instructors and business executives for suggestions on material that could be added or deleted and on ways the text could be improved in clarity, teachability, and timeliness. We would like to express our thanks to all those who helped us in this edition and in the previous editions.

FERDINAND F. MAUSER
DAVID J. SCHWARTZ

contents

1

the economic and social setting of business   2

chapter **1**   **THE AMERICAN BUSINESS ENVIRONMENT**   4

Objectives of Business   Business Efficiency and the American Standard of
Living   Business Enters a New Evolutionary Phase   Business as an
Academic Study   Supplementary Academic Study   Planning for a
Management Career   People and Their Ideas: Joseph P. Kennedy
Contemporary Issues   Business Chronicle

chapter **2**   **THE PRIVATE ENTERPRISE SYSTEM**   34

Characteristics of Private Enterprise and Why They Are Considered Beneficial
Growth and Private Enterprise   The Role of Government in Private Enterprise
The Nature of Capitalism   Capitalism, Socialism, and Communism Compared
The Challenge of Capitalism   People and Their Ideas: John Harold Johnson
Contemporary Issues   Business Chronicle

chapter **3**   **THE SOCIAL RESPONSIBILITY OF BUSINESS**   60

How Business and Society Are Related   Criticisms Directed toward Business
How Business Relates to Social Problems   Confrontations Created by
Environmental Programs   Ethics in Business   Facilitating High Ethical
Standards   People and Their Ideas: Andrew Carnegie   Contemporary Issues
Business Chronicle

2

the structure of business   86

chapter **4**   **THE FORMS OF BUSINESS**   88

Sole Proprietorship   General Partnership   Limited Partnership
Corporations   Organization of the Corporation   Control of the Corporation
Other Forms of Ownership   People and Their Ideas: Robert Chase
Townsend   Contemporary Issues   Business Chronicle

ix

112   chapter **5**   **SMALL BUSINESS, SERVICES, AND FRANCHISING**

The Value System of the Entrepreneur   Small Business: What It Is and Does
Conditions Conducive to Small Business   Operating Disadvantages of
Small Business   Causes of Small Business Failure   Service Businesses
Franchising   Aid for Small Business   People and Their Ideas:
Colonel Harland Sanders   Contemporary Issues   Business Chronicle

chapter **6**   **INTERNAL MANAGEMENT AND ORGANIZATION OF**
138   **BUSINESS**

Universal Need for Management   Forms of Organization   Organizational
Charts and Manuals   Levels of Management   Functions of Management
Communication and Management   The Theories of Management
People and Their Ideas: Alfred Pritchard Sloan, Jr.   Contemporary Issues
Business Chronicle

164   **financing a business**

166   chapter **7**   **LONG- AND SHORT-TERM FINANCING**

Long-Term Capital   Financing through Bonds   Financing through Stock
Short-Term Capital   The Trends toward Bank Loans of Longer Duration
Leasing and Conservation of Working Capital   People and Their Ideas:
J. Paul Getty   Contemporary Issues   Business Chronicle

194   chapter **8**   **FINANCIAL MANAGEMENT AND INSTITUTIONS**

Credit Management: Commercial   Sources of Consumer Credit
Credit Bureaus   Protecting the Consumer   Putting Idle Money to
Productive Use   Financial Institutions   Investment Banks   Mutual
Savings Banks   Savings and Loan Associations   Other Financial
Institutions   Security Exchanges   The Securities Exchange Act of 1934
Guidelines for Beginning Investors   People and Their Ideas: Amadeo Peter
Giannini   Contemporary Issues   Business Chronicle

230   chapter **9**   **READING BUSINESS AND FINANCIAL NEWS**

Why Read Financial News?   Types of Business and Financial News
Statistical News   Nonstatistical News   People and Their Ideas: Bernard
Kilgore   Contemporary Issues   Business Chronicle

252   chapter **10**   **RISK MANAGEMENT AND INSURANCE**

Methods of Meeting Risk   Types of Insurance Companies   Types of
Insurance   Fire Insurance   Marine Insurance   Automobile Insurance

Liability Insurance   Criminal Loss Protection   Workmen's Compensation
Insurance   Health Insurance   Life Insurance   The Purchase of Insurance
Pension Plans   People and Their Ideas: Asa T. Spaulding   Contemporary
Issues   Business Chronicle

management of human resources   284

chapter 11   MANAGEMENT AND MOTIVATION OF PERSONNEL   286

The Changing Nature of the Work Ethic   The Problem of Worker Discontent
Personnel Management   Functions of the Personnel Department
Employee Motivation   Morale   People and Their Ideas: John D. Rockefeller
Contemporary Issues   Business Chronicle

chapter 12   LABOR IN THE ECONOMY   318

Labor Economics   Unemployment   History and Organization of Labor
Union Objectives   Workers' Attitudes toward Unions   People and Their
Ideas: David Dubinsky   Contemporary Issues   Business Chronicle

chapter 13   LABOR-MANAGEMENT RELATIONS   346

Cost of Labor-Management Unrest   Management Versus Labor   How
Management Attempts to Restrain Labor   Labor Versus Management
How Labor Attempts to Further Its Interests   The Collective-Bargaining
Procedure   Labor Legislation   Current Labor Objectives   People and
Their Ideas: Henry Ford   Contemporary Issues   Business Chronicle

production and the physical environment   372

**chapter 14   GOODS AND SERVICES: THEIR PRODUCTION AND
PRODUCTION AND PROCUREMENT**   374

Characteristics of our Production System   Product Design   Production
Planning   Production Control   The Metric System   Purchasing, Buying,
and Procuring Goods and Services   Industrial Purchasing   Buying for Resale:
Resale and Industrial Buying Compared   Government Procurement
People and Their Ideas: Harley J. Earl   Contemporary Issues
Business Chronicle

404   chapter **15**   PHYSICAL DISTRIBUTION AND SPACE LOGISTICS

Economic Significance of Transportation   Classification of Carriers
Railroads   Motor Trucks   Water Transportation   Pipelines   Air
Transportation   Selection of Specific Carriers   Transportation and Traffic
Management   Intermodal Transportation and Containerization
The Future of Transportation   People and Their Ideas: Edward Vernon
Rickenbacker   Contemporary Issues   Business Chronicle

432   chapter **16**   BUSINESS LOCATION, LAND USE, AND ECOLOGY

Importance of a Good Location   Locating Manufacturing Facilities
Location of a Retail Store   Land Use and Ecology   People and Their Ideas:
William D. Ruckelshaus   Contemporary Issues   Business Chronicle

458   **management of the marketing function**

460   chapter **17**   THE MARKETING PROCESS: AN OVERVIEW

Marketing Defined   Is Marketing More Important Than Production?
Basic Elements in the Marketing Process   Consumers   Products
Functions of Marketing   Channels for Marketing Consumer Goods
Brands and Marketing   Marketing Industrial Goods   Retailing
Wholesaling   People and Their Ideas: Estée Lauder   Contemporary
Issues   Business Chronicle

484   chapter **18**   MARKETING AND THE ULTIMATE CONSUMER

The Marketing Concept   Why People Buy What They Do   Why People
Buy Where They Do   The Relation of Income to Consumption   The Relation
of Population to Consumption   Other Factors Affecting Consumption
People and Their Ideas: James Cash Penney   Contemporary Issues
Business Chronicle

512   chapter **19**   DEMAND CREATION FUNCTIONS AND PRICING

Selling   Sales Management   Advertising   The Socioeconomic Effects of
Advertising   Public Relations   Pricing   Pricing: Theoretical
Considerations   Pricing: Practical Considerations   Does Marketing Cost
Too Much?   People and Their Ideas: Frank Winfield Woolworth
Contemporary Issues   Business Chronicle

544   chapter **20**   INTERNATIONAL BUSINESS

The Importance of International Trade   International Trade and Specialization
International Trade and the Company   Problems of International Trade
Facilitating International Trade   Organization for Exporting   Organization

for Importing   Government Control and World Commerce   World
Economic Communities   Multinational Corporations   People and Their
Ideas: Keiji Kawakami   Contemporary Issues   Business Chronicle

7

management control and use of information   572

chapter **21**   **ACCOUNTING AND BUSINESS MANAGEMENT**   575

Functions of Accounting   Accounting as a Professional Field   Accounting
Procedures   Cost Accounting and Standard Costs   Budgeting
Accounting Statements   Ratio Analysis   Auditing   Accounting—More
Than Figures People and Their Ideas: Clarence C. Finley   Contemporary
Issues Business Chronicle

chapter **22**   **COMPUTERS AND ELECTRONIC DATA PROCESSING**   603

The Development of Electronic Computers   Background Information for
Understanding Computers   How the Computer Works   Applying the
Computer in Business   People and Their Ideas: Thomas J. Watson
Contemporary Issues   Business Chronicle

chapter **23**   **QUANTITATIVE ANALYSIS AND THE PRESENTATION OF
BUSINESS INFORMATION**   635

How Statistics Serve Management   Statistical Devices and Techniques
Statistics, Electronic Data Processing, and Systems Analysis   Presentation
of Statistical Data   The Business Report   Caution in the Use of Statistical
Analysis   People and Their Ideas: Louis I. Dublin Contemporary Issues
Business Chronicle

chapter **24**   **BUSINESS RESEARCH AND SOURCES OF INFORMATION**   659

What Is Research?   Types of Research   Research Methodology: The
Scientific Method   Steps in the Research Procedure   Sources of Business
Information   People and Their Ideas: David Sarnoff   Contemporary Issues
Business Chronicle

8

business, government, and the future   681

chapter **25**   **LEGAL CONSIDERATIONS IN BUSINESS**   683

Why Be Familiar with Business Law?   Business Law Defined   Contracts
Law of Agency   Law of Employer and Employee   Bankruptcy   Sales of

Personal Property   Law of Real Estate   Law of Negotiable Instruments
Trademarks, Patents, and Copyrights   Combining a Business Degree with
a Law Degree   People and Their Ideas: William Randolph Hearst
Contemporary Issues   Business Chronicle

709   chapter **26**   **BUSINESS AND GOVERNMENT**

Government Regulation of Business   Business Legislation   The Present
Status of Government Regulation   Government Regulation of Public Utilities
Taxation and Business   The Governmental Role in Perspective   A Look
at National Priorities   People and Their Ideas: Ralph Nader   Contemporary
Issues   Business Chronicle

737   chapter **27**   **THE FUTURE AND BUSINESS**

Is Business Qualified to Deal with Social Change   The Spectrum of
Corporate Social Activities   Dynamic Characteristics and the Challenge of
Change   Changes Related to Business   Changing Attitudes of Business
Management   The Opportunity   People and Their Ideas: John H. Dessauer
Contemporary Issues   Business Chronicle

767   **APPENDIX: CAREER SELECTION**

797   **GLOSSARY OF BUSINESS TERMS**

811   **INDEX**

american business
an introduction
third edition

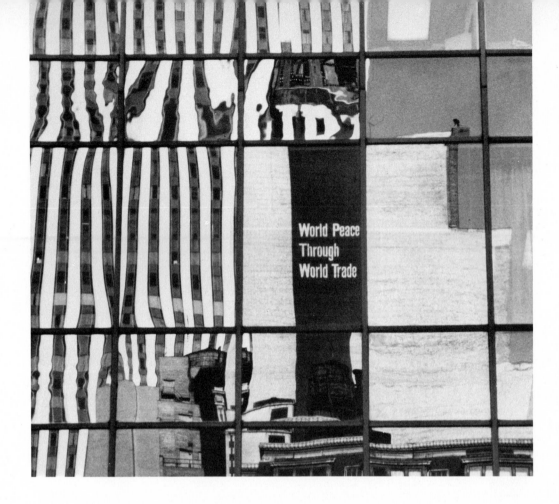

World Peace
Through
World Trade

You are about to embark on an extensive study of a fascinating subject — American business. In the United States, business is strong and vital: It is the social institution that contributes most to the nation's ever enlarging material wealth.

What are the characteristics of the environment surrounding American business? How does this environment differ from that provided by other economic systems? What are the important influences of business on our social system? How is the business environment related to you? What advantages can you obtain from a conscientious academic study of business?

In dealing with questions such as these, Part 1 sets the stage for your study of American business. The three chapters in this section are concerned with:

1

the economic and social setting of business

1

the American business environment

2

the private enterprise system

3

the social responsibilities of business

1

CHAPTER 1

OBJECTIVES OF BUSINESS
   Service. Profit. Service and Profit Related.

BUSINESS EFFICIENCY AND THE AMERICAN STANDARD OF LIVING
   The Problems of an Increased National Standard of Living. Allocating the Wealth.

BUSINESS ENTERS A NEW EVOLUTIONARY PHASE
   Creativity. Conceptualization.

BUSINESS AS AN ACADEMIC STUDY
   Can Business Be Learned in School? Advantages of a Broad, Formal Study of Business. A Liberal Approach to Business Education. Why Study Business?

SUPPLEMENTING ACADEMIC STUDY
   Systematic Reading of Business News. Observation. Discussions with Other People. Work Experience.

PLANNING FOR A MANAGEMENT CAREER
   Self Evaluation: A Useful Key. Success and the Building of a Business Vocabulary.

the American business environment

The word *business* is used in two ways. First, it may be used to designate any establishment, regardless of size, that serves the public through the manufacture or distribution of goods or through the provision of services. Thus, the U.S. Steel Corporation and the nursery you may buy plants from in the suburbs are *production businesses;* the Great Atlantic & Pacific Tea Company and the newsstand you see on a downtown street are *distribution businesses;* the Hertz Corporation that rents automobiles and the Laundromat in your shopping center are *service businesses.*

Second, the word *business* refers to the commercial life of a nation. In this sense, business includes the sum total of all economic activity — banking, production, distribution, transportation, and the various other economic pursuits undertaken by man to provide himself with a standard of living. When we say "business is up," meaning economic activity is brisk, we are using the term in this second context.

OBJECTIVES OF BUSINESS

Any individual business under the American system has two major objectives — service and profit. These objectives apply whether the

Figure **1–1**
Population and Economic Projections, 1970–2000[a]

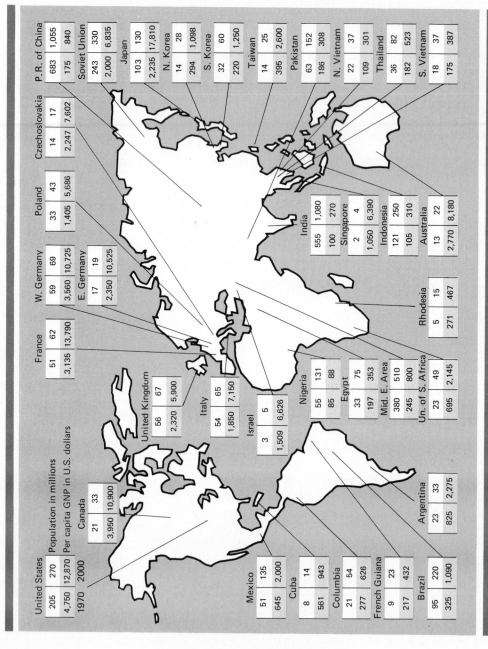

[a] These figures do not take inflation into account, they are based on constant or real 1970 dollars.
Source: 1970 figures from *United Nations Statistical Yearbook*; projections for 2000 were developed by David P. Harmon, Jr., for the Hudson Institute, Inc. Croton-on-Hudson, New York.

Many call population pressures the "doomsday clock." Can industry and agriculture provide for everyone?

business is a small neighborhood dry cleaner or a mammoth organization such as General Motors, which in 1972 employed approximately 760,000 men and women throughout the world and had a total payroll of approximately $8,668,000,000.

Service

Every business must satisfy human wants if it is to continue; simple as this may seem, it is the underlying reason for the very existence of business. Human wants are both *unlimited* and *varied*. We can say this because the satisfaction of one want leads to the creation of another. The creation of a stool to fill the want for something to sit on led to the want for a stool with a back—a chair. That led to the chair with a cushion, and that, in turn, led to a chair with a more comfortable design, and so on.

Food, clothing, shelter, television sets, vacation trips, ships, medical care, writing materials, oil paintings, space capsules, and antibiotics are examples of the literally thousands of things that are used to satisfy human wants. When a business ceases to satisfy a human want, consumers stop buying what is offered, and the business is forced to close its doors for lack of sales.

Profit

The second objective of American business is to make a *profit*. Very simply, this means that the business must operate in such a manner that income exceeds expenditures over a period of time. The two goals—service and profit—are closely related, since business must fulfill its "want-satisfying," or service, objective successfully in order to realize its profit goal. Providing everyone who wishes it an opportunity to try to earn a profit is the American system's way of harnessing human energies. The desire to *maximize* profits provides the incentive to operate with greater efficiency and to expand productivity.

Throughout the world, the United States is recognized for its exceptional business vitality. This country, having less than 6 percent of the world's population and occupying only 7 percent of the world's land area, enjoys more than 33 percent of the world's goods and services; our business system makes that possible. Figure 1–1 dramatizes the fact that the U.S. business system produces the world's highest per capita gross national product. The productivity of some technically advanced nations (such as Japan, Israel, West Germany, etc.) is catching up with or even overtaking the rate of increase of productivity of the United States. An even more alarming factor, which has grave implications, is that the gap between the so-called "have" and "have not" nations is widening.

Unfortunately, the part profit plays on the American economic scene is only vaguely understood. Profit is frequently criticized by reform-minded spokesmen who do not fully comprehend the subtle part it plays in generating economic action. Frequently you may read that certain people advocate economic systems that eliminate profit as a motivating economic element. Such critics claim that profits benefit a privileged few and exploit the majority.

No one can ignore economic reality and survive. Even "anti-establishment" enterprises understand the need for profit when it concerns their own activities. They soon learn that their income must exceed their expenditures if they wish to survive and expand. Otherwise they must curtail their services, or fail, or make up the difference with donations or subsidies. Thus the *Chicago Tribune* reported that the revolutionary New York underground newspapers *East Village Other* and *The Rat* hired Dun & Bradstreet's collection division to hound delinquent subscribers! Those who run such papers should realize that the factors which apply to their own enterprises also apply to the institutions they attack and criticize.

It is interesting to note that many communist countries, after years of denunciation of profit, have established variations of profit accountability for their managers and enterprises. In 1968, for example, the Hungarian chamber of commerce, in a publication printed in English, issued the following explanation of the "new" communist use of profit.

> The new system of interestedness (incentive) is based on the volume of profit. The first half of profit — after taxation — is turned over for the increase of personal incomes (divisible fund), while the second half of profit is allocated for company development (development fund) . . . which promotes the more vigorous development of the companies earning higher profits.[1]

The profit motive is a great economic power, and, like any power in society, it can corrupt if used improperly. But, as will be made clear later, the American system provides some safeguards against the corruptive use of profits.

Service and profit related

Satisfying human wants and making a profit are interdependent, as we have said. Consider for a moment the operation of a pharmacy. The store satisfies a human want by providing consumers with prescriptions and drugs of desired quality, variety, and price in a convenient location. It also satisfies secondary consumer wants, such as the customer's desire to shop in a clean store staffed with courteous employees. The customer

[1] Information on Matters Relating to the Hungarian Economic Management Reform, Part II, *Economic Information*, Section 221 (Budapest: Hungarian Press, 1968), p. 4.

may also wish to make purchases on credit and, in some instances, to have prescriptions delivered. These, then, are important wants the druggist attempts to satisfy, and his chances of earning a profit depend in large part on how well he can fulfill such wants. Ordinarily, he cannot expect to accomplish his second goal—profit—if he is out of stock on wanted items, if his goods are overpriced, or if his employees are rude and unfriendly.

It is important to note that a businessman must maintain a balance among the wants he tries to satisfy. The man who runs a successful business does not attempt to fulfill *all* customer desires. The novice may be tempted to do so, but if he actually tries to meet all consumer needs, he soon fails. If, for example, the druggist decides to offer credit and free-delivery services, he cannot sell his merchandise at prices as low as those of the discount operator who offers fewer services. The businessman intent on staying in business—and he can do this only by earning a profit—must decide which wants it is most strategic for him to satisfy. There is much practical significance in the words of Herbert Bayard Swope, a successful editor and publicist: "I cannot give you the formula for success, but I can give you the formula for failure—try to please everybody."

BUSINESS EFFICIENCY AND THE AMERICAN STANDARD OF LIVING

Basically, the only purpose of any kind of human activity is to fulfill physical wants and to provide psychological and spiritual satisfactions. Since the latter are subjective, they cannot be measured precisely. Unfortunately these areas are poorly understood and consequently too much ignored. But it is a fair assumption that business in the future will focus on psychological and even spiritual factors as more people realize the ambiguity of the fact that a growing abundance of physical wherewithal in and of itself is not creating a contented society.

It is possible, however, to measure the physical or material satisfiers of human wants. Clothing, food, homes, automobiles, bicycles, vacation travel, and so forth, when considered quantitatively and qualitatively, constitute a nation's *standard of living*—the measure of success of any economy. Generally, the more efficiently businesses convert raw materials into finished products and economically distribute output, the higher is the standard of living.

We can measure our standard of living in two ways. We can compare our material possessions today, first, with those of earlier periods and, second, with those of other nations. By either method, we find that the current American standard of living is very high: It has improved tremendously since earlier periods, and it is much higher than that of any other major country.

The chief factors that helped raise our standard of living, all of which are discussed in later chapters, seem to be the following:

1. A technological economy. Emphasis is on developing technical devices that help maximize use of human effort. Our leads in auto-mation and computerization illustrate this.

2. The principle of mass production, which makes possible the manu-facture of standardized products at relatively low cost.

3. A marketing system devoted to selling more goods at a small profit per unit rather than fewer goods at a large profit per unit. This marketing effort is keyed to mass selling to large markets.

4. A competitively-oriented business system under continuous pres-sure to react and adjust quickly and to rely for survival on creative and innovative abilities. Weak and inefficient businesses must give way to strong ones. Emphasis is on growth and expansion.

5. Superior executive leadership, which plans, organizes, controls, motivates, and staffs our business enterprises.

6. The economic philosophy of the people. Under the capitalistic, private enterprise system, individuals are motivated to work and to improve their skills.

Our economy is not perfect. There is much waste of physical and human resources. Business executives make many mistakes in judgment; conflicts between labor and management sometimes result in wasteful strikes; manufacturers still occasionally produce goods that the public does not want or finds to be inferior. Part of any background for the study of American business should include a careful examination of our economic system's weaknesses as well as its strengths. This examination is the substance of Chapter 2, The Private Enterprise System.

The problems of an increased national standard of living

An overriding goal of both American business and our national govern-ment continues to be to raise the standard of living, or, as the economists say, to increase the gross national product (GNP), which is the sum total of all goods and services produced in an economy.

But trying to achieve this goal is like courting a fickle woman. Suc-cess itself creates problems—certainly in the 1970s the United States has both record-breaking affluence and record-breaking social unrest. As the GNP rises, individuals and interest groups ask: "How can we get a larger

Table **1–1**
Per Capita GNP in Dollars for Top Ten Nations in 1970 and Estimates for 2000

TOP TEN	1970	TOP TEN	2000
1. United States	$4,750	1. Japan	$17,810
2. Canada	3,950	2. France	13,790
3. West Germany	3,560	3. United States	12,870
4. France	3,135	4. Canada	10,900
5. Australia	2,770	5. West Germany	10,725
6. East Germany	2,350	6. East Germany	10,525
7. United Kingdom	2,320	7. Australia	8,180
8. Czechoslovakia	2,247	8. Czechoslovakia	7,602
9. Japan	2,235	9. Italy	7,150
10. Soviet Union	2,000	10. Soviet Union	6,835

Note: Not shown in the table but of additional interest are the total world GNP figures—
1970, $3.35 trillion and 2000 estimate, $16.3 trillion.
Source: 1970 figures from *United Nations Statistical Yearbook;* projections for 2000 were developed by David P. Harmon, Jr., for the Hudson Institute, Inc., Croton-on-Hudson, New York.

What factors do you feel may be responsible for the projection that the U.S. will lose its leadership in per capita productivity by the year 2000?

slice of the larger economic melon?" Increased demand of labor, lobbying for lower income tax, pressures from abroad for aid to underdeveloped countries, pressures at home for aid to the underprivileged—these are but a few examples of the desire to share in the enlarging wealth. The questions for society as a whole are: "How should this increasing wealth be divided?" and "Does unlimited economic growth in an advanced technical society create more problems (pollution, congestion, crass materialism, and so on) than it solves?"

A body of thoughtful criticism is emerging that is questioning business and government's dedication to the growth and increase of the GNP. In fact, the very idea of GNP is being challenged. Some argue that GNP is not a proper measure of a nation's success for it records only the material dimensions of life. These critics feel we should develop a measure of national welfare that encompasses more than a mere count of the value of products produced. This new measurement would be called gross national welfare (GNW) and would include "nonmaterial" indicators such as number of hospital beds, nurses, and physicians per 1,000 population; acres of land devoted to parks; and per capita expenditure for education. Some critics propose to include such statistics as air and water pollution indexes and crime rates.

How to evaluate and report the corporation's positive and negative effects on society is becoming a subject of major interest. The accounting profession, government agencies, managers of investment funds, and some directors of corporations increasingly are concerning themselves with social measurement of economic activity. The American Institute of Certified Public Accountants has, for example, organized a Social

Figure **1–2**
Social Measurement Statement
XXXX Corporation
Socioeconomic Operating Statement for the Year Ending December 31, 1971

I RELATIONS WITH PEOPLE:
A. Improvements:
   1. Training program for handi-
     capped workers $ 10,000
   2. Contribution to edu-
     cational institution   4,000
   3. Extra turnover costs be-
     cause of minority hiring
     program   5,000
   4. Cost of nursery school for
     children of employees,
     voluntarily set up   11,000
Total Improvements $ 30,000

B. Less: Detriments
   1. Postponed installing new
     safety devices on cutting
     machines (cost of the de-
     vices) $ 14,000
C. Net Improvements in People
   Actions for the Year $ 16,000

II RELATIONS WITH ENVIRONMENT:
A. Improvements:
   1. Cost of reclaiming and
     landscaping old dump on
     company property $ 70,000
   2. Cost of installing pollu-
     tion control devices on
     Plant A smokestacks   4,000
   3. Cost of detoxifying waste
     from finishing process
     this year   9,000
Total Improvements $ 83,000

B. Less: Detriments
   1. Cost that would have been
     incurred to relandscape
     strip mining site used
     this year $ 80,000

   2. Estimated costs to have in-
     stalled purification
     process to neutralize
     poisonous liquid being
     dumped into stream $100,000
         $180,000

C. Net Deficit in Environment
   Actions for the Year   ($ 97,000)

III RELATIONS WITH PRODUCT:
A. Improvements:
   1. Salary of V.P. while
     serving on government
     Product Safety Commission $ 25,000
   2. Cost of substituting lead-
     free paint for previously
     used poisonous lead paint   9,000
Total Improvements $ 34,000

B. Less: Detriments
   1. Safety device recommended
     by Safety Council but not
     added to product   22,000

C. Net Improvements in Product
   Actions for the Year $ 12,000

Total Socioeconomic Deficit for the
Year   ($ 69,000)

Add: Net Cumulative Socioeconomic
Improvements as at January 1, 1971 $249,000

GRAND TOTAL
Net Socioeconomic Actions to
December 31, 1971 $180,000

Source: The Conference Board *Record*, November 1972, p. 60.

Is this an improved measure of corporate performance?

Measurement Committee. Corporate annual reports, discussed in Chapter 21, in the future may well reflect the social dimensions of their activities. Figure 1–2 shows a tentative social measurement statement prepared by a member of an accounting firm.

Allocating the wealth

Gross national product is divided among three principal groups. First, part of it is paid to individuals in the form of wages, dividends, or interest. They in turn will either save it or, more likely, spend it for housing, clothing, appliances, recreation, and a host of other goods and services. Second, part is retained by industry, where it is invested in new plants, machinery, and various innovations. Third, part is siphoned off by government in the form of taxes to be used for schools, roads, defense, social programs, and so on.

How the GNP is allocated greatly influences society, and today there is much debate as to which of the three segments should have the controlling share of the increasing GNP. One of the most widely read economists, John Kenneth Galbraith, discusses this topic in his best-selling books *The Affluent Society* and *The New Industrial State.*** He argues, for example, that the government should spend more of the GNP for socially desirable projects such as hospitals, recreational facilities, poverty relief, and better airports. According to Galbraith, when individuals obtain an increased share of the GNP, they tend to use it for frivolous things—for example, late-model cars, private swimming pools, fashionable clothing (which is seldom worn and soon thrown away), and second television sets—all which, he contends, dissipate much of our dwindling resources.

SPECIAL READINGS
**The New Industrial State by John Kenneth Galbraith. Boston: Houghton Mifflin Company, 1967. Widely quoted and discussed, it is possibly Mr. Galbraith's most important work. It is humanistically written with clarity and wit, and knits the great changes of the past fifty years into a comprehensive view of modern industrial society. Mr. Galbraith argues that no society, whether capitalist or communist, can resist the impact of industrial development.

BUSINESS ENTERS A NEW EVOLUTIONARY PHASE

For the first time in history we live in what is often called an *affluent society,* meaning that we produce a great abundance of goods and services. Scarcity of food, shelter, clothing, other basic necessities and communal facilities are no longer overall *economic* social problems (though they remain real enough problems for some segments of our populations). Through the application of advanced technology and intelligent

Figure **1–3**
Governments Rather Than Private Individuals Are Spending
an Increasing Share of GNP

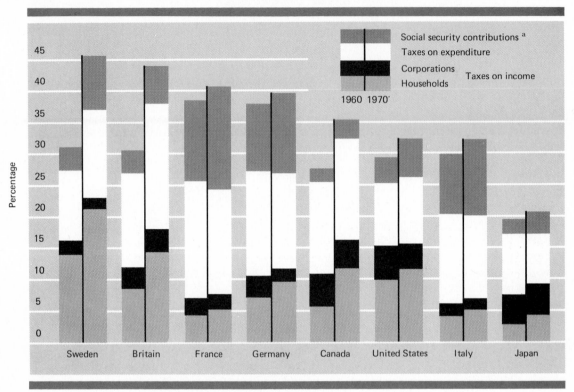

^aEmployers' and employees' contributions. Employees' contributions are sometimes thought of as taxes on income.

Source: *The Economist*, September 16, 1972, p. 69.

Are U.S. taxes high?

management, it is now *possible* for business to mass produce and mass distribute enough to satisfy all basic personal and social needs.

Among man's new prime preoccupations will be conserving and restoring the environment, which has been exploited and dislocated in the process of harnessing natural resources by means of technology. Furthermore, the consequences of the technology that produced our affluence are now being reviewed, for they have completely changed the way man lives and works. In preparing himself for a career in a technical society, man is required to spend inordinate amounts of time in school. As a worker, he is no longer part of a simple system that he can understand. He must work in the huge, impersonal, technical facilities that are required to produce and distribute our abundance. He can no longer work in the proximity of his family. He is forced to spend one-fifth of his working day (8 hours working, 2 hours traveling) commuting long distances by mechanical means over roads and railways that further complicate and dehumanize life.

Since it is the industrial corporation that provides most jobs and has brought these changes about, society now demands that it broaden its concerns and deal directly with human factors. The feeling is growing that technology should serve man—not dominate him.

Numerous problems—some new, some familiar, many relating to what is commonly called "life style"—challenge this age of affluence. They include:

1. Inflation, which leads to economic instability and creates economic hardships for those who have low or fixed incomes.

2. Unemployment, which averaged more than 5 percent between 1968 and 1972 and which, for the first time in the nation's history, included large numbers of highly trained and educated people.

3. Racial discrimination, which, while not as great as in the past, continues to deprive minorities of equal opportunities to share in our affluence. Furthermore, by not putting all of our human resources to the best possible use, society as a whole loses what they cannot contribute.

4. The struggle of women to change their position in society, including their efforts to move into higher managerial and technical job classifications at an accelerating rate.

5. Urban decay, with accompanying population shifts, polarization of society, increased crime, social unrest, and decline of central city property values with concomitant tax base erosion.

6. Continued poverty for a significant portion of our population—an estimated 20 million people, or almost 10 percent of the total population in 1972.

7. Changes in social mores regarding, for example, drug use, sexual behavior, abortions, and rights and privileges of youth.

8. The increasing impersonal nature of society exhibited by the feeling on the part of many that the work they do is unimportant, unappreciated, and even unnecessary.

9. Intensified foreign competition, especially in manufactured products such as automotives, electronics, and photographics.

10. Concern for the environment, with special consideration to pollution and land usage.

11. The changing role and priorities of government with regard to such broad matters as national defense, welfare, and tax policies.

12. The slowdown in population growth, which has resulted in a decline in the relative numerical importance of the very young category and a corresponding increase in the relative numerical importance of older age segments.

Business is showing some concern to solve such problems. To illustrate: annual reports of America's leading corporations only a decade ago were concerned almost entirely with sales, expenses, profits, and other financial data. By contrast, these reports today contain much information relating to what the companies are doing to advance social goals. Just a few headings from the 1972 General Motors Annual Report provide an example of such concerns: "Pollution Control," "Plant Safety," "Youth Activities," "Efforts on Behalf of Minorities," "Charitable and Educational Assistance," and "Employee Benefit Programs."

Whereas the problems of harnessing technology to produce abundance have been monumental, the problems of humanizing technology will be even greater. A very high order of creativity and conceptualization will be required in the years ahead.

Creativity

The most vital factor for solving tomorrow's problems and, hopefully, expanding human happiness is *creativity*. It is closely allied to other important factors. *Education* exposes man to ideas and to the experiences of others; *specialization* enables him to study a given activity in more detail; *team effort* (cooperation) enables him to combine his ideas and efforts; *computerization* directly helps to store information and to solve actual problems; and *conceptualization* enables him to concentrate on concepts instead of specific and ever-changing details. Taken together, these factors release the individual from the mental drudgery that impedes creativity. These factors, many of them created or expanded by technology — with the application of creativity — may well bring about a renaissance more impressive than any other in history. In other words, technology has given us more powerful tools than we have ever had before. Creativity is the key that will unlock their potential.[2]

Creativity is not restricted to the scientist or the engineer or the artist or the executive. Creativity can, and should, be engaged in by individuals at all levels and in all functional areas. Whether it results in new or improved products, processes, or procedures, creativity is essential to busi-

[2] Young people should be encouraged by the fact that the future will increasingly emphasize creativity. Research on the subject of creativity confirms that it is the special domain of the young. Few have quarreled with Francis Bacon's observations (1561–1626) made in his *Of Youth and Age*, "Young men are fitter to invent than to judge, fitter for execution than for counsel, and fitter for new projects than for settled business."

ness and social advancement. Since it is so uniquely human and so essential to future economic progress, creativity receives great emphasis throughout this book. In your study, bear in mind that there is nothing mysterious about creativity. In the words of the Nobel Prize winner Albert Szent-Györgyi, "Creativity is seeing what everyone else sees, but thinking what no one else thinks."

Is there a place for creativity in business? Table 1–2 shows the results of an extensive survey taken among college graduates, in which respondents revealed why they were drawn to their career fields. Originality rated high in practically all categories except business. This indicates that there may be widespread misunderstanding about the importance of creativity in business. While many nonexecutive and even some executive positions may not place high creativity demands on the individual, certain functions of business (research, advertising, planning, problem solving) place a premium on originality. Many corporation presidents will say, "My only competitive advantage is the capabilities of the people who make up my organization." This statement is really a testimony to creativity. Buildings

Table **1–2**
Occupational Values by Career Field as Judged by College Students

BUSINESS		ENGINEERING		PHYSICAL AND BIOLOGICAL SCIENCES		SOCIAL SCIENCES AND HUMANITIES		OTHER	
Value	Endorse-ment	Value	Endorse-ment	Value	Endorse-ment	Value	Endorse-ment	Value	Endorse-ment
Leader	62%	Originality	68%	Originality	74%	Originality	75%	Helpful	71%
People	54	Leader	49	Ideas	58	Helpful	73	People	54
Money	48	Ideas	44	Helpful	50	Ideas	73	Leader	46
Helpful	43	Helpful	42	Progress	31	People	51	Originality	45
Originality	40	Progress	40	Leader	30	Leader	40	Ideas	36
Progress	37	Money	33	Freedom	30	Freedom	33	Progress	29
Ideas	27	No Pressure	19	Money	28	Progress	26	Money	25
Freedom	22	Freedom	17	No Pressure	24	No Pressure	20	Freedom	25
No Pressure	17	People	16	People	12	Money	17	No Pressure	15
N	5,737	N	3,655	N	3,384	N	2,372	N	11,664

Percentage of total responses	21.4		13.6		12.6		8.8		43.5

Total responses 26,812

DEFINITION OF VALUES ENDORSED

Leader: chance to exercise leadership   Originality: opportunities to be creative   Progress: opportunities for promotion
People: work with people rather than things   Ideas: staying in the world of ideas   Freedom: flexibility in what one can do
Helpful: to others and useful to society   Money: chance for high earnings   No Pressure: relaxed atmosphere

Source: *Attitude of College Students Toward Business Careers,* Report No. 1, College Placement Council, Inc., Research Information Center, Bethlehem, Pa., © 1968.

Why do college students think business is least receptive to ideas and originality?

and machines can be duplicated by competing organizations, as can a run-of-the-mill executive team. The factor that distinguishes one team from another is its ingenuity.

Conceptualization

In view of the current information explosion, the question that inevitably comes up is: "Since there is a limit to an individual's mental capacity and to the time he has for study, what kind of information is most important for him to have?"

There is a definite shift today away from learning facts and figures, and from descriptive education, because data quickly become obsolete and methods are rapidly altered. Facts relating to population size, personal income, GNP, and miles of paved highway, for example, are literally obsolete by the time they are made public. Further, since such information can be stored in computers, why store it in the human brain? It seems far wiser to learn concepts that apply regardless of changing socioeconomic conditions or scientific and technological advances. A concept is a generalization or distillation of knowledge that can be useful today as well as twenty years from now. Throughout this textbook, emphasis is placed on presenting knowledge in a conceptualized form. Examples of concepts are given below. Watch for others as they appear in the chapters that follow.

1. International trade is a two-way street. Nations from whom we buy most tend to be our own best customers.

2. Status-minded people often purchase goods or services just to impress others.

3. In business, if service is given first priority, the profit rewards take care of themselves.

BUSINESS AS AN ACADEMIC STUDY

It is logical—and a good sign of intelligent self-concern—for you to ask yourself at the beginning of any educational effort, "Should I study in this area? Can I best prepare for a career by learning on the job or by going to school?" The information provided in Table 1–3 may help you arrive at the answer.

Table **1–3**
Family Income by Education of Head of Family, 1970[a]

RACE AND YEARS OF SCHOOL COMPLETED	NUMBER OF FAMILIES (1,000)	PERCENT DISTRIBUTION BY INCOME LEVEL						MEDIAN INCOME
		UNDER $3,000	$3,000– $4,999	$5,000– $6,999	$7,000– $9,999	$10,000– $14,999	$15,000 AND OVER	
1970								
WHITE FAMILIES	**43,209**	**7.2**	**9.0**	**10.7**	**19.6**	**28.4**	**25.2**	**10,545**
Elementary school	10,603	16.2	18.6	15.6	20.7	18.9	9.9	6,933
Less than 8 years	4,977	20.9	20.9	16.7	18.4	15.8	7.3	5,953
8 years	5,626	12.1	16.5	14.9	22.6	21.6	12.2	7,882
High school	21,098	5.2	7.1	11.0	22.3	32.3	22.2	10,579
1–3 years	6,902	7.6	10.1	12.7	23.5	27.9	18.3	9,509
4 years	14,196	4.0	5.8	10.1	21.7	34.4	24.0	11,054
College	11,508	2.6	3.4	5.6	13.6	30.0	44.9	14,127
1–3 years	5,091	3.6	4.5	6.8	17.8	32.6	34.6	12,487
4 years or more	6,417	1.9	2.5	4.6	10.3	27.9	52.9	15,841
NONWHITE FAMILIES	**4,993**	**19.5**	**16.7**	**16.0**	**18.5**	**17.7**	**11.6**	**6,692**
Elementary school	2,022	29.7	20.9	16.7	16.6	11.2	4.8	4,930
Less than 8 years	1,508	31.4	21.8	15.8	15.7	11.0	4.5	4,684
8 years	514	25.0	18.5	19.3	19.6	11.7	5.6	5,570
High school	2,377	14.2	15.2	16.9	20.4	22.0	11.2	7,492
1–3 years	1,149	18.3	18.7	16.4	19.0	18.8	9.0	6,563
4 years	1,227	10.4	11.9	17.5	21.9	25.1	13.2	8,239
College	596	5.5	9.0	10.0	17.3	22.7	35.4	11,573
1–3 years	314	7.1	11.5	12.1	19.5	25.6	24.2	9,968
4 years or more	282	3.6	6.5	7.6	15.0	19.4	48.0	14,470

[a] Columns may not add up to 100 percent because of rounding.
Source: *Statistical Abstract of the United States,* 1972.

What investment can you find that pays a better return?

Can business be learned in school?

The answer to this question is a qualified one. Business *methods* and *principles* can indeed be learned academically just as surely as those of medicine, law, education, engineering, or any other discipline. Persons in these occupations do not become skilled, of course, until they have acquired practical experience. The doctor fresh from medical school knows the latest medical techniques, but it takes years of additional learning under the guidance of capable people before he becomes an expert practitioner. Similarly, the young man with a business education knows the essentials of business, but experience in business itself is needed before he becomes proficient.

Actually, it is not a question of education *or* experience; both are essential for a successful career in business. While in the past many people rose to very high business positions with little or no formal education, today academic preparation in business is becoming increasingly necessary. Competition for a "start" at junior executive levels of business is keener, and business itself continually grows more complex.

Advantages of a broad, formal study of business

First, education makes later experience more rewarding and more meaningful. Business education shows how the various departments within an enterprise function, individually and together, and how one business is affected by other businesses and by the economy as a whole. While specialization in various phases of business organization is essential, promotions to the highest ranks go to those who understand a wide range of company operations. Thus, a broad view, best obtained from a well-rounded education, is extremely helpful in preparing for future opportunities.

A second reason for taking a broad approach to business education is that the term "business career" has many facets. Companies vary in size and deal with a multitude of products, services, and functions; and individuals employed by them perform a wide range of activities. Consequently, many educators feel it is educationally unsound to concentrate on the specifics of airline operation, appliance distribution, or insurance selling. Because of the breadth of business, business education should be concerned with the similarities rather than the dissimilarities, with broad principles rather than exceptions.

A third advantage of a broad, formal business education is that it arouses one's curiosity—it makes you want to learn more and investigate deeper. One has to know, for example, that there is such a thing as marketing research, and to know something about it, before he is able to look at a product or business activity from the research point of view. One important mark of the professional man is that he never stops learning.

Fourth, formal education, with its systematized approach, provides the framework for continuing education. This framework is especially important in American business—a field that is intensely dynamic, constantly changing. Today's method of marketing a product, for instance, may be obsolete tomorrow. Yet the basic principles behind marketing are not changed but only modified. Significantly, those who learn only from experience are usually slow to change methods as circumstances change, while those who learn the basic theory behind business practices are more sensitive to new approaches and changed conditions. In American business, speed in perceiving and adjusting to change are key factors in success.

Finally, formal study is needed to prepare for an increasingly complicated business environment. Sophisticated business activities, such as electronic data processing, operations research, and aptitude testing of employees, which help increase business efficiency, would be beyond the grasp of yesterday's business hero, who may have been indeed an uneducated, rags-to-riches Horatio Alger. The great men and women of tomorrow will most likely be well educated, for they will have to understand and be able to use the refinements of mankind's rapidly accumulating knowledge.

A liberal approach to business education

Often, college students question and even rebel against a broad or liberal approach to education for business. Frequently they ask, "Why should I have to take courses unrelated to business? Shakespeare won't help me balance a set of books. Considering my goals, am I using my time effectively by listening to an anthropology professor? He talks about apes and the Neanderthal man; I'll be dealing with twenty-first century man as a future business executive."

This sort of distress is understandable. Because it is natural to worry about immediate problems, it is easy to focus attention on one's first job rather than on long-range goals. True, a beginning position is often easier to secure when one has specific skills or training. The student worries about how he is going to answer the inevitable question, "What can you do?" when he applies for his first job. He feels he would be much more certain to get a job if he could say, "I can keep an accounts receivable ledger" or, "I've had two courses in salesmanship, so I can sell." He finds small comfort in being able to say, "I've had a fine liberal education. I can speak a foreign language, and I have a good understanding of American history and economics."

Perhaps the difficulty here is that the student confuses education with training. Note these three differences: First, training is a process whereby one learns to perform by imitating, while education teaches ways of analyzing problems one has never experienced before. Second, education in its truest sense takes the long view, training takes the short; training can become obsolete, education cannot. Third, an individual can be overtrained (like the muscle-bound athlete) but never overeducated.

Because there is no limit to education — it is a never-ending process — there is no limit to how far the educated man can advance. The liberal education seeks to impart wisdom and knowledge, with which students can ultimately become capable and discerning managers.

Management may be viewed as the ability to maximize human effort. At higher levels especially, management requires vision. The behavioral sciences (psychology, sociology, anthropology) are particularly valuable foundations, for they deal with human action and aim to establish generalizations about man's behavior in society — the precise concern of management.

Clarence B. Randall, an eminently successful industrialist and statesman, said:

In my own case, chance plunged me into the steel industry without warning. Looking back from the high plateau of retirement, I am glad that it happened that way. Had I even dreamed that steel might be my career, I would have concentrated on metallurgy, chemistry, mechanical engineering, and geology, and would have missed Shakespeare, philosophy, economics, prose composition, public speaking, and law. No amount of technical training, for example, would have served to help me play my part in dealing with the labor problems of my generation; but law, and learning how to speak and write the English language, did.

The young man who knows but one subject, even though he has completely mastered it, takes a frightful risk when he applies for his first job. He may be handcuffing himself into a situation where the future is limited, from which there will be no escape. He may rise rapidly at first, only to hit a ceiling which he cannot pass. Or he may have chosen a specialty that will eventually lose importance because of the changes that come in industry.

Just as a matter of prudence, it would seem to be safer to sign on as a utility infielder who can play any base and hit a long ball against all kinds of pitching, than to be the best shortstop and able to hit only a pitch that is low and outside.

Why study business?

Following are six important reasons why the study of business is valuable for a young person:

1. It offers an opportunity for personal economic gain
2. It helps one to make an intelligent career choice
3. It is useful in starting one's own business
4. It helps one better manage his personal affairs
5. It aids in understanding our society
6. It is in itself an interesting subject

Opportunity for personal economic gain   Young people sometimes complain that the great American frontier has disappeared, that the really exciting eras are past, that Horace Greeley's "Go West, young man, go West" has no analogy in twentieth-century America. While the West has been won, the American *economic* frontier has not vanished; in fact, the economic frontier is as young as each new generation. In competitive business, personal achievement and initiative are as important for success now as they were in frontier days.

Business is quick to reward ability that leads to efficiency, profits, and successful innovations. While it does at times appear to place undeserving individuals in high positions, by and large it has a way of moving the fit and the prepared to positions in keeping with their capabilities. A study of outstanding business people reveals that ordinarily their rise to fortune has been grounded in solid ability sparked with genuine initiative.[3]

Gustavus F. Swift, a cattle buyer, succeeded over a hundred years ago because he seized the idea of putting an icebox on wheels—a bold concept in those days—to ship refrigerated meat from the then largely unpopulated West where the cattle were to the populated East where the consumers were. This is the innovation upon which Swift & Co., America's biggest meat packer, was built. Alexander Graham Bell invented the telephone, and the business initiative of Theodore N. Vail turned the idea into a business—AT&T. An anecdote told about John D. Rockefeller, Sr., illustrates another kind of initiative. While visiting a Standard Oil Company processing plant, Rockefeller noticed an operation in which a machine dropped solder on tin cans to seal them. On inquiry he discovered that nobody had ever determined exactly how many drops of solder were necessary to seal the can tops adequately. The research that he then instituted revealed that forty drops of solder, rather than the forty-four used, were sufficient. It is said that the reduction of four drops of solder per can saved the Standard Oil Company more than $50,000 annually. To men with alertness, the "frontier" of business will always offer ample rewards.

Career choice[4]   Unfortunately, many people give too little thought to the kind of career they would like to have. As a result they often find themselves in occupations in which they lack interest and ability, and they usually discover too late that they have chosen the wrong career. Changing a specialized career in later life means that a person must start over at the bottom when he has already assumed family and financial responsibilities. Naturally, he hesitates to switch careers and may be forced to endure a lifetime of discontent.

There are two major reasons for mistakes in selecting careers. First, many young people are not acquainted with the variety of career opportunities that exist. An important objective of this book, therefore, is to present information about many different career opportunities in business.

Second, many people err in their career choice because they fail to analyze themselves objectively. Interests, temperament, abilities, and desired income are some of the elements one should consider. Career determination is a matter of matching one's own abilities and needs with the job requirements and environmental circumstances under which the job will be performed. To properly fit the individual to the job, one must painstakingly analyze both.

---

[3] This point will become increasingly apparent as you study the profiles, People and Their Ideas, found at the end of each chapter.

[4] The career selection appendix in this book provides an extended discussion of this important subject.

In reading about the various phases of business in the chapters that follow, students intent on selecting a career should try to identify themselves with the phase of business being discussed. Whenever a particular aspect of business appears especially interesting or attractive, why not investigate further—at first through additional reading and then, if the interest persists, by consulting people familiar with the activity? Once a career is decided on, it is possible, of course, to prepare for it through specific courses and work experience.

Starting one's own business   The American economy has always provided opportunity for individuals to "go into business for themselves." In fact, approximately four out of five business organizations are individually owned. Thousands of retail stores and service establishments belong in this category. Most businesses are small and can be acquired with relatively little capital. In many instances, such businesses are family enterprises. There are always many of these concerns for sale, as an inspection of the business-opportunities section of a newspaper will reveal.

It is interesting to note that practically all large corporations were once small businesses. Sears, Roebuck and Company was started by a young man who sold watches by mail. The Fuller Brush Company began as a very humble, one-man organization. The H. J. Heinz Company was started by a man in Pennsylvania who sold the first of his fifty-seven varieties, pickles, from a wheelbarrow.

Management of personal affairs   Another reason for studying business is to help one better manage his personal affairs. Individual persons and the family group are each small economic units. Like the business organization, the family must balance income and expenditures. Two families identical in income and other respects may maintain different standards of living simply because one family manages its income better than the other. A study of finance should help one make wiser decisions in securing credit for financing the purchase of a home or an automobile. A knowledge of marketing should make people better shoppers. Likewise, knowing the fundamentals of accounting is an aid to better budgeting and control of personal expenses. The large number of individuals who purchase stocks and bonds issued by corporations certainly can benefit from a study of business fundamentals.

It can be said that the goal of a student studying business is first to learn to manage his time and personal affairs in a businesslike manner as a practical preamble to practicing management in business. The person who cannot manage his own affairs can hardly expect to be entrusted with management responsibility in a business.

Social understanding and contribution   A knowledge of business contributes to one's understanding and interpretation of the numerous

Table **1–4** The Cost of "Only" Five Minutes Lost Each Day for Two Years[a]						
HOURLY RATE	NUMBER OF EMPLOYEES					
	FIVE	TEN	TWENTY-FIVE	FIFTY	ONE HUNDRED	FIVE HUNDRED
$1.50	$318.80	$ 637.50	$1,594.00	$3,180.00	$ 6,376.00	$31,880.00
2.50	531.30	1,062.50	2,656.50	5,313.00	10,626.00	53,130.00
3.50	743.80	1,487.60	3,719.00	7,430.00	14,876.00	74,380.00
4.50	956.30	1,912.60	4,781.50	9,563.00	19,126.00	95,630.00

[a] Based on eight-hour day, five-day week, 255 working days per year.

Time is a valuable asset to both individuals and business. How do you manage your time?

rumors, generalizations, and opinions that are expressed about the functioning of our society. Both print and broadcast media take definite stands on economic problems. Business executives, politicians, labor officials, and others often advance contradictory proposals for dealing with pressing economic issues. Examples of generalizations that are widely debated are given below.

1. Advertising is a form of brainwashing that creates unnecessary wants.
2. Labor is too strong and should be curbed.
3. Government is too deeply entrenched in business.
4. The stock market is really a form of gambling.
5. Costs of distribution are too high in relation to costs of production.
6. Many corporations are too large and should be broken up.

The ability to think intelligently about these and countless other questions can be improved if one is thoroughly grounded in the principles of how our economy functions. As our study of business progresses, it will become apparent that issues of this nature have no simple answers. But education does much to make one more objective and less limited by personal feelings.

The French have a saying—*Tout comprendre c'est tout pardonner*—which means roughly, "To understand is to be in sympathy with." Business in the United States, which so effectively brings together resources, labor, and management to produce so much, receives distressingly little sympathy from its beneficiaries. The functions and needs of business must be understood so its vitality is not destroyed to the detriment of society. The more people there are who understand the complexities of business, the more certain it is that continual improvement will be made. Indeed, reform-minded students especially should seek careers in business. Concerned individuals who enter and participate in business can help reshape business and give it new impetus to respond to social needs.

Inherent interest of subject   Quite apart from the career, personal, and other advantages that come from a study of business, the subject itself is interesting, even fascinating. Business is dynamic; each year brings new products, new ideas, new styles, and new business techniques, many of which can be very exciting, even to those who are not business-oriented.

American business is particularly interesting because of the keen competition that is involved. It is not unlike a professional football game. Each organization tries to surpass its competitors, and the battle for leadership never ceases. Each manufacturer is constantly trying to produce a superior product at a lower cost than his competitors; each retailer attempts to gain a larger share of the consumer market. "Avis is only number two, so we try harder," is a colorful phrase that is a familiar part of business vernacular. It attests to the quality that makes the field lively and intrinsically stimulating.

Many other aspects of business are equally interesting: the smooth functioning of the assembly line, the sensitivity of the stock market to business news and rumors, the creativeness of many advertisements and window displays, the huge automated factories and skyscraper office buildings. To those who understand something about it, business presents a never ending, highly fascinating drama.

SUPPLEMENTING ACADEMIC STUDY

Every effort is made in this book to present the fundamentals of business as clearly and concisely as possible. It should be remembered, however, that it is impossible to learn in one course, or one hundred courses, all there is to know about business. In common with students in other academic areas, those who aspire to success in business should build on the foundation laid by studying and by working in the classroom.

But the business student has many more opportunities to add to his academic knowledge than do students preparing for work in most other fields. Business permeates nearly every phase of our lives. In America the business world is everywhere; thus, our surroundings constitute an excellent laboratory for learning and understanding business methods, skills, and techniques. Following are described four specific ways you can supplement your academic study.

Systematic reading of business news

Business sections of newspapers and magazines are rich in current events concerning all phases of business. A later chapter, "Reading Business and Financial News," shows how a great deal of useful information can be obtained by reading business news regularly.

Observation

Scarcely a day passes without the average person shopping for food, clothing, other items, or services. The business student can train himself to look for indications of efficiency and inefficiency. Developing a "why" and "how" attitude is essential. The inquisitive person will ask, when watching a television commercial, "Why was an appeal to status selected to sell the product?"; when looking out a plane window, "Why is the electric company's generating plant located next to the river?"; when visiting the variety store, "Is there a reason the front counter is used for drug sundries?"; when reading a magazine, "How does it happen that General Foods always has the same page position for its advertisement in every issue of this magazine?" Each shopping trip can be a lesson to anyone who plans a business career. Contacts with banks, insurance companies, recreational establishments, and other types of business institutions can be rewarding experiences.

Discussions with other people

Much can be learned by talking to people who are specialists in certain phases of business. College professors are glad to offer advice or explain puzzling situations. Interviews with people in business are very helpful. Discussing business problems with fellow students, employees, and others gives one fresh insight. The special situations entitled Contemporary Issues, which appear at the end of each chapter, raise issues that are especially stimulating and easy to talk about.

Work experience

Actual work experience is one of the very best ways to expand one's knowledge. To many, a job is just a job; but to the interested business student, even the most menial work provides an opportunity to broaden his understanding of business. Employers place much value on actual work experience. Part-time selling in a retail store, soliciting magazine sub-scriptions house to house, or making deliveries for a business concern impresses employers; they realize how much the alert young person can learn from such job experience.

Other ways in which to take advantage of the business laboratory are through clubs, societies, and similar organizations. Experience in organizing and in working with people is valuable training for future leaders.

PLANNING FOR A MANAGEMENT CAREER

Forward-looking business management realizes that the continuation of the firm is guaranteed only if a new crop of efficient managers is constantly coming up. Plans for providing a "young crop" of executives are often informal and loosely defined; however, most larger companies have executive-trainee programs.

A wise step for the young person deciding whether or not he is fitted for a management career is to find out what personal characteristics business seeks in potential executives. These characteristics apply rather universally to business success; they are desirable attributes not only for corporation executives but also for those training to go into business for themselves or to take positions in smaller companies.

When personnel directors recruit young people for careers in management, the most important factor they look for is a *demonstrated ability to work effectively with other people.* In school the young person first encounters many extrafamily group situations; employers therefore give particular attention to an individual's participation in school and community activities. It is a good idea for a young person to keep a record of his student accomplishments for incorporation later into a formal résumé. Such evidence is valuable in applying for jobs, admission to institutions of higher learning, and so on. Note also that your résumé can be an excellent self-study device. By reviewing it periodically, you can determine the direction your life is taking and plan your personal progress more intelligently.

Business concerns also value highly a number of other factors including honesty, intelligence, integrity, emotional control, conscientiousness, promptness, and health. As he talks with you, your prospective employer is likely to want answers to questions such as:

How did you spend your spare time and vacations while in school?

Is your interest in this job long-range and sincere, or do you overemphasize immediate and monetary gains?

What career goals do you have?

Where do you want to be ten years from now?

Will you respond well to training so that you will grow and develop?

Will you accept routine assignments as part of the training process, so that you may learn quickly what is expected of you?

If advancement is regular but slow, will you become impatient?

Self-evaluation: a useful key

Honest self-analysis helps one to see if he has leadership ability. A next step is to talk with successful and experienced business people and school counselors. Students should seek frank opinions about whether or not to consider a career in management. Aptitude tests are also helpful.

With determination, some persons can acquire management skill even if tests reveal areas of weakness. A person truly interested in attaining an executive position should seek leadership positions in the school, church, and community to gain experience. Once he discovers that he has definite managerial ability, he can then undertake an appropriate training and educational program.

Success and the building of a business vocabulary

A precise knowledge of business terminology and a good general vocabulary do much to facilitate the study of business. But knowledge of words does more than aid study. It is actually a determinant of success. Johnson O'Connor, a psychological researcher, found that major executives scored higher in English vocabulary tests than any other professional group tested. (In selecting those tested, major executives were individuals who held the position of president or vice president in an organization.)

There is significant evidence that ability to comprehend words clearly and to absorb knowledge through reading is tied directly to business success. For this reason, business students should concentrate on learning the definitions of terms and their proper usage. To make word study easier, the special business terms in this book have been italicized and defined carefully, both within the text and in a glossary at the back of the book.

PEOPLE AND THEIR IDEAS
Joseph P. Kennedy

The self-made millionaire who was father of a president and two senators

Joseph Patrick Kennedy, a self-made millionaire, created a fortune estimated at $500 million. His genius in commercial and investment banking, in industry, and in real estate accounted for this fortune. He showed his business acumen early by earning $5,000 as entrepreneur of a tourist-bus

enterprise during summer vacations at Harvard. He told friends that he would be a millionaire before he was 35, and he kept his promise. At the close of his life he discounted his wealth and said, "The measure of a man's success in life is not the money he's made. It's the kind of family he's raised."

Kennedy was born in Boston, Massachusetts, in 1888, the son of a saloon owner who became a state senator and a power in local politics. He entered Harvard University and concentrated on history and economics. He was always interested in finding ways to make money (as a boy he sold newspapers); it is interesting to note, however, that he was not adept at accounting and was forced to drop that course in college.

Kennedy was graduated from Harvard in 1912. He began his career as a bank examiner, and within two years he became president of the Columbia Trust Company — at twenty-five, the nation's youngest bank president. He set about making a series of financial mergers that astounded the staid, dignified bankers of Boston. As a result of his success, he was offered the position of assistant general manager of the Fore River (Massachusetts) plant of the Bethlehem Shipbuilding Corporation. Kennedy's acceptance was a pivotal decision in his life, for it brought him into contact with Charles M. Schwab, one of the nation's leading industrialists, and Franklin Delano Roosevelt, then Undersecretary of the Navy.

His first venture in the stock market was disastrous: Stock he bought for $160 plummeted to $80. But this was almost his only failure; with uncanny foresight, he accumulated a larger and larger fortune, and in 1929, weeks before the crash, he sold all his stock holdings. When asked the reason for this decision, he replied with a story about a shoeshine boy who knew as much about the market as he did; if that was the case something had to be wrong, so he got out.

In the late 1920s, he turned his attention to the movie industry and again demonstrated his "Midas touch." The early 1930s saw him engaged in yet another and vastly different business venture. Anticipating the repeal of prohibition, Kennedy organized a new company, Somerset Importers, and became exclusive U.S. agent for Haig and Haig Ltd., John Dewar and Sons Ltd., and Gordon Dry Gin Company Ltd.

In 1932 Kennedy actively supported Franklin D. Roosevelt for President. In Kennedy's words, "I'm the only man with more than twelve dollars who is for Roosevelt." Following the passage of the Securities and Exchange Act in 1934, President Roosevelt, despite strong opposition, appointed Kennedy a member of the Securities Exchange Commission, and he was elected the commission's first chairman. In this post he was responsible for writing the stern regulations that outlawed irresponsible buying on margin and that protected investors from sharp Wall Street practices. When he resigned in 1935, he received high praise from his former critics for his outstanding work on the commission.

His most famous appointment, was as Ambassador to the Court of St. James, and in 1937 he left for England with his wife and nine children.

He resigned in 1940 amid great controversy brought about by the publication of a newspaper interview in which he was highly critical of the British war effort and strongly opposed to American intervention.

Joseph P. Kennedy, banker, industrialist, financier, and public official, died in November of 1969. He had seen one son become President of the United States and two others become United States senators.

CONTEMPORARY ISSUES
Situation 1

Is a college education really necessary for a career in business?

In discussing today's assignment with his friend, Ray remarked: "You know, John, our professor made a good case for a college education as preparation for a career in business, but I think he was exaggerating."

"What do you mean by that?" asked John. "I'm convinced no one can expect to get anywhere today without a good education."

"Well," responded Ray, "take my uncle as an example. He finished only the eleventh grade and then went into the Army for eight years. When he got out, he went to work for Sears. He's been there ever since and he's worked his way up to manager of the sporting goods department in one of their largest stores. In three more years he is going to retire, and he's got a bundle of cash in the profit-sharing program."

"Okay," admitted John, "I agree your uncle has done pretty well, but wouldn't he have done even better with a college education in business?"

"No, I don't think so. I think the most important things are experience and a willingness to work. At least, that's what made him successful."

"I'll buy the idea that willingness to work and experience are important for success," agreed John, "but if your uncle had gone to college, he might have become manager of an entire store or maybe a key executive in the Sears home office, instead of being sporting goods' manager."

"All I can do is go by what my uncle thinks," answered Ray. "He told me he has never missed not going to college, and even if he had gone, he probably would have made less money than he has."

"Well," John countered, "since I'll be working in the year 2000, I'm convinced that a college education will be an absolute necessity by then."

SITUATION EVALUATION

1. Are there any conditions under which it is advantageous for an individual to go directly into business instead of studying business in college? Explain.

2. What are the flaws in Ray's argument?

3. How does the necessity of a higher education relate to the year 2000?

BUSINESS CHRONICLE

A special feature titled Business Chronicle appears at the end of each chapter. Each chronicle portrays a business situation in a realistic manner; each is part of a continuing story and is related to the subject matter in the chapter. The questions that follow the chronicle should help you develop an understanding of the more typical ways of reaching business decisions.The name of our imaginary company is Kingmaker Estates, Inc.

Which is better, a career in business or government?

Allan King, president of Kingmaker Estates, Inc., and his son, Dennis, a sophomore at Midland Junior College who is completing a general business course, are discussing Dennis' future.

Dennis: "You know, Dad, I just can't make up my mind about what to major in when I go on to senior college. I have always been interested in medicine, but I wouldn't be interested in having my own practice. I'd rather work in research, perhaps for the government or for some foundation or university. Then, on the other hand, I feel that maybe I should forget about medicine and get a business degree. You and Granddad worked all your lives building up this company and at times I feel I should carry it on. I don't know what to do.

Mr. King: Well, we certainly were counting on having you carry on the family business. But it's your life, Dennis. You've got to get inner satisfaction from your work or you're never going to be truly happy. But exactly what don't you like about business?

Dennis: Well, I guess I'm turned off by all the problems. I notice that you have to expand and curtail your activities according to how good business is. Your life in business is too complicated and distracting for me. When you want to expand, you've got to get building permits, raise capital, face increased taxes, get insurance, and what not. These are all matters that are a strain and are diverting and I want to avoid them.

QUESTIONS

1. Is Dennis right in his conclusions in being in business versus working for the government?

2. Which do you feel is likely to be more demanding over the long run—a career in medicine or a career in business? Which do you feel will have more (a) monetary satisfactions (b) psychological satisfactions?

3. What are the advantages and disadvantages of going into a family controlled business? Does Dennis have a moral obligation to go into the business his grandfather and father developed?

APPLICATION EXERCISES

1. An out-of-town friend has heard that you are studying business admin- istration. He is just about to enter college himself to study business. He writes to you, telling you that his uncle has offered to take him into his business, a profitable electrical-supply house. The uncle is a high school graduate who has done well. He has told your friend that the best way to learn business is to start at the bottom and work your way up. He promises your friend an eventual share of this business since he has no sons of his own. Write a letter giving your friend your views.

2. Consult a daily newspaper and select three articles that report different special-interest groups seeking a larger share of the GNP. For each article, write a paragraph in which you discuss the merits of the case and relate it to society as a whole.

QUESTIONS

1. How are providing a service and earning a profit related?

2. What is meant by "standard of living" and why is it difficult to express it qualitatively? What specific factors are responsible for the compara- tively high standard of living achieved in the United States?

3. What is GNP? GNW? What is a proper measure of social progress of a government? A corporation?

4. Is it wasteful, in your opinion, for society to allow individual con- sumers, rather than the government, to spend our increased GNP?

5. How can someone interested in achieving an important position in business most quickly attain his goal: by pursuing a college level course of study in business administration or by starting out at once in a business position? Discuss.

6. What is meant by the phrase "a liberal approach to business educa- tion"? Why is such an approach recommended?

7. Which is sounder for a business school graduate who wants to become a top executive in a corporation: to start out and travel along a special- ized route and become an accountant or salesman for a company, or to seek to enter a company's program for management trainees?

8. What is meant by "business is America's twentieth-century frontier"?

9. Learning about business is more than a matter of going to school. What besides studying business in a formal way can a student do to prepare himself for a business career?

CHAPTER 2

CHARACTERISTICS OF PRIVATE ENTERPRISE AND WHY THEY ARE CONSIDERED BENEFICIAL

The Right to Own Property. The Right to Compete Freely. The Right to Become an Entrepreneur. The Right to Choose an Occupation. The Right to Make Decisions Freely. The Right to Sell Goods and Services in a Free Market. The Obligation to Incur Risk.

GROWTH AND PRIVATE ENTERPRISE

THE ROLE OF GOVERNMENT IN PRIVATE ENTERPRISE

Objectives of Government Intervention. Government Regulation of Business. Government Promotion of Business. Government Protection of Business. The Future of Government Intervention in Business.

THE NATURE OF CAPITALISM

CAPITALISM, SOCIALISM, AND COMMUNISM COMPARED

Socialism. Communism.

THE CHALLENGE OF CAPITALISM

the private enterprise system

American business, with its philosophy of efficiency and expansion, enables us to enjoy a standard of living that is the envy of the world. What is there about American business that from the outset makes it so vital and productive as compared to the business systems of most other countries?

The answer to this question is clear: The vigor of American business lies in its economic environment, an environment called the "private enterprise system." This and other phrases used to describe our economic system—the "profit system," the "free enterprise system"—are convenient labels, but they do not explain the true nature of our business climate. The principal purposes of this chapter are to define the private enterprise system and to examine its chief characteristics in the American context.

The thrust of American business, its inventiveness, its strengths because of competition, and its phenomenal accomplishments all become clear as we look more closely at the private enterprise system.

While the material attainments of the private enterprise system are obvious to many Americans and many citizens of other countries, the system is criticized by some nations with different economic systems, as well as by a minority of our own citizens. It is significant that the most out-spoken critics of our economic system—those who would replace private enterprise with something substantially different—are often those who least understand the actual functioning of private enterprise. Business-men and students are frequently drawn into critical discussions about the free enterprise system. Certainly they should be able to explain it and compare it with the two current alternatives, socialism and communism.

CHARACTERISTICS OF PRIVATE ENTERPRISE AND WHY THEY ARE CONSIDERED BENEFICIAL

The right to own property

An inherent characteristic of private enterprise, often taken for granted, is the right of individuals to own property. The right to private ownership of property carries with it the right to control that property in any way not detrimental to the public welfare—the owner may use it, sell it, alter it, bequeath it to heirs, or give it away. Most property in the United States—oil wells, factories, mines, office buildings, stores, farms, homes—is owned by individuals, singly or in groups (corporations and partner-ships), rather than by the government.

Benefits of private property   Private ownership of property affects the economy in several ways. First, the wealth of the nation generally receives better, more conscientious care under private ownership than it would under public ownership. Owner-occupied homes usually are better main-tained than are dwellings rented from the government. Post offices and public school cafeterias are generally not as well maintained as corporate business offices and privately owned restaurants. There is, in brief, a natural tendency to protect and care for one's own possessions. Private property, with the individual's natural inclination to protect and care for his own property, provides a natural means for preserving and maintain-ing the wealth of the nation; no bureaucratic superstructure or sanction is required.

Second, the right to private ownership of property encourages people to accumulate property. When individuals know that what they earn can be used as they wish, they are encouraged to work hard and to save. Busi-nessmen, in the same context, have an incentive to expand operations and make larger profits. These factors lead to greater production for a society as a whole. The private enterprise system harnesses a natural human tendency for the good of society as a whole. In brief, people work harder and are more ambitious when they know that their labor will yield property that they and their families can enjoy, take pride in owning, use to provide further income, and pass on to their heirs as they choose.

Third, private ownership results in relatively efficient use of property. Under the private enterprise system, ownership and control of property tend to gravitate toward those who can use property efficiently.

Fourth, ownership of property provides a base for taxation. Part of the theory behind the property tax is that, as property is improved, a larger tax base is developed for local and state governments to use to provide public services. The merits of this theory and tax source are being reevaluated and increasingly debated. Among the criticisms is the argument that the property tax penalizes instead of rewarding those who improve property, and thus it contributes to the chronic problems of urban decay, which in the long run erodes the tax base.

The right to private ownership of property, like any right, can be abused. To prevent excesses on the part of the few and to protect the welfare of society as a whole, such measures as inheritance taxes, conservation laws, and building codes have been established.

The right to compete freely

Probably the outstanding characteristic of private enterprise is competition—the independent effort of two or more businesses to attempt to secure the patronage of the same customers. Competition thrives under private enterprise because each businessman knows that, in general, the more successfully he competes with other businessmen, the larger his profit will be. Competition occurs in practically every type of business, regardless of the size of the firm. Although the means may differ, huge automobile companies engage in just as intense competition as do smaller manufacturers and retailers.

The most obvious evidence of competition is found in selling and advertising programs. Competition between business organizations usually begins, however, long before finished products are offered for sale. Two manufacturers, for example, will compete with each other for the best raw materials at the lowest cost, the best factory sites, the best wholesale and retail outlets, the most satisfactory equipment, and the best engineers, designers, and other employees. Only by competing successfully on these and other levels will a business be in a position to compete successfully in the market place.

Not all business firms have equal opportunities to compete successfully. Some have greater capital resources, an established reputation with the public, or more experience. New firms, as might be expected, often meet with severe competition from firms that are already established. While a definite handicap to the beginning firm, inequalities at the starting level do serve society, for only those survive that are qualified and satisfy real needs.

Competition benefits both the business and the consumer in several ways.

Lower prices to consumers   Other things being equal, consumers generally buy from the seller who offers a product or a service at the lowest price. Consequently, all concerns have a compelling incentive to eliminate waste and inefficiency in production and sales so that their products can be offered to the public at a competitive price.

Better service   Under competitive private enterprise, better service, like lower prices, is used to lure consumers. To win more customers, a department store, for example, will provide credit, attractive interiors, free delivery, and numerous other services for the comfort or convenience of shoppers. Were it not for the competitive urge to earn larger profits, there would be little incentive to provide desirable services.

New and better products   The desire to secure an ever larger share of the market—an especially potent incentive under private enterprise—causes firms to try to build products superior to those of their competitors. As a result of competition, practically all products—tires, gasoline, aircraft, refrigerators, and thousands more—are now markedly better than when first developed.

Competition also encourages the development of new products and of substitutes for old. The Pharmaceutical Manufacturers Association reports that new medicines become outdated so quickly by better ones that nearly two-thirds of the normally stocked 6,200 prescription items are withdrawn over a ten-year period.

Alertness to possibilities for improvement is one of the most interesting characteristics of American business and surely accounts for much of the tremendous progress brought about through private enterprise. For example, several years ago Alex Lewyt, the industrialist who invented the canister-type vacuum cleaner, was almost run over by a boy's homemade scooter. The near accident gave birth to an idea that brought about a new feature incorporated in models of the Lewyt Corporation's cleaners—the large-sized wheels that make it possible for the cleaner to be moved easily from place to place in the home.

Elimination of the inefficient   Inefficient businesses that cannot compete must either improve their methods of operation or forfeit their right to be in business. This weeding-out process, sometimes dubbed the "right to fail," is a self-regulating, unbureaucratic method that free enterprise has for shifting resources and manpower to where the need exists.

Opportunity for talented and industrious employees   Competition reduces the human tendency of those in power to play favorites among employees or to practice nepotism. When profits turn to losses or when a competitor gets an uncomfortably larger share of the market, management takes a hard look at the performance record of its staff, including friends, relatives, and heretofore bureaucratically entrenched employees, and makes changes as needed.

Under private enterprise, competition exists among individuals, and, like businesses, they must work efficiently to compete successfully with their fellows. Ambitious employees work hard, get further training, and in other ways prepare themselves for additional responsibilities. Ambitious hourly workers, for example, compete with one another for the opportunity to become foreman; salesmen compete with other salesmen for the position of sales manager.

In this manner, the strongest, most capable, and most promising individuals eventually rise to positions of leadership. The opportunity to make progress within the organization and, conversely, the ever-present threat of the loss of pay or job that may result from poor performance contribute greatly to the success of private enterprise.

The right to become an entrepreneur

Another important feature of the private enterprise system is the right of an individual to launch his own business.[1] The individual who initiates a business enterprise — who secures the necessary capital and assumes the risks involved — is called an *entrepreneur*. While licenses may be required for certain businesses, there are relatively few obstacles in the way of an individual who wishes to become an entrepreneur.

Entrepreneurship gives our system vitality. Each year literally thousands of individuals enter business, for they feel they have found a gap in what people require and hope to supply the goods or services that will fill that gap. Thus, the economy is provided with innumerable centers of initiative that create new businesses and keep existing companies from stagnating.

The right to entrepreneurship does not carry a guarantee of success. Because people differ greatly in aptitude, training, and experience, the degree of success achieved will also differ. In some cases, the decision to go into business for oneself may be foolish, but it is better for society to suffer the effects of some foolish decisions of this nature than to have a governmental agency specify who may and who may not enter business.

---

[1] The appendix lists references on starting a business.

The right to choose an occupation

Because of specialization, mass production, and the growth of large-scale industry, most people do not enter business for themselves but become employees. The same principle of private enterprise that permits entrepreneurship also guarantees an individual the privilege of selling his services to whomever he chooses.

Individuals who know that they are free to choose their work have the incentive to prepare themselves, through education and training, for more responsible positions than they otherwise would. The ambitious clerk, for example, who realizes that he can improve his income and obtain more job satisfaction if he becomes a junior executive, can prepare himself in various ways for more responsibility. If individuals were denied the right to improve their work situations, incentive for self-improvement would be lacking. When the ambitious clerk reaches his goal, society also benefits since he has become a more productive individual. It follows that when anyone produces more, he makes himself more valuable to society. He is, in brief, making the maximum contribution to the national welfare when he makes maximum use of his own talents.

The right of individuals to sell their services freely serves also to improve the quality of business employment. Employers recognize that to retain the services of qualified individuals, they must provide promotions, pay increases, and other rewards.

The right to make decisions freely

Perhaps the major task in the operation of any business, large or small, is formulating sound decisions. Should production be increased or decreased? Should the present building be remodeled or a new one erected? Through what sales techniques can a larger share of the market be won? Will new laborsaving machinery pay for itself? Should a computer be installed?

The private enterprise system assures businessmen the right, under normal conditions, to resolve such questions as they see fit without an appeal to some "higher authority." Under our economic system it is accepted that businessmen, who stand to gain or lose by the decisions they make, are best qualified to make them.

The right to sell goods and services in a free market

The existence of a free market for goods and services is another characteristic of private enterprise. Basically, a free market functions in the following manner. Owners of goods and services seek to *sell* them at the highest possible price. Bidders for goods and services seek to *buy* them at the lowest possible price. Before a sale can be made, buyer and seller must agree, often on a compromise price. According to the law of supply and demand, if the supply is great in relation to the demand, the advantage is on the side of the buyer, and a relatively low price will result. If, on the other hand, supply is short in relation to demand, the seller has the advantage, and a higher price is set.

Prices determined in a free market are a gauge for making future production plans. If a producer is selling his product at an advantageous price, he is encouraged to produce it in larger quantities. But if he thinks that the price is not advantageous—that is, if it does not cover costs and result in a profit—then he refrains from further production. In this way, the free market directs resources into the making of those things people want and away from unwanted items.

A free market, then, is the best assurance consumers have for obtaining the full value of their dollars and for securing what they want when they need it. When prices are controlled by a government agency, the law of supply and demand does not function. In the end, the price of the finished product is artificially high or low and there is an over- or underproduction of goods. In other words, supply does not match demand, and resources are poorly allocated.

The obligation to incur risk

The assumption of *risk*, which, for purposes of this discussion, is defined as the *chance of loss*, is inherent in the private enterprise system. Some risks, such as fire, theft, and embezzlement, can be shifted to insurance companies, which assume them for a price, called a *premium*. Many other business risks, however, such as the danger of price changes and managerial errors, must be borne by the business organization.

A business may risk thousands of dollars on research and development of a new product, never knowing with absolute certainty whether the public will accept or reject it. Or it may expand its productive capacity without complete assurance that the additional facilities will be used. And the very act of going into business carries with it a chance of failure.

The fact that a multitude of risks are present in practically every business situation works to the benefit of the economic system. Knowing that risks exist, businessmen tend to exercise greater care in making business decisions. The more successful organizations precede each important business venture with extensive research, which helps reduce errors in judgment.

The presence of risks serves also as an incentive to conserve. In a planned economy, property is owned by the state, and it matters less to the individual whether this property is lost or mishandled than it would if the property were privately owned.

The complicated decisions and risks that businesses face and the rewards that accrue to society as a result of sound judgments are dramatically demonstrated in the story of the Du Pont Company's development of nylon. It took ten years and $27 million worth of difficult and sometimes bitterly disappointing research to develop this product. Its successful development, however, gave rise to many new businesses. Crawford H. Greenewalt, former chairman of the Du Pont Company, fills in a little-known part of this fantastic private enterprise story by pointing out that for every $6 million his company risks in research that leads to a success such as nylon, perhaps $24 million is spent on unsuccessful ventures that must be paid for by the one successful product. Greenewalt is careful to point out, too, that there is no guarantee that the new products, when they are developed, will be accepted by the customer. According to Greenewalt, "The only power corporations have, whether large or small, is the right to stand in the market place and cry out about their wares."

GROWTH AND PRIVATE ENTERPRISE

A characteristic of private enterprise has been a relentless dedication to economic expansion and growth. Growth of GNP, expansion of markets, and increase in sales have traditionally been viewed as highly desirable. Lately, the desirability of unabated economic growth and industrial expansion has been questioned.** The consequences of pollution and resource depletion have become matters of serious concern. Even garbage is a problem; on the average, six pounds of garbage a day are produced for every person in the United States, which costs $4.5 billion a year to remove. With added growth, this kind of problem accelerates. In addition, urging people to consume indiscriminately can make them less well off. *Science*, the official publication of the American Association

SPECIAL READINGS
**The Limits of Growth by Denis Meadows, et al. New York: Universe Books, 1972. The book reports the findings of the Club of Rome's project investigating the "predicament of mankind." The Club of Rome, an informal organization, consists of up to one hundred persons from over twenty-five countries with a wide variety of cultures, nationalities, and value systems. The impact of the group has been impressive. The Club's report was mentioned by the *New York Times* as ". . . likely to be one of the most important documents of our age."

The volume explores the "complex of troubles affecting men of all nations" that, in the authors' view "threaten the survival of our species." The book is a statement of the Club's computerized findings worked out at MIT. It warns of the "lethal consequences in the near future unless human needs receive priority over continued industrial expansion." When the *New York Times Book Review* ran a critique of the book (July 30, 1972), it reported that "A record outpouring of letters was received . . . pro and con." Many governments and international agencies are since shaping policies in terms of the Club's findings.

for the Advancement of Science, reported (May 5, 1972) that forces in the marketplace are creating an overmedicated and drug oriented society — sources of reduced human welfare. A per capita increase in prescription drug expenditures from $6.74 in 1950 to $19.31 in 1969 is reported. If price increases are considered, this is an increase of 33.3 percent in real per capita expenditure. These consequences and others from unlimited growth may lead to a reversal of attitudes toward growth.

THE ROLE OF GOVERNMENT IN PRIVATE ENTERPRISE

Objectives of government intervention

Private enterprise encourages each individual or business to advance its own interests — but only so long as what is done also advances the welfare of the whole society. The public bestows on the individual or business the privilege of working for its own ends, but at the same time it assumes that the individual or business will act responsibly. To further the general welfare of the nation, the government, elected by the citizens, is empowered to intervene in business when intervention is believed essential for the good of all.

The general goal of the greatest good for the greatest number is made up of several specific objectives. These include (1) full employment of the nation's manpower and resources, (2) maintenance of free competition, (3) development of new businesses, and (4) enforcement of contracts.

The government attempts to accomplish its objectives in four general ways: It *regulates* certain business activities and methods to ensure that competitive private enterprise is just and fair; it attempts to *promote* the growth and development of business; through various agencies and laws, it seeks to *protect* business organizations; and it *manages* economic activity through fiscal policy, monetary controls, and wage and price administration. How these are done is discussed in detail in Chapter 26.

Government regulation of business

As noted, one major purpose of government regulation of business is to preserve free competition. In the latter half of the nineteenth century it was not uncommon for a giant industry to lower its prices and deliberately sell below cost, if necessary, to drive out small competitors. Then, after the small business had failed, the industrial giant would raise its prices to a much higher level than originally. While the consumer benefited as long as the "price war" lasted, in the long run he was at the mercy of a monopolist's price. Laws have been enacted to prevent this and other forms of unfair competition such as bribery, intimidation, and discriminatory pricing (charging one customer less than others in the same category).

In some types of business, government regulation is much more evident than in others. Government regulation of public utilities, such as electricity, gas, communications, and certain forms of transportation, for instance, is quite pronounced. In these industries the government determines the conditions of doing business, reserves the right to limit the number of firms in operation, and approves rates and prices charged for services. A railroad, for example, cannot terminate its services on a branch line without approval from a regulatory agency, even though it may incur a loss in the operation of the branch line.

The great majority of businesses—manufacturers, retailers, service establishments, and others—are not, however, subject to such extensive regulation: The guiding principle in determining the extent of regulation is the importance of the business to the public. Regulation tends to increase as the number of individuals directly dependent on the business for essential goods and services increases. Government regulation is also important in other business-related areas, such as interest rates, wages and hours, and labeling of goods.

Government promotion of business

It is essential to a private enterprise system that an economic climate exist in which new businesses can begin and prosper. It is also desirable that business organizations be encouraged to grow, provided, of course, that the power that comes from size is not permitted to stifle competition or cause public injury.

Government facilitates the development of business in numerous ways. Some of these are (1) tariffs on foreign imports in order to protect domestic producers; (2) direct or guaranteed loans to businesspeople and farmers; (3) urban renewal programs designed to improve business conditions and create employment; (4) subsidies to certain types of producers; (5) public works programs, which are intended to prevent prolonged and severe economic depressions; (6) aid to education, which trains future workers and businesspeople; (7) maintenance of harbors, highways, and airports; and (8) the activities of the Department of Commerce.

Government protection of business

Government protection of business takes several forms. Perhaps the most important of these is the *guarantee that contracts between individuals and between businesses can be enforced.* Without enforceable contracts, business could not extend beyond personal relationships; for obvious reasons, businesspeople would refrain from making transactions with other businesspeople whom they did not know. Modern business as practiced in the United States would be impossible. The government thus provides a protective service by maintaining the legal framework within which contracts can be enforced. The government also defines what is and what is not a legal contract and prevents the enforcement of contracts made under compulsion or threat, contracts made by minors and others not qualified, and contracts in restraint of trade or in violation of existing law.

Other government action that indirectly protects business includes health and sanitation laws, provisions for national defense, and fire protection. Business law will be discussed in detail in Chapter 25.

The future of government intervention in business

One of the most controversial questions of the day concerns the *future* relationship of government to business. At one extreme are those who say that the nation is drifting toward socialism, that self-regulation is adequate, and that government regulation of business should be curtailed. At the other extreme are the advocates of increased government intervention in business. These people point out that capital and opportunity are not divided equitably, with the result that segments of the population are poorly clothed, sheltered, and fed; that resources are being wasted; that numerous public improvements are needed; and that many unfair business practices exist. In particular, critics point to pollution and social unrest as proof of the need for increased government involvement.

Most businesspeople take a position between these two extremes. What future action should be taken by the government in economic affairs is a very difficult problem. Each contemplated governmental activity warrants special, detailed consideration, for once a step is taken, it is very hard to rescind it.

THE NATURE OF CAPITALISM

The simplest definition of *capital* is that it is *wealth used to produce more wealth.* Clothes, homes, furniture, cars, and similar goods constitute wealth but are not capital, since they are not used to produce more wealth. On the other hand, machines, tools, equipment, and supplies are both wealth *and* capital, for such goods are used in the production of additional wealth. Capital is essential to the economic development of every nation, whether its economic system is capitalism, communism, or socialism. The significant economic question is: Who owns the capital—individuals or the government?

Figure **2–1**
The Expansion of Share Ownership in the United States (in Millions of People)

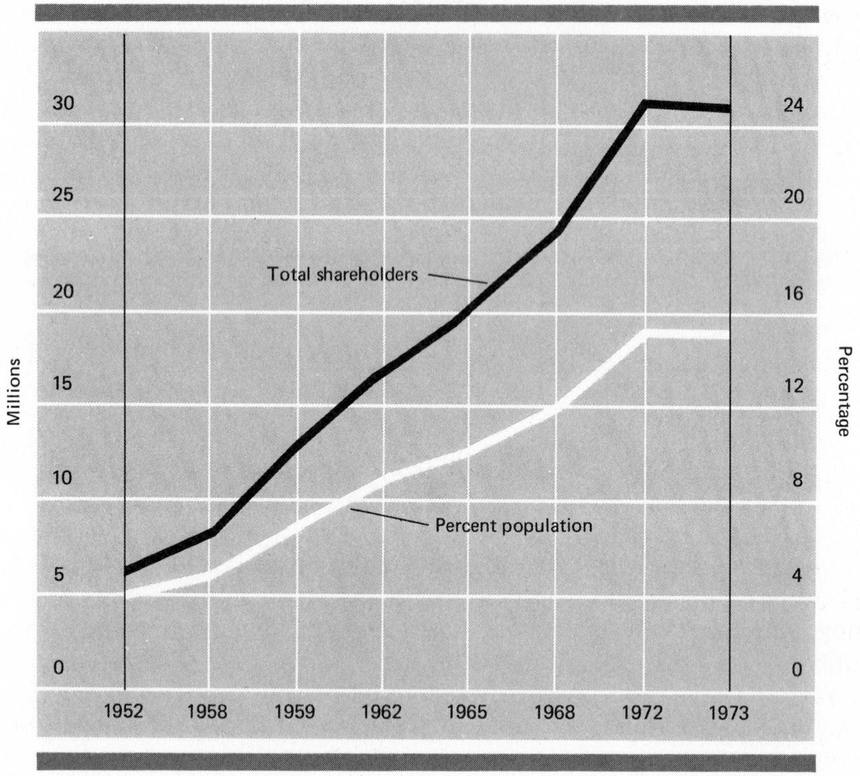

According to New York Stock Exchange estimates, there were 31.7 million shareholders in the United States as of January 1973. The exchange estimates that one out of every eight Americans now owns stock. Of the 31.7 million shareholders, approximately 50 percent are women. The figure also shows the slight decline in the number of shareholders between 1972 and 1973.

Source: New York Stock Exchange.

Capitalism is an economic system in which the bulk of the capital is privately owned by individuals and corporations and not publicly owned by the government. The communist often pictures the capitalist as a greedy, pot-bellied, cigar-smoking man who is enormously rich and treats his employees like slaves. He believes that capital is unduly concentrated in the hands of a few, with resulting oppression of the masses of people.

There is ample statistical evidence to prove this is not so, evidence that is borne out by a comparison of the standard of living of the average American citizen with that of the average citizens of other countries. Let us consider this question: Exactly who are capitalists?

Three broad classes of capitalists can be distinguished. First, there

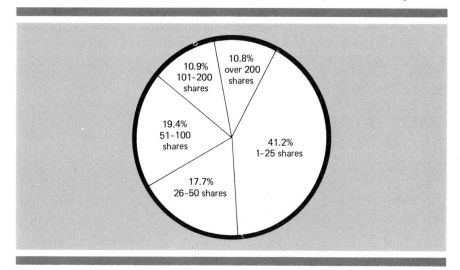

Figure **2–2**
General Motors Common and Preferred Stockholders by Size of Holdings

Source: General Motors Annual Report, 1972, p.22.

are the men, women, and children who own stock in corporations. In 1952, an estimated 6.5 million Americans owned shares in the nation's publicly held companies. By 1972, that figure had grown to 31.7 million. In 1972, the American Telephone and Telegraph Company (AT&T), for example, was owned by 2,991,620 stockholders. The Exxon Corporation, owned by 755,000 stockholders in 1972, grew out of an organization that traces its origin to the Standard Oil Trust, which was once owned by fewer than a dozen millionaires. The ownership of General Motors was divided among 1,235,000 stockholders at the end of 1972. They came from every state of the United States, from each of the Canadian provinces and territories, and from more than 90 other countries. Of the preferred and common stockholders, 69 percent are individual accounts, 20 percent joint tenant accounts and 11 percent institutions and groups, such as colleges, pension funds and insurance companies. Of GM's owners, 41 percent own 25 shares or less, and 78 percent own 100 shares or less. Most of the stockholders in American corporations would not be classified as wealthy; the average annual household income of 60 percent of shareholders is under $15,000.

A second classification of capitalists includes the millions of independent farmers and proprietors of small, unincorporated business establishments. These people are capitalists in every sense of the word, for they own, control, and use wealth to produce more wealth.

A third group of capitalists is composed of the millions of individuals who own savings accounts and life insurance policies. In 1971, 84 percent of all family units owned assets. The median holdings were

$700. Their savings were invested, in part, in savings banks, pension funds, insurance companies, and other financial institutions that, in turn, invested in stocks and other capital securities.[2]

Thus, almost everyone in our modern economic system is a capitalist. The paperboy who buys his papers and sells them at a profit, the aged widow who lives on the dividends she receives from stock in the local utility company, and the late John J. Raskob, who risked his money to build the Empire State Building, all are capitalists.

CAPITALISM, SOCIALISM, AND COMMUNISM COMPARED

Variations of two other economic systems, socialism and communism, compete with capitalism. As mentioned earlier, capitalism is frequently criticized by people who propose these systems as alternatives to our own. It is wise, therefore, to understand the economic strengths and weaknesses of socialism and communism as compared with those of capitalism. It is important, moreover, to realize that capitalism is in a slow but steady state of evolution. To fashion the capitalism of the future requires a broad appreciation, not only of our own economic system as it exists today, but also of those systems in operation elsewhere. Here we limit ourselves to comparing capitalism, socialism, and communism as economic systems and not as political dogmas. Political discussions do not fall within the province of this book.

Bear in mind that these economic systems differ in some respects depending on the nation. Capitalism in the United States is not the same as capitalism in West Germany; socialism in Sweden differs in some significant ways with socialism in Britain; and communism in Russia is not the same brand as in China. Our aim in the discussion that follows is to show the classical distinctions between the three systems.[3]

Socialism

The essential difference between capitalism and socialism is the amount of economic freedom extended to individuals. While there is little agreement on a precise definition of socialism, it is generally held to be an economic system in which the country's major resources and industries — minerals (coal, oil), communications (radio, telephone, television), trans-

---

[2] *Statistical Abstract of the United States,* 1972, p. 335.

[3] The question is sometimes asked why systems such as fascism and Nazism are not discussed at this point. They are political rather than economic systems. Hitler and Mussolini called the economic side of their system national socialism. The word Nazi is short for *nationalsozialismus.* Also, only the economic side of communism is discussed in this book.

Table 2-1
Comparison of Capitalism and Its Competitors

ECONOMIC FACTORS	CAPITALISM	SOCIALISM	COMMUNISM
Ownership of production capacity	Private ownership under constitutional guarantee of certain inalienable human rights.	State converts basic industries, such as utilities, transportation, steel, etc., to state-owned industries.	State owns all productive capacity.
Incentives	Wages and profits in direct relationship to one's ability to compete in a free market.	Wages according to the principle: from each according to his ability, to each according to his need.	Work norms plus bonuses for exceeding norms; appeals to produce effectively for glory of state; fear of legal action; public acclaim, medals.
Competition	Competition an inherent right established by custom and upheld by law. Determines efficiency, prices.	Basic production according to national economic plan. Privately owned industries sometimes pressured to comply with state plans.	Prohibited. State cooperation and state planning enforced by law. Legal action against competition.
Labor	Complete freedom in choosing place and kind of work.	Through planning, state attempts to encourage certain employment and discourage others. People allowed free choice of kind of work.	Amount and kind of work ordinarily prescribed and provided by state. State the only employer. Legal action against individuals attempting to employ labor.
Management	Management selected largely on basis of ability. Must have acceptance by employees, owners, and customers to survive.	Stress laid on nonmonetary incentives, prestige, privileges. Dangers of political bureaucracy inherent in management.	Party membership required of key managers. Political considerations cause management deficiencies. Authority backed by legal action. Highly bureaucratic.
Capital	Dependent on private investment, profits, and credit reliability of responsible business.	Comes from citizen investment in state bonds and from prices paid for goods.	Comes from state-levied turnover taxes on all goods sold. Some limited interest bonds.
Relation of government to business	Government's broad function is to foster individual initiative. The purpose of regulation is to prohibit acts that would stifle economic freedom.	State develops a master plan to which most economic activity is geared.	Government owns and operates all economic units according to plans.
Risks and losses	Assumed by private investors.	Assumed by the people of the entire state for state-owned industries. Losses are made up by taxes or higher prices.	Assumed without choice by the people of the entire state. Losses curtail standard of living.

portation (railroads, airlines, marine shipping), utilities (gas, electricity), and major manufacturing establishments (steel, automobiles) — are owned by the government. Whereas under capitalism government intervention in business is designed primarily *to further competition* (on the theory that competition enhances efficiency and stimulates progress), the government in a socialist economy is intended to *eliminate* most forms of competition (on the theory that competition is ruthless and wasteful).

Under socialism, individuals are permitted to own personal property, small businesses, and land, and they are free to choose their own occupations. However, since the major parts of the socialist economy are controlled by the state, government leaders have much more direct economic power over industries than do government leaders in capitalist countries.

Advantages claimed for socialism   The advocates of socialism claim it has four major advantages over capitalism. First, they believe that socialism results in more stable employment than does capitalism. According to the socialist theory, creation and maintenance of employment can be controlled, since the government is free to regulate the kind and amount of goods and services to be provided.

Second, socialists argue that their system eliminates the wastes and ruthlessness of competition. They ask why there should be four service stations at one intersection when one would be sufficient and why there should be more than one dairy delivering milk on the same street. Socialists believe that under capitalism there are too many competing stores, factories, transportation agencies, and other forms of business establishments. They contend that by eliminating duplication of effort, their system is more efficient.

Third, they maintain that socialism results in a more equitable distribution of wealth than does capitalism. Large inheritance taxes, maximum wage ceilings, minimum wage rates, and limitations on profits through price control are some of the ways socialism tries to equalize the distribution of wealth.

Fourth, proponents contend that socialism is better able to provide for the welfare of all the people than is a capitalistic system. For example, they feel that it is the obligation of the state to provide hospital and medical care, housing, and distribution of goods and services by cooperatively owned,[4] noncompeting stores rather than through privately owned competing stores.

Weakness of socialism   Socialism has two major weaknesses. First, government management of business institutions is inclined to be less efficient than private management. Some portion of the economy's avail-

---

[4] A *cooperative* is a socialistic enterprise owned by and operated for the benefit of those using its services.

able manpower is wasted, because a sizable bureaucracy that is non-productive and tends to favor the status quo is needed to make, control, and administer the plans of the state. Government management can lead to purely political appointments to responsible positions and can result in favoritism and bureaucratic empire-building. Thus, executive leadership tends to be weak. Under capitalism, leaders are selected by the competitive process. Employees compete with employees until the best-qualified eventually directs the enterprise.

Second, socialism is less effective than capitalism in stimulating individual incentive. Capitalism assumes that an individual is interested primarily in his own personal well-being and that he will work harder and produce more if he can reap the full reward of his effort. Thus, capitalism stimulates each individual to develop his skills and abilities so he can be of greatest value to society. Under socialism, an "I don't care" attitude can develop because individual effort is not related directly to reward. This tends to result in laxness, a lessening of self-reliance, and less stress on getting things done.

When socialism's weaknesses are pointed out to socialist supporters they are inclined to reply that the price that free enterprise pays for its superior productivity and efficiency is too great. To make his point, a socialist from a Scandinavian country that is largely socialistic said, "If forced to choose, traditional free enterprise Americans would prefer property rights over human rights, competition over cooperation, secrecy over openness, technology requirements over human needs, and puritanism over hedonism. The ideal of socialism is to reverse these choices."

Communism

Communism is an economic system that relies to an even greater degree than socialism on a planned and controlled economic order. Under communism, (1) all industries and resources are owned by the government, and (2) individuals have little economic freedom. A completely communist society is one in which all property, including farms and distribution facilities, is owned by the state. Russia and China, the leading communist nations, permit virtually no private ownership of property. The state dictates not only what will be produced but who will produce, and labor has no freedom to strike.

The chief distinguishing feature of communism is that the freedom of the individual is severely limited. The state leaves little opportunity for removal from office of those in power. Individuals conform to what the state prescribes. Under capitalism and socialism, the democratic processes are preserved.

The economic weaknesses of communism include all those inherent in the planned state. Capitalism makes each individual a center of initiative; communism makes the individual a part in a vast plan. Under capitalism, consumers dictate to business what is to be provided in the market place; under communism, state planners dictate the nature of all economic activity.

Many students wonder, as they observe Russian scientific progress, whether a communist system is perhaps more capable of achievement than is a capitalistic society. A totally state-dominated society that exercises absolute control over all economic resources can, at least in the short run, "out-accomplish" a private enterprise economy in the pursuit of a clear-cut, specific objective. Under a planned economy, such as communism, national priorities can be controlled. For example, planners in Russia could decide in any year to produce 500,000 cars and send three missions into space. Comparably, in the United States, planners similarly could decide on three space missions for the year because the space program is a government effort. It falls under the jurisdiction of NASA, the National Aeronautics and Space Administration. In peacetime, however, government control over the number of cars produced would not be possible. Furthermore, NASA must compete with private industry for material resources and personnel. In Russia, the government allocates materials and assigns personnel.

Our capitalist society has demonstrated an ability to function effectively in many economic directions at once. No comparison between these other two economic systems is valid unless it considers all forms of economic achievement, and, when this is done, capitalism produces and distributes most.

THE CHALLENGE OF CAPITALISM

Our past generations have used capitalism successfully to develop our nation's resources, to create our tremendous industrial capacity, to free human beings from physical drudgery, to wage various cold and hot wars, and at the same time to help underdeveloped nations throughout the world gain a secure economic footing.

Only the very naive would say that we have learned to practice capitalism perfectly. Our economic system has its shortcomings, and it is the task of this generation and future ones to alleviate these shortcomings while advancing on many new and exciting social and economic fronts. Specifically, the economy faces the challenges of helping to (1) remove the persistent unemployment that tends to plague our capitalist system, (2) eliminate poverty wherever it exists, (3) preserve our natural resources through elimination of water and air pollution, and (4) remove the dirt,

Figure **2-3**
The World in Miniature

If we were to imagine a world population of approximately 3,419,420,000 compressed into a single town of 1,000 people, the following picture of contrasts would emerge:

   61 persons would represent the United States.
939 would represent other countries.

   36 Americans would be church members.
   25 Americans would belong to no church.
300 of the town's population would be Christians.
639 would have other beliefs.

   80 of the town's population would be card-carrying Communists.
370 would be under Communist domination.

303 would be white.
697 would be nonwhite.

The 61 Americans would have a life expectancy of 70.
The life expectancy of the others would average under 40.

The 61 Americans would receive half the income of the town.
The 939 other people would share the other half.

Of the town's total resources, the average American would
have 15½ times as much as the average other person.

The Americans would produce 16½ percent of the town's food supply
and would consume 15 percent, storing the 1½ percent.
Most of the 939 non-Americans would be hungry most of the time.

The 61 Americans would have
     12 times as much electricity
     22 times as much coal
     21 times as much oil
     50 times as much steel
     50 times as much general equipment
as the 939 remaining persons in town.

The lowest income group of Americans would be better off
than the average of the other 939.

Source: Reprinted by permission of the Development Division, Research Institute of America, Inc., 589 Fifth Avenue, New York, N. Y.

noise, excessive commercialism, and plain ugliness that characterize such large parts of our cities and suburbs.

With technological breakthroughs in virtually every direction — space exploration, medical research, development of new sources of energy, and great advances in all phases of education — by use of our business acumen, we can do much to improve our physical, cultural, and spiritual environment.

PEOPLE AND THEIR IDEAS
John Harold Johnson

The builder of a black communications empire

John Harold Johnson is the founder and principal owner of a $20 million-a-year publishing company. The country's largest Negro publishing empire, its publications have made a major contribution to the advancement of the civil rights movement.

Johnson was born in Arkansas City, Arkansas, in 1918. When he was fifteen he moved with his family to Chicago, where he attended DuSable High School, graduating in 1936. At his graduation ceremonies he drew the attention of the president of Supreme Life Insurance Co., Harry Pace, who offered Johnson part-time employment while he attended the University of Chicago and, later, Northwestern University at Evanston, Illinois.

It was while working at Supreme Life that Johnson decided to try his hand at publishing. In November 1942, using $500 he had borrowed, Johnson published the first issue of *Negro Digest*, a monthly collection of articles about Negroes. With the help of friends, who made the rounds at newsstands and asked for the magazine, Johnson sold five thousand copies, and *Negro Digest* was thus established.

In 1945, Johnson began publishing *Ebony*, a monthly magazine with a pictorial format, "to emphasize the brighter side of Negro life and success." By 1951, he had launched *Tan* (now called *Black Stars*) and *Jet* magazines as well. *Negro Digest*, which was discontinued in 1951, was reinstated in 1961 to provide an outlet for original works by Negro authors, a service Johnson does not want to stop rendering and is now called *Black World*. In 1973, a new magazine, *Ebony Junior*, was published.

In 1971, the Johnson Publishing Company opened a new 11-story headquarters, the first Chicago Loop building exclusively designed and constructed by a Black-owned corporation. At the opening ceremonies, Mr. Johnson said, "From the beginning I considered the company as a vehicle for building and projecting the image of black people in America, an image that had been distorted by media oriented primarily to non-blacks. I felt then, and I feel now, that every man must have a wholesome image of himself before he can demand respect from others." Mr. Johnson said that his company had "changed with the changing aspirations of the people it serves."

In 1951, Johnson was named one of the ten outstanding young men of the year by the U. S. Junior Chamber of Commerce, the first black businessman so honored. He accompanied Vice President Richard M. Nixon in 1957 on a good-will tour of Africa, and two years later he visited Russia and Poland. During the Kennedy Administration, Johnson served as a member of special delegations representing the United States at independence celebrations in the Ivory Coast and Kenya.

In addition to the Johnson Publishing Company, Johnson owns a cosmetic firm and is chairman of the board of the Supreme Life Insurance Company. He became a member of the national board of the Urban League in 1958, lending increasing support, both personally and through his magazines, to the struggle for an integrated America. Further deepening its commitment in communications, in 1972 his company bought radio station WGRT, Chicago, for $1,800,000.

CONTEMPORARY ISSUES
Situation 2

Do all nations need the American type of capitalism?

One day Ray and John were trying to figure out why the United States enjoys a higher standard of living than do other countries.

"Well," said John, "the answer is perfectly obvious. The private enterprise capitalist system of doing business is the key. If other nations were to adopt our system, they too would soon have a much more productive economy."

"I don't see how you can say that," responded Ray. "Private enterprise capitalism simply won't work in many nations."

"What makes you say that?" asked John.

"For example, look at some of the new nations in Africa. Here the people don't yet have the education and the know-how for capitalism to work. The same point is true of China and even some parts of Europe. Private enterprise assumes that the masses of people are reasonably well educated and that the country has a stable political situation."

"Well, then," John asked, "are you saying that socialism or communism is better for some nations than capitalism?"

"Perhaps so. I repeat," said Ray, "for a private enterprise system to work, there must be certain basic ingredients. First, the people must have capital. Second, they have to be reasonably well educated. Third, they must have a stable political government. Fourth, they've got to be at the right stage in their economic development."

"Your argument shocks me," commented John. "As a nation, we should do everything we can to encourage other nations to adopt our economic philosophy."

SITUATION EVALUATION

1. Do you believe that private enterprise capitalism, as we know it, could work in underdeveloped nations? Why?

2. Do you agree that the four conditions proposed by Ray are essential for private enterprise capitalism to function?

3. If private enterprise capitalism is so successful, why do you think the more highly developed communist nations, such as Russia and eastern European nations, do not adopt our systems?

BUSINESS CHRONICLE

Are profit and social welfare incompatible?

Dennis continues his conversation with his father.

Dennis: Another reason I feel I'd like to go into either medical research or public health service is that I don't want to spend all of my time worrying about profits. I want to feel that the work I do helps people. Simply making profits is not really that rewarding.

Mr. King: You seem to feel business doesn't serve society. Look at it this way: people buy what they feel they need. If a company provides a service or product they don't want, or if the price is too high, or the quality is inferior, they don't buy it. This weeds out inefficient companies and those that produce what people don't want. Profit keeps business on its toes. Profit assures that companies produce what people want. As a business manager, I prefer having profit accountability. Because of it, I know whether I am efficient or not—or, as you'd probably put it, whether I am serving society or not.

Dennis: Your system's okay for providing for most of the material needs of people—housing, clothing, food, and so on. But because of profit, business only caters to man's tangible needs.

Medical, spiritual, aesthetic, and educational services are ignored. In seeking profit, business, through advertising, makes people focus too much on cars, television, and toiletries. If people spent money wisely, I'd agree with you. But, Professor Galbraith points out in *The New Industrial State* that society in general votes for what it selfishly wants and not for what's best. People bought more chrome for their cars instead of safety belts until the government finally stepped in and made seat belts mandatory.

Mr. King: I'm inclined to agree with you on that point, and that's exactly why I would like you to make a career with our company. In our land development company we want to work toward providing for man's total environment. People can and will spend wisely, but it's up to business to show them how. We want to make our land development projects attractive both from the individual's and society's points of view. I think we can be profit oriented and also provide people with greater spiritual and aesthetic satisfactions.

QUESTIONS

1. Will people spend more wisely if business shows them how? Or, as Professor Galbraith suggests, should the government intervene to assure that expenditures are socially more sound?

2. Kingmaker's land development projects would be much cheaper if environmental factors were ignored. Can they maintain a competitive position and even make a profit if they attempt to provide for the total environment?

3. The profit system is often criticized because it tends to make people want products that supply personal satisfaction but create social problems. For example, some people want high-powered automobile engines which increase pollution and consume gasoline, a non-replenishable resource. Is the profit system guilty? Explain.

APPLICATION EXERCISES

1. Ask four people you know (preferably in different professions) the following question: "What do you believe are the chief reasons the people of the United States enjoy the highest standard of living in the world?" Write a summary of the answers you receive. As a conclusion, write your reactions to the answers you received.

2. Assume that you visited a foreign country and got into a discussion with a citizen of that nation who made the following charges:
   a. Americans are too preoccupied with making money to enjoy life.
   b. The measure of one's success in the United States is based on such things as the size of his home, the kind and model of his automobile, and which country club he belongs to.
   c. The American economy makes people feel that they must "keep up with the Joneses."
   d. The strength of capitalism is eroding because the work ethic that built America is eroding.
   e. Free will is an illusion for most Americans.
   Write a paper in which you evaluate each charge.

3. Prepare a paper in which you describe (a) several specific instances you have observed in which individuals give less care to public property than to their own and (b) several instances in which you have observed that individuals give less care to others' property than to their own. What general conclusions can you reach regarding private ownership?

QUESTIONS

1. Do you think that any one of the six basic individual rights on which the private enterprise system is based is more important than the others? Why?

2. In what specific ways does private ownership of property benefit the economy?

3. How might a business manager handle the element of risk? How is risk tied to the private enterprise system?

4. Explain how practically everyone in the United States is a capitalist.

5. What is meant by the statement that capitalism, socialism, and communism are in competition with one another? Which system do you believe will ultimately be most widely adopted? Why?

6. How does it happen that the Soviet Union, a communist nation, is able to achieve such an impressive record in space technology while experiencing great difficulty with farm productivity?

7. Students tend to know more about the minuses than the pluses of our economic system. Why is this?

8. Do you believe, as some people do, that the price we pay for high productivity and efficiency is too great? What are some of the social costs?

9. What do you think the future holds for capitalism? How will it change?

10. There is evidence that resource allocation and national priorities will have to be more stringently controlled in the future. Why will this be necessary? How can this be accomplished under our economic system?

CHAPTER 3

HOW BUSINESS AND SOCIETY ARE RELATED
Business in a Society of Contradictions.

CRITICISMS DIRECTED TOWARD BUSINESS
Increased Pressures on Business.

HOW BUSINESS RELATES TO SOCIAL PROBLEMS

CONFRONTATIONS CREATED BY ENVIRONMENTAL PROGRAMS
The Environmental Factions. The Anti-Environmentalist Sentiments.

ETHICS IN BUSINESS
Should Students of Business Be Concerned with Ethics? Just How Ethical Is Business? Ethical Behavior and Legal Behavior Are Not Synonymous. The Unethical Side of Business. Unethical Behavior Is Not Restricted to Business. The "Game" Aspects of Business.

FACILITATING HIGH ETHICAL STANDARDS
Guidelines for Businesspeople. A Final Perspective on Business Ethics.

the social
responsibilities
of business

A society can be defined as a large number of people having common traditions, institutions, collective activities, and interests. Chief components of American society include—in addition to the business community—governmental bodies, religious organizations, labor unions, the communications media, family units, educational establishments, and the military. These and numerous other groups influence the way we believe, think, behave, and work.

HOW BUSINESS AND SOCIETY ARE RELATED

The various segments of society are highly interdependent. Business, for example, depends on schools and universities to prepare people to work; on religious communities to instill moral concepts so people may live and work together in harmony; on government to enact, enforce, and interpret laws relating to the conduct of business affairs; and on many other institutions.

Business is a dominant social force. It provides most of the jobs, owns much of the property, pays a large share of the taxes, makes virtually all the products we use, and in numerous other ways influences the patterns of American life. The effects, for example, of merely one aspect of business — R & D (research and development) — are incalculable. From artificial heart valves to new chemicals that increase agricultural production, discoveries flow continually from the research facilities of corporations, many as incidental sidelines. For example, a group of engineers working for a Rochester, N.Y., corporation, were trying to assist a blind fellow employee, and found that a computer system developed for the company could be adapted to provide on-line[1] Braille information to blind persons. The Association for the Blind of Rochester and Monroe County, which underwrote development costs in return for the marketing rights, stated that the Braille device would "help any blind person secure employment or vastly improve the quality of work on the job."

Business in a society of contradictions

Today, the eighth decade of the twentieth century, we live in a society of contradictions. On the one hand, we have developed a material standard of living that only a short time ago seemed beyond the dreams of most people; on the other hand, there is considerable discontent with the economic and social systems that have produced the unprecedented wealth we enjoy.

Thoughtful citizens ponder contradictions like the following that are found in society:

1. Why do so many young people reject the orderly, linear, high standard of living that business has for so long been so forcefully promulgating as the American ideal?

2. Why, with so many people realizing the ideal of two cars in every garage, one bedroom per person, college education for their children, and other evidences of material well-being, do we find violence, crime, school dropouts, alcoholism, and drug addiction on the increase?

3. Why, despite continued and impressive annual gains in the GNP, do ghettos, poverty, and opportunity lag still exist?

[1] See Chapter 22, Computers and Electronic Data Processing.

4. Why, when we know better than ever before how to solve technical problems, are large sections of our cities blighted, air and water more and more polluted, and traffic accident rates increasing?

Other contradictions include:

1. Record-breaking college enrollments . . . , *but* rising dropout rates in high school.

2. Rising membership in organized churches . . . , *but* mushrooming crime rate—up 353 percent between 1960 and 1971.

3. Teenagers with more money to spend than ever before . . . , *but* each year many thousands run away from home and reject material wealth as a legitimate goal in life.

4. More evidence associating cigarette smoking with major illness . . . , *but* continuing high per-capita consumption of cigarettes.

5. Record-breaking per capita income . . . , *but* 1 million people added to welfare roles in 1971 alone.

6. The evidence of wealth in millions of families—typified by the two-car, split-level, electronically wired, wall-to-wall carpeted suburban home . . . , *but* 182,869 personal bankruptcies in 1972.

These contradictions concern business executives deeply—as they do all of us. At stake is both a way of doing business and the well-being of society.

CRITICISMS DIRECTED TOWARD BUSINESS

Spokesmen representing religious, academic, government, and other institutions are increasingly critical of the way business seems to take advantage of people. Indeed, the Ninetieth Congress was dubbed "The Consumer Congress" because it was so concerned with the Truth in Lending Act, the Truth in Packaging Bill, and automobile safety legislation—measures designed to protect the consumer from irresponsibilities of business.

Criticisms of business cannot be taken lightly. The whole of society is more important than any segment of it, and, in the final analysis, the main purpose of business is to serve society.

Students who take an introductory course in business must be concerned with this criticism. The thoughtful student asks, "How can I, in good conscience, consider a career in business when it is accused of so

much wrong?'' Even when the student understands the essential construc-
tiveness of business in society, he is aware that some of his friends may
make charges that he is expected to answer.

A general criticism frequently leveled at business is that it values
money first and human welfare second. Some of the specific criticisms in
the area of social responsibility include:

1. Business is too profit-oriented, with the result that employees are
frequently exploited.   For example, a business may not improve its
working conditions because such an expenditure of money would
adversely affect the profit statement. Critics also charge that business frequently replaces a worker with a machine without concern
for the worker and his family.

2. Business discriminates against individuals on the basis of age, sex,
color, nationality, or religion.   While there appears to be ample federal and state legislation against outright discrimination, critics
claim that more subtle forms of discrimination still exist.

3. Business is guilty of polluting the environment.   One of the most
serious problems in today's society is air and water pollution.
Business has been accused of aggravating the problem by dumping
noxious waste materials into waterways and allowing its smoke and
soot to contaminate the air. Critics claim that business is shirking
its social responsibility because of the cost involved: Filtering
equipment and other pollution control installations are expenses
that would cut into profits.

4. Business is overly concerned with efficiency.   When building a new
factory or automating an operation, business tends to give priority
to efficiency factors, often to the neglect of other considerations—
among them, beautification, worker comforts, human values, and
conservation of resources.

5. Business will not act unless pushed.   Business is frequently casti-
gated for failing to act in society's best interests until pressure is
applied by consumers, critics, or government. The automobile
industry, for example, failed to take proper safety precautions until
critic Ralph Nader dramatically informed the public about the lack
of safety in automobiles.

Some drug manufacturers, consumer finance companies, and
meat packers also have been accused of putting their self-interest
above that of the public. They have tended to ignore the welfare of
consumers unless an aroused public or a government agency pressures them into taking appropriate action.

6. <u>Business misuses the communications media.</u> Most communications media—newspapers, magazines, radio, and television—are themselves business organizations supported largely by advertising revenue from other businesses attempting to sell their goods or services.

Advertisers are increasingly criticized for appealing to the baser human emotions in order to gain the largest possible audience and to influence people to buy their products. Critics claim that business disregards the social dangers inherent in the misuse of all media, particularly television—probably the most powerful force today in shaping opinion.

There are three specific areas of concern. First, television has been accused of contributing to crime and violence through daily programs that portray murder, cruelty, and intrigue and that idealize heroes who take the law into their own hands.

Second, television, in the opinion of many, promotes excessive self-indulgence. "Fly now, pay later"; "You owe it to yourself to own a new car"; "Why cook, sew, or bake (or do anything constructive or creative yourself) when business can do it for you"—these enticing invitations to self-indulgence come across the screen repeatedly and forcefully, dissuading the individual from taking the initiative or making any personal sacrifices.

Third, television is guilty, critics add, of over-stressing materialism and economic affluence to the extent that many people lose sight of humanitarian and spiritual values.

Increased pressures on business

Today American business finds itself in a paradoxical position. Although eminently successful—in fact, the economic envy of the world—business is under attack at home. But this should not be too surprising. As long as industry did not produce enough material wealth to meet all of society's needs, the people were reasonably content to let business pursue its singleminded goal—the one it has had since the Industrial Revolution—of striving to increase production. Now business has reached a high production level and is capable of providing enough goods and services to satisfy every citizen's material needs. But incomes are not distributed evenly (essentially because of political reasons); therefore, everyone does not share in the business community's achievement.

Success brings with it social responsibilities. No longer can business concern itself only with greater material wealth without regard for the consequences to the urban and rural areas, unmindful of air and water pollution, and at the expense of material and human resources. Society now demands a social accountability of business. The pursuit of material wealth is an empty goal if it does not bring with it a measure of happiness and fulfillment. Man is both emotional and physical. Also it is with the spiritual or "soul" side of man that many of this generation are most concerned.

The question now being raised is: Can the business community, which has been so successful in providing the quantitative material needs of life, also contribute to the spiritual, artistic, and psychological needs?**

SPECIAL READINGS

** *Getting Involved, A New Challenge for Corporate Activists* by the Editors of the *Wall Street Journal*. Princeton, N.J.: Dow Jones Books, 1971 (paperback). This book examines the new role of the corporation in our changing society. The preface states that "the central question . . . is the matter of just why the corporation exists: Does it exist solely for the profit of its owners and the employment of its workers, or does it owe a responsibility to the larger society? If so, just how far does that responsibility go?"

HOW BUSINESS RELATES TO SOCIAL PROBLEMS

Since business is an integral part of our society its success is closely tied to the solution of social problems. Why, for example, would a department store be concerned with maximum employment in the community? Because poverty and crime that stems from it are both costly to the store. Poverty limits the store's sales, while more employment means stepped up business. And the retailer bears a considerable portion of the costs of crime.

If only two of these interrelated social problems were solved—unemployment and underemployment—a more positive economic and moral climate would result. Unemployment cannot help but have a negative social effect. People willing and able to work would be spared the hardships and indignities of being unemployed. The huge sums of tax monies that now go into unemployment related welfare programs could be used for broader social programs. As a prominent political figure once stated so well: "Our objective is to make tax *payers* out of tax *eaters*."

A composite of views gleaned from the *Wall Street Journal* describes various opinions related to the corporation assuming a greater social role. These comments about the corporation's social commitment cluster around six areas of concern as indicated. . . .

WHY DOES THE CORPORATION EXIST?

Corporations are still supposed to produce profit, but more and more executives share the sentiments expressed in a directive sent recently to local plant managers and supervisors of Owens-Illinois, Inc.: "It is not enough merely to make a good product, deliver it at a good price and earn a good profit."

The central question they must ultimately face, of course, is the matter of just why the corporation exists: Does it exist solely for the profit of its owners and the employment of its workers, or does it owe a responsibility to the larger society? If so, just how far does that responsibility go?

SHOULD THE CORPORATIONS EMBRACE SOCIAL GOALS?

A determination to play some sort of social role still leaves many questions unanswered. Who pays for social projects: The stockholders through lower dividends? Customers through higher prices? Workers through forgone wage increases? Probably everyone. Yet some corporate executives now are arguing that this search for an economic rationale for social involvement may be not as difficult as it appears.

. . . the appropriateness of this development is a matter of debate. Economist Milton Friedman, for one, still argues that the corporation's responsibility is to produce profits and that the cost of corporate social goals amounts to a hidden tax on workers, customers, and shareholders.

WHAT IS THE DEPTH OF CORPORATE SOCIAL COMMITMENT?

As for corporations themselves there are still many that haven't succumbed to the notion that they're obliged to do anything but turn a profit. Others profess a social conscience but don't really mean it; they just recognize a public-relations fad when they see it.

Standard of Indiana's Mr. Drotning, looking back over the past five years says: "My own feeling is that we've been dispensing Band-Aids. We've used corporate resources to deal with symptoms of urban problems without really getting to the basic causes."

. . . behind the ballyhoo of anti-littering campaigns, self-congratulatory advertisements, and hot air from all sides, some major corporations are taking steps that they contend represent sincere efforts to gear social dimensions into their day-to-day operations.

"We are slowly moving to the real world from our earlier, overconfident rhetoric," says Thomas M. McMahon, Jr., executive vice-president of Chase Manhattan Bank. "All the way up and down the line, corporate responsibility must be treated as an integral corporate goal, just like profitability or efficiency."

In taking such a step, altruism is rarely a true motive. Most executives acknowledge they are acting from "enlightened self-interest." They see changing public opinion, growing pressure from activist groups, and the threat of ever tightening regulation of hiring, pollution, and product safety as good reasons to take the initiative themselves. As economist Paul A. Samuelson has put it: "To advance the good cause, one must not expect too much of altruism."

MEASURING THE CORPORATE COMMITMENT

If businessmen are to change their goals, the ways in which they measure their achievements must change too. Already, there is talk of finding ways to quantify the good (or bad) a company does as well as the profit (or loss) it achieves. Soon, many experts believe, there will be a system of "social accounting" that will make this possible.

One important measure of the commitment of companies to social causes is the amount of money they are willing to donate, and at the moment that amount is less than impressive. Under federal tax law, they are allowed to deduct from their taxable income donations of up to 5 percent of profits. But currently it is estimated that overall corporate philanthropy amounts to only about 1 percent of profits annually. If corporations all gave the maximum 5 percent, following the lead of Dayton-Hudson, Cummins Engine, and a few other companies—they could "create four or five Ford Foundations," one analyst figures.

ORGANIZING FOR SOCIAL COMMITMENT

For many companies, the first step in formalizing a social commitment is to put someone in charge of "public affairs." The Public Affairs Council, a Washington-based group, estimates there are now more than 200 corporate public-affairs directors, compared with only a handful a few years ago.

Often the person holding such a title is merely a recycled public relations man with little contact with top officers of the company and little effect on policy. "The standard situation is that the public-affairs director is not a guy who talks to the chairman or the president or even the executive vice president," says Michael Taylor, an official of the Council on Economic Priorities, a non-profit group that reports on corporate practices in social areas. Yet even Mr. Taylor doesn't fault the dedication of most public-affairs directors. "These are motivated guys who do have some really strong commitments. If they can get in a position of influence they can motivate everybody else."

ADVANTAGES OF SOCIAL COMMITMENT

John R. Bunting, president of First Pennsylvania Corp., a socially-involved Philadelphia bank holding company, thinks the fear of shareholder complaints is largely a myth. "Shareholders do not seem to react adversely to aggressive corporate social policies," he said recently in a speech. "Moreover," he said, "social involvement has clear immediate advantages for a company that we do not often articulate. For example, it may avert harrassment by critics. Secondly, social involvement will help attract the 'best young talents' to the corporate payroll," he said. "Finally, 'doing something' tends to energize the whole corporation and the revitalizing spirit generates easily to all corporate activities." Also, and very important, if social problems are not solved, business can expect the government to exert ever-increasing influence over its fate. If a socialist environment resulted, business would lose its privilege of operating in the free enterprise environment it has traditionally coveted so highly.

CONFRONTATIONS CREATED BY
ENVIRONMENTAL PROGRAMS

Programs intended to improve the environment[2] do not cause confrontations only between individual businesses and concerned citizens. Three other groups—government agencies, trade associations, and labor—are also involved in the broad-based movement to improve the environment. Many factions are usually represented in environmental matters. Representatives from each group, for example, attended the first large-scale national conference on the environment held in San Francisco in 1972; the topic was "Jobs and the Environment."

The environmental factions**

SPECIAL READINGS

** A Sand County Almanac by Aldo Leopold. New York: Ballantine Books, 1966 (paperback). A best-seller classic that is a joy to read; it describes the beauty found in a lifestyle that protects the environment. The preface states that "Americans proposing, agreeing to, and carrying out plans for industrializing will defend their actions on financial grounds, when economics should not be the deciding factor, especially when other alternatives are available. What better way to fight the destruction of nature than to place in the hands of the young this powerful plea for a land ethic?"

The environmental factions that are usually represented in confrontations and program development may be characterized as follows:

Government Environmental Agencies. Numerous environment-oriented government agencies now exist and have been given extensive powers. There are national agencies, such as the Environmental Protection Agency, established in 1970. There are also state and local environmental agencies—for example, Pennsylvania's Department of Environmental Resources and Allegheny County's Bureau of Air Pollution Control forced U.S. Steel into a vast anti-pollution program estimated to require an $86 million outlay over a period of six years. Government agencies such as these have proliferated and have been given more power because citizens have been electing candidates who take strong stands on environmental matters. (Chapter 26 discusses areas of responsibility of many additional environment-related agencies.)

Industry. Large corporations now tend to have departments of community relations and environmental control. At present, Du Pont has invested about $190 million in pollution control facilities. For the period

---

[2] According to the President's Council on Environmental Quality, the amount of private and public money that will be spent on environmental improvement between 1971 and 1980 will total $287 billion.

1971–75, the company has allotted nearly $600 million for new pollution control facilities and for operation and maintenance. Manpower has also increased; today Du Pont has the equivalent of nearly 1,900 full-time employees engaged in pollution control work. Trade associations also are taking an increasingly active role in social and environmental matters. Whenever environmental legislation is considered, lobbyists for industry participate actively.

Labor. Labor is strongly represented when environmental matters are at issue. Perhaps surprisingly, labor often sides with management in fighting environmental legislation, but the reason it does so is because such legislation is often a threat to jobs.

Concerned Citizens' Groups. Citizens' groups have been exceptionally active and unusually successful in environmental matters. The Sierra Club, a conservationists' organization, has been very successful in getting action for its many programs. An organization called GASP (Group Against Smog and Pollution), whose membership includes doctors, scientists, and engineers from the University of Pittsburgh and Duquesne University, was instrumental in initiating the action against the U.S. Steel Corporation cited previously.

It seems probable that no one in our society, certainly not leaders of the four power factions just mentioned, wants to see polluted air, deforested landscapes, or dirty rivers and streams. Since environmental improvements cost money, however, there is considerable disagreement as to how fast environmental improvement should take place and what specific programs should carry priority.

The anti-environmentalist sentiments

Pro-environmentalist sentiments are widely publicized. Because the arguments in favor of improving the environment are well known and often obvious, there is no need to review them here. However, the nature of the anti-environmentalist arguments are far less familiar because the forces against environmental improvement and conservation tend to work behind the scenes. Because pro-environmentalist emotions are easily stirred up and because passions of those concerned run deep, those opposed try to avoid publicity and confrontation. The nature of their views, excerpted from the San Francisco proceedings, also deserve thoughtful and unemotional consideration. Study of the comments vividly illustrate that anti-environmentalist feelings are also intense and that environmental matters are indeed complex.

An AFL-CIO Lobbyist: You are for trees or you are for jobs. It's that simple.

State Council of Carpenters Executive: If you do not have a job, you do not have a paycheck. A man's personal environment can become hell when he is out of work.

UAW President: Labor must insist upon the widely accepted but rarely practiced principle that the burdens and sacrifices required by an action taken in the service of the interests of the whole society should be shared equitably by all who benefit from that action and not be allowed to fall disproportionately on some who are made victims of the action. Workers displaced by pollution-related plant shut-downs should be indemnified for lost wages and fringe benefits, and they should be paid for retraining, relocation, and other expenses incurred in job prospecting and in selling a house. A corporation should be required to prove a plant shut-down was due to pollution standards.

University Professor: If industry merely passes its cleaning-up costs along to the consumer it will widen the gap between the rich and the poor. The distribution of the costs of anti-pollution measures is critical whether the cost is a man's job, in the price of the food he buys, or in the determination that industry might have to make decisions for the common good rather than for the profit motive.

AFL-CIO Lobbyist: The environmentalists have not recognized the needs and aspirations of people. This no-growth nonsense, this feeling that society cannot grow further, is strictly an upper-middle-class view of society, a view of those seeking to preserve their piece of turf. The need now is to develop an overall, integrated approach to job replacement and job creation. The basic gut commitment must be to broaden the job base.

AFL-CIO Spokesman: It's been a continuous battle against the environmentalists—the freeways, the coastline, timber cutting. Each threatens the jobs of labor. Now it's the no-growth prescription, which is really a prescription for greater social strife. Furthermore, should minorities be expected to accept the lowest rung to help the environment?

Teamsters' Union Representative: All of the talk about creating new jobs to take care of air and water pollution, to build mass-transit systems instead of freeways, and to retrain workers is "pie-in-the-sky."

California AFL-CIO Executive: We are in unions for job security, wages, hours, working conditions. Whether the assault on our jobs comes from industry or from academic liberals who have a contempt for the working man, we'll fight.

Steel Company Executive: We will not spend money to clean the environment; we will only spend money to bring ourselves into compliance with the law.

ETHICS IN BUSINESS

Ethics is a branch of philosophy that deals with values relating to human conduct—that is, with what is "right" or "wrong," "good" or "bad," "moral" or "immoral."

The study of business ethics is particularly difficult because no two people or groups of people have identical concepts of right and wrong. Moreover, people frequently find their values changing over time. In business, for example, the qualities of acumen, shrewdness, and cunning may be both admired by some and questioned by others.

Historically, concern about business ethics goes back to the very beginning of commercial activity. One of the early meanings of the word "business" was "a mischievous or impertinent activity." Rome, Greece, Phoenicia, and other early commercial societies considered business the lowliest of occupations. In Roman mythology, Mercury was the god of commerce, gymnastics, and thieving—in short, the god of those things that required manipulation and dexterity. Centuries later, when Napoleon wanted to insult the British, he called them a nation of shopkeepers. Only in relatively recent times has business been accorded a position of social respectability.

In many ways, the ancient suspicions still prevail. Attention still focuses on the "bad" image of business, first, because by common standards some business behavior is unethical, and, second, because more than ever before, business has assumed responsibility for a growth in our standard of living, thereby overshadowing other institutions in the impact it makes on society. It is to be expected, therefore, that clergymen, social scientists, educators, government officials, and other critics and observers in our society should make value judgments about business ethics.

Should students of business be concerned with ethics?

There are some who believe that because ethics is concerned with subjective concepts, it has no place in the formal study of business. Their arguments run as follows: Business is an amoral subject. Business skills can be taught in the classroom, but morality, being personal, is best taught at home or in church. Today, however, the widely held view is that students of business should be concerned with the ethics of business. As Dean Nathan A. Baily of the American University stated:

> . . . I believe few educators in . . . [the business] field are concerned about their graduates proving themselves *technically* competent.
>
> But what about their *ethical* competence? How well do alumni of schools of business administration—and university graduates in general—know the difference between right and wrong (and not merely in the legal sense), and how willing are they to practice what they believe is right and to suffer the consequences for doing what they believe is wrong?
>
> Until recently, very few schools of business administration offered formal courses in business ethics. It was generally felt that such courses would be largely ineffectual preaching or scholastic regurgitation of formal

rules. It was argued that ethical problems and considerations should be taken up wherever appropriate as part of the subject matter.

Further, educators in business administration felt that they did not have a good answer to a basic dilemma. If they educated for an ideal world, for the kind of world that we could dream about for some distant days in the future, their students would enter business naive, impractical and unsophisticated. They would not even be able to see the feet outstretched to trip them.

On the other hand, if students were educated for the present world (or at least the academic image of it), if they were taught today's (or more frequently yesterday's) tricks of the trade, how would they later become ethical? How would they change their day-to-day habits after years of perfecting them upon reaching the top positions in which presumably they could alter the patterns of behavior of the organization? How would graduates educated in this "realistic" fashion become the instruments for achieving a better world as our catalogs so grandiosely proclaim?[3]

Just how ethical is business?

Oscar Wilde made the point that temptation is the great defiler. "I can resist anything but temptation," he said. Business produces most of the wealth of the country, and those who sit at the source of that wealth are probably tempted most. Nevertheless, integrity is an integral part of business; in fact, without it, modern business, which is based almost entirely on credit, could not be transacted. Millions of bushels of grain and millions of dollars of securities are sold each day on the basis of oral agreements. Billions of dollars worth of goods annually are transferred between businesses on the basis of unwritten contracts. Most wholesalers and retailers allow suppliers' salesmen to write their own orders, trusting them to ship proper amounts at the prevailing prices. A money-back-guarantee from a Sears or Montgomery-Ward store has real meaning, as does the policy of "We will not be undersold," which prevails at numerous stores, large and small.

On the other hand, the business firm is a mirror of society: it reflects the morals of the society in which it functions. A corporation, like a human being, may be honest and law-abiding or greedy, shady, and chiseling.

Ethical behavior and legal behavior are not synonymous

It is important to note that something can be legal but not necessarily ethical. For example, there may be no law that says tickets to popular

---

[3] "Teaching Business Ethics," Dr. Nathan A. Baily, Dean, School of Business Administration, The American University, Washington, D.C., *Dun's Review*, January 1968, p. 20.

events must be sold on a first-come, first-served basis, but is it ethical for promoters to sell certain customers in preference to others?

Critics of business behavior claim that executives tend to question the legality of a situation far more often than they question the ethics involved.

Henry Ford II addressed himself to this point as follows:

> I suggest we . . . [business] . . . look not only at the obvious areas of danger, where we may run afoul of the law, but also at those borderline areas of corporate action which might have unfortunate social consequences for our fellow man.
>
> Morality is not just avoiding price-fixing or conflict of interest. Obedience to the law is not enough. The law is negative. It tells us only what we must not do. As Crawford Greenewalt, President of DuPont, has suggested: we in industry must be concerned more specifically with "obedience to the unenforceable—the things we do, not because they are required but because they are right. This strength is more potent and compelling than the law."
>
> A corporation may be primarily a producer of goods, but it is more than just that; it is a small society within society, one with motivations, with rules and principles of its own. It is a purposeful organization that can and must give more than just money to those who serve it, and those it serves. It should reflect in its daily actions the principles and aspirations of our society in its finest tradition.[4]

The unethical side of business

Ethical considerations are involved in all business policies and actions, whether they relate to consumers, employees, the government, or competitors. The following article from *Sales Management* provides specific examples of flagrant business practices.[5]

THE TEN MOST WANTED LIST

In the past five years the following types of businesses have been involved in the greatest number of legal violations for deceptive sales practices:

Insurance.   Major offenses: falsely stating that policies are "guaranteed renewable," using terms like "seal of approval" without explaining their meaning; alleging that policies are sponsored or underwritten by government agencies. Also: selling high-risk insurance at inflated rates, then disappearing before claims are paid out.

---

[4] From an address, "Business Ethics," delivered before the Junior Chamber of Commerce, Minneapolis, Minnesota, April 20, 1961.

[5] Reprinted by permission of *Sales Management, The Marketing Magazine.* Copyright © 1968, Sales Management, Inc.

Publishing.   Major offenses: understating the true cost of magazine sub-scriptions; selling ad space in bogus business directories designed to re-semble well-known reputable publications; approaching encyclopedia sales prospects under the pretext that they've won a contest or have been selected for "test marketing."

Mail order land sales.   Major offenses: misrepresenting tracts as "improved" when they aren't; failing to tell new owners that they must pay for future improvements; and staging bogus contests whereby "winners" of free tracts must pay "closing costs" that exceed the true value of their property.

Home improvement contractors.   Major offenses: "bait-and-switch" adver-tising, requiring customers (mainly low incomers), to sign high-interest pay-ment plans that turn out to be second mortgages, making their entire home subject to confiscation in event of default.

Automotive repairs.   Major offenses: advertising ultra-low specialty repair prices (examples: transmission, brakes), then stripping down a customer's car and suddenly "discovering" a major malfunction that requires more money to fix than the stipulated price. Also prominent: warranties that aren't honored.

Home freezer plans.   Major offenses: falsely claiming that the price of a freezer can quickly be "made up" through food cost savings; welching on promises of regular deliveries; substituting inferior products when filling orders; turning sales contracts over to finance companies without notifying the customer.

Correspondence schools.   Major offenses: offering courses falsely promising employment after graduation; offering courses of little or no value.

Vending machines.   Overestimating potential sales and profits; falsely guar-anteeing to secure the prospective franchisee's top locations; supplying franchisees with merchandise inferior to the quality promised.

Dance instruction.   Major offenses: preying upon lonely people with match-making promises; offering instruction to persons too infirm or otherwise unfit to profit by them; signing up elderly persons for future lessons which stretch far beyond their remaining life expectancy.

Medical devices.   Common offenses: inflated therapeutic claims for cosmet-ics and curative gadgets with little or no therapeutic value.

Unethical behavior is not restricted to business

Most business leaders readily admit that some unethical practices exist in the day-to-day operation of business. In fairness, however, one must point out that business is not the only area of our society in need of higher ethical standards. Several other examples are:

1. Is ghost writing of speeches ethical?

2. Is it honest for movie personalities or professional athletes to endorse products they don't use?

3. Is it ethical for a college fraternity to keep old examinations on file in an attempt to out-guess the professor? Or, is it totally ethical to sign up for professors who have a reputation for easy grades?

4. Consider the position of students who choose a university, thinking they will have a Nobel Prize winner as one of their professors; instead, he teaches only one graduate seminar, while undergraduates have teaching assistants as instructors. Would it be fair to say that the students have been cheated?

5. Think about the ethical questions involved in "featherbedding" (the deliberate slowdown of production). Is it right for a union to demand that two people be employed on one job when only one person or perhaps none at all are needed?

6. What about the publisher who uses an overly dramatic book cover, which is unrelated to the content? Is this deceiving the reader?

7. As most college deans know, there is that occasional professor who goes to an academic conference ostensibly to keep up to date in his specialty when his real motive is to try to find a better job. Is this ethical? ("No," one student remarked, "but it's pretty smart nevertheless.")

8. Is a senator acting ethically when he goes to Europe at the taxpayers' expense supposedly to investigate government spending when his real reason is to enjoy some gambling on the Riviera?

9. What ethical factors are involved for a congressman who votes on legislation that affects a corporation in which he owns stock, or a doctor who prescribes costly drugs and urges his patients to have their prescriptions filled at the pharmacy in which he is a silent partner?

By no means do the questionable actions of others justify unethical behavior on the part of businessmen. However, the fact that such practices are so widespread suggests that no one social institution (business) alone is guilty. Rather, there is a need for corrective action by all social groups—religious, educational, governmental, military, and business.

The "game" aspects of business

In baseball it is considered perfectly ethical for a manager to give the pitcher coming into the game extra warmup time by holding a "conference" with the pitcher being sent to the dressing room. In poker one is expected to bluff, deceive, and confuse the other players. In basketball the freeze or stall technique is used extensively—it is considered part of the game, and clever. In football, basketball, and hockey there are numerous "kill the clock" or stalling techniques—all considered ethical.

Some observers point out that each social institution plays its own type of "game." The comment below represents this type of thinking in regard to business:

> That most businessmen are not indifferent to ethics in their private lives, everyone will agree. My point is that in their office lives they cease to be private citizens; they become game players who must be guided by a somewhat different set of ethical standards.
>
> The point was forcefully made to me by a Midwestern executive who has given a good deal of thought to the question:
>
> "So long as a businessman complies with the laws of the land and avoids telling malicious lies, he's ethical. If the law as written gives a man a wide-open chance to make a killing, he'd be a fool not to take advantage of it. If he doesn't, somebody else will. There's no obligation on him to stop and consider who is going to get hurt. If the law says he can do it, that's all the justification he needs. There's nothing unethical about that. It's just plain business sense."[6]

The same author goes on to mention that many businessmen find it difficult to adjust to the business game and may endure personal psychological shock.

> An individual within a company often finds it difficult to adjust to the requirements of the business game. He tries to preserve his private ethical standards in situations that call for game strategy. When he is obliged to carry out company policies that challenge his conception of himself as an ethical man, he suffers.
>
> It disturbs him when he is ordered, for instance, to deny a raise to a man who deserves it, to fire an employee of long standing, to prepare advertising that he believes to be misleading, to conceal facts that he feels customers are entitled to know, to cheapen the quality of materials used in the manufacture of an established product, to sell as new a product that he knows to be rebuilt, to exaggerate the curative powers of a medicinal preparation, or to coerce dealers.[7]

FACILITATING HIGH ETHICAL STANDARDS

In 1961, President Kennedy asked his Secretary of Commerce, Luther H. Hodges, to develop some guidelines to assist businessmen seeking higher

[6] Albert Z. Carr, *Harvard Business Review*, January–February 1968, p. 146.
[7] *Ibid.*, p. 149.

ethical standards. A Business Ethics Advisory Council submitted a report to the President on January 16, 1962, whereupon he said, "I have reviewed with Secretary Hodges the report and progress you have made in the development of a program to stimulate and assist business leaders and trade association groups in attaining high ethical standards, and I am delighted."

Guidelines for Businesspeople

The Business Ethics Advisory Council report is cited below.

The following questions are designed to facilitate the examination by American businessmen of their ethical standards and performance. They are intended to illustrate the kinds of questions that must be identified and considered by each business enterprise if it is to achieve compliance with those high ethical standards that derive from our heritage and traditions. Every reader will think of others. No single list can possibly encompass all of the demands for ethical judgments that must be met by men in business.

General understanding. Do we have in our organization current, well-considered statements of the ethical principles that should guide our officers and employees in specific situations that arise in our business activities, both domestic and foreign? Do we revise these statements periodically to cover new situations and changing laws and social patterns?

Have those statements been the fruit of discussion in which all members of policy-determining management have had an opportunity to participate?

Have we given to our officers and employees at all levels sufficient motivation to search out ethical factors in business problems and apply high ethical standards in their solution? What have we done to eliminate opposing pressures?

Have we provided officers and employees with an easy accessible means of obtaining counsel on and resolution of ethical problems that may arise in their activities? Do they use it?

Do we know whether our officers and employees apply in their daily activities the ethical standards we have promulgated? Do we reward those who do so and penalize those who do not?

Compliance with law. Having in mind the complexities and everchanging patterns of modern law and government regulation:

What are we doing to make sure that our officers and employees are informed about and comply with laws and regulations affecting their activities?

Have we made clear that it is our policy to obey even those laws which we may think unwise and seek to have changed?

Do we have adequate internal checks on our compliance with law?

Have we established a simple and readily available procedure for our officers and employees to seek legal guidance in their activities? Do they use it?

Conflicts of interest.   Do we have a current, well-considered statement of policy regarding potential conflict of interest problems of our directors, officers and employees? If so, does it cover conflicts which may arise in connection with such activities as: transactions with or involving our company; acquiring interests in or performing services for our customers, distributors, suppliers and competitors; buying and selling our company's securities; or the personal undertaking of what might be called company opportunities?

What mechanism do we have for enabling our directors, officers and employees to make ethical judgments when conflicts of interest arise?

Do we require regular reports, or do we leave it to our directors, officers and employees to disclose such activities voluntarily?

Entertainment, gifts, and expenses.   Have we defined our company policy on accepting and making expenditures for gifts and entertainment? Are the criteria as to occasion and amount clearly stated or are they left merely to the judgment of the officer or employee?

Do we disseminate information about our company policy to the organizations with which we deal?

Do we require adequate reports of both the giving and receiving of gifts and entertainment; are they supported in sufficient detail; are they subject to review by appropriate authority; and could the payment or receipt be justified to our stockholders, the government, and the public?

Customers and suppliers.   Have we taken appropriate steps to keep our advertising and sales representations truthful and fair? Are these steps effective?

How often do we review our advertising, literature, labels, and packaging? Do they give our customers a fair understanding of the true quality, quantity, price and function of our products? Does our service as well as our product measure up to our basic obligations and our representations?

Do we fairly make good on flaws and defects? Is this a matter of stated policy? Do we know that our employees, distributors, dealers and agents follow it?

Do we avoid favoritism and discrimination and otherwise treat our customers and suppliers fairly and equitably in all of our dealings with them?

Social responsibilities.   Every business enterprise has manifold responsibilities to the society of which it is a part. The prime legal and social obligation of the managers is to operate it for the long-term profit of its owners. Concurrent social responsibilities pertain to a company's treatment of its past, present and prospective employees and to its various relationships with customers, suppliers, government, the community and the public at large. These responsibilities may often be, or appear to be, in conflict, and at times a management's recognition of its broad responsibilities may affect the amount of an enterprise's immediate profits and the means of attaining them.

The problems that businessmen must solve in this area are often exceedingly perplexing. One may begin his reflections on this subject by asking:

Have we reviewed our company policies in the light of our responsibilities to society? Are our employees aware of the interactions between our business policies and our social responsibilities?

Do we have a clearly understood concept of our obligation to assess our responsibilities to stockholders, employees, customers, suppliers, our community and the public?

Do we recognize and impress upon all our officers and employees the fact that our free enterprise system and our individual business enterprises can thrive and grow only to the extent that they contribute to the welfare of our country and its people?[8]

A final perspective on business ethics

Regardless of laws and guidelines, the question of ethics in business — or other social institutions — depends on individual pride and responsibility. Benjamin Franklin wrote about an experience he had when he visited Italy. He observed an Italian craftsman meticulously and lovingly finishing the wood on the back of a drawer of a beautiful cabinet he was making. Franklin asked: "Why do you take so much care to finish the back of a drawer? No one will know it is there." The craftsman paused, looked at Franklin, and said, "I'll know it is there."

PEOPLE AND THEIR IDEAS
Andrew Carnegie

The wiry Scotsman who built U.S. Steel

In 1890, the United States took the lead from Great Britain as the world's foremost producer of steel. The margin of U.S. dominance increased in the years that followed as the nation's rate of production grew rapidly, far outstripping that of any other country. No single individual did more to bring world supremacy in steel to the United States than did Andrew Carnegie. His genius for organization and his astute business judgment resulted in the creation of a vertical industry that included all phases of steel production — from the coal and ore mines to the railroads and lake steamships that transported raw materials to the great furnaces and finishing mills that turned out the final product. Carnegie was also a dedicated philanthropist. Deeply concerned with the social responsibilities of the man of wealth, he gave over $300 million back to society.

Andrew Carnegie was born in 1835 in Dunfermline, Scotland, the son of a hand loom weaver. His parents were political radicals and outspoken opponents of privilege in any form, and at an early age Andrew developed strong political and social ideals that he never lost. The introduc-

[8] U.S. Dept. of Commerce, *A Statement on Business Ethics and A Call for Action*, 1962.

tion of power looms and the Depression of 1848 left Andrew's father jobless, and so in May of that year the family sailed for America, settling in Allegheny, Pennsylvania.

Andrew soon found work in a cotton factory as a bobbin-boy at $1.20 a week. A year later he became a messenger for a telegraph office in Pittsburgh. From this time on his rise in the business world was meteoric. Thomas A. Scott, superintendent of the Pittsburgh division of the Pennsylvania Railroad hired him as personal secretary and telegrapher. When Scott moved up, Carnegie became superintendent, and when the Civil War began he went with Scott, then Assistant Secretary of War, to organize the military telegraph department.

During this time Carnegie was expanding his interests in several directions. He invested in the Woodruff Sleeping Car Company, which owned rights to Pullman cars, and introduced the first successful sleeping cars on American railroads. He also invested in the Superior Rail Mill and Blast Furnaces, the Union Iron Works, and the Pittsburgh Locomotive Works. In 1865 he formed the Keystone Bridge Company, a firm that replaced wooden railway bridges with iron; that same year he resigned from the Pennsylvania Railroad to devote more time to the expanding iron industry.

A conversation in 1873 with Henry Bessemer, inventor of the Bessemer process, convinced Carnegie that the future of industry lay in steel. He built the J. Edgar Thomson Steel Mill near Pittsburgh and from then on was involved in constant expansion. In 1899 the Carnegie Steel Company was organized with a capital of $320 million. In 1901 Carnegie sold his interests for nearly a half-billion dollars to a syndicate formed by J. P. Morgan to organize the U.S. Steel Corporation. He retired that same year.

In 1889, Carnegie wrote his well-known *Gospel of Wealth,* in which he stated his views on reconciling great wealth with social and political democracy. In keeping with these beliefs he had already begun the practice of building libraries. In his own lifetime, Carnegie provided funds for more than 2,500 libraries throughout the English-speaking world. He also created one of the largest groups of philanthropic foundations in the world. These organizations included, in Great Britain: the Carnegie Trust for the Universities of Scotland; the Carnegie Dunfermline Trust; the Carnegie Hero Fund Trust; and the Carnegie United Kingdom Trust; and in the United States: the Carnegie Institute of Pittsburgh, the Hero Fund Commission; the Carnegie Institute of Washington; the Carnegie Foundation for the Advancement of Teaching; the Carnegie Endowment for International Peace; and the largest, the Carnegie Corporation of New York, which has a basic endowment of $135 million.

In his last years Carnegie devoted much time and money to the securing of international peace. To this end he built the Pan American Union Building in Washington, D.C., and the Hague Peace Palace in the Netherlands. The outbreak of World War I touched him deeply, and he retired almost completely from public life. He died in Lenox, Massachusetts, in 1919.

CONTEMPORARY ISSUES
Situation 3

Should taxes be used to help solve social problems?

One evening Ray came across an article about the nutritionally poor eating habits of Americans.

"You know, John," he observed, "I have an idea that might help eliminate our national problem of bad diets and other bad personal health habits."

"What's that!" asked John.

"Simply this," Ray explained. "Levy a pretty stiff tax on products that aren't considered in the best interest of an individual's health. Then, rather than pay the high prices caused by the taxes, people would tend to buy better, more nutritious foods."

"Specifically, what kinds of things would you tax?" John asked.

"Well, consider candy bars, soft drinks, many kinds of precooked foods, beer, liquor, and cigarettes—now any honest person would be hard put to find much, if any, nutritional value in such products. The last time I saw him, my dentist told me that America's dental bill would be cut in half if all of us stopped eating candy."

"Okay," responded John. "I'm sure we agree that better health is a national goal. But your idea of taxing products out of the market so people won't consume them simply isn't being very realistic."

"Why?" asked Ray.

"Simply this," explained John. "If we taxed cigarettes a dollar a pack, all we would do is create a black market, and crime and corruption would be involved in the manufacture and distribution of the product."

"What about candy bars? Would a black market develop for them if we taxed each bar say ten cents or fifteen cents?" Ray asked.

"I plain don't like your idea," John affirmed. "I think we should work toward better dietary habits through education, not legislation, especially tax legislation."

SITUATION EVALUATION

1. Assuming Ray's idea would work with products that affect health, could a variation of the same idea be applied to encourage installation of safety devices on automobiles?

2. What other points could be made in support for and against Ray's proposition?

3. In effect, do we have some taxes that do attempt to give direction to human behavior? Explain.

BUSINESS CHRONICLE

Is it feasible for a land developer to provide services a community wants?

The following article appeared in the business section of the *Miami Star:*

Kingmaker Estates, Inc., has announced plans for developing 4,500 acres adjacent to the new Cyprus Creek Airport. The development will include shopping facilities, a marina, garden-style and high-rise condominiums, a hotel, private homes, and a medical center.

Allan King, president, says that the project has been very carefully planned. Included will be both a modern sewage-disposal plant, which will release no pollutants, and a pollution-free garbage disposal plant. King stated, "An ecologically sensitive approach to land development will be followed in our project." His remark has reference to the nation's newly awakened environmental awareness, which, happily, is making prospective real estate buyers look more carefully at the back-up systems that support the real estate they invest in.

Various state agencies, and in the case of the marina, the United States Army Corps of Engineers, must approve all plans for Kingmaker Estates. They are being asked to make suggestions before plans are submitted for approval. Thus far, one state agency, the Internal Improvement Trust Fund, has agreed that Kingmaker's development "is proceeding according to the ecological and developmental principles that will be considered when application for development plans are submitted for approval."

In cooperation with the Goodyear Company, Kingmaker is conducting an experimental land-fill program. Old tires donated by Goodyear are being used in the building of large artificial reefs near the proposed marina. Several recent studies indicate that fish and other marine life adapt well to such reefs. In explaining their interest in this project, Goodyear stated, "Our company must dispose of 1,000 worn tires each week. The Kingmaker project provides us with an opportunity to use these tires in an ecologically sound manner."

QUESTIONS

1. Goodyear's cooperation indicates a trend that will accelerate if society is to protect the environment for the future. What types of cooperation can Kingmaker Estates solicit from other companies in its ecological approach to development?

2. Do the plans revealed in the article appear to be overly ambitious for a land development company to undertake?

3. What sources of revenue can Kingmaker Estates tap to fulfill its plans?

APPLICATION EXERCISES

1. Discuss the subject of business and ethics with five college students and five people who have been out of school a number of years. Write

a paper on the differences in the opinions of each group. For example: Are younger people more, or less, critical of business than older people? Do the groups feel that lack of ethics in business is really an important issue? What impressed you most as a result of this assignment?

2. Once upon a time, annual meetings of America's large corporations were like genteel English tea parties. Executives who hosted stockholder meetings considered them to be required rituals that were boring to conduct. Few stockholders attended. Those who did mostly yawned while they listened to dull management reports and waited for the free lunch.

   Since the 1960s all this has changed. Many stockholder meetings are now raucous affairs. Standing room only often prevails, and they are anything but boring. The change has been brought about essentially because many factions are attempting to reshape the corporation to enlarge its social concern. Ralph Nader is representative of one kind of faction; the National Affiliation of Concerned Business Students is another. The chairman of a symposium of this latter group, S. Prakash Sethi, Associate Professor of Business Administration at the University of California, voiced the basic reason why corporations are under pressure to broaden their social mandate: "The twentieth-century corporation has replaced the church as the dominant social institution in the lives of citizens of the industrialized nations. The separation of economic enterprise from the larger social and political purposes of natural life is impossible when there is no space for separation."

   Let us consider one of the confrontations at a recent stockholder meeting. An effort called Campaign GM asked to increase the Board of Directors of the General Motors Corporation by three members who would ostensibly represent the public. The idea was to include labor unions, consumer groups, conservationists, minority groups, and others not related to ownership or management. Another of the Campaign's requests was that a special committee of the corporation be formed to oversee and evaluate the social responsibility of the corporation. Management opposed the proposals, and to nobody's surprise they were defeated by a very large margin. Nevertheless, these proposals raise questions about the nature and control of large corporations. They deserve attention because similar proposals will no doubt be made more frequently.

   Write a paper in which you answer the following questions:
   a. Is the corporation replacing the church and other institutions as the dominant twentieth-century social institution?
   b. Should the social role of the corporation be broadened, or should it follow its original mandate—the production and distribution of goods?

    c. Assuming that the role of the corporation should be changed, what is the best way for it to assume a broader orientation and desirable social goals?

QUESTIONS

1. At a time when we have reached our greatest affluence, why are we confronted with some of the most serious problems in our history?

2. How do you explain the contradictions in our society?

3. What are the most serious criticisms directed toward business?

4. Is it true that business does not become involved in social matters until it is pushed to? Discuss your answer.

5. Why are we reluctant to speak up in defense of business?

6. Is criticism of business on the increase? Is it justified?

7. Why should business be interested in solving social problems?

8. What are the confrontations created by environmental programs? How can they be resolved?

9. Does ethics have a place in the business school curriculum? Should it be part of each course or taught separately?

10. Should business be played as a game? If so, what should the rules of the game be?

2
the structure

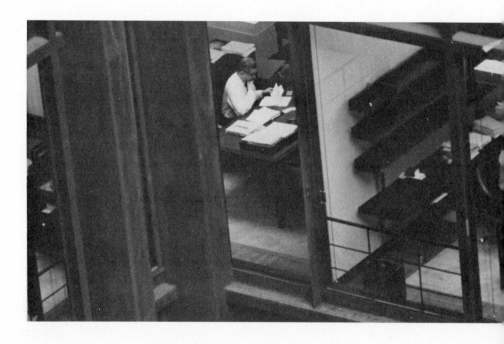

Just as a house must be built on a foundation, a business must be structured around a legal form such as a proprietorship, a partnership, or a corporation. Once the legal form is established, the business must be energized through management. And always, in every business, there is the continuous problem of how best to organize business resources. These aspects of business are discussed in the following chapters:

# of business

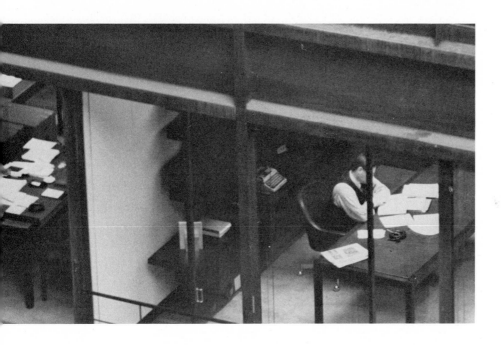

4
the forms of business

5
small business, services, and franchising

6
internal management and organization of business

CHAPTER 4

SOLE PROPRIETORSHIP
Advantages of Sole Proprietorship. Disadvantages of Sole Proprietorship. Conditions Favoring Sole Proprietorship.

GENERAL PARTNERSHIP
Advantages of General Partnership. Disadvantages of General Partnership. The Partnership Agreement.

LIMITED PARTNERSHIP

CORPORATIONS
Profit and Nonprofit Corporations. Open and Close Corporations. Advantages of Corporations. Disadvantages of Corporations.

ORGANIZATION OF THE CORPORATION
Choice of State. Corporation Charter. Board of Directors. Officers.

CONTROL OF THE CORPORATION
Separate Ownership and Management. Powers of Stockholders. The Proxy.

OTHER FORMS OF OWNERSHIP

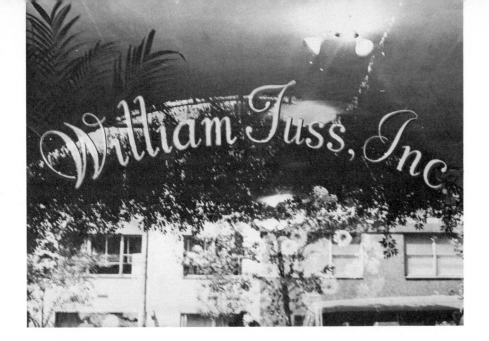

4

the forms of business

When a business is started, one key question must be answered: "What should be the form of ownership?" That is, should the business be organized as a sole proprietorship, a partnership, or a corporation?

There is no one "ideal" form of business ownership. Each has advantages and drawbacks, and which is the best choice will depend on the circumstances of the particular case at hand.

If you were considering setting up a business, basic questions that would help you decide on a form of organization would include: How complicated are the formalities for organizing? What organizational, legal, and state fees must be paid? Can the personal property of the owner be attached if the business fails? How easily is ownership transferred? How can additional capital be acquired? In case of death of an owner, how will the business be affected? To what extent will the owners participate actively in the management of the business? How does the form of organization relate to what lies ahead for the business?

SOLE PROPRIETORSHIP

Sole proprietorship—also called single proprietorship, individual proprietorship, or, simply, proprietorship—is a business owned by a single person who receives all profits and assumes all risks. We often refer to sole proprietors as being "self-employed." Usually the proprietor is also the active manager.

Sole proprietorship is the oldest form of business organization. It is also the easiest type of business to start, operate, and dissolve. Accordingly, the sole proprietorship is the most common form of business organization. It is used for 9,212,000 businesses, or about 80 percent of all business enterprises in the United States. It is especially common in retailing and personal-service industries. While sole proprietorships comprise the largest group they account for only a little more than 12 percent of all business activity.

Advantages of sole proprietorship

Simplicity of organization   To illustrate the simplicity of establishing a sole proprietorship, let us suppose you decide that your community needs an outdoor fruit market. You rent a vacant stand and purchase a supply of fruit; you are now in business as a sole proprietor. No state charter, legal agreement, or other "red tape" is involved. A state or city license may be required, but this is easy to secure. The only other requirement for starting a sole proprietorship is that the activity be legal.

Freedom and promptness of action   The sole proprietor has maximum freedom in making business decisions. He is his own boss, with no board of directors or partners to consult. The sole proprietor of a clothing store, for example, makes his own decisions on quantity, quality, and price of his stock. Since no other people are legally involved, the sole proprietor can take action more promptly than partners and corporate executives normally can.

Maximum incentive   The sole proprietorship type of organization supplies maximum incentive for business success. Since all profits accrue to the sole proprietor, he is encouraged to work hard, exercise close supervision over the business, make decisions carefully, and expand operations.

What is very significant to the sole proprietor is the fact that the business is *his* business. It is not unusual for sole proprietors to work sixty to seventy hours a week and enjoy it. These may have been the

Figure **4–1**
The Distribution of Firms by Legal Form of Organization for Each Employee Size-Class

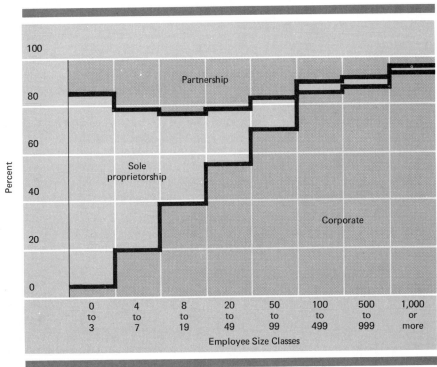

Source: Survey of Current Business.

very same people who complained about working forty hours a week before they became self-employed. In this sense, the sole proprietorship illustrates the ideal functioning of the private enterprise system.

Confidential method of operation   In some types of businesses, special or secret skills, techniques, methods of operation, production processes, and formulas constitute the chief assets of the firm. In sole proprietorships there is less danger than in partnerships and corporations that such trade secrets will be revealed.

Low organizational costs   Organizational costs are very low, frequently amounting to almost nothing. Corporations must purchase legal services in getting established and pay fees for securing a charter from the state; partnerships bear the expense of legal agreements; sole proprietorships incur neither expense.

Flexibility   Because he is operating by himself, the sole proprietor enjoys great flexibility. Methods of doing business can be altered quickly to meet changes in competition, consumer buying habits, and economic conditions.

For example, Mr. Palmer, the sole proprietor of Don's Fruit Market, can act quickly because there is no absentee ownership or partner to consult. He can switch produce shipments coming from a nearby city to neighbor Schell's truck when he hears that Schell returns with it empty from the city each day and would be willing to carry a return load of freight at half the regular rates. Such flexibility is not characteristic of the chain store competing with Don's Fruit Market.

Disadvantages of sole proprietorship

Inability to raise large sums of capital   A serious disadvantage of the sole proprietorship is difficulty in raising capital to start and expand business operations. The amount of capital that can be invested is what the proprietor is able and willing to invest and what he can borrow from banks, friends, relatives, and other sources. While the sole proprietor may have a favorable credit standing because his personal assets serve as collateral, it is difficult for him to extend his credit beyond his personal means. There is no way he can attract investors by sharing the ownership of his business, as a partnership or corporation can. Also, because the sole proprietor's credit rating is not as high as a larger firm, he usually must pay a higher interest rate on borrowed money.

Once the sole proprietorship is in operation, it may be expanded through reinvestment of part or all of its profits. But even when the business is quite successful, profits alone are usually insufficient for rapid expansion. Thus, when a sole proprietor decides to expand operations significantly, he usually finds it advantageous to change to some other form of business ownership.

Limited life   The sole proprietorship is legally terminated by the death, bankruptcy, imprisonment, or insanity of the owner. Many such businesses are terminated each year because of the proprietor's disability or advanced age. The sole proprietorship is often so much a one-man business that it is profitable only so long as the owner is active. Because of the uncertain life of the sole proprietorship, other businesses are generally unwilling to make long-term financial commitments with the sole proprietor.

Unlimited liability for indebtedness   Unlimited liability for debts is an advantage when the sole proprietor needs credit, since creditors are more willing to lend money to an individual whose personal property can be attached in the event of business failure. In one very important way, however, unlimited liability is a major disadvantage. Should the sole proprietor fail, he may lose virtually all his personal savings and possessions. This risk discourages many people from going into business for themselves and often prompts those who do establish a sole proprietorship to change it to some type of entity with limited liability.

Lack of specialized management   Typically, the sole proprietor performs all the managerial functions in the business. More often than not he serves simultaneously as general manager, sales manager, advertising manager, accountant, personnel manager, and purchasing agent. Few people are qualified by training, personality, intelligence, and inclination to perform all these tasks effectively. As a result, one or more phases of the business operation suffers or is neglected. Managerial assistance from employees is usually limited, since employees with specialized skills or those with managerial talents tend not to take jobs in businesses that have limited opportunities for advancement.

Operational disadvantages   Because of the difficulty of acquiring capital, certain operational problems are usually more acute in sole proprietorships than in other forms of business ownership. Some of them are: poor location and inadequate buildings and equipment; inability to pay wages that attract the most productive, ambitious employees; and inability to purchase merchandise in large enough volume to secure quantity discounts.

Conditions favoring sole proprietorship

The preceding review of advantages and disadvantages of the sole proprietorship suggests that this form of organization is best only for a business that (1) does not require a large amount of capital for efficient operation, (2) can be operated and managed by one person or a family, (3) does not involve a complicated and widely dispersed organization, and (4) *does* involve personal contact of the proprietor with the public. If all these conditions are not present, it is probably wise for the entrepreneur to investigate some other form of business ownership.

The sole proprietorship has special appeal when a business is just beginning—when flexibility, hard work, and a great deal of personal attention are especially important. Thus, it is often the best form of organization during the early, experimental period. Then, as the sole proprietorship proves itself, it can be discarded in favor of a form of business ownership (such as the corporation) more suitable for expansion.

GENERAL PARTNERSHIP

A *general partnership* is an association of two or more persons as co-owners of a business for profit. Most partnerships have only two or three members, although there is no limit to the number of individuals who can form a partnership. While the members of a partnership may agree to divide profits and losses in any manner they like, in the absence of a specific agreement they are presumed to share them equally. Nor is it essential that each partner contributes an equal amount of capital. In some instances, a partner contributes no capital but is brought into the organization because of his skill or specialized knowledge. Partnerships, like sole proprietorships, are found primarily in retailing, agriculture, and services such as law, accounting, and medicine. The partnership has not proved to be well suited to large businesses.

Advantages of general partnership

Financial strength   Compared with the sole proprietorship, the partnership is normally stronger financially because (1) two or more persons are usually able to invest more money in a business than is one person, and (2) the personal property and other wealth of every partner (unless a partner's liability is specifically limited in the agreement) is subject to attachment should the partnership be unable to meet its obligations.

Additional managerial skill   One of the chief weaknesses of the sole proprietorship is that the owner is solely responsible for all managerial duties, some of which he may be poorly qualified to perform. In a partnership, managerial functions can be shared. Often partnerships pool the talents of persons with contrasting skills and abilities. For example, one partner may be an expert accountant and purchasing manager, while the other may be well qualified in marketing. Division of duties in accordance with the special qualifications of each partner helps to build a more efficient organization.

Simplicity of organization   Partnerships are only slightly more difficult to organize than sole proprietorships. Essentially, all that is needed is an agreement between the partners. While legal aid is desirable in preparing such an agreement, it is not mandatory. State approval is not required, and usually no taxes are levied specifically against the partnership. Dissolving the partnership is also simple.

Personal incentive   The partnership also retains much of the individual incentive found in the sole proprietorship. What is beneficial to the partnership is obviously also beneficial to each partner.

Disadvantages of general partnership

Unlimited liability of partners   The primary disadvantage of a general partnership is the unlimited liability of each partner. Unless limited by agreement, each partner is liable for the partnership's total debts, regardless of the size of his investment. Usually, if the partnership fails, each partner assumes a loss in proportion to his share of the investment. But if one partner lacks the personal wealth to assume his full share of the loss, the other partners are required to make good the deficit.

Divided authority   The fact that each partner has a voice in the management of the business has disadvantages. The possibility of disagreements means that decisions are often more difficult to reach. The division of authority in a partnership is sometimes confusing to other business organizations, which may not be sure who the dominant partner is. Employees, too, sometimes become confused about who the boss is in a partnership. Also, because any one partner can act on behalf of the business, there is the danger that private commitments will be made by one partner without the sanction of the others.

Possibility of mutual distrust   A third disadvantage, which stems from the two above, is that a very high degree of mutual respect among partners is necessary for a partnership to function smoothly. A major mistake by any one partner can destroy the personal fortunes of the others. Unless all persons involved have full confidence in one another's honesty and business ability, a feeling of uneasiness results.

Lack of permanence   The partnership is the least permanent form of business. The death or withdrawal of a partner terminates the partnership; the remaining partners may reorganize and form a new partnership, sole proprietorship, or corporation, but in practice this is not usually done. In many cases, the remaining partner or partners lack the financial resources to buy the deceased or withdrawing partner's interest. This uncertain life, makes it difficult for the partnership to make long-term commitments to other businesses.

The partnership agreement

Fundamental to all partnerships is an agreement among the members. This agreement may be oral, written, or implied by actions of the parties. It is preferable that the agreement be written, to avoid later misunderstandings, but an oral or implied agreement can be binding. The partnership agreement should include the following items:

1. Name of the firm and name of each partner
2. Kind of business to be conducted and its location
3. Authority held by each partner
4. Duration of the partnership agreement
5. Amount of money invested by each partner
6. Description of how profits and losses are to be divided
7. Manner in which each partner is to be compensated
8. Limitation on the amount of money that can be withdrawn by a partner
9. Statement of accounting procedures to be followed
10. Procedure for admitting new partners
11. Procedure for dissolving the partnership
12. Signature to the agreement

LIMITED PARTNERSHIP

A *limited partnership* is an agreement between one or more general partners whose liability (financial obligation) is unlimited and one or more special, or limited, partners whose liability is limited to the amount of capital they have contributed to the firm unless otherwise stated in the agreement. The limited partnership is not handicapped by the unlimited liability of all the partners. A formal agreement is always required in the formation of a limited partnership. This agreement must be filed with an appropriate public official — usually the county clerk — and must specify who the general partners are and who the limited partners are. It is impossible to form a limited partnership without at least one general partner. Moreover, not all states provide for this form of business organization.

Limited partners are not permitted to exercise any managerial functions. If they do, the courts recognize them as general partners, and their liability becomes unlimited. Further, if a limited partnership wishes to do business in another state, it must comply with the statutes of that state or the limited partners will be considered general partners there.

The major advantage of the limited partnership is that it tends to attract to the partnership individuals who can contribute capital. As limited partners, they risk only their original investment. Thus, the limited partnership attracts people who want to invest but do not want to participate actively in the management of the business. Occasionally, an elderly general partner will become a limited partner on retirement, thus preserving his interest in the enterprise.

The main use of the limited partnership is that it is a means of acquiring capital. Many oil exploration companies and real estate development firms, which involve considerable risk, sell limited partnerships, usually in units of $5,000. In this way, investors can become limited partners in speculative activities with a fixed potential loss equal to the amount of their investment. Despite the apparent desirability of the limited partnership, it is not extensively used in retailing or manufacturing companies.

CORPORATIONS

The most widely accepted definition of a *corporation* is that given by Chief Justice John Marshall in 1819: "A *corporation* is an artificial being, invisible, intangible, and existing only in the contemplation of law. Being the mere creature of law, it possesses only those properties which the charter of its creation confers upon it, either expressly or as incidental to its existence."[1]

The corporation is thus a legal entity and is granted many of the same rights as individuals. These include the right to own, mortgage, and dispose of property; the right to manage its own affairs; and the right to sue. Like an individual, the corporation may also be sued.

A business corporation may apply for a charter to conduct almost any activity that produces or distributes goods or renders service. Individuals desiring to form a corporation apply for a state charter, which spells out in some detail the rights and privileges of the corporation. The corporation has continuous life for the period specified in its charter (usually 35 years) or, if no limit is indicated, for perpetuity.

Corporations comprise a relatively small percentage of the total number of business establishments; yet, the 200 largest were responsible for 60.4 percent of all business transacted in the United States in 1970. While all corporations are not big businesses, practically all big businesses are corporations.**

Profit and nonprofit corporations

Not all corporations are organized for profit. Because of the limited liability of the owners or investors (see page 99), the corporate form of organization has proved useful for government agencies, cities, towns, political subdivisions, and many charitable, religious, and educational institutions. In the discussion that follows, emphasis is placed on profit, or business, corporations.

---

[1] *Dartmouth College* v. *Woodward*, 4 Wheaton 518 (1819).

SPECIAL READINGS

** Big Business: A Positive View, by Elwood N. Chapman. Englewood Cliffs, N.J.: Prentice Hall, 1972 (paperback). Professor Chapman begins his book with this cogent observation. "Regardless of your present attitude toward the big corporations, there is no question about their importance." He points out that corporations employ more than five out of every ten graduates from our high schools and colleges and that corporations are the pillars of our production and distribution system.

Several of the books in this special readings feature dwell on the negative side of the large corporation. This suggested book helps to balance the scale, as it examines the positive side, which unfortunately is less likely to be reported. Scandal and exposé reporting is far more commonly treated because it is felt to hold more human interest.

The above book is definitely directed to students. After examining the whole idea of large corporations, it focuses attention on the problem of selecting the right company for career purposes. It asks and answers questions that students are concerned with: Are employees overregimented? Can they live in harmony with their personal values? What about the corporation's profit hang-up?

Written in a lively and contemporary style, it offers several self-tests by means of which students can match their abilities and temperaments with what large corporations seek in employees. It is generously laced with quotations from younger people who now work for large corporations. There are numerous role-playing situations and decision-making choices that enable the reader to step into a big corporation environment.

Open and close corporations

If its stock is offered for sale to the general public, the corporation is known as an *open* or public corporation. If stock is not offered for sale to the public, it is called a *close* corporation. Many businesses begin as close corporations with only a few stockholders, each of whom is active in the management of the business. Then, as the business shows promise of success and additional capital is needed, the corporation may decide to "go public" by selling shares to other investors. Practically all large corporations are open, since it is generally advantageous to a corporation for its stock, or shares, to be widely owned.

Advantages of corporations

Limited liability of owners   A very serious weakness of the sole proprietorship and the general partnership is that the owners' personal wealth can be attached should the business incur debts it cannot meet. This disadvantage is eliminated under the corporate form of organization. Owners of a corporation, called *stockholders* or *shareholders*, can, in most cases, lose no more than the value of their investment. Thus, if an individual purchases a $100 share in a corporation that subsequently fails, the most that individual can lose is $100. (An exception to this may be in the

Table **4–1**
The 50 Largest Industrial Corporations (Ranked by Sales)

RANK 1972	RANK 1971	COMPANY	SALES ($000)	NET INCOME ($000)	RANK
1	1	General Motors (Detroit)	30,435,231	2,162,807	1
2	2	Exxon (New York)	20,309,753	1,531,770	2
3	3	Ford Motor (Dearborn, Mich.)	20,194,400	870,000	5
4	4	General Electric (New York)	10,239,500	530,000	9
5	7	Chrysler (Detroit)	9,759,129	220,455	19
6	5	International Business Machines (Armonk, N.Y.)	9,532,593	1,279,268	3
7	6	Mobil Oil (New York)	9,166,332	574,199	6
8	8	Texaco (New York)	8,692,991	889,040	4
9	9	International Tel. & Tel. (New York)	8,556,826	483,303	10
10	10	Western Electric (New York)	6,551,183	282,941	13
11	11	Gulf Oil (Pittsburgh)	6,243,000	197,000	24
12	12	Standard Oil of California (San Francisco)	5,829,487	547,070	7
13	13	U.S. Steel (New York)	5,401,773	156,988	33
14	14	Westinghouse Electric (Pittsburgh)	5,086,621	198,667	23
15	15	Standard Oil (Ind.) (Chicago)	4,503,372	374,740	12
16	17	E. I. Du Pont de Nemours (Wilmington, Del.)	4,365,900	414,500	11
17	16	Shell Oil (Houston)	4,075,898*	260,480	15
18	19	Goodyear Tire & Rubber (Akron, Ohio)	4,071,523	193,159	26
19	18	RCA (New York)	3,838,180	158,104	32
20	21	Procter & Gamble (Cincinnati)	3,514,438	276,310	14
21	20	LTV (Dallas)	3,514,181	8,838	385
22	26	International Harvester (Chicago)	3,493,274	86,554	60
23	28	Eastman Kodak (Rochester, N.Y.)	3,477,764	546,250	8
24	23	Continental Oil (Stamford, Conn.)	3,414,984	170,181	30
25	22	Atlantic Richfield (Los Angeles)	3,320,793	195,561	25
26	32	Tenneco (Houston)	3,275,411	203,017	22
27	25	Union Carbide (New York)	3,261,322	205,241	21
28	27	Swift (Chicago)	3,240,931	37,003	172
29	30	Kraftco (Glenview, Ill.)	3,196,789	88,335	56
30	29	Bethlehem Steel (Bethlehem, Pa.)	3,113,602	134,584	38
31	33	Greyhound (Phoenix)[18]	2,903,607	66,848	90
32	45	McDonnell Douglas (St. Louis)	2,725,684	111,675	51
33	34	Firestone Tire & Rubber (Akron, Ohio)	2,690,957	135,773	37
34	40	Caterpillar Tractor (Peoria, Ill.)	2,602,178	206,445	20
35	35	Litton Industries (Beverly Hills)	2,558,456	1,118	466
36	37	Phillips Petroleum (Bartlesville, Okla.)	2,512,742	148,428	35
37	36	Occidental Petroleum (Los Angeles)	2,487,247	10,419	367
38	31	Lockheed Aircraft (Burbank, Calif.)	2,472,732	16,211	300
39	38	General Foods (White Plains, N.Y.)	2,423,816	66,185	92
40	52	Xerox (Stamford, Conn.)	2,419,103	249,507	16
41	46	Dow Chemical (Midland, Mich.)	2,403,709	189,189	28
42	53	Beatrice Foods (Chicago)	2,384,410	77,944	71
43	24	Boeing (Seattle)	2,369,580	30,405	194
44	39	North American Rockwell (El Segundo, Calif.)	2,362,938	86,083	61
45	47	W. R. Grace (New York)	2,315,144	63,471	98
46	42	Monsanto (St. Louis)	2,225,400	122,000	46
47	41	Singer (New York)	2,217,500	87,500	58
48	44	Borden (New York)	2,192,919	65,992	94
49	43	Continental Can (New York)	2,192,672	(39,293)	485
50	53	Honeywell (Minneapolis)	2,125,445	82,327	65

Source: *Fortune*, May 9, 1973, p. 222.

case of bank stocks, where liability can be twice as much as the amount invested.) Creditors of the corporation can acquire the assets of the corporation but cannot claim the assets of the stockholders.

Transfer of ownership is easy   A second important advantage of the corporation is the ease with which ownership can be transferred. Organized markets for corporate securities, called *stock exchanges* (such as the New York Stock Exchange and the American Stock Exchange), enable the stockholder to sell his shares or buy additional shares quickly and simply. In addition, there are over-the-counter markets that deal in shares of thousands of relatively small corporations. In cases of stocks listed on exchanges, it is necessary merely to place an order with a stockbroker, who completes the buying or selling transaction in a matter of minutes. Millions of shares of stock are sold daily. This ease of ownership transfer contrasts sharply with the difficulty often experienced by the sole proprietor or general partner who wishes to dispose of his interests. It should be noted, however, that many close corporations do not have sufficiently widespread ownership to make an active market in their shares. In such cases, disposal of stock is not always easy.

Continuous life   Corporations can be dissolved in only four ways: (1) by court order—for example, when the business goes bankrupt or engages in illegal activity; (2) by the approval of the owners of a majority of the shares; (3) by the expiration of the corporate charter; or (4) by the state, which may revoke the charter for nonuse or misuse of its franchises and powers. Generally, however, courts are reluctant to revoke a charter unless it can be proved beyond question that the public interest is adversely affected by the corporation's activities. Corporations are rarely dissolved. The third proviso above is only a legal formality in most cases, since corporate charters are easily renewed. For all practical purposes, corporations have perpetual life.

The death of a stockholder in no way affects the life of the corporation as it does the sole proprietorship or partnership. When a stockholder dies, his stock passes on to his heirs in the same manner as other assets that make up his estate.

Ability to acquire capital   The corporation usually can acquire capital more readily than any other form of business organization. Several reasons for this—limited liability of owners, ease of transferring ownership, and permanent life of the corporation—have already been noted. Two additional factors make the acquisition of capital relatively simple. First, shares of ownership generally have a relatively small dollar value. Most stocks, when first issued, sell for less than $20. This feature attracts many people of average and even below-average income who want to invest in a business but find it difficult to raise the larger amounts of money usually required for sole proprietorship or general partnership. Second, corporations can issue different types of stock (preferred and common stock, discussed in Chapter 8) that appeal to different types of investors.

Specialized management Because corporations are generally larger than sole proprietorships or partnerships, they can be staffed with specialists to a much greater extent. In a sole proprietorship and partnership, one or a few individuals must perform all managerial functions; in the corporation, experts can be placed in charge of production, marketing, finance, accounting, research, and other functions.

Disadvantages of corporations

Cost and difficulty of organization It is technically more difficult to organize a corporation than either a sole proprietorship or a partnership. Since state approval is mandatory for incorporation, legal aid is necessary in the formation of a corporation. While legal fees may be small for setting up a simple type of corporation, they may run to thousands of dollars if the corporation is large. Certain state fees or taxes must be paid at the time of incorporation. In some cases, several weeks or even months may elapse before the corporation is formally organized. The costly legal procedures and time involved undoubtedly deter many small businesses from incorporating.

Legal restrictions on business activities The corporation is permitted to engage in only those activities stated or implied in its charter. If a business incorporated to *sell* paint and related products should later decide to *manufacture* these products as well, an amendment to the corporation charter would be required. While amending a corporate charter is usually a relatively simple process, state approval must be obtained and certain legal expenses met. To compensate, at least in part, for this limitation, lawyers are careful to define the purposes of the corporation as broadly as possible in the original charter.

Taxation The most important disadvantage of the corporation is that it must pay a federal income tax, in much the same manner as an individual. This results in "double taxation" of corporation income. First, the net profits are taxed, and, second, that portion of the profits distributed to individuals is subject to the individual income tax. Neither the sole proprietorship nor the partnership must pay the federal income tax. The practice of double taxation on corporations has been severely criticized, usually by those who receive income from dividends.

In addition, many states levy an annual franchise tax[2] on all corporations doing business within the state. A corporation doing business in many states may be required to pay a franchise tax in each state.

Lack of personal interest of owners and employees   Many corporations have thousands of owners, most of whom own a very small part of the business. These small shareholders have little interest in the management of the business. Many small investors owning shares in large corporations do not even know the names of the company president and the other corporate officers. Their interest is confined to two questions: first, will the company pay dividends and how much will they be, and, second, will the stock increase in value?

As a result of lack of owner interest, corporations sometimes come under the control of self-perpetuating hired management who have only a small ownership interest in the business. The impersonal character of the corporation also may cause employees to feel less responsible and less loyal to their company than they normally would in a proprietorship or partnership.

Other disadvantages

1. Corporations are required to submit various reports to state and federal authorities at regular intervals.

2. Before a corporation can establish a branch business in a state other than the one in which it is organized, approval by that state may be required.[3]

3. Business details in a corporation are more difficult to keep private because of legal requirements that certain records be kept and disclosures be made in order to sell stock.

4. Corporations are difficult and costly to dissolve.

ORGANIZATION OF THE CORPORATION

Choice of state

After the decision to form a corporation has been made, the next step is to select the state in which to incorporate. If a small corporation expects to

---

[2] Legally, a franchise is a privilege granted by a sovereign power. A franchise tax is levied by a state on corporations for the privilege of operating as a corporation in that state.
[3] What constitutes a branch business varies from state to state.

operate primarily in one state it is convenient and advantageous to incorporate in that state. If the undertaking is large and business is to be transacted nationwide, it is wise to compare the relative advantages and disadvantages of incorporating in various states. State laws differ widely as to taxes, types of stock that can be issued, restrictions on corporate debt, restrictions on the kinds of business that can be transacted, and the breadth of power granted to corporations.

Corporation charter

The incorporators must submit a written application to the appropriate state official, usually the secretary of state. When approved, the application is recorded and filed; it then serves as the corporation charter, or certificate of incorporation. The charter becomes a three-way contract: between the state and the stockholders, between the stockholders and the corporation, and between the incorporators and the state. Ordinarily, the charter contains the following information:

1. Name and address(es) of the proposed corporation
2. Names and addresses of the incorporators and directors
3. Purposes for which the corporation is formed
4. Amount and kind of capital stock to be authorized
5. Privileges and voting powers of each kind of stock
6. Duration of the life of the corporation

Board of directors

The chief governing body of the corporation is the board of directors, elected by the stockholders, with a minimum of three directors. Some states require that each director own stock in the corporation, but ownership of a single share usually satisfies this requirement. In small corporations, though, the board of directors is usually composed of the chief stockholders.

Directors are in a position of great trust and may be held personally liable to the stockholders for fraud, gross negligence, or use of the corporation for personal gain to the detriment of the firm. They cannot be held liable for honest mistakes in business judgment.

New directors in a corporation are proposed by the present directors, not necessarily for their knowledge of the details of the business, but for their specialized business experience and for their integrity, vision, philosophy. They are often successful people of widely different backgrounds in fields such as law, finance, and accounting. It would be not unusual, for example, for a major retailing executive to be asked to serve on the board of directors of a carpet manufacturing company. The question of how much prestige the individual will lend to the corporation also enters into the selection of corporate directors.

The board of directors is responsible for the following major activities.

1. Appointing corporate officers.   Directors of the corporation are responsible for the appointment of a president, secretary, treasurer, and other executive officers who will handle the actual details of management. The board often elects some of its own members to fill these posts.

2. Making major policy decisions.   The board of directors decides such fundamental business questions as: Should the business be expanded? Should another plant be purchased? Should the product line be changed? The *implementation* of major policy decisions, however, is a function of the corporation officers, not the board.

3. Declaring dividends.   The board of directors has sole responsibility for the declaration of dividends. The basic decision about a dividend involves allied decisions, such as what percentage of the year's earnings should be retained for company use and whether the dividend should be paid in cash or in stock.

4. Other duties.   Additional duties of the board of directors are financial planning, authorizing unusual business expenditures or transactions, and calling special meetings of stockholders when deemed necessary.

Officers

Officers of the corporation are responsible to the board of directors for carrying out business policies. The essential corporate officers and their duties are usually defined by law. A typical state statute generally stipulates that every corporation organized in the state shall have a president (chief executive officer of the corporation), a secretary (recording officer), and a treasurer (chief financial officer). In addition to the legally prescribed officers, the board of directors may appoint an executive vice-president and a number of additional vice-presidents who are responsible for various divisions or functions of the business.

CONTROL OF THE CORPORATION

Separate ownership and management

In a sole proprietorship or general partnership, the owners of the business are usually also its managers. In a corporation, on the other hand, the owners (stockholders) usually exercise only indirect control over the actual management of the firm. They elect a board of directors, which is responsible for making basic policy decisions for the business and providing for competent management. In addition, they vote on major issues such as stock splits and compensation plans for top management.

One should note, however, that in a very small corporation or in a large corporation owned by a single family, the owners do exercise close control over the management of the corporation. In such cases, the principal stockholders commonly elect themselves to the board of directors and then appoint themselves to key executive positions.

Powers of stockholders

Corporation stockholders tend to meet annually for the purpose of electing a board of directors. In the election of each director, a stockholder usually has the right to cast one vote for each share of stock he owns. Thus, if a stockholder owns ten shares and there are five directors to be elected, the stockholder can cast ten votes for each directorship, or fifty votes.

To give minority stockholders some power, a single stockholder is sometimes allowed to cast all his votes for one director, so that, in the example cited, all fifty votes could be cast for a single director. While grouping of minority votes is seemingly a very democratic procedure, in actual practice the individual stockholder exercises very little power in choosing directors and in voting on major issues. This is true for two reasons:

First, most stockholders in a large corporation own only a small amount of stock, and their vote is therefore too small to be significant.

Second, many stockholders are indifferent toward the corporation's management. If they do vote, they usually give rubber-stamp approval to the recommendations of the entrenched management because they feel it knows most about the business. The average stockholder is more concerned with the profits made by the corporation than with the individuals who direct it. When he has reason to believe that the corporation is slowing down or losing money, his first inclination is to sell his stock rather than to try to influence management in any way.

In addition to electing directors, stockholders have the right to receive dividends when declared, to inspect corporation records, to vote on amendments to the bylaws and amendments to the corporation charter, and to share in the assets of the corporation on its dissolution.

The proxy

A *proxy* is a legal statement by which a stockholder transfers to someone else the right to cast his votes. When stockholders are notified of a forthcoming meeting, they are given a proxy, sometimes called "management's proxy," since, if signed and returned, it authorizes the existing management to, in effect, vote for itself. Such proxies are prepared and distributed by existing management at the expense of the corporation.

Proxies are used because it is impractical to expect more than a handful of stockholders (usually only a fraction of 1 percent for large corporations) to attend stockholders' meetings.

Sometimes a group of larger stockholders becomes dissatisfied with the existing management and attempts to gain control by asking fellow stockholders for their proxies. Business history contains interesting stories of bitter "proxy wars" that have been fought for control of corporations.

OTHER FORMS OF OWNERSHIP

While the forms of ownership discussed above are the major ones in the United States, there are several other types that warrant mention. The most important of these is the *cooperative*. The cooperative operates on simple socialistic principles with the primary aim of rendering a service to its members rather than earning a profit. Farmers' cooperatives are the most common. They are either retail cooperatives that sell fertilizers, seeds, and other farm materials to members or producer cooperatives that buy what the farmers produce.

Capital is raised by selling shares to people who become members of the cooperative and use its services. Interest is paid on money invested in shares. Earnings, if any, are returned to the members as a rebate on their purchases rather than being retained as profits. Each member of the cooperative has one vote, regardless of how many ownership shares he may have purchased.

Cooperatives have not been notably successful in this country, chiefly because of their inability to compete successfully with more efficiently operated profit-making organizations. However, there are some exceptions to this generalization, such as the Sunkist Growers, Inc., and the Land O'Lakes Creameries, Inc. Incorporation by special charter is commonly allowed and in some instances is required. Cooperatives have experienced most success in rural and agricultural areas.

There are still other forms of ownership arrangement, such as trusts, joint-stock companies, authorities, and variations in forms of partnership, but they are not widespread and tend to be highly technical. More detailed information on the provisions and purposes of all forms of ownership, a complicated matter at best, can be found by consulting standard library references.

PEOPLE AND THEIR IDEAS
Robert Chase Townsend

"when the system is fair, it will be more efficient"

Robert Chase Townsend was born in Washington, D. C., in 1920. He attended Princeton University, where he majored in English, minored in French, and received his B.A. degree in 1942. He saw action as a Navy gunnery officer in the Pacific during World War II.

After the war Townsend furthered his education at Columbia University, taking graduate courses in business administration while he worked for a Wall Street brokerage firm. For fourteen years, beginning in 1948, he was with the American Express Company, as director of Hertz American Express International, Ltd., and, later, as senior vice-president in charge of the company's investment and international banking operations.

Townsend left American Express in 1962 to become President and Chairman of the Board of Avis. Avis had been a distant runner-up to Hertz and had been floundering in the car rental field for thirteen years. In 1962 alone it lost about $3,000,000. The directors of Avis wanted to pay Townsend $50,000 a year but Townsend insisted that his salary be not more than $36,000 "because that's top salary for a company that has never earned a nickel for its stockholders."

Avis staged a brilliant recovery under Townsend's leadership. After firing the company's advertising department and ad agency, Townsend turned the account over to Doyle Dane Bernbach, then leader in Madison Avenue's trend toward imaginative but low-pressure and basically honest advertising, with the understanding that no one at Avis would be allowed to tamper with their work. Doyle Dane Bernbach invented the slogan, "When you're only number two, you try harder," and within three years the company's sales growth rate increased from 10 to 35 percent, and its ledger began to show a profit ($2.8 million in 1965). The ultimate testimonial to the advertising campaign's success was reference to it in retaliatory Hertz ads.

Townsend resigned in 1965 on the day AVIS was acquired by the International Telephone and Telegraph Company. His resignation was prompted, first, by his belief that no chief executive should serve more than 5 or 6 years because by then he is stale and bored and, second, by his antipathy toward conglomerates.

Townsend's book *Up the Organization* is summarized by William A. McWhirter. "His view is that business has swollen into a pompous, posturing, self-perpetuating fraternity at the top, layers like frosting of executive vice-presidents spilling down over senior vice-presidents and vice-presidents over assistant vice-presidents over assistants to vice-presidents. The positions, Townsend says, have largely been created to save feelings and salaries of men who no longer serve any function within a company, but this form of corporate benevolence at the top has resulted only in memos flowing from decorated offices along with costly make-work projects concocted in the executive suites. Townsend feels that life inside these places has become fraudulent, wasteful, and, in a term he uses frequently and feels deeply, 'soul-destroying.' Townsend insists . . . that when the system is fair it will become more efficient."

CONTEMPORARY ISSUES
Situation 4

Should huge corporations be broken up?

Ray and John acquired a copy of *Fortune* magazine's directory of the five hundred leading industrial corporations, which provides extensive data on corporate assets, sales, and profits.

"It seems to me," commented Ray, "that entirely too many economic resources are concentrated in too few companies. Just imagine the economic power these companies have. I'm amazed that any small business survives."

"There's no doubt about it," agreed John. "A lot of power is concentrated in relatively few business organizations, and I think this is good. Big business can spend more on research and development. If you're going to have mass production and mass distribution, then you must have giant businesses. You can't construct a jet airliner in your garage."

"Yes, but these five hundred corporations are so big that they can stifle competition, and you know how vital competition is in our type of economy," Ray argued.

"But don't you agree," asked John, "that the fact that these companies grew so big proves they're efficient and successful competitors? If one pro-football team wins several superbowls in a row, are you going to break it up to give other teams a chance? Read the list carefully. You'll see that not one of the companies has a monopoly. Consider just two of them—General Motors and Ford. Can you visualize any other two companies of any size competing more fiercely?"

"I still say," contended Ray, "that these businesses are too big. They make it almost impossible for small businesses to get started, let alone survive. And those giants are able to exercise monopoly power over our economy. If we don't watch out, we'll be in real trouble."

"Perhaps we both have tunnel vision. I guess a good case could be made that we need *both* big businesses and small businesses," replied John.

SITUATION EVALUATION

1. Does the existence of mammoth corporations in fact make it difficult for small businesses to get started and succeed?

2. Assume it were desirable to "break up" some of our giant corporations. How could this be accomplished?

3. Is it likely that the number of billion dollar corporations will continue to increase in this decade? Explain why or why not.

4. Is bigness in itself bad? What are the arguments in favor of bigness?

BUSINESS CHRONICLE

Forming businesses to accomplish objectives

Allan King was interested in what he called a "total systems" approach to business. He felt that his enterprise should try to meet the needs of those who invest and live in his company's communities. King provided for more community needs by undertaking new ventures. Starting different business activities is always risky. A wrong decision about a new venture can bankrupt even a sound company. Last year, the directors of Kingmaker Estates decided to expand into the rental field by establishing Rent Anything, Inc., a separate corporation, owned entirely by the parent company. In this way, if the venture failed, only the venture capital of the subsidiary would be risked. The assets and credit rating of the parent company would not be jeopardized.

Rent Anything, Inc., was doing well. It was already well established and making a profit. One reason Rent Anything prospered so quickly was that Kingmaker Estates sold all of its equipment (bulldozers, road graders, etc.) to Rent Anything on a lease-back arrangement. Kingmaker was now paying Rent Anything monthly rent on equipment they once owned. There were certain tax advantages because rent became a cost of doing business and Kingmaker was freed from having capital tied up in equipment.

Allan King felt another subsidiary company should be established in a similar fashion. He proposed Service All, Inc., a company to provide intangibles for those who live in the property developments (for example, maid and house-cleaning services, baby sitters, pest control, lawn and tree services, and so on).

One of the directors suggested that Rent Anything should not expand into these new fields. His feeling was that too many subsidiaries would complicate matters and add unnecessarily to executive and other overhead. Another director felt differently. He reasoned that a separate corporation would establish a separate profit center and would more clearly fix responsibility for those in charge of the new venture. The new company would sink or swim on its own and hopefully would build a stronger management team.

QUESTIONS

1. What does the formation of separate companies accomplish?

2. What are the pro and con considerations in the new company proposals?

3. It is said that such organizational arrangements (establishing separate companies) preserve the advantages of the private entrepreneur. Discuss how this may be true.

APPLICATION EXERCISES

1. Traditionally, physicians, dentists, lawyers and other professionals have organized their practices as sole proprietorships or partnerships. Recently there has been a trend toward incorporation by professionals. The Tax Reform Act of 1969 included a provision that corporations organized by professionals would be treated tax wise the same as other corporations. In a brief paper explain, in addition to possible tax savings, what other reasons might justify incorporating by professionals.

2. Based on library research (you may want to consult legal references), prepare a paper in which you explain the procedure that must be followed to dissolve a business corporation in your state. To what extent is the dissolution procedure a factor in deciding which form of ownership to use? Is a corporation more difficult to dissolve than a sole proprietorship? Explain.

3. A frequent criticism of tax policy in the United States is that profits earned by corporations are taxed twice. First, the corporation itself must pay taxes on profits earned. Second, that portion of after-tax profit which is paid as dividends is also taxed to the shareholder.

In a brief report, explain whether or not you feel this procedure is fair since profits earned by sole proprietorship or partnerships are taxed only once as ordinary income.

QUESTIONS

1. Why are most small businesses sole proprietorships?

2. Suppose that you, as the sole proprietor of a clothing store, were considering formation of a partnership. What personal characteristics would you look for in a partner?

3. What are the provisions usually found in a partnership agreement?

4. How does a limited partnership differ from a general partnership?

5. Why are practically all large businesses organized as corporations?

6. What are the advantages and disadvantages of (1) the sole proprietorship, (2) the general partnership, and (3) the corporation?

7. If you were establishing a small corporation, what kind of specialists would you appoint to the board of directors? Discuss.

8. Experienced business managers, who are desirable employees, view companies differently, depending on the manner in which they are organized. How might a sole proprietorship, partnership, and corporation attempt to appeal to high-caliber potential management employees? How would the appeals they might use to attract good managers differ?

small business, services, and franchising 5

CHAPTER 5

THE VALUE SYSTEM OF THE ENTREPRENEUR

SMALL BUSINESS: WHAT IT IS AND DOES
What Is Small Business? Small Business Facilitates Big Business. Characteristics of Small Business. Small Business and Opportunity. Small Business and Creativity.

CONDITIONS CONDUCIVE TO SMALL BUSINESS

OPERATING ADVANTAGES OF SMALL BUSINESS
Independence of Action. Adaptability to Local Needs. Public Favor. Lower Operating Costs.

OPERATING DISADVANTAGES OF SMALL BUSINESS
Difficulty in Attracting Employees. Lack of Specialized Management. Incompetent Management. Personal Disadvantages. Financial Difficulties. Sensitivity to Economic Fluctuations.

CAUSES OF SMALL BUSINESS FAILURE

SERVICE BUSINESSES
Characteristics of Service Establishments. Development of Service Industries. The Future of Services in Our Economy.

FRANCHISING
How a Franchise System Functions. Contractual Arrangements. An Evaluation of Franchising.

AID FOR SMALL BUSINESS
The Small Business Administration. Other Sources of Assistance.

Many young men and women dream of eventually owning their own businesses. For thousands, this dream comes true. Although "big business" makes most headlines, a close examination shows that "small business" is also extremely important in our society.

Most of today's big businesses started from humble beginnings — from the dreams and dedication of perhaps one person. Nor is this growth phenomenon something that was possible only in the far-distant past. The founders of several of America's top corporations are still active in the corporations they started — Dr. Edwin C. Land, founder of the Polaroid Corporation, and Norton Simon, founder of the company that bears his name, are two outstanding examples.

While the backbone of our economic system is big business — automobile manufacturers, steel companies, airlines, and similar organizations of necessity are big — small business constitutes the muscles that enable big business to move. For example, Lockheed, which obtained a multibillion dollar contract to build the C5 airplane, in turn subcontracted a large part of this business to small firms. Western Electric purchases goods and services from more than forty thousand businesses and requests price quotations from more than 120,000 qualified companies in a single year.

It is obvious, however, that small business cannot compete directly with big business. The independent food store that tries to imitate an operation like A & P is doomed to fail. Experience shows that the small businessman is most successful when he fills a need that cannot be, or is not currently being, supplied by his big-business competitor. This seeking to provide something better or different gives American business vitality.

Our business history is full of small business success stories—Leon Hess, Chief Executive Officer of Amerada Hess Corporation, O. J. Rollins, founder of Rollins, Inc., Abe Plough, founder of Plough, Inc., and Kemmons Wilson, who established Holiday Inns, are examples of contemporary business leaders who started small businesses that grew into giant organizations. Coca-Cola got its start in 1886, when John S. Pemberton, a pharmacist, lighted a fire under a cast-iron pot to brew a batch of syrup that included extracts from coca leaves and kola nuts. A friend, F. M. Robinson, a bookkeeper, tasted the results and gave the drink its name. And so, in the American tradition, from a humble start a mammoth business grew.

There are two ways for the ambitious to work to the top in the business world: by advancing through the ranks of an established company or by starting their own enterprise. To the rugged individualist, small business is the more attractive way, because it allows greater independence and freedom of action. It is an arena for those who thrive on challenge and enjoy taking risks.

THE VALUE SYSTEM OF THE ENTREPRENEUR

Much of American history is the story of entrepreneurs—people who possess a pioneer spirit and believe in self-help and hard work. The word *entrepreneur* indicates an individual who organizes, owns, manages, and assumes the risks of a business. The entrepreneur is the center of initiative in American society.

Our birthright is that it is possible for any man or woman to invent something, try something new, or do something old in a better way. Someone has said, "Every generation produces people who seek after new lamps, and some are as fortunate as Aladdin."

What factors in the environment produce the entrepreneur? Certainly, discontent or dissatisfaction is an essential factor. Because discontent is at the root of innovation, some people believe that the United States stands at the threshold of a renaissance. Discontent can be constructive because it prompts people to search for better ways for doing things.

The entrepreneur is a pioneer, one who begins or helps develop something new and prepares a way for others to follow. This entrepreneural spirit was expressed by the explorer Charles S. Miller in "Cannibal Caravan": "It was my intention to press on to the snow line. Not that I had any particular business up there, but it is one of the rules of the explorer to go where you have no particular business to be."[1]

Entrepreneurs vary on many factors. They may be of either sex or any color; have any religion; be short or tall, young or old, fat or skinny; be Democrats or Republicans. But all entrepreneurs seem to have two things in common: *initiative* and *inspiration*.

Initiative is doing something without being told; the entrepreneur is a self-starter. Of course, initiative must be constructive if it is to lead to a successful end. To break out of the rut, the entrepreneur must investigate, plan, experiment, and work.

Inspiration, the creative idea, is not as spontaneous as some fables would have us believe. The person aspiring to become an entrepreneur must saturate his mind with knowledge, for we cannot discover or create except by going from the known to the unknown. History is full of examples of people who made a chance observation that lead to something important. However, such observers had mastered their field so completely that they could notice an unusual incident, no matter how trifling, and also see its implications.

Thus Rudolph Diesel, while examining the bamboo flame-makers used by Samoan natives, got the idea for his compression ignition engine. Charles Goodyear noticed what had happened to a piece of raw rubber smeared with sulphur when it was left near a hot stove. He thus discovered vulcanization.

The entrepreneur has no manual of instructions to turn to for answers to his questions.

He is curious and searches for answers on his own.

He is stubborn and refuses to accept defeat.

He is prepared to be misunderstood and expects to encounter opposition.

He continually asks himself, "I wonder what would happen if . . . ."[2]

SMALL BUSINESS: WHAT IT IS AND DOES

What is small business?

Most people use the term "small business" to describe small drugstores, beauty shops, laundries, restaurants, insurance agencies, and other small

---

[1] Charles S. Miller and Natalie J. Ward, *History of America: Challenge and Crisis* (New York: Wiley, 1971).

[2] The authors are indebted and wish to express thanks for the inspiration and information used in preparing this section to The Royal Bank of Canada Monthly Letter, Montreal, June, 1972.

enterprises. The meaning of the term seems clear to most people, yet it is difficult to define precisely. Since it is necessary for businesses to be defined by size in order for them to obtain loans, Public Law 85–536, an amendment to the Small Business Administration (SBA) Act of 1953, was passed on July 16, 1958, establishing certain limits—admittedly arbitrary—that distinguish small from large businesses. The act states in general that "a *small business* concern shall be deemed to be one which is independently owned and operated and which is not dominant in its field of operation." In addition, the SBA sets criteria for specific fields; for example, a manufacturing establishment is small if its employees do not exceed 250 persons, a wholesaler if its annual sales do not exceed $5 million, and a retail store or service establishment if its annual sales do not exceed $1 million.

Small business facilitates big business

The remarkable economic strength enjoyed by the United States is often credited to our large, mass-production industries. While much of this credit is deserved, it is important to note that big business, as it is known in the United States, could not exist without large numbers of small businesses.

This is true for several reasons. Small businesses help link big businesses with the consuming public. Tires, refrigerators, electrical appliances, and hundreds of other mass-produced consumers' goods, though produced by industrial giants, are distributed and serviced largely by thousands of small businesses. Further, small businesses are the suppliers of big businesses. It is generally impossible (and often it would be uneconomical even if it were possible) for a big business to produce all the parts, supplies, services, and raw materials it needs to carry on its operations.

Characteristics of small business

Small businesses usually have three distinguishing characteristics apart from size.

First, capital is supplied by one person or a small number of persons. Absentee ownership is rare.

Second, management is generally independent, reporting only to itself and not to a board of directors or a distant "home office." Most small businesses are sole proprietorships, partnerships, or family-owned corporations. In most instances, the manager or managers are also the owners. Therefore, there are usually only a few people who have a voice in management.

Third, the area of operations is local. The employees and employer usually live in the community in which the business is located. The *mar-*

ket for the business is usually local, although it need not be. Mail-order houses, for example, may be small businesses but may sell to dispersed markets.

Small business and opportunity

In many cases, persons who own and operate their own businesses have more incentive to work harder than those who are employees. Self-employed persons often enjoy greater economic and psychological rewards than do persons of equal ability who are not self-employed. When each person is engaged in work that allows him to make his greatest contribution, the entire economy benefits. Centered around the small business is a way of life that most of us would not like to see disappear from the American scene.

Small business is important to physically-handicapped people, widows, and others who would be unable to find satisfactory employment. For example, a bed-ridden mother in Texas runs a successful telephone answering service, and a twenty-three year old former secretary is president of a financial company that specializes in lending money to working women only.

Small business and creativity

A business often starts with a new idea. Some of America's most successful industrialists are men who preferred to start small. Polaroid, which started its initial marketing in the late 1940s, had sales in 1972 of about $559 million. Xerox Corporation, which introduced its first commercial xerographic products in 1950, had sales in 1972 of over $2 billion.

Best-selling books such as *The Man in the Grey Flannel Suit* and *The Organization Man* dwell on the conformist and constrictive nature of large corporations. By implication, then, the proving ground and stimulator of the individualist and innovator is frequently the small business. Big business all too often becomes wedded to the status quo. The motel revolution, for example, was started by small, undercapitalized "Ma and Pa" type operators, not by Hilton or Sheraton. Likewise, not the giants Nabisco or Ward Baking, but Sara Lee, then a small Chicago baker, devised the frozen cake idea.

CONDITIONS CONDUCIVE TO SMALL BUSINESS

People sometimes debate whether big or small business is more important to the American economy. The answer is that both are essential. If markets are very large, products are highly standardized and can be mass produced, large sums of capital are essential, extensive division of labor is possible, a large labor force is needed, and demand is steady, then big business best serves the public interest. However, under certain conditions, such as those listed below, a small business has definite advantages over a big business.

1. When a market is limited.   Small stores are best for the thousands of communities that cannot support a large business—a department store, for example—because the market is too small.

2. When craftsmanship is important.   Small businesses are particularly well suited to provide custom-made goods. Examples of such businesses are tailor shops, custom furniture manufacturers, interior decorators, and watch repair shops.

3. When service is personal.   Beauty salons, landscapers, and optometrists, for example, provide services of a highly personal nature. It is clear that the smaller businesses have a great advantage in providing such services.

4. When convenience is important.   The small party store around the corner that remains open during the late hours has a convenience feature that enables the owner to compete successfully with larger stores.

5. When demand is irregular.   Businesses of a seasonal nature often do not lend themselves to large-scale organization. The Dairy Queen ice cream stores are owned locally, as are boat concessions in the park, winter and summer resort facilities, and roadside produce markets.

OPERATING ADVANTAGES OF SMALL BUSINESS

Independence of action

In the typical small business, management hierarchy need not be considered, which means quicker action and more flexible operation. The alert independent retailer, for instance, can often move faster than the chain store. Suppose that an independent shoe retailer learns of a newly developed architectural design for shoe-store fronts that will attract customers and increase store traffic. He can call in a builder and have the entire conversion completed within days. When the independent's chain-store competitor, which operates hundreds of stores, learns of such a development, it often takes months to reach a policy decision to make the changeover—and more months to remodel several hundred stores.

Adaptability to local needs

The small businessperson is ideally situated to study the desires, preferences, customs, spending habits, and other characteristics of the local market. Thus he is in a position to adapt his business methods to local peculiarities. Large businesses generally must be governed by regional or national market characteristics rather than by those existing in any one community. Successful national companies sometimes find themselves virtually shut out of certain markets because local retailers can make a more direct appeal to customers.

Public favor

Public attitudes in the United States lean toward protecting and furthering the interests of small business. This is partly because of the American impulse to "stick up for the little guy." Public favor finds expression in legislation designed to aid rather than obstruct small business. Small business is subject to fewer regulations and lower taxes than is big business. Big business, as will be noted in Chapter 26, has often been the target of legislation intended to restrict growth.

Lower operating costs

The small business typically has relatively lower operating costs than the large business. Factors accounting for this are comparatively lower wages, rent, investment in plant and equipment, administrative costs, and employee benefit costs. Often the owner's family contributes much labor for which no direct charge is made.

OPERATING DISADVANTAGES OF SMALL BUSINESS

Difficulty in attracting employees

Small businesses generally are at a competitive disadvantage with big business in securing the most efficient and productive employees. The typical small business pays relatively low wages, provides less secure employment, gives no formal training, and offers few fringe benefits like paid vacations and pension programs. Since there are only a few positions in the small business, chances for promotion are limited. Also, many people feel that employment is more prestigious with a large firm than with a small concern. For these reasons, college graduates and other well-qualified individuals do not as a rule work permanently as employees in a small business unless it shows definite promise of growth.

Lack of specialized management

In the small business, usually one person is responsible for all major business functions, such as setting policies, selling, buying, personnel management, advertising, and accounting. Obviously, no one person can be expert in all of these areas. This puts the small business at a disadvantage, for the large business can employ people with specialized training and experience for each important business function. In addition, research, which is considered essential for maximum success in many businesses is too expensive for most small firms.

Incompetent management

Relatively little capital is needed—and little "red tape" must be untangled—to start a small business. There are always many small businesses for sale. The fact that the field can be entered easily attracts many people who lack the necessary training, education, personality, enthusiasm, intelligence, and other qualifications for success. Such individuals generally do not appreciate how hard it is to make a profit. Incompetent management is one of the major factors in the high failure rate of small businesses. Table 5–1 shows the failure rates.

Table 5–1
Business Population and Business Failures, 1946–70

YEARLY AVERAGE	TOTAL CONCERNS IN BUSINESS (1,000)	FAILURES			
		NUMBER	RATE PER 10,000 CONCERNS	CURRENT LIABILITIES (MIL. DOL.)	AVERAGE LIABILITY ($1,000)
1946–1950	2,493	5,652	21	213	44,733
1951–1955	2,635	9,317	35	370	39,322
1956–1960	2,674	14,177	53	708	49,576
1961–1965	2,565	14,849	57	1,261	86,219
1966–1970	2,481	10,993	44	1,324	121,296

Source: *Statistical Abstract of the United States, 1972*, p. 485.

Personal disadvantages

In most small businesses, the owner-manager *is* the business. The very nature of a small business operation creates numerous personal problems. The individual in business for himself faces long hours, sole financial risk, responsibility and worry, and irregular income. His mistakes in business judgment often work a hardship on his family. As a result, individuals without self-reliance and a cooperative family seldom succeed in a small business.

Financial difficulties

Since the chance of failure is considerably greater for the small business, it has greater financial problems. Long-term capital is difficult to secure, since the small business does not normally enjoy as high a credit rating as the larger firm; and, as a result, when money is available to the small business, it usually is lent at a higher interest rate. Under these circumstances, business expansion is difficult.

Sensitivity to economic fluctuations

Because the typical small business has inadequate financial reserves, it is particularly sensitive to economic fluctuations. It cannot continue operations for long without earning a profit, and even a minor recession forces many small businesses to close their doors. A large business, on the other hand, ordinarily can operate, through deficit financing, for months or years without profits.

CAUSES OF SMALL BUSINESS FAILURE

An analysis of the causes of small business failure led O. D. Dickerson and Michael Kawaja to the following conclusions:[3]

1. The rate of closures bears an inverse relationship to the age of the firm's owner. (In other words, older persons are less inclined to fail.)

2. The survival experience of female business owners differs little from that of male owners.

[3] "The Failure Rates of Business," O. D. Dickerson and Michael Kawaja in *The Financing of Small Business: A Current Assessment*, Irving Pfeffer (ed.), Macmillan, 1967, pp. 82–94.

3. Owners with less formal education (measured in terms of years of schooling) have a higher rate of business discontinuance.

4. There is little relationship between previous experience in the same line of business, taken by itself, and the discontinuance rate.

5. Various combinations of education and experience were studied and it was found that inexperienced and uneducated managers are the least likely to succeed, whereas educated and experienced managers have the highest success rate.

6. Individuals who previously owned a business have a much lower failure rate than those who have never been in business before. Thus the single experience factor which appears to matter most is not experience in the same occupation but rather whether the person has had *entrepreneurial* experience.

7. Management teams of two, three, or four persons have a much higher success rate than single managers.

8. In general, the larger the amount of invested capital, especially in the $1,000–$25,000 range studied, the lower is the failure rate. Further, the source of initial capital appears to have a bearing on failure rate. Lower failure rates were found among firms which had a higher proportion of initial capital in equity form (where owners invested a lot of their own capital).

SERVICE BUSINESSES

The service sector of our economy consists of businesses that provide intangible products, or services, such as recreation, electricity, and education. It is not always easy to differentiate between goods and services. One observer explained the difference this way: "When you purchase 'goods' (a car), you acquire an asset; when you purchase 'a service' (car repairs), you incur an expense."

About one-third of all business establishments in the United States do not mine, manufacture, process, produce, or distribute goods. Rather, these businesses specialize in selling services to ultimate, industrial, or commercial consumers.

Types of service industry

Often service activities in large businesses are turned over to small businesses (protection, janitorial, and maintenance) or are leased concessions in department stores (shoe repair and photography). Inspection of the yellow pages in a telephone directory will indicate the wide range of such businesses. Leading services include:

1. <u>Amusement services</u>, such as theatres, bowling alleys, and golf courses
2. <u>Repair services</u>, such as watch, television, and automobile repair shops
3. <u>Personal services</u>, such as barbershops, photography studios, and mortuaries
4. <u>Transportation services</u>, such as airlines, railroads, transit companies, and taxicab companies
5. <u>Communications services</u>, such as telephone, electrical, and broadcasting companies
6. <u>Lodging services</u>, principally hotels and motels
7. <u>Real estate services</u>, that sell, rent, or manage property for clients
8. <u>Bank services</u>, including commercial, trust, and savings and loan establishments
9. <u>Brokerage services</u>, that buy and sell stocks, bonds, and commodities for clients
10. <u>Insurance services</u>, that sell and service insurance policies covering a wide variety of risks
11. <u>Accounting services</u>, that provide a wide range of services related to taxes, financial controls and business management assistance

Other important services include education, religion, medicine, and law — as well as government — but these are not normally considered commercial and are not included in this discussion.

While much has been written and a good number of educational courses developed to deal with producing and marketing products (tangibles), the marketing of services (intangibles) has been slighted. This oversight is because the field is less well organized and is made up of businesses smaller than those dealing in goods, as well as because only recently has a significant percentage of consumer income been spent for services. The trend toward greater expenditures for services will continue, for as income increases, the household spends more of its money for intangibles.

Almost half our labor force is employed in the service industries; almost 42 cents of every consumer dollar are spent for services. Table 5–2 shows how expenditures for services account for an increasing share of personal consumption expenditures. As you can see, the amount of money spent for services has almost doubled since 1960.

Table **5–2**
Personal per Capita Consumption Expenditures

	1950	1955	1960	1965	1968	1969	1970	1971
TOTAL EXPENDITURES	1,259	1,539	1,800	2,224	2,663	2,842	3,002	3,198
DURABLE GOODS	201	240	251	341	418	443	435	486
NONDURABLE GOODS	647	746	837	982	1,144	1,210	1,289	1,346
SERVICES	412	553	712	902	1,102	1,189	1,279	1,367

Source: *Statistical Abstract of the United States,* 1972, p. 315.

Characteristics of service establishments

No merchandise inventory   Service establishments are unique in that they have no need for merchandise inventories in the literal sense. A barber cannot store a haircut and issue it to a customer, nor can amusement establishments store fun to sell later. Service establishments require supplies and essential equipment, but these are not comparable to the inventories of goods and raw materials needed by other types of business.

Large number of sole proprietorships   With the exception of the electric power and communications industries, most service establishments are small business organizations, often operated as family enterprises. Because little or no inventory is required, relatively little capital investment is needed.

Difficulties in transportation   Again with the exception of electricity and communications, it is difficult and sometimes impossible to transport services to the consumer. Instead, the consumer visits the vendor selling the service. As a result, such establishments generally have a small trade area, a fact that discourages the development of large single-unit and chain organizations.

Specialized skills   Most proprietors of service establishments possess a certain degree of skill. This skill may be acquired from training at special schools, such as beautician, mortuary, or dancing schools, or from apprenticeship and experience. If the service establishment cannot provide expert service, the consumer will go elsewhere or will attempt to do the work himself. Skill is often much more important than capital in establishing a service business.

Labor cost predominant   Since no tangible goods are sold, the basic business cost of the service establishment is labor. In many cases the price of a given service, such as that of the taxidermist, seems to a consumer unproportionate to the time spent in giving or providing the service. In this and many other examples (plumbers, electricians, and, to a limited extent, even shoe repairmen), the labor cost includes a price for the skill of the individual who provides the service.[4]

Development of service industries

Services, taken collectively, now occupy a much more important place in our economy than at any time in the past. This is so for several reasons.

New industries   Each new industry paves the way for new types of service. The invention of the airplane led to the development of a new form of travel service. The automobile was soon followed by repair shops, rental services such as the Hertz Rent-A-Car, and other services. Indeed the "after-business" for an automobile—repair services, insurance, gasoline, etc.—costs more than the new car itself. The development of the computer resulted in schools for programmers, service bureaus, and other services. New industries in the future will continue to open the door for other types of service.

Increased prosperity and change in living standards   In general, the lower the portion of income people spend for necessities, the more money they have to buy nonessentials, many of which are services. The high-income family spends much more for amusement, travel, medical care, long distance telephone calls, dry cleaning, and repair services than the low-income family.

Prosperity has enabled more people to buy many services that once were regarded as luxuries, and it has also nurtured new luxury services. It is doubtful that many "pet heavens" providing burial services for cats and dogs exist in underdeveloped nations!

Increased business complexity   Many services, such as professional accounting and advertising services, have developed because of the increased complexity of business. Some phases of business are now so technical that the businessman must either employ specialists to do this work or rely on outside service establishments.

---

[4] A story is told about a machine that ceased to function. No one in the plant could fix it. Finally, the company called in a repair expert. The expert walked over to the machine, took a quick look, hit it three times with a hammer, and, behold, the machine began to function perfectly. Soon the manufacturer received a bill for $100. "This is terrible," he thought, "all he did was hit the machine three times with a hammer." So he requested an itemized statement. The itemized statement read, (1) Hitting machine with hammer—$1, (2) Knowing where to hit machine—$99, (3) Total—$100.

The future of services in our economy

One of the most significant economic trends in the United States during

Figure **5–1**
How the United States Became the World's First Service Economy

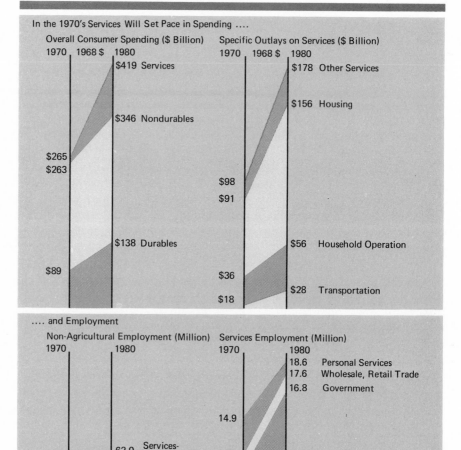

In the 1970's Services Will Set Pace in Spending ....

Overall Consumer Spending ($ Billion)   Specific Outlays on Services ($ Billion)
1970 | 1968 $ | 1980   1970 | 1968 $ | 1980

$419 Services $178 Other Services

$346 Nondurables $156 Housing

$265
$263
                                              $98
                                              $91

$138 Durables $56   Household Operation

$89
                                              $36
                                              $28   Transportation
                                              $18

.... and Employment

Non-Agricultural Employment (Million)   Services Employment (Million)
1970 | 1980   1970 | 1980

                                              18.6 Personal Services
                                              17.6 Wholesale, Retail Trade
                                              16.8 Government

                                              14.9

62.0 Services-   12.5
      Producing   11.6

47.3

                                              Transportation, Public
26.9 Goods-   4.7   Utilities, Communications
23.3 Producing   4.5
                                       3.7   4.3   Finance, Insurance
                                                    Real Estate

Note: Projections are based on 3 percent unemployment.

Source: *Sales Management* estimates; Commerce Department, "Survey of Current Business: National Income Issue";
Bureau of Labor Statistics, "The U.S. Economy in 1980."

<table>
<tr><th colspan="5">Table 5-3
Consumer Spending on Services</th></tr>
</table>

SERVICE CATEGORY	SHIFTS IN SPENDING ON SERVICES CONSUMER SPENDING 1970 ($ MILLION)	PERCENTAGE GAIN 1960-70	PERCENTAGE OF TOTAL 1970	1960
Housing	$91,190	117.9	34.4%	33.1%
Medical Care	38,684	168.8	14.6	11.4
Household Operation	36,113	83.5	13.6	15.6
Personal Business	35,497	127.6	13.4	12.3
Transportation	17,893	76.3	6.8	8.7
Recreation	11,148	76.1	4.2	5.0
Private Education and Research	10,353	133.0	3.9	3.5
Personal Care	9,772	60.1	3.7	4.8
Religion and Charities	8,826	87.9	3.3	3.7
Foreign Travel	5,445	133.6	2.1	1.8
TOTAL	**$264,921**	**109.6**	**100.0%**	**100.0%**

Note: Figures may not add to 100 due to rounding.

Source: *Sales Management* estimates; Commerce Department, "Survey of Current Business: National Income Issue"; Bureau of Labor Statistics, "The U.S. Economy in 1980."

the last two decades has been a gradual transition from a production-oriented to a service-dominated economy. (See Figure 5–1.) Between 1947 and 1967, man-hours worked in personal services increased 50 percent; in financial services, 74 percent; and in state and local government, 170 percent. Meanwhile, during the same twenty-year period, man-hours worked in manufacturing and mining increased only 20 percent, and in agriculture there was actually a drop of 59 percent despite an increase of 42 percent in output.[5]

A major problem concerns the lag in services' productivity growth (2 percent per year) as compared with that of production industries (4 percent per year). Because of the relatively low productivity and its low growth rate, service workers earn less ($5,568 in 1970 as compared to $8,036 for all occupations).

Wages for service jobs could be raised without pricing services out of the market if productivity could be increased. Following are two examples of experimentation that may increase productivity.

First, the National Committee on Household Employment, in cooperation with the U.S. Department of Labor, has developed pilot projects to upgrade household employment standards and opportunities. Employees are trained for "day work" and often cleaning "teams" are used. The worker is employed, not by the housewife directly, but by a special company that shares profits with the employee.

[5] Gilbert Burck, "The Still Bright Promise of Productivity," *Fortune*, October 1968, p. 134.

Second, franchised house-cleaning service on a contract basis has been initiated by a large national retailer. Relatively little capital is required to enter the business. The franchise serves as a link between working for wages and outright ownership.

FRANCHISING

The careful observer of business practices will note the appearance of new approaches to meet changing conditions. One of these is called the *franchising system*. While the franchising idea is not new, widespread application of it has occurred largely since 1950.

A franchise is an exclusive — that is, protective — arrangement binding parties, usually a manufacturer or operating company and a private investor. The manufacturer or operating company supplies, on an exclusive-territory basis, nationally-known brands, advertising, and well-tested business methods. In return, the private businessman agrees to provide local managerial skill and at least part of the capital. He also promises to deal exclusively with the franchisor and to operate the business in the manner prescribed by him. Since a Supreme Court decision in the case of the Federal Trade Commission versus the Brown Shoe Company ruled that certain controls violated antitrust laws, the whole matter of franchises and restriction of freedom of choice has been up in the air.

The franchise method of organization has grown more rapidly in recent years than any other type of distribution arrangement. It is estimated by The Conference Board that franchises account for $100 billion in sales annually, which represents 25 percent of total retail sales and 10 percent of the GNP. There are some 500,000 franchised businesses in the United States, with new franchises being added at the rate of 21,000 a year.

How a franchise system functions

Franchising systems vary widely in operational procedures, but a generalized pattern can be identified.** The most common franchise arrangement is one in which a *franchisor* (sometimes referred to as the seller or licenser), who has systematized a method for the production and/or distribution of a product or service, extends to a *franchisee* (variously identi-

SPECIAL READINGS

** Profits from Franchising, by Robert M. Rosenberg and Madelon Bedell. New York: McGraw-Hill, 1969. This book covers some history of franchising and discusses its future, gives advice on getting financing, explains how to judge the validity of franchise offers, and explains the franchising control systems. Included is a roster of franchisers, along with a sample franchise contract.

fied as dealer, outlet, associate, licensee, or member) the right to carry on the business, subject to a number of restrictions and controls. The franchisee uses the franchisor's name as a trade name, which gives the public the impression that the business is a corporate chain-type operation. Sometimes the franchisor will own some of his own outlets and franchise others. Automobile dealerships and Coca-Cola distributors and bottlers are widely known franchises. Such diverse outlets as Mary Carter Paints, Shakey's Pizza, Western Auto, Walgreen's, Hertz Rent-A-Car, Kelly Girl, Aamco Transmissions, Kentucky Fried Chicken, H & R Block, and Holiday Inns are also franchising operations.

The franchisor and the franchisee work together in this general manner: The franchisor advertises his products or services nationally (or in the area where the franchisees are located) and also attempts to create public recognition of the franchised outlets. The franchisee, following the merchandising and business procedures outlined by the franchisor, proceeds to operate his outlet as an independent establishment.

The net effect of this cooperative action is to develop a "chain" of independent businesses. *In an ideal situation, the franchise system combines the advantages of large and small business while avoiding weaknesses of each.* Extensive public recognition, standardized procedures, and known merchandise plus the enthusiasm and devotion of independent owner-operators often result in a very successful marketing approach.

Contractual arrangements

Formal contractual agreements are usually drawn up to define the rights and responsibilities of the franchisor and the franchisee. In the typical agreement the franchisor agrees to:

1. Grant an exclusive selling territory to the franchisee

2. Supply merchandise to the franchisee at a "competitive" price

3. Create and maintain good will for the benefit of the franchisee

4. Furnish trademarks, signs, and other materials that will identify the franchisee as an affiliate of the franchisor

5. Provide assistance in the management of the franchisee's business

The franchisee generally agrees to:

1. Invest a certain sum in his business

2. Purchase all or a specific portion of his supplies and merchandise from the franchisor

3. Pay the franchisor a certain amount (usually a percentage of gross volume) at regular intervals for services rendered

4. Identify his outlet with signs, posters, etc., in *exactly* the manner prescribed by the franchisor

5. Operate the business according to policies recommended by the franchisor

Success within these contractual arrangements requires the cooperation of both parties. A major problem in building a successful franchising system is helping highly individualistic businessmen adapt to procedures and techniques developed by the franchisor. Franchisors are aware that the public regards a franchising system as a chain and that the business behavior of one unit in that chain is a reflection on all units. That is why many franchisors prefer dealers who have had no related experience. Unlearning preferences and prejudices pertaining to business procedures is sometimes impossible for the individual with extensive experience. The attitude, "Teach me the franchise way—I'll do everything possible to learn it," seems to be the prime quality needed by those who choose to operate a franchised outlet.

As we have said, to achieve maximum success, both parties must make concessions. Franchisees must be willing to sacrifice some independence of action and to conform substantially to the franchisor's methods. By the same token, the franchisors must accept the fact that complete control over the franchise outlet is impossible because it is an independent business.

An evaluation of franchising

While franchising systems appear to be an excellent means of developing and stimulating small business, their future has become quite clouded. Once thought to be the answer to many marketing problems, the method in recent years has encountered numerous difficulties. Laws are being enacted to control them in virtually every state. A law school dean said at a recent conference that "There are at present lawsuits against virtually every major franchisor in the United States."[6]

The following franchisor practices come in for criticism:

1. Canceling franchise agreements for minor contract infringements

2. Limiting the right of the franchisee to transfer ownership of the franchise

3. Charging franchisees excessive fees and demanding royalty payments out of proportion to sales

[6] *The New York Times*, July 18, 1971.

Figure **5–2**
Franchising Encompassed Thirty Percent of Retail Sales in 1973

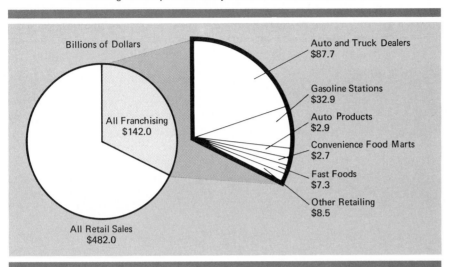

Do you anticipate franchising to account for an even larger percentage of retail sales in the future? Why?

4. Requiring franchisees to buy merchandise, supplies, and equipment from franchisors at prices above what the franchisees would have to pay elsewhere

5. Demanding control of the selling price regardless of local conditions

6. Putting intense pressure on franchisees to expand

Despite unfair and occasionally illegal practices on the part of some franchisors, it seems that franchising will continue to become more important in the years ahead. In those fields where it is feasible, it remains, in theory at least, the best means for combining the advantages of both big and small business.

AID FOR SMALL BUSINESS

Individuals considering going into business for themselves frequently ask, "Where can I get advice?" "How can I learn more about the business I want to start?" Assistance is available from both public and private sources.

The Small Business Administration

The Small Business Administration (SBA) is a permanent, independent government agency created by Congress to advise and assist small business enterprises. The agency was established by the Small Business Act of 1953.

In expressing the policy of Congress with regard to small businesses and the SBA, Section 202 of the Small Business Act states:

> It is the declared policy of the Congress that the Government should aid, counsel, assist, and protect insofar as is possible the interests of small-business concerns in order to preserve free competitive enterprise, to insure that a fair proportion of the total purchases and contracts for supplies and services for the Government be placed with small-business enterprises, and to maintain and strengthen the overall economy of the Nation.

The SBA provides the following services:

1. Government contracts. The Small Business Act states that "a fair proportion of the total purchases and contracts for supplies and services for the Government" should be placed with small business concerns. In carrying out this objective, the SBA gives counsel to small business on different methods for obtaining government contracts.

2. Financial assistance. The SBA renders financial assistance to small business in the form of loans to finance various aspects of doing business.

3. Managerial and technical assistance. The SBA provides managerial advice through administrative-management courses, supplies leaflets covering a wide range of practical business problems, and offers management counseling.

Other sources of assistance

In addition to the SBA, people interested in going into business for themselves may obtain assistance from a variety of other organizations such as: commercial banks; trade associations; colleges and universities; periodicals; persons already in business; and wholesalers, manufacturers, and others who supply small business. The career appendix provides some guidelines for going into business for oneself.

PEOPLE AND THEIR IDEAS
Colonel Harland Sanders

The franchising method's most colorful character

At the age of sixty-five, when most people are thinking about retirement, Harland Sanders was embarking on an entirely new business venture—franchising other restaurants to use his southern fried chicken recipe. Today, the Kentucky Fried Chicken Corporation is one of the largest food franchise operations in the world.

Colonel Sanders (the title of Colonel is honorary) was born in Henryville, Indiana, in 1890. His early career included such diversified jobs as farm hand, streetcar conductor, carriage painter, railroad fireman, soldier, ferryboat operator, insurance salesman, service-station operator, and motel-keeper. For twenty-five years, he operated a successful roadside restaurant just outside Corbin, Kentucky. Then in 1952 a new expressway was built, diverting traffic away from the restaurant; within three years Sanders was bankrupt. It was at this point, in 1955, that he decided to start a new business. Equipped with a $105-a-month social security check, a pressure cooker, and his "secret blend of herbs and spices," Sanders set out in a 1946 Ford to sell his recipe. In the first two years of door-to-door canvassing, he sold only five franchises. Gradually, however, his efforts gained momentum and his Kentucky-colonel image caught on. Ten years later he had acquired over seven hundred franchises.

In 1964, Sanders began to realize that the business was outgrowing his capacity to run it. He sold the company, including title to patents, trademarks, and his image, to three investors for $2 million, plus a $40,000-a-year lifetime contract to act as good will ambassador for Kentucky Fried Chicken. (This contract has subsequently been raised to $60,000.) He retained control of some two hundred Canadian outlets, whose profits are turned over to the Harland Sanders Foundation, an educational philanthropy.

In his capacity as roving ambassador, Colonel Sanders travels 250,000 miles a year, acting as the company's spokesman and chief promoter. Commenting on his success at an age when most men retire, the Colonel remarked, "Anyone who has reached sixty-five years of age has a world of experience behind him. He ought to be able to gather something valuable out of that." As the world's best-known salesman of fried chicken, he predictably has also been interested in the production of chickens. He once claimed that he had produced a chicken with four legs. "Why not market them?" he was asked. "Because the damned things run too fast to catch," he said.

CONTEMPORARY ISSUES
Situation 5

Should retailers be required to pass an "entrance examination"?

After class, Ray expressed his amazement that two out of every three small retailers who start a business each year fail.

"But don't you know why?" asked John. "Most people who go into retailing on their own simply do not have enough capital, experience, education, or training. It isn't surprising that they fail."

"I heard one fellow in class say that the state should give a licensing examination to people who want to set up their own retail stores," said Ray. "If they don't get a high enough score on the test, then they can't start the business. What do you think about that?"

"You miss the whole point about private enterprise, Ray. It means you're free to start your own business any time you want. If you fail, that's your problem. We need risk-takers."

"I partially agree with what you say," admitted Ray. "But when one business fails, other businesses are hurt too. Think of the manufacturers and wholesalers who lose money because retailers fail. And think of the individuals themselves who often lose their lifetime savings in just a few months or years."

"You have a point there," agreed John, "but suppose you did have an 'entrance exam,' who would make up the questions? What would be considered a passing grade? And how could you be sure that the person who made that grade would also make a good retailer? You've known people who have made straight A's in school and were failures in the business world. There are also those who flunked in school who were successful when they got out."

"Besides," John insisted, "the government already has far too much control over business. Sure, we don't like to see retailers fail and lose their hard-earned savings, but that still doesn't justify setting up an examination hurdle. And besides, would such an examination be practical?"

"I think so," persisted Ray. "At least it would show whether the individual knew how a business should be run. The CPA exam keeps the unqualified out of public accounting. And other types of businessmen such as stock brokers and real estate salesmen must pass an exam. Granted, an exam won't tell whether a person will, in fact, run the business as he should, but it will tell whether he has the potential to do it if he really tries."

SITUATION EVALUATION

1. What do you think of an "entrance exam" for retailers?

2. What practical considerations were overlooked by both John and Ray?

3. Do you anticipate that some day an "entrance exam" will be required? Explain why or why not.

BUSINESS CHRONICLE

Considerations in expanding Rent Anything, Inc.

Rent Anything, Inc., became so successful that the company began receiving inquiries to extend the operation in other localities. Prospects for successful expansion were indeed promising. Rent Anything's executive group was ambitious, young (average age 28), and already had accumulated considerable experience. The big question was whether to expand by establishing company-owned outlets in promising territories, or whether it would be better to franchise, whereby others would own and manage the outlets.

Some of the problems discussed by management were:

1. Lack of experience in other territories

2. Large demand for capital required to expand

3. Loss of control for a type of business that needs extensive, detailed supervision

4. Lack of knowledge of laws, taxes, personnel problems, and competition in other states

5. Lack of experience in franchising

QUESTIONS

1. What are the primary factors that must be considered in deciding whether to expand on a company-owned outlet basis or to use a franchise arrangement?

2. Which method of expansion would you advise—company-owned outlets or franchises?

APPLICATION EXERCISES

1. One aid in determining whether or not a new business venture should be started is a *feasibility study*. Such a report gathers all available information about the business potential in an area and balances the pros and cons so an objective decision can be made. Select a business of your choice and draw up a table of contents that shows what information you would include in a feasibility study for the business you selected.

2. Cable television is a rapidly expanding industry. Make a list of at least 10 new types of service businesses that have resulted or will result from this new industry.

3. Review recent issues of the *Wall Street Journal* and inspect the advertisements that sell franchises. Make a list of those offered, the products involved, and the price of the franchise (if it is given). What conclusions can you draw about (a) the variety of franchises available, (b) the types of product suitable for franchising, and (c) the capital required.

4. In a recent issue of the *Wall Street Journal*, review carefully the advertisements selling franchises. Then, (a) select the one which you feel is most promising, and (b) select the one you feel is least promising. In a short paper, explain your choices.

QUESTIONS

1. What contributions does small business make to the American economy?

2. What is meant by the statement, "Small business is free enterprise's way of establishing new centers of initiative"? Do you think the statement is true? Why?

3. What can an independent food store do to meet customer needs usually not met by chain grocery competition?

4. Consider three small businesses with which you are familiar. Summarize what you think are their chief strengths and weaknesses.

5. In what ways can the intelligent, independent businessman put to good use his opportunities for personal contact with his customers?

6. How do service establishments differ from consumer-goods businesses? In which of the two areas is the greatest opportunities for small business? Why?

7. How do you account for the growth of service establishments? Will this growth continue? Explain why or why not.

8. Define a franchise. Explain how franchising ideally combines the advantages of both the large business and the small business.

9. What is the Small Business Administration? Why was it established, and what does it do?

10. Is government assistance to small business inconsistent with free enterprise? Should all businesses rise or fall on their own merits alone?

CHAPTER 6

UNIVERSAL NEED FOR MANAGEMENT

FORMS OF ORGANIZATION
　　Line Organization. Line-and-Staff Organization.

ORGANIZATIONAL CHARTS AND MANUALS

LEVELS OF MANAGEMENT
　　How the Levels of Management Interrelate.

FUNCTIONS OF MANAGEMENT
　　Business Objectives. Planning. Policies. Controls. Procedures.

COMMUNICATION AND MANAGEMENT
　　The Communication Process. Effective Communication.

THE THEORIES OF MANAGEMENT

internal management and organization of business

Management is often considered the most attractive area of business by those who find leadership challenging and enjoyable.

Management is the activity that determines the objectives or goals of the business; plans what to do, when to do it, and how and by whom it will be done; establishes work procedures; and fixes controls to make certain that the work is performed correctly. Management may also be defined as the selection, assignment, and organization of individuals for the efficient use of materials, money, machines and methods. It is well to consider still another definition, that of Lawrence A. Apply, president of the American Management Association (AMA): "Management is not the direction of things; it is the development of people."

Management consists of all people who perform a management function, from foreman or supervisor to president. Specific types of management are usually indicated by adjectives. Thus, *personnel* management is responsible for manpower; *marketing* management directs company distribution; *production* management is in charge of manufacturing com-

139

pany products; *traffic* management oversees the shipping of goods from suppliers to the factory and from the factory to customers; and *office* management controls the records and communications within the business.

UNIVERSAL NEED FOR MANAGEMENT

The need for management exists in all businesses and, indeed, in each phase of human activity. The federal government—a huge, complex system of legislative bodies, agencies, and departments—obviously requires management talents and skills. In fact, special commissions are frequently appointed to study government functions with a view toward streamlining—eliminating unessential activities, combining certain functions, and so forth.

Such widely different institutions as the armed services, colleges, churches, hospitals, and political parties also require management. The management process is not restricted, therefore, to business, but is needed in all situations in which group effort is expended. *Organization* can be defined as the process of logically grouping activities, delineating authority and responsibility, and establishing working relationships that enable the employees, and thus the company, to work with maximum efficiency and effectiveness. More specifically, those in charge of organization must

1. Decide exactly what work each individual in the enterprise shall perform and apportion this work among the employees

2. Fix responsibility and authority for each employee

3. Decide to whom each employee will report—that is, establish the chain of command

4. Determine how the work done by individuals and groups of individuals shall be coordinated so that the desired goods or services can be produced and marketed economically and effectively

The organization process is essential in all businesses, large or small. The food-store proprietor with only two employees is organizing his business when he says, "Jack, you're in charge of all meats and produce; handle them the best way you can. When you have problems, bring them to me. And, when I'm not here, you're in charge of the entire store. Bill, your job is to handle all canned and packaged groceries. When I'm here, bring your questions to me, but when I'm gone, ask Jack what to do."

While this example is oversimplified, even for a small store, it does show how organization involves the assignment of responsibility and delegation of authority. In the large company, where hundreds or thousands of jobs must be performed, organization is naturally much more complicated. It is highly formalized, and most job assignments are clearly defined, often in writing.

When everyone in a company knows exactly what is expected of him, to whom he reports, and how far his authority extends, and when the work of everyone is coordinated properly, an effective working organization exists. If these conditions are not present, the company is not well organized; in an extreme case, instead of resembling a team, the employees would be simply a confused mob. Though inefficient organization is not obvious to the untrained eye, it often causes friction among employees or customer vexation because of late deliveries or shipment of wrong merchandise.

Andrew Carnegie, one of America's early business geniuses, once said, "Organizing power, upon the development of which my material success in my life has hung [is] a success not to be attributed to what I have known or done myself, but to the faculty of knowing and choosing others who did know better than myself. Precious knowledge this for any man to possess. I did not understand steam machinery, but I tried to understand that more complicated piece of mechanism—man."[1]

FORMS OF ORGANIZATION

Line organization

In *line organization*, orders and authority flow in a straight line from the chief executive to lower management levels. The concept of line organization stems from the military, where authority is based solely on rank—the corporal has authority over the private, the sergeant over both corporals and privates, and so on. In business each line executive has authority over certain segments of the business. The president issues orders to his subordinates, who either execute them or pass them on to their subordinates. In addition to the president, there are usually line executives in a manufacturing establishment who are in charge of marketing and manufacturing. They give orders and make decisions about the function for which they are responsible.

The line form has certain advantages.

1. It is easily understood by all employees and executives. There is no question as to who is in charge over a certain segment of the business.

[1] *Autobiography*, Houghton Mifflin, 1920, p. 24.

2. Decisions can be made and carried out quickly. This is true because one man can make any given decision.

3. Executive overhead expense is kept low because there are no executive specialists.

Despite these advantages, the line form of organization in its purest form is used only in small companies. As a business grows larger, certain weaknesses begin to appear in the line structure, chiefly because line executives often lack both the time to study problems and the specialized training needed to make wise decisions on complicated business matters. Also, as a business grows larger, the chain of command lengthens and direct orders cannot be executed quickly enough for maximum effectiveness. To compensate for these weaknesses, the line-and-staff organization is used by larger concerns.

Line-and-staff organization

The *line-and-staff* structure is similar to the line arrangement in that line executives still make all major decisions and issue orders. But, since the work of a larger concern is more complex, no one line executive can become expert in all its details. Thus it has been found desirable to use the services of specialists, none of whom has direct line authority except in his own department. These specialists are called *staff executives.*

Staff executives are usually technically trained and are employed to advise and inform line and other staff executives on the many complicated problems of the larger business. "Line" and "staff" are among the most perplexing business terms for students to understand. For clarity, substitute terms like "operating" for "line" and "service" for "staff" are sometimes used. Examples of staff executives and the line executives whom they usually assist are:

STAFF EXECUTIVE	LINE EXECUTIVE ASSISTED
Marketing research director Advertising manager	Vice-president in charge of marketing
Legal counsel	→ President and other line executives
Industrial relations director Quality control head Chief designer	Superintendent in charge of manufacturing
Public-relations director	→ President and his assistants

Observe that *line executives still make all basic decisions and issue all orders.* The staff executive can only recommend; he cannot enforce.

The obvious advantage of the line-and-staff organization structure is that technical problems are delegated to experts. On the negative side, the line-and-staff organization results in slower decisions and increases the executive overhead expense.

ORGANIZATIONAL CHARTS AND MANUALS

The *organizational chart*** is a visual device that shows how the various departments of the business relate to each other. Figure 6–1 is an example of a highly simplified organizational chart, which serves two chief purposes. First, it provides employees, executives, and stockholders with a readily understandable picture of the divisions of responsibility and lines of authority. Second, it aids in studying how to modify or improve relationships and areas of responsibilities within the organizational structure.

SPECIAL READINGS

** Up the Organization by Robert Townsend. New York: Knopf, 1970. The maverick author of this best seller was the spectacularly successful president of the Avis Corporation. His book is a tongue-in-cheek, yet deadly serious, satire of corporation organizational matters. Here are two typical barbs: (1) "Organization charts: rigor mortis: draw them in pencil, never formalize, print and circulate them . . . in the best organizations people see themselves working in a circle as if around one table." (2) "Directors are usually the friends of the chief executive, put there to keep him safely in office." William Benton, former U. S. Senator who reviewed the book wrote, "In mavericks like Townsend lies the vitality of our economy and the hidden future of our business destiny. I believe our country will continue to produce them."

In large companies, organizational structures are very complex and cannot be committed to memory. If the structure is in chart form, top executives can more readily determine, for example, where a new department should be placed or whether a span of control is too broad or too narrow. (Span of control refers to the number of employees under the supervision of an individual manager.)

Organizational charts, while very helpful in presenting a general view of the organizational structure, only present that structure in skeleton form. A review of the chart will not, for example, reveal the exact functions of the various departments. To provide such detailed information, *organization manuals* are often prepared. These manuals usually include the following:

1. Summaries of the functions and operations of each department in the company

Figure **6-1**
A Simplified Line-and-Staff Organization

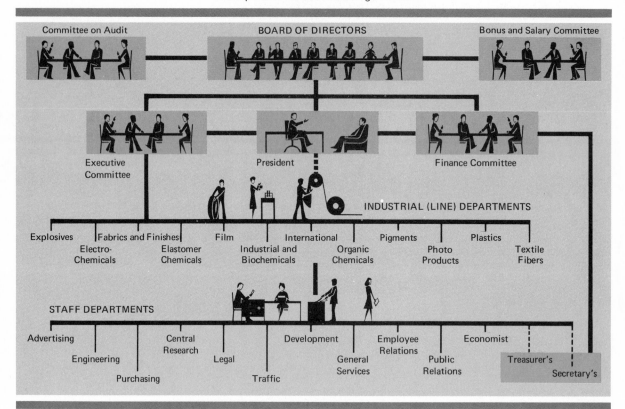

Source: E. I. DuPont de Nemours.

2. Job descriptions and responsibilities of all key executives and their personnel

3. Information regarding company policies, rules, fringe benefits, and regulations.

LEVELS OF MANAGEMENT

As we observed earlier, the overall authority and responsibility for management of a corporation rests with the stockholders, who delegate them to the board of directors. Actual direction of the large corporation is then assigned to what may be called professional, or hired, management. Company management can be divided into three levels: top management, middle management, and operating management.

Top management is the highest level of management in the organization. Top-management personnel usually have many years of varied business experience. Often called key or senior executives, they usually bear

Table **6-1**
The Amount of Time Executives Spend on the Job and at Leisure

	HOURS PER WEEK
On the job:	
At office or place of business	42.7
At home (paperwork, etc.)	6.8
Business travel	6.6
Travel between home and office	5.3
Business social functions outside home	2.8
Business entertaining	2.6
Total	66.8
At leisure:	
Hobbies, sports, relaxing, etc.	21.8
Literary and cultural activities	5.2
Study to further career	3.5
Civic and political activities	2.4
Church activities	2.1
Total	35.0

Source: Data provided by Twentieth Century Fund.

Is this profile of the executive at work and at play your idea of "the good life"?

the title of president or vice-president. Specifically, the term refers to the highest echelon—those who exercise command—regardless of title.

Top management determines the broad objectives, policies, and procedures of the company and makes the larger decisions such as whether to issue stock, establish a foreign subsidiary, buy out a competitor, or manufacture a new product.

Top executives, as a class, enjoy special benefits such as options to purchase company stock at especially favorable prices, pension plans, life insurance paid for by the company, opportunities to travel extensively, and prestige.

Middle management, the second level of management, is responsible for developing operational plans and procedures to implement the broader ones conceived by top management. Middle management is often given much leeway in the development of plans, so long as the end result is in keeping with top management requirements. Decisions on which advertising media to use, how many new salesmen to hire, what new equipment to purchase, and how to develop new machinery are examples of the matters concerning middle management.

Middle management includes superintendents and managers of various units and departments. The term "junior executive" generally refers to younger members on lower levels of middle management who are being groomed for higher management positions.

Operating management is the lowest level in management. It includes foremen and supervisors immediately responsible for directing the work of employees. Members of operating management are concerned primarily with putting into action operational plans devised by middle management; generally they do not initiate plans of their own.

How the levels of management interrelate

Because the direction a business takes is established by top management, this level is most important. Top management makes policies, middle management makes plans to carry out the policies, and operating management sees that the work called for is done. Top management is secure only as long as the profit picture is favorable. To illustrate, when a business is in serious trouble and losses instead of profits appear, the board of directors may make changes in the top echelon. Sometimes a new president

Figure **6–2**
The Management Activities Pyramid

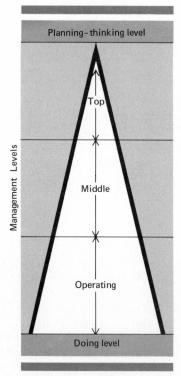

The bottom portion of the pyramid indicates time spent performing "doing" kinds of work, such as gathering statistics, writing letters, inspecting work, issuing orders. The top area of the pyramid indicates activities such as conferring, planning, formulating policy, and thinking. As the manager advances from one level to another, his activities change in a manner corresponding to that shown in the illustration.

and key assistants are employed. When this is done, changes at other management levels are not always made by the new top management, for middle management can still make plans to carry out policy, and operating management can still implement plans. The nature of activity carried on at each management level is illustrated in the Management Activities Pyramid (Figure 6–2).

In business, major changes in managerial thinking are made at the top. Without sound top-management policy, long-range profits and a smoothly functioning business cannot be provided even by the most competent middle and operating management. In a very real sense, top management casts a shadow that affects the behavior of the lower levels of management.

FUNCTIONS OF MANAGEMENT

The work of management can be appreciated more fully by a study of its chief functions, some of which are:

1. Establish objectives   **5.** Develop procedures
2. Make plans   **6.** Motivate employees
3. Develop policies   **7.** Staffing
4. Establish controls   **8.** Public relations

The first five of these are discussed below. The others are taken up in later chapters.

Business objectives

A business concern, like an individual, must have definite goals or purposes to be successful. The successful engineer makes proficiency in engineering his goal; the management of a successful chemical company makes the efficient production and distribution of chemicals its goal. Objectives should be established for the business as a whole, for each department or unit in the business, and for many individual activities.

Examples of objectives   Company-wide objectives embody the general aims of the business. For example, such an objective might be to produce clothes washers and dryers for the widest mass market possible. Such a goal describes in very broad terms the essential work to be performed in the organization. However obvious or even trite it may seem, there is an advantage in preparing a written expression of company objectives. It is useful for a company to say, "This is what, in general, we are trying to do," for then it can ask, with greater acuteness, "Does this policy we are considering further that general aim?"

The overall objectives, in addition to stating the purpose of the business, may include specifics that give the company its character and designate what the company considers of major importance. The following excerpt from the executive manual of a large department store illustrates the point.

It shall be our objective to be an "ACE" organization. An "ACE" organization is alert, courteous, and efficient.

An alert organization is wide-awake, open-minded, always eager to learn more, enthusiastic, and aggressive in the best sense of the word. We want to be an aggressive, hard-working, fast-moving organization, without the usual politics, bickerings, and petty conflicts so commonly found in organizations.

We want to be a courteous organization. We must always find time to be courteous to our associates, to our customers, and to our market resources. A courteous, considerate manner is the mark of a good executive. A truly courteous, tactful manner will smooth the way for a happy, smoothly operating organization. Courtesy is the lubricant which eliminates friction in human contacts, as oil does in a motor. Our executives are expected to be just as courteous to their subordinates as to their superior officers. We want executives who can be unselfish enough to find satisfaction in contributing to the happiness and welfare of others.

We must be an efficient organization. It is not enough to be merely "nice"; we must also be efficient or we are one-sided. Efficiency and happiness in work go hand in hand. It is seldom that one is found without the other. It shall be our policy to strive for both.

Objectives established for the various departments should be related to the general company-wide objectives. In the example above, one of the controller division's objectives is "to provide every department with accurate and prompt statistical information on its operations." The production department in a manufacturing plant might have as an objective the production of appliances in the most efficient manner possible. A sales department's objective could be to sell 500,000 clothes dryers annually.

Objectives can also be established for subdivisions and for individual activities in the organization. The head of the sales department, for example, may establish quotas for each regional sales division. Thus, an objective of the Midwest division of the business might be to sell 120,000 dryers in the next year. Each salesman, in turn, may have a specific sales quota assigned to him.

Because objectives are generally ideals, they must be altered as new circumstances arise. The sales department, for example, may sell 300,000 units, 200,000 under its goal of 500,000 units; the following year the goal might consequently be lowered to 400,000 units. Even though they may have to be modified, objectives must always be set; the members of an organization are inclined to work more realistically and effectively when they can aim at specific goals or quotas.

Planning

Planning is the management function of determining what should be done and how, when, and by whom.

Examples of planning   The purpose of planning is to facilitate the accomplishment of company objectives. For example, a company objective might be to double production within a five-year period. To accomplish this objective, a vast amount of planning is necessary. First, top management must determine what has to be done to double production. Numerous major matters, such as obtaining additional capital, increasing plant capacity, and expanding the selling program, must be considered. Second, management must decide how to expand plant facilities by choosing from such alternatives as buying additional plants, building an addition to the present factory, or using some other means; and how to expand the sales program by choosing to add more salesmen, increase advertising, and so on. After such decisions have been made, management must establish a timetable showing when the various activities are to take place. Finally, management must decide who will be in charge of each project.

Once a general blueprint has been created, a great amount of detailed and routine planning is also necessary. For example, if it is decided to expand production facilities by acquiring additional plants, detailed plans for such acquisitions must be developed. Other detailed planning will be required to obtain the necessary capital and to sell the increased output. Actually, many separate plans must be created to accomplish major objectives.

For the objectives of each department to be accomplished, planning must also be a day-to-day activity. Indeed, the overall plan itself should be reviewed regularly and revised as necessary.

Policies

Another very important function of management is to establish *policies*, or rules of action, to guide the company in the achievement of its objectives. Examples of specific policies that a company might adopt are listed below.

1. Product policy. The product manufactured must meet quality specifications at least equal to competition in its price range.

2. <u>Credit policy</u>. Credit is extended only to customers approved by the credit manager. Payment must be made in 60 days, with a 2 percent discount for payment in 10 days.

3. <u>Price policy</u>. Prices stated in the company's catalog are not subject to change, except by the general manager.

4. <u>Employment policy</u>. Close relatives of present employees are not eligible for employment in this company.

5. <u>Returned-goods policy</u>. Goods returned by customers are accepted only within 10 days of the time of purchase and only if not soiled or damaged by the customer.

Hundreds of policies are in effect in any company, and those of a very broad character are established by top management. Power to make specific policies for the guidance of each department usually is delegated to department heads.

Importance of policies   Policies are essential to the organization for several reasons. First, they save time; problems frequently can be solved quickly and easily if a policy has been established to cover the situation. For example, a credit-department policy might be to send reminder letters to customers whenever an account is thirty days overdue. This assures that all accounts are reviewed regularly for payment delinquencies and routinely prodded when necessary.

Second, policies make for fairness in dealing with the public. It is never wise to give one customer special favors or advantages that are denied another who is equally deserving. For example, if credit is extended to one person but withheld from another who is equally qualified, resentment on the part of the latter, if he finds out, is sure to result. Questions as to who can and who cannot receive credit are easily handled if a definite policy has been created.

Third, policies build confidence on the part of employees. Policies clarify rules of procedure, make it easier to train employees, and keep morale high, for employees know what they are supposed to do.

Characteristics of sound policies   For a policy to be of maximum benefit to the organization, the policy-makers should follow these guidelines:

1. <u>Put them in writing</u>. An objective that is stated in writing has a clearer meaning than one that is only verbalized.

2. <u>Make them as simple as possible</u>. A policy or procedure that is not understood causes misunderstandings and mistakes.

3. <u>Make them comprehensive.</u> Ideally a plan or procedure should cover every possible situation, not only the purely routine conditions.

4. <u>Make them flexible.</u> No rule or procedure or control can reach the ideal of covering every situation. Therefore, objectives, plans, and the other management functions should be adaptable to unusual circumstances.

5. <u>Review and amend them regularly.</u> Because conditions change rapidly, a good practice is to review all conceptual work of management at least annually and to revise where necessary.

Controls

Once objectives are determined and plans have been made to achieve them, management must exercise the *control function*. No plan, no matter how carefully conceived, is of value unless it is carried out properly. Control requires:

1. General supervision of all those who perform tasks related to carrying out the plan

2. Scheduling of work so that the plan is executed on time

3. Regular or periodic review of work to make certain it is being performed properly

4. Corrective action when needed. Management, of course, is responsible not only for tracking down mistakes but also for correcting them

Procedures

A fifth major function of management is to reduce to a simple routine as much of the company's work as possible by establishing systems, or procedures. A procedure is like an "umbrella" covering company activities so that routine tasks can be effortlessly carried out. The need for procedures is apparent in all business organizations. For example, every major company receives and sends large quantities of mail. Unless some procedure is developed for receiving and sorting incoming mail and collecting and stamping outgoing mail, confusion obviously results.

Procedures should be established in all departments in the business. An accounting department needs a procedure for classifying and recording income and expenses. A supply room needs a procedure for supplying other units in the organization with equipment, tools, paper, and other goods. Incoming orders and the purchasing of raw materials should be handled according to a definite procedure. Procedures are necessary for recording the amount of time employees work, for filing, for handling correspondence and customer complaints, for greeting visitors to the company, and for dozens of other functions in the business.

Characteristics of good procedures   Unless they are carefully conceived, procedures can result in needless paperwork and excessive red tape. If there is no sound reason behind the system, employees tend to resent it. Therefore procedures should be based on actual need, and they should be simple, easily understood by all employees, and amended only when necessary.

Consider the value of the following written procedure as part of a department store's protection instructions:

> No person other than a detective shall stop, question, or detain a person suspected of taking the store's property. All cases of suspicion must be immediately reported to the detective, either in person or over the phone. No person shall attempt to assist the detective unless called upon by him. A detective should never be recognized when he is on duty. He should always be a "customer" to fellow employees.

A clearly defined procedure like this spells out how an employee should behave in a specific situation. The problems and embarrassment that could result if a workable procedure were not developed and applied are easy to imagine.

COMMUNICATION AND MANAGEMENT

Plans, policies, controls, and procedures developed by management have no value until put into operation. Before they can be activated, information about them must be transmitted to other levels of management and to employees. Transmission and interpretation of information in business is called *communication*, which the American Management Association defines as "any behavior that results in an exchange of meaning."

The communication process

Company communication is both external and internal. *External* communication is with customers, stockholders, unions, and others outside the organization and will be discussed in later chapters. *Internal* communication involves transmission of information inside the company. It is a three-way process: upward, downward, and horizontal.

The need for upward communication (keeping the boss informed about what's going on) and downward (letting those who work for you know what's happening so they can perform efficiently and aren't demoralized) is more obvious than the need for horizontal, or "crosswise," communication between individuals of different departments, divisions, or branches. Activities in large businesses are complex, and few major decisions are made by one manager alone. The effective manager must use the skills, advice, and experience of others. To do this he gathers information and consults other management-level personnel before making decisions. Indeed, decisions increasingly are made by a group rather than by a single individual. The theory is that the larger the number of ideas and information considered, the sounder the decision.

Intelligent management understands that no one has a monopoly on ideas or knowledge. Further, as a business grows in size it becomes more and more divided into specialized parts. Specialization in turn lessens

Figure **6–3**
A Directional Chart of Internal Management Communication

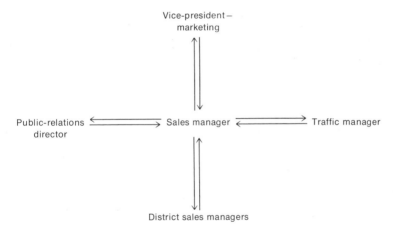

What types of communication would take place with the sales manager in each of the directions shown? What are the difficulties of communicating, and how does management overcome them?

the ability to understand the other fellow's job. Specialized vocabularies result, and conflicting ways of thinking emerge. Managers find that many of their administrative problems come from the inability to communicate in three directions. Overcoming the problem is far from simple, for the work of people with such diverse backgrounds as computer programmer, warehouse superintendent, public relations director, union steward, chief accountant, and sales manager may have to be coordinated in order to achieve a company goal.

Numerous studies show the types of communication utilized in the day's work of a typical manager. They include:

1. Interpret objectives, plans, policies, procedures, and controls to others

2. Make assignments and issue instructions

3. Encourage others to perform their jobs well

4. Give advice and opinions

5. Make short talks and speeches

6. Mediate disputes between subordinates

7. Initiate memos and letters to gather information or provide information

8. Prepare reports

9. Attend meetings and conferences

10. Negotiate with suppliers and/or customers

It is apparent from the above that an effective manager needs skill in both oral and written communication; and the higher one goes in management the more necessary the ability to communicate becomes.

Effective communication

Proper communication is vital to effective management, and great skill is needed by those responsible for communications. Even the corporate name is closely linked to communication. This is evident from the large number of firms that change names each year so that the name will communicate the company's image in keeping with the times. (See Table 6–2.)

Communication of any kind is a difficult art, since it involves many variables and intangibles. The starting place for those intent on communicating well is to recognize its importance—that it can either contribute to effective management or handicap and demoralize an organization. As is usually the case in dealing with business problems, no one set of rules can be applied to all communications problems. There are, however, points that should be kept in mind.

Table **6–2** Name Changes for Companies Listed on the New York Stock Exchange	
FROM	**TO**
American Radiator & Stand. Sanitary Corp.	American Standard Inc.
Bangor Punta Alegre Sugar Corp.	Bangor Punta Corp.
Bath Iron Works Corp.	Bath Industries, Inc.
California Packing Corp.	Del Monte Corp.
De Soto Chemical Coatings, Inc.	De Soto, Inc.
Diamond Alkali Company	Diamond Shamrock Corp.
Electric Storage Battery Co.	ESB Inc.
Engelhard Industries, Inc.	Engelhard Minerals & Chemicals Corp.
General Baking Co.	General Host Corp.
Hammond Organ Co.	Hammond Corp.
Hayes Industries, Inc.	Hayes-Albion Corp.
McDonnell Co.	McDonnell Douglas Corp.
Meredith Publishing Co.	Meredith Corp.
Natco Corp.	Fuqua Industries, Inc.
National Aeronautical Corp.	Narco Scientific Industries, Inc.
North American Aviation, Inc.	North American Rockwell Corp.
Oxford Manufacturing Co., Inc.	Oxford Industries, Inc.
Seaboard Air Line Railroad Co.	Seaboard Coast Line Railroad Co.
Studebaker Corp.	Studebaker-Worthington, Inc.
U. S. Plywood Corp.	U. S. Plywood-Champion Papers Inc.
United States Rubber Co.	Uniroyal, Inc.
Wayne Knitting Mills	Wayne-Gossard Corp.

The company name is a form of communication. Can you conclude from studying this list why companies change names?

1. Try to keep everyone as well informed as possible

2. Follow the chain of command

3. Adapt yourself to the language level of the recipient and use simple, clear English

4. Organize thoughts logically

5. Consider timing—time the communication for when the recipient will be most receptive

6. Remember that written communication is more reliable than oral

7. Treat only one subject in each written communication

8. Make summaries and headings in written communications meaningful

9. Consider attractiveness and appearance of written communications

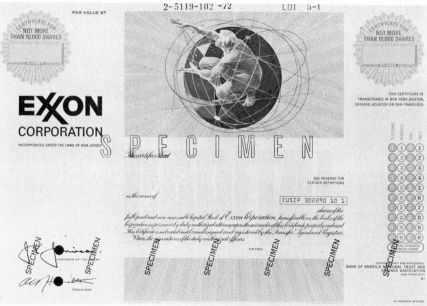

Figure **6–4**

Common-Stock Certificates, Old and New, for a Company that Changed Its Name

In 1972 the Standard Oil Company of New Jersey changed its name after 97 percent of its stockholders voted to do so. The new name is said to be more efficient. When anti-trust action broke up the Standard Oil trust in 1911, Jersey Standard was allowed to use the Esso name in only 18 states. Elsewhere, the company used the trademarks Enco or Humble. Exxon will be used in all areas, eliminating the need to prepare separate advertising for separate regions and eventually eliminating ''the confused image the public has of the corporation.''

Source: Exxon photographs.

THE THEORIES OF MANAGEMENT

The mastery of management is a complex matter for which there is no single formula. There are as many management styles as there are managers; yet there are elements that good managers share and which are elucidated by theory.

There are numerous theories with which serious students intent upon becoming managers should familiarize themselves. Detailed discussion of even the major theories are beyond the scope of an introductory textbook on business.

The Conference Board queried companies about management theories that influenced management most. In 302 replies received, those persons whose theories were mentioned most were McGregor (134); Herzberg (96); Likert (88); Argyris (85); Maslow (54); and Blake and/or Mouton (52). The gist of the major theories, along with the books and persons responsible for them, follow.

McGregor: Theory X and Theory Y. Douglas McGregor's *The Human Side of Enterprise* (1960) is probably the most widely read work in its field. McGregor describes two views about men and their relation to work which have become part of the vocabulary of management: "Theory X" (employees are headstrong, lazy, capricious, and in need of constant watching) and "Theory Y" (employees like to work, seek responsibility, and are capable of self-control).

Herzberg: Motivation Hygiene Theory. Frederick Herzberg's *Work and the Nature of Man* (1966) stresses his motivation-hygiene theory. The factors that motivate men are responsibility, achievement, recognition, and growth opportunities. The "hygiene factors"—fringe benefits, working conditions, holidays, and so on—are essential but are not motivating.

Likert: Organizational Model Systems. Rensis Likert, in his *New Patterns of Management* (1961) and *The Human Organization* (1967), maintains that the value of people can be measured and that they can be managed as carefully as physical assets. Instead of Theory X and Theory Y, he describes four organizational model systems.

Argyris: T Group Training. Chris Argyris, in his *Interpersonal Competence and Organizational Effectiveness* (1962) and *Integrating the Individual and the Organization* (1964), is widely known for recommending T-groups (for training) and for developing new organizational designs and controls.

Maslow: Hierarchy of Needs. Abraham Maslow, in his *Motivation and Personality* (1954), is best known for his "need hierarchy" theory, which states that there is a progression of human needs that motivate people. He stresses growth opportunity and involvement as prime motivators.

Blake and Mouton: Stress-Balance. Robert Blake and Jane S. Mouton wrote *The Managerial Grid* (1964), in which they integrate theories of others and stress a balance between concern for production and concern for people.

PEOPLE AND THEIR IDEAS
Alfred Pritchard Sloan, Jr.

The genius who steered GM into its position as the world's largest corporation

Alfred P. Sloan, Jr., was born in New Haven, Connecticut, in 1875 and graduated from the Massachusetts Institute of Technology at twenty. Four years later he was general manager of the Hyatt Roller Bearing Company. When Hyatt was combined with several other automotive suppliers to form the United Motors Corporation, Mr. Sloan was named president of the new company. In 1918 United Motors became part of General Motors, and Mr. Sloan joined General Motors as a director and vice-president. At that time General Motors was a sprawling, loosely organized company headed toward severe financial and management crises. So effective was he in resolving problems that Sloan was made president and chief executive officer in 1923 and was elected board chairman in 1937, a post he held until 1956, when he was named honorary chairman.

His autobiography[2] is refreshing to read, partly because his career does not fit the usual formula: for example, he did not start by working for the pittance that is orthodox for future tycoons taking their first jobs. Indeed, he started in a responsible position at a good salary. Let us consider some of the ideas of this man who accomplished so much in business.

> On intuition: An essential aspect of our management philosophy is the factual approach to business judgment. The final act of business judgment is of course intuition.

> On change: Some of the biggest [company losses of position in an industry] came about because someone got an idea he thought was eternal.

> On competition: I believe in competition as an article of faith, a means of progress, and a way of life.

> On people: No organization is sounder than the men who run it and delegate others to run it. . . . One of the corporation's great strengths is that it was designed to be an objective organization, as distinguished from the type that gets lost in the subjectivity of personalities. . . . The role of personality can be so important that sometimes it is necessary to build an organization, or rather perhaps a section of it, around one or more individuals rather than fit individuals into the organization.

> On committees: It is doctrine in General Motors that, while policy may originate anywhere, it must be appraised and approved by committees before being administered by individuals.

---

[2] The quotations in this sketch are from *My Years with General Motors,* Alfred P. Sloan, Garden City, N.Y.: Doubleday, 1963.

<u>On size</u>: I am glad to meet the issue of size, for to my mind size of a competitive enterprise is the outcome of its competitive performance; and when it comes to making things like automobiles and locomotives in large numbers for a large home country and the world market, a large size is fitting. . . . I do not regard size as a barrier. To me it is only a problem of management. . . . I have always believed in planning big, and I have always discovered after the fact, if anything, we didn't plan big enough.

<u>On problems</u>: Obstacles, conflicts, new problems in various shapes, and new horizons arise to stir the imagination and contribute to progress of industry.

<u>On self-satisfaction</u>: Success, however, may bring self-satisfaction. . . . the urge for competitive survival, the strongest of all economic incentives, is dulled. The spirit of venture is lost in the inertia of the mind against change.

<u>On being number 1</u>: The perpetuation of an unusual success or the maintenance of an unusually high standard of leadership in any industry is sometimes more difficult than the attainment of that success or leadership in the first place.

In 1934, Sloan established the Alfred Pritchard Sloan Foundation, with an original grant of $500,000. Additional gifts have increased assets to over $200,000,000. In 1945, the foundation set up the Sloan-Kettering Institute for Cancer Research as part of the Memorial Cancer Center in New York City. Its funds support scholarship programs at about thirty-five colleges and universities, and it emphasizes support to education and research projects in mathematics, engineering, science, and economics.

CONTEMPORARY ISSUES
Situation 6

Do women have equal opportunities in management?

One afternoon Ray appeared quite agitated. "You know, sometimes I think some of our instructors have their wires crossed. Remember that discussion we had in our sociology class yesterday—the professor said that women don't really have much of a chance to get to the top in business? Yet today our professor for our introduction to business class said just the opposite—that women do have an opportunity to work their way into management. Whom do you think is right?"

"Well, as I remember it," John replied, "the sociology professor made three points: First, society expects women to rear children and maintain a home; second, men who now almost totally control the power in business, are prejudiced toward women; and third, women really don't want the responsibility that goes with management."

"Yes," Ray responded, "and then our business professor said women are going to become a really significant factor in management. As I recall, he advanced four key reasons: First, there is an ever-increasing shortage of management talent, and so, for practical reasons, women will be promoted to high-level jobs; second, planned parenthood gives women control over rearing a family; third, the government will increasingly work to enforce Title VII of the Civil Rights Act which guarantees women equal employment rights; and fourth, women are just as capable as men in performing management functions."

"I still have mixed feelings," said John. "I ask myself if I would work for a woman executive, and I confess I don't think I'd like it."

"Why?" asked Ray. "I've never seen any evidence that proves women can't do just as good a job in management as men. If you're smart, John, you'll get used to the idea of women in management, because they will be there—whether you like it or not."

SITUATION EVALUATION

1. What additional points can you make to support the sociology professor's views? The business professor's views?

2. Which viewpoint do you feel is the stronger and why?

3. In what types of management job do you feel women would stand the best chance of success? Explain your answer.

BUSINESS CHRONICLE

Organizational problems of expansion

The management of Rent Anything, Inc., decided to experiment and expand in two ways. Two franchises would be granted and two company-owned units would be opened. One of each type would be opened in northern Florida and would provide experience in another part of the home state. The other two would be opened in Georgia and would provide out-of-state experience.

It was felt that the same supervisors could establish both operations. In each case, a team from the home office would search for and develop a location, and then work with the unit until it was operating smoothly. It was felt that, after a few years, it would be clear which organizational arrangement—franchising or company-owned—was better.

QUESTIONS

1. Is the test a good one? What are its advantages and disadvantages?

2. Which system do you think is best for this type of business—company-owned or franchise? Why?

3. What organizational and management problems will likely be encountered? What steps should be taken to prevent a occurrence of the same problem at another time?

APPLICATION EXERCISES

1. Jim Brown owns a heavy-machinery leasing company that rents steam shovels, bulldozers, and construction- and road-building machinery to contractors. He employs 25 people: 2 salesmen, 5 mechanics, 3 clerical workers, 12 laborers, and 3 skilled machinery-maintenance men. Brown is a large, roughly dressed, uncouth man. He speaks sharply to his employees and often uses abusive language. He gives his employees little responsibility and insists on making virtually all business decisions himself. He prides himself on being a "self-made" man. He never takes a vacation and is always present on the business premises during business hours. His employee turnover is low, however. While his employees do not like him, they consider him fair, and he pays wages as good as, and often better than, those of his competitors. His firm shows above-average profits for his line of business, and his customers recommend him because his equipment is commendably maintained and his technical knowledge and that of his staff enable him to provide his customers with excellent advice on how to use equipment for economical and efficient operation. Is Jim Brown a good manager? Could he become a better manager? If so, explain how.

2. Not many years ago, a very large company that manufactured and distributed soaps, paper products, and similar items sold in food stores was in need of a new president. The board of directors, feeling that none of the company's own executives was competent to fill the position, hired a man whom we shall call Mr. Wright. Wright was the outstandingly successful president of a smaller concern that processed and sold meat products to food stores and meat markets. He had been associated with the meat-packing company during his entire business career. Wright tackled his new job with vigor. Almost immediately he replaced about 60 percent of the company's key executives with men with whom he had had business contacts or who had worked with him in the smaller company. He also introduced what he called an efficiency program and within three years closed several of the smaller plants, built two new, larger plants, and consolidated and reorganized the branch sales offices. He expanded the company by buying several firms that produced lines not previously handled by the parent company. At the end of the fifth year, this large and once profitable company was losing money and had slipped from the number two position in the industry to fourth position. How could the few moves described have contributed to the company's loss of position?

3. Mr. Landis is vice-president in charge of marketing for ABC, Incorporated, which is a manufacturer and distributor of air-conditioning equipment. In less than 10 years, the company has grown from a relatively small organization into one of nationwide importance.

The record of the company indicates that Landis and the marketing division have been able to meet the increased responsibilities to a reasonably successful degree. Recently, however, Landis has found that his marketing staff has not been functioning effectively. The morale of the executives seems low, accounts are being lost, and expenses are rising, often without apparent reason. Some of the specific troubles are: (1) The capable southern division branch manager has resigned, stating that the general office insists on selling goods in his branch directly without crediting the branch with these sales. (2) A purchasing agent in the northern division refuses to deal with the local ABC salesman because in several cases he has been able to receive a lower price quotation by phoning his order to ABC's assistant sales manager. (3) When Landis traced an overextension of credit made to a questionable account, the credit manager blamed the local sales manager and the sales manager blamed the local credit manager. (4) An important account has been lost because of a delayed shipment caused by a jurisdictional argument between the traffic manager in charge of truck shipments and the traffic manager in charge of rail and water shipments. (5) Salesmen in the eastern division have presented a demand for wage increases arguing that wages for the same work in the central division are higher. (6) When the southern division branch manager resigned, there was no suitable replacement.

Clearly, Landis is in serious difficulty. He needs help, and he engages a consulting firm, which, after study, submits a report. The chief recommendations in the report call for construction of an organizational chart and assignment of responsibilities accordingly.

Show how lack of organization was responsible for each specific difficulty enumerated above.

QUESTIONS

1. Define the term "management" and explain the different levels of management. What are the responsibilities of each level?

2. Explain the statement: "What is everyone's responsibility is no one's."

3. There is both formal and informal organization in any business. Sometimes the informal organizational power structure is more effective than the formal. Explain why.

4. Every individual in an organization, from the lowest-paid employee to the president, is accountable to some other individual. Discuss this statement.

5. Define business policy. What are the advantages of carefully conceived policies? Devise three examples of ill-conceived policies?

6. What can be done to assure flexibility in organization? Why is it dangerous for a business not to have flexibility?

7. Draw an analogy between a good organization and a good athletic team.

8. Differentiate between line and staff executives. Which would you rather be? Give reasons for your answer.

9. Explain the different theories of management. What do you believe is a good theory of management?

10. In what ways does management in the small company differ from management in the large company? Is management less important in the small company? Explain why or why not.

3

financing

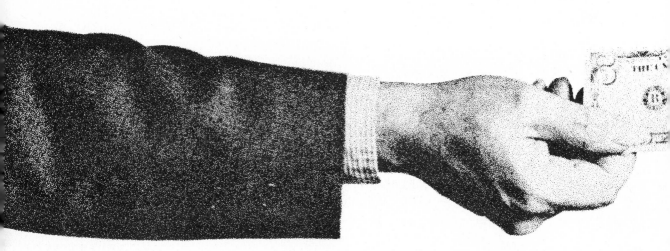

Money is to the economic system what blood is to the human body. Without money, or capital, business could not function. Money is needed to establish, operate, and expand the business.

How does one obtain capital to start and expand a business? How is working capital secured? How do banks and other financial institutions function? How do the securities markets operate? These and other interesting questions are dealt with in this section.

The following four chapters serve as an introduction to the financial aspects of business:

a business

7

long- and short-term financing

8

financial management and institutions

9

reading business and financial news

10

risk management and insurance

long- and short-term financing 7

CHAPTER 7

LONG-TERM CAPITAL

Internal versus External Financing. Obtaining Long-Term Capital Externally.

FINANCING THROUGH BONDS

What Determines Bond Interest. Bond Indenture. Trustee. Denominations. Interest. Maturity Date. Why Bond Prices Fluctuate. Types of Bonds. Methods of Retiring Bonds.

FINANCING THROUGH STOCK

Authorized Stock. Par and No-Par Value Stock. Market Value, Sale of Stock and Pre-Emptive Rights. Preferred Stock. Common Stock.

SHORT-TERM CAPITAL

Types of Short-Term Obligation. Open-Account Credit. Other Unsecured Obligations. Collateral-Supported Short-Term Loans.

THE TREND TOWARD BANK LOANS OF LONGER DURATION

LEASING AND CONSERVATION OF WORKING CAPITAL

All business organizations, large and small, need capital to operate. This capital can be divided into long term and short term. *Long-term capital* is needed for relatively permanent investments, such as new equipment, additional manufacturing plants, stores, warehouses, or land. *Short-term capital* is needed to finance the current operations of a business, such as payment of salaries and wages and purchase of inventories.

LONG-TERM CAPITA

Internal versus external financin

In studying methods of financing, note that both internal (within the business) and external (outside the business) sources are used to provide capital. Long- and short-term capital are generated both externally from loans and internally from profits. Most businesses attempt to meet capital needs out of earnings or profits. When internal funds are insufficient, money is borrowed—or, to use business vernacular, the business "goes into the money market."

Figure **7–1**
Sources of Corporate Funds

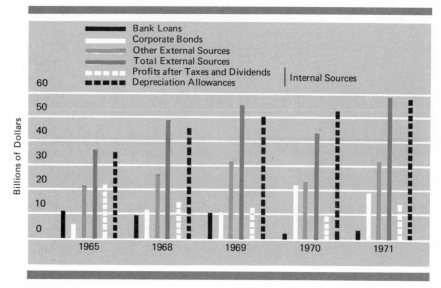

Source: Federal Reserve *Bulletin*.

How profits are to be distributed is an important decision. The individual owner of a business decides how much profit to pay himself and how much to plow back into his business. Corporation officers decide what percentage of earnings they should pay to the stockholders and what percentage they should retain for operations, debt retirement, and expansion.

In recent years America's larger corporations have increasingly generated their capital needs internally. Even corporations with large capital requirements, such as electric utilities, manage to accumulate a large share of their needed capital internally, as indicated in Figure 7–1.

Just one example should serve to indicate how important financing is to a business and its profitability. A new airplane, for example, is valued at $20 million. The interest on that amount, at just 8 percent per year, is $1,600,000; per day it amounts to $4,383.56 for interest. If we assume the plane depreciates over a 10-year period, depreciation costs alone are $2,000,000 per year, or $5,479.45 per day, in addition to interest. No wonder airline executives say that "the only plane making money is the plane that's in the air." Financially, they certainly cost a lot to keep on the ground.

Obtaining long-term capital externally

The methods used to obtain long-term capital externally depend in large part on whether the business is established as a sole proprietorship, partnership, or corporation. The unincorporated business generally does its long-term financing in two ways. First, the owners can invest their personal savings. Second, if the business owns real estate, it may obtain a mortgage (a form of loan on the property) from a bank or an insurance company.

Neither of these methods, however, normally provides sufficient capital for large-scale business operations. Partly for this reason, unincorporated businesses that plan expansion programs generally incorporate. The corporate form of organization facilitates procurement of capital through two methods not available to sole proprietorships and partnerships—the sale of corporate bonds and the sale of stocks. Since long-term financing is a concern primarily of corporations, our discussion will deal with corporate structures.

The basic types of securities used in raising long-term funds are bonds and stocks. Deciding which type of security to issue involves many factors. In reaching a decision, a company gives careful consideration to such important questions as:

1. Which type of security will be easiest to sell in the current money market?

2. How do the different types of financing compare in long-run and immediate costs?

3. Which financing plan will achieve the company's goals and, at the same time, be acceptable to those who already have a financial interest in the corporation?

4. How will the program affect ownership control of the business?

5. What repayment method should be provided for?

Nonequity securities (debt obligations) still are the major source of long-term capital. However, equity securities (which share in corporate ownership) are growing in importance (see Figure 7–2).

FINANCING THROUGH BONDS

A *bond* is a long-term credit instrument that contains promises to pay (1) a specific sum, called the "principal," to the bondholder at a specified

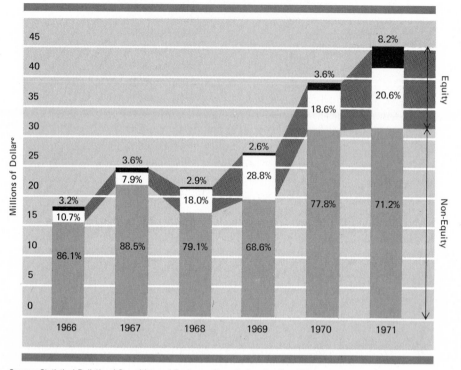

Figure **7–2**
Gross Proceeds of Corporate New Issues
(Equity-Type Securities and Recently Preferred Stocks
Account for Growing Share of New Issues)

Source: Statistical Bulletin of Securities and Exchange Commission, October 1972.

future date, and (2) a definite rate of interest until the principal is repaid when the bond is redeemed. An example that meets these requirements is a $1,000 bond paying 6 percent interest each year until 1990 (the maturity date), at which time the loan would be repaid. Financing through the sale of bonds is a method of borrowing money. Each bond sold by the firm represents a part of the total loan. The firm uses the money as capital for its business. Many types of corporations — industrial, railroad, utility, as well as municipal, state, and federal governments — use bonds extensively to raise capital. Legally, there is no reason a sole proprietor or partnership could not issue bonds; however, because only the corporation has continuity of life, bond financing is almost exclusively used as a corporate method of financing. Four important advantages of bonds are:

1. The sale of bonds does not affect control of the corporation, since bondholders, unlike stockholders, have no voting power. Stockholders are *owners*, while bondholders are *creditors*.

2. Although many of the largest corporate investors, such as banks and insurance companies, are prohibited by federal legislation from buying certain stocks, they can buy bonds. The corporation that sells bonds can therefore tap these large sources of capital.

3. Because they are generally secured (backed) by company assets, bonds can frequently be sold at low interest rates. Thus, money obtained by bond sale may cost the corporation less than that obtained by other methods.

4. Bonds have great tax advantages to the corporation, since interest on debt is a cost of doing business and is deductible from taxable income.

Practically all bonds issued by business corporations are *negotiable*, which means that the original purchaser can sell them to someone else. During the course of its life, a bond may be bought and sold many times.

What determines bond interest

In general, the interest rate paid on borrowed money is determined by two factors: conditions in the money market and the financial condition of the business. Suppose Company A wishes to borrow money by selling bonds secured by certain company assets. The price it will have to pay — that is, the *interest rate* — will depend on conditions in the money market (whether or not money is in short supply) when the bonds are offered for sale. Bonds offered one year may have to pay a rate of 7 percent in order to sell. The same bonds offered two years later might sell paying only 5 percent. It is obvious, therefore, that long-range fiscal planning is quite important to large corporations. Fiscal officers try to time the securing of funds in order to take advantage of the cheapest interest rates.

As would be assumed, financially strong, profitable corporations can sell bonds at lower interest rates than financially weak companies. The price (interest rate) a company must pay to borrow money is related directly to its risk rating. A *risk rating* refers to how able the issuer is to meet the promises specified on the bond. Judging what the chances are that the bond's obligations will be met is done by independent rating agencies to facilitate trading in bonds. The agencies used in U.S. financial circles, along with their rating codes, are given on page 172.

Bonds that earn one of the agency's top four ratings are considered to be investment-grade securities, which means that the speculative, or risk, element is almost nonexistent. By the fifth rating (BB, Ba, BB), the risk element becomes significant, and by the seventh rating (CCC, Caa, CCC), the bond is out-and-out speculative.

FITCH'S	MOODY'S	STANDARD & POOR'S
AAA	Aaa	AAA
AA	Aa	AA
A	A	A
BBB	Baa	BBB
BB	Ba	BB
B	B	B
CCC	Caa	CCC
CC	Ca	CC
C	C	C
DDD		DDD
DD		DD
D		D

Bond indenture

Before a corporation issues bonds to the public, it must prepare a detailed statement called a *bond,* or *trust, indenture,* which describes the rights and privileges of bondholders and the rights, privileges, and responsibilities of the issuing corporation. The indenture includes: (a) specific information about the purposes of the bond issue, (b) the denomination of the bonds, (c) the number of bonds to be issued, (d) the security behind the bonds, (e) the rate of interest and method of payment, and (f) action to be taken in the event the corporation defaults payment. The indenture also indicates the name and responsibilities of the trustee.

Trustee

Since most bond issues are sold nationwide to hundreds or thousands of individuals and organizations, the individual bondholder would be almost powerless to enforce his rights and privileges were it not for the *trustee.* The trustee may be an individual but is usually a bank or other financial institution specializing in this work, and is appointed by the issuing corporation to represent all bondholders. The trustee's duties are listed below.

1. He certifies the bonds—that is, he verifies that the bond is provided for as described in the indenture. This certification affords some protection against overissue or forgery of bonds.

2. He sees that the corporation carries out its obligations to the bondholders. The trustee studies bondholder complaints and, if necessary, brings action against the corporation.

3. He represents the bondholders should the issuing corporation default in payment of interest or principal or engage in some activity that jeopardizes the ultimate repayment of the bonds. The trustee acts as liaison between the corporation and the bondholders. Interest payments and bond redemptions are commonly handled by the trustee, who also sees that the property backing the bond is in safe custody.

Denominations

Most corporation bonds are of $1,000 denomination, although larger bonds of $5,000 or $10,000 denominations are not uncommon. Occasionally bonds will be issued for $100 or $500; however, small denomination bonds are not popular because the more certificates issued, the larger the expenses incurred in handling the issue.

Interest

All bonds bear an interest rate expressed as a percentage, such as 2⅞ percent, 3¼ percent, or 6 percent. Interest is usually paid semiannually. Interest payments on bonds are a fixed charge to the company and so are not dependent on fluctuations in company earnings; nor does payment require action by the board of directors as in the case of stocks.

The method used to pay interest depends on whether the security is a coupon bond or a registered bond. *Coupon bonds* have interest coupons attached to the bond. When interest is due, the bondholder detaches the appropriate coupon and presents it to a bank for payment. He receives payment in much the same manner as when he cashes a check. The bank then collects from the corporation that issued the bonds. The corporation selling coupon bonds does not keep a record of each owner. Holders of *registered bonds* receive their interest payments by check directly from the corporation. Names of these bondholders are registered by the issuing corporation. If the bond is sold, the new owner's name is recorded.

Maturity date

The *maturity date* is the time at which the principal of a bond is due. It is always stated on the bond certificate. Bonds may have a life ranging from five to one hundred years or, in unusual instances, even longer. However, most bonds have a maturity date of twenty or thirty years.

Many bond issues are listed on the stock exchanges. The price of a bond is nearly always quoted as a percentage of face value. To illustrate:

if the bond is quoted at 98½, this means that a bond whose face, or stated, value is $1,000 is being sold at $985. Usually, in the bond price quotations given in newspapers, it is customary to designate each bond issue by short abbreviations — for example, "XYZ corporation 1st 5s." In this case the "1st" indicates first mortgage bonds (having first claim on the property used as backing), and "5s" means a 5 percent interest rate.

Why bond prices fluctuate

Even though bonds have a stipulated interest rate, prices paid for outstanding bonds on the securities exchanges may vary significantly even if the company's basic financial standing is constant. Prices of outstanding bonds tend to fall when money is in great demand and to rise when money is plentiful.

Assume that a company found the going interest rate to be 5 percent a few years ago and issued a bond under agreement to pay that rate. A few years later, interest rates advanced, and the same company now has to pay 9 percent to borrow money under identical terms. It stands to reason that people would rather have the new 9 percent bond than the old 5 percent bond. As a result, the market price of the old bond moves downward so that its yield is comparable to that of the new bond.

Types of bonds

Over the years, financial planners have devised numerous types of bonds to raise capital. Some of the most important types are mortgage bonds, debenture bonds, convertible bonds, warrants, and municipal (tax-exempt) bonds.

Mortgage bonds   *Mortgage bonds* are secured by a mortgage on assets owned by the issuing corporation. A detailed description of the pledged property is included in the indenture. The company maintains control over the property, but title is vested in the trustee, who holds it for protection of the bondholders. When the bonds are redeemed, title reverts to the issuing corporation. If the company fails, the property backing a mortgage bond can be liquidated (sold) and the proceeds used to pay the bondholders.

Mortgage-bond issues may be either *closed* or *open-end*. A closed-mortgage bond issue is one in which a limit is placed on the number of bonds that can be sold. This provision benefits bondholders, since the security behind their bond cannot be offered as a pledge for additional bonds. Obviously, this is a disadvantage to the issuing corporation, since it cannot use that security to borrow more funds.

The *open-end mortgage* does not specify a limit on the number of bonds that may be issued. This form of issue is usually preferred by industrial corporations, railroads, and public utilities, since it permits greater flexibility in future financing and enables the companies to take advantage of increased property values.

Debenture bonds   *Debenture bonds* are direct obligations of the issuing corporation and, unlike mortgage bonds, are not secured by any specific property. The only security is the general credit or financial condition of the company. Since no property is pledged, the company has greater control of its assets. Industrial corporations, traditionally opposed to placing mortgages on manufacturing plants, and companies (notably service companies) with limited tangible assets make wide use of debenture bonds.

Convertible bonds   Broadly speaking, a *convertible bond* can be exchanged for other securities, usually common stock, at a set rate of exchange. Terms of conversion usually stipulate when the conversion option can be exercised and what the conversion rate will be—that is, how many shares of stock will be given in exchange for each bond.

There are two reasons for issuing convertible bonds. First, the bonds are usually easier to sell than ordinary stocks and bonds. Second, when bondholders convert to stock, the corporation frees itself from the responsibility of paying fixed interest charges. However, there are two major disadvantages of such bonds. One is that if many bondholders decide to convert to voting common stock, control of the corporation may be shifted. Another disadvantage is that widespread conversion means a large increase in the number of shares of stock outstanding; this, in turn, reduces per share earnings, which may depress the price of company stock.

Warrants   Akin to the convertible bond is the bond issued with *warrants* (see Figure 7–3). Warrants, which are usually detachable from the bonds, entitle the holders to purchase the common stock of the company at specified prices through the payment of cash and the surrender of the warrants rather than through the surrender of the bonds. If the price of the company's stock advances beyond the price indicated in the warrant, the bondholder can exercise his warrants or sell them at a profit.

When the future of the economy appears more uncertain than usual, the two-way appeal of convertibles and warrants is greatly enhanced. On the one hand, the buyer is comforted by his assured interest payments and the limited risk involved. On the other hand, since convertibles and warrants can be exchanged for common stock, there is a chance for him to share in any subsequent rise in the company's fortunes.

Figure **7–3**
A Warrant

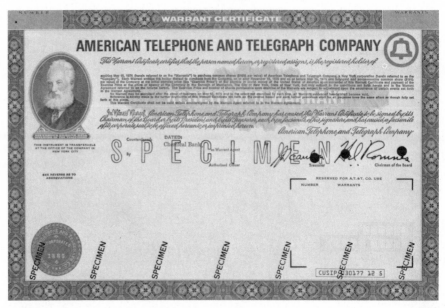

Source: American Telephone and Telegraph Company.

Municipal (tax-exempt) bonds   State and local governments are permitted to issue bonds on which interest is exempt from federal, and usually also from state and city, income tax. *Tax exempts*, as they are called, are used to finance the building of schools, water systems, roads, and other public projects. The tax-exempt feature enables municipalities both to secure money they would otherwise have difficulty obtaining and to do so at the lowest possible interest rates.

Methods of retiring bonds

The issuing corporation must provide for the eventual repayment of its obligation. One or more general provisions for redemption may be indicated in the bond indenture; for example:

1. The call option provides the right to retire bonds at the convenience of the issuing corporation *before* the maturity date.

2. The sinking-fund plan calls for periodic deposit with the trustee of an amount that will assure that money is available to retire bonds at maturity.

3. The serial-plan method stipulates that a certain number of bonds will be retired each year according to the numbers on the bonds, running in sequence from the lowest to the highest.

FINANCING THROUGH STOCK

The second basic method used by corporations to acquire long-term capital is to sell capital stock. Unlike the money secured from bonds, money acquired by the sale of stock is not borrowed. Purchasers of stock become owners of the business. Actual title to specific assets is held by the corporation, and the stockholder has a pro rata ownership interest in the corporation (that is, an ownership proportionate to the number of shares he owns). The corporation will not at a later date, as in the case of bonds, refund money invested by stockholders, although the investor can sell his stock to another investor if he so desires.

Authorized stock

Authorized stock is the maximum number of shares that can be issued as specified in a company's articles of incorporation. If, at a later date, management wishes to increase the amount, it is required by law to secure the approval of the stockholders. In practice, newly formed corporations authorize considerably more stock than they plan to issue in the foreseeable future so that if additional financing eventually becomes desirable, it can be accomplished with a minimum of difficulty.

Authorized stock should not be confused with issued stock. *Issued* stock is that portion of authorized stock that has been sold; *unissued* stock is authorized stock that has not been offered for sale.

Par and no-par value stock

Par value stock is assigned a fixed dollar value, which is printed on the stock certificates. This printed value may be any amount, ranging from one cent to $100 or more. The par value suggests the original price, although more often than not stock is originally sold for less or more than the printed amount.

No-par-value stock, unlike par value stock, does not have a printed value on the stock certificate. Accordingly, it does not suggest a fictional value. It can be sold for any amount without subjecting the purchaser to an assessment at a later date.

Market value

Market value is the price stock commands on the market at a given time. The price others are willing to pay depends on a host of factors, all related in some manner to the anticipated earning power of the corporation. Holders of stocks in major corporations can check their market values daily by reading stock quotations on the financial pages. This procedure is described in Chapter 9.

Sale of stock and pre-emptive rights

Original stock in a new corporation is either sold openly to the investing public or restricted to limited numbers of investors. Subsequent stock issues are, in many instances, offered first to current stockholders. This privilege, called the stockholders' *pre-emptive right*, is intended to protect the stockholder from losing his proportionate interest in the corporation. For example, if an investor owns 5 percent of the stock in a corporation that later doubles its outstanding stock, the investor's proportionate interest drops to 2½ percent if he does not purchase any of the new stock. Pre-emptive rights exist only when required by state law or when provided for in the company's certificate of incorporation.

Where pre-emptive rights exist, stockholders are mailed *stock-subscription warrants* in advance of the issue date of a new offering. These warrants describe the new issue and tell the stockholder the number of new shares he is entitled to buy. Usually this number is determined on a pro rata basis. To refer to the previous example, the owner of 5 percent of the shares would be entitled to buy 5 percent of the new issues.

Such new stock is almost always sold below the current market price of the company's outstanding stock. Therefore, the stock-subscription warrant or right has value: The stockholder can, if he chooses, buy the new stock at less than market value and resell it at the higher market price, or, under most circumstances, he is permitted to sell the stock-subscription warrant or right to someone else if he does not choose to exercise it. A distinction is made between warrants and rights. Rights typically have a life of only a few months. A warrant is a certificate issued by the company and typically has a life of 5, 10, or even 20 years. Thus a Textron Corp. warrant does not expire until 1984, and an Indian Head Corp. warrant in 1990.

Preferred stock

One type of capital stock is *preferred stock*, or "stock that has a preference." The term preferred stock has no particular meaning in itself; the specific preferences are always spelled out in the stock certificate. Usually, however, preferred stockholders are given the following two preferences: (1) the right to receive a fixed dividend before common stockholders receive any and (2) a prior claim on assets (prior to that of common stockholders) in the event the corporation is dissolved. (Common stock will be discussed shortly.)

The right to convert preferred stock to common stock is frequently granted. Preferred stock carries a predetermined, stated dividend rate, which is much like interest payment on bonds.

Preferred stock is not used by all corporations, but corporations that issue it do so for several reasons. First, it is a method of acquiring capital from the more conservative investors who would not invest in common stock. Second, capital can be acquired without affecting the control of the corporation, since preferred stock may be issued so it does not dilute ownership of the common stockholders. Third, preferred stock, because of preferences that may be established for it, is often easier to sell than common stock.

Cumulative and noncumulative preferred Dividends on preferred stock may be either *cumulative* or *noncumulative*. To illustrate, suppose that a corporation fails to earn a profit one year but in the following year earns $120,000, just twice the amount needed to pay one year's dividends on the preferred stock. Under the noncumulative arrangement, the preferred stockholders receive only one year's dividend—$60,000—just half the earnings of the company. The common stockholders are then entitled to receive the remaining $60,000, less any amount the directors feel should be reinvested in the business or held as a cash reserve. If the stock is cumulative, however, the preferred stockholders receive the entire $120,000, and those owning common stock receive nothing.[1]

Participating and nonparticipating preferred Preferred stock is said to be *participating* if it carries a provision that its owners, after receiving their regular, predetermined dividend, will participate, or share, in the remaining earnings of the company with the common stockholders. There are many plans for participation, but the one most commonly used permits the preferred stockholder to share equally with the common stockholders on a per-share basis in the undistributed earnings—unpaid profits—*after* (1) the preferred stockholders have received their stipulated per-share dividend, and (2) a dividend has been declared on each share of common stock, as the example will illustrate.

Nonparticipating preferred limits the preferred stockholder to the specified dividend. This type of preferred stock is the most widely used.

Let us suppose, by way of illustration, that Corporation X has (1) 2,000 shares of preferred stock on which the established dividend is $6 and (2) 2,500 shares of common stock. The corporation declares total dividends of $45,000. If the preferred stock is nonparticipating, the total

[1] It should not be inferred that a corporation distributes all its profits to stockholders; a certain percentage is almost always retained for use in the business or is held as reserve.

payment will be $12,000 to preferred stockholders, and $33,000 to common stockholders. If the preferred stockholders participate equally, the payments will be in this order: $12,000 to preferred stockholders, $15,000 ($6 times 2,500) to common stockholders, and the remaining $18,000 to both preferred and common stockholders—that is, $4 per both preferred and common share.

Voting privileges   Preferred stock may have no voting rights, full voting rights, or voting privileges limited to important company matters. The complete absence of voting rights is not common. Stock with limited voting privileges is the most customary. In this type of stock the right to vote is usually restricted to proposals that directly affect the stock value, such as selling or mortgaging company property, changing preferred stock provisions, and voluntarily dissolving the company.

Common stock

Common stock is the primary source of capital for most corporations. In terms of cash dividends, common stocks on the New York Stock Exchange paid out $20.2 billion in 1971, while preferred stocks paid out only $1.3 billion.

In a sense, common stock is risk capital in that it is capital that is never paid back and pays returns to the investor only if the business prospers. Frequently, it is called "equity capital." Common stock, unlike preferred, does not specify a definite rate of return. Whether or not dividends are paid depends largely on the amount of net profit earned and the decision of the board of directors on how much profit shall be declared as dividends. Common stockholders are the *residual* owners of the business. They receive no dividends until all interest is paid on the "funded debt" (debts, like bonds, that are a fixed cost of doing business) and until preferred stockholders have received their dividends. If the corporation fails, a similar priority exists for the proceeds of liquidation. Holders of common stock have only residual claim on all assets—that is, they receive only what remains after creditors' and preferred stockholders' claims have been satisfied.

From the standpoint of the investor, common stock has four advantages that make it an attractive method for corporations to use to raise capital. First, it is not, as is often the case with preferred stock, limited as to dividends and, consequently, under favorable conditions, may yield a high rate of return. Second, if the corporation is successful, common stock tends to *appreciate* in value. Thus, stock in a new corporation purchased for $10 per share may, some years later, be worth several times that amount. Third, common stockholders usually have full voting power so that, collectively, they control the management of the corporation. Fourth, common stock, especially of major corporations, is easily bought and sold.

Advantages to the corporation The most significant advantage of common stock is that no fixed financial burden is placed on the corporation. Unlike financing by bond issues, there is no interest that must be paid in bad times as well as good. Furthermore, the management of the corporation is free to use profits, if it seems advisable, to expand business operations rather than to pay dividends as it normally would on preferred stock.

Disadvantages to the corporation The acquisition of capital by the sale of common stock has, however, certain disadvantages. First, increasing the amount of common stock may extend voting power to a larger number of people so that the original organizers may lose control. Second, it is often impossible to obtain all the desired capital through common stock. Third, it may be more costly in the long run to issue common stock than to sell bonds, since common stock is a permanent investment, while bonds are paid off at some point in the future.

SHORT-TERM CAPITAL

Several reasons account for the widespread borrowing of short-term, or working, capital, which is usually borrowed for periods of anywhere from 30 days to several years. First, nearly every business has seasonal peaks of activity; in the off sales periods, unusually large inventories of raw materials or merchandise must be held pending sale. Retailers, for instance, may have to buy large quantities of goods in, say, September and October that will not be sold until the Christmas season.

Second, manufacturers, farmers, and other producers may possess raw materials or livestock but lack cash funds to prepare them for market. The farmer, for example, may have cattle on hand that, unless he can borrow money for feed, cannot be fattened.

Third, some unforeseen event may throw a business into temporary financial difficulty. A strike, for example, may make it impossible to ship goods. In such an event, access to short-term capital may help the organization weather the business curtailment.

Another reason for the extensive use of short-term financing is that it is not considered good management to keep an unusually large amount of cash in reserve. The financial health of business is best when the flow of money is vigorous. Cash lying in a strong box is just as undesirable as an employee playing cards instead of working, a machine gathering dust instead of producing, or a building idle instead of earning rent.

Short-term financing is a common business procedure, not an indication of financial weakness. Commercial banks, which directly or indirectly grant most short-term credit, *want* to loan money, for that is their business. A statement such as "Use our money to expand your business; see us for money to finance your inventory and take care of your short-term needs," briefly describes the position of commercial banks.

Types of short-term obligation

Short-term obligations can be divided into two broad categories: unsecured and secured. *Unsecured obligations*—promissory notes, commercial drafts, trade acceptances, and bank acceptances—involve no collateral (no assets used to guarantee repayment of the loan). Money is loaned on an unsecured basis only if the business has a high credit rating. *Secured obligations* are those backed by the pledge of some asset. Accounts receivable, warehouse receipts, bills of lading, and chattel mortgages are commonly used assets to back loans.

Open-account credit

A large part of the working-capital requirements for most business firms is supplied by *open-account credit*. This form of credit is not a cash advance; rather, it is the sale of goods by one business to another, with payment expected at a later date. Since no security is required, a careful investigation of the business seeking credit must be made. Almost all transactions among industrial organizations, wholesalers, and retailers are made on an open-account basis. The end result is that most business firms both *grant* credit and *receive* it.

Credit terms In selling goods on open-account credit, vendors normally make certain stipulations called *credit terms*. Customarily these terms state the length of the credit period and offer a form of reward, called the cash discount, for prompt payment of the bill.

The length of the credit period, though usually 30 days, depends mainly on the custom in the particular industry. The cash discount specifies the amount that can be deducted from a bill if payment is made on or before the designated due date. A very common credit term is 2/10 net 30. The "2/10" means that the buyer is entitled to a 2 percent discount if the goods are paid for within ten days; "net 30" signifies that if the discount is not taken, the entire bill must be paid within 30 days. Assume that a retailer receives a $100 shipment of goods billed 2/10 net 30. If he pays for the merchandise before the tenth day, he deducts 2 percent, or

Figure **7-4**
A Promissory Note

$ 1,200.00	NEW YORK, _____ January 5 _____ 19 __

-------------------Thirty days-------------AFTER DATE THE UNDERSIGNED PROMISE(S) TO

PAY TO THE ORDER OF ------------------Wilbur Wright--

Twelve hundred--- DOLLARS
                                                                                    100

AT FIRST NATIONAL CITY BANK   Washington Square Branch
                                                          OFFICE OR BRANCH

WITH INTEREST AT RATE OF ____ 12 ___% PER ANNUM,

INTEREST PAYABLE ___ Feb. 4, 19 _____

VALUE RECEIVED

No. ____ 15 _____   DUE __ Feb. 4, 19 ___   J. C. John _____

SF 1242A (L) 7-63
PRINTING OF 5-64

Source: First National City Bank, New York, N.Y.

$2, and remits $98. If he waits until after the tenth day, the full $100 is due on or before the thirtieth day.

There are several reasons for offering cash discounts:

1. Prompt payment allows sellers to operate with less working capital.

2. Less billing and collection expense is necessary when goods are paid for promptly.

3. Losses from bad debts tend to be lower.

The buyer also benefits from cash discounts. If a merchant buys $100,000 worth of merchandise from a manufacturer and the terms are 1/10 net 30, he saves $1,000 by paying within 10 days. The manufacturer is saying in effect, "If you pay me 20 days before the bill becomes due, I will give you a 1 percent discount for paying promptly." It is the same as saying, "I will give you 1 percent for the use of that money for 20 days." This is equivalent to an annual interest rate of more than 18 percent (360 divided by 20 equals 18). Obviously, it is better for a merchant to borrow from the bank in order to discount bills than to delay payment. Further, buyers who take cash discounts are regarded as preferred customers. If, at some future date, such a buyer experiences temporary financial difficulty, the vendor is likely to be especially understanding.

Other unsecured obligations

Promissory notes   A *promissory note* (usually referred to simply as a note) is an unconditional promise in writing made by one individual or firm (the *maker*) to another. It is signed by the maker, who agrees to pay

Figure **7–5**
A Sight Draft

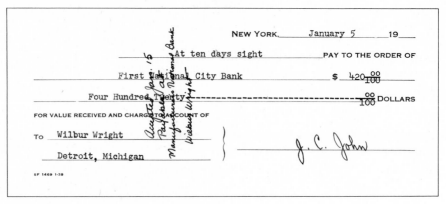

the bearer on demand, or at a stated future date, a specified sum of money.

Short-term business obligations are usually *negotiable*—that is, they can be legally transferred and are therefore saleable. For example, the ABC Manufacturing Company sold a shipment of window frames to the Brill Lumber Company, which agreed to pay for the shipment within 90 days. The ABC Manufacturing Company turned the claim into a tangible security by means of a promissory note payable within that time. Before the note became due, the ABC Manufacturing Company sold it (discounted it) to the First National Bank.

At the end of 90 days, when the note became due, the First National Bank said, in effect, to the Brill Lumber Company, "Here is the note you gave the ABC Manufacturing Company. We now own this note. It is due; pay us." If the Brill Lumber Company had failed to pay, the bank would have returned the note to the ABC Manufacturing Company, which would have been legally obligated to pay the bank. Legal action for non-payment would then have been initiated by the ABC Manufacturing Company against the Brill Lumber Company.

Frequently, banks or business establishments ask the maker to have someone else guarantee the note. In the event the original maker cannot pay as agreed, the second signer, called an *accommodation endorser*, is then held liable. Another common method for adding security to the note is to require two people, called "comakers" or "cosigners," to sign the note. On such a note, each comaker is equally liable for payment.

Drafts   A *draft* is an unconditional written order made by one party (the *drawer*) addressed to a second party (the *drawee*) that orders the drawee to pay a specified sum to a third party (the *payee*). A draft differs from a promissory note in that it is an order rather than a promise to pay. A draft is drawn by a creditor, whereas a promissory note is drawn by a borrower. Three parties are always involved in a draft, but two of them may be the same person. When the drawer orders payment to himself, drawer and payee are the same. For example, a business can order itself to pay itself $1,000 in ninety days and then use the order at the bank to borrow the money for ninety days. Whoever holds the note at the end of ninety days gets paid for it. In other cases the payee may be the drawer's bank; in such an event, three different parties may be involved. If the draft is payable on demand, it is called a *sight* (or *demand*) *draft*; if it orders payment at a future date, it is known as a *time draft*.

Trade, or bank, acceptances Bankers' or trade acceptances are used almost exclusively to finance trade, mostly foreign. Highly popular, their volume has increased fourfold in the past ten years. They are bought primarily by businesses to earn a return on temporarily idle funds.

In simplest terms, a trade acceptance is a draft that a bank promises to honor at maturity, usually 60 to 90 days. Recently investors could earn $5\frac{5}{8}$ percent for 1-to-30-day acceptances, $5\frac{3}{4}$ percent for 31-to-90-day, and $5\frac{7}{8}$ for 91-to-180-day maturities.

Let us take a typical example to see how this works. Suppose a U.S. importer wishes to purchase cocoa beans from a Central American exporter. The U.S. importer asks his bank for a letter of credit that gives the details of the transaction and states the amount the Central American can collect on a time draft that the U.S. bank will be willing to pay. The U.S. importer agrees to pay his bank at maturity, which will be after he has received the cocoa beans. Meanwhile the Latin exporter gets his cash from his bank when he gives them the shipping documents (title to the cocoa beans) and the U.S. bank draft. The Latin bank sends the draft to the U.S. bank for collection. If it finds the shipping documents in order (it keeps them for security), it stamps the draft "accepted" and pays the Latin bank. The draft has now become an acceptance and is the irrevocable obligation of the U.S. bank, which may hold it in its own loan portfolio or sell it to a dealer in such securities, who in turn sells it to

Figure **7–6**
A Trade Acceptance

TRADE ACCEPTANCE

No 75 Jacksonville, Fla., (CITY OF DRAWER) Jan. 5 19 (DATE)

To J. C. John and Son (NAME OF DRAWEE) New York, N. Y. (ADDRESS OF DRAWEE)

On January 31, 19-- (DATE OF MATURITY) Pay to the order of Ourselves (NAME OF PAYEE)

Nine Hundred Ninety-------------------------00 Dollars ($ 990 00/100)

The transaction which gives rise to this instrument is the Purchase of Goods by the Acceptor from the Drawer. The Drawee may accept this Bill payable at any Bank, Banker or Trust Company in the United States which he may designate.

Accepted at New York (CITY) on Jan. 9 19 (DATE)
Payable at First National City Bank (NAME OF BANK)
Location New York City
J. C. John (SIGNATURE OF ACCEPTOR)

Florida Linen Service Co. (SIGNATURE OF DRAWER)
By R. W. Payne

★ WILSON JONES CO. U.S.A.

business investors who wish to put idle funds to use. Over $3.5 billion of trade acceptances can be outstanding in world trade at any time. A big plus which makes acceptance drafts so attractive is that there is no record of any investor ever having suffered a loss of principal on an acceptance of a U.S. bank.

Collateral-supported short-term loans

Some loans are made by banks and other lending agencies only if collateral is pledged. The purpose of collateral is to give the lender a lien on certain property that can be seized if the borrower fails to repay the loan. As an extra precaution, most lending agencies insist that the marketable value of the collateral leave a margin of at least 20 percent more than the amount of the loan. Thus, if a business wanted to borrow $1,600 on a secured loan, the lender would probably require at least $2,000 worth of collateral.

A lending agency is likely to require collateral if (1) the borrower has only a fair credit rating, (2) the borrower is not known to the lending agency, (3) an unusually large sum is involved, (4) the lender questions the use to be made of the money, (5) collateral is required on all loans as a matter of policy, or (6) secured loans are easier to rediscount. (See page 210.) Some common forms of collateral offered to support short-term loans are accounts receivable, bills of lading, warehouse receipts, chattel mortgages, and stocks and bonds.

Accounts receivable   Very frequently a business pledges its *accounts receivable* (money customers owe the company) as collateral for a loan. Lending money on accounts receivable, often called *factoring,* is done by a number of commercial credit companies who specialize in making such loans and, increasingly, by commercial banks.

Many large retailers finance their installment business by selling their accounts to banks. Under this plan, the accounts are sold outright, although the retailer continues to service them. The customer never knows that his account has been sold to a bank, since the company makes all collections. At the end of a given accounting period, the retailer settles with the bank, selling it new accounts placed on the company books during the period and remitting to the bank collections received on old pledged accounts during the period.

Bills of lading   Another form of collateral for loans is the *bill of lading,* a receipt issued by a transportation agency for merchandise to be transported from a named shipper (the consignor) either to a specified consignee or to the order of any person. A bill of lading stating that the goods are being shipped to a specific person is called a *straight bill* and is nonnegotiable. If the bill of lading does not specify the consignee, it is called an *order bill* and is negotiable. The holder of either type of bill of lading holds the title to the merchandise and can offer it as security for a loan.

Warehouse receipts   One of the most common types of collateral for loans is the *warehouse receipt*, which is used in the following manner. A business firm stores merchandise or other goods in a public warehouse that specializes in storage for a fee. The warehouse issues a warehouse receipt, which is title to the stored merchandise described in the receipt. If the business needs funds, it can present the receipt to a bank and usually obtain a loan for up to 70 or 80 percent of the goods' market value. Until the loan is repaid, the borrower cannot withdraw the merchandise from storage. If he defaults in payment, the bank takes possession of the goods. Warehouse receipts are usually negotiable.

Chattel mortgages   Another form of acceptable collateral for short-term loans is the *chattel mortgage.* This security can be given on almost any *movable* property that has a market, such as motor vehicles, tractors and other farm machinery, furniture, livestock, appliances, and grain. Chattel mortgages are especially common in the financing of motor vehicles. A business purchasing a truck, for example, can make the customary down payment and then sign a note backed by a chattel mortgage on the truck for the balance.

THE TREND TOWARD BANK LOANS OF LONGER DURATION

As a borrowing arrangement, the short-term loan is more and more being replaced by what is called the *term loan.* There are several types of term loans, their common characteristic being a contractual agreement stating that the bank will supply credit for longer than a year. The particular type of arrangement usually reflects the purpose of the borrowing and the length of time the user will need credit. Banks make such arrangements only for "qualified" customers—those with well-established relations with the bank and with financial conditions and prospects that meet rigid standards.

Reports made to the Federal Reserve by 150 of the nation's largest banks indicate that more than 45 percent of their outstanding commercial and industrial loans were made under agreements that provided the borrower with credit for more than a year—in many cases, up to seven or eight years. There has been a trend toward longer loan maturities since the mid-1950s.

LEASING AND CONSERVATION OF WORKING CAPITAL

Since 1960, leasing has become an important business practice designed, among other things, to reduce operating-capital requirements. Businesses today frequently lease automobiles, trucks, data-processing equipment, copying machines, and many other items. Kodak, for example, both sells and rents its KOM-90 Microfilmer, a complex machine that sells for $117,000 or rents for $3,660 a month.

Under a lease arrangement, the lessee (firm granted the lease) needs less capital than if it were making an outright purchase. There is also a tax advantage in leasing. A rental fee is a business expense that is paid for *before* taxes. A piece of equipment is paid for *after* taxes; that is, with dollars that are left over when perhaps as much as 52 percent has been paid out for income tax.

Companies employing outside salesmen frequently lease, rather than purchase, a fleet of cars and make monthly rental payments. The principal disadvantage of leasing to the lessee is that no equity is built up. It is a situation similar to the individual renting an apartment compared with the individual buying a home. Under some lease arrangements, however, the lessee can apply part or all of the lease payments to the purchase of the item at a later date.

PEOPLE AND THEIR IDEAS
J. Paul Getty**

The richest American businessman

He has preserved the virtues of "rugged individualism" and grafted them onto the "know-how" of the Planning Age. This is how one of his biographers explains J. Paul Getty. Born in 1892, he earned a diploma from Oxford University and attended the University of California and the University of Southern California. As a young man, he once floored his friend Jack Dempsey, who said if he had become a professional boxer, he might have been the world champ.

An internationalist who believes he can view his business ventures

SPECIAL READINGS

**How to Be Rich by J. Paul Getty. Chicago: Playboy Press, 1965. This book reveals insights about business by the nation's richest businessman. Some of its chapter headings are: The Wall Street Investor, The Millionaire Mentality, Business Blunders and Booby Traps, The Psychology of Sound Personnel Management, A Real Approach to Real Estate, and The Morals of Money. Among the controversial ideas in this book is the following: "The conformist is not born. He is made. I believe the brainwashing process begins in the schools and colleges . . . [which] seem hell-bent on imbuing their students with a desire to achieve 'security' above all — and at all — costs."

with better perspective from abroad, he speaks seven languages, which he taught himself by listening to records and reading foreign newspapers aloud. Thus, for example, when he negotiates with the Arabs for oil rights, he speaks Arabic. A rich man's son, he made his own fortune because his father distrusted his business ability and so failed to provide for him in his will! Getty made his first million by investing a monthly allowance of $100. In 1958, when it was determined that he was America's richest businessman, he commented, "I don't know of anybody who could sell out for more than I could."

In amassing his fortune he has been in the middle of many proxy fights. He had this penetrating comment to make about the difficulty of winning a proxy fight. "The press in the United States thoughtlessly aids an entrenched Board. The press comes out with headlines that so-and-so is trying to get control. Those who seek reform and protest against infringements of stockholder's rights are pictured as opportunists. The merits are not discussed. That is just selling newspapers."

A former President of Tidewater Oil had this to say, "The greatness of J. Paul Getty is that he knows how to wait. He is so patient. He doesn't jump into hasty actions, but waits for something good to turn up, calculates all the hazards and only then moves." Another man who knows him well said, "He is first and foremost a deep thinker—all intellect and basically a scholar. He confounds experts with thousands of questions and sometimes spends months in the library studying." Getty himself has said, "I have a blinding, restless urge to see and participate in everything that's happening."

Deeply interested in art and history, he has written several books on those subjects. A passionate worker—"sixteen hours a day—that's my minimum"—he states that his business is to "think and plan. I am a businessman before all else. [He is said to have outstanding instinct for identifying capable men.] I delegate authority whenever I feel it's justified, but there are moral responsibilities I can't ignore. I can't remain a member of the leisured classes for more than a couple of weeks. If there is midnight oil to be burned—well it's burned until my desk is clear." "What have you achieved today?" is a catch-phrase that is part of the lore of the Getty empire. Getty is frequently teased about having so much money. When the President phoned him to congratulate him on his 80th birthday in December 1972, he was asked whether he was offered the job of Secretary of the Treasury.

He married many times; all of them ended in failure. He once said, "I hate being a failure. I hate and regret the failure of my marriages. I would gladly trade my millions for just one, lasting marital success." Ralph Hewins, one of his biographers and obvious admirers concluded: "J. Paul Getty's quest led not to happiness but to wisdom."[2]

---

[2] *The Richest American: J. Paul Getty*, Ralph Hewins, New York: E. P. Dutton.

CONTEMPORARY ISSUES
Situation 7
A perplexing question: to specialize or generalize?

"Now that we're studying finance in our textbook," Ray observed, "we're getting into the areas of business specialization. My problem is, quite simply, that I haven't yet decided what to major in. You don't have that problem, John. You like accounting, you're going to major in it, and you will end up a CPA earning a good salary and doing work you know you like. That's nice, and I envy you. But what about me? I'm interested in everything in general and nothing in particular. That worries me — to say nothing of my parents."

John was surprised at Ray's point of view. "Look, there are two roads: that of the specialist, and that of the generalist who really enables the specialists to work together. I'd say being interested in a lot of things is an asset. It takes *both* specialists and generalists to make a business go. The specialist needs a thorough, detailed knowledge of a specific function like computer programming, personnel management, or financial analysis. But the people who head big departments or the entire business need to have a broad understanding of all functions and how they fit together."

However Ray was still not convinced. "You have a specific target in mind, but I don't. And that worries me. I don't know yet where I can fit in and be happy. I'm thinking too of what C.P. Snow, the English philosopher, said in his book *The Two Cultures: And a Second Look*;[3] namely, that the specialist and the generalist are ending up unable to talk to each other, and that this could lead to the downfall of the Western World."

"Well," responded John, "whether to specialize or generalize is a question each student must answer for himself. One thing I'm sure of, however, is that the work of the generalist is going to become more difficult in the future as new specialties are developed. Today, many senior executives who manage computer operations went to college before the first computer was developed."

SITUATION EVALUATION

1. What are the bases for Ray's unrest and how would you answer him?

2. How would you evaluate C.P. Snow's thesis?

3. What are some examples of emerging new fields of specialization?

---

[3] Cambridge University Press, 1969.

BUSINESS CHRONICLE

Planning for and considering financing

Financing was a problem for Rent Anything, Inc., for two reasons: locations had to be purchased and, in each case, a specifically designed building had to be constructed. Fully-developed locations consisted of parking and drive-in facilities, equipment storage areas, display rooms, a parts depot, and a repair and maintenance facility. Because properties were developed in such a highly specialized manner, experienced investors, such as insurance and mortgage companies, shied away from financing them through mortgages. Specialized or single-purpose properties usually have a low resale value; hence they are avoided by institutional investors.

Rental equipment inventories (the company's stock in trade) required large amounts of capital. Fixtures, signs, repair equipment, and tools also required financing. Initial working capital needs were great for there were heavy advertising expenses, personnel hiring and training costs, advanced payment for insurance and licenses, and other expenses.

QUESTIONS

1. Why does "special purposes" real estate often present difficult problems for financing? Is there anything that can be done to reduce this problem?

2. Classify the various capital needs of Rent Anything into short-, intermediate-, and long-term categories. Suggest how each category could be financed — for company-owned outlets and franchises.

3. Credit is also a form of financing. What credit arrangements might be used to provide financing?

APPLICATION EXERCISES

1. Sam and Sally Brown are about to purchase a $25,000 home. They plan to make a down payment of $5,000 and borrow $20,000 from a lending institution to be repaid over a 20-year period. They visit two banks, A and B, and a savings and loan association. Bank A offers to make them a loan at $8\frac{1}{2}$ percent, bank B offers them a loan at $8\frac{3}{4}$ percent, and the association promises them a loan at 9 percent. Sam and Sally, both intelligent consumers, then compute that over the full 20-year period the $8\frac{1}{2}$ percent loan will cost a total of $21,656.80 in interest, the $8\frac{3}{4}$ percent loan will cost $22,420.00, and the 9 percent loan will cost $23,188.00.

   a. How do you account for the substantial difference in cost for only a fraction of one percent difference in the interest rate?

   b. Obviously, it pays to shop when borrowing money. Why is it then that many people pay little attention to the interest rates that are charged?

2. Assume long-term credit would be required in each of the following instances. In each case suggest a logical method for financing—that is, by issuing stocks or bonds. (1) A retail appliance store wishes to sell refrigerators on terms payable in 120 days. Capital is needed to finance customer accounts. (2) The Barton Tractor Company, a farm implement manufacturer, wishes to build a branch factory. (3) A retail hardware chain wishes to buy the buildings that house the stores it now rents. (4) An airline wishes to finance the purchase of additional airplanes. (5) A tobacco company wishes to finance tobacco inventories that must be cured and stored for a period of nineteen months.

3. Red Top, Inc., canners of tomatoes, have a problem of short-term financing. Their season of operation is short. They buy fresh tomatoes from farmers and pack them in August and September, and they sell and ship their entire pack during the months of October and November. Describe the collateral that could be used and the methods available for securing capital to be paid out over a period four months for such direct costs as (a) fresh tomatoes brought from farmers, (b) wages paid to cannery employees, and (c) tin cans and labels. Assume that at the end of four months—that is, by November 1—the entire pack is sold on terms that mean the company can pay its debts in full no later than November 15.

QUESTIONS

1. What is meant by "plowing money back" into a business? What is meant by "milking a business"? Who decides which one of these courses is to be followed?

2. Why is it necessary to name a trustee for a bond issue? What are the trustee's duties?

3. What is the difference between interest and dividends?

4. Since a corporation does not have to repay funds raised through issuing stock, why does it bother to issue bonds, which have fixed interest rates and which must be repaid?

5. Why does a young corporation usually depend on the sale of stock rather than bonds to obtain long-term capital?

6. What is the difference between par value and market value of stocks?

7. What are the advantages and disadvantages of common stock from the viewpoint of the corporation?

8. Why may it be "poor business" for a company to pay for everything it buys on a cash basis? Why is it often "poor business" to sell on a cash-only basis?

9. What are the distinguishing characteristics and uses of a promissory note? A draft?

10. What is a cash discount? Is it always wise for a business to take the cash discount? Discuss why or why not.

financial management and institutions

CHAPTER 8

CREDIT MANAGEMENT: COMMERCIAL
Objectives of Credit Management. Investigating Credit Applicants. Establishing Credit Limits. Collection Procedures.

SOURCES OF CONSUMER CREDIT
Retailers. Outside Agencies—Credit Card Companies. Sales Finance Companies. Commercial Banks. Consumer Finance Companies. Credit Unions.

CREDIT BUREAUS

PROTECTING THE CONSUMER
Fair Credit Reporting Act. Consumer Credit Protection Act.

PUTTING IDLE MONEY TO PRODUCTIVE USE
Negotiable Certificates of Deposit.

FINANCIAL INSTITUTIONS
Commercial Banks. The Federal Reserve System. The Federal Deposit Insurance Corporation.

INVESTMENT BANKS / MUTUAL SAVINGS BANKS / SAVINGS AND LOAN

ASSOCIATIONS / OTHER FINANCIAL INSTITUTIONS

SECURITY EXCHANGES
Membership. Functions. Listing of Securities. Brokerage Houses. Over-the-Counter Markets.

THE SECURITIES EXCHANGE ACT OF 1934
Major Regulatory Provisions.

GUIDELINES FOR BEGINNING INVESTORS

Financial and credit management and the institutions that facilitate such management are the subject of this chapter. Money and credit management is often considered dull. Bankers are often stereotyped as arch-conservatives with stuffy personalities. Such assumptions are totally misleading. The management of money and credit can be very exciting. The Finance Committee (see Figure 6–2, page 146) is always of crucial importance to the corporation. One can be sure that the important financial decisions are made by the highest ranking executives in the corporation.

Finance is at the forefront of change, for changes cannot be implemented unless you plan and provide for financing. Money, even historically, has been associated with change. The Great Seal of the United States that is found on our one-dollar bills, bears the motto "Novus Ordo Seclorum," which means "a new order of the century." The first appeal of our continent lay in its newness, and money was the implementer of opportunity. This applies as much today as it did back in the days when the Great Seal was first placed on our dollars.

CREDIT MANAGEMENT: COMMERCIAL

The wide use of open-account and other forms of credit has created a need for credit management specialists. Medium-sized and large companies generally establish a separate credit department headed by a credit manager; in the small business, credit decisions are made by the manager or his assistant. The following discussion is confined to credit extended by one business to another. Because of several important differences, consumer credit will be discussed separately later in this chapter.

Objectives of credit management

Credit management has two basic, sometimes conflicting, objectives: first, to minimize bad debt losses and, second, to maximize sales volume. Minimizing bad debt losses requires that all credit applicants be screened carefully to avoid extending credit to business firms that may not meet their obligations. To achieve maximum sales, however, it is necessary to be reasonably lenient in extending credit. If credit policies are too rigid, customers will take their business elsewhere. So it is apparent that realizing both objectives—that is, both minimizing bad debts and maximizing sales—is not easy. Credit managers, who want strict control, and sales managers, who want lax control, frequently lock horns!

To make wise credit decisions it is ordinarily necessary to investigate credit applicants, establish credit limits, and follow an orderly collection procedure.

Investigating credit applicants

The basic purpose of the credit investigation is to determine whether the applicant can pay for goods bought on credit. Each applying company is normally evaluated in accordance with what are popularly known as the "four C's" of credit. These are:

1. Character: the applicant's reputation for honesty, integrity, and responsibility

2. Capacity: the applicant's business ability as measured by efficiency, methods, and history

3. Capital: the applicant's ability to pay (so that his company could be made to pay if the company failed to pay as agreed)

4. <u>Conditions</u>: the probable economic trends and competitive position of the credit applicant

To evaluate each applying business on the basis of the four C's, information concerning the business is collected from one or more of the following sources: Dun & Bradstreet, Inc., specialized mercantile agencies, other creditors, and miscellaneous sources. These are discussed below.

Dun & Bradstreet, Inc.   This organization, at one time called the "Mercantile Agency," specializes in gathering credit information about manufacturers, wholesalers, retailers, and other businessmen throughout the United States and in many foreign countries. This information forms the basis for "Business Information Reports," which are available on a confidential basis to businesses, banks, and insurance companies that are D&B subscribers. Services of Dun & Bradstreet include:

<u>Reference books.</u>   These contain pertinent credit information on close to three million businesses in the U. S. and Canada. Each listing includes the name of the business, the line of business, the year started, and a credit rating. In addition, similar reference books are published for South America and Europe. These books are confidential for the use of D&B subscribers only and are rented, not sold. They are under constant revision and are published every sixty days. The rating for each business is given in code form and serves as a quick guide to the credit manager for checking routine orders. On marginal, very large, or complicated accounts, however, it is recommended that the full "Business Information Reports" be obtained before reaching credit opinions.

<u>Special reports.</u>   In exceptional situations when large sums are involved or unusual factors exist that make it necessary for the credit man to have specific data not normally included in the regular D&B Business Information Report, specialized reports can be ordered. These reports are tailormade for the sole use of the inquiring subscriber and are usually very comprehensive. They are priced in accordance with the extent of investigation required to complete them. (See Figure 8-1.)

<u>Other services.</u>   Dun & Bradstreet offers numerous other services not necessarily related directly to the investigation of a specific credit risk. They include publication of various credit periodicals, a service for collecting accounts, a special service for the building and construction industries, and a credit advisory service designed specifically for the apparel trades.

Specialized mercantile agencies   Specialized mercantile agencies perform many of the same activities as Dun & Bradstreet, but they usually restrict their analyses to firms in one type of business. Examples are Credit Exchange, Inc., headquartered in New York, which gives credit ratings on

Figure **8-1**

A Sample Information Summary Used by Credit Managers

Dun & Bradstreet, Inc.

Please note whether name, business and street address correspond with your inquiry.

BUSINESS INFORMATION REPORT

BASE REPORT

SIC	D-U-N-S	© DUN & BRADSTREET, INC.		STARTED	RATING
34 69	04-426-3226	CD 13 APR 21 19--		1957	DD 1
	ARNOLD METAL PRODUCTS CO	METAL STAMPINGS			

53 S MAIN ST
DAWSON MICH   49666
TEL 215 999-0000

SAMUEL B. ARNOLD)
GEORGE T. ARNOLD) PARTNERS

SUMMARY

PAYMENTS	DISC
SALES	$177,250
WORTH	$42,961
EMPLOYS	10
RECORD	CLEAR

CONDITION	STRONG
TREND	UP

PAYMENTS

HC	OWE	P DUE	TERMS	APR 19--	
3000	1500		1 10 30	Disc	SOLD
2500	1000		1 10 30	Disc	Over 3 yrs
2000	500		2 20 30	Disc	Over 3 yrs
					Old Account

FINANCE

On Apr 21 19-- S. B. Arnold, Partner, submitted the following statement dated Dec 31 19--

Cash	$ 4,870	Accts Pay	$ 6,121
Accts Rec	15,472	Notes Pay (Curr)	2,400
Mdse	14,619	Accruals	3,583
	----------		----------
Current	34,961	Current	12,104
Fixt & Equip ($4,183)	22,840	Notes Pay (Def)	5,000
CSV of Life Ins	2,264	NET WORTH	42,961
	----------		----------
Total Assets	60,065	Total	60,065

Annual sales $177,250; gross profit $47,821; net income $8,204. Fire insurance mdse $15,000; fixt $20,000. Annual rent $3,000.
Signed Apr 21 19-- ARNOLD METAL PRODUCTS CO by Samuel B. Arnold, Partner.

-----0-----

New equipment purchased last Sep was financed by bank loan. Monthly payments on loan are $200.

Arnold reported sales for the three months ended Mar 31 were up 10% compared to the same period last year. Increase was attributed by management to additional capacity provided by new equipment.

Profit is being made and retained resulting in an increase in net worth. Current debt is light in relation to worth. Inventory turnover is rapid.

BANKING

Balances average high four figures. Loans granted to low five figures, secured by equipment, now owing high four figures. Relations satisfactory.

HISTORY

Style registered Feb 1 1965 by partners. S. ARNOLD, born 1918, married. 1939 graduate of Lehigh University. 1939-50 employed by Industrial Machine Corporation, Detroit, and 1950-56 production manager with Aerial Motors Inc., Detroit. Started this business in 1957. G. ARNOLD, born 1940, single, son of Samuel. Graduated in 1963, Dawson Institute of Technology. Served U.S. Air Force 1963-1964. Admitted to partnership Feb 1965.

OPERATION

Manufactures perforated metal stampings for industrial concerns. Sells on Net 30 day terms. Has twelve accounts. Territory greater Detroit area. Employs ten including partners. LOCATION: Rents 5,000 square feet in one story cinder block building in normal condition. Located in central business section of main street. Premises neat.
4-21 (803 77) PRA

Source: Dun & Bradstreet, Inc.

businesses associated with the apparel industry; and the Packer Produce Mercantile Agency, which specializes in credit data on firms distributing vegetables, butter, eggs, and other produce. These agencies have the advantage of specialization, so their reports can be more meaningful than those issued by Dun & Bradstreet.

Creditors and other sources   The most specific information concerning a credit applicant's paying habits can be obtained from businessmen who have made credit sales to the applicant. Sometimes a telephone call or letter is sufficient, though some larger organizations employ credit investigators whose main job is to inquire about an applicant's paying habits. Groups of businessmen selling to the same accounts sometimes form credit exchange bureaus for the purpose of sharing credit information. Other sources of credit information are financial statements, personal interviews, banks, attorneys, and the sales representatives who call on applicants.

Establishing credit limits

The investigations described above supply an answer to the question, "Should credit be extended to the applicant?" In a general way, the investigations also reveal how much credit can safely be granted. The fixed maximum amount of credit permitted to be outstanding at any given time is called the *credit limit* or *line of credit*. The credit limit is determined by several factors, but basically, if the applicant is found to be a good credit risk, the limit will be relatively high, while if he is found to be a questionable risk, the limit will be low.

While numerous formulas have been designed to fix such limits on a semi-scientific basis, the judgment of the credit executive remains the most important factor in deciding the limit. As the credit applicant's circumstances change, so will the credit limit accorded him.

Collection procedures

It is estimated that more than one-third of all business failures can be traced to inadequate working capital. This is often the result of a failure to collect accounts promptly. There are several advantages in prompt collection: (1) Working capital keeps coming in, enabling the creditor to pay his own bills on time. (2) Bad debt losses are reduced; experience shows that the longer a bill remains outstanding, the less likely it is that it will be collected. (3) Better customer relations are maintained; once an account falls behind in payment, the debtor tends to take his business where his credit is less apt to be questioned.

To make certain that as many accounts as possible are collected promptly, or at least eventually, a planned collection procedure is essential. This consists of a series of steps, ranging from mild reminders that the account is due, through more drastic notices that suggest some legal action may become necessary, to legal action itself. Common steps in an efficient collection procedure (applied in the following order) include statements or bills stamped "overdue," collection letters, personal calls, action by attorneys or collection agencies, and lawsuits. Any collection procedure should attempt to collect accounts and still retain the good will of the customer.

SOURCES OF CONSUMER CREDIT

Consumer credit, or, as it is often called, retail credit, is credit extended to ultimate consumers. As one humorist put it, "You must give the American people credit for their standard of living." Actually, this remark is an accurate comment on the American economic scene.

Consumer credit first began to enable purchases of so-called big-ticket items — hard goods that are relatively expensive, such as major appliances and furniture. Today, much consumer credit is extended in the sale of so-called soft goods.[1]

There are two forms of consumer credit: charge-account credit and installment credit. *Charge-account credit* resembles the open-account credit extended by business firms. At the end of a given period, usually 30 days, consumers are billed for all purchases. Approximately 76 percent of all retail credit sales are made on this basis. *Installment credit* differs from the charge account in that the customer's obligation is repaid in fractional amounts at stated intervals after the purchase is made. This method is known by various names — "easy-payment plan," "budget plan," "deferred-payment plan," and "time sales."

A number of different businesses extend consumer credit. Here we discuss the following sources of consumer credit: retailers, outside agencies, sales finance companies, commercial banks, consumer finance companies, and credit unions.

---

[1] This is common business vernacular. *Soft goods* are clothing, shoes, furs, and linens made from textiles and soft material; *hard goods* are appliances, furniture, batteries, and so on. The division has significance in business because of differences in handling each class. Credit practices, for example, may vary because one class has repossession value while the other does not.

Retailers

Many retail and service establishments extend credit, both charge account and installment, to their customers. For example, in 1971, 52.7 percent of all Sears, Roebuck and Co. sales were sold on an installment basis.[2]

Outside agencies — credit card companies

In recent years an ever increasing share of consumer credit is supplied by outside agencies such as American Express, Diners' Club, Carte Blanche, Master Charge, and Bank Americard. Retailers who honor these cards receive payment from the credit card companies minus a certain percentage (ranging from 3 to 8 percent), which goes to pay the credit card company for its risk, operating costs, and profit. Credit card companies greatly simplify the retailer's credit granting problem, since the retailer does not have its own money tied up and can operate with relatively less working capital. Furthermore the retailer bears no risk and dispenses with the expense of certain credit department overhead such as credit investigations, billing, etc.

Sales finance companies

Sales finance companies specialize in financing the sale of automobiles and other durable goods, such as sewing machines, refrigerators, and television sets. They perform a useful service for businesses by relieving them of the financing burden. Examples of sales finance companies are the General Motors Acceptance Corporation (GMAC), which does most of the financing of General Motors' cars; the Universal CIT Credit Corporation; and the Commercial Credit Company. There are also hundreds of smaller sales finance companies.

Some sales finance organizations make cash loans directly to individuals. Most of them, however, engage chiefly in buying consumer installment contracts from dealers and providing financing for these dealers at the *wholesale* level.

About half the total installment sales in the country are made by automobile dealers. To maintain working capital, the retailer often uses the services of sales-finance companies to which time-payment accounts are sold. For example, a motorcycle dealer sells a bike for $1,500. He offers the customer an installment plan which, in this assumed case, calls for a down payment of 20 percent or $300, leaving a balance of $1,200. To this

[2] See the Sears case in the Manual of Student Assignments accompanying this text.

balance the dealer adds a finance charge of 18 percent per year, or $216.[3] Then, the customer signs a contract to pay a total of $1,416 ($1,200 + $216) in 12 monthly payments of $118 per month. The motorcycle dealer then sells this contract to a financing organization for $1,200 which, with the down payment, equals the full price of the bike. By selling the customer's account, the dealer gets the full amount of the sale in cash and thereby maintains his working capital. To maintain working capital, retailers often use the services of sales-finance companies or banks to which time-payment accounts are sold.

Commercial banks

Commercial banks are involved in consumer credit in three ways. First, like finance companies, banks buy installment accounts from retailers. To the bank, this is wholesale business. Second, commercial banks loan money to consumer finance and sales finance companies, which in turn loan it to customers — also wholesale business. Third, commercial banks are increasingly aggressive in loaning cash directly to consumers to finance cars, make home improvements, consolidate small accounts into a single account, and finance other purchases on a time-payment basis. To the bank, this is retail business.

Consumer finance companies

Consumer finance companies, often called "small loan companies," specialize in making cash loans to consumers for almost any worthwhile purpose. These loans are repaid in installments. Frequently they are signature loans with no cosigners, although household furniture is sometimes required as collateral.

Consumer finance companies charge considerably higher interest rates than other financial institutions because their risk is greater and because the size of the loan is small.

Credit unions

A credit union is a group of people who have a common bond (they are usually employees of the same company or members of the same union,

---

[3] The amount of down payment and the percentage of interest charged varies from time to time depending on government fiscal and monetary policies.

church, or fraternal order) and who agree to save their money together and to make loans to members at low rates of interest. All members are required to purchase one or more shares in the credit union, which provides funds for future loans. Most loans are small—generally up to $750—and are intended for personal needs. The interest rate charged is about 1 percent per month of the unpaid balance, and such loans are less costly than most other sources of credit. Larger credit unions also make real-estate loans when capital reserves are high enough for them to do so. Funds not needed for loans are usually invested in government bonds.

Credit unions, organized under law, are often composed of relatively large groups of people, usually more than one hundred. The growth of this type of financial institution has been quite significant. In April 1973, it is estimated there were 23,081 such organizations, with assets of $26.1 billion.

CREDIT BUREAUS

Managers of consumer credit rely heavily on credit bureaus for information on credit applicants. These bureaus are organized by various "member" businesses, which extend considerable consumer credit. Each member is required to furnish credit information on each of his credit customers to the bureau. In this way credit files are established for all consumers who buy on credit. The various bureaus in the United States and Canada cooperate closely, so an individual's credit history follows him wherever he goes.

The consumer-reporting industry, composed of several thousand credit bureaus maintains records on the bill-paying habits and financial status of more than 100 million Americans.

PROTECTING THE CONSUMER

Fair Credit Reporting Act

In 1970, Congress passed the Fair Credit Reporting Act, which protects consumers from inaccurate or obsolete information in reports used to determine eligibility for credit or employment. Basically, the law guarantees the consumer's right to know what personal data is being reported by a credit bureau; and it gives the applicant the right to correct any false information. If rejected for a loan, job, or insurance because of an un-favorable credit report, the applicant must be told so by those refusing him.

Whoever uses credit information must have a bona fide business interest in the individual's background. Retail stores are acceptable; lawyers seeking evidence for a divorce case are not. The FBI and Internal Revenue Service must secure a court order to get access. The congressman who sponsored the bill said, "At some point, the individual's right to privacy must take precedence over the creditor's right to obtain information."

Consumer Credit Protection Act

The purpose of the Consumer Credit Protection Act, which became law on July 1, 1969, is "To assure meaningful disclosure of credit terms so that the consumer will be able to compare more readily the various credit terms available to him and to avoid the uninformed use of credit." The act does not attempt to fix maximum finance charges; it relates only to what and how information must be disclosed to borrowers. Commonly referred to as the "Truth-in-Lending Act," it requires extenders of consumer credit to provide detailed information on the dollar amount and annual percentage rates of finance charges. In addition to setting criminal penalties, it also has provisions relating to credit advertising, wage garnishments, and extortionate credit transactions.

It applies to credit sales and loans to individuals for personal, family, household, or agricultural purposes where the amount financed is less than $25,000. It does not apply to commercial or business transactions.

Nine federal agencies enforce the law (see Table 8–1). The Board of Governors of the Federal Reserve System was asked to specify the rules all creditors must follow. Regulation Z resulted, which spells out the provisions of the Consumer Credit Protection Act. Regulation Z applies to every firm and individual regularly extending credit to consumers.

PUTTING IDLE MONEY TO PRODUCTIVE USE

Thus far, the different means companies have for securing funds and credit have been discussed in detail, for the primary concern of a company's financial management is to have adequate funds available at the time they are needed. While it is important to have enough money on hand at a given time, it is economically unsound and undesirable to have too much money that is idle. Therefore, when excess money cannot be

Table **8–1**
Agencies Responsible for Truth-in-Lending

TYPE OF CREDITOR	ENFORCEMENT AGENCY
National Banks	Comptroller of the Currency United States Treasury Department Washington, D.C. 20220
State Member Banks	Federal Reserve Bank serving the area in which the State member bank is located.
Nonmember Insured Banks	Federal Deposit Insurance Corporation Supervising Examiner for the District in which the nonmember insured bank is located.
Savings Institutions Insured by the FSLIC and Members of the FHLB System (except for Savings Banks Insured by FDIC)	The FHLBB's Supervisory Agent in the Federal Home Loan Bank District in which the institution is located.
Federal Credit Unions	Regional Office of the Bureau of Federal Credit Unions, serving the area in which the Federal Credit Union is located.
Creditors Subject to Civil Aeronautics Board	Director, Bureau of Enforcement Civil Aeronautics Board 1825 Connecticut Avenue, N.W. Washington, D.C. 20428
Creditors Subject to Interstate Commerce Commission	Office of Proceedings Interstate Commerce Commission Washington, D.C. 20523
Creditors Subject to Packers and Stockyards Act	Nearest Packers and Stockyards Administration area supervisor
Retail, Department Stores, Consumer Finance Companies, and All Other Creditors	Truth in Lending Federal Trade Commission Washington, D.C. 20580

Source: Board of Governors of the Federal Reserve System.

used profitably in the business, the efficient manager will invest those funds to earn interest. Because the working capital needs of most businesses fluctuate so widely, usually owing to seasonal factors, a great need exists to put money to work for short periods.

Assume a corporation has $500,000 in idle cash that it does not need for a few months or even a few weeks. This sum invested at 6 percent would produce $2,500 per month in interest (see Table 8–2). The company can put the money to work in several profitable ways: It can lend the funds to a bank and receive a promissory note; it can buy some commercial paper, such as short-term negotiable promissory notes; or it can deposit the money in a bank by buying certificates of deposit. A word of explanation is in order regarding certificates of deposit.

TIME INVESTED	PERCENTAGE RATE OF RETURN				
	SIX	SEVEN	EIGHT	NINE	TEN
One day	$ 82.20	$ 95.89	$ 109.59	$ 123.29	$ 136.99
One week	575.40	671.23	767.23	863.03	958.63
One month	2,500.00	2,916.67	3,333.33	3,750.00	4,166.67
One year	30,000.00	35,000.00	40,000.00	45,000.00	50,000.00

Table **8–2**
How Much Is $500,000 Worth Invested
for Different Time Periods and at Different Interest Levels?

Negotiable certificates of deposit

Before 1961, certificates of deposit were always "time deposits" — that is, they had to be left in the bank for a specified period of time. That year, however, the First National City Bank of New York introduced two major innovations: It made the certificates negotiable, and it arranged for a securities dealer to buy and sell certificates. As a result, if a company's financial manager incorrectly estimated his cash requirements, he could get his money any time he needed it — not from the bank that issued the certificate, but by selling the certificate through a dealer. It is said that these innovations revolutionized American banking in the 1960s; CD's, as they are popularly called, grew to a peak of $18.5 billion in August 1966.

FINANCIAL INSTITUTIONS

The United States has an effective system of financial institutions that is used by many financial and credit managers. A description of these institutions and a brief explanation of their primary services follows.

Commercial banks

Commercial banks have two distinguishing features. First, they accept *demand deposits* — that is, deposits that can be withdrawn by the depositor at any time, with no advance notice; and, second, they specialize in making loans to businessmen and individuals.

Functions   One important service rendered by commercial banks is that of <u>checking accounts</u>, whereby deposits in the form of cash, notes, drafts,

Figure **8–2**
Negotiable Time Certificate of Deposit

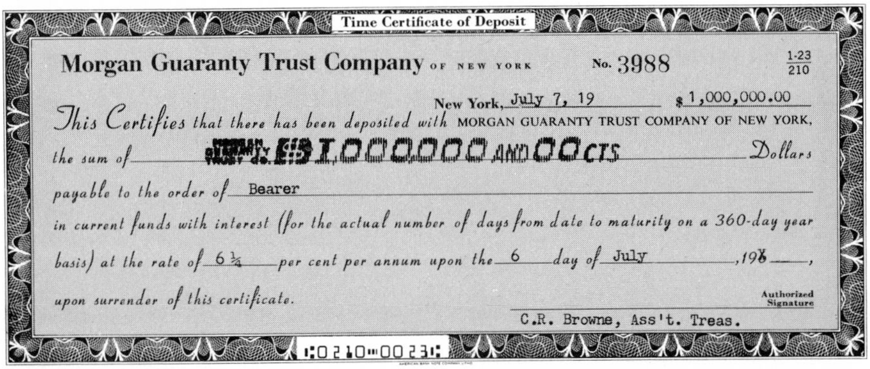
Time Certificate of Deposit

Morgan Guaranty Trust Company OF NEW YORK No. 3988 1-23/210

New York, July 7, 19 $1,000,000.00

This Certifies that there has been deposited with MORGAN GUARANTY TRUST COMPANY OF NEW YORK,

the sum of $1000000 AND 00 CTS Dollars

payable to the order of Bearer

in current funds with interest (for the actual number of days from date to maturity on a 360-day year basis) at the rate of 6¾ per cent per annum upon the 6 day of July, 198_,

upon surrender of this certificate.

Authorized Signature
C.R. Browne, Ass't. Treas.

:0210:0023:

Source: Morgan Guaranty Trust Company, New York, N.Y.

or similar instruments are accepted; the depositor then can withdraw or transfer the money at will by the simple process of writing checks. The safety and convenience of checking accounts so facilitates business that their use is now almost universal.

The procedure for opening a checking account varies, depending on whether the applicant is an individual, a corporation, or a partnership. *Individual* checking accounts are opened with a minimum of difficulty. Opening a *corporation* checking account is more involved. The bank requires the corporation to prepare a formal resolution that (1) authorizes the opening of the account, (2) specifies the officers who are entitled to sign checks, and (3) indicates which officers have authority to borrow money in the name of the corporation. Sample signatures of the company officials authorized to sign checks must accompany the resolution.

Partnership accounts are opened in much the same manner as individual accounts. The bank may request a copy of the partnership agreement, however, to protect itself from making unauthorized payments.

Loans A second and very important service of commercial banks is making loans to depositors and other customers. Loans fall into two general classes: commercial and personal. Only the former apply to business purposes.

Commercial loans. These are loans made to businesses. Interest charged on commercial loans is the bank's chief source of revenue, and for this reason banks are eager to make good loans. Traditionally, commercial bank loans have been for short periods, usually 90 days or less. In recent years, however, banks have frequently made loans for much longer periods.

Commercial loans may be secured or unsecured. As already noted, security, or collateral, can be almost any tangible or intangible property — stocks, bonds, merchandise, grain, equipment, real estate, mortgages, life insurance policies, accounts receivable, royalties, and so on. Unsecured loans are available only to well-established businesses that have demonstrated high financial reliability.

To avoid delays in borrowing funds, a qualified commercial depositor who borrows frequently often establishes a *line of credit*, which is a predetermined limit up to which a bank will lend.

Other services   Commercial banks offer a number of other important services to business and nonbusiness customers; savings-account facilities, certified checks, payroll service, and business counsel are a few examples.

Savings accounts.   Commercial banks encourage the opening of savings accounts. These are opened in much the same manner as checking accounts. They differ, however, in three respects. First, funds placed in savings accounts cannot be withdrawn by check; withdrawals are permitted only on presentation of a passbook. Second, the bank reserves the right to require a notice, usually of thirty days, of intention to withdraw funds, although this rule is seldom enforced. Third, money placed in savings accounts customarily earns interest. Because of the length of time money is kept in savings accounts, banks usually invest a substantial part of it in longer-term loans.

Certified checks.   A certified check is one for which payment is guaranteed by the bank that issues it. An officer of the bank does the guaranteeing by writing "accepted" or "certified" on the face of the check and then signing his name. A sum equal to the amount of the check is immediately withdrawn from the depositor's account and held by the bank pending cashing of the check. In this manner the bank agrees unconditionally to honor the check when it is presented. Certified checks are used when personal checks might not be accepted, as when large amounts are involved — in real estate and securities transactions, for example.

Payroll service.   For a fee, many banks prepare a depositor's payroll. The bank, on presentation of the names of employees and the amounts earned, prepares either cash pay envelopes or, if the depositor prefers, checks.

Also, for a fee, many banks will handle a company's payroll deductions for U.S. Savings Bonds, keeping track of the deductions and issuing and sending the bonds to the employees when they are paid for. Arrangements can also be made whereby employees can, if they like, have their checks sent directly to their bank for deposit. Some of the larger banks provide an account-reconciliation plan for businesses that issue a substantial number of payroll checks. The service provides that the business has cashed payroll checks returned from the bank, sorted and totaled, with indications of missing checks that have not been cashed. This enables the company to balance its accounts quickly and accurately.

Business counsel.   Because bank officials are in daily contact with a wide variety of business matters, are trained in finance, and have an extensive knowledge of local economic conditions, they usually possess financial knowledge that can be of value to customers. Many businessmen rely on their banker's advice in the purchase of securities and real estate, methods of acquiring additional capital, and other important financial matters. Large banks often employ economists who specialize in interpreting business trends.

Trust services.   Most commercial banks maintain a trust department to manage funds owned by individuals or businesses. Most of the work of a trust department is in managing estates. When the bank is named trustee, it carries out the provisions of an individual's will, and prudently invests the money left in the estate. Other services of the typical trust department are to (1) serve as trustee in a bond issue, (2) act as registrar and transfer agent for stock issuance, and (3) serve as trustee for employee pension plans.

The Federal Reserve System

All national banks (those with a federal charter) and many state banks (those with a state charter) belong to the Federal Reserve System. This system, established by the Federal Reserve Act of 1913, is managed by a Board of Governors, the seven members of which are appointed by the President. The nation is divided into twelve districts with a Federal Reserve Bank in each.

The Federal Reserve System has an enormous influence not only on commercial banking but also on economic affairs in general. Its broad objective is to regulate the supply of money and credit in such a manner as to contribute to a high level of employment, economic growth, and price stability. The Federal Reserve System seeks to achieve its objective in three ways.

1. Regulation of bank reserves.   In banking, *reserves* refers to that portion of deposits withheld from loanable funds to meet the withdrawal demands of depositors.

The Federal Reserve System determines the size of cash reserves that member banks must maintain, thereby regulating the percentage of deposits that banks can loan to borrowers. Reducing reserve requirements enables banks to use more money for loans and investments, with a resulting inflationary effect on the economy. An increase in reserve requirements decreases the money available for credit purposes, and this is deflationary.

2. Regulation of the discount rate. In banking, a discount is a charge, similar to interest, except that it is deducted from a loan in advance of payment. In practice, a bank which is a member of the Federal Reserve System may need, say, $1,000,000 to bring its cash reserves against deposits up to a level required by the Federal Reserve System. (Unless a bank's cash reserves equal a certain percentage of the money on deposit, it is prohibited from lending money.) To obtain the $1,000,000, the commercial bank deposits collateral (mainly U.S. Government securities, although high quality commercial notes may be accepted with the Federal Reserve Bank). Then the Federal Reserve Bank will advance the commercial bank the $1,000,000 minus the discount. Usually, the loan is made for only 15 days.

In this example, assuming the loan is for $1,000,000, the discount rate is 6.5 percent and the length is 15 days, the bank receives $1,000,000 minus interest of $2,551.23 or $997,448.80.

Discounting is profitable to banks because it provides them with money which in effect enables them to make loans to their customers at a higher interest rate than the discount paid to the Federal Reserve Bank.

The Federal Reserve Board is empowered to raise or lower the discount rate. When it raises the rate, it slows down borrowing. When the rate is lowered, the cost of money to the banks is reduced and they have more incentive to borrow, thus helping to expand economic activity.

3. Open-market operations. These operations refer to purchases of federal government securities, primarily bonds, on the open market by Federal Reserve Banks. When government bonds are purchased, new deposits and reserves are created. Money that the Reserve uses for these purchases is new money (money they print) that is put into circulation. When these bonds are sold, reserves and deposits are destroyed, because money is taken out of circulation.

For the Federal Reserve, the purpose of buying and selling government securities is not to invest but to cause the supply of money to contract and expand.

In summary, it may be said that the Federal Reserve System deals directly with the supply of money, by adding to or subtracting from it, and indirectly with the demand for it, by making money cheaper or more expensive to secure. Thus, if we seem to be heading into inflation, the Federal Reserve System restricts credit in order to decrease the amount of money in circulation. It does so by raising reserve requirements, by selling government securities and withholding the proceeds, and by raising discount rates.

If we seem to be sliding into a recession, the Federal Reserve expands credit in order to increase the amount of money in circulation. It does so by lowering reserve requirements, by buying government securities, and by lowering discount rates.

The Federal Deposit Insurance Corporation

In the depression of the 1930s, numerous banks in all parts of the country became insolvent—that is, the banks were unable to pay depositors the full amount they had placed on deposit. To prevent a recurrence of this and to restore public confidence in our banking system, the government established the Federal Deposit Insurance Corporation (FDIC). All banks belonging to the Federal Reserve System are required to belong. Nonmember banks may join if they can pass a careful examination conducted by the FDIC.

The FDIC insures each deposit account up to $20,000. In the event a member bank fails, the FDIC pays off each account up to that amount while it simultaneously takes possession of the bank's assets. Funds for the operation of the FDIC are obtained by assessing each member bank an annual fee that equals one-twelfth of 1 percent of all money on deposit in that bank.

INVESTMENT BANKS

The investment banker is a middleman between a corporation that wants to sell securities and the investing public. Investment banks do not purchase stocks and bonds for their own investment; rather, they make a business of reselling long-term securities. Investment banks relieve corporations of the burden of selling their own stocks and bonds. They serve not only corporations but various governmental units wishing to sell bonds for such public improvements as new schools or sewage systems.

The business or government body wishing to raise capital by issuing securities establishes contact with the investment banker. The investment banker then makes a careful analysis of the issuing company to determine whether the proposed security issue is sound. Extensive information is obtained concerning the company's financial status, profit possibilities, products manufactured or sold, legal status, labor relations, competitive strength, and the qualifications of its executives.

If the investment banker is satisfied that the issuing corporation is sound, he may decide to bid on the entire issue of securities. When the amount involved is large, he usually invites other investment bankers to join in the venture. Such an arrangement, called a "purchase group" or "underwriting syndicate," spreads the risk among all who participate.

A selling price for the securities, based in large part on the judgment of the investment banker, is then set. Consideration is given to prices of similar offerings, general market conditions, and prominence of the issuing firm. When the deal is closed, the investment banker pays the issuing corporation the full price of the securities *less* a commission (or "spread," as it is called), which serves as the investment banker's compensation for selling the securities. On very high-grade bond issues, the commission rate is often less than 1 percent. On other issues, depending on their size, type, and quality, the spread may be anywhere from 2 to 10 percent. From this commission, the investment banker pays his expenses and takes his profit.

Investment bankers maintain a sales department, which is in charge of distribution of the securities. Part of a given issue may be sold directly to individual investors, though securities usually are sold to institutional investors, such as commercial banks, insurance companies, and mutual funds. Part may also be sold through brokerage houses.

MUTUAL SAVINGS BANKS

A mutual savings bank accepts savings deposits of individuals, pools them, and then channels them into real-estate mortgages and other productive loans and investments. Mutual savings banks are the nation's oldest type of savings institution. The first savings banks in this country were formed in Philadelphia and Boston in 1816, more than a century and a half ago. There are at present more than five hundred mutual savings banks located in eighteen states and in the Commonwealth of Puerto Rico, with total assets in excess of $70 billion.[4]

The majority of mutual savings banks are located in the Northeast, where the institution historically originated. In several of these states, including New York, Massachusetts, and Connecticut, where four-fifths of such banks' resources are located, the volume of savings held at mutual savings banks is greater than the combined volume held at commercial banks and savings and loan associations.

In contrast to commercial banks, savings and loan associations, and credit unions, mutual savings banks do not operate under a state-federal system of dual chartering and regulation but are chartered solely by the state. Unlike commercial banks, mutual savings banks have no stockholders. All earnings, after expenses and taxes are deducted, accrue to the benefit of depositors and are paid in the form of interest or are added to reserves.

[4] The eighteen states in which mutual savings banks are chartered and operate are Alaska, Connecticut, Delaware, Indiana, Maine, Maryland, Massachusetts, Minnesota, New Hampshire, New Jersey, New York, Ohio, Oregon, Pennsylvania, Rhode Island, Vermont, Washington, and Wisconsin.

Mutual savings banks are a valuable source of long-term capital. Depending on provisions of state laws, mutual savings banks may invest in residential and nonresidential mortgages, corporate stock, and corporate and government bonds.

SAVINGS AND LOAN ASSOCIATIONS

Savings and loan associations, known also as building and loan associations, operate in much the same manner as savings banks. The owner of the account is given a passbook in which additions and withdrawals are entered as they are made. Lump-sum investments can also be made, for which certificates are issued. Dividends on savings are paid regularly. Federal Savings and Loan Insurance is also available to qualifying savings and loan associations, which assures their solvency in much the same manner as the FDIC protection that is available to banks. Funds from small savers are pooled and used for investment.

Approximately 30 percent of all savings and loan associations are incorporated under federal law; the remaining 70 percent have state charters. Those chartered under federal law must use the word "federal" in their names. In 1971 the number of loan associations was more than 5,544 with combined assets of more than $206.3 billion.

Savings and loan associations invest most of their capital (85 percent) in local home mortgages, and they account for more than 40 percent of all the home-mortgage investment in the United States. These mortgages, usually amortized (retired) on a monthly installment basis, are long-term, running from five to twenty years or more.

OTHER FINANCIAL INSTITUTIONS

Insurance companies   In 1971, life insurance companies had assets of more than $222 billion invested in real estate and real estate mortgages; state, local, and government bonds; corporate bonds; and selected preferred and common stock. Today, life insurance companies are one of the most important sources of capital used to finance housing developments, shopping centers, and major commercial buildings.

Mutual funds   Sometimes called "investment companies," mutual funds are an important financial institution controlling more than $50 billion in assets and representing more than 3.5 million individual and institutional investors. Most of these assets are invested in corporate stocks and bonds. Mutual funds are discussed further in Chapter 10.

Pension funds   While not separate companies or organizations, pension funds are a rapidly growing source of capital for investment, with well over $100 billion in assets. Pension funds invest their assets about equally in common stocks and corporate bonds.

SECURITY EXCHANGES

One hundred years ago, only 6 percent of American productivity was provided by machines. Animal muscle provided 79 percent and human labor 15 percent of total productive energy. It is estimated that in 1980, human labor will contribute less than 3 percent to productivity, animal power virtually nothing, with machines taking care of a staggering 97 percent!

Huge capital investment per worker characterizes American industry (see Figure 8–3). (Capital investment per worker is the amount the business has invested in buildings, equipment, machinery, and plant facilities for each worker employed.)

Because of the large capital investment required by mechanization, certain financial agencies are obviously needed in order to provide, on a large scale, an organized means for businesses to raise money. Security exchanges (or stock exchanges) offer the elaborate marketing apparatus needed for people to buy and sell securities.

Despite their prominence for generations, security exchanges are poorly understood by the public. At the one extreme they represent to many people a sort of casino where gamblers meet daily to win or lose fortunes. At the other extreme, they are regarded as unusually complicated institutions that only expert financiers understand. Neither view is correct.

Stock exchanges are organized markets that provide a meeting place for buyers and sellers of stocks and bonds. The most important are the two New York exchanges: the New York Stock Exchange and the American Stock Exchange. Smaller exchanges are located in some of our other large cities. The trading done outside New York is, for the most part, in issues of local corporations or for those listed on both the local and a New York exchange. In addition to organized exchanges, there are over-the-counter markets (see page 222).

While exchanges differ in some respects, all tend to follow the methods and procedures established by the New York Stock Exchange. The

Figure **8-3**
Capital Invested per Employee in Manufacturing
(in Thousands of Dollars)

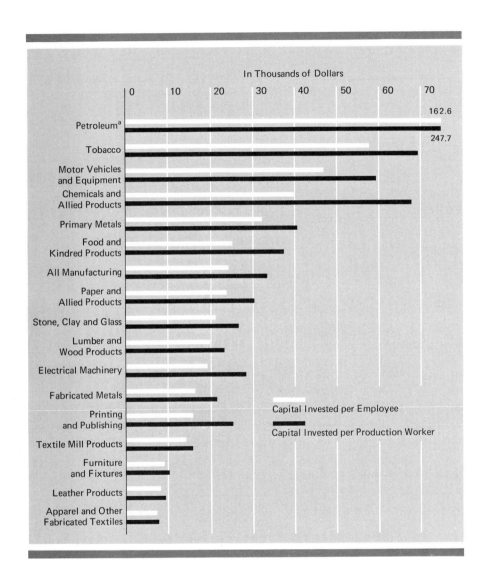

In Thousands of Dollars

Petroleum[a]   162.6   247.7
Tobacco
Motor Vehicles and Equipment
Chemicals and Allied Products
Primary Metals
Food and Kindred Products
All Manufacturing
Paper and Allied Products
Stone, Clay and Glass
Lumber and Wood Products
Electrical Machinery
Fabricated Metals
Printing and Publishing
Textile Mill Products
Furniture and Fixtures
Leather Products
Apparel and Other Fabricated Textiles

☐ Capital Invested per Employee

■ Capital Invested per Production Worker

Note: Data are for 1969.
[a] Petroleum extraction, refining, and pipeline transportation.
[b] Includes ordnance and accessories.

Source: "Capital Invested in Manufacturing," Road Maps of Industry, No. 1707, The Conference Board, February 1, 1973.

following discussion is confined to the New York Stock Exchange, since it serves as a prototype for the others.**

SPECIAL READINGS

** Forty Years on Wall Street by George Shea. Princeton, N. J.: Dow Jones & Company, 1968 (paperback). As its long, secondary title indicates, this book consists of "Appraisals of the economic scene from 'The Outlook' columns written by the Wall Street Journal's long-time financial editor." Among other things, the preface promises that "Readers will learn . . . why there are no 'free lunches' in the business world."

Mr. Shea is able to take complex subjects like stocks and inflation, the automation fallacy, the gold problem, devaluation, interest and inflation, money and credit, and the input-output tool and make them both understandable and entertaining. He examines the reasons for stock market rises and crashes and concludes that most of the time, the cash position of investors seems to be the deciding factor. His approach is forthright, and he does not hesitate, when necessary, to attack some of the sacred cows of finance, as when he says that "the banking system must also be blamed at least in part for the stock price decline."

Many interesting questions are discussed in the columns that were chosen for this book. One example appears in a column titled "Small Investors' Record." It examines the popular myth "that the odd-loters (those who buy less than 100 shares) are probably wrong most of the time — that is, they buy stocks at high prices, and then get scared and sell at low prices, losing money most of the time on their stock transactions."

Membership

The exchange currently has 1,366 members. Each member must be an individual, not a corporation. He may be a partner or an officer in a brokerage firm, which, by virtue of his exchange membership, is known as a member firm. A member firm may be a sole proprietorship, a partnership, or a corporation.

To become a member, one must arrange to purchase a membership, called a "seat," from an existing member or from the estate of a deceased member. Prices paid for seats on the exchange vary greatly, depending mainly on the volume of business transacted. In 1929, a very active year, seats sold for as much as $625,000, whereas in 1942, a relatively slow year, seats sold for as little as $17,000.

Functions

Security exchanges have several functions useful to both investors and corporations. First, they make available an immediate market for the purchase and sale of securities. This fact gives people confidence in making investments, since they realize they can sell their securities for cash in a very short period of time.

Second, security exchanges enable individuals to purchase shares in large corporations.

Table **8-3** Fifty NYSE Companies with the Largest Number of Common Stockholders of Record, Early 1973			
COMPANY	**STOCKHOLDERS**	**COMPANY**	**STOCKHOLDERS**
American Tel. & Tel.	3,010,000	Standard Oil (Indiana)	168,000
General Motors	1,261,000	Pacific Gas & Electric	167,000
Exxon Corp.	755,000	Detroit Edison	167,000
Int'l Business Machines	558,000	Philadelphia Electric	166,000
General Electric	527,000	Greyhound Corp.	164,000
General Tel. & Electronics	494,000	Niagara Mohawk Power	162,000
Ford Motor	329,000	Westinghouse Electric	159,000
U.S. Steel	325,000	Transamerica Corp.	158,000
Gulf Oil	307,000	Phillips Petroleum	153,000
Texaco Inc.	301,000	Northeast Utilities	150,000
Consolidated Edison	287,000	International Tel. & Tel.	150,000
RCA Corp.	283,000	Xerox Corp.	144,000
Sears, Roebuck	262,000	General Public Utilities	141,000
Standard Oil of California	259,000	Atlantic Richfield	141,000
Tenneco Corp.	235,000	Penn Central	137,000
Eastman Kodak	230,000	Pan Amer. World Airways	134,000
Mobil Oil	223,000	International Harvester	131,000
E.I. duPont de Nemours	222,000	American Brands	130,000
Bethlehem Steel	202,000	Cities Service	129,000
Occidental Petroleum	202,000	Southern Co.	129,000
Union Carbide	200,000	American Motors	128,000
Chrysler Corp.	189,000	Litton Industries	127,000
Columbia Gas System	175,000	El Paso Natural Gas	122,000
Public Service Elec. & Gas	171,000	R.J. Reynolds Industries	120,000
Commonwealth Edison	169,000	American Can	120,000

Source: New York Stock Exchange Fact Book, 1973.

Large corporations prefer to have wide distribution of their stock. Why?

Third, because small investors have the opportunity to purchase securities, corporations have an additional source of capital for development programs.

Fourth, security exchanges provide a marketplace where investors' opinions determine stock prices. Someone is always ready to buy if the price is low enough, and someone is always ready to sell if the price is sufficiently high. This results in prices being set on a "free-market," or supply-and-demand, basis.

Listing of securities

Trading on the floor of the New York Stock Exchange is restricted to securities that have been approved for coveted listing that is gained only

Figure **8–4**
Videomaster Used for Stock Quotations at New York Stock Exchange

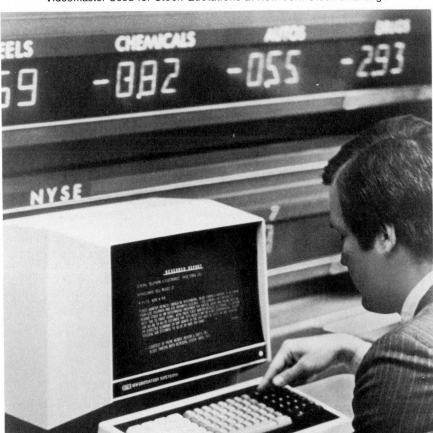

Source: General Telephone & Electronics Information Systems.

after a long and tedious process. The exchange lists more than 2,700 stocks and bonds issued by over 1,300 corporations. While securities of the largest corporations are generally listed, only a small portion of all corporate securities are traded on this exchange.

There are several reasons why a corporation would want its securities listed. (1) Investors generally prefer listed securities to unlisted ones. (2) Such securities can be traded quickly and at fixed commission rates. (3) They are more acceptable than unlisted securities as collateral for loans. (4) At the time of listing, each company must comply with certain standards established by the exchange, including the publication of

Table **8–4** Stocks and Symbols			
All stocks are referred to by symbols—either initials or combinations of letters. Here, for example, are the symbols for ten widely owned companies.			
American Telephone and Telegraph	T	General Telephone & Electronics	GEN
General Motors	GM	Ford	F
EXXON [Standard Oil (N.J.)]	XON	U.S. Steel	X
International Business Machines	IBM	Gulf Oil	GO
General Electric	GE	Texaco	TX

quarterly and annual earnings reports and prompt dissemination of information concerning dividend action. The fact that it has complied with these provisions strengthens a company's stock. (5) Listing gives the security a national market; the corporation whose securities are traded becomes better known, with the result that future security issues are less difficult to sell.

Brokerage houses

Buyers and sellers of securities place their orders through brokers. The broker's office is connected with the trading floor of the exchange by a direct wire system. The basic service of these institutions is demonstrated in the following example of a business transaction:

Suppose Mr. Brown of Indianapolis decides to purchase one hundred shares of Coca-Cola stock. He telephones a local brokerage house and places his order. The account executive may ask, "Do you want to buy this at the market?" (This is the common way of saying "current market price.") If the customer says yes, the order, called a *market order*, is wired directly to the floor of the exchange and delivered to the firm's floor member. Since it is a market order, the member executes it immediately at the prevailing market price and confirms the transaction by wire to his office, stating the exact price that was paid. Often the entire transaction is completed in a matter of minutes.

If the customer wants to buy his one hundred shares of Coca-Cola not at the current price of, say, 100 (that is, $100), but at, say, 96, he may place a *limited order* which applies for one day only unless a longer time period is specified. The shares will not be purchased unless the price goes down to 96. If no time limit is specified the order is called an *open order* and will be held until the purchase is made or the order canceled.

The same procedure is followed if the order is to sell rather than to buy. It is not necessary for the customer to visit the brokerage house in person; orders can be given by telegraph, telephone, or mail.

Rates as shown in Table 8–5 are the rates most brokers charge their customers for stocks traded on the New York Stock Exchange.

Other brokerage-house services

<u>Advice and counsel.</u>   Brokers, being trained in the field of investment, help customers reach decisions regarding the purchase and sale of specific security issues.

Table **8–5**
Commission Charges on New York Stock Exchange Securities

STOCKS

RATES ON ROUND LOTS (ORDERS OF 100 SHARES)

MONEY INVOLVED	MINIMUM COMMISSION[a]
Under $ 100	As mutually agreed
$ 100—but under $ 800	2.0% plus $ 6.40
$ 800—but under $2,500	1.3% $12.00
$2,500—and above	0.9% $22.00

EXAMPLES

PRICE PER SHARE × 100 SHARES		CALCULATION	COMMISSION CHARGE FOR 100 SHARES
$ 7	$ 700	2.0% of $ 700 = $14 + $6.40	Total: $20.40
$20	$2,000	1.3% of $2,000 = $26 + $12.00	Total: $38.00
$45	$4,500	0.9% of $4,500 = $40.50 + $22.00	Total: $62.50

RATES ON ODD LOTS (ORDERS OF 1–99 SHARES)

MONEY INVOLVED	MINIMUM COMMISSION[b]
$ 100—but under $ 800	2.0% plus $ 4.40
$ 800—but under $2,500	1.3% $10.00
$2,500—and above	0.9% $20.00

EXAMPLES

NO. OF SHARES	PRICE PER SHARE	MONEY INVOLVED	MINIMUM COMMISSION	
20	× $20	= $ 400	2.0% of $ 400 = $8 + $4.40	Total: $12.40
50	× $25	= $1,250	1.3% of $1,250 = $16.25 + $10	Total: $26.25
70	× $65	= $4,550	0.9% of $4,550 = $40.95 + $20	Total: $60.95

[a] The minimum commission on an order for 100 shares will not exceed $65. Lower rates apply on orders involving multiples of 100 shares (200, 300, etc.).
[b] The minimum commission on an odd lot order will not exceed $65.

Source: Merrill, Lynch, Pierce, Fenner & Smith, Inc.

Figure **8–5**
How Stocks Are Bought and Sold on the New York Stock Exchange

1. An account executive receives a round-lot market order from an investor by telephone.

2. The order goes to the wire room of the local office, where it is sent by teletype to the New York headquarters . . .

3. . . . and simultaneously to the floor of the New York Stock Exchange . . .

4. . . . where it is given to the firm's floor broker . . .

5. . . . who executes it, bargaining for the best possible price, at the appropriate trading post.

6. Confirmation is teletyped to the local office . . .

7. . . . where it is received . . .

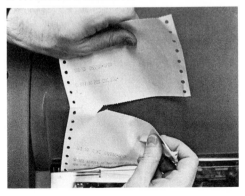

8. . . . and relayed to the account executive so that he can notify the customer of the price he paid—or received—for the stock. It takes only two or three minutes to buy or sell a popular stock.

Source: Merrill Lynch, Pierce, Fenner & Smith, Inc.

Statistical analyses.   Most brokerage houses publish statistical reports describing different securities. These reports frequently are quite detailed, giving such information as the price fluctuation of the security, dividend and earnings records, and other important facts. Often these reports analyze an entire industry, such as apparel or electronics, and attempt to show what is likely to happen to securities in these industries.

Advance funds to customers.   Most brokerage houses arrange to help customers buy securities *on margin.* Buying on margin means that the customer pays for a certain portion of the purchase and secures credit through the broker for the balance. Margin requirements are subject to regulation and change from time to time because of federal credit policies. If, for example, the current margin requirements set by the Federal Reserve Board is 75 percent, $25 in credit may be secured through the broker for each $100 worth of stock purchased. Under a margin or credit arrangement, the securities are held by the brokerage firm until full payment is made.

Over-the-counter markets

The term *over-the-counter market* refers to trading in unlisted securities outside the organized security exchanges. These markets provide trading facilities for an estimated 50,000 securities, as compared with 2,700 for the New York Stock Exchange. Many security issues traded in this manner are small, but, taken collectively, the volume of trading greatly exceeds that on the organized exchanges. Most bonds also are traded in this way.

On the organized exchanges, securities are traded by the auction method, with offers to buy and sell being quoted openly. In the over-the-counter market, transactions are negotiated privately. An investor who wants to buy an unlisted security consults a broker, who then contacts other brokers dealing in this particular security. When he learns which one is offering the security at the lowest price, he places an order.

THE SECURITIES EXCHANGE ACT OF 1934

The stock market collapse of 1929, which meant financial ruin for thousands of investors and contributed to the economic chaos of the entire nation, revealed certain weaknesses and abuses in securities trading. To help remedy the situation, Congress passed the Securities Exchange Act in 1934. Specific purposes of this law are to

1. Provide the investing public with reliable information concerning securities that are listed on the security exchanges

2. Prevent manipulation of security prices (deliberate, unethical action on the part of individuals or brokerage houses to cause prices to rise or fall and thus create an artificial market)

3. Control the use of credit for financing the purchase of securities on margin

Major regulatory provisions

Registration of securities   All securities listed for trading on national exchanges must be registered with the Securities and Exchange Commission (SEC). This makes available to the investor pertinent and reliable information about the securities.

Accounting and financial reports   Corporations whose securities are listed on the exchanges must submit periodic reports that describe their current financial condition. This gives the investor information concerning the financial condition of the company in which he has invested or may invest.

Registration of securities exchanges   Each interstate securities exchange must file information concerning its constitution, bylaws, requirements for membership, and regulations. The SEC is especially alert to make certain that methods of soliciting business and commission rates are in the public interest. The SEC is empowered to compel the exchanges to adhere to desirable practices.

Prohibition of unfair dealings   Such tactics as dissemination of false or misleading information about securities, price fixing, and collusion in stock transactions are prohibited.

Regulation of brokers   Brokers' activities are subject to certain controls by the SEC. In addition to curbing unfair or fraudulent practices, SEC regulation prevents excessive use of credit for the purchase of securities.

GUIDELINES FOR BEGINNING INVESTORS

1. Invest in stocks only with extra cash; you should have at least half a year's living expenses in a bank account or government bonds for emergencies.

2. Never invest with borrowed money.

3. Never invest for or press advice on friends or relatives, as such practices breed enemies.

4. Investigate before investing. Before you buy or sell a stock, obtain the advice of three proven brokers or experts. Do not buy or sell on the basis of tips that have not been checked.

5. Study financial reports issued by companies in which you invest.

Relate what you read to reports on the company's industry so you can determine how your company's progress compares with that of the industry in which you invest.

6. Do not generalize about an industry. There can be great differences among companies in the same industry. In 1965 in the rubber industry, Uniroyal went up twenty-five points and Goodyear went down five points.

7. Invest in different companies in different industries, instead of putting all your money in a single firm or even a single industry.

8. Think twice before rejecting a stock simply because it pays small dividends. Consider the outcome of IBM, Xerox, and Polaroid over the long run.

9. Invest only in stocks listed on organized exchanges, because they must comply with various government and exchange regulations designed to protect the investor.

10. Do not buy stock in a company that does not have an earnings record for at least five years. Consult cumulative financial records found in investor's service references, such as Standard & Poor's and Moody's.

11. If you insist on putting your money into speculative situations, discipline yourself to hold the amount to no more than 20 percent of your total investments, and then be prepared to lose it. If you cannot afford to lose it, do not speculate!

12. Do not become enchanted with a stock. If you do, your decisions about it will be based on emotion instead of logic, and you will soon be separated from some of your money.

13. Review your portfolio regularly. Sell those stocks that appear weakest, *even at a loss*, and replace them with stocks that show more promise.

14. You will not improve a bad decision by spending more money on it. If a stock drops below what you paid for it, reevaluate the whole situation before you buy more of the same stock.

15. Remember that, ultimately, earnings or prospective earnings determine the value of a stock. Consider selling when price-earnings ratio is "too high." Consider buying when price-earnings ratio is "too low."[5]

16. Regularly read respected financial publications such as the *Wall*

---

[5] The *price-earnings ratio* is the ratio of a stock's market price to the company's earnings for the year. Whether that ratio is too high or too low depends in large part on how it compares with other ratios *in the same industry*.

Street Journal, Barron's, or *Forbes,* and consult an advisory service such as Value Line or Moody's.

17. Buy only stocks of leading companies, in sound and essential industries, and buy them only when they are attractively priced. GM may be a very fine company, but the stock is not a good buy if its price is exhorbitant.

18. Consider your *aggregate* gains or losses and what they will be in a year's time. Do not worry about day-to-day losses on individual stocks or become disenchanted with a broker if a stock he recommends drops the day after you buy it. In the long run, if the decision is sound, the investment will pay off.

19. Jumping in and out of the market may make the broker rich on your commissions, but it will not help you!

20. Do not buy just because you happen to have some extra cash. Wait until the right opportunity presents itself or until the market is depressed.

PEOPLE AND THEIR IDEAS
Amadeo Peter Giannini

The founder of America's largest bank—Bank of America

Amadeo Peter Giannini's major contribution to American banking was the concept of branch banking. His policy of buying small banks and converting them into branch banks resulted in the formation of the Bank of America, one of the largest banking systems in the world.

Giannini was born in San José, California, in 1870, the son of Italian immigrants. He left school at the age of 12 and went to work for a produce company. His rise was meteoric; he was a partner at nineteen and retired at thirty-one, when the firm had become the largest business of its kind in San Francisco.

In 1901, Giannini was elected to the board of directors of the Columbus Savings and Loan Society in San Francisco. He resigned in a dispute over policy and, in 1904, organized his own bank, the Bank of Italy. An important function of the Bank of Italy was to assist people of small means in need of loans—at that time an unprecedented service for the laborer, farmer, or merchant.

The public began to hear of Giannini in the months following the great San Francisco earthquake and fire of 1906. Giannini had managed to salvage the gold and securities from his bank and began making loans for the rebuilding of the city.[6] His reputation gained stature a year later when he anticipated the panic of 1907. While other banks used clearing house certificates that year, the Bank of Italy paid its depositors with the gold that Giannini had been careful to accumulate before the crash.

The panic convinced Giannini that only big banks were secure enough to withstand monetary fluctuations. Thereafter he bought small banks and converted them into branches of the Bank of Italy. In 1919 he founded Bancitaly Corporation as a holding company for his financial interests; it was succeeded in 1928 by the Transamerica Corporation. The following year he purchased the Bank of America, and in 1930 he consolidated his banks into the Bank of America National Trust and Savings Association, which by 1948 had become the largest bank in the United States, with 517 branches and assets of more than $6 billion.

Giannini gave much of his fortune to the University of California and to various other philanthropies. He died in 1949.

CONTEMPORARY ISSUES
Situation 8

Is it better to use credit or to pay cash?

"That section on short-term financing started me thinking about the whole question of going into debt. I've decided, John, I'm going to avoid using credit or borrowing money. Someone has to pay for credit and borrowed money and the person who avoids both is going to be ahead."

After listening thoughtfully, Ray said, "I'm not sure you're right. Naturally you'll be saving interest and credit charges, but it is possible to use credit intelligently. Inflation allows you to pay back with cheaper dollars, and you can use other people's money to make money. The man who buys a house on credit builds up an equity, but the fellow who pays rent only ends up with a box full of rent receipts. When a good opportunity presents itself, buying makes much more sense than waiting until you have the money saved up."

"But consider peace of mind," interjected John. "The cash buyer doesn't worry about making payments."

"Well," retorted Ray, "that's just a hunch. I'll trade a little worrying for being able to have something *now* rather than waiting months or years."

John smiled. "I'll bet you lunch that at our 1990 class reunion I'll be farther ahead by paying cash."

---

[6] The story is told that Giannini, in order to save the bank's assets from plundering hordes, put all the money and securities in a wagon, heaped vegetables on top, and then calmly drove his horse and wagon through the frenzied mobs.

"I doubt it," said Ray. "You'll not only be behind me, because I'm going to use credit and borrow wisely, but you'll delay making use of a higher standard of living. I'll be glad to take that bet."

SITUATION EVALUATION

1. Who will pay for the lunch in 1990 and why?

2. What do you feel is the best policy for yourself: to use credit or to pay cash?

3. What is "intelligent" use of credit?

4. What did Ray mean when he said John would "delay making use of a higher standard of living"?

BUSINESS CHRONICLE

Condominiums[7] versus rental properties

The directors of Kingmaker Estates, Inc., planned to build four multiple-dwelling buildings consisting of twelve units each. The units would be four to seven rooms in size. The buildings would be located in a Kingmaker Planned Community and serviced by community facilities.

The directors were trying to decide whether to offer the units for sale as condominiums or whether to maintain them as company-owned rental apartments. If they were offered as condominiums, each building would net $600,000 (each unit would sell for an average of $50,000). Under the condominium plan, the directors figured that the company would have all of its money within a year after construction started. Mortgage money for condominiums buyers who needed financing would be made available by the First Federal Savings and Loan Association at 9 percent per year, the going rate that Kingmaker directors used in their calculations.

If the company kept and operated the buildings, the average rental per unit would be $450 per month. Taxes, caretaker, maintenance, and other costs would be 40 percent. The vacancy factor (rents lost when the apartments became empty) was estimated at 5 percent per year.

QUESTIONS

1. What are the advantages of selling the units as condominiums versus maintaining and renting them as apartments?

2. Which plan should the directors decide to use? Why?

3. For the family who needs housing, which plan would you recommend? Why?

[7] An apartment house where units are owned separately by individuals and not by corporation or cooperative.

APPLICATION EXERCISES

1. Evaluate the following two cases according to the "4 C's" of credit. Under each "C" rate the example as good, fair, or poor. After you have made the ratings, give your decision as to whether or not you would grant the credit requested.

   a. The Florida Linen Service Company, supplier of linens to hotels, restaurants, and other business establishments, has been asked by a Mr. Payne to supply linen to his new resort hotel, which operates for five months a year—from November 15 to April 15. This is Mr. Payne's first business venture; however, he has a good record of successfully managing a much larger resort hotel where he dealt with the Florida Linen Service Company. In these dealings, bills were paid promptly. Mr. Payne has rented this new business and has invested his entire savings of $15,000 in it. He asks that he be granted credit for the full season. He estimates that he will need credit of from $2,000 to $2,500, to be paid on April 15. He claims that this, his first season, is the only time he will need such extensive terms and that he will in following seasons be a good cash customer.

   b. The Bar X Lumber Company, a lumber yard and mill supply house established five years ago with a net worth of approximately $85,000, has received a request for credit for a period of 90 days from J. C. John and Son, a carpenter contractor for lumber and mill supplies. The credit would amount to $35,000. J. C. John and Son has been a customer of the yard for three years, has had credit for amounts up to $5,000, and has always paid its bills promptly. There is no credit record previous to the three-year period because, until then, the men always worked for someone else rather than contracting for themselves. They have just received a contract, from a large company with a good credit standing, that is approximately five times larger than any handled before. Mr. John and his son live in their own home, which is worth $20,000 and which carries a mortgage of $8,000. They have approximately $1,700 in the bank and own a late model car, a company truck, and tools that have a total market value of $6,700. There are no other assets. The John family is well respected by neighbors.

2. Assume you are now a stockbroker. Next week you have appointments with the following individuals to help them devise investment programs to suit their needs.

   a. Abe Brown, age 27. Single. Income, $11,200 per year. Amount available for investing, $3,600.

   b. Fred Green, age 47. Married. Three dependents. Income, $42,500. Amount available for investing, $40,000.

   c. Ida Blue, age 66. Widowed. Income from other investments and Social Security, $6,200. Amount available for investing, $75,000.

For each individual, explain what general types of securities you would advise be purchased. You need not name specific stocks. Why would the same investment program not be wise for all three individuals?

QUESTIONS

1. What is open-account credit? Why is security or collateral generally not required?

2. How does the management of a business decide how much credit to extend when a business is the customer? When a private individual is the customer?

3. Define the "4 C's" of credit. Which of these do you feel is most important and why?

4. What is Dun & Bradstreet, Inc.? What service does it provide its business subscribers?

5. What economic functions are performed by investment bankers?

6. Explain the major differences between mutual savings banks and savings and loan associations.

7. A banker's interests are a lot broader than many people suspect. What are the less evident aspects of a banker's career activities? What kinds of training, other than finance, would be of value to the banker?

8. Suppose one of your friends told you that security exchanges are nothing but legalized gambling establishments. What, as a student of business, could you answer to refute this charge?

9. Describe the various federal regulations that relate to finance. What do they intend to accomplish? What additional legislation is needed, if any?

10. How does one go about buying stock on a stock exchange? What happens if you place an order in New Orleans for a stock traded on the New York Stock Exchange? Describe the procedure.

11. What should your policy be in advising people about how to invest? Explain.

reading business and financial news 9

CHAPTER 9

WHY READ FINANCIAL NEWS?
Investment Information. Guidance for Business Decisions. Education in Business.

TYPES OF BUSINESS AND FINANCIAL NEWS
Profit Yardsticks.

STATISTICAL NEWS
Stock Quotations. Bond Quotations. Stock and Bond Averages. Over-the-Counter Quotations. Mutual Funds Information. Commodity Information. Production News and Indices. Consumption News and Indices.

NONSTATISTICAL NEWS
Corporation News. Government News. News about International Markets. Financial Reporting Services.

The stock market crash that occurred on Thursday, October 24, 1929, and the Great Depression of the ensuing years focused the attention of the world on the New York Stock Exchange. Masses of people who had hardly realized that the exchange existed were shocked into concern about it. Wall Street became a symbol somehow related to their economic welfare. Naturally, people wanted to learn more about it. In the depression that followed the economic collapse, unbelieving citizens saw wheat selling at $.44 per bushel, a price so low that historians had to go back to the days of Sir Walter Raleigh and Queen Elizabeth to find its equal. Cotton went begging at a nickel a pound. New York Central Railroad stock dropped from its 1929 high of $256 a share to a 1932 low of $8.75. Radio Corporation of America, a high flyer that hit $570 in 1929, could be purchased in 1932 for $2.50.

Wealthy investors were made penniless overnight. All around them, people saw banks closed, mortgages foreclosed on their homes or those of their friends, and bankruptcy courts swamped with business failures. A Broadway comedian in 1930 evoked bitter laughs when he told the story of the ruined speculator who asked a hotel room clerk for a room on the twentieth floor. The clerk replied, "Certainly sir—for sleeping or jumping?"

Since 1929, people have been increasingly interested in business and economics. Political campaigns today hinge largely on such economic and financial considerations as farm support prices, price controls, welfare, poverty programs, import controls, subsidies, and foreign aid. Workers find their weekly pay envelopes affected by cost-of-living and price-index figures. Homemakers know that personal economics is tied closely to national economics and that this in turn is affected by the people we elect to political office. All these considerations serve to arouse the interest, not only of the businessman, but of individual citizens in economic news.

To satisfy the wide demand for up-to-the-minute financial and business information, practically all daily newspapers publish several pages of news relating to finance and business. Several newspapers, such as the *Wall Street Journal, Barron's,* and *Women's Wear Daily,* are devoted to the presentation and interpretation of such information. Numerous magazines—*Business Week, Fortune, Financial World, Dun's Review,* a great many trade association journals, and others—devote extensive space to reporting and analyzing the myriad factors relating to business.

WHY READ FINANCIAL NEWS?

Financial news presents an overall picture of the nation's economic activity. Any event that affects a single major corporation, an entire industry, or the whole economy is reflected in the mass of statistics and editorial comment. A premature frost in the Midwest, for example, usually results in an increase in corn prices. The threat of shortages may send prices of certain products skyrocketing, and news of surpluses may send prices down. New legislation, trade restrictions, the introduction of new products, even a speech by a major political or business leader are all likely to affect, favorably or unfavorably, certain business interests.

We can say that information results in good luck, for clearly the informed individual is best able to anticipate change and to capitalize on it. Baron Rothschild greatly increased his wealth by buying British Government bonds in 1815, after he was informed by carrier pigeon of Napoleon's defeat at Waterloo.

Specifically, there are three reasons why it pays to read financial news: (1) Such information serves as a guide in *choosing investments.* (2) It can be very helpful in *making business plans.* (3) It has *general educational value* in that it keeps the reader informed of the economic state of the nation and the world.

Investment information**

Wise investors study financial news diligently. As a basis for deciding which securities to buy or sell, this news is far superior to "hot tips" or "hunches." Each day extensive reports appear concerning the activity of the leading securities, market trends, business expansion, and corporate organizational shifts, as well as commentaries on many business events and trends. From this information, the intelligent investor can glean facts useful in selecting the most appropriate investments.

SPECIAL READINGS

** The Innovators by the *Wall Street Journal* staff. Princeton, N. J.: Dow Jones Books, 1968 (paperback). The foreword to this collection of articles on innovation from the *Wall Street Journal* points out that "Almost daily we are comforted with reams of statistics proving we are the richest, most diverse society that ever was. And yet the statisticians overlook one of the most valuable of our resources—the inquiring mind and inventive spirit."

This book examines aspects of the creative effort behind some of the statistics and actions reported in financial publications. Stories of personalities and discovery processes are featured —Peter Carl Goldmark of CBS Laboratories; the development of cortisone, which revolutionized the pharmaceutical industry; and Donald Wilkes, who invented rolamite, an important device for reducing friction.

There is an article devoted to innovators who are so-called loners—inventors and developers who work and create alone. Also explored is the newer approach to innovation—group thought. Such subjects as the government's activities in research, the theft of ideas, accidents that have made millions, and today's kooks—tomorrow's geniuses—are treated in an interesting and revealing manner. This is a lively volume that stimulates the imagination.

For example, if the financial news reveals that stocks in the electronics industry have been rising and that prospects are good for expansion, the investor may seriously consider an investment in that field. Once an investment is made, the investor should continue to evaluate news that may affect the price of his security and its earning power. If at a later date he finds news unfavorable to the electronics industry, he may prevent or minimize a loss by selling his holdings. In short, keeping abreast of the financial news is essential to intelligent management of an investment portfolio.[1]

Despite the daily publicity given the securities industry and despite the broadly based costly advertising programs of leading brokerage houses, the majority of the American public has little interest in the stock market. A study conducted by Opinion Research Corporation of Princeton, New Jersey, in 1972 involving 2,200 interviews revealed that (1) 6 out of 10 people know little or nothing about the securities industry, (2) 8 out of 10 do not read any financially oriented news, (3) 5 out of 10 feel it takes a lot

[1] The term *portfolio* refers to the total investment holdings of the individual investor.

of money to invest in the stock market, and (4) 3 out of 4 have no under-standing of the fees charged by stockbrokers.[2]

Guidance for business decisions

Financial news is of great value in making business plans. Decisions about such matters as whether to expand or contract manufacturing facilities, whether to add to or reduce merchandise inventories, and whether to increase or decrease production schedules and sales quotas are usually best made in the light of data appearing in the business pages. For example, if prices of certain raw materials show a downward trend and the analysts who interpret this news see no immediate signs of a reverse, businessmen who purchase these raw materials may decide to buy only for their immediate needs and to postpone large-scale purchases.

Education in business

Education for those aspiring to become entrepreneurs or executives involves more than completing a prescribed number of business courses or serving an apprenticeship with a business concern. Business is exceptionally dynamic; it is in constant flux. Business information quickly becomes obsolete, so the student of business must read regularly to stay up to date.

Success in business often stems directly from decisions based, not on the situation of one's own business alone, but on an interpretation of the total current economic situation. A single firm plays only a small part in the overall business picture, but businesses are interdependent and exceedingly sensitive to economic trends. The alert executive knows that a *combination* of general economic and commercial information from specific business news and reports is of most value to him in the conduct of his own segment of business operations. Sales increases in the automobile industry reflect favorably in rubber, glass, steel, and other related industries. An extended new federal highway construction program means increased use of cement, heavy trucks, and earth-moving equipment.

There is an additional reward for those who devote time to reading and understanding the business and financial pages. These pages, perhaps forbidding to the uninitiated, are interesting in and of themselves. To a businessman the financial section contains as much excitement as any other section of the daily newspaper.

[2] As reported in "The Invisible Brokers" by Terry Robards, *New York Times*, December 10, 1972.

The student developing the habit of reading financial pages might well select several stocks, bonds, and commodities and follow them in their daily ups and downs. Keeping informed on corporate and other news that concerns the investments selected may prove, over a period of several months, quite revealing.

Such a system of study can lead to worthwhile conjecture and discussion. If a stock goes up, why? If an industry becomes depressed, why? Why does a rise in grain prices affect livestock shipments? The business and financial pages open the door to the complex commercial world; reading them is sound business education in an attractive and interesting way.

TYPES OF BUSINESS AND FINANCIAL NEWS

Business news can be classified as statistical or nonstatistical.

Statistical news is a factual summary of what has already happened in the business world. It is the combined record of thousands of transactions and reflects the actions of the thousands of individuals who, collectively, compose the market. Such news is our most accurate business barometer.

Statistical news is supplied in tabular form. It includes stock and bond quotations, commodity prices, carloadings,[3] money exchange rates, bank clearings, steel production, electric power output, and similar economic indices. Most statistical news is presented in the same form day after day, sometimes even on the same page position. Thus, it can be found quickly and be interpreted easily by the trained eye.

Nonstatistical information includes articles and analytical reports that explain past business activity and try to predict future trends. The range of articles is great and covers such topics as governmental action and policies, trends in and predictions of industrial and agricultural production, foreign trade, trends in consumption and prices, notes on the affairs of individual companies, briefs on market opinions, and trends within a single industry.

The reports, editorials, and articles have a different significance to different individuals. The same news may be beneficial to one group and harmful to another. For example, reports of airport congestion can be bad news for those with investments in airlines and good news for those holding shares in companies providing airport facilities. What happens in the political and business worlds has a direct or indirect influence on the fate of some company or on the values of some security. The problem for the reader is to pick out the news that is most crucial for his particular areas of interest.

[3] Number of railroad cars of freight shipped.

Figure **9–1**
Which is Most Meaningful, Percentage Return on Sales
or Percentage Return on Net Worth?

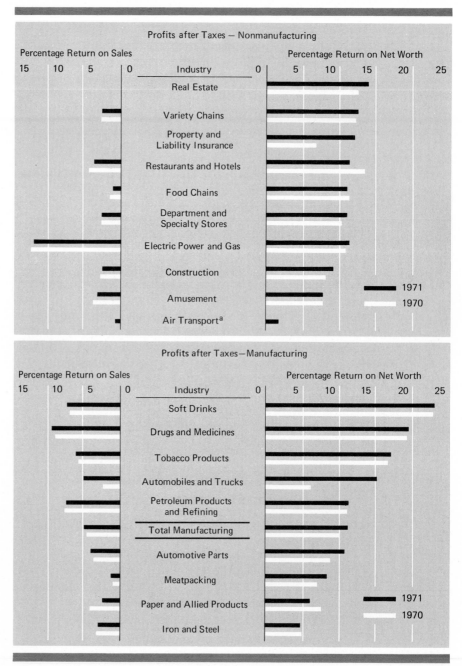

a Figures for 1970 are not shown because of deficit in that year.
Note: Net worth (or shareholders' equity is the excess of the book value of the assets over liabilities; book values are not necessarily the same as current value.

Source: "Corporate Profit," Road Maps of Industry, No. 1691, The Conference Board, June 1, 1972.

Note that nonstatistical news influences what *will become* statistical news. Many readers evaluate the various articles and make their plans accordingly; their collective action affects the sales, purchases, and prices of commodities and securities.

Profit yardsticks

All industries and companies within an industry are far from being equally profitable. Figure 9–1 shows profit differences between the manufacturing and nonmanufacturing sectors of industry and also shows significant differences between profit return on sales versus profit return on net worth. The figures are important references to keep in mind when reading profitability reports of companies and industries in financial journals.

STATISTICAL NEWS

Stock quotations

An important part of the statistical news is the quoting of stock transactions and prices on the New York Stock Exchange and the American Stock Exchange. Large city newspapers also provide records of transactions on smaller exchanges. The method for presenting stock quotations, however, is reasonably uniform throughout the United States. Figure 9–2 presents a partial list of stock transactions as published in the *Wall Street Journal*.

The first two columns in the figure (under the heading "1973 High Low") show the range in selling price for each listed security to date in that year. For example, the price for the first stock listed ranged from 80⅞ to 61 per share. Stock quotations always indicate dollars per share (although the dollar sign is omitted). Further inspection of these two columns shows that stocks are quoted in fractions of ⅛, ¼, ⅜, ½, ⅝, ¾, and ⅞ of a point or dollar. Thus, a stock price of 124¼ means $124.25 per share. Generally, the higher the price of the stock, the greater the dollar range in high and low selling prices. More significant, however, is the range in percentage terms: a stock that has ranged from 4 to 2 in price (50 percent) is more likely to be subject to speculation than one that has ranged from 101 to 87 in price (16.7 percent).[4]

---

[4] Speculation is the willingness to assume larger risk for larger gain. People who speculate, or speculators, are important in the commercial world, for they often "make a market"—that is, they buy or sell in anticipation of profit when conventional traders are not interested in buying or selling.

Figure **9–2**

Stock and Bond Quotations Printed in the *Wall Street Journal*

A-B-C

-1973- High	Low	Stocks Div.	P-E Ratio	Sales 100s	High	Low	Close	Net Chg.
80⅞	61	AbbtLb 1.20	21	41	66¼	65½	66	.....
49¾	40½	ACF Ind2.40	10	6	43¼	42¾	43	+ ¼
17⅛	12¼	AcmeClv .88	7	8	13½	13	13	.....
26	16½	AcmeMkt 1	9	17	19¾	19½	19½	− ¼
14¾	12	AdmE 1.15e		4	12⅜	12¼	12⅜	+ ⅛
8½	5½	Ad Millis .20	8	1	6	6	6	.....
34	11½	Addrsso .60	7	97	13¼	12¾	13¼	+ ¼
18	7¼	Admiral	5	17	10⅝	10½	10⅝	+ ⅛
13¾	10½	AdvInv .02e		36	11⅛	10⅝	11	+ ¼
76¾	57½	AetnLf 1.76a	11	164	75½	74¼	75½	+ 1½
31⅛	11½	Ahman .10e	7	76	15	14¼	15	+ ⅝
9	3⅞	Aileen Inc	14	15	4½	4⅜	4½	..
45¾	37	AirProd .20	26	126	44⅝	44⅛	44⅝	+ ⅜
18¼	10¾	Airco .80	9	29	11⅝	11⅜	11⅝	+ ⅛
3⅝	2	AJ Industris	6	24	2⅛	2	2	..
31¼	22¼	Akzona 1.10	9	4	23	23	23	+ ⅜
17½	15	Ala Gas 1.18	6	2	16	15¾	15¾	
109	98¼	AlaP pf8.28		z60	100	100	100	+ ½
37⅞	24⅜	Alaska Intrs	21	46	28½	27½	28½	+ ⅞
29¼	8⅜	AlbertoC .35	7	40	9¼	9	9⅛	− ¼
17⅜	10½	Albtsn .36a	9	1	13	13	13	.....
34	22⅞	AlcanAlu 1	17	283	33½	33	33⅜	+ ¼
10⅞	7⅛	AlcoStd .36	5	25	8⅛	7⅞	8	.....
42¾	29¼	AlconLb .16	44	12	33	32¾	33	+ ¼
9½	3½	Alexdrs .10e	38	7	5⅞	5¾	5¾	− ¼
31⅞	23¼	AlisnM 2.98e	8	13	27	26¾	27	.....
15⅛	6¾	AllALfe .24	8	25	10⅜	10⅛	10⅜	.....
14½	8⅜	AllegCp .28e	9	5	9⅛	9⅛	9⅛	− ⅛
29⅞	19¾	AllgLud 1.20	6	46	24⅜	23⅝	23⅝	− ⅝
24½	18	AllgPw 1.44	8	28	19⅝	19¾	19½	+ ⅛
19⅜	9¼	AllenGp .65t	9	5	11½	11⅜	11½	+ ⅛
36⅞	28⅛	AlldCh 1.32	11	84	35½	35⅛	35¼	− ¼
44⅞	27½	AlldMnt .48	21	23	32	31⅝	32	+ ¾
22	14⅝	AlldPd .68	5	2	16⅞	16¾	16⅞	.....
39⅜	22½	AlldStr 1.40	6	19	24	23⅞	23⅞	− ⅛
5½	3	Alld Supmkt	10	40	4¾	4¼	4¾	+ ½
..⅝	8	AllisCh	·1	133	12⅛	11¾		

CORPORATION BONDS

Volume, $13,700,000

Bonds	Cur Yld	Vol	High	Low	Close	Net Chg
AlaP 9s2000	8.5	25	104⅞	104¾	104⅞	+1⅞
Alaska 6s96	cv	3	119	119	119	.....
Alison 8¾79	8.9	12	98½	97½	97½	−1
AlldCh 3½78	3.8	7	90½	90½	90½	+ ⅛
AlldSt 4½81	cv	6	88¾	88¾	88¾	+2½
AlldSt 4½92	cv	12	65	64¾	65	+ ¼
Alcoa 9s95	8.4	10	106¾	106¾	106¾	.....
Alcoa 5¼s91	cv	197	96½	93⅞	95½	+2
AluCa 9½95	9.0	4	105¼	105¼	105¼	.....
Amerce 5s92	cv	6	68	68	68	.....
AAirFil 6s90	cv	38	91½	91½	91½	+1
AAirln 11s88	10.	29	104½	104	104½	+ ½
AAirl 10⅞88	10.	10	103	103	103	.....
AAirln 10s89	9.7	12	102½	102¼	102¼	+ ⅝
AAirl 4¼s92	cv	32	52	51½	52	+ ½
ABrnd 8⅞75	8.7	5	102	102	102	.....
ACeM 6¾91	cv	6	67½	67½	67½	.....
AExp 5¼493f	cv	48	8½	8¼	8¼	− ¼
AForP 5s30	10.	5	49¾	49¾	49¾	+ ¼
AForP 5s30r		5	49¼	49¼	49¼	.....
AFoP 4.8s87	8.8	2	54½	54½	54½	.....
AHoist 5½293	cv	1	70⅝	70⅝	70⅝	.....
Alnvt 8¾s89	9.0	2	96½	96½	96½	+1
AMF 4¼s81	cv	110	77	76⅝	77	+ ⅜
AMedcp 5s97	cv	66	43¼	42⅜	42¾	− ½
AMeCl 8½296	8.4	15	100¾	100¾	100¾	+ ¾
AmMot 6s88	cv	13	78	77½	77½	− ½
ATT 8¾2000	8.2	407	106½	106⅛	106½	+ ½
ATT 8.7s02	8.2	112	105¾	105¼	105¾	+ ½
ATT 7.75s77	7.6	46	101	100⅛	100¾	+ ⅛
ATT 7⅛s03	7.6	57	93⅝	93⅝	93⅝	+1⅛
ATT 7s01	7.5	94	92¾	91¾	92¾	+ ⅞
ATT 6⅛s79	6.8	3	94½	94½	94½	− ¾
ATT 4⅜s85	5.9	35	7⅛		73¾	74	.....
ATT 3⅞s90	4.0			43½	63½	− ¾
ATT 3½					66	− ⅝

Source: *Wall Street Journal*, September 4, 1973.

The third column, titled "Stocks Div.," gives the name of the corporation whose stock is listed and the dividend rates in dollars. Unless otherwise noted, rates of dividends are annual disbursements based on the last quarterly or semiannual declaration. Special or extra dividends or payments not designated as regular are identified in footnotes which appear at the end of the quotations. Unless the name of the corporation is very short, it is almost always abbreviated to save space; the meanings of these abbreviations will soon become clear to the regular reader of the financial news. In Figure 9–2, for example, the first stock listed is Abbt Lb, or Abbott Laboratories.

Following the name of each security is a number, such as .80, 1, 1.20, or 2.40. In Figure 9–2 the number .60 following Addrsso means that $.60 in annual dividends was paid on each share of stock, based on the last quarterly or semiannual declaration. Frequently, the symbol *pf* appears, followed by a number; the symbol indicates that the stock is preferred, and the number indicates the size of the promised dividend. Thus "du Pont pf 4.50" means that the stock normally pays an annual dividend of $4.50.

Some other of the most common abbreviations and their meanings are:

COM	common stock
CV	convertible
xd	ex dividend
ex rts	ex rights

The term *ex dividend* can be explained as follows. At the time a company declares a dividend, a *record date* is set. This means that any stockholder recorded on the company books as an owner of stock on that record date will receive the dividend, even if he sells the stock sometime between the record date and the date on which the dividend is actually paid. After the record date passes, the stock is quoted without the buyer on that day being entitled to the dividend — or it is said to be ex dividend.

The term *ex rights* indicates that stock is quoted without entitlement to declared rights. (A right could be the right to buy additional stock, for example.) Special letters or symbols, such as *a, b, c, #,* and +, the use of which varies from publication to publication, are usually explained in a legend following the quotations.

The column headed "P-E Ratio" means Price-Earnings ratio. This is a new information column added to daily stock quotations in October, 1972 by the Associated Press which is the source of stock quotations published in most newspapers. The P-E ratio is the per share earnings divided into the stock price. The per share earnings used are basically for the last twelve months the company has reported.

The column headed "Sales 100s" indicates the number of one-hundred-share lots sold during the day's trading. For example, the figure "48" means that 4,800 shares were traded, while the figure "1" means that only 100 shares were sold that day. Only *round lots* (one-hundred-share lots) are traded on organized exchanges.[5] *Odd lots* are less than one-hundred-share transactions. If only odd lots of a particular security were traded, that security is not listed in the regular place, but is shown in the "Bids and Offers" column, a feature that is included only in larger and more specialized newspapers. About one-third of the buy-and-sell orders from the general public are for odd lots.

The next three columns (labeled, respectively, "High," "Low," and "Close") indicate the highest price of the day, the lowest price of the day, and the price of the last sale before trading activities were terminated. For example, for Abbt Lb the highest price paid was 66¼, the lowest

---

[5] When the individual investor buys less than 100 shares, the stock is provided to his broker by an odd-lot broker who specializes in breaking round lots he has purchased on an exchange into odd lots.

price was 65½, and the closing price was 66. The closing price and the following day's opening price are not always the same. Some important information regarding the stock may be released during the night, causing the first transaction of the next day to be priced differently from the last transaction of the day before.

The last column shows the "Net Chg" (net change) between the closing price of the day and the previous trading day's closing price. A plus (+) symbol indicates an increase in price and a minus (−) symbol shows a decrease in price. Thus, Admiral increased ⅛ point, or 12.5 cents per share. Dots or a blank in the "Net Change" column indicate that, although the price of the stock may have fluctuated during the day, the closing price is the same as the previous day's.

Bond quotations

The second most important group of statistical quotations pertains to records of bond sales. For quotation purposes, bonds are generally classified as domestic, foreign, utility, and U.S. Other classifications, such as World Bank Bonds, Municipal Bonds, and Federal Land Bank Bonds, are given in some financial publications. Figure 9–2 shows how results of bond trading are presented in the *Wall Street Journal*.

Bond prices are quoted somewhat differently from stock prices. Bonds generally have a par, or stated, value—usually $1,000. So, a quotation at 96 means that the current price of a bond is $960[6], a quotation at 103¼ indicates a current selling price of $1,032.50. Any interest that has accrued since the time of the last interest payment must always be added to the price of the bond. U.S. government bonds are quoted in thirty-seconds of a point. Almost all other bonds are regularly quoted in eighths of a point.

In the first column the name of the issuing corporation and several symbols are listed. Such symbols as 5s, 3½s, and 8⅜s refer to the interest rate, 3s meaning 3's, or 3 percent; 5s, 5 percent; and so forth.

The figures after the interest rate, such as 87, 81, 78, indicate the maturity date of the bond. Thus, 87 means that the bond will be paid off by the issuing company in 1987. On occasion there is a single capital letter after the maturity date, such as 2010A. This identifies the series of the bond. Series letters are used to identify the separate issues of companies issuing many series of bonds. Lower-case letters following the maturity date are usually explained in a legend that accompanies the quotations.

---

[6] The broker receiving an order from a customer for two bonds @ 96 will buy two bonds @ $960. In contrast, a stock order for two shares of stock @ 96 would secure for the customer two shares of stock @ $96.

The next column "Cur Yld," means current yield, or the approximate interest rate based on the price quoted. The "cv" which sometimes appears instead of a yield means that it is a convertible bond.

Total sales for bonds are reported in $1,000 units. The figure "10" under "Vol" (volume) means that $10,000 worth were traded or sold. The figure "1" means that only one $1,000 bond was sold or traded. The remaining columns are the same as for the previously explained stock quotations.

Stock and bond averages

To understand general market behavior by studying hundreds of individual security transactions would be an impossible task. Accordingly, several indices have been developed to show the general activity of the securities markets. Two better known are the *Dow-Jones* averages and the *New York Times* indices. They furnish a quick answer to the question, "How did the market do today?" Alert businessmen read at least one of these sets of averages regularly to keep abreast of the overall market movement.

The Dow-Jones averages include four stock and five bond price indices. The four stock indices are based on the average of: thirty representative industrial stocks, twenty representative railroad stocks, fifteen representative public utility stocks, and a composite of all sixty-five representative stocks.

The bond indices consist of the average prices of: ten representative high-grade railroad bonds, ten representative second-grade railroad bonds, ten representative public utilities bonds, ten representative industrial bonds, and a composite of the forty representative bonds. The Dow-Jones stock and bond averages are published in many newspapers and are broadcast daily by many radio and television stations.

The *New York Times* indices also cover both stocks and bonds. The stock averages are based on: twenty-five representative railroad stocks, twenty-five representative industrial stocks, and fifty representative stocks. Bond averages are prepared for: public utility bonds, railroad and industrial bonds, and a composite of the bonds of all three groups.

Over-the-counter quotations

The over-the-counter market comprises the stocks and bonds sold outside the organized exchanges. Price quotations for such transactions are found in very large and specialized financial journals. Since the volume of many such securities is not so great, they are often reported only on a weekly rather than daily basis.

Mutual funds information

One way for people and institutions to invest in the stock market is in mutual funds. Financial pages contain daily quotations, references, and news regarding these funds. A mutual fund pools the money of a large number of investors and then uses that money to purchase securities of many different corporations. Stated briefly, mutual funds offer the investor three major services:

1. <u>Professional management.</u> Securities are selected and supervised by experienced investment managers.[7]

2. <u>Diversification.</u> Investments are spread among many different companies, thereby reducing risk.

3. <u>Convenience.</u> A ready market is available if the investor wishes to sell his shares.

The overall objective of a mutual fund is the profitable investment of money entrusted to it by investors. How this objective is to be achieved varies. Some funds stress long-range gain by concentrating on growth industries; others concern themselves with immediate income. The investor reviews fund objectives and selects the fund that mirrors his own aims.

[7] Senator Thomas J. McIntyre, economist Paul Samuelson, and others testified at committee hearings that random selection of stocks produces results equal to those of mutual fund investment managers. Members of the committee contended that throwing darts at the New York Stock Exchange listings would produce results as good as those produced by the funds. Arthur Wiesenberger & Co., a brokerage firm, had a computer fly 1,000 sorties at the dart board. In the following table of results, the percentages relate to appreciation shown on the average for 1,000 hypothetical dartboard selections for 55 growth and income funds and 37 maximum gains funds.

YEAR	DART BOARD SELECTION	GROWTH AND INCOME FUNDS	MAX. CAP. GROWTH FUNDS	MAX. CAP. GAINS FUNDS
1957	− 8.2%	− 7.4	− 10.7	− 12.2
1958	+35.0	+34.5	+44.2	+47.5
1959	+ 14.5	+ 9	+ 16.2	+23.9
1960	− 1.0	+ 3.4	+ 4.7	+ 7.8
1961	+ 0.31	+23.4	+23.7	+27.4
1962	− 16.0	− 7.9	− 15.7	−21.6
1963	+ 19.0	+ 16.8	+ 18.9	+23.1
1964	+ 18.3	+ 14.1	+ 12.8	+ 13.0
1965	+37.7	+ 14.2	+23.8	+40.6
1966	− 6.0	− 6.5	− 3.0	− 1.7

Clearly, from the above evidence, investors are well advised to look into performance records of the "professional management" of various mutual funds before buying.

Proceeds to shareholders in mutual funds may be distributed from (1) dividends earned on the corporate securities owned by the fund or (2) capital gains distributions coming from sales of securities that have increased in value. It is important, for income tax reasons, to distinguish between the two sources of payment made to shareholders. Dividends from investments are taxed at regular income tax rates; capital gains distributions are taxed at (normally lower) capital gains rates.

The first mutual funds were formed in the early 1920s. By 1972 the number of mutual shareholders had grown to more than 11 million. Prices of mutual fund shares are computed each day. They are based on prices of all securities held by a fund. A charge of 7.1 to 8.5 percent is usually added to these prices to cover costs of distribution and to pay for the professional management fees. A special kind of mutual fund called the "no load" employs no salesmen and therefore makes no sales charges.

Commodity information

Prices of many commodities or raw materials, such as wheat, corn, soybeans, sugar, copper, cotton, silver, dairy products and livestock are reported daily. Raw materials are bought and sold through *commodity exchanges*, which function in much the same manner as stock exchanges. The Chicago Board of Trade, the Chicago Mercantile Exchange, and the New York Mercantile Exchange are some of the best-known commodity exchanges.

Trading may be either on a (1) cash basis, called *spot trading*, for immediate delivery or (2) contractual basis, called *futures trading*, for future delivery.

Businesspeople who purchase large amounts of raw materials read commodity news carefully, as do speculators who hope to gain by buying at one price and selling at a higher price. Surprisingly, the dollar volume of trading on the commodity markets is larger than the volume of trade on the security exchanges.

Production news and indices

Economic prosperity is related to the nation's productivity. High-level production results in high employment and large purchasing power. Low production normally means unemployment for many people and so reduces purchasing power. Because of its importance, production news is treated in detail in the financial pages.

Numerous indices have been developed to help businesses analyze production figures. These are reported in the financial pages in the form of tables, charts, or graphs. In many cases production in selected years, such

Figure **9-3**
Production Reports Printed in *Barron's*

PULSE OF INDUSTRY AND TRADE

	Latest date	Latest period	Preceding period	Year ago
Production—What They Make: Weekly:				
Auto output, U.S. .... Aug. 24		p132,890	r89,019	153,331
Bituminous coal prod, th tons ...... Aug. 18		p11,900	r12,300	11,645
Electric power prod, mil kw hrs .... Aug. 18		39,633	40,276	36,733
Paper prod, th tons .... Aug. 18		p517	r506	490
Paperboard prod, th tons .... Aug. 18		594	582	567
Petroleum, dly avge prod, th bbls .. Aug. 17		13,473	13,587	11,857
Petroleum, refinery operations, % .. Aug. 17		99.6	100.5	89.0
Steel production, th tons .... Aug. 18		2,781	2,771	2,461
Steel prod index (Am Ir & Stl Inst)a Aug. 18		114.0	113.6	100.9
Monthly:				
Boot and shoe prod, th pairs .... June		41,513	41,669	46,224
Wool, mill consumption, th lbs ..... June		9,623	r10,146	15,472
Distribution—What They Sell: Weekly:				
Carloadings, th cars .... Aug. 18		540	533	518
Intercity tr ton (% chge fr yr ago) .Aug. 18		+6.9	+5.6	+2.4
Retail store sales, mil $ .... Aug. 18		9,470	9,468	8,470
Inventories—What's Left on Hand:				
Crude oil, th bbls .... Aug. 17		244,807	243,549	262,556
Gasoline, th bbls .... Aug. 17		201,234	202,714	199,714
Failures (D. & B.)				
Business failures, no .... Aug. 16		192	182	183
Purchasing Power:				
Whlesle Food Price Index (D&B) $ .Aug. 21		11.84	12.07	7.62
Monthly:				
Cons Price Index (USBLS) a .... July		132.7	132.4	125.5
Construction: Weekly:				
Advance Planning (ENR), mil $ ....Aug. 23		1,655.6	1,335.8	1,108.9
a-1967 equals 100. p-Preliminary. r-Revised.				

Source: *Barron's*, August 27, 1973, published by Dow Jones & Co., Inc.

as the period 1967–69, is used as a reference for comparison, and it is represented by the number "100." Current production is then presented as a percentage of 100. Showing production of a certain commodity as 130, for example, means that output is 30 percent greater than the average for 1967–69. In other cases, production is reported in units and then compared with the number of units produced in a corresponding period some time ago. Automobile production is usually expressed in this manner. Figure 9–3 shows some of the common production reports.

Specific products and commodities for which up-to-the-minute production figures are kept include motor vehicles, steel, coal, oil, lumber, paperboard, electric power, and new construction. Many of these figures are used as a basis for business forecasting. Businessmen are naturally most interested in production figures for their own industry. The steel manufacturer, presumably, looks first at steel output. But productivity trends in one industry may correspond to trends in another. Steel production, for example, corresponds to automobile production. Careful reading, therefore, includes checking the productivity of other industries and relating it to the industry of one's own concern.

Consumption news and indices

For high production to be maintained, high consumption is essential. Much consumption news is statistical. Wholesale sales, retail sales, carloadings, and inventories are presented in tabular form for quick reading. These indices show whether or not the goods produced are moving into the hands of users. In addition to actual consumption data, there is information that gives a clue to future consumption. Savings deposits, consumer debt, consumer incomes, and unemployment statistics, properly interpreted, help reveal what consumption will be in the weeks and months ahead.

The Consumer Price Index (CPI) is perhaps the most highly publicized and closely watched economic series in the United States. It is released frequently and furnishes the basis for automatic wage increases for thousands of unionized wage earners under contracts tied to cost of living. It is considered as a measure of inflation and the erosion of the dollar. Because of its importance, it receives a great deal of attention from businessmen. CPI is based on price information gathered in urban portions of 39 standard metropolitan statistical areas (see Chapter 17) and 17 smaller cities. Approximately 18,000 establishments are included in the sample. The CPI measures *changes in price*; it does not give *level* of prices. It cannot be used to compare the cost of living of one city with that of another.

NONSTATISTICAL NEWS

Corporation news

Financial pages usually contain news about individual corporations — information which indicates whether a corporation is making forward strides or is regressing. Corporation news is of most interest to stockholders, investors, and competing businesses. Information about specific companies can be divided into four categories.

Changes in personnel Promotions, terminations, new appointments, and deaths of key executives are reported. Some of this information is purely routine, having human rather than business interest. But if a business has been on the downgrade, the appointment of a capable, widely respected executive as head of the corporation may inspire confidence in investors. On the other hand, if a business loses a major executive, such news may possibly depress the price of stock in the corporation.

New products   Publicity is often given to the development of new products. When, for example, a manufacturing concern announces its intention to market a new machine, numerous people are interested. The investing public may interpret this as a sign of greater prosperity for the company; competitors may take it as a signal to be on the alert.

Corporate expansion programs   News that a company plans to expand is of major interest. Normally it indicates the corporation expects further growth, which is welcomed by its stockholders and perhaps feared by its competitors. Suppliers dealing with the expanding company may adjust their sales strategy toward this customer accordingly.

Corporate mergers and conglomerates   News of company mergers has an impact on investors and businessmen. One of the glamour words in Wall Street news in recent years has been *conglomerate*. The term has no precise meaning. It usually refers to a company that grows quickly by acquiring other companies in completely unrelated fields of business. J. A. Livingston, a financial columnist, offers this definition of conglomerate: "A collection of corporations mixed together as opportunity offers."

Antitrust enforcement had much to do with fostering the conglomerate trend in company mergers. Company diversification, either horizontally (acquiring companies in the same or related fields) or vertically (acquiring companies from the raw-materials end through the distribution of the finished product), has been viewed skeptically by the Justice Department and the Federal Trade Commission. However, there appeared to be no legal barriers when a company took over a business unrelated to its own. Whether extension of conglomerates will continue is open to question.

Government news

In recent years, actions of the federal government have had an increasing influence on prices, investment, production, and business activity in general. Decisions made by Congress, federal courts, and various governmental agencies affect corporations as well as industries. Certain high-level business decisions cannot be made without consideration of existing or proposed governmental policies and projects.

News about international markets

Many businesspeople have a keen interest in news that concerns foreign markets. There are six principal reasons for this interest.

1. Certain businesspeople are involved in domestic corporations with interests in foreign countries.

2. Many people who live in the United States own stocks and bonds in foreign corporations.

3. Foreign countries purchase a significant volume of domestic products and materials.

4. American corporations purchase large quantities of foreign-produced raw materials and manufactured articles.

5. Foreign and domestic corporations compete to sell to other nations. The United States, for example, competes with West Germany in selling automobiles in Brazil.

6. The development of the European Common Market and the internal economic welfare of various countries have a strong bearing on our political as well as business climate.

As a result of the close economic and political interactions between the United States and other countries, many newspapers and magazines devote space to foreign commerce and economic matters. Such news is varied in character. Foreign trade is regulated by all countries, and since the governments in some nations are relatively unstable, foreign trade is an intricate and sometimes confusing study. Its complexity is not lessened by the fact that our own government's policies regarding imports and exports necessarily change from time to time (see Chapter 20).

Financial reporting services

In addition to the customary financial and business news found in newspapers and magazines, there are detailed analytical reports, compiled by special investment advisory services and sold on a subscription basis, that project the probable performance of specific securities. Trendline, Dow Theory Forecasts, and Security Research Company are examples of such services. The *Wall Street Journal*, *Barron's*, and other financial publications carry considerable advertising of firms selling financial advice.

Brokerage house information service   Merrill Lynch, Pierce, Fenner & Smith, Inc.; Paine, Webber, Jackson, and Curtis; Bache & Co., and other brokerage houses provide investors with extensive information about specific companies and industries as well as the total economy. This information is available at no charge to investors and prospective investors.

PEOPLE AND THEIR IDEAS
Bernard Kilgore

The guiding genius behind the *Wall Street Journal*

Bernard Kilgore was named managing editor of the *Wall Street Journal* in 1941. He was only thirty-two at the time. The paper was small, with a circulation of only 33,000; under his direction, it became the nation's leading financial newspaper, with a circulation, at the time of his death in 1967, of over one million.

Kilgore was born in Albany, Indiana, in 1908 and grew up in South Bend, Indiana. In school he earned top grades, was a skilled debater, and was a ragtime jazz pianist. He graduated Phi Beta Kappa from De Pauw University with a degree in political science.

In 1929 Kilgore joined the *Wall Street Journal* as a reporter. He was transferred to San Francisco in 1931 and there began a "Dear George" column in which he explained complex financial and economic problems in easy-to-understand English. The column was a tremendous success, and Kilgore was soon brought back East as a regular editorial-page columnist.

When Kilgore, as managing editor, took over the task of reorganizing the *Journal*, he began with the front page. There he developed the kind of background, in-depth story that now distinguishes the paper (since 1960, the *Journal* has won five Pulitzer Prizes). He expanded the scope of the paper without minimizing the chief reason for its being — its full and accurate coverage of the stock market and corporate affairs. He developed the concept of delivering the same comprehensive news and editorial coverage each morning to subscribers throughout the United States, while continuing to emphasize the importance of simplifying the complicated — of keeping readers interested. "The easiest thing in the world," he often said, "is to stop reading."

In 1945 Kilgore became president of Dow Jones and Company, Inc., the parent corporation, which, in addition to the *Wall Street Journal*, publishes *Barron's*, a leading financial weekly, *The National Observer*, the nation's first weekly newspaper, and the *Dow Jones News Service*. He was instrumental in the creation of *The National Observer* in 1962 — a family-oriented newspaper printed on Saturday, when the *Wall Street Journal* is not. At the time, critics were doubtful of the paper's future, but its circulation is now a healthy 500,000. In 1966, he was elected chairman of the board of Dow Jones, a position he was to hold for only a year.

In spite of his ability as an executive, Kilgore regarded himself primarily as a newspaperman. He was dedicated to the idea that the quality of journalism could always be improved. He often warned his staff of the dangers of standing still, and his constant reminder to them was, "We don't want to pattern tomorrow's paper on yesterday's." Kilgore frequently encouraged his staff to argue their points of view. "One of my big jobs," he said shortly before his death, "has been to make certain that no one is indispensable. And I think I have done that job."

CONTEMPORARY ISSUES
Situation 9

Is the stock market right for the small investor?

Ray and John continued discussing the wisdom of investing in the stock market after class. "You know, I'm not so sure I think buying common stock is such a good idea for people of modest means," observed Ray. "Do you realize on odd-lot purchases and sales, the economics of the marketplace are against the little guy. Just to break even on a four-hundred-dollar investment, for example, the stock must appreciate nine percent, while on a five-thousand dollar investment—the kind more substantial investors make—it must appreciate only two and one-quarter percent."

"I agree," commented John, "that people who buy or sell less than a hundred shares are hurt most by the commission charged by the brokers. But what the small investor can do is save enough money so he can buy round lots. Aside from the commission, I like to see small investors in the stock market. Widespread stock ownership lends an equalizing effect to the distribution of wealth. And just about everybody I know wants to own something. Ownership of corporate securities is good for the society."

"I like what they say in theory, but I can't quite buy it in practice," interjected Ray. "The small investor generally loses. He tends to exaggerate his ability and underestimate his weaknesses. My uncle told me the way to make money in the stock market is to 'buy low, sell high, fast.' Perhaps professional investors can do this but the average amateur can't."

"Well, what do you recommend we do to protect the small investor?" asked John.

"One idea I have," answered Ray, "is to prohibit transactions of less than one hundred shares of any stock. Also, I feel they should do away with margin trading for small accounts. I think small investors should pay the full amount in cash for the stock they purchase."

SITUATION EVALUATION

1. Do you agree that small investors should not buy corporate securities? Why or why not?

2. Evaluate Ray's proposed solutions.

BUSINESS CHRONICLE

Decision-making under conditions of uncertainty

Kingmaker Estates, Inc., had an option to buy 900 acres of undeveloped land for $1,200 an acre. A major problem was servicing the site with water and sewers. The company invited contractors to bid on providing these services. The lowest bid was $800,000, an amount so large that it would place a strain on the company's finances and credit standing. If Kingmaker decided to provide the services, it was estimated that it would take three years to have the first parcel of land ready for sale to pay off the $800,000 investment in services.

The alternative was to work with the county and get them to provide the needed services. This was considerably less certain, since Kingmaker, of course, had no control over the local government. Discussions with county officials indicated that if Kingmaker petitioned for services it would take from four to five years to provide them.

The taxes on the property, which generated a net $50 an acre per year when rented for farming, were $20 an acre. It would cost Kingmaker 9 percent to finance the purchase investment once it exercised its option to buy at $1,200 per acre. The option to buy was good for six months. After that time, the price of the land could be raised or it might be sold to someone else. Kingmaker directors felt that when developed, the land would net $3,000 per acre over purchase price and expenses.

QUESTIONS

1. What are the variables that must be considered in this proposition?

2. Is it safe to plan in terms of what the county officials estimate?

3. What should Kingmaker management do?

APPLICATION EXERCISES

1. Consult the financial pages of a recent copy of your newspaper and list the current price, yearly range, and number of sales made for each of the following stocks listed on the New York Stock Exchange: IBM, common; Procter & Gamble, common; Du Pont, preferred; American Telephone and Telegraph, common; United Air Lines, preferred. Which do you feel is the best investment? Why?

2. Clip six nonstatistical news articles from the financial pages of your newspaper. Explain how each would be of interest to a businessman.

3. Consult the "dividends declared" listings in the financial pages of a recent issue of a large city newspaper. Explain what the different items in the listing mean.

QUESTIONS

1. Some people contend that those who read financial news are too materialistic and that this is an undesirable aspect of our society. Do you agree or disagree with this contention? Explain your answer.

2. How do you account for the fact that the *Wall Street Journal* is one of the fastest growing national newspapers, and can be found on many newsstands all over the United States, when many daily newspapers in large cities are disappearing?

3. Differentiate between statistical and nonstatistical news. How do they relate to each other?

4. How do bond quotations differ from stock quotations?

5. What are the Dow-Jones averages? How are they compiled?

6. What reasons can you think of to explain the rapid growth in acceptance of mutual funds?

7. Why are local wholesale egg, butter, fresh fruit, and vegetable prices published regularly in virtually every newspaper in the country?

8. Why does government news appear on the financial pages?

9. Even if they were not interested in investments, might an anthropologist, a sociologist, a psychologist, a chemist, and an English teacher find the financial pages of interest? In what ways?

risk management and insurance

CHAPTER 10

METHODS OF MEETING RISK
Reducing the Chance of Loss. Good Management. Self-Insurance. Insurance.

TYPES OF INSURANCE COMPANIES
Stock Companies. Mutual Companies. Stocks and Mutuals Compared.

TYPES OF INSURANCE

FIRE INSURANCE
Direct Losses. Consequential Losses. Coinsurance Clause.

MARINE INSURANCE
Ocean Marine. Inland Marine.

AUTOMOBILE INSURANCE
Collision. Fire and Theft. Automobile Liability. No-Fault Auto Insurance—
A Key Issue.

LIABILITY INSURANCE

CRIMINAL LOSS PROTECTION
Other Crime Protection Coverages. Government Involvement in Crime
Insurance.

WORKMEN'S COMPENSATION INSURANCE

HEALTH INSURANCE

LIFE INSURANCE
Mortality Table. Premiums. The Natural Premium Plan. The Level-Premium
Plan. Types of Life Insurance Policies. Comparison of the Four Policies.

THE PURCHASE OF INSURANCE

PENSION PLANS
Types of Pension Plans.

Perhaps the only certain thing in business is uncertainty. Since uncertainty, or risk, can at any time weaken or destroy a business, risk must be managed by carefully anticipating and providing for it.

Business risk is, in simplest terms, the chance that something will happen to cause a financial loss. The following are examples of common business risks.

1. Property may be damaged or destroyed by fire, windstorm, flood, hail, explosion, riot, vandalism, or earthquake

2. Merchandise and other property may be stolen by employees, customers, or others

253

3. Company funds may be embezzled by employees

4. Accidents may injure employees, customers, or others, posing a threat of lawsuit

5. Goods may spoil or deteriorate, or they may become obsolete because of changes in customer preferences

6. There are a large variety of miscellaneous risks, such as the death of key executives, drought in the grain and cattle areas, strikes, changes in the price of goods, credit losses, new competition, new legislation, and decrease in demand for a firm's products

Lack of preparation for such contingencies is both a major cause of business failure and a significant factor in reducing profits. Wise businesses face risks realistically and minimize the chances of loss in every way possible.**

METHODS OF MEETING RISK

There are four general ways to meet risk: (1) reduce or eliminate the chance of loss, (2) practice good management, (3) self-insure—that is, establish a reserve for contingencies, and (4) transfer risk to insurance carriers.

SPECIAL READINGS

** Riding the Pennsy to Ruin, A Wall Street Journal Chronicle of the Penn Central Debacle, edited by Michael Gartner. Princeton, N. J.: Dow Jones Books, 1971 (paperback). Because America's huge corporations are so powerful, they often seem invulnerable and not subject to great risks. This book tells the story of one of America's recent spectacular bankruptcies.

One of the big corporate news stories in 1968 was the merger of two huge U.S. railroads, the Pennsylvania and the New York Central, which by combining gave the new company a virtual monopoly on service in the nation's richest and most concentrated industrial area. The behemoth that was created was supposed to realize efficiencies and help revolutionize U.S. railroading. Less than three years later, in 1970, the merged railroad went broke.

The editors of the Wall Street Journal launched an investigation to answer questions like:

"How did it happen? How did one of the largest corporations in America end up in bankruptcy court? How could any company lose $431 million in one year? And, equally important, how could this gigantic company go down without pulling a lot of other corporations down with it?"

In their investigation, reporters discovered quite a scandal. It was found that a group of officers of the Penn Central unloaded 40,000 shares in the road just before the company's troubles were made public. They uncovered the fact that a large and respected Philadelphia brokerage house that had close ties with the Pennsy led two lives (the respectable facade for public consumption and another behind-the-scenes life) before Penn's financial disaster hit. They also found how the nation's banking system closed ranks helped avert further disaster.

While probing for the causes of the collapse, reporters saw how deeply a corporation affects other elements in the community. The Penn Central debacle turned neighbor against neighbor and even had ramifications at the Philadelphia Museum of Art and at the University of Pennsylvania, all of which is chronicled in this interesting book.

Reducing the chance of loss

The chance of loss can be reduced through preventive and protective measures. These include fireproof buildings, safety equipment, and safety education for employees. Automatic sprinkler systems, regular inspection of movable equipment (such as elevators), employment of guards in industrial plants and detectives in stores, special locks on safes and vaults, adequate lighting, electronic surveillance systems, and careful selection of employees who will handle money are all calculated to reduce risks.

Such measures, while valuable, *do not eliminate the chance of loss.* Numerous "guaranteed fireproof" hotels burn; shoplifting goes on in stores staffed with detectives; thieves break into "unbreakable" vaults; and machines "just inspected" break, injuring employees. It is necessary, therefore, for a business to do more than take preventive and protective measures against risks.

Good management

All business organizations face a number of risks that can be met, if at all, only through good managerial practices. For example, risks of product obsolescence, population movements that reduce the value of a given business location, price changes, and economic recession can be dealt with only if the organization anticipates these changes and prepares for them. Many large organizations maintain research departments to study trends and guide management decisions. For example, research can measure in advance customer reactions to new product ideas, changes in business procedures, advertising, and so forth, helping management to minimize costly wrong commitments.

Self-insurance

A third method of meeting risk is to set aside a financial reserve that can be drawn on when losses occur. Self-insurance is simple and appeals to some businesses; it is not, however, a practical method for most. Suppose, for example, that the owner of a $10,000 building decided to put $100 per year into a reserve to protect his property against fire. It would obviously take more than a lifetime before sufficient funds could be accumulated to cover a total loss.

Self-insurance is sometimes used successfully by organizations that operate several hundred similar, widely scattered establishments. A contribution by each unit to a general fund might be sufficient to meet certain losses that occur.

The self-insurance method may be used for protection against only some risks. For example, a taxicab company operating a large number of cabs may self-insure against the risk of collision, since this risk is reasonably easy to predict. The same company would not, in all probability, self-insure against the risk of injuring a third party, since losses from such a risk are much more difficult to estimate. Thus, even for large organizations, self-insurance is usually not a complete answer to the problem of risk.

Insurance

The methods of meeting risk discussed above provide only partial protection against the chance of loss. The most popular and effective method is to *transfer* the risk to professional risk bearers — insurance companies.

Insurance, explained simply, is a process in which one party (the *insurer*) agrees, for a sum of money (the *premium*), which is paid by a second party (the *insured*), to pay the second party a certain sum if he should suffer a specified loss.

Suppose that A owns a building worth $10,000. B, the insurance company, agrees, for a $80 annual premium paid by A, to insure against the risk that A's building may be destroyed by fire. If the building should burn, B will pay A the amount of loss up to $10,000. If the building does not burn, B keeps the premium and uses it, together with premiums from other insureds, to reimburse those who do experience losses and to pay his own operating expenses. Thus, insurance does not *prevent* loss. Rather, it *shifts the burden of risk* to someone better qualified to assume it.

The question of which kinds of risks can be insured is significant. Insurance concerns itself only with pure risks — that is, risks where there is a chance only to lose. Speculative risks, where there is a chance to gain or lose, as in fluctuations of stock prices or in horse races, cannot be insured. Insurance offsets risks that are already present. It always involves the *transfer* of these risks.

Claims beyond the amount of risk that can be transferred are not insured. Claims for a burned down building cannot be for more than the value of the building. If the owner received more than the value, the risk principle would be violated. All insurers would suffer in the long run through higher premiums because the unscrupulous would be encouraged to destroy property deliberately for money gain.

Further, to obtain insurance, the applicant must have an *insurable interest* in the property insured. Ownership of property is an obvious example of insurable interest. But one cannot, for example, purchase insurance on property belonging to someone else.

Law of large numbers   How can an insurance company afford to assume a $10,000 risk for a seemingly small premium of $80? The explanation lies in the law of large numbers, commonly referred to as the law of averages. According to this mathematical law, out of a very large number of similar risks, only a certain number of losses will occur. By studying the experience of, say, 10,000 similar buildings over a period of years, actuaries[1] are able to predict with surprising accuracy how many of these structures will be destroyed by fire in any one year. When this number is known, the insurance company can determine how much money it must collect in the form of premiums to have a sufficiently large fund to pay all losses, meet its own operating expenses, and realize a profit.

If, for example, of the 10,000 insured buildings it was determined that 250 would be damaged by fire to the extent of $1,000 each in a normal year, the company would need to collect $250,000 to cover losses and, we may assume, $50,000 for expenses and profit, for a total of $300,000. Prorating this cost equally among all those buying the insurance would mean that each would pay a $30 premium.

The necessity for large numbers in predicting losses must be emphasized. The same actuaries who can predict almost the exact number of fires in a large group of buildings could not predict the number of losses in a small group of one hundred buildings.

The law of large numbers can be used to predict losses other than those from fire. All insurance coverage is based in part on this law. As will be shown later, life insurance estimates are very exact.

What constitutes an insurable risk?　Several qualifications must be met before an insurance company will insure a given risk.

First, as implied above, *the chance of loss must be predictable with reasonable accuracy.* Without such predictions, companies simply do not know how large the premium should be. An example of risk that cannot be predicted is error in decisions made by executives. Occasionally, insurance companies do assume risks for which little or no statistical evidence is available. In such cases, however, very careful judgment is used, and a relatively large premium is charged.[2]

---

[1] An actuary is a person who calculates insurance premiums and determines acceptable risks based on estimates of interest that the premiums will earn, mortality rates, and the like.

[2] The oldest and most famous insurers are Lloyd's of London, which acts as a sort of stock exchange for the buying and selling of insurance risks. They do not themselves underwrite insurance. Lloyd's has long been a leader in providing marine insurance but is best known for the fact that it specializes in arranging to insure risks that are not acceptable to conventional insurance companies. Insurance of a baseball player's arm or a piano player's hands and insurance against a change in the weather or the danger of war are examples of unique risks insured by Lloyd's.

The foremost American insurer of unusual risks is the St. Paul Fire and Marine Insurance Company of St. Paul, Minnesota. It pays if Lassie is ever unable to go before the cameras and insures a particular store owner on a loss-of-business policy on a bridge so that if it ever collapses (and customers cannot patronize him), he can collect.

Sometimes risks move from the uninsurable to the insurable classification. Risks associated with air transportation, for example, were once uninsurable, but, as experience accumulated, coverage became available and at progressively lower premiums.

Second, *the risk must concern possible financial loss.* Sentimental losses, such as the destruction of a child's painting, cannot be insured, because there is no objective way to evaluate sentiment.

Third, *the company or individual that applies for insurance must not be a "moral hazard."* A moral hazard exists when there is danger that the property will be deliberately destroyed by the insured to collect the insurance. The moral hazard is particularly important in fire insurance. Over the years a substantial body of evidence has accumulated that the number of business properties that burn increases greatly during a business depression. Unfortunately, some individuals apparently set fire or hire others to set fire to their businesses to get themselves out of debt. A number of state insurance commissioners estimate that 25 percent or more of all fires involving business property are intentionally started.[3]

To minimize the moral hazard, insurance companies conduct investigations of applicants. Particular attention is given to the applicant's character, to his previous insurance-loss record, and to the profitableness of his present business operation. Sudden eagerness for large insurance coverage by a hard-pressed business not previously heavily insured would be suspect. Life insurance policies generally include a "suicide clause," which states that, in the event the insured commits suicide within two years after purchasing the policy, the company will pay the beneficiary only the amount of the premiums paid, not the face value of the policy. The purpose of this clause is to reduce the moral hazard.

TYPES OF INSURANCE COMPANIES

Stock companies

This type insurance company is a corporation owned and operated by stockholders for profit. The stockholders are not necessarily purchasers of insurance. Rather, they act in the capacity of investors hoping to earn dividends. Stock companies attempt to earn a profit in two ways: (1) by charging premiums that exceed the combined costs of claims and business expenses, and (2) by investing their assets in securities of prosperous companies.

[3] Insurance commissioners have also noted an increase in fire losses in businesses, located along older highways, that were bypassed by the new interstate highway system.

Stock companies write most of the insurance in all lines except life. In fire insurance, for example, more than 75 percent is written by stock companies.

Mutual companies

Mutuals are a form of cooperative. There are no stockholders, and the companies are owned by the policyholders; hence there can be no dividends on stock. Mutuals can be divided into two classes: *assessment mutuals* and *full-advance premium mutuals*. In the assessment type, a relatively low premium is charged. Then, if losses exceed premiums collected, each policyholder is assessed an amount to make up the deficiency. Assessment mutuals are most successful in farm areas, especially for fire insurance.

The full-advance premium mutual operates in much the same manner as a stock company except that there are no stockholders and, of course, no stock dividends. Premium rates are set sufficiencly high to meet all expected losses. In some cases these rates are higher than those charged by stock companies. If a surplus accumulates, the policyholders receive a rebate, commonly called a dividend. This is not to be confused with the dividend of a stock company paid out of profits. The world's largest life insurance companies are full-advance premium mutuals.

Stocks and mutuals compared

At first glance, one would assume that, since profits are eliminated, mutual companies should be able to provide insurance at lower cost than stock companies. In the case of life insurance, the evidence suggests that this may be true. Proof regarding other types of insurance is lacking. Proponents of the stock companies insist that profit-motivated management is naturally superior to the nonprofit-minded management found in mutuals. Advocates of the mutual organizations say this is not true. One can conclude only that individual evaluation should be given each company when one is considering insurance purchases.

TYPES OF INSURANCE

Insurance can be divided into eight broad classifications: fire, marine, automobile, liability, criminal loss protection, workmen's compensation, health, and life.

FIRE INSURANCE

Direct losses

One of the oldest and most essential types of insurance is that against losses due to fire. All fire insurance is written on one basic contract form called the "standard policy." Blank spaces are provided for describing the property to be insured. Fire insurance policies are written for one to five years. Rates vary according to the risks involved. Frame buildings carry higher rates than brick and steel structures. Well-protected areas in cities have lower rates than rural areas. The type of occupancy in the buildings is also a factor, with more hazardous operations paying higher rates.

The policy pays for actual value of the loss up to the face value of the policy. If, for example, the face value of the policy is $5,000 and the amount of the loss is $2,000, the most that can be collected is the latter sum. Adjustments downward are made for depreciation. That is, if a destroyed building was originally worth $5,000, the insured normally receives $5,000, less the estimated depreciation. The insured is never intentionally allowed to profit as a result of a loss covered by fire or any other type of insurance.

A very common supplement (called a rider) to the standard fire insurance contract is one covering losses from wind, hail, explosion, riot, falling aircraft, and smoke.

Consequential losses

The fire insurance contract reimburses the insured only for losses that can be traced directly to fire. When all or part of a business is destroyed, however, the business will experience indirect losses resulting from the inability to conduct normal operations. These are called "consequential losses," for they arise as a consequence of fire. The more important endorsements appended to the regular fire insurance contract to cover such losses are:

1. Loss resulting from vandalism, water damage, sprinkler leakage, collapse, falling objects, weight of snow, ice, or sleet

2. Loss of earnings and rent payments to be made while building is being repaired or rebuilt

3. Loss resulting from destruction of accounts receivables, records, and other valuable papers

Coinsurance clause

Because most fires result in only partial loss of property, there is a natural temptation for businessmen to insure property for considerably less than its total value. A businessman's reasoning might be: "My building is worth $40,000. The odds are very great that if I should have a fire it would destroy only part of the building. Therefore, I'll purchase only a $20,000 policy and take my chances that a total loss will never occur."

This reasoning tends to work to the disadvantage of the insurance company, for it reduces premium income. Insurance companies have therefore adopted the coinsurance clause, which states, in effect: "In the event of loss, this company shall be liable for no greater proportion thereof than the sum hereby insured bears to ——— (usually 80 percent, although other percentages are used) of the cash value of the property described herein at the time when such loss shall happen."

The coinsurance clause operates as follows: Assume that Mr. Smith, owner of a building worth $40,000, insures it with a fire insurance company under a contract containing an 80 percent coinsurance clause. A policy is written for $32,000. Later, a $24,000 fire occurs. Since the property owner had met the requirements of the 80 percent coinsurance clause, the full amount of the loss, $24,000, would be paid. However, if the owner in this case had obtained insurance for only $20,000, and a $24,000 fire had occurred, the owner would only receive $15,000 in settlement of the loss. In this case the owner must share the loss, because he has failed to meet the requirements of the 80 percent coinsurance clause.

The settlement is determined in the following manner: Smith had purchased $20,000 worth of insurance, which is five-eighths of the amount ($32,000) needed to be fully insured against partial losses. Therefore, he is reimbursed for only five-eighths of the $24,000 loss, or $15,000.

MARINE INSURANCE

Marine insurance, sometimes called transportation insurance, took its name from the fact that it was first used to insure ships and cargoes at sea. It has the distinction of being the oldest type of insurance; it existed in an elementary form five thousand years ago. Marine insurance covers two broad areas: ocean marine and inland marine.

Ocean marine

Ocean marine insurance, as the name suggests, is used to protect shippers while goods are on the sea or temporarily in port. Protection is against losses resulting from sinking, capsizing, stranding, collision, bad weather, and theft. While all ocean marine policies tend to follow the same form, there is no standard policy, as there is in fire insurance. Time policies are used when shipments are made regularly, while single-voyage policies are issued when shipments are made at infrequent intervals. Rate-setting is complicated, since many variables must be considered: route traveled, season of the year, type of cargo; thus judgment ratings, which are arbitrary, are used.

An actual example will serve to illustrate why insurance is an integral part of business planning. General Electric once undertook a most complex shipping assignment. From its plant in Schenectady, N.Y., General Electric shipped a 130-ton stator and a 64-ton steel drum halfway around the world to Baghdad. The mammoth equipment was loaded on the SS *Weisenfels*, which delivered the cargo to Basrah, Iraq, for the 350-mile trip by barge up the Tigris River. There, a three-story steel framework was erected to hoist the stator and drum to shore. In view of the transportation and construction risks involved in this complicated operation, General Electric arranged for the necessary marine and erection insurance coverage with Marsh & McLennan, insurance brokers in New York.

Inland marine

Of more significance to most businessmen is inland marine insurance, which is made up of two major divisions: inland transportation insurance and personal property floaters.

Inland transportation insurance is not restricted to inland water transportation but covers risks while goods are being transported by truck, plane, and railroad. Inland insurance contracts were originally very similar to ocean marine, but with the extension of coverage to many new risks the contract has been modified substantially to cover plate glass, signs, bridges, and other things indirectly related to transportation.

The usual policies cover almost every conceivable accidental loss, such as fire, lightning, flood, windstorm, earthquake, collision, derailment of trains, and overturning of trucks. Generally, however, risks such as theft, robbery, strikes, and riot are covered only if specifically endorsed.

A *personal property floater* is a type of coverage that protects personal property in the home, away from home, or in transit. It is comprehensive, covering fire, theft, and other hazards.

AUTOMOBILE INSURANCE

Automobile owners face two major kinds of risk: (1) that the automobile will be damaged or destroyed through collision, fire, or theft, and (2) that

Figure **10-1**
Age and Driving Accidents

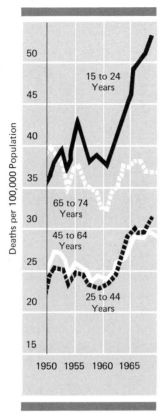

Source: Natural Transportation Safety Board.

How do the statistics above relate to insurance rates?

the automobile may be responsible for injury or damage to other people or property. To protect himself from loss, the automobile owner needs three types of coverage: collision, fire and theft, and liability.

There are approximately 109 million motor vehicles registered in the United States, and 108.3 million licensed drivers. Automobile insurance coverage is provided by more than 1,000 property and casualty insurance companies. To arrive at equitable rates, these companies classify drivers according to the risk they are likely to encounter. Rates depend on a number of factors: usage of car (business or pleasure), city versus rural driving, age, sex, marital status, occupation, number of miles driven and value or age of the auto itself. Insurance studies relate measurable differences in accident potential to the rate structure. For example, it is found

Figure **10–2**
Rates Go Down As Young Drivers Grow Older[a]

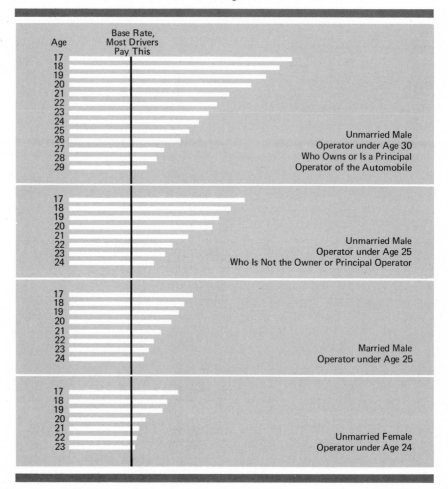

[a] Based on a driver classification plan used by a large segment of the insurance businesses in many states. These comparisons of gradations are for private passenger cars used for pleasure where all operators have "clean" driving records. Adjustments in premiums are made for cars used to drive to work, used for business, or used on a farm. Adjustments are also made for youthful operators with driver training credit, drivers with "unclean" driving records, and owners of more than one car. In many states, premium discounts are available to students with outstanding scholastic records.

Source: Insurance Information Institute.

that the frequency of accidents is extremely high when drivers are young, but that the frequency declines steadily as these drivers gain maturity and experience (see Figure 10–1).

A National Transportation Safety Board study notes that insurance companies have for a long time offered premium reductions to persons completing driver education courses. Interestingly, the study states that "the insurance companies have never ascertained whether driver education is the cause of a better accident rate." The study found that alcohol plays an important role in auto accidents among young people — more than 60 percent of 16- to 24-year-old drivers killed had measurable amounts of alcohol in their systems. "The young driver has a double hazard. He is an inexperienced driver and an inexperienced drinker," states the report. It recommends more thorough licensing examinations and a two-year probationary license for all drivers under 21, which would facilitate placing offenders in improvement programs.

Collision

This coverage protects against losses from collision with other automobiles or with other objects, either moving or fixed. Collision insurance may be either full-coverage or deductible. Under full-coverage, the insurance company indemnifies (compensates) for all losses, regardless of amount; under deductible coverage, the insurance company is liable (responsible) only for losses over a specified sum, such as $50, $100, or $150. Since most automobile accidents involve relatively small losses, premium rates for deductible collision insurance are much lower than for full-coverage.

Fire and theft

Fire and theft coverage indemnifies for losses caused from fire or theft. This coverage can, for an additional premium, be extended to cover losses resulting from windstorm, riot, flood, or almost any other risk not covered under the collision policy. Such additional coverage is called *comprehensive coverage.*

Automobile liability

Automobile liability insurance is issued to cover property and personal liability. If the driver of a car is found to be responsible for an accident, a very expensive lawsuit can result. Automobile liability coverage is very similar to the public liability coverages. The company investigates claims made by the parties, defends the insured in lawsuits, and pays damages to the limit of the policy.

Standard policy limits are set at $10,000 for death or injury to one person and at $20,000 for death or injury to more than one person. The maximum that can be collected for one accident by one individual is $10,000. Frequently, however, this is insufficient to pay the costs of damages; accordingly, for a higher premium, the automobile owner can get insurance for larger amounts, such as $20,000/$40,000, $50,000/$100,000, and $100,000/$200,000.

So serious have automobile lawsuits been that most states now have financial responsibility laws that require all automobile owners either to carry automobile liability insurance or to prove that they have sufficient financial resources to pay for the costs of accidents caused by their negligence.

Judgments as high as several hundred thousand dollars have been rendered in automobile liability cases, and in recent years the trend has been for jury awards to increase. Some indication of the hazards in this field is the fact that large trucking companies operating multimillion dollar businesses often pay 5 percent or even more of their gross revenues for insurance premiums of this type.

No-fault auto insurance—a key issue

On August 13, 1970, Massachusetts enacted the nation's first "no-fault" automobile insurance plan. A widespread dissatisfaction with automobile insurance exists because of the frequent inability to get insurance and rising premium rates. The present system for allocating costs of automobile accidents is based on *fault*, or *tort*, law. Fault law involves determining who is legally responsible for the losses suffered. Criticisms of the system are (1) it assumes that driver error is the only cause of accidents, (2) when the system pays, it is inequitable—some are overpaid, others underpaid, (3) many automobile accident victims go unpaid entirely, (4) it is incredibly slow in paying benefits because of litigation, which may take 4 or 5 years, (5) it is inefficient and wasteful—legal and administrative costs are so high that only 40 cents of every dollar paid goes to the victim, and (6) it encourages routine exaggeration of claims.

The Department of Transportation and the FTC did a multimillion dollar study of the automobile insurance system. As a result, the abolishment of automobile fault law may be expected, substituting a "compensation" insurance plan. The principle of the plan is that the victim is entitled to receive specified benefits from his *own* insurance company without regard to fault. Several states have already passed laws switching to variations of "no fault." Most other states have plans pending. Also pending are two federal measures in the House and Senate.

LIABILITY INSURANCE

With the exception of automobile liability insurance, the coverages discussed thus far have pertained only to direct loss or damage to the insured's property. Another major class of risk to which all businesses and individuals are exposed is the chance of loss resulting from injury to another person or damage to his property. For this reason, liability insurance is also called *third-party insurance*.

Under our legal system, one is liable for any damage done to another person through some *negligent act*. Exactly what constitutes negligence is usually a matter for the courts to decide. In general, "failure to exercise caution or prudence" is considered negligence, but this broad generalization obviously leaves much room for legal interpretation.

Some of the more common instances in which liability may arise are the following: Restaurants may be liable for illness resulting from spoiled food. Farmers may be liable for accidents caused by livestock that wander onto a highway. Pharmacists who make a mistake in compounding a prescription might be sued. Homeowners may be liable for injuries suffered by guests from accidents. Manufacturers may be liable if the public suffers injury from using their products. Contractors erecting a building may be liable for injury caused by materials that fall and strike someone. Doctors are sometimes held liable under malpractice charges.

There are many different liability coverages. Most of the policies have fairly uniform, standardized provisions. The insurance company agrees to indemnify the insured, up to the amount of loss or limit of the policy, for liability claims on the insured adjudged *by law*. The insurance company automatically provides legal defense for the insured when he is accused of causing an accident.

Insurance companies exercise a constant lookout for fake claim artists. To protect themselves against these dishonest individuals, the insurance companies maintain the *National Casualty and Surety Underwriters Bureau,* which, in addition to other activities, keeps a record of all liability claims.

CRIMINAL LOSS PROTECTION

Insurance is available to cover burglary, which is marked by forcible entry; robbery, which is the taking of property by violence or threat of violence; and theft, which is stealing property while it is unprotected. Businesses face many risks both from dishonest employees and from criminals. Protection against possible loss from criminal acts can be covered through fidelity bonds, surety bonds, and a variety of other coverages.

Fidelity and surety bonds are issued by bonding companies to protect a business against the acts of a third party or against a third party's failure to act. *Fidelity bonds* indemnify employers against theft, forgery, and embezzlement by employees who handle company funds or company property.

Fidelity bonds can be purchased for individuals or for groups. A fidelity bond can be purchased to equal the maximum amount of cash or property an employee may have access to at any time or an amount that might possibly be misappropriated by several employees acting in collusion.

Surety bonds insure not only against dishonest acts but also against the failure of a third party to fulfill a contractual obligation. They are used to insure the completion of contracts made with building contractors, suppliers, and other parties. If the third party does not carry out the agreement, the bonding company then pays the amount specified in the bond.

Other crime protection coverages

Insurance policies are available to protect businesses from other crime-related losses, including: (1) robbery of money and securities inside company premises, (2) robbery of money and securities outside company premises, (3) depositor's forgery and use of counterfeit paper currency, and (4) storekeeper's burglary and robbery.

Government involvement in crime insurance

The Department of Housing and Urban Development (HUD) has set up a federal crime insurance program because many businesses in central city high-crime areas had closed or moved when they were unable to get insurance they could afford against losses from robbery and burglary. In the program, the government is the insurer, but private agents and brokers sell the insurance and handle the paper work. The program offers insurance where it is not available privately or where the cost is prohibitive.

WORKMEN'S COMPENSATION INSURANCE

Until about 1910, if an employee suffered injury while at work or, as a result of work-related circumstances, contracted an occupational disease, his only chance for obtaining compensation was to prove that the employer was negligent, which, in practice, was nearly impossible to do.

After considerable unsatisfactory experience with this system, the point of view developed that, since accidents are bound to occur in industry, insurance should be provided to cover injuries regardless of who is at fault—the employer or the employee. This view is basic to the compulsory workmen's compensation laws now in effect in all states. These laws require that almost all employers carry workmen's compensation insurance. The major exceptions are employers of agricultural workers or of domestic and casual labor and those who employ only a small number of people.

In some states, workmen's compensation insurance is underwritten by the state, while in others, private insurance companies provide the coverage. A few states permit large businesses to self-insure their own workmen's compensation risks. Premiums for workmen's compensation insurance amount to a certain percentage of the company's total payroll, the percentage depending on the hazards involved. In many cases special allowance is made for companies that experience less than average losses. Supervision of workmen's compensation insurance is usually the responsibility of a state agency established for this purpose.

Policy provisions in general provide compensation to the employee, after a waiting period of several days to two weeks, for (1) medical and surgical aid, (2) fatal injuries (the insurer pays last-illness expenses and makes a weekly payment to the dependents for a specified period), and (3) temporary total disability (the employee receives as much as $66\frac{2}{3}$ percent of his weekly wage at the time of the injury up to a specified amount). Usually the same rate applies when permanent total disability results.

HEALTH INSURANCE

The purpose of health insurance is to pay the insured for expenses resulting from sickness and to reimburse him for lost earnings. Many health insurance plans are available, but, in general, they provide the following benefits.

1. Payment of all or part of medical, hospital, and surgical expenses

2. Loss of income payments for a certain period of time when the insured is unable to work

3. A specified sum for the loss of an eye, hand, foot, and so on

4. Death benefits, if death results from an accident

The Blue Cross Plan, which pays hospital bills, and the Blue Shield Plan, which pays surgical expenses, are the best known of such plans. Both are nonprofit organizations established by citizens, hospitals, and the medical profession itself.

Much health insurance is purchased under group plans for employees, of which the employer generally pays all or part of the cost.

In addition to private insurance carriers the federal government is deeply involved with health insurance through Medicare, Medicaid, and by virtue of certain other provisions of the Social Security Act. And it appears increasingly likely that a national health insurance law will be enacted in the years ahead.

LIFE INSURANCE

All insurance contracts discussed thus far indemnify the insured only when some uncertain event happens. Life insurance, however, deals with a certain risk—death.

Basically, life insurance offers financial protection to dependents when death of the breadwinner occurs. Further, it can be used (assuming a sufficient amount was purchased) to provide a monthly income for the family, to pay for the education of children, and to repay long-term loans such as home mortgages. It should not be concluded that one must "die to win" in life insurance. Many life insurance policies contain investment features that provide for the policyholder's retirement.

The popularity of life insurance among families has grown dramatically in the last decade, although amounts held per family vary considerably from state to state (see Table 10–1).

Business life insurance is used to protect a business, or the family of a businessman from the financial loss that often results from the death of someone associated with the business. It gives assurance of business continuity and can protect value of the business' equity for the family of the deceased. In other words, if there is insurance, the business does not have to be sold to meet expenses that accrue at the time of death.

Business life insurance is written for numerous specific purposes, chief among them are:

Table **10–1**
Average Amount of Life Insurance in Force per Family
in the United States by State, 1967 and 1971

	1967	1971		1967	1971
Alabama	$16,500	$21,500	Montana	$13,900	$17,400
Alaska	14,600	20,000	Nebraska	16,700	21,200
Arizona	15,100	20,100	Nevada	13,300	18,000
Arkansas	10,300	14,000	New Hampshire	16,700	21,400
California	16,700	20,300	New Jersey	20,200	26,600
Colorado	18,100	22,600	New Mexico	15,700	20,400
Connecticut	22,000	27,600	New York	18,100	23,100
Delaware	25,000	32,900	North Carolina	15,200	19,600
D.C.	23,200	29,100	North Dakota	14,700	18,300
Florida	14,100	18,300	Ohio	18,400	23,600
Georgia	17,400	23,400	Oklahoma	15,000	18,800
Hawaii	26,100	36,000	Oregon	14,500	17,800
Idaho	14,400	18,100	Pennsylvania	18,500	22,600
Illinois	19,500	24,900	Rhode Island	18,000	22,000
Indiana	18,500	22,700	South Carolina	15,800	20,700
Iowa	16,400	20,300	South Dakota	13,800	18,000
Kansas	15,900	20,600	Tennessee	15,500	20,200
Kentucky	13,200	17,500	Texas	16,100	21,300
Louisiana	15,100	20,400	Utah	17,600	22,300
Maine	14,400	18,200	Vermont	15,300	19,800
Maryland	17,500	22,300	Virginia	17,500	23,100
Massachusetts	18,100	22,500	Washington	15,800	18,700
Michigan	19,600	24,900	West Virginia	13,400	16,200
Minnesota	16,500	21,200	Wisconsin	16,600	20,800
Mississippi	11,000	15,100	Wyoming	16,900	18,900
Missouri	16,800	21,200	Total United States	17,200	21,800

Source: *Life Insurance Fact Book 1972.* Institute of Life Insurance. New York, p. 24.

Key man protection — to reimburse a company for loss or provide for replacement in the event of the death of a key employee

Partnership insurance — to retire a partner's interest at death

Corporation insurance — to provide for maintenance of a business upon the death of a key stockholder

Credit status insurance — to cover the owner or key man during the period of a loan or the duration of a mortgage on property

Business estate insurance — to provide heirs with cash and to aid in liquidating a business when the businessman's estate consists largely of his interest in a business

Mortality table

The Commissioners' 1958 Standard Ordinary Mortality Table shown in Table 10–2, which is the official table still used in 1973 by the insurance

Table 10-2
Mortality Tables

AGE	COMMISSIONERS 1958 STANDARD ORDINARY (1950–1954)		AGE	COMMISSIONERS 1958 STANDARD ORDINARY (1950–1954)	
	DEATHS PER 1,000	EXPECTATION OF LIFE (YEARS)		DEATHS PER 1,000	EXPECTATION OF LIFE (YEARS)
0	7.08	68.30	50	8.32	23.63
1	1.76	67.78	51	9.11	22.82
2	1.52	66.90	52	9.96	22.03
3	1.46	66.00	53	10.89	21.25
4	1.40	65.10	54	11.90	20.47
5	1.35	64.19	55	13.00	19.71
6	1.30	63.27	56	14.21	18.97
7	1.26	62.35	57	15.54	18.23
8	1.23	61.43	58	17.00	17.51
9	1.21	60.51	59	18.59	16.81
10	1.21	59.58	60	20.34	16.12
11	1.23	58.65	61	22.24	15.44
12	1.26	57.72	62	24.31	14.78
13	1.32	56.80	63	26.57	14.14
14	1.39	55.87	64	29.04	13.51
15	1.46	54.95	65	31.75	12.90
16	1.54	54.03	66	34.74	12.31
17	1.62	53.11	67	38.04	11.73
18	1.69	52.19	68	41.68	11.17
19	1.74	51.28	69	45.61	10.64
20	1.79	50.37	70	49.79	10.12
21	1.83	49.46	71	54.15	9.63
22	1.86	48.55	72	58.65	9.15
23	1.89	47.64	73	63.26	8.69
24	1.91	46.73	74	68.12	8.24
25	1.93	45.82	75	73.37	7.81
26	1.96	44.90	76	79.18	7.39
27	1.99	43.99	77	85.70	6.98
28	2.03	43.08	78	93.06	6.59
29	2.08	42.16	79	101.19	6.21
30	2.13	41.25	80	109.98	5.85
31	2.19	40.34	81	119.35	5.51
32	2.25	39.43	82	129.17	5.19
33	2.32	38.51	83	139.38	4.89
34	2.40	37.60	84	150.01	4.60
35	2.51	36.69	85	161.14	4.32
36	2.64	35.78	86	172.82	4.06
37	2.80	34.88	87	185.13	3.80
38	3.01	33.97	88	198.25	3.55
39	3.25	33.07	89	212.46	3.31
40	3.53	32.18	90	228.14	3.06
41	3.84	31.29	91	245.77	2.82
42	4.17	30.41	92	265.93	2.58
43	4.53	29.54	93	289.30	2.33
44	4.92	28.67	94	316.66	2.07
45	5.35	27.81	95	351.24	1.80
46	5.83	26.95	96	400.56	1.51
47	6.36	26.11	97	488.42	1.18
48	6.95	25.27	98	668.15	.83
49	7.60	24.45	99	1,000.00	.50

Source: Institute of Life Insurance, *Life Insurance Fact Book 1969*, pp. 106–07.

Figure **10–3**
Expectation of Life at Birth in the United States (All Citizens)

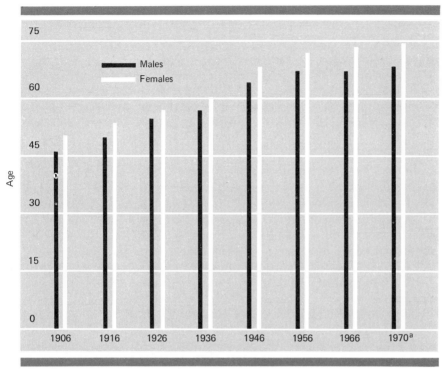

ᵃ In 1970, the difference in life expectancy between white and nonwhite persons at birth was 6.5 years for females and 7.6 years for males. The difference between white and nonwhite persons at age 45 was smaller than at birth, with life expectancy at that age being 3.3 years greater for white males and 3.8 years greater for white females.

Source: Institute of Life Insurance, *Life Insurance Fact Book 1972*, p. 90.

industry in determining premium rates, is an excellent example of the practical application to life insurance of the "law of large numbers." The table is based on accurate statistical findings of previous death rates and shows how many deaths will occur at each age each year. At age twenty, for example, 1.79 people per thousand will die. The further life expectancy at this age is 50.37 years. It is quite apparent that the death rate slowly but surely increases as age advances. While an occasional individual will live to be one hundred or more, for practical reasons the table assumes that no one will reach this age. As life expectancy is increased through preventive medicine and the discovery of new cures for illness, the mortality table will be revised. Longer life expectancy will mean lower premiums at each age. Trends in longevity appear in Figure 10–3. The insurance industry is slow to adopt new official mortality tables since it is to their advantage to use older tables when longevity increases.

Premiums

The major use of the mortality table is to compute life insurance premiums on a scientific basis. A simple illustration will indicate how this is done. Suppose that 100,000 college students, all twenty years old, decide to form an insurance company, with each student purchasing a $1,000 policy. Reference to Table 10–2 shows that 1.79 persons per 1,000 in this age group will die. So, 179 persons in the 100,000 student group can be expected to die during the first year. Claims will total $179,000, for which each of the 100,000 students will be assessed $1.79 for the one-year policy.

The company will, however, have other expenses—managers' salaries, clerical costs, sales commissions, printing expenses, and office costs. Let us assume that these costs, which are called the "loading," equal $71,000. This amount must be added to the $179,000 needed to pay claims. The total premium needed now stands at $250,000, or $2.50 for each $1,000 policy.

This premium may be slightly reduced because of interest that is earned on the money received before claims are paid. The amount of the reduction will depend on how successful the managers are in keeping funds invested and on how much interest is received from the investments. In practice, life insurance companies assume that all premiums are paid at the beginning of the year and all claims at the end of the year, giving the company full use of the money for one year.

The natural premium plan

Under the *natural premium plan,* a person purchasing life insurance at, say, age twenty would pay a progressively higher premium to renew it each year, since the chance of death increases with age. Thus, disregarding loading and interest income, the premium for a $1,000 one-year policy would be $1.79 at twenty, $2.13 at thirty, $3.53 at forty, $8.32 at fifty, $20.34 at sixty, $49.79 at seventy, $109.98 at eighty, $228.14 at ninety, and $668.15 at ninety-eight.

The level-premium plan

A constantly increasing premium rate, as indicated in the natural premium plan, is statistically sound and fair to all concerned, but it is not popular because the income of most people tends to reach a peak some-where between the ages of fifty and sixty and then to decline, making the higher premiums at older ages an unusually heavy burden. To over-come this disadvantage, practically all policies are now sold on a *level-premium* basis, which means that the insured pays the same amount each year. The level premium is computed by averaging the premiums for all ages the insured is expected to reach.

Under the level-premium plan, the insured actually pays more than his pro-rata share during the early years of the policy and less than his share when he is older. Part of the excess paid during the early life of the policy, together with interest earned on it, is a reserve that actually be-longs to the insured and that, as will be noted later, constitutes the cash surrender value of the policy.

Types of life insurance policies

Straight-life policies   The straight-life policy requires that premiums be paid from the date of purchase until death. The level-premium plan is used so the insured pays the same amount each year. The full amount of the policy is payable to the beneficiary.

Straight-life policies include a savings feature, which means that, in effect, part of each premium is placed in a fund and invested by the insurance company. This fund, which increases each year, is the *cash surrender value* of the policy. The insured can terminate his policy at any time and receive this amount in a lump sum, or, if he prefers, he can borrow this amount from the insurance company.

The ordinary life policy gives the greatest amount of *permanent* insurance protection for a given premium. It is the most popular life insurance contract written.

Limited-payment policies   The limited-payment policy resembles the straight-life policy in all respects but one. Premiums are paid, not for an entire lifetime, but for a definite number of years—usually twenty. Limited-payment policies appeal to people who prefer to complete pay-ment for their insurance during the prime of life, when income is near its peak, rather than to continue to pay premiums after the beginning of old age. Further, the policyholder knows exactly the number of pay-ments that must be made. The cash surrender value of the policy also builds up more rapidly than in ordinary life policies. The policy does not, however, mature until death.

The disadvantage of the limited-payment plan is that relatively less insurance protection can be purchased for a given premium. This is an important consideration for those who have lower incomes and important financial responsibilities, such as a large family.

Endowment policies   Endowment policies provide for the payment of the full value of the policy to the insured at the end of a definite number of years or to his designated beneficiary at his death if that occurs before the end of the endowment period. To illustrate, assume that a man of twenty-five purchases a $10,000, thirty-year endowment policy. If he lives to age fifty-five, he will then be paid $10,000 by the company. If he dies any time before age fifty-five, his beneficiary will receive $10,000. Endowment insurance thus combines protection with savings, and premiums for endowment policies are, accordingly, much higher than for any other form of permanent insurance.

Endowment policies may be written for almost any number of years, such as ten, twenty, or thirty. Often the policies are issued to endow at sixty or sixty-five. Thus, an individual at age thirty-eight who purchases a policy of endowment at sixty-five pays premiums for twenty-seven years.

Endowment insurance is a popular coverage, appealing especially to people who want to save money as well as have insurance protection. Such insurance is used widely to provide for the education of children. However, as insurance it gives the least coverage per dollar spent.

Term policies   Term insurance affords "pure protection," there being no savings element. Term policies guarantee to pay a given sum of money to the insured's beneficiaries if death occurs during the term of the policy. Since no savings accumulate, it has use only in the event of death.

Term-insurance policies are generally issued for five or ten years and usually carry the stipulation that they can be renewed (at a higher premium) or that they can be converted into other types of policies if desired. Term insurance is relatively inexpensive during early years but more and more expensive as age and the possibility of death increase.

Term insurance appeals to people who want the maximum amount of insurance protection at the lowest possible cost. Its great advantage lies in giving inexpensive temporary protection during times when greatest protection is needed—for example, when children are young or when a business is being started. How great a disadvantage the lack of savings is remains an open question (see below).

Comparison of the four policies

Most people understand clearly the need for life insurance but are perplexed by the question, "Which type of policy is best for me?" One im-

Table **10-3**
Typical Annual Premium Rates for $1,000 of Insurance
Under Selected Insurance Plans[a]

AGE	ORDINARY LIFE	TWENTY-PAY LIFE	TWENTY-YEAR ENDOWMENT	FIVE-YEAR RENEWABLE TERM INSURANCE
20	$10.83	$18.66	$42.12	$ 4.01
30	14.99	24.00	46.50	5.57
40	27.45	40.10	51.86	8.61
50	33.50	46.20	56.60	13.62

[a] All premiums given for standard risks—that is, persons in satisfactory health.

portant consideration is cost. Table 10–3 compares premiums for $1,000 worth of insurance under the four major plans discussed.

There is no intention to imply that one plan is a greater "bargain" than another. In the case of life insurance, one must always choose between savings and protection. Since the country has experienced continuous inflation, the value of the savings aspects of insurance is open to serious question. As we have noted, the maximum amount of savings is provided by the endowment policy, whereas the maximum amount of protection is provided by term insurance.

Each individual case requires separate study. Age, income, family responsibility, future job prospects, and health are some of the factors modifying any particular need for insurance. Choosing a policy contract is an important matter, for while the initial premium is relatively small, the contract usually exists for a long period of time.

THE PURCHASE OF INSURANCE

Because of the technical nature of insurance and the fact that adequate insurance involves a large outlay of money, large organizations often employ insurance experts, whose chief functions are to determine the nature of company hazards, study ways to reduce them, decide what risks should be insured, determine what specific insurance programs should be followed, and select the insurance carriers that are best qualified to assume risks.

For obvious reasons, the small business cannot afford to maintain an insurance department. The manager of a small business must rely heavily on the advice of insurance agents or on professional insurance consultants.

Life insurance should be purchased on a businesslike basis. Too often, however, personal friendship with an agent will be the basis for buying. A wise procedure is to ask for proposals from two or more companies. While the difference in annual premiums may be small, the total difference over a period of time can be significant. Moreover, it is often difficult to get objective advice about insurance matters from those who sell insurance. Various consumer organizations and publications can be of assistance in helping one make prudent decisions about what to buy.

PENSION PLANS

About 30 million workers in private employment, almost half the total number employed, are now covered by pension plans. While pension plans as such are not a form of insurance, they are often provided through the assistance of insurance companies and they partake of many aspects of insurance. The Federal Reserve reports that pension funds are now larger than savings and loan associations or life insurance companies.

Pension funds are rarely administered by employers. Where insurance companies are not involved, larger banks administer funds. The Morgan Guaranty Trust Company, the largest manager of such investments, is trustee for $16 billion in pension funds. Because the amounts involved are becoming so large, pressures are mounting in Congress for pension fund reforms. Reform centers on two major issues (1) federal insurance for private pension plans and (2) portability, which would allow an employee to transfer his plan from one employer to another.

Types of pension plans

Trust fund pension plans   These involve setting up a trust fund that is administered by a bank or trust company, from which pensions are paid. The company makes regular contributions to the fund. Normally, the employee makes no contribution and, therefore, may receive nothing from the fund should he die or leave the company before retirement.

Contributory pension plans   These call for contributions by both employer and employee. Should the employee resign or be discharged, he receives his own money back with interest. Many pension plans give employees what are called "vested rights." This means an employee will receive a pension at retirement age based on the company's contributions as well as on his own, even if he leaves the company prior to retirement age.

Profit-sharing pension plans   These are created from a certain percentage of the company's profits that is put in the plan each year. The employee's share is based on his length of service and his earnings. In some cases, the employee also makes a cash contribution to the fund, usually under a payroll deduction arrangement.

PEOPLE AND THEIR IDEAS
Asa T. Spaulding

Mediator and insurance leader

Asa T. Spaulding attributes his successful business career to the fact that he was taught responsibility early in life. As a boy, he had to plant and tend a one-acre cotton patch on his parents' small farm. Today he is president of the North Carolina Mutual Life Insurance Company, a firm with assets of over $130 million, and sits on the board of directors of four other corporations.

Born in 1902 in Whiteville, North Carolina, Spaulding attended high school in Durham, North Carolina, while supporting himself with a job as a stock clerk at the North Carolina Mutual Life Insurance Company. He attended Howard University for a time, but his savings ran out and he went back to work at North Carolina Mutual for three years. Eventually Spaulding was able to borrow enough money to attend New York University, from which he graduated *magna cum laude*. From there he went to the University of Michigan, where he received a degree in actuarial science and mathematics. In 1932, at the age of thirty, he returned to North Carolina Mutual to become the company's first black actuary.

By 1959, Spaulding had worked his way to the presidency of North Carolina Mutual. Since then he has kept the company expanding—largely by showing his agents that their standard of living is restricted only by the amount of insurance they sell.

In 1967 he became co-chairman of a group of successful blacks enlisted by the NAACP's Legal Defense and Education Fund, which formed the National Negro Business and Professional Committee. The group's aim was to raise funds for use in financing lawsuits over enforcement of civil rights legislation.

Spaulding has long been active in the attempt to solve interracial problems in Durham. When asked to comment on his role as mediator, he replied: "You listen to the grievances, real or imaginary, and make a decision that is fair to both sides. There are always three sides to every story: your side, my side, and the right side. The truth is usually in between."

CONTEMPORARY ISSUES
Situation 10

Retirement should be compulsory at age sixty

One day after class, Ray and John discussed a problem all organizations must deal with—at what age should employees be retired?

John is opposed to compulsory retirement at age sixty. "As I see it," he noted, "since we still have many unfilled needs in our society, we should encourage people to work as long as they can and want to. Besides, many individuals at age sixty are still mentally and physically capable of effective work for ten to fifteen more years. Compulsory retirement just results in wasting many years of valuable experience and knowledge. All of us are hurt by early retirement, since as a society we can't consume more than we collectively produce."

"But, John," commented Ray, "you're missing the point. Compulsory retirement opens the door for younger people and improves their morale by keeping promotion channels open. Also, a compulsory retirement program is fair to all. It avoids stigmatizing a worker or an executive as being washed up while someone else the same age is kept on with the company."

"I go back to a basic concept I've believed for a long time," continued John, "work is good, not bad. Rather than make everyone retire at an arbitrary age—whether it is sixty, fifty-five, or sixty-five—we should make jobs more interesting so people *want* to work as long as they can still perform their job efficiently."

"What's more," observed John, "is that if we retire people at age sixty, younger people will be forced to carry a larger burden in the form of taxes for pensions for older people. If older citizens work beyond age sixty, younger people will have more of their incomes to spend on themselves.

"Of course," Ray interjected, "if you believe what you read, a great many jobs in our economy are very dull and boring, and I am sure in a way it's like slavery to keep people working."

1. What other arguments, either pro or con, can be made regarding the proposition that all employees be retired at age sixty?

2. Do you feel compulsory retirement at age sixty is a good idea? What about any fixed age?

BUSINESS CHRONICLE

Risk management and protection

Insurance was a subject that top management of Kingmaker Estates was especially sensitive about. Two unfortunate experiences in the early history of the company taught Mr. King a bitter lesson. A building contractor failed to complete a shopping center development on time. He dragged out the completion date for four months and then finally defaulted on his contract when construction was 60 percent completed. This experience cost Kingmaker management considerable anguish and the company lost an estimated $170,000. Store openings of tenants were delayed. In addition to the monetary losses, much ill will against Kingmaker resulted.

In another situation, a Kingmaker real estate salesman showed a potential customer a piece of property that contained an old warehouse that Kingmaker planned to tear down *if* Kingmaker bought the property the warehouse stood on. When the potential customer returned to look at the property (which Kingmaker did not own), he tripped and broke his leg while walking through the warehouse. He sued Kingmaker, and the court awarded $20,000 damages, since Kingmaker offered the property as being potentially for sale. Kingmaker found that its insurance policies did not provide coverage for this eventuality.

QUESTIONS

1. What kinds of insurance would cover these situations?

2. What kinds of insurance would a real estate development company like Kingmaker carry to fully protect itself?

3. What kinds of personnel training programs should Kingmaker have to reduce hazards?

APPLICATION EXERCISES

1. Ralph Watts, a Pittsburgh warehouse operator, has twice suffered extensive losses caused by floods. He has attempted to secure insurance to protect himself against the flood hazard but finds that no insurance company will sell him such coverage. What is there about the nature of flood risks that makes them generally uninsurable?

2. Bruce Brooks has been successfully operating his own self-service food market for the past five years. Prior to this time he worked as manager of a chain supermarket. Holdup men recently caused Mr. Brooks a $2,700 loss. He had failed to protect himself against this loss with insurance because when he worked as a chain store manager he knew that this two-hundred-store organization did not carry insurance to protect itself against holdups. Since the chain's practices seemed sound, Mr. Brooks followed their example. Was he right or wrong in doing so?

3. The following news item appeared in the November 29, 1972, issue of *Computerworld*:

> Too Much Earthquake Coverage, Firm Finds
>
> Riverside, Calif. A computer model of a building's susceptibility to earthquake damage was a manufacturing firm's impetus to change insurance policies, for a savings of about $45,000 a year.
>
> The analysis of the building's construction indicated the new $5 million plant had a 90% chance of suffering $10,000 in earthquake damage over the 25-year life of the building, a 40% change of $50,000 in damages, and a 4% chance of $800,000 in repair costs.
>
> The building owner had been paying $54,000 annually on earthquake insurance, but his policy had a $1 million deductible proviso.
>
> Using the analysis developed by Albert C. Martin & Associates, the owner decided to underwrite his own insurance.

   a. How can the use of computer models be applied to other types of insurance that a business carries?
   b. Under what kinds of circumstances would management decide to underwrite its own risks?

QUESTIONS

1. What are the possible business risks to which the owner of a gasoline station is exposed? A department store? A factory?

2. What is an insurable risk? What is an uninsurable risk?

3. What might be done to reduce automobile insurance costs for younger drivers?

4. What are the different types of marine insurance? Why is the name "marine insurance" applied to all of them?

5. Describe the different kinds of casualty insurance. From the business viewpoint are some kinds more important than others?

6. Explain the pros and cons in the controversy about no-fault automobile insurance. What stand do you take in the matter? Why?

7. What factors should an individual purchasing life insurance consider in choosing a specific form of coverage? How can he get objective information to assist him?

8. Consider the following argument: The American people have been oversold on life insurance. Because of steady inflation, policies are always paid off with dollars of less value than those paid in by the policyholder. In addition, the American male pays so much money for insurance that he denies himself the pleasures he is entitled to. His family sees little of him because the pressures of financial commitments make him work too hard and die too young. Is he really doing the best thing for his family by taking out so much insurance? What do you think of these arguments?

9. The responsibilities of the company insurance executive should extend beyond the mere purchasing of insurance. He should be the company's risk education expert. In this broad context, what could such responsibility include?

4

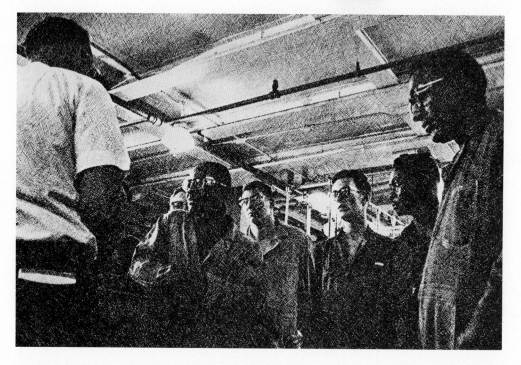

Stated simply, a business is a group of people working toward a common goal. It follows then that the principal asset, the key competitive advantage of any business, is its human resources—the intelligence, skill, motivation, and loyalty of its personnel.

People, not machines, are the paramount contemporary problem. We can design machines to perform exactly and precisely as instructed. But fortunately man is singular and emotional; he differs widely in ability, skill, desire, and personality, and he cannot be programmed.

Much of management's work, therefore, is centered around getting people to cooperate and to work to achieve desired goals. How can people be made more productive? How can each person in the organization be given the maximum opportunity for self-fulfillment? These questions, typical of those management continuously asks, are explored in the following chapters:

management of human resources

11
management and motivation of personnel

12
labor in the economy

13
labor-management relations

management and motivation of personnel 11

CHAPTER 11

THE CHANGING NATURE OF THE WORK ETHIC

THE PROBLEM OF WORKER DISCONTENT
Social Costs of Worker Malcontent. Actions and Findings Regarding the Problem. The Road to Solving Worker Discontent.

PERSONNEL MANAGEMENT

FUNCTIONS OF THE PERSONNEL DEPARTMENT
Employment. Training. Compensation. Employee Services and Fringe Benefits. Health and Safety and OSHA. Transfer, Promotion, and Discharge.

EMPLOYEE MOTIVATION
Importance of Motivation.

MORALE
How to Gauge Morale. Steps in the Motivation Process. Motivation and Leadership. Basic Principles of Leadership. Experimental Approaches to Employee Motivation.

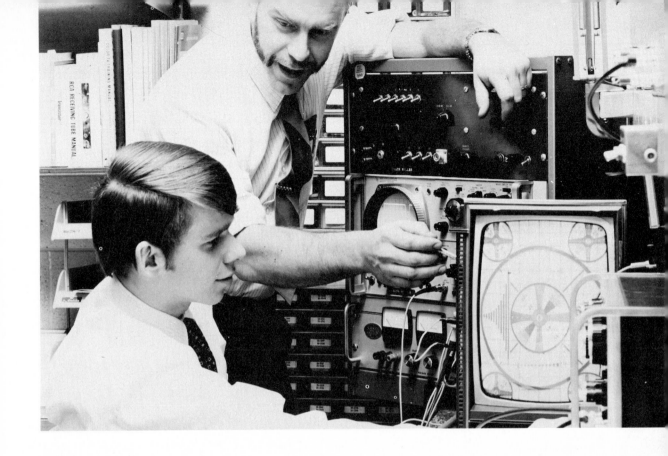

Today, enlightened managements realize that a company's greatest competitive advantage can be the people who work for it. Technological advantages over competition are not easy to maintain. A company's advances in production and materials are soon copied. But human performance varies widely, and superior personnel performance is not easy to duplicate. It follows that the company with the most effective personnel has a competitive advantage. Competition among employers for talented personnel is often keen. For example, on occasions companies in technical industries are so desperate for qualified employees that they advertise not only regionally but nationally and internationally to attract people.

THE CHANGING NATURE OF THE WORK ETHIC

The evolution of the work ethic provides insight about one of our largest contemporary socioeconomic problems: the desire of people to work.

The ancient Greeks thought that there was more honor in leisure than in work. According to Aristotle, "Paid employment absorbs and degrades the mind."

Emergence of the Judeo-Protestant ethic changed attitudes toward work. St. Paul held that slaves and free men are one in the eyes of Jesus Christ and that "if one will not work, let him not eat." Later, John Calvin advocated that acquisition of material wealth was a worthy objective in line with the Divine plan — indeed, a visible sign of Divine grace.

The Puritans believed in Calvin's attitude toward hard work and brought the work ethic to America. They equated idleness with sin and in many ways promoted hard work as God's plan for men. The work ethic as developed by the Puritans holds that labor is good in itself and that the human being is made better by the act of working.

In more recent times, the Puritan concept of the work ethic was much in evidence. It flourished during the Great Depression because, without work, people faced destitution. And during World War II, hard work was equated with patriotism. Able-bodied people who did not work were considered to be not helping America in a great crisis period.

Now, thirty years later, the American attitude toward work has changed. Work is held in lower esteem than ever before. In part, this may be due to the vast expansion in welfare programs, or it may also be related to higher levels of education and affluence. Today young people are much better educated than their parents and thus they are turned off by boring, routine jobs that permit little self-expression.

THE PROBLEM OF WORKER DISCONTENT

Management in recent years has been concerned about alienation of the work force, which has resulted in, among other things, rising absenteeism, lower production, and deterioration of the quality of work performed. So serious have disruptions been in some plants that industry spokesmen are speaking out on the subject, which they questionably view mainly in terms of increased labor costs.

Social costs of worker malcontent

Richard C. Gerstenberg, Chairman of General Motors, in a talk about worker discontent cautioned about what he termed misleading publicity about drudgery on the assembly line which in turn creates an atmosphere in which the public begins to approve working without relating what

they do to production. "All of these efforts (that do not relate to production) involve extra costs," he said, "which must inevitably be reflected in the price of the product — that is, the price the consumer must
pay."

Findings in a government report had this to say about social costs.

> Because work is central to the lives of so many Americans, either the
> absence of work or employment in meaningless work is creating an in-
> creasingly intolerable situation. The human costs of this state of affairs are
> manifested in worker alienation, alcoholism, drug addiction and other
> symptoms of poor mental health. . . .
>
> A great part of the staggering national bill in the areas of crime and
> delinquency, mental and physical health, manpower and welfare are
> generated in our national policies and attitudes toward work.

Actions and findings regarding the problem

The problem has become so serious that some senators have drafted
legislation calling for ways to humanize jobs. The Department of Health,
Education and Welfare (HEW) commissioned a huge study on the subject, which resulted in a report titled *Work in America*. It found that
monotonous tasks and dreary regimentation are common to both factory
and office, to men and women, to black and white, and that a growing
body of research suggests that the cost to the nation is large. Changes
should be made, because if the alienation of workers is allowed to grow,
workers could become ripe for totalitarian political movements.

Findings in the report are mixed. Attitudes toward work are by no
means uniform. One survey found, for example, that 79 percent of college students feel that a meaningful career is an important part of a
person's life. Another study, dealing with longevity, discovered that
people who are content with their work live longer. Also indicated was
that "work is a critical variable in mental health problems."

Blue-collar workers feel their jobs have little variety and fail to provide them an opportunity to use their skills. Significantly, however, there
is no greater dissatisfaction among blue-collar workers than among other
workers. The report cites evidence that increasing numbers of the nation's
4.5 million middle managers are seeking mid-career changes or are showing willingness to join a union. "A general feeling of obsolescence appears
to overtake middle managers when they reach their late thirties. Charac-
teristically middle managers perceive that they lack influence on organizational decision-making, yet they must implement company policy —
and often without sufficient authority or resources to effectively carry it
out."

The road to solving worker discontent

Happy workers had jobs where they had a chance to use their skills, to be creative, had enough help to do their best work, to learn new things, and had supervisors who left workers alone unless they asked for help. Interestingly, it was also found that workers were happiest in jobs where they had to work fast and hard.

What solutions does the HEW report recommend? It talks about "Job Redesign." It suggests experimentation with a team approach to work so workers feel less alone in exerting effort. Workers should be given a chance to perform varied tasks, to shape a whole product and not just a part of it, to share in decisions that affect them, and to participate in profits that result from extra effort on their part. It also proposes to subsidize (1) study for new careers and prevent obsolescence of skills, and (2) more on-the-job training for welfare recipients who want to work.

PERSONNEL MANAGEMENT

Personnel management concerns the selection and training of employees and the development of employees' abilities and attitudes so they will be productive, contented, and loyal to the company.

In large organizations, the individual in charge of personnel is commonly given the title of "personnel director," or sometimes "personnel manager" or "vice-president in charge of personnel." Since the personnel director is a staff executive, he does not issue orders to anyone other than employees in the personnel department itself. Rather, he acts as an adviser to line and other staff executives on problems concerning employees. For example, the personnel director may recommend a three-week vacation for employees, but the final decision on whether or not the vacation policy will be adopted is made by a line executive.

FUNCTIONS OF THE PERSONNEL DEPARTMENT

Six major functions are performed by the personnel department: (1) employment, (2) training, (3) compensation, (4) employee services and fringe benefits, (5) health and safety programs, and (6) transfer, promotion, and discharge. To perform these functions satisfactorily, the personnel director and his assistants need access to facts concerning the specific kind of work performed by each employee. The method used to gather necessary job information is called "job analysis."

Job analysis is a detailed study of a job to learn what duties are performed, what equipment and tools are used, what physical and mental abilities are needed, the nature of the working conditions, the responsibilities of the worker, and the relationship of the job to other jobs in the company.

Job analyses usually are made by a trained specialist called a "job analyst." The analyst may use one or several methods to make the appraisal: observation of employees on the job, personal interviews with supervisors and employees, questionnaires completed by employees. Pertinent facts about the job are set forth in a "job description."

This description serves as a source of information whenever specific facts about a given job are needed. For example, from the job description it is possible to prepare a "job specification," which shows what physical, mental, educational, and other qualifications must be possessed by the worker. Originally, job analyses were made only of factory jobs, but now they are used widely in banks, stores, offices, and sales organizations.

Employment

There are three major phases of the employment process: (1) determining the source of new employees, (2) selecting employees, and (3) introducing new employees to the job.

Sources of employees   Job applicants can come from either internal or external sources; most companies use both.

Internal sources: present employees.   Companies frequently encourage employees to recommend job applicants, especially when the opening is difficult to fill. Some companies give an employee an award or a bonus if the individual he recommends is accepted.

One advantage of this method is that it is inexpensive. Also, it has a positive effect on morale, for employees feel, and rightly so, that they are participating in management. The chief disadvantage is that it can lead to inbreeding and sometimes to cliques within the organization.

Many companies prohibit hiring close relatives of key personnel, fearful that such a practice could lead to, or be interpreted as, nepotism.

External sources.   External sources of job applicants include public employment agencies, such as the various state employment services; trade schools, which train people for specialized skills, such as stenography or television repair; private employment agencies; colleges and universities; unions; and unsolicited applications. Advertising in newspapers and trade magazines is, of course, a very common method of obtaining new employees.

Figure **11–1**
Median Income of Women and Men, 1970 (Year-Round Full-Time Workers)

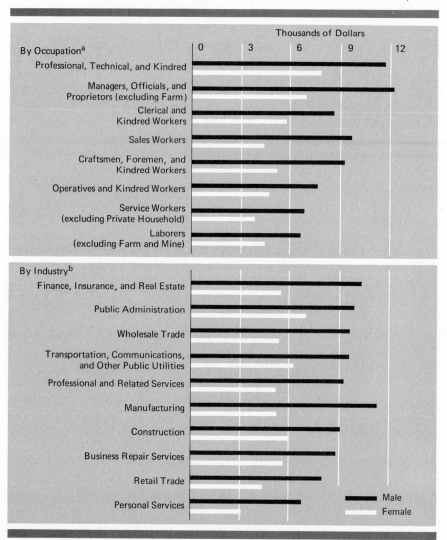

In 1970, the median income for all women who were year-round full-time workers was $5,440, compared with $9,184 for men. Thus women's earnings, on the average, were 41 percent below those of men, virtually the same ratio as in 1939.

[a] Excludes farm workers and managers and private household workers.
[b] Excludes agriculture, forestry, fishing, mining, entertainment, and recreation services.

Source: "Earnings Profile of Working Women," Road Maps of Industry, No. 1704, The Conference Board, December 15, 1972.

How will the changing status of women affect management?

Selection of employees   The second step in the employment procedure is selecting applicants who are best qualified. Personnel directors use every disposable means, including tests and guided interviews to procure qualified employees. In large companies, several well-defined steps are usually followed in the selection process.

Initial screening.   If the job specification is clearly understood, it is often possible for a trained receptionist or interviewer to eliminate the obviously unqualified applicants. For example, if the job calls for a high school graduate in excellent physical condition with at least two years' experience in certain work, the preliminary interviewer can politely eliminate those who do not meet these basic requirements.

The application form and résumé.   Applicants who pass the original screening are then asked to complete an application form. The applicant is generally asked to give his name, age, marital status, address, telephone number, work history, military record, education and training, and several references. Other information such as membership in organizations, hobbies, and goals in life, is sometimes requested.

It is wise for personnel people to inform the applicant that it is to his advantage to fill out the application form completely and accurately. The applicant should realize that it is just as important for him to be in the right job as it is for the company to have the right person for the job.

It is common for those seeking management-level positions to provide employers with a résumé (see Figure 11–2). This is an outline of one's career aspirations, employment history, educational achievements, skills and job qualifications, references, and vital statistics. A résumé is normally prepared by the applicant before he starts looking for a job. By submitting such a document, the applicant shows foresight. Although he will still have to fill out a company's application form for employment, he does not limit himself to the confines of the company's standardized form.

The completed application form, as well as the résumé, serves four purposes. First, the act of filling out the application blank or organizing material for a résumé is itself a test of the applicant's suitability, since it reveals something of his ability to follow directions, to express himself, and to give facts neatly and correctly. Second, it is a guide for the interviews that follow. Third, if the applicant is hired, the forms become a part of his permanent work record and are used for reference when promotion, transfer, discharge, or similar actions are considered. Last, if there are no immediate job openings for an applicant, the forms may be filed and referred to when appropriate openings do occur.

The Federal Civil Rights Act of 1964 makes it illegal for employers to request a personal picture or information on race, creed, religion, national origin, or ancestry on an application form or in a "help wanted" advertisement. However, an exception is made when such information relates to a *bona fide* requirement for the job.

Figure **11-2**
A Well-Written Résumé Provides the Job Seeker with a Competitive Edge

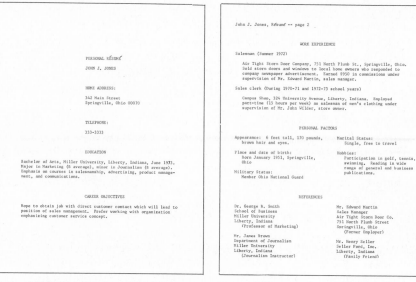

Source: Adapted from *Marketing Insights/Dart 1968–69,* December 9, 1968, p. 13.

Testing the applicant. Tests are frequently used to determine whether the applicant would be a useful employee. Tests attempt to measure the applicant's mental and mechanical abilities, skills, personality and attitudes, and vocational interests. *Tests, however, are only a guide to selection.* They show what an applicant is able to do, but they do *not* indicate what he will actually do when assigned to a job. Ambition, for instance, cannot be measured by a test.

The interview.   The most important stage in the selection process is the personal interview, which is usually conducted by the person the applicant will work under if employed. The applicant may be asked to explain or expand statements made on the application form. For example, the interviewer may want the applicant to explain in detail the work performed in his previous employment. The interview reveals what sort of general impression the applicant will make in personal-contact situations. This is especially important if the employee is expected to meet the public. Specific traits noted by the interviewer are use of language, neatness, posture, mannerisms, and grooming. Further, the personal interview is the appropriate time to answer the applicant's questions and explain facts to him about the job and the company.

Checking references.   It is good practice to obtain as much information about a prospective employee as possible. Personnel departments may ask outside private investigators to check the claims and background of applicants, or they may do the checking themselves. Credit ratings are established, police and court records are checked, educational claims are substantiated, and former employers are questioned to determine how the applicant performed on his previous job and how he was regarded by associates.

Experienced personnel administrators know that applicants sometimes try to obtain jobs by exaggerating their qualifications or falsifying their credentials. For instance, college registrars report that attempts at deception about educational backgrounds are frequent. Such deception, however, can usually be uncovered through in-depth interviews with applicants and careful investigations. Major falsifications on an employment application or on résumés are grounds for immediate dismissal if the applicant is already on the job or refusal to consider his application if he is not.

Introducing new employees to the job   After an employee has been hired, the next step is to introduce him to the job. This is an important matter, for the first impression of the working environment often has long-lasting influences on an employee. Everything possible, such as explaining "coffee-break" policies, health services, and names of supervisors and co-workers, should be done to make the new employee feel welcome and at home in his new job.

Training

Another major responsibility of the personnel department is to plan, organize, and control the company's training programs. Training, which is the process of supplying employees with the knowledge and skills they need to do their work effectively, has several objectives. These are to

1. Minimize the amount of time required to learn the job

2. Increase the productivity of employees and improve the quality of their work

3. Prepare employees for more responsible positions

4. Reduce accidents

5. Lessen wear and tear on equipment

Since the ideal of training is to approach perfection, the training should be continuous, either formal or informal. Practically every employee can benefit from learning improved methods for performing tasks. Most large, progressive companies have several different types of training programs in operation at the same time—training for plant employees, office workers, salesmen, supervisors, and executives.

Many companies have special introductory programs, which often require the trainee to spend several weeks or months in each of several departments to gain an overall view of the business before a permanent assignment is made.

Compensation

Every compensation plan—whether for unskilled labor, office workers, salesmen, or executives—should meet three objectives.

1. It should attract well-qualified, willing workers to the company. This means that the wages and salaries normally should be at least equal to those paid by similar businesses in the same geographical area.

2. It should help keep workers satisfied in their jobs. Wages should be fair to all employees, with consideration being given to the difficulty of the job and the special qualifications required of the employee.

3. It should inspire employees to produce. To accomplish this, special wage incentives (discussed below) are often used.

Four factors that determine any firm's wage policy are the wages paid by concerns competing for the same labor, the cost of living, government legislation, and the financial status of the firm.

There are several methods for compensating workers. What method should be used in any one case depends largely on the nature of the job and on the custom of the company.

Time-payment wages   The time-payment wage plan is the simplest and easiest to administer. A certain amount is paid the employee per hour worked. Thus, if the wage is $3.63 per hour and the employee works forty hours, the gross income for the employee is $145.20. Wages are paid on an hourly basis when the work done by an individual is difficult to measure. For example, assembly line workers, plant guards, and plumbers are generally paid a straight hourly rate. The disadvantage of the time-payment plan is that there is no direct incentive for the employee to produce the maximum amount possible.

Piece-rate plan   Under the piece-rate plan, workers are paid a certain amount for each unit of work accomplished. Usually, employees paid in this fashion are guaranteed a certain minimum hourly rate. The piece-rate plan acts as an incentive, for the harder and faster the employee works, the more he earns. This plan is used only when the work is standardized and when the output of each employee can be measured.

Figure **11-3**
Do Executives Prefer More Time Off or More Money?

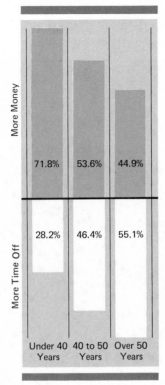

Source: Adapted from Twentieth Century Fund data.

How could differences in what motivates people at various ages affect corporate personnel policies?

Commission system   The commission payment system is used extensively in personal selling. Under this arrangement a salesman is paid a certain percentage of his sales volume. If, for example, a salesman's commission rate is 5 percent of sales he receives $5 on each $100 sold. This plan is similar to the piece-rate system, for the more a salesman sells, the more he earns.

Frequently, salesmen paid on a commission basis are given a certain sum at regular intervals, which is called a drawing account. A drawing account is charged against future commissions.

Salary   The salary plan is generally used to compensate white-collar workers, such as office help, executives, and supervisors. Salaries are calculated on a weekly, monthly, or annual basis. Salaried employees normally have considerably more job stability than hourly rated personnel. In times of business recession for example, many hourly rated workers are

Figure **11–4**
Comparison of 1951–71 Employee Benefits

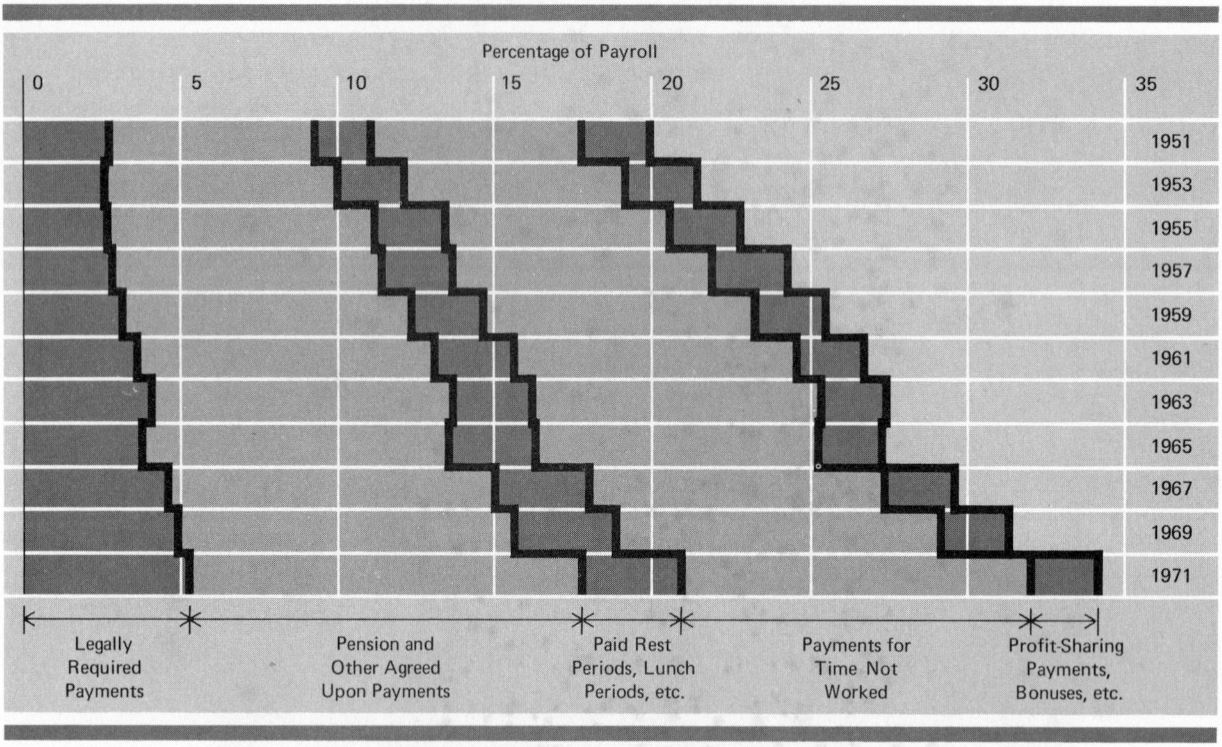

Note: Data are from 137 companies.
Source: U.S. Chamber of Commerce, *Employee Benefits 1971*, p. 26.

What are the effects of these increases on employees?
On companies? On the economy?

laid off, but salaried employees tend to retain their jobs unless the recession becomes very severe.

Profit sharing   Profit sharing is a plan for sharing some of the company's profits with employees after the stockholders have received their returns. The purpose of profit sharing is to develop greater loyalty toward the company and teamwork among employees, which in turn should spur them on to greater effort.

An example of a profit-sharing plan, that of the Pacific Finance Corporation, is shown below.

If you are a regular full-time employee and are working on December 31, you qualify for participation in the company's profit-sharing contribution for that year. After the close of each year, the company pays into the profit-sharing fund, a sum equal to 5 percent of its consolidated income for the past year before income taxes are deducted. . . . You will be credited with a share of the company's contribution, prorated according to the proportion your base salary for the year bears to the total of the base salaries of all participants. Your share of each year's profits will be credited to an account which will be set up for you. . . . If you should leave the company with less than ten years of service, you would forfeit a part of your share in the fund.

Since the share in the profits is not fully available to the employee until he has worked for ten years, the plan above has the added feature of helping reduce turnover among employees.

Employee services and fringe benefits

A fourth major function of the personnel department is to provide employees with special financial services, such as credit unions and insurance and pension plans, and with nonfinancial services, such as cafeterias and recreational programs. These services are necessary because the welfare of the company cannot be separated from the welfare of individual employees. To the extent that greater efficiency results, these services are economically justified.

It is important that employees have a voice in deciding what services should be offered. When management alone determines the kinds of services to be extended, employees can become resentful. Complaints and suggestions of employees sometimes reveal what kinds of services would be valuable to both the employee and the company. Figure 11–4 indicates types and extent of employee benefits.

Suggestion systems   Suggestion systems are commonly used both to build morale and to improve operations. United Air Lines explains its employee suggestion system as follows: "An employee making a suggestion that is adopted receives 10 percent of the value of the idea's net benefit during the first year. The program has grown rapidly since October 1940, when it was first established. In that year, 70 suggestions out of 400 were adopted, and a total of $862 was paid in awards. By comparison, in 1970, there were 27,114 suggestions submitted, 6,229 were adopted, and $371,745 was paid in awards. Since the program was established, a total of 325,000 suggestions have been submitted, and 75,000 have been adopted. From these, United has realized first year net benefits of $25 million, and employees have been awarded $2.5 million.

The suggested improvements came from various types of employees of United Air Lines. For example, a stewardess earned $1,170 for an idea for combining beverage lists with dinner menus. An office worker designed a form letter and postcard to replace costly telegrams and earned $1,280. In another case, a mechanic devised a way to inspect jet engines without disassembling them and became $14,645 richer. The largest single award to date (April 1971) has been $45,850 to a pilot who developed an improved cargo loading method that shifts an aircraft's center of gravity slightly aft, resulting in a substantial reduction in fuel consumption.

There are opportunities to suggest improvements or modifications in al-most every job, whether or not an award system exists.

Financial services   Financial services are intended to help employees attain a greater degree of financial security. Credit unions—discussed in Chapter 8—help employees to obtain loans at low rates of interest and to invest savings.

Two very important fringe benefits in many companies, discussed in Chapter 10, are *group insurance,* which protects workers against the risks of death, illness, or accident, and *pension plans,* which provide retire-ment income.

Nonfinancial services   Nonfinancial services are devised to improve the mental and physical fitness of employees and thus to encourage higher morale. Which services are offered depends largely on the philos-ophy of company top management. Company-subsidized food services, recreational programs, libraries, legal aid, retirement and religious coun-seling, and employee discounts on company products are examples of services that may be offered.

Health and safety and OSHA

There are practical as well as humanitarian reasons for protecting the health and safety of employees. Company health and safety programs in-crease the production of employees by reducing working time lost be-cause of illness and accidents.

The National Safety Council estimated that in 1972 there were 14,100 workers killed while at work and 42,500 died from off-the-job accidents—a death toll of 56,600. Worker injuries numbered about 5,700,000. Where-as the number of deaths and injuries increases as the number of people employed increases, the rate of death and injuries is decreasing because we are gaining greater insight into accident causes and use of safety meas-ures. Costs of work-related accidents, including loss from business fires, amounted to $9.8 billion in 1972.

In response to growing concern about the social and dollar costs of job-related accidents and illnesses, the highly controversial Occupational Safety and Health Act (OSHA) was passed in 1970. As the nation's first federal safety and health law its stated goal is "to assure as far as possible to every working man and woman in the nation safe and healthful work-ing conditions and a right to a workplace free from recognized hazards that are causing or likely to cause death or serious physical harm." Re-sentment arises because the law requires inspectors to show up without any advance notice. Anyone who tips off a company that the OSHA in-spector is coming is subject to a jail sentence. Under the law, an employee can write to OSHA and complain about a safety or health hazard without having his name revealed.

The law has had considerable impact. In 1973, expenditures to improve health and safety conditions were estimated to be $3.2 billion—an increase of 26 percent over 1972. There has been a proliferation in communications and training about safety—house organs, bulletin boards, meetings, and so on. Some companies now have a director or department of safety. Another result has been sterner discipline. In the past, management may have overlooked a situation where an employee refused to wear a hard hat or goggles; today the employee would be fired unless he complied.

According to figures released by OSHA after the first year of operation, 32,701 inspections were made and 23,231 citations were issued covering an alleged 120,861 violations of the standards set by OSHA.

Transfer, promotion, and discharge

"Transfer" is the assignment of a worker to another job; it may be necessary for any of several reasons. He may have been placed originally in a job for which he was not suited, or he may be unable to get along with fellow workers. Management may also transfer employees to build a more flexible working force or to meet a change in work requirement. Transfer may be at the request either of the worker or of management.

"Promotion" means advancing the employee to a position requiring more skill and responsibility. Usually, a promotion carries an increase in pay. Promotions are a great incentive to employees and, when administered properly, favorably influence employee morale. Extreme care must be exercised, however, in awarding promotions, lest hard feelings result among employees who are not promoted but feel they deserve more recognition.

Usually, promotions are awarded for a consistent display of ambition, initiative, high productivity, and ability to assume leadership. Often, however, promotions are automatic when a specialized course of study or training is completed. In any event, it is essential that all employees understand clearly the bases for promotion; otherwise, resentment, accompanied by lowered morale, results.

Occasionally it is necessary to dismiss employees for various reasons: for intoxication on the job, incompetence, insubordination, or because business is curtailed. It is interesting to note that most discharges are the result of personality factors, not incompetence.

As with promotion, caution must be exercised in discharging employees, regardless of the reason. Unless the remaining employees see the wisdom of dismissing the individual in question, lower morale may result. Numerous strikes have occurred because workers believed management unfair in discharging workers—unions are quick to protest in such situations. Some companies have a policy of requiring a committee to approve each dismissal, which eliminates the danger of an employee being fired merely because his supervisor dislikes him.

EMPLOYEE MOTIVATION

Fair wages, good working conditions, and relatively short working hours, although unquestionably important, do not guarantee the attainment of such management objectives as high worker productivity and labor peace. Some of our worst strikes and other labor difficulties occur in companies that pay the highest wages, provide a comfortable working environment, and supply employees with many fringe benefits.

Money is not as important a motivating factor as many people believe. The University of Michigan Survey Research Center asked 1,533 working people to rank various aspects of work in order of importance. "Good pay" came in a distant fifth, behind "interesting work," "enough help and equipment to get the job done," "enough information to do the job," and "enough authority to do the job."[1]

Otherwise excellent managers sometimes overlook the human factors in dealing with employees. While concentrating on motivating employees to perform their tasks more economically and effectively, managers fail to consider the attitudes, desires, and basic interests of the employees.

Motivation is also important outside the business setting. For example, as every student knows, there is a great difference among professors. All agree that college work can be an enjoyable experience under one instructor and a real chore under another. While the subject matter, the textbooks, the personalities of other students in the class, and the physical makeup of the classroom itself do, to a certain extent, influence the class's enthusiasm and willingness to work, the factor that looms largest in the success or failure of a class is the instructor.

The psychological relationship established between the students and the professor is the determining factor. Even if students were paid to go to class and do homework, a good teacher would still have higher student motivation and get more and better work from a class than would a poor teacher. Similarly, in industry, the supervisor in charge is often the variable that determines the degree of employee productivity.

Importance of motivation

Clarence Francis, the former chairman of the board of directors of the General Foods Corporation, has ably expressed the problem of motivation:

[1] "Is the Work Ethic Going Out of Style?" Donald M. Morrison, *Time*, October 30, 1972, p. 97.

You can buy a man's time; you can buy a man's physical presence at a given place; you can even buy a measured number of skilled muscular motions per hour or day. But you cannot buy enthusiasm; you cannot buy initiative; you cannot buy loyalty; you cannot buy the devotion of hearts, minds, and souls. You have to earn these things. . . . It is ironic that Americans — the most advanced people technically, mechanically, and industrially — should have waited until a comparatively recent period to inquire into the most promising single source of productivity; namely, the human will to work. It is hopeful, on the other hand, that the search is now under way.

The need for more attention to psychological factors in business is predicated on two basic truths. First, human behavior, although infinitely more complicated than machinery, has in the past received relatively less study. Second, business is becoming increasingly impersonal, so employees often feel lost and unimportant. In large plants most employees may never have seen the company president or his top executives. The owners, who were once also the managers, are now unknown to most employees.

The machinist says, "I get tired of doing the same thing day in and day out"; the executive says, "I find myself critical of my steady job and the built-in opportunity the firm thinks it has sold me — an opportunity that is as standardized as the monthly issue of the employee magazine and the electric clock on the wall." An all too common cry is, "I feel lost in this large organization; what do *they* care whether or not I do a good job." Motivation is needed to help employees in circumstances such as these.

MORALE

Attention to psychological factors has one major objective: to develop, maintain, and improve the morale of employees so they will be more enthusiastic about their work and, consequently, more productive.

How to gauge morale

Three of the most important morale indicators are cooperation of employees, loyalty and organizational pride, and discipline.

Cooperation   No organization can run smoothly, efficiently, and effectively unless employees on all levels cooperate with one another. Willing cooperation, however, is often difficult to achieve, since it requires the individual to place his personal interests second to those of the organization.

For example, a worker on an assembly line may be asked to cooperate by temporarily filling the job vacated by a sick employee. If he does not

Table **11-1**
Indications of High and Low Morale

EVIDENCES OF HIGH MORALE	EVIDENCES OF LOW MORALE
Excellent cooperation between employees at all levels	Unwillingness to cooperate
Loyalty and pride among employees	Employees' distrust of each other and management
Willing compliance of employees with rules, regulations, and policies	Deliberate disobedience of rules, regulations, and policies
Sincere enthusiasm of employees for their work	Employee attitude of "do as little as possible"
Punctuality and willingness to work over-time as needed	Tardiness and high rate of absenteeism
Careful treatment by employees of company property	Careless treatment of company property; conceivable theft
Low employee turnover	High employee turnover
Principal allegiance to the company	Principal allegiance to the union

What other evidences of high and low morale can you think of?
How much responsibility for morale rests with management?

cooperate willingly, other workers will be resentful. Retail salespeople must cooperate in a similar fashion. An employee may prefer to take her lunch break at twelve o'clock, but since store traffic may be particularly heavy during this hour, she may be asked to cooperate by waiting until one o'clock.

Cooperation at the executive level requires sacrifices also. When forming company policies, various officials often must compromise their ideas in the best interests of the company. Those who hesitate to place the welfare of the company above their own wishes breed low morale and dissension among fellow executives.

Loyalty and organizational pride An example of disloyalty is the employee who quits his job without giving reasonable notice to his employers. This inconveniences other employees in the company and has a negative effect on their morale. Another example of disloyalty is the employee who speaks disrespectfully about his company to outsiders.

Pride is evidenced by the confidence employees have in their leadership and company — do they speak well of their company to their friends? Employees who feel their company is a good place to work are the best advertisers a business can have.

Discipline Morale can be judged also by the degree to which employees conform to company rules and regulations. In every organization, it is essential that there is obedience to rules and regulations pertaining to such things as taking rest periods, smoking, wearing safety devices, and caring for equipment.

Discipline can be lax or strict. Contrary to popular opinion, strict discipline does not always cause low morale. For example, very high morale often exists on athletic teams, which have very rigid regulations. At the other extreme, it has been found that unusually lax discipline can contribute to low morale.

Evidence of effective discipline is the willing obedience of employees to rules, while examples of ineffective discipline are loitering on the job, excessive talking instead of working, late arrival at work, quitting before closing time, wasteful use of supplies, failure to follow instructions, and insubordination.

Steps in the motivation process

The study of behavioral sciences has shown that human beings have two basic incentives for work. The first is material, which in business takes the form of wages, profit sharing, bonuses, and prizes for outstanding performance. The second is nonmaterial, the personal satisfaction a worker gets from his job. This satisfaction comes from the worker's pride in his work, his feeling of loyalty toward the company and his co-workers, his pleasure in associating with the people that make up his working environment, the intellectual stimulation his work offers, and a feeling of getting ahead by being recognized and appreciated.

We have always understood the material incentive and have recognized the importance of incentive wages, commissions, profit sharing, bonuses, and the like. However, the potency of the nonmaterial incentive is underestimated. The issue is not one of material incentives *versus* psychological satisfactions. Rather, it is a question of integrating the tangible and intangible rewards. Three ways to develop greater motivation among employees are instilling in them a feeling of recognition, fairness, and personal identification.

Recognition   Consider this actual case involving a bank teller. The teller compared the way certain things were handled in two banks—the one for which he had formerly worked and the one where he was currently employed. He was antagonistic toward his former employer and enthusiastic about his present employer.

"It's a lot of little things that make the difference," he said. "For example, when I was working at X bank, I got a pay increase. Sure, I liked the money, but I didn't like the way they handled it. I found out about it from a printed form that appeared in my pay envelope one day. Now, instead of having his own signature, the name of the president of the bank was *printed* on the bottom of the form! But when I got a raise at this bank, the president came down to tell me about it and shake my hand. He told me

I was doing a good job. That really made me feel good. I like working for this kind of outfit."

The use of recognition in the morale-building process is predicated on the fact that individuals crave personal attention and are willing to work hard to earn this attention.

Recognition may be simple or elaborate, informal or formal, ranging from a pat on the back with a few words of praise to a banquet or party in honor of some individual or group. Regardless of the type of recognition, it is essential that it be sincere. Just about anyone can spot the false compliment.

Fairness   Favoritism, the opposite of fairness, lowers morale. Under favoritism, promotions, vacations, transfers, extra work assignments, and the like are given to individuals whom the supervisor personally likes or dislikes. These conditions cause employees to lose respect for the leader. Usually even the minority of employees who receive the favors, while pretending to admire the leader, actually disrespect him.

Another aspect of fairness is observance of the individual's self-respect. Regardless of his education, intelligence, or type of work, each individual has pride. In particular, an employee resents being criticized before his fellow employees. Criticism is sometimes necessary, but it should always be given in private.

Personal identification   One valuable method of stimulating job interest is to let the employee see how his work contributes to the finished product. Actual displays of the product can be used to convince the employee that his effort is absolutely essential. Showing the product in its final form is an excellent way to impress on workers the need for high-quality work.

Employees tend to take more interest in their work when they are reminded that promotions depend on how well they perform their present tasks. Individuals must often start much lower in the organization than they would like, so unless they are encouraged, there is real danger that they will lose interest.

Motivation and leadership

To most employees, the "boss" is the company. If the worker respects his superior, he tends to be more productive than if he does not respect him. The results of a study made by a large public utility company conclusively demonstrate that "good" supervisors have low absence rates, while "poor" supervisors have high absence rates. In that study, a total of 163 white-collar men and 251 blue-collar men were examined. Workers in groups with lower absence rates were found to be more satisfied with their supervisors, associates, wages, and promotional opportunities, as well as with their jobs and the company in general.

Basic principles of leadership

Whether employees fully perform depends largely on those who lead them. Knowledge of leadership and its relationship to employee motivation is essential for anyone aspiring to a management position.**

SPECIAL READINGS

**The Young Executives, How and Why Successful Managers Get Ahead by Walter Guzzardi, Jr. New York and Scarborough, Ontario: Mentor Book, New American Library, 1965 (paperback). This remarkable volume, written by a director of the editorial board of *Fortune* magazine, is an exhaustive study of about 100 executives who submitted to lengthy interviews and of another several thousand who answered extensive questionnaires.

In the introduction, Peter F. Drucker states that the book in effect asks: "How can the next generation of leaders, the generation now growing into manhood, add to the solid foundation of competence, effectiveness, and professionalism what today's Young Executives lack: wisdom, values, and commitment?"

Written in a journalistic style by an experienced journalist, the book is highly readable and is generously laced with direct and surprisingly frank quotes from executives.

The study concludes that the young executives feel that the large organization offers freedom of action, opportunities for advancement, and room for self-expression. Furthermore, "An amazingly large number [of young executives] attribute their success to their opposition to higher authority or to their defiance of company tradition."

Though the basic principles of leadership are listed below in a simple manner, please note that, in practice, they are indeed difficult to follow.

1. Know your job.

2. Know yourself and seek self-improvement.

3. Set the example you want followed.

4. Take responsibility for your actions, regardless of their outcome.

5. Know your subordinates and look out for their welfare.

6. Use the capabilities of each employee.

7. See that the work assignment is understood; supervise and follow through to see that it is carried out.

Figure 11–5

Leadership Style of Five Presidents in Action

PRESIDENT	NO. 1 60 YEARS OLD $365 MILLION SALES SINGLE PRODUCT FUNCTIONAL ORGANIZATION	NO. 2 45 YEARS OLD $225 MILLION SALES MULTIPRODUCT DIVISIONALIZED ORGANIZATION	NO. 3 63 YEARS OLD $425 MILLION SALES SINGLE PRODUCT FUNCTIONAL ORGANIZATION	NO. 4 61 YEARS OLD $785 MILLION SALES MULTIPRODUCT DIVISIONALIZED ORGANIZATION	NO. 5 53 YEARS OLD $325 MILLION SALES SINGLE PRODUCT FUNCTIONAL ORGANIZATION
LEADERSHIP IMAGE	Inspires by deep concern for others, apparent sincerity, and unquestioned ethics. Evokes a feeling of deep respect.	Sparks subordinates by questioning mind, youthful energy, ideas, and efforts to "stretch" executives. Considered tough but fair.	Inspires through his own loyalty and devotion to company. Respected for judgment and common sense. Informal and friendly, the "old shoe" type.	Moves by his shrewdness and detailed knowledge of all operating aspects of business. Held in fear and not well-liked.	Drives others by the sharpness and toughness of his thinking. Sets the climate by his own drive for perfection. Respected, but not held in affection.
PERFORMANCE STANDARDS AND EVALUATION	Appeals for improved performance but does not make tough, specific demands. Will tolerate mediocrity.	Pushes executives to set high standards. Tough evaluator. Will replace mediocrity.	Varies between being very demanding and quite permissive. Some standards set but he judges more on "belly feel." When pushed, removes poor performer.	No formal or general setting of standards. Will "chew out" executives for performance in specific situations, but will tolerate overall mediocre performance.	Highly demanding and critical. Generally imposes own standards. Critical evaluator on both results and methods. Highly emotional over tough "people decisions." Will bypass but not fire the mediocre performer.
DECISION-MAKING TECHNIQUES	Based primarily on experience mixed with some fact and intuition. Will listen, then make decisions. These are rarely challenged.	Fact-based. Discusses decisions in advance with subordinates. Willing to change his mind.	Based on mixture of experience, some facts, and much intuitive feel. Unusual mixture of group and unilateral decisions. In group decision making, heavily influences results.	Heavily weighted on experience. Will listen, but decisions generally unilateral and are not challenged.	Goes heavily on intuition and long experience. While he does consult with key people, in the main makes most decisions himself and holds fast to them.

	NO. 1 60 YEARS OLD $365 MILLION SALES SINGLE PRODUCT FUNCTIONAL ORGANIZATION	NO. 2 45 YEARS OLD $225 MILLION SALES MULTIPRODUCT DIVISIONALIZED ORGANIZATION	NO. 3 63 YEARS OLD $425 MILLION SALES SINGLE PRODUCT FUNCTIONAL ORGANIZATION	NO. 4 61 YEARS OLD $785 MILLION SALES MULTIPRODUCT DIVISIONALIZED ORGANIZATION	NO. 5 53 YEARS OLD $325 MILLION SALES SINGLE PRODUCT FUNCTIONAL ORGANIZATION
USE OF AUTHORITY	Permissive on performance. Established mores of organization exert control over operating methods. Rarely exhibits raw authority.	Reasonably permissive within limits of achieving goals. Authority more implied than overtly used.	Alternates between being permissive and highly authoritative.	Permissive on overall performance but highly authoritative in individual situations where he has particular interest.	Highly authoritative. Strong and positive in viewpoints, which he imposes with force.
ATTITUDE ON CHANGE	Has experienced little. Is cautious but modestly willing to try change. Becoming more desirous to make changes.	Seeks change and pushes others. Thorough in programming to carry it out.	Does not seek change, but when thrust upon him will accept and move quickly.	Generally resists strongly but is beginning to make changes of substance.	Intellectually ready for change, but fearful that organization cannot cope with resulting problems. Fear of mistakes further holds back some change.
NATURE OF INVOLVEMENT	Involved in individual incidents. Follows up on specific events that come to his attention or that he finds of particular interest. Major concern operational.	Deeply involved in planning, goal setting and evaluation against targets. Has deep understanding of each business; thus has close, frequent contact with each key executive.	Manages by incident for short-term results. Deeply involved in all aspects of business. Has established formal planning but does not follow in practice.	Heavily involved in individual incidents, primarily in areas of own background.	Has made strong effort to delegate responsibility widely but continues "over the shoulder" control. Gives much thought to strategy, but also holds on to operations.

Source: From Robert P. Neuschel, "Presidential Style: Updated Versions," *Business Horizons*, June 1969, p. 22. Copyright 1969 by the Foundation for the School of Business located at Indiana University. Reproduced by permission.

What does this tell you about leadership?

8. Seek responsibility and develop a sense of responsibility among subordinates by delegating; supervise, but intervene only when necessary.

9. Keep your employees informed.

10. Train your employees as a team whenever you can.

Experimental approaches to employee motivation

A number of companies are experimenting with ways to motivate employees. Some examples are given below.

Give workers a totality of tasks.   In compiling its telephone books, Indiana Bell used to divide 17 separate operations among a staff of women. The company gradually changed, giving each worker her own directory and making her responsible for all 17 tasks, from scheduling to proofreading. Results: work force turnover dropped, and errors, absenteeism and overtime declined.

Break up the assembly line.   A potentially revolutionary attempt at change is under way in the Swedish auto industry. Volvo and Saab are taking a number of operations off the assembly line. Some brakes and other sub-assemblies are put together by teams of workers; each performs several operations instead of a single repetitive task. In the U.S., Chrysler has used the work team to set up a conventional engine-assembly line; two foremen were given complete freedom to design the line, hand-pick team members and use whatever tools and equipment they wanted.

Permit employees to organize their own work.   Polaroid lets its scientists pursue their own projects and order their own materials without checking with a supervisor; film assembly workers are allowed to run their machines at the pace they think best. A T & T eased supervision of its shareholder correspondents and let them send out letters to complainants over their own signatures, without review by higher-ups. Absenteeism decreased and turnover was practically eliminated. Syntex Corp. allowed two groups of its salesmen to set their own work standards and quotas; sales increased 116% and 20% respectively over groups of salesmen who were not given that freedom.

Let workers see the end product of their efforts.   Chrysler has sent employees from supply plants to assembly plants so they can see where their parts fit into the finished product. The company has also put assembly-line workers into inspection jobs for one-week stints. Said one welder: "I see metal damage, missing welds and framing fits that I never would have noticed before."[2]

---

[2] "Is the Work Ethic Going Out of Style?" Donald M. Morrison, *Time*, October 30, 1972, p. 97.

As shown throughout this chapter, the art of leadership is the great intangible that effectively develops the most valuable of all business assets—the human resource. A great business leader, emphasizing the importance of personnel, said that he could lose all other assets of his business and still be able to rebuild quickly as long as the personnel he had selected and developed remained.

The building of an effective business organization is only possible through leadership, and only the person who understands human behavior can be a successful leader. This, undoubtedly, was the kind of person the Chinese philosopher Lao-tse had in mind some 2,500 years ago when he wrote:

A leader is best when people barely know he exists,
Not so good when people obey and acclaim him,
Worse when people despise him.
Fail to honor people, and they fail to honor you.
But when a good leader, who talks little,
Has done his work, fulfilled his aim . . .
They will all say . . . "We did it ourselves."

PEOPLE AND THEIR IDEAS
John D. Rockefeller

U.S. history's most influential businessman

From his vast interests in oil, railroads, iron and steel, and other industries, John D. Rockefeller amassed a personal fortune estimated at $1 billion. After his retirement from active business, he devoted most of his time and energy to philanthropy, giving away, largely through a group of foundations he created, more than $530 million. He established a tradition of generous support of worthy causes that has been actively continued by his son and grandsons.

Born in 1839 in Rickford, Tioga County, New York, Rockefeller moved with his family to Cleveland, Ohio, in 1853 and graduated from a local high school there. After taking a business course, he was employed as a clerk and later as a cashier and bookkeeper in the Cleveland commission house of Hewitt and Tuttle. In 1859 he and Maurice B. Clark became partners in the produce commission business. The first oil well was drilled that year in Titusville, Pennsylvania, and in 1862 Rockefeller and Clark formed the firm of Andrews, Clark and Co., petroleum refiners. In 1866 Rockefeller joined with his brother William and Samuel Andrews in establishing William Rockefeller and Company. The various interests of John D. and William Rockefeller were combined in 1867 as

Rockefeller, Andrews, and Flayer, with Henry M. Flayer as a general partner and S. V. Harkness as a special partner. In 1870 the business was incorporated as the Standard Oil Company of Ohio, with a capital of $1 million.

Through mergers with other companies, favorable railroad rates, and other devices, the Standard Oil Company eliminated most of its competition and by 1879 controlled over 75 percent of the total refining capacity of the country. Trustees were appointed to hold properties that could not be held under the company's Ohio charter. These properties were combined in 1882 to form the Standard Oil Trust, which was declared illegal by the Supreme Court of Ohio in 1892. The trust was not actually dissolved until 1899, when it was replaced by the Standard Oil Company of New Jersey, capitalized at $110 million. This maneuver caused violent public reaction, and the company was ordered by the Supreme Court, in an antitrust suit decided in 1911, to cease operations.

Rockefeller retained the title of president of the Standard Oil Company until its dissolution in 1911, but from 1895 on he gradually turned over its direction to his associates and began to concentrate on the establishment of foundations through which he could channel his fortune to those areas where it would be most beneficial. He created the Rockefeller Institute for Medical Research in 1901, the General Education Board in 1902, the Rockefeller Foundation in 1913, and the Laura Spelman Rockefeller Memorial, later combined with the Rockefeller Foundation, in 1918. He was also instrumental in founding the University of Chicago, to which he donated approximately $35 million.

Rockefeller died in 1937 at the age of ninety-seven. Far outliving his associates and his opponents, he came to be thought of more as a philanthropist than as an oil magnate. His son, John D. Rockefeller, Jr., devoted most of his life to his father's philanthropic and civic activities, especially to those intended to advance human welfare and promote harmony among people of different nations, races, and creeds. He was deeply interested in the conservation of natural resources and contributed liberally to this cause. Among his important undertakings was the restoration of Williamsburg, to which he gave over $60 million. Of his sons, John D. Rockefeller III has been chairman of the Rockefeller Foundation since 1952 and is chairman of the Lincoln Center for the Performing Arts and Chairman and Trustee of the Asia Society; Nelson A. Rockefeller is now serving his fourth term as governor of the State of New York; Laurance S. Rockefeller is honorary chairman of the Rockefeller Brothers, Inc. and Rockefeller Center, Inc.; Winthrop Rockefeller was former governor of the state of Arkansas; and David Rockefeller is chairman and chief executive of Chase Manhattan Bank and chairman of Chase International Investment Corporation.

CONTEMPORARY ISSUES
Situation 11

Are we ready for a four-day, thirty-two-hour work week?

During class the question of a four-day work week arose and resulted in a heated debate. Later, John and Ray continued the discussion.

"What America needs," observed John, "is a four-day week. Just imagine how much more time consumers would have for shopping and how much more free time there would be for recreation and education. A four-day work week would also mean full employment for everybody, since the maximum work week would be thirty-two hours, and more people would have to be hired."

"You're overlooking a great deal," interrupted Ray. "Do you honestly believe people would enjoy life more if they worked only four days instead of the conventional five? All the professional people I know— doctors, lawyers, executives, self-employed business people—work fifty to seventy-five hours a week. Maybe the main reason they work so much is that they like it. Besides, these people sometimes depend on the amount of time they work for the bulk of their livelihood. What we need to do is to make ordinary jobs more challenging, so people would find more enjoyment in working instead of sitting around watching television or being bored."

"You may be right," replied John, "but you are not being practical. Look, with more and more automation there will be less for individual workers to do. We will have to have a shorter week so we can spread around what work there is."

"That's nonsense," Ray contended. "We learned early in the course that all human wants can't be satisfied. That means there will always be more work to do than there are talented people to do it. And besides, John, a shorter work week could result in increased crime, violence, fighting and all the other negative aspects of modern-day living. You and I know that when people are idle they are much more likely to get into trouble than if they are kept busy."

"You may or may not be right," responded Ray, "but making more of our holidays fall on Monday so people will have three-day weekends in my opinion is a prelude to the day when most people will work only a four-day, 32-hour week."

SITUATION EVALUATION

1. Who do you feel has the better argument and why?

2. What points can be made to support Ray's argument? John's argument?

3. Do you feel that the four-day work week will become a reality? What problems will it produce for company management?

BUSINESS CHRONICLE

Team spirit and business

King was chatting in his office with Gary Adams, his personnel manager, about the fine record of Clancy Bacon, one of the company's young real estate salesmen.

King: Clancy's really a gem. He's not thirty years old; yet he accomplishes twice as much as anyone on the sales staff.

Adams: I'm really proud of him and impressed with his record, too.

King: What is it that makes him so successful?

Adams: Above all, he's so devoted to his job. He finds it fascinating. Because he thinks about it so much, he's much more creative than other salesmen.

King: That's so true. He came up with that terrific idea that the company should buy the old Southern Railways station and turn it into a restaurant and mini amusement park. That's one of the company's most profitable operations. We were able to turn a community eyesore into a recreation area that the city is proud of. It isn't Clancy's job to think up business opportunities, yet he does it right along. Why?

Adams: For one, he feels it is his company as well as ours and he wants the company to do things he can be proud of. He knows that if the company prospers and gains prestige that he and the rest of the employees benefit too.

King: Unfortunately most employees think only of themselves and not of the company as a whole. Clancy seems to be a team worker. He feels I'm the captain and you're a coach and that it's up to him as one of the players to help everyone to score more points.

Adams: Younger employees sometimes have that spirit when we first hire them. I wish we could encourage it more and not lose it.

King: That's your job. What do you suggest? As president, what can I do?

QUESTIONS

1. Why are some employees enthusiastic about their jobs and others not?

2. What can be done to encourage the kind of attitude Clancy seems to have? Especially, what can be done to encourage creativity?

3. What can Mr. King, as president of the company, do to improve employee attitudes?

APPLICATION EXERCISES

1. Many people believe money is the primary source of motivation for human beings, and they feel that the more you pay people, the harder they will work. In a brief report, answer the following questions:
   a. Most senior executives in our 500 largest companies earn well in excess of $100,000 each year and most of these people work very hard. Assume that you doubled their pay, would you expect even better job performance?
   b. Who is likely to be most motivated by money—the individual earning $7,500 or one earning $75,000? Why?
   c. How do you account for the fact that some of our most highly motivated individuals, especially those in certain religious orders, receive very little money?
   d. Based on your reflection, what is the proper role of money as a motivator?

2. People in highly developed countries become less enthusiastic about working for they seem to take their affluent and technical societies for granted. Working becomes both a strain and a bore for many. Thus, motivating employees becomes a serious problem.

   An idea to make the everyday work experience more interesting and efficient is making inroads in Europe. The plan, called "flextime," gives employees extraordinary freedom to begin and finish their work day. Formerly, Herr Meier, for instance, in his purchasing job at the Lufthansa Cologne office, was required to be at his desk punctually at 7:30 A.M. Now he can arrive any time between 7:00 and 9:30 A.M. and leave anytime between 3:30 and 7:00 P.M. He is required only to get his work done and to accumulate a fixed number of hours each month. No one's permission is required if he wants to leave early Friday to beat the weekend traffic crush.

   European managements using the system claim that it increases efficiency. Employees can take it easy on days they are not up to par. The office atmosphere is said to be more relaxed. Flextime is said to cut absenteeism, increase productivity, reduce paid overtime, and probably cut down on the incidence of ulcers.

   The key to the system is "core time." In the above example, everyone must be at his job from 9:30 A.M. to 3:30 P.M., except for lunch and coffee breaks. During core time, meetings are held, and employees are sure to be able to catch one another for needed communication. During non-core hours, the phone rings less, and other people are not apt to be underfoot. So the employee has time to concentrate and thus accomplish things more efficiently.
   a. What advantages and disadvantages do you see in this system from the business viewpoint?

b. What effects would widespread use of the system, which is said to be crossing the Atlantic, have outside of the company? Are these effects good or bad?

c. Do you approve or disapprove of the system? How would you argue for your point of view?

3. Anthony Pitkin, a college senior in business administration, had an interview for a job as a management trainee. Following are some of the things that occurred in the interview. How would you analyze each of them?

a. The interviewer was not smoking. Pitkin asked if he could smoke. The interviewer said, "Go ahead, if you wish."

b. The interviewer asked Pitkin a hypothetical question, "As a future manager, what is your philosophy of management?" Pitkin replied, "I believe in the Golden Rule—Do unto others as you would have others do unto you." The interviewer responded, "That philosophy assumes that everyone is like you."

c. Pitkin said he was a good writer, when actually he was only fair; he said he had been president of his high school class when he had been secretary; he said he earned his own way through college when his parents provided his room and board.

d. Pitkin wanted to know company policies on raises and time off.

e. Since the interview was on campus, Pitkin did not wear a suit and tie. He dressed neatly in a sport shirt and sweater.

f. When asked whether he would consider relocating from time to time, Pitkin said he preferred to stay in the large city where he would start work.

g. When asked whether his wife would assist him in getting ahead in a business career, Pitkin refused to answer saying that he felt it was a personal question.

QUESTIONS

1. Why are the attitudes toward work in our society changing? How does deterioration in our willingness to work relate to our balance of payments problem, domestic welfare, and personal life? What would you suggest to counteract this trend?

2. In the final analysis, the relative success of two companies can be explained by the quality of their personnel. Do you agree with this statement? Explain your answer.

3. As an applicant for a job, should you fill out the employment application completely and truthfully or should you "play down" certain undesirable things about yourself? Give reasons for your answer.

4. Some companies give polygraph tests (lie detector tests) and psychological tests to applicants for executive positions. Do you feel this is wise? What factors do you feel explain this trend?

5. Does a humanistic view toward personnel conflict with the theory that labor is a cost of production and should be carefully managed to avoid overpayment? Explain carefully.

6. What is meant by "employee services"? Should the trend toward more so-called fringe benefits be encouraged?

7. What do you think the advantages and disadvantages of basing a company promotional policy on merit alone might be?

8. What has brought about the increased emphasis on human relations in business?

9. It is said that a good manager can tell by observation whether the morale of people who work for him is good or bad. What indicators does he look for?

10. Do you feel all employees of, say, an automobile manufacturer should be required to use the cars manufactured by that company? Suppose you observe that 50 percent of the employees of one company drive cars produced by another company. Would you conclude a morale problem is involved?

12

CHAPTER 12

LABOR ECONOMICS

Labor Production and Labor Productivity. Trends in Productivity. Labor as a Cost of Production. Earnings of Labor. Women in the Labor Force.

UNEMPLOYMENT

Causes of Unemployment. Remedies for Unemployment. Do We Need a New Measure of Unemployment?

HISTORY AND ORGANIZATION OF LABOR

Early History of Unions. American Federation of Labor (AFL). Congress of Industrial Organizations (CIO). Merger of the AFL and CIO. Unaffiliated, or Independent, Unions. White-Collar Unions. Current Trends.

UNION OBJECTIVES

WORKERS' ATTITUDES TOWARD UNIONS

Why Workers Join Unions. Why Workers Do Not Join Unions.

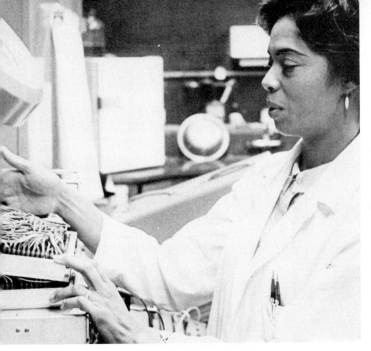

labor in the economy

Labor is the interest of everyone. Almost every day newspapers carry banner headlines such as "Real Wages Up Over Last Year," "Thousands Idled By Strike," "Unemployment Creates Concern," "Union Demands Recognition," and "Hard-Core Unemployed Training Program Initiated." It is a rare political speech that does not dwell on problems concerning labor. When businesspeople meet, various labor topics — strikes, productivity, automation, efficiency and cost of labor, unions, unemployment — are commonly discussed.

Labor, in the broadest sense, is human energy expended to perform the various tasks associated with the production and distribution of goods and services. The labor force, as defined by the U.S. Bureau of the Census, includes all people over sixteen[1] years of age who are willing and able to work and who are either employed or seeking employment. This definition includes executives, self-employed persons, professional people,

[1] The lower limit for official statistics on the labor force was raised from 14 to 16 years of age in January of 1967.

Figure **12–1**
Trends in the Labor Force, 1959–72

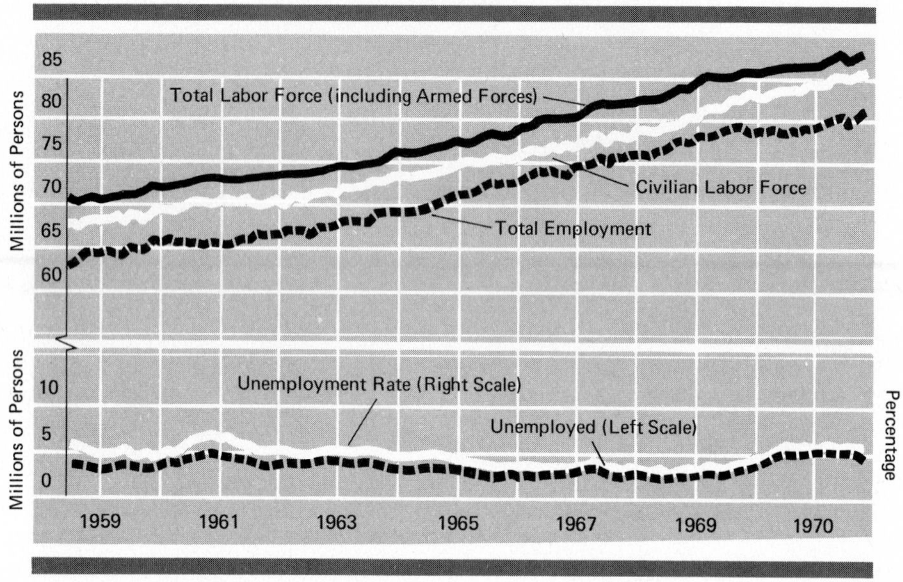

Source: *Statistical Abstract of the United States, 1972,* p. 212.

Is it possible to eliminate unemployment?

farmers, wage earners, and all others who devote a portion of their time to some activity for which they are compensated. (See Figure 12–1 for trends in the labor force.)

There are a number of classifications of labor. One division is "white-collar" and "blue-collar" labor. White-collar refers to office workers, managers, and those self-employed persons who do not perform manual tasks. Blue-collar includes those who engage in manual activity, such as factory workers, truck drivers, tool-and-die makers, and farm operators.

Blue-collar labor is sometimes further classified as skilled, semi-skilled, and unskilled, depending on the qualifications, training, and capabilities of the worker. Labor may be described as unionized (organized), and nonunionized (unorganized), depending on whether the employees do or do not belong to a labor organization.

LABOR ECONOMICS

Labor production and labor productivity

Labor production, in simplest terms, is the amount of work of an acceptable quality produced by an individual or group of individuals in a given period of time. For example, the number of bricks laid per hour by a bricklayer is an indication of his production, or output. Production of

Figure **12–2**
Farm Productivity Figures

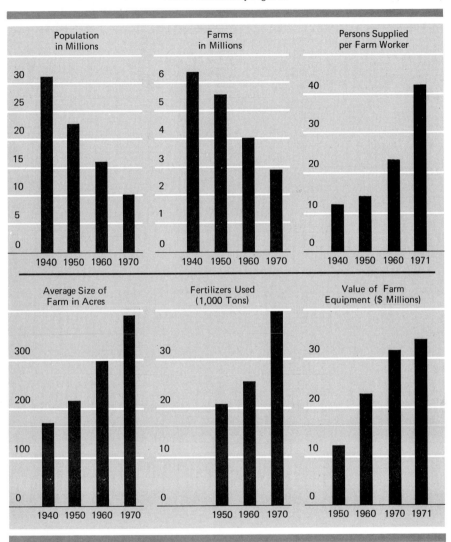

Source: *Statistical Abstract of the United States, 1972*, p. 580.

Comparing the United States with Other Countries					
PERSONS SUPPLIED PER FARM WORKER	**1940**	**1950**	**1960**	**1965**	**1971** (Prel)
AT HOME	10.3	13.8	22.3	30.8	42.0
ABROAD	0.4	1.7	3.5	6.2	7.0

How do you explain these statistics?

Figure **12-3**
Wages, Prices, and Productivity for the Total Private Economy (1967 = 100)

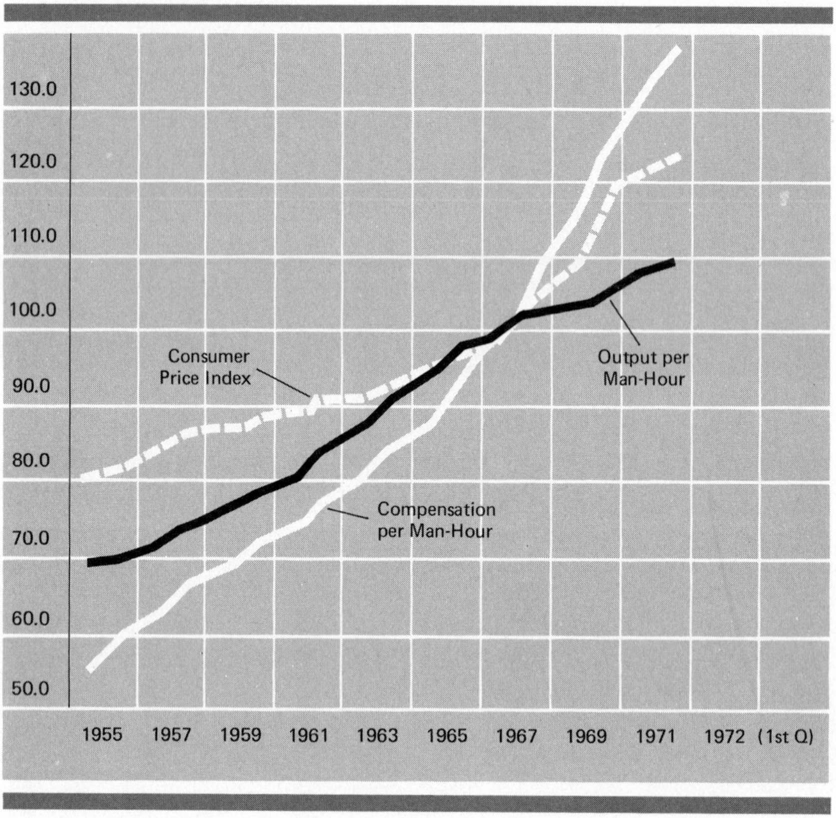

Source: The Conference Board, U.S. Bureau of Labor Statistics.

What is the consequence of compensation rising faster than man-hour output?

employees often can be measured with a certain degree of precision, but in many occupations it is difficult to determine. How can one measure precisely the "production" of ministers or engineers? One of the most dramatic productivity accomplishments in the world is that of the U.S. farmer (see Figure 12-1).

Productivity is important when employees ask for wage increases. New labor-saving equipment, research, development of new methods, greater specialization, and better management all contribute to increased output. While workers should be paid more for increased productivity, some of the benefits resulting from more efficient operation should be passed on to the management and owners, who provide the ingenuity and capital and who take the risks involved.

Table **12–1**
Productivity in Manufacturing
YEAR	PERCENTAGE GAIN	YEAR	PERCENTAGE GAIN	YEAR	PERCENTAGE GAIN
1961	3.5	1965	3.4	1969	0.4
1962	4.7	1966	4.0	1970	0.7
1963	3.6	1967	2.1		
1964	3.9	1968	2.9		

Source: Bureau of Labor Statistics.

Trends in productivity

Figure 12–3 reveals trends in wages, prices, and productivity for the economy. The year 1967 is the index year (index numbers are explained in Chapter 23), which is the base that all other years are compared with for purposes for revealing trends.

The United States has prided itself, with measurable justification, in its ability to out-produce all other countries. In fact, after World War II, a chief preoccupation of America was to assist war-torn countries with industrial reconstruction and modernization. Many of the countries that the United States coached and assisted learned all too well. They have become so proficient that a study made by the Argus Research Corporation notes that the United States has fallen behind other major countries in raising manufacturing productivity (that is, output per man-hour). From 1965 to 1970 productivity in the United States increased only about 2 percent. "This performance," states Argus, "put the United States dead last among the leading industrial countries." (See Figure 12–4.) The extent to which productivity in manufacturing deteriorated in the last decade is shown in Table 12–1.

When workers in the United States produce less than workers in countries we compete with in international markets and when we fall behind others in technology, modernization, and resourcefulness, the value of the dollar is eroded, which in the long run affects our standard of living adversely. Chapter 20 on international trade considers these matters further. Fortunately our record for productivity in agriculture has been more distinguished than in manufacturing (refer back to Figure 12–2 on page 321). The country owes a great debt to farmers who can, from an international viewpoint, be said to be the nation's unsung heroes.[2]

---

[2] This is not to infer that farmers today are by any means among the nation's underprivileged. Someone recently pointed out that Corn Belt farmers are following a new classic "c. s. M. rotation system"—corn and soybeans in the summer and Miami in the winter!

Figure **12–4**
Output per Man-Hour: Manufacturing (1965 = 100)

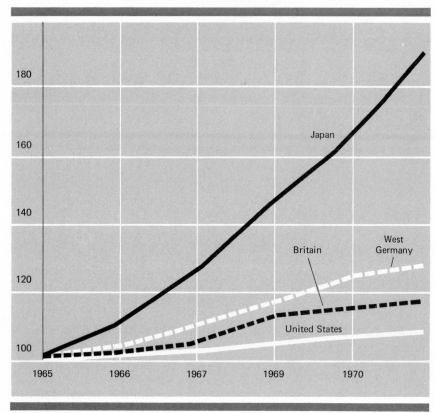

Source: U.S. Bureau of Labor Statistics.

What accounts for this lag on the part of the United States?

Labor as a cost of production

For the total economy, labor is the major expense incurred in production and distribution. For some products, such as cigarettes, wages represent only a very small percentage of the total selling price. Accordingly, an increase in wages in the tobacco industry would probably not materially affect the prices paid by consumers. On the other hand, the labor cost of manufacturing pottery is very high, and any substantial increase in pottery workers' wages would be reflected in higher prices for pottery.

Salaries and wages in most nonfarm industries range from 10 to 45 percent of sales. Furthermore, the supplies and machinery these indus-

Table **12–2**
Corporate Profits
(Quarterly Data at Seasonally Adjusted Annual Rates)

YEAR OR QUARTER	CORPORATE PROFITS: ($ BILLIONS)		CORPORATE PROFITS AFTER TAXES AS PERCENTAGE OF:				
	BEFORE TAXES	AFTER TAXES	GNP	NATIONAL INCOME	INCOME ORIGINATING IN CORPORATIONS[a]	CORPORATE GROSS PRODUCT[b]	SALES[b] (MANUFACTURING CORPORATIONS)
1929 ...	$10.5	$ 9.1	8.8%	10.5%	19.8%	16.9%	n.a.
1939 ...	6.3	4.9	5.4	6.7	13.2	10.5	n.a.
1961 ...	50.3	27.2	5.2	6.4	10.5	8.5	4.3
1962 ...	55.7	31.5	5.6	6.9	11.3	9.1	4.6
1963 ...	58.9	32.6	5.5	6.8	11.1	9.0	4.7
1964 ...	66.3	37.9	6.0	7.3	11.9	9.6	5.2
1965 ...	76.1	44.8	6.5	7.9	12.9	10.5	5.6
1966 ...	82.4	48.1	6.6	7.8	12.7	10.4	5.6
1967 ...	78.7	45.5	5.7	7.3	12.4	10.1	5.0
1968 ...	84.3	44.5	5.1	6.2	11.1	9.0	5.1
1969 ...	78.6	39.0	4.2	5.1	9.2	7.4	4.8
1970 ...	70.8	36.7	3.8	4.6	8.5	6.8	4.0
1971 ...	81.0	43.2	4.1	5.1	9.3	7.4	4.2
1969 First	82.7	40.9	4.5	5.5	9.8	7.9	5.0
Second	80.7	39.6	4.3	5.2	9.3	7.5	4.9
Third	78.0	39.8	4.2	5.2	9.3	7.5	4.8
Fourth	73.3	35.6	3.8	4.6	8.3	6.7	4.5
1970 First	69.8	35.7	3.7	4.5	8.3	6.7	4.0
Second	71.5	37.1	3.8	4.7	8.6	6.9	4.4
Third	73.0	37.4	3.8	4.7	8.5	6.8	4.3
Fourth	69.0	36.6	3.7	4.6	8.5	6.7	3.7
1971 First	79.5	41.3	4.0	5.0	9.1	7.3	3.9
Second	82.5	43.4	4.0	5.1	9.4	7.4	4.5
Third	80.0	42.4	4.0	5.0	9.2	7.3	4.1
Fourth	82.0	45.6	4.3	5.3	9.7	7.7	4.1
1972 First	86.0	46.7	4.2	5.2	9.5	7.6	n.a.

Source: The Conference Board, U.S. Dept. of Commerce.
Note: Profits are after inventory valuation adjustment. n.a.—Not available.
[a] Excludes branch profits remitted from abroad net of corresponding U.S. remittances to foreigners. [b] Cents per dollar of sales.

tries purchase also have substantial labor input. Altogether, wages and other compensation of employees amount to about 65 percent of the industrial sales dollar. The rest of the corporate product income is paid out in taxes, investment in capital goods and property, and profits.

There is widespread and gross misunderstanding about where corporate income goes. A survey made among employees of a Wall Street bank showed that 63 percent thought profits were about equal to or greater than wages. Actually this is far from the truth, for employees receive nearly fifteen times as much in compensation as stockholders get in dividends (see Table 12–2).

Table **12–3**
Hours Worked and Gross Earnings Received
by Production Workers, 1940–72: Manufacturing

PERIOD	AVERAGE WEEKLY EARNINGS (CURRENT DOLLARS)	AVERAGE NUMBER OF HOURS WORKED	AVERAGE HOURLY EARNINGS (WITH OVERTIME)
1940	$ 24.96	38.1 hrs.	$ .66
1945	44.20	43.5	1.02
1950	58.32	40.5	1.44
1955	75.70	40.7	1.86
1960	89.72	39.7	2.26
1965	107.53	41.2	2.61
1970	133.73	39.8	3.22
1972	152.69	n.a.	3.59

Source: U.S. Department of Labor, Bureau of Labor Statistics.

Earnings of labor

The wages and salaries paid to individuals are important in the economy for two principal reasons. First, as has already been shown, wage payments to individuals represent one of the major costs of production. Second, the amount paid to individuals in wages determines in large part the quantity of goods and services that will be consumed. As income goes up, consumers spend more; and as income decreases, so does spending.

Average hourly earnings since 1945 have increased greatly (see Table 12–3). The wages paid to specific groups of labor vary considerably, depending on such factors as skill, experience, and training of the individual, bargaining power of labor unions, minimum-wage legislation, supply of and demand for labor, and financial strength of the employer.

Wages also vary in different geographical regions. In 1970, for example, production workers in Tennessee earned $2.73 per hour, while similar workers in Michigan earned $4.15 — a difference of $1.42. In the same year, construction workers were earning $5.22 per hour — more than twice the hourly wage of workers in the retail industry.

Two types of income can be distinguished — money income and real income. *Money income* is the actual amount earned by a worker in a given period. When tax, social security, and other deductions are made, the amount remaining is referred to as *take-home pay*. But the dollar amount of the paycheck does not always indicate its true economic value to the individual. During a period of inflation, prices of goods and services the worker buys may increase faster than his wages, with the result that his earnings are relatively less valuable. What is more important than money income is *real income*, which indicates how much the money income can actually buy.

Women in the labor force

Participation of females in the labor force has been increasing steadily from less than 28 percent in 1947 to 36.4 percent in 1970. Participation rates for women have risen for all age categories, except for those over sixty-four. Rates are considerably higher for nonwhites, especially for those of age twenty-five and over. The difference indicates a greater need for income.

Whereas the percentage of women in the work force is increasing, it can be said that their potential is not being properly tapped. While there are more women in professional and semiprofessional fields than ever before, their *proportion* of the total *is less*. Marriage and resulting pregnancies sometimes cause employers to discriminate against women because their span of employment may be short. Yet according to a study made by the Department of Labor, 51 percent of the women who graduated from college in June 1957 were in the labor force seven years after graduation. The report noted that the number of women entering the labor force after four years of college had risen from 50 percent in 1952 to 59 percent in 1965. It forecast that "increasingly larger numbers of women will enter the work force in the coming decade. The trend appears not to be a temporary phenomenon."

A survey issued by the Department of Labor revealed that American women not only earn less than men, but the gap between the sexes had been widening in the last 15 years.[3] In 1955, the median wage of a working woman was nearly 64 percent of that of her counterpart. But in 1970, despite the passage of civil rights legislation banning pay discrimination and the rise of women's liberation movement, the median earnings of females were only 59.4 percent of a male's salary. In 1970, median earnings for males was $9,184, whereas females received only $5,440. The greatest imbalance was in the sales field, where female earnings were 43 percent of male earnings. In professional and technical fields females were paid 67 percent as much as males. The survey concluded that, not only were women usually employed in less skilled, lower paying jobs, but they often got unequal pay for equal work. Women do have one small advantage over males: since women work at either white-collar or service jobs, their positions are less likely to be affected by economic fluctuations. Unemploy-

---

[3] Other agencies report different percentages, however conclusions are the same. Statistical studies, even for governmental agencies, do not always agree. This is to be expected since different sets of assumptions, samples, and estimates are used in making compilations.

ment rates for males often rise earlier than that for females, since males tend to get laid off first.

A study made by the government's Commission on the Status of Women found that in the better jobs women differed very little from men in turnover, length of service, and reliability. While employers are discovering that a prime source of brainpower is the female college graduate, and laws are being passed against discrimination, what really is needed is a new attitude. Women must be encouraged to enter nontraditional fields and to enlarge their horizons. Ways should be found to help them continue their education during the time they are away from work for childbearing and rearing, so that they will be up to date with technological changes when they are ready to re-enter the job market. Stubborn traditions must be broken if the country is to benefit from a crucial resource that is now not fully utilized.

UNEMPLOYMENT

At any given time there are a certain number of people who are willing and able to work but cannot find employment. (See Figure 12–1.) The extent of unemployment is important for several reasons. First, the unemployed individual and his family endure financial hardship and deprivation.

Second, unemployment is a social waste. Productive time is forever lost, for the productive resource of labor cannot be stored. Society suffers also because the unemployed must be cared for. Those who are employed must contribute to the support of the unemployed, many of whom could support themselves if they had employment.

Third, the number of unemployed is a reliable indicator of the nation's economic health. When unemployment is negligible—that is, roughly, when it is under 4 percent—business is generally good, for there is sufficient purchasing power to stimulate business activity. As unemployment increases, purchasing power decreases, and production is curtailed. Business becomes depressed and is described as "bad," and people talk about depression and recession.

It is fallacy to view unemployment as a problem that only concerns labor and government. Actually management is usually deeply concerned since unemployed workers are poor customers, and hiring, firing, or laying off people is costly. Unfortunately demand fluctuates widely. For example, the sale of farm machinery depends largely on how good farm crops and prices were for the year. It is to the advantage of all manufacturers to get maximum use of plant capacity. As a hedge against bad

Figure **12–5**
Unemployment Rates for Persons 16 Years of Age and Over, 1971

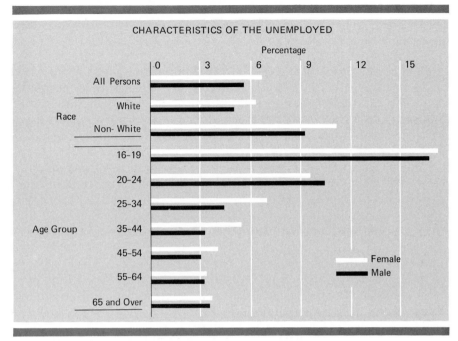

Source: The Conference Board, *A Guide to Consumer Markets 1972/1973.*

years, farm equipment manufacturers try to use some of their manu-facturing capacity to produce non-farm related goods. International Harvester Company, in addition to its line of pickup and heavy-duty trucks, makes four-wheel drive station wagons, sit-down lawn mowers, mining and quarrying equipment, and highway maintenance machines. Deere & Co. produces snowmobiles, snow blowers, and a line of home gardening equipment. Allis-Chalmers makes minibikes and amphibious, all-terrain vehicles.

Causes of unemployment

Unemployment is often categorized by its causes, which are several: unemployment owing to personal difficulties (characteristics such as irre-sponsible behavior, emotional instability, or low mentality that render an individual unemployable); technological unemployment (resulting from automated techniques and changes in production methods); seasonal un-employment; and economic or cyclical unemployment (caused by a general business contraction during periods of depression or recession). In addition, a more or less temporary form of unemployment results from strikes, business failures, business mergers, model changeovers, plant relocations, and catastrophes (fire, flood, etc.).

The incidence of unemployment falls most heavily on certain groups and regions. Unemployment is greater for nonwhites, teen-agers, older people, and the unskilled and poorly educated (see Figure 12–5). In certain geographic areas it has been alarmingly high—for example, in large city slums and in Appalachia and other depressed rural areas.

Unemployment is definitely related to age. For example, currently there is a shortage of experienced, middle-aged workers because of the low birth rates of the 1930s. On the other hand, there is an excess of inexperienced workers because of the large number of teen-agers from the postwar baby boom who are now entering the job market.

Studies show that at any given time, half or more of the unemployed have been out of work for less than five weeks. Most are between jobs and are definitely not hard-core unemployed. Sometimes workers refuse job opportunities until they get the job offer they want. They can do this without suffering undue hardship because of their ability to draw on savings and to collect unemployment compensation, union payments, and severance allowances. Indirectly, then, cash unemployment benefits contribute to unemployment in those cases where people work until they are eligible for benefits, then lay off, and return to work only when the benefits run out. This "work-then-don't-work-while-you-can-get-benefits" cycle is repeated chronically by a number of people.

Hard-core unemployed are those individuals who seek, but are chronically unable to find, employment. Many are not employable because of physical handicaps, obsolete skills, police records, inadequate educations, antisocial attitudes, or poor work records. A large percentage of the hard-core unemployed are high school dropouts or substandard graduates; the requirements of the jobs they seek are too high for their experience and abilities. In other words, because of technology there aren't enough jobs with low requirements.

Remedies for unemployment

The government has become increasingly active in attempting to provide employment. Two pieces of legislation should be noted.

The Manpower Development and Training Act of 1962 (MDTA) was passed by Congress in 1962 in a time of high unemployment, a growing labor force, and a widening impact of technological change on employment.

Amendments to the act since 1962 have reflected an improved employment situation for the general population but persistently high unemployment rates for many special groups, including teen-agers, nonwhites, older workers, the handicapped, and the unskilled. Recent changes place a greater emphasis on serving the disadvantaged and on coordinating manpower programs.

MDTA covers a broad and comprehensive range of programs. Its primary purpose is to train people for jobs that may exist or be developed. It can provide needed basic education; institutional training in the form of classroom instruction; preapprenticeship training; on-the-job training (OJT), which takes place at the employer's place of business; and coupled training, which combines institutional and on-the-job training.

The Department of Labor, through its Manpower Administration, is responsible for conducting research; developing on a regular basis, experimental and demonstration projects; establishing and maintaining policies and standards; and providing supportive services. State employment service offices determine training needs, select and place participants, provide testing and counseling services, and provide certain allowances, when needed. The Department of Health, Education and Welfare, through its U. S. Office of Education, is responsible for the educational and institutional training aspects of the programs.

Those people in any age group who are unemployed or underemployed are eligible for enrollment in MDTA projects. Included are those whose skills may be becoming obsolete due to technological advances in industry; members of minority groups who may have certain cultural, emotional, social, or other handicaps; and others, including those in rural areas, whose poor education or economic situation makes it difficult for them to develop job skills.

The state employment services seek out the unemployed for participation in MDTA programs. Or they may be referred by community agency sponsors of other Manpower Administration programs.

The Emergency Employment Act of 1971 provides *transitional* public service jobs for unemployed and underemployed workers and, in so doing, helps meet the need for improved public services in states and localities. The act authorizes a federally financed two-year program of temporary jobs in state and local government agencies to go into effect when the national unemployment rate equals or exceeds 4.5 percent for a three-month period. A special program for local areas with unemployment rates of 6 percent or above is also provided.

Do we need a new measure of unemployment?

Of late there have been criticisms of how unemployment is measured. It is pointed out that more attention must be paid to the composition of the unemployed so more selective remedies for unemployment can be applied. Present measures lead to wrong diagnosis and to the application of wrong medicines. For example, a 4 percent unemployment rate in 1956 is not the same as a similar rate in the 1970s because different categories of jobless are involved. The unemployment rate of the young has risen during the past few years. The jobless rate for 16- to 19-year-old males was, for example, three and one-half times the rate of 25- to 64-year-old males in 1955. In 1970, the rate for those under 20 was five and one-half times as large as the rate for older males. Unemployment of youth cannot be solved by the customary expansionary actions of government. Instead programs of manpower training and the facilitating of job mobility must be undertaken. Discussions are now underway that may lead to the adoption of a "weighted unemployment rate" related to age, race, sex, hours and wages. Just how this may best be implemented is yet to be decided.

HISTORY AND ORGANIZATION OF LABOR**

Over twenty million workers, employed in hundreds of different types of jobs and tens of thousands of companies, have banded together into labor unions. Collectively, these workers are known as "organized labor." Approximately 23 percent of the nation's total labor force belong to a union. Unions are relatively more important in manufacturing than in other segments of the economy. Agricultural workers, domestic workers, and most professional workers are, in general, only loosely organized or not organized at all; such organization, though, is expanding somewhat.

The main reason for labor unions is the idea that an individual worker has little power but that, collectively, the voice of thousands of workers has a strength the employer cannot refuse to hear.

SPECIAL READINGS

** Toil and Trouble, A History of American Labor, Second Edition, by Thomas R. Brooks. New York: Delacorte Press, 1971. This book, probably the most readable about the American labor movement, has a misleading subtitle, for it is considerably more than a history. It devotes a sizable amount of space to current labor personalities and issues. The author is especially reflective about youth and labor. He points out that young workers have different priorities and asks, "How is this changing labor?" The young workers, he tells us, tend to prefer immediate wage gains over deferred benefits such as pension improvements. Yet early retirement is attractive as an issue because it opens more jobs for the young. Among the many interesting questions the author raises are: "Are young workers going to be more political than previous generations? If so, what kind of politics?" There is evidence that the young tend to support "more recent prominent issues—like air and water pollution control and consumer legislation."

This well-written, concise book also tells about many little known matters such as The United Farm Workers Organizing Committee negotiating a ban on "hard pesticides" such as DDT. It informs us that "The United Auto Workers joined with six conservation groups in urging Congress to set air pollution control standards so tough that they would banish the internal-combustion engine from autos by 1975." Chapters on "The Legacy of George Meany," "Black Upsurge in the Unions," "Automation," and "Bleaching the Blue Collar" indicate the scope of this stimulating book in a field where there is a lack of well-written books.

Early history of unions

There were "labor unions" even before the Declaration of Independence. Workers formed benevolent societies to help members who had suffered financial or personal misfortune. These early unions were mainly friendship organizations and were not concerned with wages, hours, and working conditions.

It was soon realized, however, that organized employees could bring about improvements in working conditions, and by 1791 some skilled workers—printers, shoemakers, carpenters, and shipbuilders—were organized for this purpose. However, early unions were weak, poorly organized, and usually short-lived. Small-scale farming and manufacturing predominated during this period, and workers, by and large, saw little reason for cohesive organization. If they were not satisfied with the treatment received from employers, they could, with very little capital, go into business for themselves or move west and farm.

During the 1820s, unionism spread rapidly. Unions were local, but they grew in power, and loud demands were made for better wages, shorter hours, and improved working environments. Over the following decades, unionism tended to grow during good times but to suffer severe setbacks when times were hard and jobs were few.

American Federation of Labor (AFL)

In 1881 several craft unions—that is, labor unions that limit their membership to workers who practice one trade or a group of related trades, even though the workers may work for a number of different employers—established the Federation of Organized Trades and Labor Unions. In 1886, it merged with several other unions. The new organization was called the American Federation of Labor (AFL). Under the leadership of Samuel Gompers, the AFL grew rapidly during the next three decades and became unquestionably the dominant labor organization in the United States. As a matter for historical perspective, it is interesting to note that Gompers made the following statement: "The worst crime against working people is the company that fails to operate at a profit."

The AFL was not interested in social or political changes. Instead, it concentrated its efforts on gaining better working conditions for its members. It always believed in collective bargaining with employers (see Chapter 13). Strikes have been called only when this method has failed. From 1920 to 1935, however, the AFL met with difficulty. It became apparent that further growth was limited by the principle of organizing labor along craft lines. As industry became more mechanized, relatively fewer employees were skilled craftsmen, and, consequently, many workers could not quality for AFL membership.

Congress of Industrial Organizations (CIO)

In the mid-1930s a major controversy arose within the AFL over whether or not the organization should extend membership to unskilled, noncraft workers. Those who argued for extending membership pointed out that (1) the growth of the AFL was near a standstill, with the result that the entire labor movement was weakening; (2) entire industries, such as steel and automobiles, were unorganized; and (3) practically no unskilled workers had any union ties.

As an outgrowth of this controversy, several unions belonging to the AFL formed the Committee for Industrial Organizations, with the stated purpose of promoting organization of the workers in mass-production and unorganized industries and encouraging their affiliation with the AFL.

The committee organized workers in many industries without the approval of the AFL and formally organized the Congress of Industrial Organizations (CIO). The CIO was successful from the start. Workers were organized in the steel, automobile, newspaper, cannery, and communications industries. Soon the CIO was almost as strong as the AFL.

Merger of the AFL and CIO

During and after World War II, efforts were made to unite the AFL and CIO. Success was finally achieved in 1955. George Meany, president of the AFL, was named to head the huge consolidation. A policy-making and administrative structure for organized labor is shown in Figure 12–6. In 1971 there were a total of 234 unions in the United States, 120 of which were AFL-CIO affiliated.

Unaffiliated, or independent, unions

Approximately three million workers belong to unions not affiliated with the AFL-CIO. One important reason for independent unionism is the AFL-CIO's policing of its own ranks. AFL-CIO expulsions account for about two-thirds of the total membership of unaffiliated national unions.

Company unions are independent organizations limiting membership to employees of individual companies. Originally company unions were dominated by management, but this practice was declared illegal by the Supreme Court in 1937. Although there are hundreds of company unions in the United States, their total membership is a small fraction of the number belonging to all unions.

Figure **12–6**
General Structural Arrangements of Organized Labor

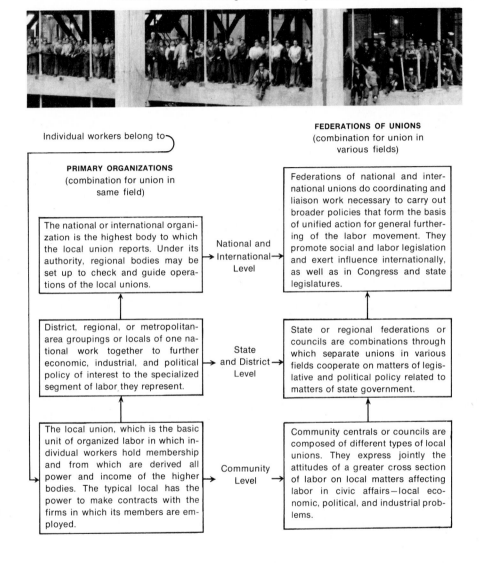

Individual workers belong to⌐

FEDERATIONS OF UNIONS
(combination for union in
various fields)

PRIMARY ORGANIZATIONS
(combination for union in
same field)

The national or international organization is the highest body to which the local union reports. Under its authority, regional bodies may be set up to check and guide operations of the local unions.

National and
→ International
Level

Federations of national and international unions do coordinating and liaison work necessary to carry out broader policies that form the basis of unified action for general furthering of the labor movement. They promote social and labor legislation and exert influence internationally, as well as in Congress and state legislatures.

District, regional, or metropolitan-area groupings or locals of one national work together to further economic, industrial, and political policy of interest to the specialized segment of labor they represent.

State
→ and District →
Level

State or regional federations or councils are combinations through which separate unions in various fields cooperate on matters of legislative and political policy related to matters of state government.

The local union, which is the basic unit of organized labor in which individual workers hold membership and from which are derived all power and income of the higher bodies. The typical local has the power to make contracts with the firms in which its members are employed.

Community
Level

Community centrals or councils are composed of different types of local unions. They express jointly the attitudes of a greater cross section of labor on local matters affecting labor in civic affairs—local economic, political, and industrial problems.

White-collar unions

There is an unmistakable trend toward unionizing white-collar employees —clerical employees, salesmen, insurance agents, musicians, teachers, engineers, and retail clerks. Though only somewhat more than 10 percent

Figure **12–7**
Thirty Largest National Unions, 1970
(Thousands of Members)

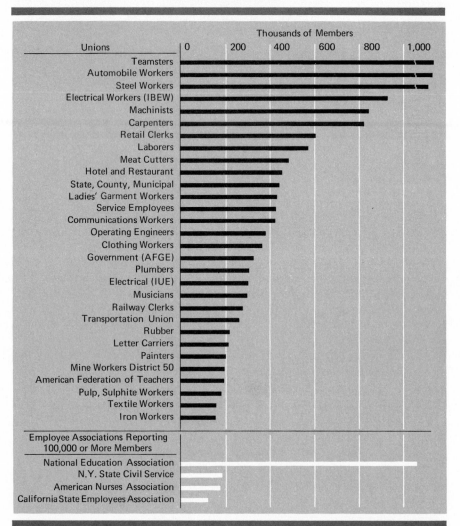

Source: Bureau of Labor Statistics; Road Maps of Industry, No. 1702, "Union Membership," The Conference Board,
November 15, 1972.

of all clerical and professional employees are unionized, the evidence
indicates that this percentage will increase.

White-collar unions are traditionally more reluctant than industrial
unions to resort to strikes. In the early 1970s, however, strikes by white-
collar unions were numerous, principally because of the lag of wages and
salaries behind the cost of living and the failure of white-collar unorgan-

ized workers to keep up with the organized blue-collar workers in wages
and benefits. Important white-collar and public servant strikes in recent
years include those of industrial insurance agents, newspaper employees,
teachers, firemen, and policemen.

Current trends

The Conference Board, in its Road Maps of Industry No. 1702,[4] had this
to say about union membership growth:

> Union membership in the nonmanufacturing sector has been growing at a
> faster pace than in manufacturing; gains in membership of government em-
> ployees, however, have outstripped those of the private sector. Between
> 1968 and 1970, membership in manufacturing — where unionization has
> been historically strongest — declined by 44,000. In the nonmanufacturing
> sector, 361,000 employees were added to union rolls during the same two
> years. In 1970, 47 percent of employees in manufacturing industries and
> 24 percent in private nonmanufacturing industries were unionized. Trans-
> portation continues to be the most unionized of all industries; the propor-
> tion unionized has, however, fallen from 98 percent of all transportation
> workers in 1966 to 91 percent in 1970.
>
> Union membership among government employees — federal, state, and
> local — increased by 162,000 between 1968 and 1970. Since 1962, when
> collective bargaining became permissible for government employees, the
> unionization of these workers has increased considerably. Virtually one-
> third of all government employees were unionized in 1970, including half
> of all Federal Government workers. Over the decade 1960–1970, the Ameri-
> can Federation of Government Employees has more than quadrupled in
> size and grown to be the seventeenth largest nation in the country.
>
> Employee associations, which are functionally the same as labor unions
> but not included in the discussion above, have grown substantially in recent
> years. These associations, almost entirely groups of professional or state
> and local government employees, had a total membership of 1.9 million in
> 1970. Their members constitute a growing proportion of all workers covered
> by formal and informal collective bargaining agreements. The largest group
> is the National Education Association (NEA) with 1.1 million members. In
> 1970, only three unions — the Teamsters, the United Auto Workers, and the
> United Steelworkers — had larger memberships than the NEA.

UNION OBJECTIVES

The specific aims of organized labor can best be understood by studying
the objectives of a large union. Below are quoted the objectives of the

[4] The Conference Board, Road Maps of Industry, No. 1702, "Union Membership," November
15, 1972.

International Union, United Automobile, Aircraft, and Agricultural Implement Workers of America (UAW, which stands for United Auto Workers), taken from their constitution:

OBJECTIVES

SECTION 1. To improve working conditions, create a uniform system of shorter hours and higher wages; to maintain and protect the interests of workers under the jurisdiction of this International Union.

SECTION 2. To unite in one organization, regardless of religion, race, creed, color, political affiliation or nationality, all employees under the jurisdiction of the International Union.

SECTION 3. To improve the sanitary and working conditions of employment within the factory, and in the accomplishment of these necessary reforms, we pledge ourselves to utilize the conference room and joint jurisdiction of this International Union to advocate and support strike action.

SECTION 4. To educate our membership in the history of the Labor Movement and to develop and maintain an intelligent and dignified membership; to vote and work for the election of candidates and the passage of improved legislation in the interest of all labor. To enforce existing laws; to work for the repeal of those which are unjust to labor; to work for legislation on a national scale, having as its object the establishment of real social and unemployment insurance, the expense of which to be borne by the employer and the Government.

SECTION 5. To engage in legislative, political, educational, civic, welfare and other activities which further, directly or indirectly, the joint interests of the membership of this organization in the improvement of general economic and social conditions in the United States of America, Canada, and generally in the nations of the world.

SECTION 6. To work as an autonomous International Union affiliated with the American Federation of Labor and Congress of Industrial Organizations and the Canadian Labour Congress together with other International Unions for solidification of the entire labor movement; and provide assistance, financial and otherwise, to labor and other organizations in the United States, Canada, and other parts of the world having purposes and objectives similar or related to those sought by this organization.

WORKERS' ATTITUDES TOWARD UNIONS

Why workers join unions

The union record. Unions have been important in helping secure higher wages for workers, the reduced work week, paid vacations and holidays, pensions, better working conditions, and other benefits. The individual worker, interested in securing the highest possible standard of living, joins an organization whose programs help achieve this.

Educational, social, and political benefits.　Unions frequently provide members with educational programs, sickness and accident benefits, pensions, legal advice, and other forms of assistance. Union social events give workers opportunities for relaxation. Aggressive political activity of unions also holds appeal for some.

Membership as job requisite.　Some skilled occupations, such as motion picture projection and printing, are so highly organized that nonmembers cannot secure employment.

Self-respect.　In a civilization of large-scale industry and mass living, unions provide a sense of security, participation, and belonging. They help to satisfy psychological, social, and even ethical needs. An individual feels pride when he knows he is allied with a movement in which he can express himself and further the worker's point of view.

Why workers do not join unions

Despite the growth of labor organizations, approximately three-fourths of all workers are still unorganized. Several reasons for this are stated below.

Communications difficulties.　The physical distribution of workers sometimes makes their organization difficult. This is true of traveling salesmen, for example, whose employment ordinarily does not bring them into close communication with one another.

Barriers to joining unions.　Unions may limit membership by setting up complicated membership qualification requirements such as long apprenticeship periods. Barriers to membership are sometimes raised to retain more work and privileges for present members.

Union dues and financial assessments.　Some workers think union membership costs more than it is worth. Initiation fees range from $5 to $100 and more, while monthly dues usually begin at $2.50 and occasionally exceed $25. Some unions also levy assessments when a financial emergency is occasioned by a major strike or a special union activity, such as lobbying for favorable legislation.

Fear of restrictions on individual freedom.　Some workers believe that union leaders are dictatorial and as a result the individual has no more control over his own destiny than if he were to bargain individually with his employer. Workers sometimes feel that union leaders place their own interests above those of the group.

Fear of job loss.　In companies where unions do not exist or are weak, employees sometimes feel they may be discriminated against if they join a union. While this argument rarely holds true for factory personnel, numerous cases of discrimination have been reported in the case of office workers, retail employees, and other white-collar workers.

<u>Need to join not felt</u>.   Some companies have treated employees with such fairness that workers do not feel the need for union membership. Indeed, the threat of a union being formed is a strong factor in motivating management to provide employment benefits.

<u>Incompatibility with professional status</u>.   This argument is offered by many people in professional work, including doctors, teachers, and lawyers.

PEOPLE AND THEIR IDEAS
David Dubinsky

A production-minded union leader

David Dubinsky assumed the presidency of the International Ladies' Garment Workers' Union (ILGWU) at the height of the Depression, when it was scant in membership, disrupted by Communist factionalism, and virtually penniless. He stepped down from the office in 1966, having built an organization with a membership of 363,000 and resources amounting to $571 million.

Born in Poland in 1892, Dubinsky was an apprentice in his father's bakery at the age of eleven and a qualified baker at fifteen. He joined the bakers' union and shortly after was arrested for leading strikes. He was sentenced as a "revolutionary conspirator" and banished to a labor camp in Siberia. He escaped from the camp and, in 1911, immigrated to the United States.

Dubinsky quickly found work as a cloak cutter in New York City's garment center. His sense of injustice, first aroused by the czarist police in Poland, was strengthened by the plight of thousands of men, women, and children laboring up to seventy hours a week in the dim light of steamy sweatshops. He joined the cutter's local union of the ILGWU, soon became head of it and, after a succession of jobs, was elected president of the entire ILGWU in 1932.

For the next two decades, Dubinsky fought and won a battle against Communist efforts to take over his union. He also fought steadily to improve working conditions for union members. In 1933, he won an unheard-of 35-hour work week for the union, and ILGWU members were the first to receive such fringe benefits as employer-financed vacations, medical and retirement plans, and severance pay.

As the ILGWU's funds grew, Dubinsky invested them in a number of different projects: low-cost housing in Puerto Rico, cooperative apartments on New York's Lower East Side, union buildings, and the 1,000 acre vacation resort for members in the Pennsylvania Pocono Mountains.

Always deeply involved in politics, Dubinsky helped organize the

American Labor Party in 1936 and New York's Liberal Party in 1944. He joined with John L. Lewis and others to form the Congress of Industrial Organizations (CIO) in 1935, but resigned when the American Federation of Labor (AFL) voted to suspend CIO unions. The ILGWU reaffiliated with the AFL in 1940. One of Dubinsky's primary concerns was to keep racketeering out of the unions, and it was partly due to his efforts that, in 1957, the AFL-CIO adopted its anti-racket codes.

CONTEMPORARY ISSUES
Situation 12

Does pressure by organized labor increase real income?

John came across an item in the *Wall Street Journal* about a recent 9.4 percent wage increase won by a labor union. A companion article discussed price increases that seemed certain to follow.

"You know, those labor guys must be shortsighted. They use their pressure to get big wage increases and then management simply turns around and raises prices. The net result is that labor simply helps to create inflation and doesn't get anything in terms of real income. It's a silly game."

"I agree," admitted Ray, "and there's a subtle point most people don't notice. When labor gets a big increase, in addition to raising prices, management also tries to figure out ways to cut costs. Why do you think we have so much automation in our economy? Because labor is pricing itself out of the market. When labor gets a big increase, management puts the engineers to work to develop automated equipment so they can reduce the number of workers needed."

"Okay, let's assume we're right—that most wage increases are reflected by price increases. What can be done about it?" asked John.

"One idea," answered Ray, "would be to let the federal government continue to experiment with wage-price guidelines. In this way government would set a formula as to how much wages could be raised each year and at the same time would impose another formula determining how much prices could be raised during the same period."

"Another idea," Ray continued, "would be to give all employees a course in "honest" economics. They would soon see there's no point in getting higher pay without a corresponding increase in productivity."

SITUATION EVALUATION

1. Is it true that many labor wage increases are offset by corresponding price increases?

2. What solutions do you see to the problem John and Ray discussed?

3. In view of wage increases, is inflation inevitable? Why or why not?

BUSINESS CHRONICLE

Trouble in paradise

Mr. King was shocked by two developments involving personnel. One concerned employee turnover, the other unionization. The company lost three good employees within a month. Sylvia Barrows (his talented advertising director), John Pitt (a promising young civil engineer), and Phil Cleaver (his assistant sales manager), all quit to take jobs with other companies. Furthermore, the office staff was considering whether to vote to join a union.

King was greatly disappointed because he felt he was a fair employer. He provided employees with attractive benefits few other companies offered. All employees lived in Kingmaker developments and paid about 40 percent less rent than the going rate. Also they had free use of facilities in all developments — parking, swimming pools, garden plots, tennis courts, etc. King felt that employees would identify more with the company if they lived on its premises so he made it more attractive for them to do so.

He interviewed each employee that left and also the spokesman for the office staff that had voted to consider unionizing. Key remarks from the interviews were:

> Sylvia Barrows: As a creative person, I don't feel happy in an environment that's so peaceful. I need turmoil, excitement, and interesting people around me if I am going to be creative. Living in a garden-type community is stifling.

> John Pitt: I feel forced to live in a Kingmaker development. As a result, I feel captive so I was just not happy. I want the feeling of being completely independent.

> Phil Cleaver: As a member of the sales department, I'm showing and praising Kingmaker developments all day long. When I go home at night, I just can't face up to more of the same.

Office Employee Representative: Sure we want the union, even if it costs the dues. It's not so much that we're unhappy, it's that we want what we're entitled to and not what is given to us paternalistically. We have no rights. We just have your charity.

QUESTIONS

1. Evaluate each response. What is the problem in each case, and what can be done about it?

2. Is this a case of dealing with each incident separately, or is overall company policy involved? If the latter, what policy changes do you recommend?

3. When valued employees quit, should management try to induce them to change their minds, or should it do nothing and let them leave?

APPLICATION EXERCISES

1. Below are given average weekly earnings in 1971 for production workers for selected states.

LOW-INCOME STATES		HIGH-INCOME STATES	
STATE	AMOUNT	STATE	AMOUNT
Mississippi	$103.83	Michigan	$188.19
West Virginia	104.00	Ohio	167.28
Arkansas	104.94	Washington	166.57
New Mexico	106.31	Indiana	161.20
South Carolina	108.38		

Prepare a paper in which you
  a. Explain the significant differences in wages for the production workers in different states despite the fact that the minimum wage law applies in all states.
  b. Explain how, if at all, wage differentials might be a factor in plant location.
  c. Discuss whether wage differentials among states are likely to increase or decrease in the years ahead.

2. Management and labor are constantly in conflict. Frequently each argues an exaggerated and totally selfish point of view. This not infrequently gives rise to proposals (and even actual legislation) that have the welfare of a vested interest at their base to the detriment of the welfare of citizens in general and the country as a whole. Identify the vested interest in each of the following, and discuss the probable impact of the proposal or action.

a. Last week Senator Blair introduced a bill to raise tariffs (a tax on imports) on steel. In the testimony he argued that Japanese steel is flooding the U.S. market. Steel is produced in Japan in plants that are more modern and more highly automated than are those in the United States.

b. Kent Allenson, a candidate for elective office in Akron, Ohio, proposes that all union wage agreements should contain an automatic cost-of-living increase clause so the value of the workingman's weekly paycheck is not eroded.

c. Keith Stanton, a junior in a liberal arts college, in a debate argued that labor unions are monopolies just like telephone companies and electric power companies; therefore the rates they set for wages, fringe benefits, and worker privileges should be regulated by the state as are utilities.

d. Whenever the XYZ rubber processing plant has a fire, which is frequent because rubber is shaped with heat and is flammable, the company policy is for workers to be laid off until the damaged section of the plant is able to produce again.

QUESTIONS

1. Explain the statement: "The only way the American standard of living can advance is through increases in per capita productivity."

2. What causes increased productivity? Explain why productivity has increased more significantly in some industries than in others.

3. How do you explain the fact that the United States has fallen behind other advanced nations in increases of output per man-hour? What can be done to remedy the situation?

4. Should women receive the same wages for the same work as men? Give the reasons for your stand on this matter.

5. How does it happen that so many people assume that corporate profits are as high as corporate wage payments? What can be done to correct this erroneous impression?

6. It is agreed that unemployment is wasteful and a national tragedy in any country where it exists to an appreciable degree. What can business do to prevent unemployment? What can the government do to prevent unemployment?

7. Trace the history of the American labor movement.

8. Do you feel it is ethical for white-collar employees such as school teachers to join unions? Give reasons for your position.

9. What prompts workers to join unions? Why do some workers prefer not to join unions? Do you expect unions to expand or decline in importance in the future?

13

CHAPTER 13

COST OF LABOR-MANAGEMENT UNREST
Issues and Duration of Work Stoppages.

MANAGEMENT VERSUS LABOR
Attitude of Management toward Labor. Union Policies Disliked by Management.

HOW MANAGEMENT ATTEMPTS TO RESTRAIN LABOR
Employers' Associations. Lobbies. Blacklists. Discrimination against Union Members. Lockouts. Strikebreakers. Injunctions.

LABOR VERSUS MANAGEMENT

HOW LABOR ATTEMPTS TO FURTHER ITS INTERESTS
Lobbies. Strikes. Boycotts.

THE COLLECTIVE-BARGAINING PROCEDURE
Preliminaries. The First Meeting. Subsequent Meetings. Mediation. Arbitration. The Union Contract.

LABOR LEGISLATION
The Wagner Act. The Taft-Hartley Act. The Future of Taft-Hartley: Labor's Prime Issue. State "Right-to-Work" Laws.

CURRENT LABOR OBJECTIVES
The Guaranteed Annual Wage. The Shorter Workweek.

labor - management relations

An interesting story about the late United Auto Workers' president, Walter Reuther, subtly illustrates one kind of labor-management conflict. When Reuther was being shown through an ultramodern Ford plant, a Ford official proudly pointed to some new automatically controlled machines and jokingly asked, "How are you union people going to collect union dues from these guys?" Answered Mr. Reuther, "How are you going to get them to buy Fords?"

Questions regarding the cost of labor unrest, the reasons behind strikes, how labor-management conflicts are resolved, and the role of government in settling labor-management differences deserve careful analysis by business students.

COST OF LABOR-MANAGEMENT UNREST

In 1971, more than 62 million man-days were lost because of strikes and related work stoppages. This enormous waste of human productivity has severe negative effects. Not long ago, a longshoremen's strike lasting ninety-four days cost the nation $100 million each day by government estimates. The strike hurt not only labor and management; it also had a serious negative effect on our international balance of payments, which in turn affects the value of the dollar.

While on strike, workers endure financial hardships. As a strike wears on, debts accumulate, buying is postponed, and the worker and his family must do without goods and services they normally enjoy. Even if higher wages—the most common goal of strikes—are attained, it may be months or even years before the added income equals the wages lost during the strike.

The owners of a strike-bound business suffer too, because profits cannot be made when production is stopped. Even in productive periods, the difference between profit and loss is often small, and if there is a strike, the affected business may close its doors.

The effect of a strike in a major industry, such as steel, causes thousands of other businesses to suffer. Retailers feel an economic pinch because of workers' decreased purchasing power. Since a firm on strike has no need for raw materials, parts, and new machinery, companies that sell these products must often curtail their production.

Issues and duration of work stoppages

As shown in Table 13–1, the major issue in most work stoppages is general wage changes. The number of persons involved and the number of idle man-days are also given in the table. Other major causes of work stoppages are other union contractual matters, union organization and security, dissatisfaction with plant administration, and interunion or intraunion matters.

MANAGEMENT VERSUS LABOR

The fundamental reason for disputes between labor and management is the difference in viewpoints. Management, which represents stockholders, feels obligated to earn the greatest possible profit. Management knows that profits are essential to the very life of the business and to the private enterprise system, for without them business cannot compete, modernize, or expand.

Organized labor, being responsible to employees, is concerned with obtaining concessions from management in the form of higher wages, shorter hours, better working conditions, and other benefits. Since these concessions, if granted, often reduce the profit possibilities of the business, management, remembering its primary responsibility to the welfare of the business and its owners, tends to resist the demands of organized labor.

Table **13–1**
Work Stoppages—Major Issues and Duration: 1971

MAJOR ISSUES AND DURATION	WORK STOPPAGES	WORKERS INVOLVED (1,000)	MAN-DAYS IDLE DURING YEAR (1,000)
MAJOR ISSUES			
All issues	**5,135**	**3,263**	**47,417**
General wage changes	2,598	2,133	31,693
Supplementary benefits	40	77	2,800
Wage adjustments	159	94	575
Hours of work	5	2	4
Other contractual matters	116	50	5,048
Union organization and security	482	179	3,327
Job security	210	105	1,007
Plant administration	904	507	2,300
Other working conditions	155	41	267
Interunion or intraunion matters	415	72	350
Not reported	51	4	46
DURATION			
All stoppages	**5,150**	**3,273**	**62,101**
1 day	673	185	185
2–3 days	688	769	1,374
4–6 days	642	252	895
7–14 days	886	741	4,099
15–29 days	788	614	7,192
30–59 days	734	385	11,034
60–89 days	364	174	7,527
90 days and over	375	153	29,795

Source: *Statistical Abstract of the United States, 1972*, p. 244.

What conclusions can you draw from the issues for striking?

Attitude of management toward labor

Management is somewhat divided in its attitude toward labor. At one extreme, some business leaders feel union activity is fundamentally wrong. These executives regard labor as a commodity to be purchased and used in much the same manner as machinery and raw materials. They agree that employees should be provided with adequate working conditions and a reasonable income; but they feel that basic decisions pertaining in any way to the operation of the business, including policies regarding hiring, compensating, and supervising workers, should be made exclusively by management.

After all, they contend, the business belongs to the owners, and decisions on how it is run are an inherent right of ownership. Those who have provided the capital assume the financial risks of business failure and often deprive themselves so that the business can grow and prosper. Therefore, management should refrain from giving anything to labor that would adversely affect the best interests of the stockholders or the future growth of the business. When management views organized labor in this manner, it will go to great lengths to prevent unions from being formed in its company.

At the other extreme, many businessmen accept labor unions as an integral part of the American system and see no inherent evil in labor unions as such. These management people believe that workers deserve the right to organize and to express themselves freely on matters that concern them. Some executives feel it is more efficient to deal with labor in an organized manner than to discuss job matters with each employee.

Union policies disliked by management

Though there are different attitudes toward unions, management in general agrees that union influence is too great and should be curbed, and virtually all executives and owners of businesses are opposed to the following union tactics:

1. Strikes of all kinds

2. Deliberate curtailment of daily output

3. Interference in the hiring, promotion, transfer, demotion, and dismissal of employees

4. Interference with management's traditional rights and prerogatives pertaining to the introduction of new machinery and changes in production schedules and production methods

5. "Featherbedding," a practice that calls for employment of workers who are not needed—for example, the employment of a fireman on a diesel locomotive

HOW MANAGEMENT ATTEMPTS TO RESTRAIN LABOR

Employers' associations

The major purpose of employers' associations (groups of employers acting together) is to present a solid front in management's dealings with labor. The associations may be formed on a city, regional, or national basis. Employers' associations differ greatly in size, type, structure, and scope and are most important in those industries where workers are highly unionized. Some operate on a full-time basis, while others remain dormant until labor unrest develops. Two examples of the more than two thousand such associations are the National Association of Manufacturers and the Appalachian Coal Association — both very active.

Lobbies

Management actively promotes federal and state legislation designed to restrict union power and influence. When an important labor law is being considered in Congress, management, either through employers' associations or independently, exerts pressure on lawmakers to pass, defeat, or amend the proposed legislation. Advertisements in magazines and newspapers; letters, telegrams, and personal visits to influential people; and speeches on radio and television are some methods used to lobby for particular legislation.

Blacklists

Although illegal under federal law, the blacklist, a tabulation of the names of union troublemakers and organizers, is sometimes circulated among employers. The objective is to prevent the hiring of people who might cause employers difficulty either by forming a union in the company or by inciting existing unions to make more demands.

Discrimination against union members

Another illegal tactic sometimes used by management to curb unions is discrimination against employees who belong to unions or who are known union sympathizers. This discrimination may take one of two forms. Management may attempt to find a "reason" for discharging the suspected employee, or it may transfer the worker to a less interesting, lower-paying job. Such practices, which frighten some employees who want to keep their present jobs, are used in department stores, hotels, and other nonfactory business establishments, where labor is less likely to be unionized.

Lockouts

As the name suggests, a lockout occurs when an employer refuses to permit workers to enter the plant until they agree to withdraw their demands. Once a common management technique, the lockout is rarely used now.

Strikebreakers

While a strike is in progress, management may hire new employees in an effort to cause regular workers to return to work out of fear that their jobs might be lost permanently. The new employees are called "scabs" by the striking workers. On occasion, management personnel attempt to operate the business by doing the work of the strikers, in the hope that the strikers will ultimately concede.

Injunctions

An injunction is a court order directing a person or persons to refrain from a certain act or acts. Injunctions against labor unions are designed to protect the employer interests by holding off strikes, boycotts, or picketing that might cause injury to the employer's position and established relations with customers and employees. Though injunctions can be granted to either labor or management, they are chiefly a device of management. But legal restrictions have made it virtually impossible for private employers to obtain labor injunctions except in instances of violence or fraud.

Injunctions issued by the federal government to prevent work stoppage are fairly common, especially in industries that are critically important to the economy. The right to strike is sometimes abridged by injunction when the economic security of the nation is endangered.

LABOR VERSUS MANAGEMENT

Just as management feels it has certain prerogatives, labor also believes that it is entitled to certain rights. Workers feel they have a vested interest in their jobs. The employee who has spent months or years learning how to do his work feels that, in a sense, he *owns* his job. Consequently, he thinks that he should have something to say about such matters as the introduction of machinery or an increase in the output expected of him.

Labor feels that employees are just as essential to the success of business as are capital and management. It is obvious, labor argues, that there could be no management or owners if there were no employees.

Another right claimed by labor is equal opportunity. It is unfair, they say, to penalize a group because it does not have certain advantages, such as a college education, that others enjoy. Similarly, labor leaders contend that it is unfair for management to dictate the working policies that labor must abide by; labor too should have a voice in such policies.

HOW LABOR ATTEMPTS TO FURTHER ITS INTERESTS

Methods used by labor to further its interests closely parallel those used by management. To a much greater extent labor depends on organized strength (which it obtains through the formation of unions) to gain its objectives.

Lobbies

Like management, labor relies extensively on lobbying and various forms of propaganda to influence legislation at state and federal levels and thus gain public sympathy for its cause. Unions are active in political campaigns. Some labor organizations own newspapers and buy radio and television time to further the interests of labor.

Strikes

A strike, labor's ultimate weapon, is a deliberate work stoppage initiated by the union to force management to grant concessions. Often, strikes are called during the busiest season of the year, on the theory that at such times labor can force management's hand more quickly. For example, newspaper employees might strike or threaten to strike in December, when the newspaper stands to lose the most advertising revenue.

Early strikes were not well organized, often being spontaneous in nature. Today, however, strikes often are planned carefully. The more common kinds of strikes are the following:

1. <u>Walkout strike</u>. Workers leave their jobs and refuse to return until their demands are met. Picketing is a device used in conjunction with these strikes. The union posts members around the strike-bound company's premises in order to persuade nonstrikers and customers not to enter and also to gain public sympathy.

2. <u>Slowdown strike</u>. Workers work but only with token production.

Management is not notified officially, and therefore wages continue.

3. <u>Sympathy strike</u>. This type of strike is called (infrequently) to support workers in other strike-bound plants or industries.

4. <u>Wildcat strike</u>. This is a strike where workers walk off the job without the sanction of its national headquarters or even the local union.

5. <u>Jurisdictional strike</u>. This is a strike called by a union vying with a rival union for recognition as the sole representative of workers.

Boycotts

A boycott is a concerted effort to stop the purchase of goods or services from a company until it grants the boycotters' demands. In the case of labor boycotts, if the employees refuse to patronize only their own employer, the action is called a "primary" boycott. A "secondary" boycott occurs when employees refuse to handle, process, manufacture, or transport goods of a second employer who is accused of being unfair to his employees. A variation of the secondary boycott occurs when workers in a unionized plant refuse to use tools, parts, or equipment made by nonunion workers in a supplier plant. The secondary boycott is illegal, but nevertheless it is used.

Though boycotts and strikes may or may not occur concurrently, their purpose is the same—to force management to yield to labor's demands.

THE COLLECTIVE-BARGAINING PROCEDURE

Despite the large amount of publicity given to strikes, the great majority of all labor-management disputes are settled with no interruption of production. Differences between labor and management generally are settled by *collective bargaining*, which may be defined as the procedure in which representatives of management and labor meet to discuss and resolve their differences. It is a form of negotiation used by employers and employees in an attempt to reach agreement on mutual responsibilities and activities for a stated period of time. When such agreement is reached, it will be embodied in a written contract.

Collective bargaining is most often carried on between management and labor in a single company. Frequently, however, it is conducted between representatives of management and labor from several companies in the same industry and in the same geographical area. This is called "area-wide" collective bargaining. If the negotiations are held for an entire industry, as is the case with steel and coal, the procedure is called "industry-wide" collective bargaining.

Collective bargaining is now fully accepted by both management and labor. Although instances of failure are many, all concerned, including the public and government, see in collective bargaining a useful method for maintaining labor peace.

Preliminaries

The first step in the collective-bargaining procedure is for representatives of labor and management to agree to meet. Management in larger companies is represented by the director of labor relations or industrial relations. In smaller organizations the personnel director or a hired outside labor-relations specialist may be management's representative. Other top-management executives may also be present. Labor is represented by local labor leaders, the union business agent, and sometimes representatives from national headquarters. Each side frequently employs attorneys, economists, and other consultants to help in the negotiations.

Preparations for the negotiations usually begin far in advance of the first meeting. Each side tries to anticipate the actions of the other. Management attempts to discover the demands of labor, and the union makes an effort to learn what management's reactions will be to their demands.

To support their positions at the bargaining conference, leaders of both management and labor collect facts on a wide variety of topics such as (1) working conditions, (2) economic prospects for the immediate future, (3) cost of living and workers' real wages, and (4) conditions in other similar plants.

The information collected for each group is similar, but, for obvious reasons, interpretations differ. Management uses the data to show why concessions on its part are not practical or even needed, while labor leaders do just the opposite, attempting to show why management should make concessions.

The choice of a site for negotiations may help determine whether or not the meeting will be successful. If the bargaining is between the management and employees of a single plant, there is a choice of meeting on the company premises or at some "neutral" place, such as a local hotel. The chief advantage of meeting in company conference rooms is convenience. However, since labor representatives may not feel at home in the executive offices, a neutral location is often used.

The first meeting

The atmosphere of the first meeting between the representatives of management and labor often determines whether the succeeding negotiations will be successful. The atmosphere should be one of mutual respect; the conference should be regarded as a meeting of peers.

One purpose of the first meeting is to establish rules and policies for future conferences and to agree on such matters as the length and frequency of meetings to be held. Another purpose is to give labor leaders an opportunity to present concrete proposals to management. A short, generalized discussion of the proposals may follow, but a detailed review of labor's demands ordinarily is postponed until the second meeting of the two groups, when management may present a counterproposal.

Subsequent meetings

In its counterproposal, management may agree to minor requests by labor, but on major demands, such as wage increases or shorter hours, a compromise solution is usually suggested. The difference between the union's demands and management's response is the area of bargaining.

Tension often runs high during collective-bargaining conferences. Both sides realize much is at stake, and frequently neither party wants to make any real concessions. Usually, however, some form of compromise agreement is reached; when that happens, a strike is avoided.

Despite the usually sincere efforts of both parties, agreement on certain issues cannot always be reached. Labor may still contend that their demands are not excessive, and management may insist that granting such demands would be detrimental. When such a stalemate occurs, there are still two peaceful methods of settlement: mediation and arbitration.

Mediation

Mediation is an attempt to settle labor disputes with the assistance of a disinterested third party. The third party, which may be composed of one or several individuals, listens to the arguments of each side and attempts to reconcile the differences. Mutually satisfactory mediators are available from several sources. Frequently, community leaders, such as professors or city officials, are asked to act in this capacity. There has been a tendency for federal, state, and local government agencies to provide assistance in mediation. The Federal Mediation and Conciliation Service, an independent agency of the federal government, has a staff of several hundred mediators to help settle disputes threatening interstate commerce, national defense, or public health and welfare. Most states provide mediation services.

It is important to note that the objective of mediation is not to settle disagreements by *order,* since neither party is obligated to accept suggestions. Rather, mediators try to help labor and management reconcile their differences by suggesting compromise solutions. Mediation is not always successful, and a strike may still occur. Even after a strike is under way, however, mediators may continue to work toward a settlement, in order to prevent a long strike.

Arbitration

Arbitration and mediation are essentially the same but for one major difference: The mediator can only *recommend* solutions to labor-management differences; the arbitrator is empowered to *determine* the solution. When arbitration is used, both parties agree in advance to abide by the decision. The arbitrator plays the role of a judge. Labor and management jointly designate the arbitrator or arbitrators to ensure obtaining people who are not prejudiced. Most frequently, union contracts call for the American Arbitration Association, an independent agency for arbitration of labor disputes, or the Federal Mediation and Conciliation Service to act as arbitrators.

Ninety percent of all contractual agreements between labor and management stipulate that if the parties cannot reach an agreement, issues in dispute will be referred to arbitration. Some contracts specify which issues will or will not be arbitrated. Frequently excluded are wage issues, production standards, and other bread-and-butter issues.

There is considerable interest in legislating *compulsory* arbitration. If arbitration were compulsory, strikes would be avoided.

The union contract

Successful collective bargaining results in a set of rules and procedures that constitute a legal document known as the union contract. Once it is adopted, both parties are legally bound to abide by its terms and provisions for the life of the agreement, usually one, two, or three years. A majority of contracts provide that they shall continue in effect after their termination dates if no action is taken to amend or terminate them.

Union contracts are frequently lengthy documents ranging up to twenty pages or more. The following are some areas commonly covered:

1. Management and union rights. (Management rights include direction of the work force, determination of products to be made and their prices, and control of production methods. Union rights include solicitation for union membership, collection of dues, plant access by union representatives and use of company bulletin boards.)

2. Union security provisions such as that it must be a union shop in which specified classifications of workers must belong to unions, and the checkoff (deduction of union dues from wages by the company).

3. Wages, including clauses concerning how wages will be adjusted according to the cost of living. (Call-back procedures, shift differentials, job classifications, time-study procedures, and wage-incentive provisions are the wage areas most frequently covered.)

4. Work or pay guarantees and unemployment pay.

5. Employee benefits (most frequently, life and health insurance and pensions).

6. Standard work hours and overtime.

7. Working conditions (such as health and safety considerations, physical examinations, and guarantees against discrimination).

8. Holidays, leaves of absence, and absenteeism from work.

9. Lunch, rest, and cleanup periods.

10. Company rules.

11. Disciplinary measures (loss of seniority and suspension are the most commonly used measures).

12. Procedures for handling grievances and arbitration.

13. Strikes and lockouts.

14. Temporary employees.

15. Grounds for discharge; discharge and appeals procedure.

16. Separation pay and resignation.

17. Seniority, layoff, promotion, and transfer.

18. Retirement.

19. Provision for contract renewal.

Grievance procedure   One important provision specifies the *grievance procedure* (see Figure 13–1). Grievances or complaints are bound to arise over such matters as seniority, work assignments, transfer, and piece-

Figure **13-1**

Steps in the Grievance Machinery of Companies with Union Contracts

If grievances are not settled at one level, they are carried to the next level.

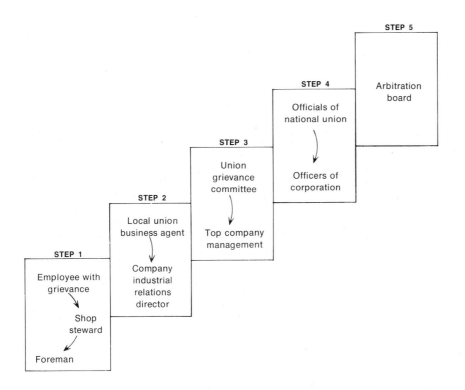

work rates. Even when these topics are discussed in the contract, arguments can arise over interpretations.

Grievance procedure usually stipulates that when there is an employee complaint, the union representatives will present the grievance to the employee's immediate superior. If the supervisor does not correct the complaint, the union official presents it to successively higher officials in the company. If the highest company official does not settle the grievance, the case is then appealed to an outside arbitration board, whose decision is final and binding on both parties.

Even in nonunion plants, wise employers establish an orderly grievance procedure so that minor dissatisfactions can be kept from becoming major issues. Grievance procedures give employees a chance to "let off steam" and tend to improve morale.

LABOR LEGISLATION

Federal legislation pertaining to labor unions dates back to the nineteenth century. Current labor policy, however, is based on two important laws: the Wagner Act and the Taft-Hartley Act. In addition, fair employment practice laws have been enacted by Congress and by some state legislatures.

The Wagner Act

The severe economic depression of the early 1930s and a concurrent increase in union membership gave impetus to the passage of the Wagner Act, also known as the National Labor Relations Act of 1935. The chief purpose of this law was to reduce strikes and industrial unrest by setting forth as a national policy the right of workers in any plant to organize and bargain collectively with their employers. The act strengthened the position of labor greatly; management regarded it as "pro-labor." The most important provisions of the act declared it unlawful for employers to

1. Interfere in any way with employees' right to bargain collectively

2. Dominate or interfere with the formation or administration of a union

3. Refuse to bargain collectively with employees

4. Discriminate in any way against employees because of their union affiliation

To administer the act, the National Labor Relations Board (NLRB) was established. This board was given two broad responsibilities. First, the board was to certify the appropriate bargaining representatives of the employees—to determine, in other words, whether the leaders were actually the chosen representatives of the majority of employees. Second, it was given authority to pass on alleged unfair labor practices. When a complaint is made, the board holds a hearing. If there is not sufficient evidence that management has acted in bad faith, the case is dropped. If the board believes management to be guilty, a cease and desist order is issued. The board has the power to call on federal courts to enforce its decisions.

From the date of its enactment, the Wagner Act was sharply criticized by management on the grounds that it was slanted in favor of labor and against management. Ultimately, agitation for a new national labor law resulted in the passage of the Taft-Hartley Act.

The Taft-Hartley Act

A major amendment to the Wagner Act, the Taft-Hartley Act, also known as the Labor-Management Relations Act of 1947, was enacted after a bitter battle in Congress. The chief objective of the Taft-Hartley Act is to equalize the rights and privileges of management and labor. The act gives management no new rights but seeks to balance power by withholding some of the prerogatives that had been extended to labor.

The Taft-Hartley Act declares that it is an unfair labor practice for an employer to

1. Encourage or discourage membership in any labor organization
2. Dominate or interfere with the formation and administration of any labor organization
3. Contribute financial or other support to any labor organization
4. Discriminate against an employee because of testimony the employee gives under the act
5. Refuse to bargain collectively with employees

Under the act, it is held unfair for labor organizations to

1. Restrain or coerce any employee in the exercise of rights guaranteed by law
2. Discriminate against any employee who has dropped out of the labor organization or who has been denied membership in the organization, unless the employee has failed to live up to an agreement requiring membership in a labor organization as a condition of employment
3. Attempt to cause the employer to discriminate against any employee in any way that would make him guilty of an unfair labor practice
4. Attempt to cause the employer to pay for services not performed (commonly called "featherbedding")
5. Refuse to bargain collectively with the employer

The Taft-Hartley Act, like the Wagner Act, is administered by the NLRB. In effect, the federal government now has more control over labor-management relationships than ever before. For instance, the President of the United States now has the power to ask for an injunction against strikers when the strike would endanger the health and welfare of the citizens.

The future of Taft-Hartley: labor's prime issue

The Taft-Hartley controversy is destined to become the major labor issue
in the years immediately ahead. In 1972, the Taft-Hartley Act was 25 years
old. The occasion of the silver anniversary caused many spokesmen concerned with the act to reflect about it. The *New York Times*[1] stated,
"Even though outright repeal was scrapped long ago as a primary labor
goal, the focus on political involvement and Congressional lobbying gets
stronger every year." The *Times* goes on to say that despite the feverish
conflict that surrounded the birth of Taft-Hartley, most authorities are
convinced that the law is an insignificant factor in basic industries. The
ban on the closed shop (where *prior* union membership is required for
employment) has become almost meaningless in certain industries with
strong unions. Court rulings have negated the supposed bans on featherbedding.

George Meany, President of the AFL, said, "The main impact of the
Taft-Hartley Act has been its adverse effect upon new organizing, and it
has had relatively little effect where unions were already strongly established by 1947. The act is largely concerned with regulating the conduct
of employees and unions during organizing campaigns."

R. Heath Larry, vice-chairman of the Board of United States Steel Corporation, made these observations:

> During the last 25 years, the United States has moved from the postwar time
> during which it seemed to have unquestioned industrial and economic
> superiority in the non-Communist world to a today in which its com-
> petitiveness in world markets is most seriously challenged. . . . The evidence
> is clear that real wages in the long-term improve only in relation to produc-
> tivity improvement, no matter how much dollar wages increase. . . . Our
> country is at a point where better economic results must be expected from
> the institution of collective bargaining — in terms of reducing the economic
> damage of strikes and strike threats, and in terms of achieving more con-
> structive trends in unit-labor costs.

State "right-to-work" laws

Growing out of the Labor-Management Act of 1947 are the so-called
right-to-work laws, which in 1972 were active in nineteen states. A right-
to-work law bans the union shop and all other forms of compulsory
unionism. Under these laws a person cannot be required to join a union
as a condition of employment. In the absence of such laws, union membership can be a condition of employment.

[1] The views quoted in this section appeared in "Taft-Hartley at 25 — How It Has Worked,"
New York Times, June 18, 1972.

Figure **13–2**
Twenty States with the Highest Union and Employee Association Membership

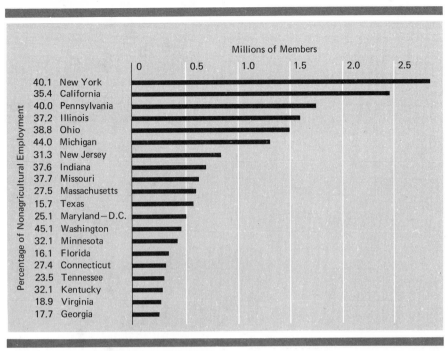

Source: U.S. Bureau of Labor Statistics; Road Maps of Industry, No. 1702, "Union Membership," The Conference Board, November 15, 1972.

Unions have bitterly assailed right-to-work laws and have kept them out of the most heavily industrialized states.

CURRENT LABOR OBJECTIVES

In addition to its major aim of changing the Taft-Hartley Act already discussed, labor focuses on the issues of the guaranteed annual wage and the shorter workweek.

The guaranteed annual wage

One of organized labor's objectives has been to secure guaranteed annual wage (GAW) agreements or guaranteed employment agreements with management. While various plans have been presented, all have one central purpose: to secure an agreement with management that all hourly

Figure **13-3**
Distribution of Labor Union and Employee Association Membership, 1970

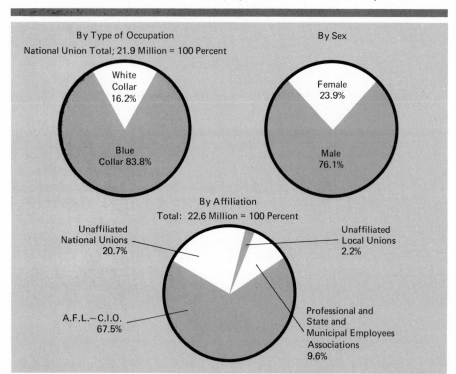

Source: U.S. Bureau of Labor Statistics; Road Maps of Industry, No. 1702, "Union Membership," The Conference Board, November 15, 1972.

paid employees will have steady, year-round work with a guaranteed minimum annual income.

Organized labor supports the philosophy of the guaranteed annual wage for two basic reasons: (1) A guaranteed annual wage would add security to the wage earner's job. (2) Such a plan would tend to stabilize income and thus increase and stabilize the demand for goods and stimulate employment. The result would be a higher standard of living for all.

Management presents forceful arguments against the guaranteed annual wage. A guaranteed annual wage is impractical, management argues, because it is often not feasible to schedule production at the same rate the year round. The demand for many products is seasonal, so that there are periods when production (and employment) are higher than at other times. It is economically unsound to pay workers when they are not working. A guaranteed annual wage would tend to raise production costs, and this would raise the price of goods to consumers. Labor costs, management continues, should vary in accordance with the amount of goods produced.

It is difficult to predict the future of the guaranteed wage. The increasing pressure of unions and the trend toward year-round buying of many products, however, are two important factors that suggest the guaranteed annual wage in a variety of forms will certainly be more common in the years ahead.

The shorter workweek

For many years unions have been very active in promoting shorter workweeks. Emphasis now is on reducing what has become the traditional forty-hour workweek to thirty-five, or even thirty-two, hours. Labor leaders contend, first, that a shorter workweek can be one important answer to the unemployment problems created by automation and, second, that a shorter workweek is deserved on the basis of great advances in worker productivity.

In all probability, the workweek will be shortened in the decade ahead. However, this trend is not necessarily in our best economic interest. A shorter workweek may lower productivity and productivity is linked to ability to compete in international markets, which in turn affects the strength of the dollar and inflation. A further shortening of the workweek may serve to increase the erosion of the value of the dollar and the deteriorating U.S. position in international markets. Furthermore, a nation's standard of living depends on how much it produces. In other words, production determines the size of the pie to be divided. When the pie gets smaller, the pieces that can be consumed are also smaller.**

SPECIAL READINGS

** Struggle for Identity: The Silent Revolution Against Corporate Conformity by Roger M. D'Aprix. Homewood, Ill.: Dow Jones-Irwin, Inc., 1972. D'Aprix maintains that the basis of unionism is partially a dissatisfaction with and a questioning of corporate practices — in other words, that joining a union is a form of rebellion. He maintains further that discontent occurs because employees are fighting to retain their individuality in an age of mass production, of look alikes and think alikes. The book attempts to assist the employee to deal with the corporation on a personal level.

The author states that, "The fundamental problem with our organizations today is the absence of the all-important feeling of belonging to a worthwhile enterprise where one can grow and contribute, where one can feel he is part of a cause to which he can dedicate his talents and energies. The crisis is a crisis of spirit, a crisis of meaning, a crisis of alienation from the task and from the other people in the organization." Although the author has a penchant for over-dramatizing, what he says and has assembled is well worth considering.

The book has four parts, the last of which is "A montage of ideas and actual experiences to contemplate." These consist mostly of ideas from people employed in corporations and provide a valuable insight into matters that concern the corporate employee. The book has a modern approach and discusses many changes that are currently taking place in the corporation.

PEOPLE AND THEIR IDEAS
Henry Ford

The father of mass-produced automobiles

Henry Ford's strategy of growth through mass production resulted in changes in the economic and social life of the United States and the world that were nothing short of revolutionary. It created a new system of transportation, ended rural isolation, and radically altered the lives of millions of people. By producing a cheap but efficient car that would sell to millions and by raising wages so that his employees would have greater purchasing power, Ford made lasting contributions to society. In realizing his first objective, he developed the moving assembly line and other methods of modern manufacturing procedures, thereby creating the modern automobile industry. In achieving his second goal, he helped to increase the consumer market for industrial products.

Henry Ford was born on a farm near Dearborn, Michigan, in 1863. After finishing grade school, he left the farm to work as a machinist's apprentice at the James Flower & Brothers machine shop in Detroit, and then at the Detroit Drydock Company. He returned to Dearborn to try his hand at farming but found it unrewarding and came back to the city in 1891 as an engineer for the Edison Illuminating Company. Ford began spending all his spare time experimenting with his plan for a horseless carriage. In 1896, he hade a successful trial run with his vehicle and acquired a reputation for making and driving racing cars. By 1902, he had become associated with two automotive companies, the Detroit Motor Company, which failed, and the Henry Ford Company, which later was reorganized as the Cadillac Motor Company.

In 1903, with the aid of Alexander Y. Malcolmson, a Detroit coal dealer, Ford formed the Ford Motor Company. For 25.5 percent of company stock, Ford contributed some patents and a new, unfinished car. Other stockholders included James Couzens, who became the business brains of the company, and the Dodge brothers, who built the engines for the car.

Before long, controversy struck the company. Malcolmson wanted the firm to produce a high-priced, six cylinder Model K, while Ford insisted that they concentrate on his light, low-priced car. The issue was resolved in 1906 when Malcolmson sold out to Ford, thereby giving him control of 58.5 percent of the company's stock.

In 1908 the first Model T appeared for sale, and in 1913 in a new plant in Highland Park, Michigan, it became the first car to be produced on a moving assembly line. By 1914, the plant was turning out over one thousand vehicles a day, and the average labor time for assembling a chassis had dropped from twelve hours and twenty-eight minutes to one hour and thirty-three minutes. The company's profits had become so large that in January 1915, Ford announced a sensational 5-dollar-a-day minimum wage for his employees. But when he proposed to plow all earnings back into the company, the Dodge brothers brought suit against him. In 1917 the Supreme Court ruled that profits permitted both expansion and payment of dividends. After this decision Ford announced he would form a new company; in 1919, he purchased all minority stockholdings and became sole owner of the half-billion dollar company.

During the early 1920s Ford commanded over 55 percent of the automobile market. As the decade progressed, however, the demand for cars leveled off, and marketing became a more serious challenge than production—a fact Ford refused to accept. Moreover, Ford's competitors were making advances in appearance, comfort, and technology that Ford was slow to adopt. In 1927 and 1928 management and marketing weaknesses finally overwhelmed the company. The Model T was abandoned, and the assembly plants were closed for retooling for at least six months and did not return to full-scale production for more than a year. Ford never fully recovered from the changeover. The new Model A was not able to achieve the popularity of the Model T, and General Motors obtained a foothold in the market it has never lost.

In 1936 Ford established the Ford Foundation, which, on his death and the deaths of his wife Clara and his son Edsel, received control of resources in excess of half a billion dollars. Ford died in 1947; the foundation continues today as a powerful force in our society and an impressive memorial to his accomplishments.

CONTEMPORARY ISSUES
Situation 13

Is stronger anti-strike legislation needed?

John was shocked when he reviewed the statistics in Table 13–1. "Imagine, in nineteen seventy-one, more than sixty-two million man-days were lost because of strikes, and three-hundred and seventy-five strikes lasted three months or more. Something must be done to reduce this enormous economic waste. Just look at what strikes cost us: lost production, lost income, reduced consumption, plus a lot of unpleasantness between workers and the employers. And strikes hurt other industries because they don't get deliveries of component parts and raw materials on time.

"In a nutshell," he continued, "strikes go against free enterprise, and all of us suffer. I think we need really strict anti-strike legislation."

"Well, first of all sixty-two and a half million lost man-days is only a very small fraction of one percent of the total," Ray countered. "Anyway, if unions couldn't strike, what power would they have left? If you believe in our system, then you've got to have a labor movement with real power, and the strike is the most potent weapon they have. Besides, within the framework of our system, we have ways to settle differences without resorting to the power of the federal government."

"I think my rights are being violated when I can't buy something because labor in a certain industry called a strike," John replied. "And strikes are grossly unfair to the management of the company involved, the stockholders, other industries, and employees who work for other companies. I'm in favor of stopping strikes and will support any legislation needed to do it."

"You don't realize how you would upset the system's balance," said Ray. "You've got to allow labor unions freedom to act aggressively. Management, stockholders, the public, all have potent weapons too. Our balance of power has done very well for this country in the past, and it will continue to do so in the future, if people like you don't tamper with it."

SITUATION EVALUATION

1. What are the economic losses and gains that result from strikes?

2. Estimate the probable long-run results of a law to prohibit strikes.

3. Who do you feel has the better argument — John or Ray? Why?

BUSINESS CHRONICLE

Fight the union or what?

Mr. King called a meeting of his key executives to decide what to do about the office workers' interest in unionizing. The highlights of the opinions that were expressed are:

Gerry Adams, Personnel Manager: If they want to unionize, it's their business. They know they may lose some benefits they now have, but they probably feel they'll get others they don't have. I don't think it will make any difference in how well they do their work. Good employees are good; weak ones aren't. It has nothing to do with unions, so let

them do what they want. Furthermore, there is no saying they will
vote for the union. They may reject
it.

Cliff Brown, General Manager: I hate to see them pay dues when
they won't get anything for it. It's up
to us to present the other side of the
coin. The union organizers are feeding them their slanted version —
we've got to at least balance that out.

Mildred Payton, Office Manager: They really don't know when they
are well off. I think if we'd let just
two ring leaders go, we'd have heard
the last of this. We'll lose control if
the union comes in here.

Stanley Mitkopf, Chief Accountant: Mildred's right. We can stop the
union coming in here. We've got a
good office force. They aren't really
unhappy. They know that basically
they're well off. There's just a couple
of rotten apples in the barrel. Let's
get rid of them and save the rest the
union dues. We'll save ourselves the
headaches that come with having a
union.

QUESTIONS

1. Appraise each view. What is the strength and weakness of each argument?

2. What position should the company take? Explain.

3. Does a union have an affect on the morale and performance of employees? Explain.

APPLICATION EXERCISES

1. Between 1955 and 1970 membership in white-collar unions increased
   by 26.5 percent while membership in blue-collar unions gained only
   12.1 percent. Prepare a paper in which you:

a. Explain why white-collar unions are growing faster than blue-collar unions, and

b. Discuss whether this trend is likely to continue.

2. A growing complaint about labor unions is that in the last 30 years there has been a general shift in power and control from the rank and file to the leaders, who keep themselves entrenched. As one critic put it, "Today a handful of old men in their 60s and 70s are the guardians of the welfare of millions of union members, about half of whom are under 40, and by 1980 the median will be 35." Another critic said, "Sure there are some leaders who want to bring young people into the labor movement, but there is a fear of strength of young people." Interview ten young people and discuss the following:

a. Are they pro- or anti-labor?

b. Why?

c. Should young people become active in the labor movement?

d. What can be done to make the labor movement of interest to young people?

Summarize your findings, and conclude with your own beliefs about labor.

3. In 1971, man-days idle during the year expressed as a percentage of estimated working time ranged from only 0.04 percent in New Hampshire to 2.06 in West Virginia. (Only one other state, Montana, with 1.12 percent had more than 0.5 percent lost time due to work stoppages.) How do you account for the significant time lost in West Virginia?

QUESTIONS

1. What methods are used by management to restrain labor power? Which of these methods seems most ethical to you? Why?

2. Define walkout strike, slowdown strike, sympathy strike, wildcat strike, jurisdictional strike, and boycott.

3. Do nonunion workers benefit in any way from gains made by union workers? Explain.

4. Define collective bargaining. What is its chief objective?

5. What is the difference between mediation and arbitration?

6. Should the trend toward a shorter workweek be continued, or should it be reversed in light of our balance of payments problem and the competition we face in world markets? Explain your answer.

7. What are the major provisions of the Taft-Hartley Act?

8. Are labor unions too powerful? What new labor legislation do you think is needed?

9. What does the government do to aid employment? Evaluate these measures. What else could be done?

10. What should the main thrust of labor demands be in the future?

5

production and the physical environment

Much of our most important production-related and environment-shaping activities—manufacturing, assembly of goods, a vast transportation network, spatial planning—takes place behind the scenes. It is not surprising then that most citizens do not know how we produce goods and how we shape our environment. The following chapters will acquaint you with the essentials of production and spatial manipulation needed to understand American business more fully.

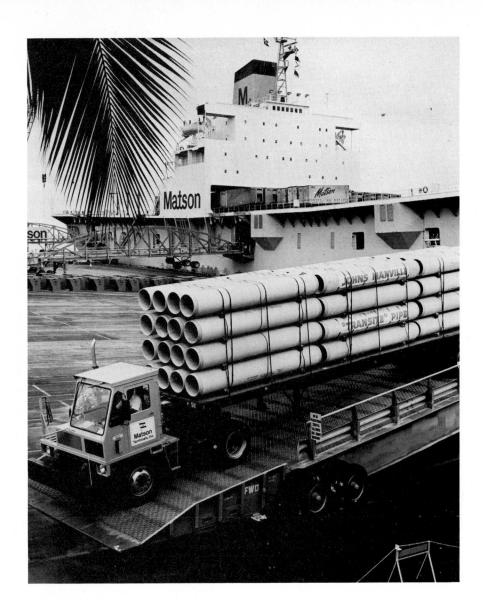

14
goods and services: their production and procurement

15
physical distribution and space logistics

16
business location, land use, and ecology

goods and services: their production and procurement 14

CHAPTER 14

CHARACTERISTICS OF OUR PRODUCTION SYSTEM
Mechanization. Automation. Standardization. Specialization.

PRODUCT DESIGN
Functional Design. Style Design. Package Design.

PRODUCTION PLANNING
Key Decision Area.

PRODUCTION CONTROL / THE METRIC SYSTEM

PURCHASING, BUYING, AND PROCURING GOODS AND SERVICES
Importance and Complexity of Acquiring Goods and Services.

INDUSTRIAL PURCHASING
Organization for Industrial Purchasing. The Purchasing Function. The Conceptual Change in Industrial Purchasing.

BUYING FOR RESALE: RESALE AND INDUSTRIAL BUYING COMPARED
Differences in Terminology. Differences in Buying Organization. Differences in Responsibility. Differences in Buying Methods.

GOVERNMENT PROCUREMENT
How Government Purchases Differ from Purchases by Private Businesses. Federal Procurement Policies. Notifying Prospective Suppliers of Government Needs. What Constitutes a Responsible Supplier? Prime Contractors and Subcontractors.

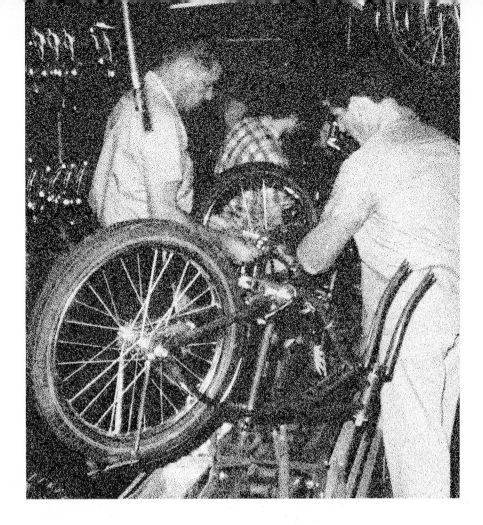

Production can be defined as the process by which raw materials are converted into useful goods capable of directly or indirectly satisfying human wants.

Our highly developed civilization is dependent on the nation's productive capacity. Almost everything we use in daily living has been manufactured, processed, or treated in some manner. Much of our food, which was once consumed in its natural form by primitive man, now goes through numerous manufacturing processes before it is consumed. Even commodities that do not change form, such as milk and meat, are processed. It is significant that the variety of products needed to satisfy human wants increases steadily, so there is a constantly increasing emphasis on production.

We depend on production, too, because manufacturing industries provide employment for approximately 30 percent of the total labor force. More people in the United States depend on production for income than on any other type of work activity. Retailers and wholesalers also depend on production, for without the output of factories there obviously would be no manufactured goods to sell.

In brief, the United States today enjoys its high standard of living largely because of its tremendous industrial productivity. But, why has the United States traditionally been a leader in production? An answer to this question is found in an analysis of the characteristics of our industrial system.

CHARACTERISTICS OF OUR PRODUCTION SYSTEM

Key factors that contribute to the efficiency of our production system include mechanization, automation, standardization, and specialization.

The term "mass production" refers to the large-scale production of goods using standardized, interchangeable parts. The objective of mass production is to lower costs of production.

Mechanization

The Machine Age is a relatively recent period in the history of man. In 1850, the average worker worked seventy hours a week and, chiefly with his muscles and those of animals, produced roughly 27 cents worth of goods per hour. The average worker in 1965, using virtually no animal muscle and a great deal less human physical effort, produced $2.70 worth of goods per hour. By 1975 each worker will be producing almost twelve times as much as the worker of 1850 (see Figure 14–1).

Almost all industries are now highly mechanized. Increased mechanization leads to greater worker productivity, which in turn leads to lower production costs. Moreover, in most instances, machines produce superior, as well as more uniform, products.

Automation**

A relatively new term in industry is *automation*, which can be defined as the complete performance of a complex mechanical process without human intervention. The objective of automation is to eliminate as much hand labor and manual operation of machines as possible. In a sense, automation is an extension of mechanization. Mechanization substitutes mechanical effort for human effort, but man must still operate and control the machine. In true automation, the manual control of machines is eliminated. For example, machines start and stop themselves automatically, and the levels and weights of packages they fill are checked and corrected

Figure **14–1**
Trends in Productivity

In rate of increase, U.S. productivity lags behind other advanced countries.

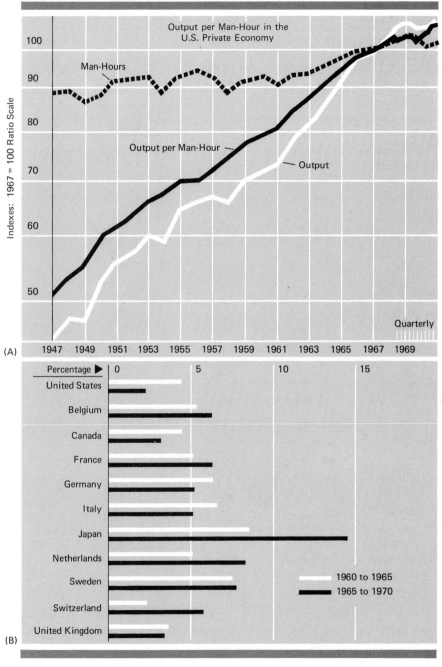

Source: "Trends in Productivity," Road Maps of Industry, No. 1675, The Conference Board, October 1, 1971.

How do you account for the fact that the United States is
lagging in rate of productivity increase?

by electric eyes. Under automation then the machine not only does the work, but it controls and checks what is done as well.

Automation is spurred on by several factors. First, human labor is the most expensive manufacturing element. Thus, anything that can reduce the labor needed to produce goods tends to lower cost. As unions demand higher wages, management turns more and more to automation.

Second, many jobs have become too complicated for human beings to perform competently and efficiently; many industrial operations are much too rapid for the human eye to observe and react to. Human beings are less accurate than carefully constructed machines.

Third, some industrial activities are harmful or unsafe. Chemical industries, munitions factories, and the new atomic energy installations, especially, have potential hazards. Automation reduces the potential number of accidents.

Nevertheless, the spread of automation is still feared by many, especially some labor leaders, who express concern that it may cause mass unemployment. In this context, the following two historical examples from publications of the times may be illuminating.

COTTON TEXTILES, 1760–1835

At the accession of George III (1760), the manufacture of cotton supported hardly more than 40,000 persons; but since machines have been invented by means of which one worker can produce as much yarn as 200 or 300 persons could at that time, and one person can print as much material as could 100 persons at that time, 1,500,000 or 37 times as many as formerly can now earn their bread from this work.

And yet there are still many, even scholars and members of Parliament, who are so ignorant or so blinded by prejudice as to raise a pathetic lament over the increase and spread of the manufacturing system . . . there are persons who regard it as a great disaster when they hear that 150,000 persons in our spinning works now produce as much yarn as could hardly be spun with the little handwheel by 40,000,000.

These people appear to cherish the absurd opinion that if there were no machines, manufacture would really give employment to as many millions as now; nor do they reflect that the whole of Europe would be inadequate for all this work; and that in that case a fifth of the whole population would need to be occupied with cotton-spinning alone! Both experience and reflection teach us just the contrary; and we should certainly maintain that, if we still had to spin with the handwheel today, cotton manufacture would employ only a fifth of the present number.[1]

DIAL TELEPHONES, 1920–60

Since 1920 the Bell System has been building the world's largest computer—the nationwide dial telephone system. About 96 percent of the 59 million Bell System telephones are now dial operated.

The 730,000 men and women now working for the Bell System companies are more than two and one-half times the number employed in 1920, when dial conversion began.

Service has improved tremendously. A three-minute cross-country call costs $2.25 today [1960]. In 1920 the price was $16.50.

Without automation, telephone service long ago would have been priced out of reach of a large portion of present subscribers. It is also a fact that, had automation not taken place, it would not now be possible to get enough qualified people to provide the volume and scope of telephone service which the public, industry and government need and have today.[2]

Despite examples such as these, there are very real, very serious problems that arise when large numbers of workers are replaced by machines. However, automation is a manifestation of a basic drive in American business—the drive to do things better at a lower cost—and it would certainly be foolhardy to throttle a drive that can produce such abundance. Furthermore, production curtailment always means a parallel curtailment of standard of living, for a society cannot enjoy what it does not produce. And if the spread of automation were actively impeded and some jobs were saved, the lost competitive position of the United States in world markets to nations that do push automation would create even more unemployment and erosion of the value of the dollar.

While automation causes some to suffer short-range hardships, a convincing case can be built for its long-range benefits. Automation creates jobs for more highly skilled employees, since machines must be designed, built, serviced, and controlled by highly skilled personnel; primarily, the routine jobs are eliminated. We would do better to find solutions (such as retraining) for those whose jobs are lost than to hobble our economy by curtailing automation.

[1] Edward Baines, *History of the Cotton Manufacture in Great Britain*, 1835.
[2] Excerpts from American Telephone and Telegraph Company statement to the Automation Subcommittee of the Joint Economic Committee, July 1, 1960.

Standardization

Large-scale production depends on standardization, which concerns the product and the parts that go into it — their size and shape and the quality of materials used. A *standardized product* is one in which each unit produced is identical to every other unit. Radios, television sets, automobiles, and refrigerators are common examples of standardized products. Such products may be differentiated on some basis like color or styling, but the differentiation is usually slight, and it is added near the end of the production process. For example, automobile stylists in Detroit say they are in the business of attractively packaging the standardized automobile!

Standardization facilitates assembly line production, which in turn brings about cost reductions for the following reasons:

1. Longer production runs. Once a machine is set up, it can run for days turning out the same item.

2. Purchasing advantages. Greater quantities of identical materials can be purchased, with resulting lowered unit prices.

3. Less time lost. Workers do not have their routines interrupted when switching machines, nor do they have to stop for training.

4. Better quality control. It is economical to set up automatic checking devices, such as electric eyes, that assure accurate testing and checking.

5. Less paper work. Fewer shop orders and specifications are required. This reduces not only costs but possibility of error.

6. Lower production costs. There is less tooling, which is an expensive process, since fewer dies, molds, and so forth are needed. Maintenance costs are also lower.

Standardized products are easier to sell, because consumers know that thousands of similar products are sold and give satisfaction. Service problems are vastly simplified because of interchangeability of parts. (Imagine the chaos that would exist in the automobile repair shop if each automobile of a given make had a different kind of motor.)

Specialization

The whole field of production is pervaded by the principle of specialization, which, in its simplest form, means dividing work into separate jobs.

But specialization in other forms appears at all levels in our industrial economy.

Geographical specialization reflects the nation's division of labor for transformation of resources—Grand Rapids for furniture, Pittsburgh for steel, Corning (New York) for glass, Minneapolis for flour milling, and Detroit for automobiles.

Specialization by process divides establishments into machine shops, product-engineering concerns, processing plants, and commercial testing laboratories.

Work specialization separates workers into job groups, such as tool-and-die makers, electricians, drill-press operators, inspectors, assemblers, and the like. Within the plant itself, organizational specialization is accomplished by dividing activities into departments, departments into sections, sections into operations. Operations in turn are divided, until a single machine, tool, or worker performs only one task.

Specialization yields enormous benefits—but at a price. With specialization, industries become highly interdependent. Delivery failure from one plant curtails production in another. A strike among crane operators once shut down operations of an entire automobile factory. So intertwined are the various departments within a large company that a miscalculation or disruption anywhere along the line can easily throw an entire plant into confusion. It becomes the responsibility of management to decide how far specialization should be carried and to balance the good and bad effects.

PRODUCT DESIGN

The purpose of manufacturing is to produce goods that either give satisfaction to consumers or can be used in the manufacture of other products. In the language of the layman, the manufacturer is expected to produce a "good" product. Fundamental to the manufacture of such a product is product design, which may be divided into mechanical design and style design, and is a first step in the manufacturing process.**

Functional design

Functional design is that phase of product design which gives the product its operational characteristics. Its objective is to build a product that will provide the desired service and satisfaction. For example, the vacuum cleaner manufacturer is concerned with designing a product that picks up dust and dirt effectively, can be emptied easily, is light and easy to handle, will reach into corners and under furniture, has attachments that can be used to clean, say, a venetian blind, will fit in small closets, is safe, and is durable and capable of long service. If these product characteristics are not provided, the vacuum cleaner will soon be labeled "inferior" by the consuming public, and sales will drop.

In many industries, such as automobile manufacturing, functional design is a complicated function usually performed by several design groups. There may be separate groups of designers for the chassis, engine, electrical assembly, body, and transmission.

The need for functional design is apparent in the so-called engineering industries, such as the aircraft industry. For producers of petroleum products, chemicals, clothing, or other products that are not assembled, functional design, sometimes called "product development," is equally important. The oil refinery strives to "design" an oil that gives lasting engine protection; the textile manufacturer attempts to produce fabrics that will be wrinkle proof and repel water.

Style design

That a product is highly satisfactory from a functional standpoint does not assure its public acceptance. Unless consumers are also satisfied with its appearance, sales will be limited. Some years ago, the Ford Motor Company produced a car that was widely acclaimed as an excellent vehicle mechanically. It was probably as safe, dependable, and economical as any other automobile in its price range then being manufactured. Despite this fact, the Edsel did not sell because the public was not impressed with the size or style of the car.

Style design, then, is that phase of product design that adds attractiveness, distinctiveness, and aesthetic value to the product. Whereas functional designers are usually trained in engineering, style designers are usually trained in the fine arts.

Package design

A separate phase of style design is package design. With many competing brands on the market, and with self-service, the need for attractive packaging is great. Tests conducted in retail stores, where competing products are displayed side by side, show that often a change in the package design affects consumer preference. A cigarette manufacturer once spent $250,000 and two years in developing a package.

PRODUCTION PLANNING

Production planning, the next major step after product design, involves determining where and how to manufacture a product. Costs are estimated, so decisions can be made as to which parts should be manufactured "at home," which should be purchased from others, and what plant facilities should be used. This step is commonly referred to as the "make or buy" decision.

Key decision area

Planning for production centers around five key elements sometimes called the "five Ms"—methods, manpower, machines, money, and materials. Consideration of typical questions related to each "M" identifies typical decision areas.

Methods: Can present production lines be used to produce the new product, or must other facilities be provided?

Manpower: Can present personnel be used, or must new skills be added to the work force?

Machines: What kind, capacity, and numbers will be needed?

Money: What will long- and short-term money requirements be?

Materials: How large should inventories of parts, materials, and supplies be?

Production planning also includes (1) estimating costs of materials, labor, overhead, and equipment, (2) developing work standards and schedules to indicate length of manufacturing time, (3) anticipating what factory layout changes will be necessary, (4) diagramming methods for handling materials, (5) compiling lists of tools and machinery needed, and (6) conducting motion-and-time studies.[3] Production planning should be careful and complete, for carelessness leads to losses in time and money.

PRODUCTION CONTROL

Management of the production process is called *production control,* and it involves following predetermined guidelines to coordinate the production process.

The work of a production-control group is influenced directly by the marketing department. This department, often on the basis of carefully conducted market analysis, estimates the number of units that can be sold in a forthcoming period (usually one year). Once the sales estimate is completed, the production-control group proceeds.

Suppose, for example, that the sales department of a washing machine manufacturer estimates that 250,000 units can be sold during the next year. The production-control executives then break this estimate down into the number of units that must be produced each month, week, and working day of the coming year. In this case, assuming that there are 250 working days, the daily production volume should be one thousand units. (Seasonal variations often make it necessary, of course, to adjust production schedules.) When this figure is known, it is possible to determine how many workers, how much raw material, and what parts and machines will be needed to meet the production quota.

In this illustration, production control is, of course, grossly oversimplified. Factors like consumer demand and competition affect sales volume, with the result that the original sales estimate may need modification at later dates. When changes are made in the sales estimate, corresponding changes must be made in production schedules.

In a continuous manufacturing industry various subassembly lines are employed for certain operations. Eventually, these subassemblies flow into a final assembly line, from which the finished product emerges. Production control is needed to keep production on each subassembly line flowing at the right speed, so that final assembly is in an orderly

---

[3] A *motion-and-time* study is a detailed analysis of a labor operation, broken down into its respective parts. Each motion is studied, and the time it takes is recorded. The analysis is used then to increase efficiency and to improve work procedures.

fashion. If production on any one subassembly is either too slow or too fast, the entire assembly operation may break down.

Coordination of production is particularly difficult if there is any degree of product diversification. For example, in the automobile assembly plants, different body styles and different colored automobiles are produced on the same assembly line. Extreme care is needed to assure that proper accessories and bodies are correctly positioned on the assembly line.

THE METRIC SYSTEM

The United States will most likely adopt the metric system of measurement. Such a change is more or less inevitable since the United States is now the only major nation that does not officially use it. The chief advantage of the metric system is its simplicity—everything is counted in tens or multiples of 10. In 1795, France decreed the nomenclature for each measure (meter, gram, etc.). Prefixed to these measuring units were decimal multiples: deca (10), hecto (100), kilo (1,000), myria (10,000), deci (1/10th), centi (1/100th), and milli (1/1,000th). Thus a kilogram is 1,000 grams.

The archaic system still used in the United States originated in England, which has since abandoned it in favor of the infinitely more scientific metric system. A yard, amusingly, is the distance from the tip of King Edgar's nose to the end of the fingers of his outstretched arm! An inch is the width of the thumb of some forgotten king! A mile is 1,000 paces stepped off by a Roman soldier! An acre is the amount of land that can be plowed in a day by a yoke of oxen!

The U.S. Department of Commerce recently prepared a study recommending a switch to the metric system. Although it is estimated that it will cost $11 billion and take approximately 16 years to convert, there are many reasons why the United States should do so. Educators say that $700 million can be saved each year in teachers' time if school children are not required to use the present, more complicated system of measurement. There are threats to have nonmetric goods barred from foreign markets. American firms now manufacture according to two specifications, one for export and another for domestic sale. However, many U.S. industries—space, pharmaceutical, defense—are already metric.

The United States will probably base its conversion on the experiences of the British, who recently converted as a preamble for entering the Common Market, which traditionally has been metric. American companies with overseas operations list dual dimensions, the method the United States will use in converting—initially giving measurements in both units and then gradually phasing out the old system.

PURCHASING, BUYING, AND PROCURING GOODS AND SERVICES

We have already noted that in many different ways American business is highly interdependent. No business is self-sufficient; each must buy goods and services from other businesses.

The manufacturer must purchase raw materials, equipment, and supplies in order to produce; the wholesaler must buy in anticipation of the retailer's demands; the retailer must buy merchandise that will satisfy the ultimate consumer; and local, state, and federal governments must procure goods and services in order to function. What is not so obvious and not always fully appreciated is the strategic importance and surprising complexity of the buying function.

Different terms are used for the function of acquiring goods and services. Ultimate consumers call it "shopping." In manufacturing, it is usually referred to as "purchasing," in wholesale houses and retailing establishments as "buying," and in government as "procurement." This section will discuss professional buying—industrial purchasing, buying for resale, and government procurement. It is necessary to distinguish among these three originators of orders for goods and services; though their buying has many common characteristics, there are significant differences. The ultimate consumer's buying is discussed separately in Chapter 18 because of its fundamental importance to marketing and because consumers are non-professional buyers. Buying for resale purposes, which is strictly a function of marketing rather than production, is discussed here so it can be compared with production-oriented industrial purchasing and government procurement.

Importance and complexity of acquiring goods and services

One evidence of the importance of acquiring goods is that the average business spends more each year for raw materials, supplies, equipment, or merchandise for resale than for wages, rent, insurance, advertising, and all other business costs combined. A typical retailer spends 50 percent or more of his gross income for merchandise, and the average manufacturer spends an even larger percentage of his total sales volume for materials that go into finished products. A saving in the acquisition of goods obviously affects the firm's profit favorably.

The average manufacturing company spends 53.7 percent of its sales dollar on goods and services. For example, a company with a sales volume of $60 million would spend $32,220,000 for the purchase of materials, supplies, and services. At the typical average profit margin of 8.2 percent (before taxes), it would take $6 million in sales to make a $492,000 profit. But a reduction of only 1.5 percent in purchasing costs would mean a nearly identical $483,000 in additional profit. It is no wonder that management considers purchasing so important.

Government procurement is enormous. During a recent fiscal period, for example, military inventories alone were $44 billion. During the same period, manufacturing inventories were $55 billion and retailing inventories $25 billion. The economic impact of this procurement on large concerns, as well as on the thousands of subcontractors, suppliers, and servicers (transporters, warehouses, and handlers), is tremendous.

Buying, by its nature, is a behind-the-scenes activity. Business people can compare themselves fairly easily with competitors in almost every business practice—selling, advertising, production techniques—but not in purchasing. Consequently, it is easy to overlook an advantage a competitor has when he does a better buying job.

INDUSTRIAL PURCHASING

Organization for industrial purchasing

In most industrial organizations, the purchasing function is centralized in a purchasing department. This means that all orders for supplies, raw materials, equipment, and other goods are handled by one department— a procedure that permits specialization in purchasing, with greater economy and efficiency than would be possible if each department in the company purchased individually. Other advantages include:

1. Purchasing specialists who are experts in specific markets and materials can be employed.

2. The purchasing responsibility is the sole province of one executive and is thus kept under strict control.

3. Other departments, such as manufacturing, sales, and engineering, can concentrate better on their respective jobs.

4. Records of materials and specifications, information about sources of supply, and order records and details are assembled and maintained at a central point.

5. Better coordination with the receiving, traffic, and warehousing departments is possible.

The purchasing department is headed by an executive often called the purchasing manager,[4] director of purchasing, or vice president in charge of purchasing.

---

[4] The term "purchasing agent" is still used by some companies to indicate the person in charge of that function.

The purchasing manager may be assisted by one or more assistant purchasing managers and a staff of buyers. Often a buyer is responsible for one commodity or a group of related products. In this manner, the work of purchasing benefits from specialization.

The purchasing department works closely with other departments, especially those concerned with production, transportation, storage, and maintenance. These and other departments initiate requests for goods and send them to the purchasing department. Thus, purchasing is a "service" for other departments.

The purchasing function

The ten functions most commonly performed by the purchasing department, as reported by the National Industrial Conference Board, are to

1. Issue purchase orders
2. Interview salesmen
3. Negotiate with vendors
4. Analyze bids and prices
5. Select vendors
6. Make adjustments with vendors
7. Maintain records on vendors
8. Develop new sources of supply
9. Follow up on orders
10. Maintain a catalog library

The purchase of most items is initiated by a purchase requisition. This is a request filled out by the department that needs the material or supplies. It describes the needed goods or services and includes such details as quantity, quality, and date or dates for delivery. When the requisition is received in the purchasing department, a source for the requested goods or services is contacted, and negotiations begin. Purchasing negotiations between buyer and seller are usually centered on four major factors: quality, quantity, price, and service.

Quality Those responsible for purchasing are expected to acquire the best possible goods for a specified purpose. This does not mean that the quality of the goods must necessarily be the highest; it simply means that it should be as good as needed. To purchase better materials than are needed can add unnecessary cost, and to purchase poorer quality material than necessary can result in an inferior finished product.

Worshiping quality for quality's sake can be poor business practice. A top business executive once pointed out that industry wastes millions of dollars a year purchasing things that are better than required—that is, buying expensive things when a cheaper substitute would be adequate. His criticism stressed the fact that purchasers tend to take the easy course of action—relying on brands, materials, or sources that have proved satisfactory in the past, often because it is safer and less worrisome to do so.

Quantity   Once the proper quality has been determined, the next step is to decide *how much* should be purchased. There is no simple formula for making this decision. A number of factors must be evaluated carefully.

Stock on hand.   The amount on hand is important in determining how much should be ordered. It is important to note that it costs money to store parts and supplies. Specific inventory costs are rent on storage space, record-keeping expenses, handling charges, losses due to obsolescence or spoilage, interest on monies tied up in stocks, and insurance. Carrying-costs are usually estimated as running from 10 percent to 30 percent per year, depending on the nature of the goods and on storage requirements. In well-organized plants, very careful control is exercised over inventories in order to avoid overstocking.

Rate of use.   Knowing what stocks are on hand means little unless the rate at which the material is consumed is known. When stocks on hand are divided by daily use, the number of days' supply is ascertained. The rate of use depends on production schedules and therefore varies as production is increased or decreased.

Storage facilities.   Storage facilities and storage costs also play a part in determining what quantity to buy. If more goods are ordered than can be stored in the existing facilities, extra space must be either rented or borrowed from some other department in the business. Many factors enter into deciding the amount of goods to store. Items on which quick delivery can be secured may be kept in relatively short supply. Distance between supplier and the using company may be important. Goods that are scarce may be stockpiled. Rising prices may also justify heavy purchasing.

Type and use of goods.   Consideration must be given to possible obsolescence and deterioration of goods. Obsolescence may occur if a change is made in the manufactured product. Accordingly, those responsible for purchasing materials in the automotive, appliance, and other industries producing new models at regular intervals must make certain that the model changeover does not find them stocked with parts or products that no longer are usable.

Transportation availability and costs.   Transportation costs vary appreciably with the quantity shipped. Per-unit transportation costs are substantially greater when goods are shipped in less-than-carload lots. Other things being equal, it is desirable to ship in large quantities. Availability of transportation is also a factor. Transportation equipment, such

Figure **14–2**
The Locations of the 21,074 Suppliers
of One Automobile Company

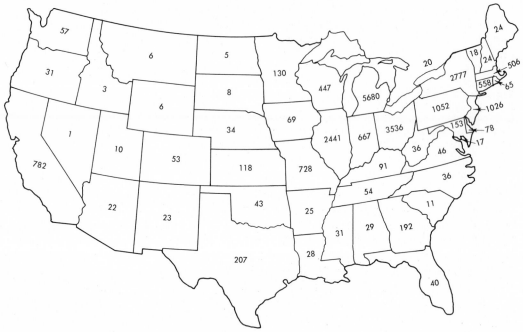

Source: Automobile Manufacturers Association.

as railroad cars and ships, is used seasonally and is not always available when desired. For example, it takes one hundred railroad cars per day, and 341 boatloads of fourteen thousand tons per season, to move the needed coal into the Ford Motor Company's Rouge Plant. It can easily be seen that should ice stay in the Great Lakes longer than usual or more cars than normal be needed to move a bumper wheat crop, Ford's transportation plans could be disrupted.

Quantity discounts. The prevailing practice in nearly all businesses is to grant quantity discounts. Such discounts are, in effect, price reductions. They are offered because the vendor's selling costs are correspondingly lowered when he can ship in larger quantities.

Quantity discounts are a temptation to most purchasing managers, but, for reasons noted elsewhere in this section, purchasing in quantity may not be economical when all factors are considered.

Price After quality and quantity have been decided, the next step is to find the most satisfactory price. What is "satisfactory" depends largely on the nature of the goods. While price certainly is a major consideration, it is not as important as one might suspect. This is true because a low price is meaningless unless suitability of quality is first assured. Reliability and assurance of supply and delivery also bear heavily on determining the "right price." Price negotiating as a modern business practice should not be considered "haggling" between buyer and seller. Sales representatives of a supplier are usually not empowered to make price concessions. Purchasing managers understand this policy and tend to accept a quotation as being "firm."

Service One of the primary responsibilities of the purchasing department is to determine before an order is placed, the prospective supplier's ability to meet requirements. Visits to vendor plants, if the size of the order warrants them, are a common method used to establish a supplier's ability to fulfill commitments. The purchasing department receives assistance from the engineering and production departments in inspecting and evaluating the vendor's plant facilities.

Most purchasing managers keep records of the performance of vendors to aid in evaluating the vendor at a later date when a new order is under consideration. The vendor's mistakes and defaulted promises, as well as his services, are not forgotten.

The specific elements of service to consider are discussed below.

Ability to deliver on schedule. A measure of the vendor's service is whether he delivers goods at the promised time. If delivery dates are not kept, the manufacturing process may have to be interrupted, idling men and machines. Purchasing management should order goods sufficiently far in advance of actual need to prevent such an occurrence. In assembly line production, failure to have crucial supplies can be so serious that it is the practice, in the case of critical parts, to spread orders between two or more suppliers, even though the cost per unit may be slightly higher. Thus when one supplier fails to deliver, there is always another to fall back on. The increased costs are considered worthwhile insurance against shutdown.

Maintenance service. Purchasers of machinery and equipment are interested in the vendor's maintenance service. Many machines are complicated and, if trouble develops, must be serviced by people with special training. Naturally, the purchaser prefers to do business with a supplier who maintains equipment in a trouble-free manner.

Engineering service. Many vendors give valuable engineering service and advice to their customers. This may be advice on how a plant can be modernized, waste effort eliminated, higher-quality products produced, and so on. Sometimes a vendor maintains a laboratory for the purchaser's testing and experimental work.

Some companies have a policy of encouraging criticisms and suggestions from suppliers. Such suggestions often lead to reductions in production costs. Some firms have requests for assistance printed on order and specification sheets. For example, one industrial machinery manufacturer states: "Any suggestions which will result in a saving to us will be appreciated. Substitutions or alterations will be considered if full information is given."

Shipping service.   Care in packing and shipment to avoid loss and breakage and to facilitate settling possible damage claims is part of satisfactory service. How materials are handled and routed is also a factor. For example, it costs approximately $700 to send a carload shipment from Detroit to Los Angeles. A single freight car holds only enough material to build ten automobiles. If the freight car is loaded to hold more or if parts are engineered so they nest when packed, impressive savings can result. Savings are realized if the receiver can unload quickly, if unnecessarily expensive and weighty crating is reduced, and if the shipment is on racks or in containers instead of in boxes so rehandling of goods by the purchaser is eliminated.

Service of salesmen.   The supplier's salesmen can be of assistance to purchasing managers. The salesman can pass along worthwhile information that goes far beyond the details of the product he sells. The salesman circulates freely in the purchaser's industry and visits many plants having problems similar to those of the purchaser. Thus he can pass along information concerning new developments in production and materials handling; and since he knows a great deal about production applications, he often can supply valuable information about business conditions. All these factors are important in making purchasing decisions, since information leads to efficiencies of value to the company.

The conceptual change in industrial purchasing

There has been a great conceptual change in how the purchasing function is considered in the company. Yesterday's purchasing manager reported to the production manager (or general manager). His function was to *save* money for the company. He received purchase orders from various departments and was to buy the best of what was wanted at the lowest possible price. Chances were that he got three bids from different suppliers and took the lowest. Today's purchasing manager probably reports to a vice president. His responsibility is much broader, for it is likely to include materials management. His function is now viewed as a way to *make* money for the company; purchasing and materials handling are now regarded as profit-making activities.

Since the purchasing/materials manager spends a large part of the company's budget, he becomes involved with the financial aspects of management problems, and he must understand the functions of all departments. To an increasing extent, he must look at each purchasing situation as a part of an integrated manufacturing process. This is verified by W. F. Rockwell, President of Rockwell Manufacturing Company, who said,

> Today's purchasing agent must be one of the most knowledgeable managers in his company. Unless he understands enough design, engineering, production, marketing, and related functions in sufficient detail, he can't possibly do his job. We insist that our purchasing people be brought into the picture in the earliest stages of design, engineering, and production. Frequently, they are able to make creative suggestions and studies that result in improved products, faster production schedules, even better design and appearance.

BUYING FOR RESALE: RESALE AND INDUSTRIAL BUYING COMPARED

Buying by resale organizations (retail stores and wholesalers) and purchasing by industrial organizations have much in common. In both cases, primary emphasis is placed on the selection of the right quality of goods in the right quantity, at the right price, and from a fair, dependable vendor who gives the desired services. In both types of organization, individuals responsible for buying occupy positions of high importance. There are, however, certain differences.

Differences in terminology

An obvious difference is in the titles given to those responsible for buying. In the retail field, they are called "buyers" or "merchandisers," while industrial purchasing executives tend to be called "purchasing managers," although their subordinates may be called "buyers."

Differences in buying organization

Industrial organizations usually have centralized purchasing departments, with one staff of executives doing virtually all the purchasing for an entire company. In large retail stores buying tends to be decentralized, with a buyer for each major line handled. In a large store there may be dozens of buyers, each responsible for a major product line, such as housewares, furs, or ladies' ready-to-wear garments. Like the purchasing manager, however, the retail-store buyer may have several assistant buyers.

Differences in responsibility

The most important difference between industrial purchasing managers and retail-store buyers is the nature of the responsibilities assumed by each.

Resale buyers determine what to buy   Most purchasing in industry is initiated by purchase requisitions submitted by those who will use the goods. The purchasing manager's main job then is to purchase what someone else in the organization needs. Retail buyers, on the other hand, buy what they personally (or in conference with others) believe can be resold successfully. A significant point is that the retail buyer has responsibility for both buying *and* selling goods. If the goods he buys prove to be unsalable, he must assume responsibility for his error. This is not true of the purchasing manager.

Resale buyers buy for reselling only   While the purchasing manager purchases for manufacturing needs, the retail buyer must select goods that appeal to the ultimate consumer. The result is a difference in the buying approach. The purchasing manager can evaluate materials, equipment, and supplies *objectively* by comparing them in price, quality, and other factors. In many cases, extensive laboratory tests can be used to judge the relative quality of different offerings. Though the retail buyer may subject merchandise to test, he also takes into account the subjective elements involved in pleasing customers—such intangibles as emotional appeal and style factors. For this reason, retail buyers, unlike purchasing managers, must be students of consumer psychology. Indeed, their success hinges to a large extent on their ability to judge taste variables.

Resale buyers must plan to resell what they buy   Another responsibility of the retail buyer (obviously never one of the purchasing manager), is planning the resale of the merchandise he buys. This responsibility may involve training salespeople, arranging attractive displays, decorating windows, planning sales-promotion events, pricing, deciding what and how to advertise, and handling customer complaints.

Resale buyers are responsible for stock-keeping   In the industrial organization, the stock-keeping function is performed by a separate department. In the retail store, stock-keeping is the responsibility of the buyer and his assistants. This responsibility requires that the retail buyer take inventory, handle returned goods, and check in the merchandise when it is delivered.

Resale buyers have direct profit-making responsibility   The retail buyer's effectiveness is easily measured, since he has full responsibility for his department's profits. In retailing, departmental profits are easily ascertained, and comparisons with previous sales records can be made. Comparisons can be made also with operations of other stores. Industrial purchasing efficiency is more difficult to evaluate.

Differences in buying methods

Industrial purchasing managers, for the most part, do their purchasing from their own offices. Orders may be placed directly with salesmen or by phone, telegraph, or mail. Retail buyers, in contrast, do a large part of their buying by visiting market centers and by looking through display rooms of manufacturers and distributors.

Sources of supply for many types of retail merchandise are concentrated in certain cities (Grand Rapids for furniture; New York for ready-to-wear garments). Retail buyers often prefer to visit the market to compare the offerings of several vendors simultaneously. Furthermore, since appearance is a major factor in determining the salability of goods in retail stores, the buyer benefits from personal inspection of the merchandise. The purchasing manager, on the other hand, can do most of his buying by specification.

GOVERNMENT PROCUREMENT

The U.S. government is the largest buyer of machinery, equipment, supplies, and services. Together with state and local governments, it offers the businessman a tremendous market for products and services.

How government purchases differ from purchases by private businesses

Government purchases differ in three essential respects from purchases by private business. First, the government buys goods mainly for use, not for resale or for use in production. (A noteworthy exception is the purchase by the government of many consumer goods for resale through post exchanges and commissaries.) Second, government purchases are not motivated by a desire for profit. Third, government purchasing is subject to many legal and budgetary restrictions intended to safeguard the expenditure of public funds.

Traditionally, it is the policy of the government not to compete with private industry in manufacturing goods or in rendering services. In fact almost all of the tremendous amount and variety of products purchased by the government are bought from private industry. It is true that the federal government does own some manufacturing plants and equipment, but such property is leased to private business for the production of defense-related products.

Federal procurement policies

Three basic principles guide government procurement. First, all known responsible suppliers are given an equal opportunity to compete for government contracts through bids or negotiations. Second, all goods and services purchased must meet predetermined specifications and standards. Third, all supplies, equipment, and commodities offered by a supplier must be inspected and approved by government inspectors before the vendor is paid.

Procurement through competitive bids   Whenever possible, the federal government encourages competitive bidding for contracts. Advertisements in various media and direct-mail announcements to suppliers are used to interest the maximum number of businesses in various contracts. A deadline is set for bids, and the lowest responsible bidder whose proposal fully meets the specifications receives the job.

Procurement through negotiated contracts   In some cases, it is neither practical nor economical for the government to use competitive bidding. Rather, purchases are negotiated with suppliers; examples of such situations are given below:

1. When the purchase is under $2,500
2. During a period of national emergency declared either by the President or Congress, when the situation demands it
3. When the contract is for property or services to be procured and used outside the United States and its possessions
4. When the contract is for subsistence supplies
5. When it is impossible to secure competitive bids because there is only one supplier
6. When appropriate government officials believe that the character, ingredients, or components of the items needed should not be disclosed publicly
7. When the contract is for equipment for which standardization and interchangeability of parts is essential

Even if the government plans to negotiate a purchase, it still attempts to encourage competition, typically by directly contacting several responsible suppliers and inviting them to make proposals. In this case, however, the government is not obligated to grant the contract to the lowest bidder since other factors such as expertise, experience, and engineering talent may be more important than price.

Notifying prospective suppliers of government needs

Because of its policy of encouraging the largest possible number of responsible businesses to bid or negotiate for contracts, the government uses a variety of publications to advise prospective suppliers of its needs. One of the most valuable is the *U.S. Government Purchasing and Sales Directory.* Published by the Small Business Administration, it contains a detailed list of products purchased by both civilian and military government agencies, the locations of government purchasing offices, and procedural information useful to suppliers, contractors, and subcontractors dealing with the government. The *Commerce Business Daily,* published each workday by the Department of Commerce, runs a list of proposed federal procurement and subcontracting leads, contract awards, sales of surplus property, and foreign business opportunities.

In addition, many federal agencies publish their own brochures outlining specific procurement needs and the procedures suppliers should follow—for example, "Selling to the Military" (Department of Defense), "How to do Business with the DSA" (Defense Supply Agency), "Selling to the U.S.D.A." (Department of Agriculture), "How to Sell to the U.S. Department of Commerce," and "Selling to NASA" (National Aeronautics and Space Administration).

What constitutes a responsible supplier?

Government contracting officers are required to make contract awards on the basis of the lowest bid by a responsible bidder, not merely on the basis of the lowest quoted price. However, it is not always easy to determine whether a supplier is responsible, as many factors may be involved. For example, the supplier may be a new firm with no track record, or it may be an established firm with no previous experience as a government contractor. And, in the case of developmental work, there may be no firm that has ever made a similar product.

Generally, the contracting officer, in attempting to determine whether the bidder is responsible, will investigate its plant, production capabilities, testing facilities, quality-control procedures, financial status, and so on. He will also consider the reputation of the bidder for honesty and dependability.

Prime contractors and subcontractors

Companies that contract directly with the government to provide products are called *prime contractors*. They in turn often farm out portions of the work to other, usually smaller businesses called *subcontractors*. A business may market its products to the government, then, in two ways: (a) directly, by arranging for a prime contract, or (b) indirectly, by selling to the prime contractor. Subcontractors greatly outnumber prime contractors, since an estimated 50 percent of all government purchasing covered by prime contracts involves subcontractors.[5]

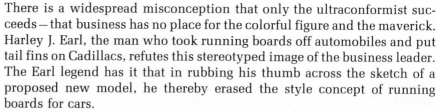

PEOPLE AND THEIR IDEAS
Harley J. Earl

The automobile industry's greatest design influence

There is a widespread misconception that only the ultraconformist succeeds—that business has no place for the colorful figure and the maverick. Harley J. Earl, the man who took running boards off automobiles and put tail fins on Cadillacs, refutes this stereotyped image of the business leader. The Earl legend has it that in rubbing his thumb across the sketch of a proposed new model, he thereby erased the style concept of running boards for cars.

Harley Earl, who died in 1969 at the age of 75, demonstrated that a businessman can be both creative and successful. When he retired in 1958 as vice-president in charge of styling for General Motors, it is estimated that he was earning $130,000 a year in salary alone and had left his imprint on more than fifty million GM vehicles. As a pioneer in the field, he also had a profound influence on the design of millions of competing cars.

A native of Los Angeles, Earl received his early training in that city, working in his father's successful carriage works. After attending Stanford University, he began designing custom automobiles for Hollywood movie stars. He once designed a special car for Tom Mix that had a real saddle fastened to the hood.

His reputation as a designer spread, and he was hired as a consulting engineer by the Cadillac Motor Car Company. Later, having proved that high styling produces high sales, he headed the industry's first staff devoted solely to automotive appearance.

During his thirty-one years as head of GM's styling department, his staff grew from fifty to more than 1,100 specialists. In addition to passenger cars, they designed trucks, buses, streamlined trains, household appliances, batteries, auto exhibits, and even earth-moving equipment.

[5] Juan Cameron, "The Case for Cutting Defense Spending," *Fortune*, August 1, 1969, p. 74.

Earl obtained his ideas from many sources. The P-35 fighter plane inspired the "fish tail" rear lights on a successful Cadillac model. GM's jet-like Firebird, the first American car with a gas-turbine engine, was designed by Earl after he saw a picture of a new airplane and decided that the design principle was applicable to automobiles.

In discussing his design principles, the six foot five inch, 235-pound Earl liked to tell the ironic story about the critic who once wrote him: "Why don't you design cars for grownups like me instead of midgets like you?" Mr. Earl summed up the rationale for his design:

> "My primary purpose has been to lengthen and lower the American automobile, at times in reality and always at least in appearance. Why? Because my sense of proportion tells me that oblongs are more attractive than squares, just as a ranch house is more attractive than a square, three-story, flat-roofed house, or a greyhound is more graceful than an English bulldog."

CONTEMPORARY ISSUES
Situation 14

Is purchasing skill underemphasized in business?

"You know, Ray," John observed, "until now I didn't really appreciate how important purchasing is. Actually, in business situations, the people in charge of purchasing can, at times, contribute even more to profit than those who are charged with the sales function. But it seems to me that business in general puts much more emphasis on selling than on buying."

"I think you are right," Ray agreed. "I have an uncle who is the sales manager for a major company, and he is conducting sales training classes and seminars almost all the time to help train his salesmen how to sell better. But from what he tells me, his company does virtually nothing to train purchasing people, other than let them subscribe to a purchasing journal and belong to a trade association of purchasing managers."

"Yes, on the face of it," John observed, "it does seem that purchasing people are neglected. Their expertise is taken for granted. Now, if we are open-minded, we have to admit that purchasing is just as important as selling because without buying there can be no selling, and vice versa."

"I'll bet," commented Ray, "that if corporations put as much emphasis on training purchasing managers as they do on training salesmen, there would be a whole lot more efficiency and less waste."

"I agree," said John, "and you know something else, the 'how' of purchasing is not only underplayed in business, it's also virtually ignored for the consumer. Most consumers that I know have never taken a course in how to buy anything. So, at all levels we seem to have trained salesmen and untrained buyers. I'm reminded of something I liked so much I memorized it 'When he wastes a dollar in poor buymanship, he deprives himself of other products that he might have enjoyed if he had purchased with greater wisdom.'"[6]

"What do you recommend be done about it?" asked Ray.

"I'm not sure anything can be done. But I know this, if I decide to go into business and ever get the authority, I'm going to be sure my purchasing people are well trained in the work they do."

SITUATION EVALUATION

1. Why is it that so much more emphasis is placed on training and educating sales personnel than is done for purchasing people?

2. What specific things might be done in business to train purchasing personnel? Can anything be done in colleges and universities?

3. Can the art and skill of negotiation be taught? What are some of the things purchasing people should be trained to do?

BUSINESS CHRONICLE

Mobile housing and the future

Management of Kingmaker Estates was inclined to discourage the use of house trailers, mobile homes, and modulars. Mr. King especially seemed to be prejudiced against them. He was proud of the solid and well-designed appearance of his developments and felt that mass, factory-built housing was poorly constructed. He believed that to include them in his housing developments would give Kingmaker an image he wanted to avoid.

Statistics on the acceptance of mobile homes could no longer be ignored, particularly in Florida. To ignore them was to be blind to the future. Not only were they growing impressively in popularity, but also on-site building was becoming prohibitively expensive and difficult because of shortages of skilled workers, high wage rates, and difficulty with quality control. Significant excerpts from planning meetings that Kingmaker management held about the subject are:

Milton Bach, Building Contractor: Modular housing is the coming thing and it certainly simplifies life for the builder. The factory solves the problems of quality control. The standardization of units makes it easy to put them up. I can teach inexperienced

---

[6] *Consumer Education*, by N. E. Brown (Canada: Macmillan Co.), 1964.

men to do it in a matter of hours, and I don't have to pay such high wages.

Shirley Swift, Architect: I think we should start thinking about how we can merge modular housing with conventional housing. I think if Kingmaker took the lead and showed how this could be done practically and artistically, the company could really make a name for itself in a field that is about to take off like a rocket from a launching pad.

Alden Parks, Architect: Modular housing has flexibility that conventional housing doesn't have. As family housing needs change as families increase and decrease in size, and as family members grow older, rooms can be added and removed easily. Modernization is also facilitated. An old kitchen unit is removed and a modern one with the latest built-in appliances is added; it's just that simple. Kingmaker could become the king of flexibility and make a name for itself.

QUESTIONS

1. Evaluate each comment and suggest policy decisions for Kingmaker.

2. What are the production advantages of modular housing over on-site construction?

APPLICATION EXERCISES

1. Robert Large is the young assistant to J. C. Stern, a seasoned purchasing manager. Attempting to teach Large how to be an effective buyer, Stern made the following statements that puzzled the young man. "Products cheapest in price may be the most expensive," and, "A penny saved in the purchase price is worth more than a penny in profit." What did Stern mean by these statements?

2. Visit one of your neighborhood stores and discuss the subject of salesmen's services with the proprietor or manager. Ask him to give examples of the services salesmen provide him. Explain what you have done

in a paper, and list the services that were mentioned. As a conclusion to your paper, indicate whether or not you believe the person you interviewed fully appreciates the value of salesmen's services.

3. Jerry Walsh is buyer for a men's clothing department in a large department store. Though the department operates successfully, it has not been able to attract young men of college age as customers. The profit of the department stems from its solid and steady clientele of businessmen. Walsh, in attempting to determine why younger customers stay away, has discussed the problem with one of his part-time clerks, John Corbett, a bright young man who is a full-time college student in business administration. Corbett has said that he will try to find out why his college classmates and fraternity brothers do not shop in the store. Corbett reports to the buyer that the consensus among college students is that the department always has last year's styles instead of what young men are interested in right now. Walsh agrees that stocking merchandise for college students is a real problem: Their tastes change quickly and commitments for purchases have to be made from four to six months in advance of the selling season. Walsh asks Corbett to suggest a program that will enable him to determine the taste of college men six months ahead of time. Prepare a suggested program that you would submit to Walsh if you were Corbett.

QUESTIONS

1. What types of workers stand to benefit most from automation? What types are apt to suffer?

2. Explain the statement: "Each department in a business is in competition with corresponding departments in other businesses in the same industry."

3. Contrast functional design with style design. Which is more important? Explain carefully.

4. Planning for production focuses on what five key elements? What else is involved in production planning?

5. What is production control? How does it relate to marketing?

6. Define purchasing, buying, and procurement.

7. Why is determination of quality often a joint decision of executives from several departments rather than an exclusive right of the purchasing manager?

8. What factors are involved in deciding on the quantity of goods to be purchased?

9. The nature of services that the vendor offers is an important consideration in selecting a vendor. What vendor services should be appraised?

10. What are the advantages and disadvantages of purchasing from a single supplier? Do you believe the advantages outweigh the disadvantages? Why or why not?

11. Which is the more specialized function—industrial purchasing or retail buying? Which requires broader knowledge on the part of the executive in charge? Explain.

CHAPTER 15

ECONOMIC SIGNIFICANCE OF TRANSPORTATION
Transportation as a Cost of Production. Transportation Makes Resources Available. Transportation Makes Specialization Possible.

CLASSIFICATION OF CARRIERS
Legal Status. Methods of Operation.

RAILROADS
Advantages. Disadvantages. Railroad Rates. Railroad Services. Railroad Auxiliaries.

MOTOR TRUCKS
Advantages. Disadvantages. Piggyback Service.

WATER TRANSPORTATION
Advantages. Disadvantages.

PIPELINES
Advantages. Disadvantages

AIR TRANSPORTATION
Products Shipped by Air. Advantages. Disadvantages.

SELECTION OF SPECIFIC CARRIERS

TRANSPORTATION AND TRAFFIC MANAGEMENT

INTERMODAL TRANSPORTATION AND CONTAINERIZATION
Obstacles to Transportation Integration. Containerization. DOT: A Systems Approach to Transportation.

THE FUTURE OF TRANSPORTATION

15 physical distribution and space logistics

The term *physical distribution* refers to the physical handling and movement of products from one business to another. Among the specific activities included are transportation, warehousing and shipping, order processing, inventory control, and protective packaging. In this chapter, main emphasis is placed on transportation, which is the most costly physical distribution function.

ECONOMIC SIGNIFICANCE OF TRANSPORTATION

The industrial power and wealth of the United States is made possible largely by our well-developed and varied transportation system. Economic development has closely paralleled the development of transportation. That this is so should not surprise us — economic progress depends on moving goods from one place to another at low cost. Resources are developed only when they can be moved to locations where they can be

Table **15–1**
A 10-Cent Candy Bar Represents a 100,000 Mile Trip

"ZERO" CANDY BAR INGREDIENTS	POINT OF ORIGIN	DISTANCE FROM MANUFACTURING PLANT (IN MILES)
Cane sugar	West Indies, Hawaii	1,900
Corn syrup, molasses	Barbadoes (B.W.I.), New Orleans	2,000
Vegetable fat	American Midwest	400
Nonfat dry and sweetened skim milk	Local suppliers	100
Almonds	Spain, Italy, California	5,200
Malted milk	Lafayette (Ind.)	150
Cocoa beans	Equador, Venezuela, Trinidad (B.W.I.), Brazil, San Domingo	2,100–5,600
Egg whites	Local suppliers	100
Salt	Salt Lake City (Utah)	1,300
Soybean lecithin	Americus (Ga.)	650
Mono and diglycerides	Lexington (Ky.)	200
Filberts	Spain, Turkey	5,000–6,800
Gum arabic	Egypt	6,700
Gum tragacanth	Iran	6,900
Oil of anise	Taiwan	8,700
Oil of rose	Bulgaria	6,600
Vanilla beans	Mexico, Madagascar	1,500–5,600
Cashew nuts	India	7,300
Maple sugar	Vermont	750
Oil of cloves	Zanzibar	5,900
Walnuts	France, Turkey, California	5,400
Approximate distance goods traveled (adjusted for routing and other factors)		90,000–110,000

processed and, in most instances, combined with other resources gathered from different locations.

Transportation as a cost of production

Transportation expenses account for anywhere from 5 to more than 50 percent of the selling price of consumer goods. The actual cost is frequently underestimated; it can, and often does, cost more to move goods from manufacturer to consumer than it costs to make them. The cost of shipping a refrigerator from producer to consumer is simple to compute. But the various costs of transporting parts and raw materials from their production points to the factory that assembles the refrigerator are easily overlooked. (See Table 15–1.)

Transportation costs incurred in producing and distributing different products vary greatly. Such costs form a relatively large part of the selling price if the commodity is bulky, requires special handling, is perishable, or is to be moved a long distance. The cost of transporting iron ore from the Lake Superior region to Pittsburgh accounts for as much as 75 percent of the wholesale price of the ore sold in Pittsburgh.

If, however, the product is nonperishable, has considerable value in relation to the amount of space it takes up, or is transported only a short distance, transportation costs in relation to selling price tend to be comparatively low.

Transportation makes resources available

Efficiency in transportation is often the key that unlocks the door to greater economic resources. One of the most dramatic examples of the 1960s was the construction of a 360-mile railroad linking Knob Lake, in the remote and wild interior of Labrador, with the town of Seven Islands on the St. Lawrence River. At Seven Islands, ore from deposits around Knob Lake is trans-shipped from rail to water transportation, which carries it to ore-hungry blast furnaces in the nation's industrial centers. The new railroad was a daring, $250 million project. Six thousand men were needed for its construction, which depended in part on air transportation for machinery, cement, steel, and other materials.

Transportation adds value to goods by bringing them from where nature provides them or from where they are produced to the place where they are needed. The iron ore in Labrador has no value to society until it is transported. Without economical transportation such resources remain useless.

Transportation makes specialization possible

Transportation makes possible territorial division of labor—that is, a geographical area can specialize in products for which its climate, resources, or skills are best suited. Transportation enables farmers in the Midwest to specialize in the production of grain and cattle; growers in California, Arizona, and Florida to specialize in citrus fruit; and various regions to specialize in manufacturing. Without fast, economical transportation, each area—even each community—would be forced to be largely self-sufficient.

Efficient transportation tends also to intensify competition, since more sources of supply can compete in many markets. If a distant seller can ship his goods rapidly and economically, he can compete with a seller located closer to the market, especially if he enjoys such production advantages as cheaper raw materials or lower wage rates.

CLASSIFICATION OF CARRIERS

Legal status

A *carrier* is a company that engages in transportation. Carriers can be classified according to legal status or according to method of operation. Legally, there are three types of carrier: common, contract, and private.

Common carriers operate on regular schedules between fixed terminals and over definite routes. The common carrier gives the same service and charges the same rates to all shippers. It is closely regulated and is required by law to give a certain minimum service. Railroads, bus lines, most airlines, and some trucking companies are common carriers.

Contract carriers are engaged in "for hire" transportation and do not offer the same service or the same price to everyone. A contract is made with each shipper. The legal obligations of the carrier are contained in the individual contract. Often, contract carriers specialize in transporting only certain kinds of products. The specialized rack and tank trucks commonly seen on highways, for example, are used only for carrying automobiles or chemicals on contract. Much trucking and inland shipping is of this nature.

A *private carrier* is part of a business. Farmers, merchants, and manufacturers who operate their own trucks in connection with their business operations are private carriers. Legal restrictions on private carriers are relatively few.

Methods of operation

As defined by method of operation, there are five types of domestic carrier: railroads, trucks, vessels on inland waterways, pipelines, and airplanes. Each offers special services and has special characteristics. They are discussed in turn below.

RAILROADS

From the standpoint of amount of freight carried, railroads are the most important method of domestic transportation. The United States owns 30 percent of the world's railroad mileage. Yet among the transportation changes that have taken place in the United States, the chief one has been the comparative decline of railroads. During the past thirty-five years, shipments of freight by railroads have declined from about 65 percent of

Figure **15–1**
U.S. Intercity Freight Ton-Mile Distribution

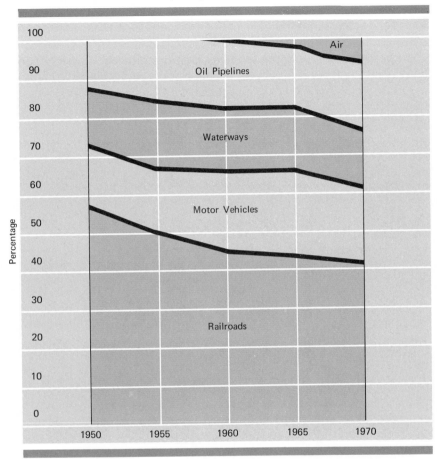

Source: *Statistical Abstract of the United States, 1972,* p. 535; *Container News,* April 1972, p. 42.

Is transportation a static field? How do you think the picture will
change by 1980?

the nation's freight total to only 43 percent. (Figure 15–1 shows trend
relationships between modes of transportation.)

Advantages

The chief advantage of rail transportation is low cost for moving heavy
goods long distances. On long hauls, trucks find it difficult to compete in
cost with railroads. While it is much cheaper to move freight by water, the
lack of waterways in much of the United States does not make this method

a direct competitor of railroads except in certain sections. Low rail-transportation costs stem from the fact that usually only one power unit, the locomotive, is needed to move a train. Trucks, on the other hand, have a smaller capacity than freight cars, and each truck must have its own power unit.

A second advantage is the relative safety of railroads. Fewer accidents occur, and these usually damage only a small part of the cargo.

Third, trains are able to maintain fairly reliable schedules. A severe snow and ice storm may upset schedules of other means of transportation, but railroads usually take all but the most inclement weather in stride.

Fourth, railroads, with almost one and a half million freight cars, usually have the capacity to accommodate peak loads.

A fifth advantage is the unusual variety of services performed for shippers; these will be discussed shortly.

Disadvantages

Slow speed on shorter distances and lack of flexibility are the chief limitations of rail transportation. Delays are often encountered along the way when it is necessary to drop off cars that have arrived at their destination or to add new cars. "Breaking up" the train, as it is called, is an expensive and time-consuming activity. When several railways are used to route shipments, this delay is repeated many times.

Another major disadvantage is lack of accessibility. Freight stations are usually located in congested areas, making them difficult to reach. Costly transfer of freight to local trucks is necessary if the pickup or destination points are not on a railroad siding. Furthermore, there are thousands of small communities that are not serviced by railroads. The problem of accessibility becomes more significant each year. This is because our network of railroads, for the most part, was built many years ago, when concentrations of populations and industries differed from what they are now. Numerous communities, especially in rural areas, which were important then are relatively unimportant today. At the same time, new communities, often far removed from railroad tracks, have sprung up.

Railroad rates

Class rates   Since there are more than twenty-five thousand different kinds of commodities, products, and articles shipped by rail, it is obvious that to establish a rate for each would be a mammoth undertaking and would result in an unwieldy schedule. Accordingly, products that are similar from a transportation standpoint are grouped and placed in classes.

All commodities in the same class are given the same rate, called the *class rate.* Factors determining what class a product belongs in are (1) value, (2) weight in proportion to space occupied, (3) condition in which shipped (whether loose, in bulk, or in cartons), (4) type of railroad equipment used, and (5) hazards involved in shipping.

Commodity rates   The *commodity rate*, lower than class rates, applies to specific commodities that move in large volume, such as lumber, wheat, coal, iron ore, or cotton. To qualify for the commodity rate, the commodity must move with some regularity and in carload lots. By far the largest percentage of railroad freight moves under this rate.

Carload and less-than-carload rates   The rates described above are subject to modification according to the volume of goods shipped. To encourage shipments in economical quantities, a wide differential exists between *carload* (c.l.) and *less-than-carload* (l.c.l.) *rates.* Carload rates, with few exceptions, cost only half (or even less than half) of l.c.l. rates. Even with these differentials railroads have all but abandoned l.c.l. shipments, since, for the most part, this business is not profitable. With l.c.l. shipments there are greater collection, billing, and checking costs, and a waste that comes from having to ship partially filled cars.

Through and local rates   Another modifying influence on rates is the distance moved. The farther goods are hauled, the less it costs per ton-mile.[1] Some of the savings achieved in this manner are passed on to shippers in the form of the *through rate.* Railroads must provide the same terminal switching, loading, unloading, storing, checking, and billing facilities whether a shipment goes sixty or six hundred miles. Clearly there is justification for charging higher rates for shorter distances. The *local rate* generally is used for a short haul of, say, seventy-five to one hundred and fifty miles, while the through rate is used for shipments of several hundred miles.

Rate-making has changed markedly since the Transportation Act of 1958. Whereas rate structures were once highly inflexible, the new act allows regulated carriers greater freedom to meet both competition and changing conditions. One manifestation of this has been the appearance of incentive-type rates. Shipping costs go down as shipper tonnage goes up. In other words, the shipper is given the incentive of lower rates to encourage him to ship in larger quantities. Early government policies, designed to encourage heavy investment in the building of railroads, canals, and other costly transportation facilities, sought to shield transportation promoters from competition. Now that the forms of transportation are fully developed (that is, our railroads and airports are built), government

---

[1] The basic unit for measuring freight shipments is the "ton-mile" — that is, the movement of one ton (2,000 pounds) of freight over a distance of one mile.

policies tend to reintroduce competition. These new policies have served in part to revitalize transportation by making the modes competitive, however it is far from certain that policy changes alone can revitalize our railroads which in many instances are chronically in serious difficulty.

Railroad services

Railroads offer various kinds of services to provide the shipper with flexibility and added convenience. The layman is inclined to think of the railroad in limited terms, as simply a means of shipping goods from one terminal point to another. The knowledgeable business, on the other hand, realizes that most carriers offer growing numbers of services that facilitate and expedite the shipment of goods.

In-transit privilege   Shippers of commodities, such as grain or lumber, often find it desirable to process or fabricate goods at a point between the origin of the shipment and its final destination. When the processing or manufacturing is completed—perhaps months later—the goods are reloaded and sent on to their destination. This would be a very expensive procedure if the shipper had to pay two local rates—that is, one local rate from point of origin to the processing point and a second from there onward. Railroads charge only a through rate for such a shipment, extending what is called the "in-transit" privilege. A service charge is applied, but the total charge is much less than the sum of two local rates.

Shippers and processors of more than three hundred commodities use this service. Examples are milling of wheat, compressing of cotton, creosoting of telephone poles, and fattening of cattle.

Diversion-in-transit privilege   A second service, particularly important in the distribution of perishable goods and in the marketing of grain, lumber, and coal, is "diversion-in-transit." This privilege enables a shipper to start a car of unsold produce toward one city and then, if it should appear wise, to divert the shipment to another city, in the same general direction, while the car is in transit. So long as the goods continue in the same general direction, the shipper pays the through rate from the point of origin to the final destination, plus a relatively small diversion charge.

To illustrate: an apple grower in Spokane, Washington, may send a shipment consigned to himself in Minneapolis, but with no *specific* market in mind. While the apples are en route, the shipper maintains close contact with the various wholesale fruit markets in the Midwest and East. As the car approaches Minneapolis, he learns that the market there is glutted. Instructions are then wired to railroad officials to divert the car to Chicago, where the market is more favorable. If the market in Chicago is unfavorable too, the apples may be diverted again — say, to Detroit, where they are finally sold.

Under the diversion-in-transit privilege, the shipper pays only the through rate from Spokane to Detroit rather than paying one rate from Spokane to Minneapolis, another from Minneapolis to Chicago, and a third from Chicago to Detroit. If, however, the car was diverted in Chicago to Omaha, Nebraska, a back haul would be involved, and the regular rate from Chicago to Omaha would apply.

Pool-car service   Frequently a manufacturer ships a carload of goods intended for several dealers located in different towns along the same railroad. The railroad grants the shipper the carload rate from the point of origin to the *first* receiver and from there charges the l.c.l. rate until the car is unloaded. This is called "pool-car" service. To illustrate, a Cleveland manufacturer of bicycles may ship a carload south to be delivered in various cities between Louisville and Nashville. The manufacturer would pay the carload rate as far as Louisville and the l.c.l. rate from there to Nashville.

Railroad auxiliaries

Freight forwarders.   Freight forwarders are transportation specialists who provide an economical, convenient, and fast service to the shipping public. The forwarder, under contract as the agent of the shipper, assembles enough l.c.l. shipments to fill an entire car and thus obtains a carload rate. He charges the shipper a higher rate, but it is less than the l.c.l. rate, the difference being his compensation. Small shippers profit from this service because it is faster than regular freight service offered by the railroads and no more expensive, and it often includes such other services as pickup and delivery. Freight forwarders now make extensive use of motor as well as rail transportation.

REA Express Agency.   The REA Express Agency, formerly the Railway Express Agency, is a premium type of transportation service owned entirely by the railroads. It deals almost exclusively in l.c.l. or l.t.l. (less-than-truckload) shipments, although it also transports carload lots of fresh produce where several shippers may fill a car with, say, fresh strawberries that must be expressed to the market as quickly as possible. REA Express shipments are usually placed in cars attached to fast trains to ensure rapid delivery. The agency also operates trucks and makes extensive use of air transportation to move goods long distances. The ratio is 35 percent truck versus 65 percent rail. Advantages of REA Express, as compared with other methods of transportation, include (1) greater speed, (2) more careful handling of merchandise, (3) pickup and delivery, (4) prompt adjustment of losses and damages, (5) low-cost insurance, and (6) shipment of any size package.

MOTOR TRUCKS

Truck transportation is the most adaptable and flexible method of moving goods. The amount of freight moved by truck has leveled out during the last decade to where it now accounts for from 21 to 23 percent of domestic transportation in any one year. This figure, however, understates the relative importance of trucks, since it does not include intracity transportation, such as wholesale and retail delivery of goods, and use of trucks by farmers.

Trucks compete directly with all other methods of transportation, but they also facilitate the use of other methods. For example, trucks are used to carry goods to and from piers, railheads, and air terminals.

Advantages

One important advantage of trucks is that they can reach communities that are inaccessible by other means of transportation. Thousands of towns have no rail, air, or water transportation facilities and, were it not for trucks, would be virtually cut off from the commercial world.

Second, trucks are adapted to an unusually wide variety of purposes. Manufacturers build trucks for almost any use, from transporting oil to mixing cement in transit.

Third, on short hauls, truck transportation is generally less expensive than other means of transportation.

Fourth, trucks are relatively inexpensive and can therefore be owned or leased by almost any business, regardless of size.

Fifth, trucks make possible frequent delivery of goods, which means that fewer goods need be kept in inventory.

Disadvantages

Truck shipping has its disadvantages. First, long-haul transportation by truck tends to be more expensive than rail transportation. Second, even very large trucks can transport less than a railroad car. Third, interstate shipments are hindered by the lack of uniformity of trucking regulations between states. These difficulties help explain the higher costs per ton-mile of shipping goods long distance by truck than by rail. It should be noted, however, that truck shipping is a major beneficiary of our tremendous interstate highway system. As this system of improved highways is expanded, trucks will become increasingly competitive with railroads for long-haul shipping. Fully loaded trucks can now span the continent in less than sixty hours.

Piggyback service

An interesting development combining rail and truck services overcomes the major shortcomings of both systems. This service, offered by many railroads, is popularly called *piggyback* or *trailer-on-flatcar*, service. Loaded truck trailers are placed on railroad flatcars. Truckers at both ends of the journey take care of pickup and delivery. The system coordinates rail and truck services utilizing the strong points of each: the truck's flexibility at the pickup and delivery points and the railroad's lower long-haul cost. The piggyback system is regarded as one of the best long-range solutions to the national transportation and fuel conservation problems.

WATER TRANSPORTATION

Our inland water transportation system consists of the Great Lakes Seaway System and the Mississippi, Atlantic Coast, Gulf Coast, and Pacific Coast river systems. Inland waterways total more than twenty-eight thousand miles, and more than fourteen thousand commercial vessels are in use on them. Waterways are a significant, though often overlooked, feature of our transportation system.

Water transportation uses a variety of equipment, and much of it quite modern. Diesel-motored or gasoline-motored towboats that push steel barges capable of carrying between two and three thousand tons are employed on rivers. One towboat can easily handle a dozen loaded barges, and each barge can carry as much as twenty-five boxcars. Loading and unloading equipment is modern; it requires only a few hours to unload a large freighter.

Water transportation is especially important in the shipment of bulky, heavy goods of low unit value, such as coal, iron ore, cement, grain, lumber, chemicals, cotton, sand and gravel, fertilizer, and petroleum products. Perishable products and manufactured goods are not transported in quantity by water. Most shipping is by contract and private carriers, though common carriers do operate on the more important inland waterways. Frequently a vessel may be a private carrier going one way and a contract carrier on the return trip.

At one time, water transportation was more important. During the eighteenth and nineteenth centuries an extended system of man-made canals was constructed to connect natural bodies of water, but the debut of the railroad made most of these canals obsolete. Since the opening of the St. Lawrence Seaway, called the "fourth seacoast," however, the inland waterways are again increasing in their attractiveness to shippers, for many of the Great Lakes cities are developing new port facilities and

Figure **15–2**
Waterborne Commerce of the United States, 1940–70

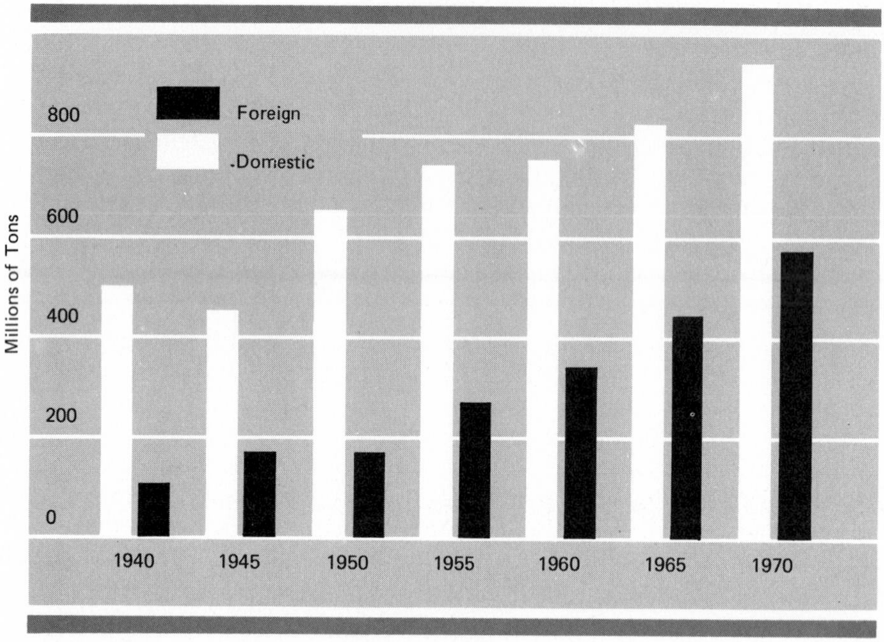

Source: *Statistical Abstract of the United States, 1972*, page 562.

are ports of call for even the largest ocean-going freighters from all over the world.

The growth and magnitude of water transportation is often overlooked because it is largely out of sight, whereas airplanes, railroads, and surely trucks are quite visible. Figure 15–2 shows the remarkable growth of water transportation within the United States in the past three decades.

Advantages

Low cost is the chief advantage of water transportation. Many goods can be shipped by water for approximately one-third the cost of rail transportation; large quantities can be transported in one vessel with less cost in personnel, motive power, and wear and tear on equipment. It is not uncommon for one ship on the Great Lakes to transport the equivalent of six or more trainloads of freight.

River traffic has been substantially restored through two innovations: the diesel towboat, which requires little maintenance, and radar, which makes it possible to operate nights as well as days. There are only 8,760 clock hours in a year, but diesel towboats are subject to so little "down time" (idleness) that some log from 8,000–8,500 hours yearly in operation.

Disadvantages

The greatest limiting feature of water transportation is that slow forward speed, plus longer, more roundabout routes, often make it the slowest method of transportation. Where an alternate railroad route exists, the water route is often 25 percent longer in miles.

Second, much water transportation is seasonal. Shipping in the Great Lakes, for example, can go on only 240 days a year.

Third, the services of water transportation are limited. Other modes of transportation must usually be used to pick up and deliver commodities shipped by water.

Fourth, the lack of waterways in many parts of the United States is an obvious disadvantage.

PIPELINES

Transportation by pipeline began in 1872, when the first oil fields were opened in Titusville, Pennsylvania. Since then, their importance has increased steadily because of the enormous demand for oil. (There are now more than 225,000 miles of pipeline in operation.) Many early difficulties, such as corrosion of pipes, leakage, and limited pumping power have been overcome. Today some pipelines are more than a thousand miles in length and are capable of transporting 300,000 barrels of oil in a twenty-four-hour period.

Pipeline transportation is highly specialized, being devoted solely to movement of petroleum products, including natural and artificial gas. It differs from other methods in that no vehicle is needed. Lines of pipe laid underground carry crude oil and gas from oil fields to refineries and from there to major points of consumption.

Most pipelines run from the great oil and gas fields of the Southwest to the industrial cities of the North and Northeast. Some pipelines function as common carriers, moving shipments of petroleum products for the public at large, but most of them operate as private carriers, being owned by petroleum companies.

Advantages

Low cost is the basic advantage of pipeline transportation. Although the construction of a pipeline is very costly, often running into tens of thousands of dollars per mile, maintenance and operating costs are low. Operation of the pipeline is largely automatic, and depreciation of equipment is slight. And, unlike all other modes of transportation, there is no movement of empty equipment, since there is no return haul. Water transportation is the only method of transportation that can compete in cost with the pipeline, and since waterways are often at some distance from points of production and consumption, pipelines remain the most practical method for transporting oil and gas.

A second advantage of pipeline transportation is safety. Dangers of fire and explosion are greatly minimized when oil, which is highly inflammable, is transported underground.

Third, unlike other modes of transportation, pipelines are not affected by weather.

Disadvantages

Pipelines suffer from several disadvantages. First, some other means of transportation is needed at the end of the line, for oil is seldom consumed at the end of the pipeline. Also, pipelines can be used only for very limited purposes. Finally, they are difficult to move; once laid, they are permanently fixed.

AIR TRANSPORTATION

Shipment of products by air is the newest form of transportation. Still an infant, air transportation accounts for less than 3 percent of the total volume (weight) of transportation. Nevertheless, it is growing lustily and promises to continue to do so. Interest in air transportation was aroused during World War II, when military aircraft carried many different types of goods previously considered unsuitable for air freight. The famous Berlin airlift in 1947, in which airplanes were used to deliver large quantities of goods such as food and fuel to the West German city, gave additional evidence of the practicality of shipping freight by air.

Products shipped by air

It has been estimated that more than two thousand different commodities have been shipped by air freight. One study indicated that 18 percent of gross air-freight revenue comes from auto parts, 17 percent from apparel, 14 percent from electrical goods, 9 percent from flowers and nursery stock, 6 percent from drugs, and 5 percent from aircraft parts. The remaining 31 percent comes from miscellaneous shipments including baby chicks, newspapers, fresh vegetables, seafood, films, and coffins.

Advantages

Several advantages of air transportation can be noted. First is speed. Major cities are only hours apart by air, which makes air transportation desirable in the case of emergency goods and perishable products. Second is safety. Products are less likely to be damaged or stolen while in transit than when shipped by rail or truck. Third is packaging convenience. Air transportation makes light packaging possible since the product is not subjected to the shocks common in surface carriage. In many instances, paper boxes replace the heavy wooden crates needed in rail or truck transportation. A large office-machine manufacturer air-ships fragile computers wrapped only in reusable blanket-type padding.

Disadvantages

High cost is the principal disadvantage of shipping by air. Though there are exceptions, the air cargo rate is generally most costly. One reason for the high cost is "directional unbalance"—that is, many planes must make return trips underloaded. A second disadvantage is the lack of airports in smaller cities. Finally, airports located from ten to fifteen miles from the city are less accessible to businesses than railroads or trucks. Transportation from the city to the airfield entails time, inconvenience, and cost.

SELECTION OF SPECIFIC CARRIERS

Choosing a carrier requires an analysis of the shipping problem at hand so the most economical means of fulfilling the overall requirements can be selected. For example, in making a shipment of machinery from Cincinnati to New Orleans, the shipper should determine:

1. Accessibility. Which carriers give service over this route?
2. Adequacy. Which carriers are equipped to handle the product?
3. Reliability. Which carriers will be sure to carry out the shipping requirement?
4. Speed. Which carriers will deliver within the time limitations?
5. Services. Which carriers provide any special services needed?

TRANSPORTATION AND TRAFFIC MANAGEMENT**

Efficient company transportation operations need an enlightened management, one alert to the costs and problems. Physical distribution is all-encompassing; it exists wherever there is flow or stoppage. As this has become more widely recognized, the trend has been to raise the traffic function in organizational level and to broaden its scope to include the entire function of materials handling, storage, packing, and transportation. Warehousing and inventory control may also be included.

SPECIAL READINGS

** The Logistics of Materials Management by Paul T. McElhiney and Robert I. Cook (eds.). New York: Houghton Mifflin, 1969 (paperback). This book deals with the integration of physical distribution, purchasing, and space and handling logistics. The book consists of articles written by various experts who, by relating their specialties to the overall problems of materials management, show how transportation, marketing, packaging, warehousing, computer applications, and inventory control are integrated in the overall process of materials management. Many of the articles are of an advanced nature; however, they serve the beginning student well by introducing him to important behind-the-scenes business functions that hold significant career possibilities.

A distribution director or a general traffic manager with the rank of vice-president is becoming common in many organizations. The stature of such titles and rank does much to assure coordination among the various departments that are related to physical distribution and to give matters of physical distribution greater consideration in the development of company policies.

Having a physical distribution director leads to efficiencies because distribution costs are analyzed as a whole. The executive in charge analyzes and thinks on a flow basis. In other words, all materials, merchandise, and services should flow uninterruptedly from suppliers through the plant to customers. He can see where coordination is lacking, where duplication occurs, where consolidations can be made, where costs pile up, and where policy is lacking or inappropriate.

When a company does not place a qualified distribution executive sufficiently high in the organization and does not give him enough responsibility so that he has a broad overview of operations, physical distribution inefficiencies are sure to arise. *Segmentation of responsibility of the functions of physical distribution lessens effective control and tends to conceal the total cost of the overall function.*

Smaller companies that do not center responsibility for overall physical distribution in a separate department headed by a key executive will have someone, usually called a traffic manager, who is responsible for all matters pertaining to incoming and outgoing shipments. In very small companies responsibility is even more limited, and there may be only a shipping clerk who dispatches and receives shipments.

INTERMODAL TRANSPORTATION AND CONTAINERIZATION

The businessperson is really not interested in transportation per se. What he is interested in is service—in getting goods from where he makes them to where his customers are. He wants to do this as economically and effortlessly as possible within his particular time limitations. In other words, he would like to use whatever mode or combination of modes will most suitably provide the solution to his particular shipping problem. Unfortunately, there is no really integrated or completely intermodal transportation system available. (See Figure 15–3.)

Obstacles to transportation integration

We have described the various modes of transportation—rail, truck, air, water, and pipeline—as they were developed historically—that is, independent of one another. The historical separateness of modes of transportation persists and hinders development of a fully integrated transportation service. Some of the factors that make integration so difficult are:

1. Rivalry.   Competition between types of carrier is fierce. Truckers have traditionally been anti-rail, railroads anti-air, and so on.[2] Physical distribution has been severely handicapped by the attitude of carriers that their form of transportation is the only one of merit.

2. Government regulation.   Government policies and regulation in the past have discouraged competition between the modes of transportation. The new modes were usually protected from competition and were even subsidized in order to get them developed. As is usually the case with protective measures, they are hard to discard once the need for them no longer exists.

3. Geographical boundaries.   Borders between states and nations represent obstacles to efficiency. There are regulations on the kind of equipment that can cross borders. Tax and paperwork also cause hindrances.

---

[2] A remark made by a crusty old railroad man who was chided about the superiority of air travel typifies the bitterness of intertransport rivalry, "Air travel? Ha, deadliest poison in the world; one drop and you've had it!"

Figure **15–3**
Intermodal Transportation

How many modes of transportation and modern facilities can you spot
in these figures?

4. <u>Labor unions</u>.   Organized labor puts many obstacles in the way of integrating transportation because, understandably, it wants to preserve jobs. Longshoremen, for example, insist on reloading any container from overseas carrying goods covered by more than one bill of lading, destined for an inland point farther than a 50-mile radius of a port.

While the obstacles that work against intermodal transportation are formidable, restrictions, attitudes, and laws in some cases are relaxing.

Containerization

A new service offered by various carriers is *containerization*, believed by many experts to be the most significant recent development in transportation. Containerization refers to the practice of packing goods in a container at the point of origin, where a seal is placed on it that is not broken until it reaches the point of destination. The bright promise of container freight is based on coordination of all kinds of shipping service, leaving each mode to the part of the job it is best able to handle. Light-weight aluminum containers (see Figure 15–4) can be cheaply transferred from truck to train, from ship to plane at lower handling costs. Containers offer many advantages that are not immediately obvious. Packages of many sizes and shapes can be packed together; because containers are sealed, shipments never get divided; and losses from pilferage and weather exposure are eliminated. Growth in use of containers and adaptations of the method can be expected in the future.

An interesting extension of the container idea is the lighter, or floating container. Lighters enable ships to load and discharge cargo independent of piers. Tugboats move cargo between ships and various locations. Port delays are eliminated, and multiple pier deliveries are possible. New ships now cross the Pacific that have a capacity of 49 lighters and 334 standard containers.

DOT: a systems approach to transportation

The Department of Transportation (DOT) was created in 1967, and includes the Office of Undersecretary of Commerce for Transportation, the Bureau of Public Roads, the Federal Aviation Agency, the U.S. Coast Guard, the St. Lawrence Seaway Development Corporation, and the Alaska Railroad. DOT has also taken over certain functions of the Interstate Commerce Commission (ICC), the Civil Aeronautics Board (CAB), and the Army Corps of Engineers, and provisions have been made for bureaus to administer motor vehicle and highway-safety legislation.

Figure **15–4**
Switching from a Labor-Intensive
to a Capital-Intensive System
through Containerization

Source: *Container News* magazine, New York.

As supervisor of the nation's transportation, DOT is authorized to:

1. Develop national transportation policies and programs conducive to the provision of fast, safe, efficient, and convenient transportation at the lowest cost consistent with other national objectives, including the efficient utilization and conservation of the nation's resources

2. Assure the coordinated, effective administration of the transportation programs of the federal government

3. Facilitate the development and improvement of coordinated transportation service, to be provided by private enterprise to the maximum extent feasible

4. Encourage cooperation of federal, state, and local governments, carriers, labor, and other interested parties toward the achievement of national transportation objectives

5. Stimulate technological advances in transportation

6. Provide general leadership in the identification and solution of transportation problems

7. Develop and recommend to the President and the Congress for approval national transportation policies and programs to accomplish these objectives with full and appropriate consideration of the needs of the public, users, carriers, industry, labor and the national defense

THE FUTURE OF TRANSPORTATION

Future U.S. historians will probably view the 1960s as the beginning of the second transportation revolution. Prior to 1960 the country was concerned with the development of the various forms of transportation. Railway, truck, waterway, pipeline, and air networks spanned the nation, and technological refinements greatly improved power units, equipment, and controls. Today, computers enable carriers to keep track of freight cars, trailers, and various containers and to operate mechanized and automated cargo terminals.

Strong-willed individuals like the railway tycoons and the airline pioneers shaped the pre-1960 destinies of transportation. Their single-mindedness provided excellent *modes* of transportation. It did not, however, provide the flexibility and efficiency in movement that could result from breaking the barriers between modes to provide unified, or intermodal, transportation service. Pressures were felt in the economy for such a unified service.

In 1968, the Secretary of Transportation stated that the job of our transportation system would double in thirteen years. Many forecasters think the freight transport job in the year 2000 will be three times as large as in 1975. In ton-miles, that would mean an increase from over 1.7 trillion to about 7 trillion.

It is of value for the student to be aware of the earlier specialized-carrier approach to transportation and the presently emerging unified-service approach. The bases for the intense rivalries between the forms of transportation, and the problems arising from unification based on a desire to provide an overall service, can thus be understood. While this chapter, of necessity, considers the various forms of transportation separately, the student is reminded to think of the advantages and limitations of each form, as would a business manager interested in using the best combination of advantages to provide the most effective transportation service for the particular shipping problem at hand.

PEOPLE AND THEIR IDEAS
Edward Vernon Rickenbacker

The World War I "ace of aces" who built Eastern Airlines

Edward Vernon Rickenbacker converted an early love for racing and flying into a distinguished career in aviation. He was among the first to recognize the tremendous potential of the airplane.

Rickenbacker was born in Columbus, Ohio, in 1890. When he was thirteen years old his father died, and he was forced to work to support the family. He had a succession of jobs for about a year and then began working in a garage. He soon knew that he wanted to work with automobiles. He took drafting and automotive engineering courses by correspondence and by the time he was twenty had become branch manager of the Columbus Buggy Company.

In 1909 Rickenbacker started auto racing and achieved fame as a driver. He drove in the 1911 and 1912 Indianapolis races and, in 1914, established a new speed record of 134 m.p.h. at Daytona Beach. When World War I broke out, Rickenbacker, too old to enter flight training, was assigned as chauffeur to Colonel William Mitchell. Through Mitchell's efforts Rickenbacker was eventually accepted into the Air Service, and he completed training and reached the front as a pilot early in 1918. He quickly became America's "Ace of Aces," shooting down twenty-six German planes and logging in more flight hours than any other U.S. flyer. After the Armistice he was awarded the Medal of Merit, the Croix de Guerre, the Legion of Honor, and the Congressional Medal of Honor.

On his return to the United States, Rickenbacker reentered the automobile business, founding the Rickenbacker Car Company in 1921. The
company failed in 1925, and two years later Rickenbacker acquired controlling interest in the Indianapolis Speedway, of which he was president
until 1945. In 1938, he bought Eastern Airlines for $3.5 million, becoming
president, general manager, and a member of the board of directors of
the company. He resigned as president of Eastern in 1953 and was named
chairman of the board.

In 1941 Rickenbacker was seriously injured in an airplane crash outside Atlanta, Georgia. Shortly after his recovery he was asked to undertake
a special mission to all Air Force combat units under final training in the
United States. This was followed by special missions to Iceland, England,
and the South Pacific, where his plane was forced down and he spent
twenty-three days in a life raft before rescuers reached him and six other
survivors. He completed his mission to Guadalcanal, New Guinea, and
other combat areas and later was sent as a consultant for the State Department to North Africa, Iran, India, and Russia.

The 1967 publication of his autobiography, *Rickenbacker*, served to
remind today's generation of a name once synonymous with trail-blazing
adventures in aviation. He died in 1973.

CONTEMPORARY ISSUES
Situation 15

How can we solve our passenger transportation problems?

One day Ray came across a newspaper item that read, "Because of surface traffic tie-ups within cities, it takes longer today to get from downtown Cincinnati to downtown Indianapolis than it took thirty years ago,
despite the air-time advantage of jets over trains."

"Why is our transportation system so fouled up?" asked Ray. "Millions of Americans, who work only eight hours a day, spend another
three going to and from work."

"Well, they seem to be trying something," John replied. "Listen to
this article. 'Amtrak,[3] a quasi-public corporation owned by the railroads,
assumed responsibility for almost all of the nation's passenger trains on
May 1, 1971. It operates over 24,000 miles of track and had a deficit of
$124.4 million in its second year of operation which was subsidized by
the government.'" John continued, "I think that transportation is a
public service that should try to pay its own way; but if it can't, then it
has to be subsidized. We've got to keep rail passenger service viable."

"But there are a lot of us who don't like the mass transit idea," re-

[3] Term used in transportation circles for the National Passenger Railroad Corporation.

sponded Ray. "I prefer to drive my own car, and I think most others do too. No mass transit system has the flexibility of the private automobile. If we build track-bound systems like subways or monorails, we permanently fix the growth patterns of our cities."

"You're using a self-centered approach, thinking only of yourself and your car. That's not going to solve transportation problems on a community-wide basis. What other alternatives do you have?"

"Well, I can think of at least two," offered Ray. "First, we can double- or triple-deck our freeways and build huge multistoried parking garages. Or we can speed up the development of practical helicopters or develop workable versions of vertical take-off aircraft for mass transit to and from multistoried parking facilities."

"Both of your suggestions are dedicated to the use of the private automobile and you haven't mentioned their polluting and congesting effects," interjected John. "Also, remember that energy sources are running out, as will your ability to pay for gasoline as prices climb, assuming you can get it at all. To have millions of separate engines consuming fuel as the private automobile does, is not efficient conservation of dwindling supplies of fuel. The days of the private automobile are numbered. Some cities are already outlawing them. We should prepare now for living without our own automobile."

SITUATION EVALUATION

1. Are modern-day workers, who spend three hours a day commuting, any better off than their grandfathers who worked twelve hours a day near their homes? What are the alternatives to commuting in the future?

2. How would a significant switch to mass transportation systems affect business? What opportunities would such a switch present?

3. Is the Amtrak approach to rail passenger transportation (modernization with government subsidies) a good idea? What would you propose?

4. Do you feel that the days of the private automobile are numbered? What should be done about the automobile and energy scarcities?

BUSINESS CHRONICLE

How real estate brokers exercise options

Most real estate companies have potential customers approach them with requests to search for special-purpose properties. Real estate agents are called brokers, and they arrange for either buying or selling real estate. Frequently, when representing a buyer, the broker does not reveal the identity of the party he represents. Also, he is inclined to work with as little fanfare as possible. The reason for this is that when a buyer wants to assemble a number of parcels of property (for, say, a trucking terminal or shopping center), he must move very discreetly; the moment property owners in an area become aware that someone is accumulating real estate for a specific purpose, prices for surrounding property rise. The option method is therefore used in real estate.

An option is a promise to sell at a fixed price within a specific time period. The broker tries to secure options for the parcels of property he needs. If he secures options for all the properties he needs (anything less is often useless) and there are no holdouts, options are exercised and the "deal" (to use real estate parlance) is made.

The real estate division of Kingmaker Estates was approached by a large earth-moving equipment manufacturer from Wisconsin. They needed a piece of property with a length of 650 feet and a depth of 250 feet for equipment assembly and equipment trans-shipment internationally to Central and South America and domestically to southern states. Ideally the property should have easy access to the interstate highway system, a rail spur, and should be on the water for marine loading facilities. Zoning of the property would have to be commercial or for light manufacturing.

QUESTIONS

1. How would Kingmaker go about getting options on this type of property?

2. How would a search for such property be conducted? Would advertising, other brokers, or government agencies be of any assistance?

3. If the zoning for a desirable parcel of property is wrong, is there any way to get the zoning changed? If so, how would Kingmaker go about this? Would it be wise to hold property while it was uncertain whether the petition for re-zoning would be granted?

APPLICATION EXERCISES

1. For each of the following indicate the type of transportation you would select and your reasons: (a) one thousand orchids from Panama to New York City, (b) a spare flywheel for a production machine in a branch factory located 175 miles away, (c) five hundred thousand bricks from Cleveland to Milwaukee, (d) six dozen expensive women's dresses made in Los Angeles but needed in Denver, and (e) oil that goes regularly from an oil well to a refinery two hundred miles away.

2. On an outline map of the Great Lakes region, draw the route iron ore takes when it is shipped from the Mesabi iron ore deposits in Minnesota to the Pittsburgh steel mills. Consult library references to secure the necessary information. How many types of carriers are used in completing a normal shipment? What seasonal and handling factors are involved?

3. In this chapter we explained that containerization is probably the most revolutionary recent transportation development. Statements of leaders representing different interests affected by this development are given below. (These views were expressed at the Baltimore Symposia on Containerization.) Study the opinions and extract from them a list of what you believe are the issues arising from containerization. How do you believe each issue either affects the future or should be resolved? Some people believe that containerization is creating more problems than it solves. What is your view?

George G. McManis, Vice-President, Trailmobile Division, Pullman, Inc. Containerization is combining new concepts and new technology, supported by multi-billion dollar outlays, to create whole new industries and revive old ones. The container age is destined to have a major impact on people and their economies around the world, providing better jobs, greater rewards and richer opportunities. . . . A crucial element arising out of this breakthrough in the transport science will be the upgrading and training of countless thousands of people who will direct the intermodal movement of goods at home and abroad.

Thomas W. Gleason, President, ILA (Longshoreman's Union). . . . Port labor is determined not to be boxed in by the container. Nor is port labor a commodity to be shifted around . . . like cargo. Management in this industry has got to learn — just as management in other industries has learned — that it must be satisfied only with its fair share of the benefits to it from containerization, unitized cargoes, and other technical innovation. Part of the gain must be shared with the dock workers. . . . Higher pay, more hours and more benefits for a dwindling labor force do not add up to true overall gains for the port labor generally. . . . The longshoreman who has lost his job has a real problem. Where is he to find a substitute for the only kind of work he knows? . . . The ILA intends to see to it that, containers or no containers, the traditional work of the dock worker shall not be taken from him.

Dudley Perkins, Director General, Port of London Authority. A key factor in making the economics of port operations of containers financially sensible is to reduce the number of men needed for the operation. The Port of London has been successful in doing this by the cooperation of the men and unions, by the introduction of a sensible and humanitarian scheme for voluntary severance and by a scheme for a reasonably highly paid, permanent body of men, who are paid just like a salaried employee — work or no work. They are guaranteed security, and in return they guarantee to turn out to work as required, day or night, on any day of the week.

Capt. G. R. William, Port Operations Consultant, London. It would be a mistake not to include the less developed countries in container planning. The experience of some African ports with pallets and fork lifts, which open the way for a much higher degree of mechanization, shows that emerging countries should not be left out of such progressive concepts.

James W. Gullick, Federal Maritime Administration. What about the future? We can and must expect a great deal in the way of systems approach, technical advances, innovation. We need management of quality, intensity, and imagination. . . . New techniques in port management and development must be found. Nowhere in the United States is there a thoroughly organized training program for port workers, to say nothing of supervisors.

QUESTIONS

1. Explain how the industrial wealth of the country is based to a large extent on its varied transportation system.

2. Define "carrier." How are carriers classified for legal purposes?

3. What are the chief factors to be considered in selecting a carrier?

4. Summarize the advantages and disadvantages of rail transportation, motor-truck transportation, water transportation, pipeline transportation, and air transportation.

5. When does a business use the services of a freight forwarder?

6. What is meant by intermodal transportation? What problems are involved in developing it?

7. Which type of carrier stands to benefit the most from the interstate highway program? Which carrier stands to lose the most? Give reasons for your answers.

8. What transportation activities are subject to governmental regulation? Why does the government regulate transportation so carefully?

9. What is containerization? Why is it considered so revolutionary, and why has it exploded so in importance?

10. One hundred years ago, three of our five transportation modes—trucks, pipelines, and airplanes—were not even in the planning stages. What distinctively new transportation modes might we find one hundred years from now? (Keep in mind that many transportation leaders believe transportation and communications will merge.)

CHAPTER 16

IMPORTANCE OF A GOOD LOCATION

LOCATING MANUFACTURING FACILITIES
Choosing a Community. Appraising the Intangible Mix of Factors in Location Selection. Selecting a Specific Site. Industrial Parks. Sources of Aid.

LOCATION OF A RETAIL STORE
Retail and Industrial Location Compared. Choosing a Community for Retail Location. Selecting a Specific Site.

LAND USE AND ECOLOGY
Land Use. Water Pollution. Air Pollution. Noise and Ugliness Pollution. Solid Waste. Some Further Questions.

16 business location, land use, and ecology

Selecting the best location for factories, retail stores, service establishments, warehouses, and other distribution and processing facilities is a critically important business and social consideration. Good location is always a great asset; poor location of physical facilities can be a severe handicap.

The purpose of this chapter is to consider the matter of location in business and relate it to the general subject of land use and ecology. Specific attention is given to the location problems of manufacturers and retailers. Analysis of these problems will also suggest most of the placement considerations for other types of business, such as banks, wholesalers, service stations, and hotels.

While a picture of the ideal location can easily be conceived in the minds of management, finding such a location is often difficult. Frequently, a location with all desired advantages is unavailable or, indeed, nonexistent. For example, a site near coal mines, with water shipping facilities, accessibility to West Coast markets, a labor supply of skilled craftsmen, and a dry climate is ideal for some types of manufacturing; however, such a combination simply does not exist. So the various alternatives must be evaluated, and the ultimate choice is always a compromise. Too often, sites are selected "by hunch and hope."

IMPORTANCE OF A GOOD LOCATION

Nearly everyone has seen a poorly located retail store and is aware that, as long as the business remains in that location, its success will be limited. Mislocation of factories is also common, although less obvious.

The best possible location is desirable primarily because it gives the business a competitive advantage. Other things being equal, the manufacturer located in a region where wage rates are low obviously has an advantage over a competitor located in a high wage-rate area. Similarly, the gas station located at a busy intersection can expect to sell much more gasoline and related products than a competitor located in the middle of the block on a street with less traffic.

The value of a location is subject to change. What was originally a good location may, several years later, become a poor one. Shifts in population, relocation of major streets and highways, and deterioration of the neighborhood are among the many factors that can destroy a location's value. Wanamaker's, once one of New York City's leading department stores, finally closed its main store in that city after fighting a losing battle for years against a location handicap. Each year hundreds of motels located along "old" highways are affected adversely by the new interstate highway system. Conversely, poor locations may become valuable sites when change works to their advantage.

Unfortunately, many locations are chosen without much consideration of their advantages and disadvantages. Often the only concern is the rent or puchase price. A low-cost location, however, is not necessarily good.

Business organizations that build plants or add new stores often research first, then decide where to locate the new units. Some organizations may have a separate department concerned exclusively with studying new business sites and evaluating present locations; others retain the service of independent research organizations. Literally dozens of locations may have to be considered and perhaps a hundred different factors for each location may be taken into account before a final selection is made. One only has to cite the example of the DuPont Corporation, with nearly one hundred plants in some thirty states as well as plants in foreign countries, to realize how vast and complex is the task of choosing locations. The president of Holiday Inns has stated that location is the most important contributor to its success, and MacDonald's, the mammoth hamburger chain, lists location as its prime consideration.

LOCATING MANUFACTURING FACILITIES

In choosing a location for a factory, first, a community must be chosen, and then a specific site within the community.

Choosing a community

The Conference Board reports that since 1940 there has been a trend toward locating plants in smaller communities, although large cities still receive the greatest share of plant expansions. Expansion activity in the large cities consists chiefly of additions to existing plants, while new plant construction is most common in the outlying communities, some of which may be in industrial parks (discussed later).

Important factors to consider in selecting a community in which to locate a factory are: (1) labor, (2) transportation, (3) power, (4) proximity to raw materials, (5) proximity to markets, and (6) local regulations (zoning, taxes, etc.) and community living conditions.

There is *no perfect location;* no one community excels in all those factors. Some form of compromise is always necessary.

Labor   In studying the merits of different plant locations, particular attention is paid to the quantity of labor, its skill, and union affiliations.

Quantity of labor.   To determine whether a new factory would be able to attract all the employees it needs, an analysis is made of the workers within a radius of twenty-five miles or so, who seek employment.

A reservoir of labor is desirable for two reasons: (1) A large supply gives greater assurance that a sufficient number of desirable workers can be found. (2) The larger the supply, the less the pressure to raise wage rates, since more people are competing for jobs. The large labor supply, with the attendant lower wage rates, is one of the major reasons that some Northern and Eastern industries build new plants in the South, where wages tend to be lower. Since labor is often the major production cost, the savings may be substantial.

Labor skill.   Many types of manufacturing require skilled workers. While factories are sometimes prepared to train new employees, they prefer to hire those who have the necessary skills. Labor productivity — which is based on how fast and well work is done as well as the quality of work traditional in the line involved—is taken into account. The need for skilled employees is one of the reasons that the automobile industry is concentrated in Detroit, St. Louis, Cleveland, and New Jersey. In these areas thousands of specialized employees with years of training can be found.

Frequently, in considering a new factory site, manufacturers investigate vocational training given in schools in the community, since the vocational-training program is related to the availability of skilled or potentially skilled employees.

Labor unions.   To many manufacturers, the type and extent of union affiliation is significant. A reason that some manufacturers have moved into the South is that labor unions there are still not strong. Without unions, management has more control over wages, hours, and working conditions.

Transportation   Most factories depend on transportation facilities to bring materials to the plant and to transport the finished product to wholesalers, retailers, or other factories. Thus, in the selection of a community for a factory, attention must be given to the types of transportation available and the competition among carriers. Communities served by several modes of transportation—water, air, rail, and motor truck—are preferred, since goods then can be shipped by a variety of means. And the more competition among carriers, the better the service will be.

The balance between freight costs for transporting *unfinished* materials *to the plant* and shipment of *finished* products *from the plant* to the market has to be considered. Bulk shipments of unprocessed materials are cheaper in most cases than are shipments of finished products. Automobile manufacturers, for example, have built assembly plants in several regions, since it is cheaper to ship carloads of parts than carloads of finished automobiles.

Power   The importance of power as a location factor varies with the type of industry. Electrochemical industries need large quantities of power and for that reason tend to be located near hydroelectric plants, where electricity is cheap. Other industries, such as furniture factories, consume relatively little power, so this is an unimportant factor for the most part.

Power supplied in the form of electricity is quoted by the kilowatt-hour. While the rate differential often appears small, the annual cost difference between two locations may be significant for large users. For example, in the aluminum industry, nine kilowatt-hours of electricity are required to produce one pound of aluminum, which equals 10 to 13 percent of production cost. A difference of one mill (one-tenth of one cent)

Figure **16–1**
The Forty-Mile Chemical Strip on the Mississippi River
between Baton Rouge and New Orleans

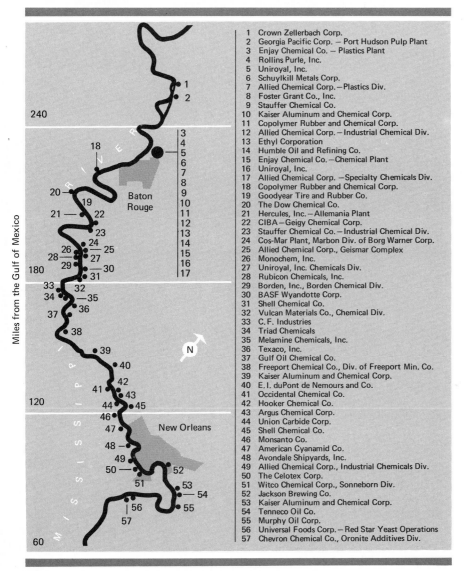

1 Crown Zellerbach Corp.
2 Georgia Pacific Corp. — Port Hudson Pulp Plant
3 Enjay Chemical Co. — Plastics Plant
4 Rollins Purle, Inc.
5 Uniroyal, Inc.
6 Schuylkill Metals Corp.
7 Allied Chemical Corp. — Plastics Div.
8 Foster Grant Co., Inc.
9 Stauffer Chemical Co.
10 Kaiser Aluminum and Chemical Corp.
11 Copolymer Rubber and Chemical Corp.
12 Allied Chemical Corp. — Industrial Chemical Div.
13 Ethyl Corporation
14 Humble Oil and Refining Co.
15 Enjay Chemical Co. — Chemical Plant
16 Uniroyal, Inc.
17 Allied Chemical Corp. — Specialty Chemicals Div.
18 Copolymer Rubber and Chemical Corp.
19 Goodyear Tire and Rubber Co.
20 The Dow Chemical Co.
21 Hercules, Inc. — Allemania Plant
22 CIBA — Geigy Chemical Corp.
23 Stauffer Chemical Co. — Industrial Chemical Div.
24 Cos-Mar Plant, Marbon Div. of Borg Warner Corp.
25 Allied Chemical Corp., Geismar Complex
26 Monochem, Inc.
27 Uniroyal, Inc. Chemicals Div.
28 Rubicon Chemicals, Inc.
29 Borden, Inc., Borden Chemical Div.
30 BASF Wyandotte Corp.
31 Shell Chemical Co.
32 Vulcan Materials Co., Chemical Div.
33 C. F. Industries
34 Triad Chemicals
35 Melamine Chemicals, Inc.
36 Texaco, Inc.
37 Gulf Oil Chemical Co.
38 Freeport Chemical Co., Div. of Freeport Min. Co.
39 Kaiser Aluminum and Chemical Corp.
40 E. I. duPont de Nemours and Co.
41 Occidental Chemical Co.
42 Hooker Chemical Co.
43 Argus Chemical Corp.
44 Union Carbide Corp.
45 Shell Chemical Co.
46 Monsanto Co.
47 American Cyanamid Co.
48 Avondale Shipyards, Inc.
49 Allied Chemical Corp., Industrial Chemicals Div.
50 The Celotex Corp.
51 Witco Chemical Corp., Sonneborn Div.
52 Jackson Brewing Co.
53 Kaiser Aluminum and Chemical Corp.
54 Tenneco Oil Co.
55 Murphy Oil Corp.
56 Universal Foods Corp. — Red Star Yeast Operations
57 Chevron Chemical Co., Oronite Additives Div.

Source: Data prepared by the Environmental Protection Agency.

How does this testify to the fact that location is a factor in
competition? What elements are present here to make the area
so attractive for chemical plants?

per kilowatt-hour in the cost of electricity would make a difference of one cent per pound in the market price for aluminum. In the Tennessee Valley Authority area, electricity runs as low as 2.1 mills per kilowatt-hour, compared with seven and eight mills per kilowatt-hour in Chicago or Pittsburgh.

Proximity to raw materials   Proximity to raw materials needed in manufacturing can be a major, sometimes a decisive, factor in selecting locations for manufacturing plants. For example, raw materials plus other factors have caused forty chemical companies to crowd onto the banks of the Mississippi from Baton Rouge to New Orleans (see Figure 16–1). Called the "chemical strip," the area has mammoth raw material resources at its disposal—water, oil and gas reserves, sulfur, salt, and limestone deposits—all accessible to inexpensive water transportation. From New Orleans there are fourteen thousand miles of inland waterways that flow to two-thirds of the nation's markets for chemicals. A chemical plant not located "on the strip" would be at a serious disadvantage competing with these fifty-seven companies, for this particular mix of essential advantages does not exist elsewhere.

In the case of steel, more than four tons of raw materials (not including large quantities of water) must be assembled for each ton of steel produced. Since the size and weight of the raw material is often reduced greatly by manufacture, it is generally wise to ship it for only short distances and, if necessary, to transport the finished product longer distances. Clay, for example, is very heavy, with the result that brick and tile factories are located close to clay deposits. Lumber mills tend to follow the forest line because a large part of the log is waste material. If logs that might be 40 percent scrap were shipped long distances, large amounts of freight would be paid on material that is simply discarded.

Proximity to markets   Ideally, all manufacturers would like to be located near the markets in which their products are sold. Many relatively small manufacturing firms that produce parts for major industries are located in the same cities as their largest industrial customers. One of the factors prompting industrial decentralization is the desire to be near markets. Accordingly, machinery manufacturers and others have established plants in various metropolitan areas in the United States. The Conference Board found that in plant expansions the desire to extend into new markets and the desire to improve customer services (quick shipments, replacement adjustments, and so on) were factors that had great bearing in one-third of all reported plant placements.

Government and community   The efficiency and cooperation of state and local governments are important factors in choosing an industrial location. City, county, school, and certain other taxes vary appreciably from one locality to another. A tax differential can mean the difference between meeting or not meeting the competition's prices. For example, practically all states levy a sales tax. However, some states exempt building materials, which means substantially lower industrial construction costs. The same applies to machinery and office equipment and regular purchases of supplies such as business forms, duplicating paper, and so on. If the state levies sales taxes on purchases used for conducting business, costs of doing business are raised accordingly.

Attention should also be given to other community factors that may be unimportant considered singly but, taken collectively, can be significant. These include civic pride; recreational, religious, educational, and financial facilities; crime rates; newspapers; radio and television stations; and percentage of home ownership. Analyzed carefully, these factors provide clues to the character and ambition of the citizens who make up the community.

Appraising the intangible mix of factors in location selection

How management arrives at a location decision depends on the nature of the business and on its priorities. It is not the tangible factors that are difficult to weigh but the intangible. The following statement by Lammot du Pont Copeland, of du Pont provides an example of how intangible values are balanced in making location decisions.

[We try to strike a balance, but] . . . the business climate which we find at the site always weighs heavily with all levels of our management. We have no desire to locate where we are not wanted, nor where it would be more difficult for us to carry on our business. We do not always realize the ideal situation, but we look for it. . . .

First, we try to appraise the nature of the people. Do they seem intelligent, alert, trustworthy, industrious, and willing to learn so that they can develop their full potential of accomplishment when given that opportunity? Are they willing and able to accept responsibility?

We seek the answers to these questions in many ways. We talk to community leaders. We look at the physical condition of homes, lawns, and parks. We are especially interested in the school system, because the kind of people we are seeking will insist upon good educational facilities for their children.

A sound education [for prospective employees] . . . is important to us, for the operations of a chemical business are highly technical. While we do our own training of employees, their educational background must be such that [they] can absorb the training, as well as have the willingness to continue to learn.

Second, we are interested in the nature of local governments. In many communities, inducements of a short-range character are offered to industries. These do not attract us—we are far more concerned with long-range values.

We try to discover, for example, whether municipal services are carried out with competence and efficiency. These services usually are not essential for the plant because we provide our own, but we must think about our employees who depend upon these services in their homes and in their travel to and from work.

We take note of the trend of the community debt, for this is a measure of the willingness of the government to live within its income. We examine the tax system with care. While we expect to assume full responsibility for our fair share of civic operating expenses, we do not think it right to expect du Pont or any other business to assume the rightful burdens of others in the community, or to bear special penalties.

It goes almost without saying that the kind of government in any community reflects the nature of its citizens. If the government is bad, you can be sure there is apathy and indifference among the people.

Finally, we are interested in the attitude of the state and local governments toward industry, and the relationships which exist among them. If this attitude is one of hostility toward business, or even indifference to its problems, we are tempted to get back on the plane and resume our search elsewhere.[1]

Selecting a specific site

Once a community has been chosen, the next step is to select a specific site. This decision depends in part on whether the concern plans to rent facilities or to erect a new structure. Choice of an ideal site is naturally limited when the business decides to rent, for usually there are relatively few sites from which to choose. Care should be exercised to choose a site near transportation facilities. Consideration should also be given to room for expansion, water supply (especially important in certain industries), zoning regulations, and waste disposal, and, if renting, condition of the building, remodeling needed, and terms of the lease. In the undeveloped areas surrounding central cities, there are many sites for manufacturing plants. For them to be good locations, however, they must be accessible, be supplied with utilities, and have other community services.

Industrial parks

Historically, factories, warehouses, and commercial areas have been synonymous with congestion, noise, and pollution. Industrial areas were

---

[1] Speech by Lammot du Pont Copeland, president of the E. I. du Pont de Nemours and Co., Governor's Conference on Business and Industry, Wilmington, Del., April, 1966.

eye-sores that people felt they had to contend with as the price for industrialization. Many firms are discovering that their ways of doing business on old sites would either (1) now be prohibited by law with the enactment of pollution and zoning standards or are (2) antiquated facilities
that defy renovation.

The development of the industrial park concept is receiving support
from many communities and businesses. Industrial parks are planned
industrial centers that often look much like university campuses. To
qualify as a planned park, the land must be controlled, either by local
zoning ordinances or by the developer, to provide suitable land-to-build-
ing ratios, building setbacks, landscaping, on-site parking, design and construction standards for all buildings, sign limitations, and restrictions
against uses that would be objectionable by reasons of noise, odor, smoke,
or vibration.

In the main, industrial parks are attracting facilities for warehousing
and distribution functions, manufacturing plants that are mainly in the
"light" industry category, and research and service companies. Recently,
some industrial parks have allowed retail businesses, office buildings,
restaurants, motels, theaters, and other nonindustrial firms to locate in
their areas. There is debate about whether this is proper, since new consumer businesses tend to create antagonism with established industrial
businesses, which results in friction between the community and the industrial park.

Sources of aid

There are several sources of assistance to help a business find and even
finance the securing of an appropriate location.

City and regional agencies   Most cities have a chamber of commerce
to promote the economic welfare of the community. Since industries are
a source of payrolls and taxes, most chambers of commerce are eager to
attract industry since most of a region's existing businesses—especially
retailers, wholesalers, and service establishments—stand to benefit (see
Figure 16–2). Accordingly, chambers of commerce often collect economic
data for those considering the town as an industrial site.

Communities are also interested in developing their areas logically
and orderly. As a result, many highly concentrated sections of the country have established regional planning commissions, whose purpose is
to plan for the long-range development of areas for both community and
industrial life. Such agencies are staffed with city-planning engineers
and other specialists who, through training and experience, can provide
assistance to businesses faced with location problems.

Figure **16–2**
What One-Hundred Factory Workers Bring to a Town

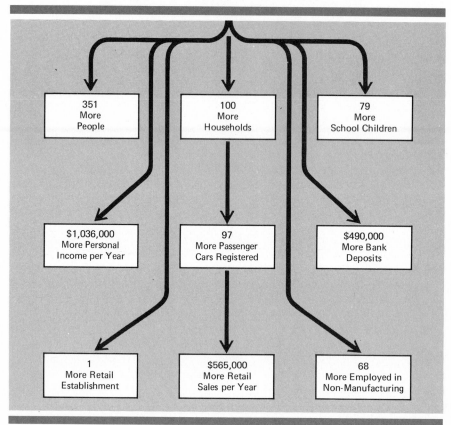

Source: *Nation's Business,* March 1973, p. 26.

Public utilities and railroads   Electric, gas and telephone companies may be eager to see new industries established in their territories, since this increases the market for their services. Power companies often prepare extensive data on the advantages of locating in their area and are generally glad to make studies for interested concerns.

Railroads are interested in seeing industries established along their rights of way, because this means more revenue for them. Like power companies, railroads prepare reports showing the advantages of their areas.

State departments of economic development   Each state government has an agency intended to attract industry. States want to attract industry, for it means more jobs, payrolls, and more tax revenue. Competition among states for new industry is keen.

Incentive financing, to encourage companies to locate in underindustrialized areas, is available through many state resources development offices. In the 1930s, Mississippi introduced financing through issuing industrial bonds. Variations of such financing are now available in over 40 states. In every case where this financing is available, the interest rate is one or two percentage points below that of conventional financing, a considerable saving. Real estate tax exemptions for stated or indefinite periods may also be granted for new plants.

LOCATION OF A RETAIL STORE

Retail and industrial location compared

Like manufacturers, retailers must choose a community in which to locate and then select a specific site. There are, however, important differences in the location problems and considerations.

Manufacturers choose locations on the basis of factors affecting production efficiencies and physical distribution, whereas retailers choose on the basis of customer potential and what will appeal to and best serve the customer. Thus the industrial concern is interested primarily in labor supply, transportation facilities, power costs, and proximity to raw materials and markets. Retailers are concerned with population, income, and competition.

Community attitudes, recreational facilities for employees, climate, and power availability, which are significant in factory location, are less important in retail-store location. Because factories tend to have large payrolls, pay sizable taxes, consume power, and ship large quantities of freight, numerous civic and private interests are eager to see them locate in their community. Retailers do not, as a rule, contribute so directly to the economic well-being of the locality and are not, therefore, so courted.

Choosing a community for retail location

Population   Specific aspects of population that warrant study are size, trend, and characteristics.

Population size.   Retail stores are interested chiefly in the number of people—and especially the number of household units—located in the area from which the store expects to draw customers. This factor varies, since the distance (in travel time) customers will go to shop varies with the type of business and section of the country. People will travel a long distance to purchase furniture, whereas they prefer to buy groceries in the nearest shopping center. Supermarkets draw about 25 percent of their customers from within a quarter-mile radius of the store, roughly 25 percent come from a quarter to half a mile, 10 percent from half to three-quarters of a mile, 7 percent from three-quarters to a mile, and slightly over 33 percent from beyond the one-mile radius.

Size of household, number of children, and age of adults all have a direct bearing on a population's shopping habits and are therefore important considerations in location selection. Moreover, the increasing mobility of our population is also important in location planning. The Bureau of the Census is now required by federal law to produce a National Travel Survey every five years that answers many questions related to the mobility of people.

Population trend. Population statistics should also be studied to learn whether the population of an area is decreasing, static, or increasing. Obviously, a decreasing population means less retail business each year. Nor is a static population desirable, since the possibility of increasing business is slight. An increasing population is most desirable, since it means that, other things being equal, the retailer can expect growth.

Data on size and trend of population can be procured from most chambers of commerce or from census figures. It is important to remember that absolute population figures alone are a dangerous yardstick—a population's characteristics must be analyzed before sound conclusions can be reached. For example, neighborhoods grow older. While the number of people living in a community may remain constant or indeed even increase, the retailer's market potential may decrease because of population aging. A neighborhood of families with many children has a greater sales potential for a store selling ice cream and soft drinks than the same neighborhood fifteen years later if by then most of the people are adults.

Population characteristics. Religious and ethnic background may be important determinants of the type of business that will be successful in an area. A kosher food store succeeds only within easy access of a Jewish population. Type of work done is also a factor, as consumption habits of blue-collar workers differ from those of white-collar workers even when income is roughly the same. Studies show marked consumption pattern differences according to occupation classifications. For example, blue-collar families buy larger refrigerators, while white-collar families eat out more often.

Income   While population size is important, sheer numbers of people do not guarantee consumption. The income of people in the community and its trading area determines how much and what will be purchased. In studying income, consideration should be given to such things as size, source, and stability. Retail trade is more stable if people in the trading area receive a year-round income and the source is from several different industries.

Selecting a specific site

Customer traffic   The number, type, and attitudes of people who pass by a given site are very important factors in store location, since they suggest customer potential. Every city, town, or shopping area has major intersections where customer foot traffic is heavier than at other locations. From these points outward, customer traffic decreases. Most retailers prefer to locate as close to these points (called the "100 percent location") as possible, since it is assumed that the larger the potential customer traffic, the larger the volume of business.

Accordingly, many retailers, especially chain stores, make scientific analyses of the traffic that passes by locations under consideration. Some of the factors considered are:

1. How many potential customers pass daily?

2. At what time of day do traffic peaks occur?

3. What distances are people traveling?

4. Why are the people passing by? Are they shopping, hurrying to buses, or going home from work?

Accessibility   Good retail locations should be easily accessible to large numbers of people. That is, the ease with which people can reach the site is important. In larger cities, an analysis of public transportation and parking facilities would be needed to judge accessibility. Parking facilities continue to be an important factor in retail locations. Shoppers are less willing to shop in a concentrated and crowded downtown area. Retailers in locations surrounded by ample parking facilities, such as suburban shopping centers, receive more favorable attention from the shopping public.

Surrounding business establishments and competition   The nature of other businesses and competitors in the immediate vicinity directly affects the value of a particular location. In the case of goods where customers make comparisons before buying (furniture, automobiles, shoes, clothing), locations close to competitors are often desirable, since customers generally prefer to visit several stores before making a purchase decision. In other cases being near a strong competitor may be undesirable.

Certain businesses tend to detract from the value of a location. Bars, mortuaries, and cheap hotels belong in this category. Furthermore, the general upkeep of the vicinity is significant.

Availability of sites   The past decade has witnessed a continued trend toward building planned shopping centers. These centers may have from as few as ten retail and service establishments to as many as two hundred. Free parking, modern stores, combined drawing power of many stores, and location away from the congested downtown areas are major advantages of the shopping centers.

The best locations may be difficult to acquire, since they are in great demand. Prime space in a shopping center is usually leased before the center is constructed, and usually to national chains. Most retailers in shopping centers lease rather than build their own structures. While rental costs are important, it should be noted that choosing a location solely on the basis of low-rent is dangerous.

Consideration should also be given to the appearance of the site, its suitability for the contemplated purposes, the remodeling that will be necessary, and leasing arrangements. In the case of a vacant store, the prospective tenant should learn how long the site has been vacant and what its history has been. If other businesses have tried a location without success, there is reason to believe that the site may be undesirable.

Whether additional space can be added at a later date is often another consideration. Some stores are built so that floors can be added if needed; supermarkets often attempt to lease adjoining property to provide additional space at a future date.

LAND USE AND ECOLOGY**

The choice of industrial and commercial locations today must take into account the overall environment. Land use can no longer be determined solely by business considerations. In the past, communities considered payrolls, taxes, and other economic benefits more significant than environmental conservation. The fundamental question now being raised is: Can both economic progress and the environment be preserved or must one be sacrificed to the other? Society's escalating concern over pollution and depletion of natural resources has resulted in various legal restraints. Furthermore, location decisions cannot, and should not, be made to avoid the costs of anti-pollution devices or to circumvent depletion of resources. Locating polluting industries in sparsely populated areas, using nighttime smokestack emissions, placing a plant on the leeward side of a city, and disguising or covering up abuses are solutions of the past.

SPECIAL READINGS

**How to Manage Your Company Ecologically by Jerome Goldstein, Emmaus, Pa.: Rodale Press, 1971 (paperback). A statement on the title page sets the stage for this book. "The paper in this book has been made from waste paper that normally winds up at the city dump. This reclaimed paper is an example of how today's wastes can be re-used, thereby helping to solve the solid waste disposal crisis and preserving the quality of our environment." The subtitle of the book reads, "Some suggestions on how to be corporately clean and profitable . . . while encouraging your suppliers, colleagues, employees, and customers to do likewise."

The main subject of the book—how to manage ecologically—is one about which little has been written. The subject looms large on the horizon, so it is safe to predict that this small volume is among the first of many that will follow. Business managers have barely started to think in terms of making decisions on the basis of what is sound ecologically. The subject is complicated and requires a nonspecialist's orientation that is yet barely understood.

The book discusses whether an ecological approach can yield profits and concludes that profits and ecology are not inconsistent. Among other things, it offers a ten-point program for chief executives and tells how to "use your company's purchasing power" to achieve results that will preserve the environment. There is also an extensive reading list related to business management and ecology.

The population explosion, especially the concentration of populations in specific areas, and increasing economic activity (see Figures 16–3 and 16–4) result in growing governmental regulation and social pressures for business to conduct itself in terms of what is best for the total environment. The complicated and increasingly popular science that deals with total environment—relations between living organisms and their environment—is *ecology*. It studies total environment in terms of human populations related to their environment, spatial distribution, and cultural needs. Some of the constraints and concerns that affect business and relate to ecology are discussed in the following paragraphs.

Land use

Any discussion of land use quickly runs to paradoxes. The most perplexing one is that 70 percent of the U.S. population lives on a scant $1\frac{1}{2}$ percent of our total land mass. This land is all in urban areas, and some of it is not used! People want to live where urban excitement, services, and opportunities are available. Urban amenities are very costly, so a great deal of effort is exerted to increase the amount of usable land in urban areas. Businesses, of course, are the leaders in this movement—Manhattan Island being the extreme example of concentrated land use promoted by business interests.

Increased utilization of land in urban areas is fostered in the following ways: (1) increases in the speed of transportation (if commuting is twice as fast, the city may be four times as large); (2) use of the third—i.e., vertical—dimension, which means skyscrapers, underground garages and utilities, structures over highways and rail right-of-ways; (3) stag-

Figure **16–3**
Man and His Environment

The biosphere, the habitat of man and 1.3 million other species, is only a tiny sliver in the universal scheme. It is sustained by limited resources and replenishing cycles. In the energy cycle, (1) animals eat plants fed by soil and air nutrients, (2) flesh-eating animals eat plant-eating animals, (3) animals defecate, die, and decompose—returning nutrients to soil, (4) with this same process occurring in the sea. (5) There is also a water cycle— evaporation, (6) which returns as rain. Unchecked population growth and pollution upset natural cycles that renew the earth's blanket of life. Business must sustain the renewal process.

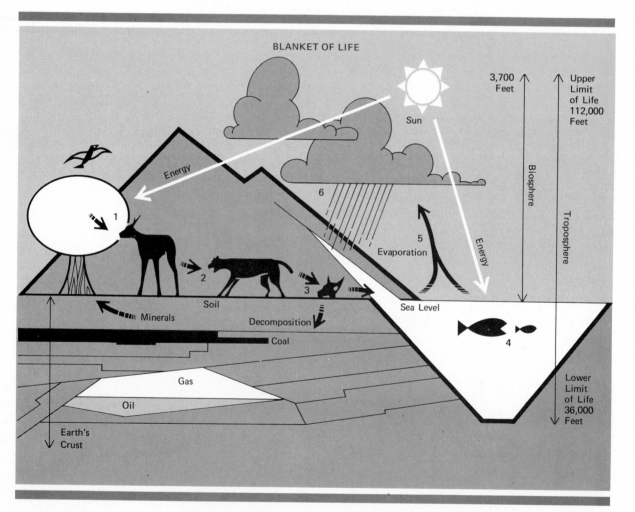

gering work hours and around-the-clock work shifts, which extend the time dimension for use of space; and (4) landfill operations and new building techniques, which permit use of difficult sites.

Most communities have regulations for land use and building. There

Figure **16–4**
The Population Bomb

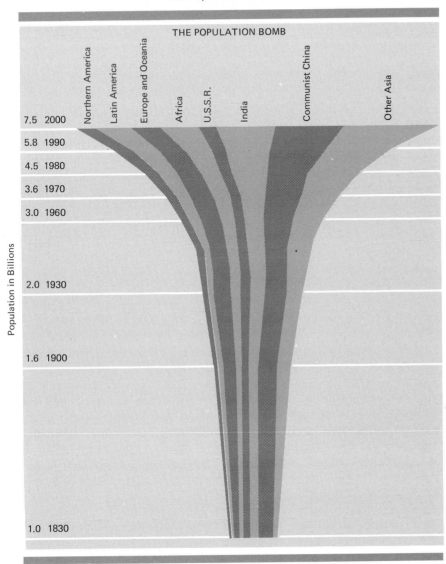

Source: Data from U.S. State Department.

are three categories: (1) zoning regulations, which deal with how land may be used; (2) subdivision regulations, which relate to such matters as sewage disposal and public facilities to be provided; and (3) building codes, which prescribe materials that can be used, fire precautions, and the like.

Recent land-use regulation reflects clearly the growing concern with

life quality and ecological matters. Regional planning authorities now prescribe such things as reduction of home-to-work transportation problems,
housing of many types that suit people in all income levels and stages of
life, and discreetly designed industrial parks for industrial activities.

Water Pollution

Every second of every day, about 2 million gallons of sewage and other
wastewater pour into our public waters. It is said that the water in the
Ohio River is used four times by communities and industries along its
banks before it even reaches the Mississippi! The Water Pollution Act of
1972 requires every company that discharges waste into any waterway
to apply for a permit and must disclose fully the amount and nature of
their pollutants. The following deadlines have been set: by July 1, 1977,
companies must install "best practical" control technology. By July 1,
1983, companies must install "best available" control technology. By
1985, the goal is zero discharge—the complete elimination of water
pollution.

Air pollution

Many communities try to control air pollution. Nationally, the Air Pollution Control Office of the Environmental Protection Agency (EPA) sets
standards (effective in 1975) and institutes controls for atmospheric conditions. Controls bring new influences into play in site selection. Availability and delivered costs of minimum polluting energy sources must be
considered. Sites must be large enough to accommodate treatment facilities. Costs for these facilities are so high that some communities feel
the burden should be shared. Indeed, if the costs are not shared, some
businesses may well have to close. As a result, tax benefits or accelerated
depreciation write-offs that encourage investment in anti-pollution
devices have been made available.

Noise and ugliness pollution

The World Health Organization (WHO) states that noise in the United
States costs $4 billion a year in accidents, absenteeism, reduced pro-
ductivity, and workmen's compensation payments. Metropolitan police
departments respond to a steady stream of telephoned and written complaints of noise. Indeed, of the many nuisances that are complained about,
noise is the overwhelming gripe. In one of the largest cities, an astounding

Figure **16–5**
Land and Solid Waste

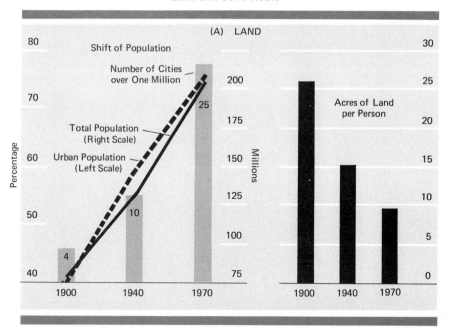

(A) LAND

Shift of Population

Number of Cities over One Million

Total Population (Right Scale)

Urban Population (Left Scale)

Acres of Land per Person

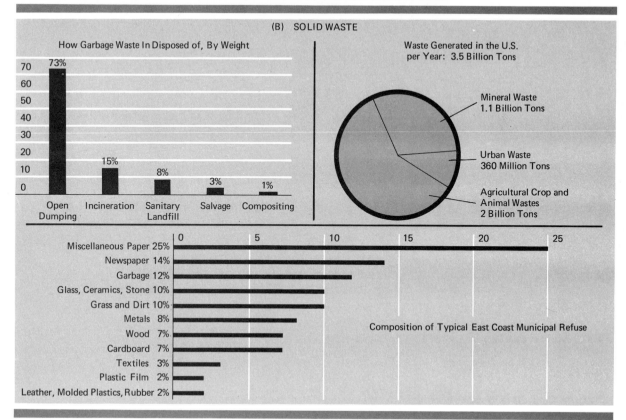

(B) SOLID WASTE

How Garbage Waste In Disposed of, By Weight

Open Dumping 73%
Incineration 15%
Sanitary Landfill 8%
Salvage 3%
Compositing 1%

Waste Generated in the U.S. per Year: 3.5 Billion Tons

Mineral Waste 1.1 Billion Tons
Urban Waste 360 Million Tons
Agricultural Crop and Animal Wastes 2 Billion Tons

Composition of Typical East Coast Municipal Refuse

Miscellaneous Paper 25%
Newspaper 14%
Garbage 12%
Glass, Ceramics, Stone 10%
Grass and Dirt 10%
Metals 8%
Wood 7%
Cardboard 7%
Textiles 3%
Plastic Film 2%
Leather, Molded Plastics, Rubber 2%

Source: Data from U.S. Public Health Service.

96.6 percent of nuisance complaints were about noise. New York City has passed a comprehensive noise control code. Congress adopted the Noise Control Act in 1972. The EPA was given broad authority to establish noise levels for new motors and engines for transportation, construction, and electrical equipment; it will also extensively study noise standards for aircraft, in particular, and submit proposals for lessening noise pollution.

In some places, planes cannot land or take off during normal sleeping hours. Billboards, junkyards, the appearance of buildings, and abandonments are increasingly being regulated to combat ugliness — a factor with which businesses must concern themselves.

Solid waste

Every individual in the United States generates about 7 pounds of trash each day. According to a major study made by the National League of Cities released in 1973, America's cities are smothering in garbage and over 45 percent of them will run out of places to dump their trash within five years. Industrial and agricultural wastes are infinitely larger. (See Figure 16–5.) Ecologists rightly ask how long we can go on using up resources and casually discarding them as if supplies were inexhaustible. Little or no regulation is in effect or is even being proposed in this area. A possible solution is to place taxes on natural raw materials so they are priced higher than similar recycled resources.

Some further questions

The technological innovations and changed laws related to land use and ecology open a new vista for business' relationship to the total environment and to the quality of life.

Many questions remain however. Among them are: How perilous are conditions in the various problem areas? How much time do we have? To what extent can man have all the material things he wants and yet maintain a livable environment? What is the "trade off" point between production and social costs? Who should make the decisions? For example, electric power demands double each decade — can this continue in terms of fuel exhaustion and pollution? When do we cut back on electric toothbrushes, sunlamps, card shufflers, and exercise bicycles? What is enough Kleenex, Coca Cola, and cars? One proposed solution is the "no-growth economy," where population and productivity are stabilized and attention is shifted from quantity to quality. Can we achieve such a situation? Do we want to?

PEOPLE AND THEIR IDEAS
William D. Ruckelshaus

The nation's first environmental enforcer

The mission of the nation's Environmental Protection Agency (EPA), established in 1970, is to restore our physical environment to a semblance of what it was like before the industrial revolution. Mr. Ruckelshaus was appointed as the Agency's first administrator and continued in that job until mid-1973. In 1972 the Agency had a budget of almost $2.5 billion and some 8,800 employees, most of them scattered throughout 10 semi-autonomous federal regions. Two billion dollars of this budget was parceled out as subsidies for local sewage-plant construction. As administrator, Mr. Ruckelshaus was the chief enforcer of federal laws on air and water pollution: pesticides, radiation, solid waste disposal, and water supply.

Ruckelshaus gained his reputation from 1960 to 1965, when, as Deputy Attorney General for Indiana, he represented the Indiana State Pollution Control Board in its vigorous program to end contamination of lakes and rivers. At the time he also drafted a historic Air Pollution Control Act, which provided state supervision and tough sanctions where localities declined to act.

Born in 1932 in Indianapolis, Indiana, he graduated cum laude from Princeton University in 1957 and took his Ll.B. from the Harvard Law School.

As head of the EPA, he had one of the toughest jobs in Washington, since environmental improvement treads on the toes of so many people with considerable influence. The pressures brought against the Agency are enormous—as in the case of the automobile industry's anguished pleas for deferment (finally granted) of pollution-control requirements set for 1975.

When asked whether his Agency was political, Ruckelshaus was disarmingly candid.

Of course we're political. Most governmental activities are accommodations of conflicting interests. What you get when you have all the facts on the table is a political judgment of what is workable. But that doesn't mean we're not enforcing the laws. It has nothing to do with partisan politics or caving in to special-interest groups. The criterion is what is in the public interest. A policeman, if he's any good, doesn't deal with a truant the same way he does with a bank robber. A program that will arouse a storm of public resentment defeats the objective. Those are the kind of "political" decisions we have to make.

When asked about the progress being made, he said, "What we're really in now is a gap between the time of commitment and progress visible to the man on the street." The year 1975 is the date he most often cites as the point where improvement of the environment should start becoming evident to citizens.

He says further, "No more than with policemen is our object to get all the traffic off the road, or to stifle technological initiative and return to the horse-and-buggy age. We do not see the choice before us now as one between a strong economy and a healthy environment. We believe we can have both."

Significantly, he has this to say about the future. "The pollution phase of environment that we're going through, I think we'll whip. But there's another whole set of problems—the energy crisis, land use, population control, the whole question of growth. Those problems will be with us a long time, and will be much more hotly debated than anything we've seen yet."

CONTEMPORARY ISSUES
Situation 16

Should tax incentives be used to decentralize industry?

After reviewing the material presented in this chapter, John and Ray debated the question of industry decentralization.

"Something should be done to stimulate industry in small towns," suggested Ray. "Besides helping the people who live there, we would reduce urban congestion and thereby help eliminate ghettos, urban sprawl, traffic tie-ups and many other problems cities face. If we gave industry tax incentives to locate in small towns, we would help people in both urban and rural areas."

"I agree urban congestion is one of our biggest problems," admitted John, "but I don't think the solution lies in giving tax incentives to industries to locate in small towns. You've got to be practical, Ray. Industry today employs location specialists. They don't simply pick a location at random—they study the local tax structure, the proximity of the area to raw materials and markets, cost of utilities, access to labor, and many other factors before they reach a decision. A lot of small towns, especially those located far from big cities, just don't measure up. If through tax incentives we encourage industry to locate in small towns that offer no economic advantages, we would impair business efficiency and everybody would be hurt."

"But you don't understand what I am saying," said Ray. "If the government would cut the tax rate for businesses that agree to locate in small towns, then it would be economical for them to do so. We would help the prosperity of our small towns. We'd slow the migration from rural areas and from small towns to big cities. If we can't do something about our small towns, one of these days the politicians will demand federal aid to help clean up small town slums. So, in the long run, I think it would be better for the nation as a whole to decentralize industry, even if all the immediate economic factors don't support it."

"Again, I say you've got to be practical," implored John. "Look, you've spent your entire life in a big city. Suppose someone offered you a job as a management trainee in a small town of say five thousand. Would you go?"

SITUATION EVALUATION

1. Who has the better argument? Explain.

2. What additional points can be offered to support the viewpoints of both John and Ray?

3. Do you anticipate that some type of federal incentive will be used in the future to encourage decentralization? Why or why not?

BUSINESS CHRONICLE

Land developing and ecology

A feature writer in a newspaper (Naples, Florida, *Daily News,* June 25, 1972) opened his column as follows: "A sure way to start an argument — or, at the very least, a heated discussion — is to place a house builder and an environmentalist in the same room. They are natural enemies. Have been for a long time. . . . Newspapers are continually recounting the battles between developers and civic groups over the proper use of land."

The sentiments expressed above highlight the growing public attitude about land development.

Let us assume that Kingmaker Estates wishes to operate so its developments will be compatible with ecological requirements and goals.

QUESTIONS

1. What environmental policies should Kingmaker Estates establish for land development projects it might undertake such as (1) slum clearance, (2) subdivision of farms into building plots, (3) shopping centers, (4) office building complexes, (5) industrial parks, and (6) recreational areas?

2. Cooperation of what agencies in the community should Kingmaker seek?

3. Would a community advisory board help Kingmaker's plan? If so, who should serve on such a board and how should it operate? What are the advantages and disadvantages of a community advisory board?

APPLICATION EXERCISES

1. Site location is a continuing problem for large chain organizations. Outline a program that would result in a continuing search for good sites for a food chain with approximately 85 stores in your state. Include in your program (a) methods of evaluating suggested locations, (b) types of information necessary for making proper evaluations, and (c) where or how the necessary information can be secured.

2. Sunday's Department Store is the largest store in Zenith, a city with a population of 160,000. It has a record of 25 years of profitable operation. The owner, Dan Sunday, has a son, Dan Sunday, Jr., a graduate of the state university with a business administration degree. The young man, who shows a great deal of promise, is working as assistant to his father and is expected to succeed him in five years. The present business is excellently located in the center of the city near the main post office and the city hall and is surrounded by many of the city's other leading businesses.

    A real estate development company has recently purchased an attractive plot of land it plans to develop as a shopping center. This land is on a main highway skirting the better residential areas of the town. It is near the area in which future residential development is most likely to take place. Sunday's, as a leading local retail organization, was the first to be offered a choice and exclusive site in the new shopping center. It is known that if Sunday's does not accept the offer, it will be made to a large national department store organization.

    Sunday, Sr., does not wish to go into the new venture. He says, "Zenith is small enough for everyone to shop at the downtown store. We now have the best location possible. Taking the new location will simply divide our present business between two stores. In the end we will increase expenses and reduce profits. We have successfully operated where we are for twenty-five years; why introduce all this uncertainty? Our customers are loyal and we know how to please them, so that we will continue to be the top business in town."

    Sunday, Jr., disagrees with his father. What would your decision be? Why?

3. An energy crisis is definitely looming most ominously. There is little question that cities, counties, and states in the future will be directed to reduce their energy consumption. Assume it is 1980 and your state is ordered to cut its energy consumption (gas, electricity, fuel oil, and gasoline) by 30 percent. The governor of your state asks you to prepare a plan of specific measures that he can implement to comply with this reduction order. Some areas of action that could be included in your plan are positive and negative tax programs, laws and regulations, educational programs, restrictions, redesigning cities, building and

centralizing or decentralizing of facilities, creation or reorganization of agencies, appointment of officials, and so forth. Your plan should contain pros and cons and alternatives so it can be debated as meaningfully as possible by the state legislature and other interested groups.

QUESTIONS

1. Explain the significance of each of the following in the selection of a community for a factory location: labor, transportation, power, proximity to raw materials, proximity to markets, and municipal government.

2. Which is the more important for an oil refinery: location near raw materials or proximity to market? For a stockyard? For a cannery? For a dairy? For a brick factory?

3. The management of a manufacturing establishment located in a large northern city has decided to build a branch plant in the South. What sources of information are available to aid in choosing a community for this new plant?

4. In what important ways do the location problems of retailers differ from those of manufacturers?

5. What are the various population factors that must be taken into consideration in retail locations?

6. The character of our large cities has changed drastically since 1950. What are the causes of these changes and how do they affect business location?

7. What is ecology, and how does it relate to business location and land use?

8. Will most people continue to live on 1½ percent of our available land? Why? What should be done about this concentration?

9. How is urban land utilization increased? Are the methods desirable?

10. What are the various pollution problems?

11. Evaluate the idea of a "no-growth economy."

management of the marketing function

American business is transacted in what is frequently termed a "market-oriented" environment. Businessmen, regardless of their specialty, know they do not succeed until consumers buy what they have to sell.

"Nothing happens until a sale is made" is a deeper concept than it at first appears to be. Production is geared to demand: If sales fall off, production—and jobs—are curtailed; conversely, if demand increases, production—and employment—increase.

Thus, sales volume determines not only the fate of a product or a company, but the state of the economy. It is not difficult to see, therefore, why marketing is such a potent social force.

In our age of advanced technological development "Can we make it?" is often an easier question to answer than "Can we sell it?"

With the arrival of consumerism, which is, in a larger sense, related to ecology, a set of even more difficult questions looms. "Should the product be made?" "If so, how can its social suitability be maximized?" These chapters explore the various aspects of marketing:

17

the marketing process: an overview

18

marketing and the ultimate consumer

19

demand creation functions and pricing

20

international business

CHAPTER 17

MARKETING DEFINED / IS MARKETING MORE IMPORTANT THAN PRODUCTION? / BASIC ELEMENTS IN THE MARKETING PROCESS / CONSUMERS / PRODUCTS
> Consumer Goods. Industrial Goods. Consumer- and Industrial-Goods Marketing Compared.

FUNCTIONS OF MARKETING

CHANNELS FOR MARKETING CONSUMER GOODS
> Manufacturer → Consumer. Manufacturer → Retailer → Consumer. Manufacturer → Wholesaler → Retailer → Consumer. Manufacturer → Agent Middleman → Wholesaler → Retailer → Consumer. Marketing Functions Are Indispensable.

BRANDS AND MARKETING
> Types of Brand. Advantages of Branding.

MARKETING INDUSTRIAL GOODS
> Major Channels for Industrial Goods.

RETAILING
> Retailers Classified by Ownership. Dynamic Developments and Trends in Retailing.

WHOLESALING
> Wholesalers. Agent Middlemen.

17 the marketing process: an overview

Production is not an end in itself; rather, consumption — the satisfaction of wants — is the ultimate goal of the economic side of our social system. While fulfillment of material wants alone does not assure a contented society, ample housing, clothing, transportation, elimination of poverty, and so on are considered in an industrial society to be essential bases upon which the more lasting mental, spiritual, artistic, and creative dimensions of life are built. Thus we assume that the just distribution of material wherewithal precedes achievement of the good life for everyone.

Production converts raw materials into what economists call form utility. Marketing adds the dimensions of time, place, and possession utility to the finished products.

We have seen that the United States has developed a reasonably efficient system of mass production. But because of this efficiency, we would soon be plagued with overproduction were it not for a correspondingly efficient system of mass marketing to move goods from producers to consumers. Factories are useless unless ways are devised to distribute their output to those who require it.

MARKETING DEFINED

Marketing is the term applied to business activities directed toward, and incident to, the flow of goods and services from producers to consumers. The word "marketing" is often used interchangeably with the word "distribution," although marketing is generally considered a more comprehensive term.

IS MARKETING MORE IMPORTANT THAN PRODUCTION?

Frequently, students and academicians debate the question "Which is more important, marketing (selling) or production (engineering)?" Objectively, such an argument is pointless. It's like trying to decide which is more vital in football, offense or defense.

On reflection, one can readily see that a society cannot have a highly sophisticated marketing system without a correspondingly sophisticated production system, and vice versa. Each is dependent on the other. Each should cooperate with the other to gain the common goal: an increase in the standard of living for the maximum number of people.

It takes highly skilled engineers to design an automated production system and highly skilled sales representatives to make sure the products are sold and the system serviced. In the ideal sense, engineering and marketing departments work together as closely as possible from the moment a new product is conceived until the product is in use by consumers—and, indeed, even after that, to see to the product's continued quality and salability and to its possible improvement.

The history of marketing somewhat parallels the history of civilization itself. In probing the very oldest civilizations, archaeologists have unearthed a variety of artifacts far from their points of production, indicating that trade was carried on before recorded history. Biblical passages written thousands of years ago describe buying and selling for profit. Specialized middlemen were common in ancient Greece and Rome. Trade flourished in the European and Mediterranean cities during the Middle Ages.

However, early commerce was confined largely to luxury products—such as spices, furs, and expensive cloth—for distribution expenses were so high that only these items could bear them. Most people were largely self-sufficient—they raised their own food, made their own clothing, and provided their own shelter. Only the very rich purchased goods that came from a distance. The few products that were purchased by ordinary people were generally made near where they lived.

The character of marketing changed drastically with the coming of the Industrial Revolution. Mass production resulted in a phenomenal increase in goods that had to be marketed, as well as in geographical specialization. People living near a factory could use only limited amounts of the factory's output, so markets located elsewhere had to be found to absorb the surplus production. Disposing of the greatly expanded output was no easy task. Accordingly, specialists in distribution developed. Thus the Industrial Revolution, along with improvements in transportation and communications, greatly enlarged the scope of marketing.**

SPECIAL READINGS

** *Social Issues in Marketing, Readings of Analysis,* by Lee E. Preston (ed.). Glenview, Ill.: Scott, Foresman and Company, 1967 (paperback). In the past, marketing was viewed as the business function that provided consumers with the products of industry. Recently, it has been suggested that marketing extend its responsibility beyond merely providing goods and services. Included in the function, it is argued, should be concerns about the quality of what is distributed, effects of marketing and advertising on society and its mores, their ethical and aesthetical impact, consumer rights, and environment.

This collection of readings brings into focus the various social issues surrounding marketing. The articles are divided into four groups: Part I, The Social Viewpoint, Part II, Efficiency: Marketing Tasks and the Cost of Doing Them, Part III, Fair Competition, and, Part IV, The Welfare of the Consumer. Works of well-known, socially conscious authors are included, such as Stanley Hollander, Eugene Rostow, William Lazer, and Reavis Cox. Some of the subjects they write on are: The Consumer and Madison Avenue, The Ethics of Competition Revisited, Changing Social Objectives in Marketing, and Size of Firm and the Structure of Costs in Retailing.

BASIC ELEMENTS IN THE MARKETING PROCESS

In this chapter we consider the five basic elements in the marketing process.

<u>Consumers</u>. All people, businesses, and nonprofit organizations, including governments, who purchase and use goods and services.

<u>Products</u>. The tangible and intangible goods and services marketed to satisfy consumers' wants and needs.

<u>Functions of Marketing</u>. The economic activities performed by middlemen and other specialists in moving goods from producers to consumers.

<u>Middlemen</u>. Businesses that link producers to consumers and perform much of the work of marketing.

<u>Channels of Distribution</u>. The path products take as they move from producers to consumers.

CONSUMERS

We can divide consumers into two categories: *ultimate* and *industrial*. The ultimate consumer classification includes each of us when we buy products for personal or family use. The industrial user category includes all businesses, nonprofit organizations and governmental agencies that consume products for a profit-making reason or to meet a social need such as education or highways.

Wholesale and retail middlemen are classed as *buyers for resale*, not as industrial users except when they purchase fixtures, equipment, and supplies to operate their businesses.

Consumers will be discussed in more detail in the next chapter.

PRODUCTS

In simplest terms, a product is that some*thing* a business sells. It may be tangible (such as a car, boat, or television), or it may be intangible (such as a movie, life insurance policy, or ocean cruise). A product may be very expensive (jet liners cost up to $30 million) or very inexpensive (bubble gum is still sold for as little as one cent). Some products are highly perishable (newspapers last about one day), while other products are durable (houses are designed to last a half-century or longer).

In an expanded sense, the term "product" includes all the peripheral factors that contribute to the consumer's satisfaction. To illustrate: when you eat in a restaurant, the product is more than just the food. It includes the quality of service and the atmosphere. Since services were discussed separately in Chapter 5, this chapter will be limited to the marketing of goods.

Just as we divided consumers into two classifications, ultimate consumers and industrial users, we can divide products into two categories, *consumer goods* and *industrial goods*.

Consumer goods

Consumer goods are purchased by ultimate consumers for personal and household use. Every person is part of the market for consumer goods. Basically there are three classes of consumer goods, each based on the buying habits of the purchaser: convenience, shopping, and specialty goods.

Convenience goods   Convenience products are purchased frequently, in small quantities, and with a minimum of effort. Common examples are cigarettes, candy, staple groceries, and gasoline. Convenience goods generally have a low unit value and are easy to carry.

Since the consumer is not inclined to go out of his way to buy convenience goods, manufacturers attempt to place them in as many retail outlets as possible. Coca-Cola, for example, is available at more than three million locations in the United States. Profit margins on convenience goods are low, and the products require little or no personal sales effort.

Shopping goods   Shopping goods differ from convenience goods in that they are of relatively high unit value, purchased less frequently, and often bought only after the customer has compared several offerings as to price, style, quality, and general suitability.

Examples of shopping goods are furniture, clothing, shoes, china, and rugs. Like convenience goods, shopping goods are often advertised nationally, but some personal sales effort is usually necessary.

The number of outlets selling shopping goods is small compared with the number selling convenience goods. Generally, retailers of shopping goods are located close to each other. Developers of shopping centers realize that customers like to inspect several brands before they purchase; they therefore arrange to have groupings of stores to attract shoppers.

Specialty goods   Specialty goods are for consumers willing to make a special purchasing effort. As compared with convenience and shopping goods, specialty products are found in few retail outlets and command much more customer loyalty. Specialty goods usually are higher priced than other goods. Examples of specialty goods are furs, expensive tobaccos, automobiles, and pianos.

What may be a convenience item to one person may be a shopping item to a second and a specialty item to a third. The *intention* is the determining factor. Take the example of a housewife shopping for roast beef for Sunday dinner. To many people, this is a simple convenience-goods purchase, to be made at a conveniently located store. Some housewives, however, may be price-conscious and visit several stores to compare prices and quality before making the purchase. In this case, the beef becomes a shopping item. To another homemaker, Sunday dinner may be a special event planned for some important guests. This homemaker may go far out of her way to purchase the beef, regardless of cost, at a store handling only the finest quality aged beef. This purchase would thus fall into the specialty-goods classification.

Goods tend to fall into the same classification for most people, however. This is important, since store location, decor, arrangement of goods, and marketing methods must be adapted to the classification of goods.

Other classifications of consumer goods   Consumer goods are also classified in other ways such as:

1. Impulse goods—low unit value items purchased with little or no forethought. Items placed at checkout stands in supermarkets and discount stores are often impulse goods.

2. Emergency goods—products purchased on an emergency basis, such as tire chains when a motorist is caught without them in a snowstorm.

3. Soft goods—clothing, rubber sheets, and other products made from textiles or other nondurable materials.

4. Hard, or durable, goods—such as home appliances.

Industrial goods

Industrial goods are used in the production of consumer goods or in business and industrial operations. Examples include parts, raw materials, various kinds of equipment, supplies, and machinery.

How goods are classified depends on how the buyer intends to use them. Oil sold at a service station for a motorist's car is a consumer item. Oil purchased for a truck or by the General Electric Company to lubricate gears on an assembly line is an industrial item.

Industrial goods can be divided into two broad categories:

1. Goods that are used in the production of other goods and/or become a physical part of another product: raw materials, semi-manufactured goods, components, and subcontracted production services.

2. Goods that are used to conduct business and do not become part of another product: capital goods, operating supplies, services for which the user contracts.

Consumer- and industrial-goods marketing compared

Consumer and industrial goods are marketed very differently. They are sold through virtually separate sets of channels and agencies. Consumer goods are sold through a much larger number of outlets and tend to have a longer channel of distribution (that is, they go through the hands of more middlemen).

Consumer-goods marketing is more widely understood; it is the phase of marketing with which the public most often comes into contact. Most people are familiar with consumer-goods marketing terms, such as "retail outlet," "soft goods," and "discounts," but they have only a hazy impression of such industrial-goods terms as "steel broker," "installations," and "basing points." The distinctions between the two fields are especially significant for those considering careers in marketing.

Industrial marketing places emphasis on inanimates—production, materials, and technical services. The successful executive in this field usually is stimulated by dealing with things in a precise manner and is adept at making judgments based on facts and analysis.

Consumer goods marketing places emphasis on animates—that is on people: how they respond and what they require. The successful executive in this field is usually stimulated by influencing people and uses psychology to achieve his ends. Whereas he also uses facts and analysis, he tends to make generous use of intuition and experience in making decisions.

Appeals used to reach customers also differ. Consumer-goods selling, to a large extent, relies on emotional appeals, whereas industrial-goods selling is directed at rational buying motives. The ultimate consumer often buys because he "likes" a product or it "looks nice"; the industrial consumer buys because the product will enable him to manufacture efficiently—because he can "depend on deliveries" or because "quality control specifications are maintained."

The ultimate consumer, by and large, has only limited knowledge about the products he buys. The industrial-goods buyer, on the other hand, is often a trained purchasing manager who requires concrete facts concerning the performance of a product before he buys.

FUNCTIONS OF MARKETING

Marketing can best be explained by describing each of the functions, or major specialized activities, that together make up the marketing process. These marketing functions are:

1. Buying.   This function (discussed in Chapter 14) is concerned with acquiring what is needed for resale or industrial purposes.

2. Selling.   The counterpart of buying, selling (discussed in Chapter 19) includes locating customers, creating demand through advertising, and helping customers use or resell products.

3. Transportation.   Often called physical distribution (discussed in Chapter 15), this function provides place utility and is concerned with transporting goods from point of production to point of consumption.

4. Storage.   This function provides time utility. Storage, or ware-

housing (discussed in Chapter 15), is necessary when there is a lag between time of production and the time of consumption.

5. Standardization. This function concerns form utility by setting uniform specifications for goods. Standardization aids in the marketing process by facilitating selling and by making sales by description possible.

6. Financing. This function concerns itself with facilitating payment for what is bought. Credit (discussed in Chapter 8) is the main aspect of market financing.

7. Risk-bearing. This function (discussed in Chapter 10) provides for transfer or minimization of risks incurred in marketing. In addition to insurable risks, it also concerns price-change protection (hedging against price fluctuations), spoilage, and deterioration of goods.

8. Market information. Marketers attempt to leave as little as possible to hunch or guesswork. Marketing requires constant sources of information, for situations in the market change continually. Changes in prices, consumer wants, supply and demand, and social trends make it essential to expend considerable effort in securing information.

9. Pricing. This function (discussed in Chapter 19) concerns the complicated art of setting prices to maximize profit.

CHANNELS FOR MARKETING CONSUMER GOODS

The route taken in the transfer of ownership of a product as it passes from producer to consumer is known as the *channel of distribution*. Most marketing functions along that route are performed by what are called middlemen, who bridge the gap between producer and consumer. Middlemen need not own or physically handle the goods in which they deal. They may do no more than negotiate contracts for purchase or sale. More than two million business organizations (approximately 300,000 wholesalers and 1.7 million retailers) function as middlemen in our economy.

One reason for our large middleman structure is that the producer is, by and large, an expert only in producing—that is what he knows how to do best. Modern business is not simple, and markets are complicated and distant. Since most producers want to give their full attention to production, they turn the highly specialized functions of marketing over to specialists.

As a specialist, the middleman provides services for many producers.

The middleman ordinarily is located where the marketing is to be done—whether in St. Louis or Millcreek Center—while the manufacturer is located in the place where he produces—say, Los Angeles. The St. Louis middleman, for instance, knows the St. Louis marketing area intimately; he has buying and selling contacts there that have been established over long periods of time; and he has access to St. Louis handling facilities. Surely the manufacturer in Los Angeles would find it difficult and expensive to learn about storage facilities, to establish contacts with buyers, and to become informed about credit ratings of business establishments in the St. Louis area. Hence, he turns to the middleman.

For the consumer, middlemen form a system through which he can purchase goods in the desired amounts and at the most convenient points.

The channels of distribution vary greatly depending on the nature of the product, the financial strength of the manufacturer, the number and kinds of consumers, and the marketing experience of the manufacturer. It is possible, however, to distinguish four major channels:

1. Manufacturer → Consumer

2. Manufacturer → Retailer → Consumer

3. Manufacturer → Wholesaler → Retailer → Consumer

4. Manufacturer → Agent Middleman → Wholesaler → Retailer → Consumer

Manufacturer ⟶ consumer

To many, this channel appears to be the most simple and logical. However, it is the least important for most consumer goods. Imagine for a moment the difficulties if manufacturers of cigarettes, soap, or chewing gum should attempt to sell their products directly to the consumer!

Some manufacturers do contact the consumer directly by selling door-to-door, by mail or telephone, or through their own retail stores.

Manufacturer ⟶ retailer ⟶ consumer

For a number of reasons, many manufacturers prefer to sell directly to retailers, who in turn sell to consumers.

First, some manufacturers believe a larger profit can be earned by not selling through a wholesaler.

Second, a manufacturer's customers may buy in large quantities. Chain organizations, discount houses, and large department stores, for example, may purchase a sizable portion of a single manufacturer's output.

Third, some manufacturers sell to retailers to retain closer control.

Because wholesalers carry many competing brands, they may not exert special effort to dispose of any single manufacturer's output.

Fourth, when fashion is exceptionally important, manufacturers tend to sell directly to retailers. Manufacturers of women's apparel are never sure where the fickle finger of fashion will point. Speed is essential in getting such goods to market, for a delay may see a change in fashion. Retailers have a saying that the "real dog" (hard to get rid of) is yesterday's fashion-goods item.

Fifth, manufacturers sometimes sell directly if retailers are concentrated geographically. Under these circumstances, salesmen can visit many stores with minimum effort and expense.

Manufacturer ⟶ wholesaler ⟶ retailer ⟶ consumer

A large volume of consumer goods is marketed through wholesalers, who sell to retailers, who, in turn, sell to the ultimate consumer. Wholesalers *do take title* to the merchandise they handle, assume risks, extend credit, and deliver merchandise. There are five reasons for the popularity of this channel.

First, the wholesaler relieves the manufacturer of the complicated and costly sales function.

Second, the wholesaler is close to the market and has many established customers who might be difficult for the manufacturer to sell to and service.

Third, it is often more economical for the manufacturer to sell to wholesalers because the wholesaler's cost of selling to retailers is spread over many different manufacturers' products.

Fourth, wholesalers accept large quantities from manufacturers and sell to retailers in smaller quantities. In many cases, it is too costly for manufacturers to ship merchandise in the quantity the retailer wants.

Fifth, the manufacturer needs less capital if he does not have to do his own marketing and he can concentrate on production without the distraction of doing his own marketing.

Manufacturer ⟶ agent middleman ⟶ wholesaler ⟶ retailer ⟶ consumer

Agent (sometimes called "functional") middlemen *do not take title* to goods. They are used extensively. In the channels just discussed, the manufacturer needs a sales force to call on wholesalers or retailers. When the agent middleman is used, the manufacturer does not need a sales force, for the agent middleman serves as a substitute, thus permitting the manufacturer to concentrate on production. Agent middlemen are usually compensated on a commission basis.

Marketing functions are indispensable

A manufacturer who sells directly to retailers or to the ultimate consumer has not eliminated the marketing functions; he simply performs them himself. The inference "buy from us and eliminate the middleman's profit" is unfair and takes advantage of the public's ignorance of marketing.

The economic activities of retailers and wholesalers can be expressed in terms of what is called "value added." Manufacturing gives a product *form* utility. It converts raw materials, such as wood or steel, into finished products, such as furniture or appliances. Making the furniture or appliances available at the *place* and *time* the consumer wants them is a considerably less obvious type of value creation. Therefore, the contribution of retailers and wholesalers to the standard of living is less fully appreciated.

Nevertheless, the existence of large numbers of middlemen such as wholesalers and brokerage houses proves that they perform economically justifiable functions. A middleman simply could not sell his services to the shrewd manufacturer if that manufacturer felt he could do the job better himself. There are always manufacturers who say, "I'm going to organize my own sales force," and retailers who say, "I'll buy in carload lots, direct." And some do find these procedures economical or advisable. However, the agent, or functional, middlemen—the manufacturer's agents, brokers, auction companies, commission merchants, and wholesalers—all flourish because they are doing a necessary job; otherwise they would be eliminated by the natural competitive forces of our private enterprise system.

BRANDS AND MARKETING

One important thing to note about consumer goods is the emphasis on branded merchandise. Brand name products are generally preferred to nonbranded and greatly exceed the latter in importance.

Types of brand

A *brand* identifies the product or products of a seller. A *manufacturer's brand*, often called a *national brand*, is one sponsored by a manufacturer. Some of the more common are Heinz 57, Zenith, Tums, and Yardley.

A *distributor's brand*, or *private brand*, is sponsored by a wholesaler and is usually known only on a regional basis.

A *retailer's private brand* is promoted by a large retailer, such as a department store, chain organization, or mail-order house. Examples are Ann Page (A&P), David Bradley (Sears, Roebuck), and French Brand Coffee (The Kroger Company).

Advantages of branding

Brands build consumer loyalty. Branding a product encourages repeat patronage—provided, of course, that the product meets with customer approval. Once a person becomes accustomed to buying a certain brand of coffee or toothpaste, it is hard for a competitor to get him to change his habits.

Second, branding makes advertising of the product more effective. Some brands, like Coca-Cola, Ford, and Bayer, have become a part of the American tradition. Many are quite old, and some have most interesting histories. A soap salesman by the name of Harley Procter, of Cincinnati, Ohio, was sitting in church one Sunday in 1882 when he was struck with the beauty of the word "ivory" as it appeared in one of the psalms. He accordingly so named his best white soap. At about the same time, George Eastman, of Rochester, New York, was puzzling out a word that would read and sound the same in any language—Kodak.

Third, brands can avoid direct price competition. Consumers, relying on the quality of a branded product, are often willing to pay more for it than for nonbranded merchandise. All aspirins are the same, but the known brands command higher prices because they command public confidence.

MARKETING INDUSTRIAL GOODS

Thus far we have considered only the channels through which goods pass from manufacturer to ultimate consumer. The public in general is inclined to think that marketing relates only to goods sold for personal use, but a large part of marketing moves industrial goods. Characteristics of industrial-goods marketing are:

Industrial purchasers require technical assistance. The industrial purchaser expects the seller to furnish technical information. Performance standards, tolerance rates, tensile strengths, and heat-resisting properties are of utmost importance in manufacturing. The fact that such knowledge is difficult to pass on reliably through a middleman is one reason for the dominance of direct selling in industrial goods.

Units of purchase are large. While industrial goods are purchased in varying quantities, almost all purchases are large when compared with purchases of consumer goods. A characteristic of industrial purchasing is that purchase contracts cover deliveries over long periods of time — often for a season, a year, or even longer.

Many enter into purchasing decisions.   Seldom is the purchasing decision vested in a single person. While the contact for the supplier seeking an order is the company purchasing manager, other people in the company, including engineers, company officers, designers, and plant superintendents, can be expected to have a voice in purchasing decisions.

The market is concentrated geographically.   Industrial business is often concentrated in a few concerns, a fact that encourages direct selling. For example, a supplier of products used in the manufacture of glass will find the bulk of his market located in just three states — Ohio, West Virginia, and Pennsylvania.

Major channels for industrial goods

Compared with consumer goods, industrial goods are marketed through relatively short channels. These goods flow to market through three main distribution channels: (1) direct from producer to user, sometimes with assistance from the manufacturer's branch operation; (2) from manufacturer to wholesaler (usually known as the "industrial distributor") to user; and (3) from manufacturer to agent middlemen, such as brokers and manufacturers' agents, to user.

It is estimated, from business census data, that more than 80 percent of industrial goods move to market in the direct manner. It is understandable that this channel is the most economical for bulky goods, such as coal, oil, telephone poles, cables, newsprint, and pig iron.

RETAILING

The broad function of retailing is to secure goods from manufacturers or wholesalers in relatively large quantities and resell them to ultimate consumers in comparatively small quantities. The retailing industry which employs some nine million people is a major source of employment and its intense competition is indicated by the high failure rate.

Retailers classified by ownership

Independent retail stores   An independent retail store is one that is separate from any other store in operation and ownership. Usually, the independent retail store is small; frequently it is small enough to be operated as a family business with no other employees. (Key advantages and disadvantages of independent retailers are those of the small business, explained in Chapter 5.)

Chain stores   Chain stores, such as Woolworth's and Kresge's, are particularly important in variety retailing, where they account for about 85 percent of the business. Chains are also widespread in the drug, food, ready-to-wear, shoe, and millinery fields.

Chain stores operate on the principle of mass (large-scale) merchandising. There must be a large demand for standardized merchandise, as opposed to technical or personalized goods that require the services of specially trained personnel. While modern chain stores may sell quality merchandise, they make every effort to keep costs down so that their appeals can be made on the basis of low or moderate price.

Major advantages of chains, compared with independent stores, include (1) large scale buying power, (2) spread of risk over a number of units, (3) use of highly skilled executives, and (4) more capital for modernization and expansion. Among the disadvantages are (1) difficulty in adjusting to local conditions, (2) impersonal relationships with customers, and (3) less motivation on the part of the store manager, since he is usually not the owner.

The following comparative sales figures for the year ending December 1972 give an idea of the size of the nation's largest general retailers:

Sears, Roebuck	$10,991,001,000
J. C. Penney	5,529,622,000
S. S. Kresge	3,875,183,000
Montgomery Ward (Marcor)	3,369,321,000
F. W. Woolworth	3,148,108,000
Gamble's–Skogmo	1,348,826,000

Dynamic developments and trends in retailing

Retailing is an especially dynamic segment of business; as such, it is always in a state of change and innovation. Some of the key trends likely in the 1970s include continued growth of the following:

Discount retailing   A discount house sells a large selection of well-known merchandise at below list (manufacturer's suggested) prices; its operation is characterized by some or all of the following: (1) limited customer services, (2) inelaborate facilities, (3) ample parking, (4) low rent locations, and (5) self-service displays. Such stores set sales records in the 1960s, and are expected to continue to show gains in the 1970s.

Controlled, or managed, shopping centers   The planned, or controlled, shopping center, developed as a unit and usually located in suburban shopping areas, is expected to become even more prominent in the decade ahead. Modern shopping centers now include ten to one hundred or more stores carefully selected so in combination they have maximum consumer drawing power. Many new centers include banks, brokerage houses, theaters, restaurants, and other commercial enterprises.

Voluntary groups   A voluntary group, sometimes called a voluntary chain, consists of independently owned retailing establishments, banded together to create the impression that they constitute a corporate chain. These retailers, usually working under the sponsorship of a wholesaler, agree to (1) buy branded merchandise from a common source, (2) advertise jointly, (3) provide similar service to customers, and (4) give their stores a standardized physical appearance. This type of cooperative arrangement, common in food marketing and to some extent in drugs, seems likely to grow in the future.

Vending-machine retailing   Vending machines, a nonpersonal service type of retailing, should have continued rapid growth, principally because of improved equipment and the continued emphasis on self-service.

Catalog/showroom/warehouse operation   Buying by catalog, also known as catalog discounting, is emerging as a significant retailing trend. The merchandise catalog—often bulky and once the mainstay of shopping by mail—is now simplifying shopping in the store. While this form of retailing is still unknown to many people, it is already a $1 billion industry with several hundred stores around the country. The operators specialize in furniture, but many sell almost everything except apparel. The customer pre-selects from a catalog at home or at the showroom. In either case, delivery is immediate—an advantage in furniture-buying, where a 6- or 8-week wait is not uncommon.

WHOLESALING

Much of the merchandise sold in retail stores passes through the hands of wholesale middlemen. Nevertheless, such large wholesalers as Hibbard, Spencer, Bartlett and Company (hardware), and Foremost-McKesson, Inc. (drugs) are virtually unknown to the general public, despite the fact their sales volume dwarfs that of many more widely known manufacturers and retailers.

Wholesalers sell to customers who buy for resale or for industrial and institutional use. Wholesale transactions include sales to retailers; other wholesalers and institutions; manufacturers and processors of all kinds of goods; building contractors, railroads, public utilities, and the U.S. government; service establishments, such as dry cleaning shops and hotels; and farmers for supplies and equipment used in farm production.

Wholesale sales ordinarily are made in quantities much larger than retail sales, but it is the *motive* of the buyer, not the *size* of the transaction, that determines whether a sale is wholesale or retail. This is an important point that bears repetition. If the purchaser is to resell the goods, use them in the manufacture of other goods, or use them in the operation of a business or institution, the transaction is wholesale. The sale of combs, clippers, and tonics to a barber, for instance, is a wholesale transaction, because the motive of the barber is to use these supplies in his business.

In normal years, the volume of goods sold at wholesale is approximately 50 percent larger than the total retail volume, first, because much merchandise sold to manufacturers and businesses is used for business operations, and, second, because wholesale sales are often made to other wholesalers. For instance, one wholesale middleman may sell a carload of oranges to another wholesaler, who in turn sells it to retailers. In this example, oranges have been sold twice at wholesale, but, as is always the case, only once at retail. In addition, wholesale trade includes export sales, and sales made to federal, state, and local governments.

Because middlemen play such an important role in our society, we shall discuss them in more detail.

Wholesalers

Wholesalers—sometimes called regular wholesalers, jobbers, or service wholesalers—are distinguished from other middlemen in that they *take title* to goods and perform wholesale functions that include (1) buying and selling goods, (2) storing merchandise, (3) maintaining a regular place of business, (4) delivering merchandise, (5) assembling merchandise in large quantities, and (6) redistributing merchandise in smaller quantities.

All wholesalers do not perform all services. Some are limited-function wholesalers, such as cash-and-carry-jobbers, who do not grant credit or make deliveries. A truck-jobber, important in housewares and frozen foods, may combine the functions of selling and delivery.

How the wholesaler serves retailers Consider for a moment what the retailer would encounter without the services of the wholesaler. For example, the ordinary independent retail drugstore stocks from six thousand to ten thousand different merchandise items produced by as many as 1,400 manufacturers. There would be utter confusion (to say nothing of the extra expense) if the druggist had to do business with each of 1,400 manufacturers! A druggist trying to deal with each of these manufacturers might receive each month about 350 separate shipments of merchandise, each with invoices requiring individual attention—separate bookkeeping, check-writing, correspondence, and so on.

Functions performed by wholesalers for retailers include simplifying buying problems, storing merchandise until needed, delivering merchandise, extending credit, and supplying market information and advice.

How the wholesaler serves manufacturers Functions wholesalers perform for manufacturers are: assuming responsibility for selling, transporting, storing merchandise, and extending credit to the retailer—thereby enabling the manufacturer to concentrate on production.

Agent middlemen

Another major group of middlemen *do not take title* to the goods in which they deal and normally perform few services. Their chief function is to negotiate a sale. These are agent middlemen, and they include brokers, selling agents, and manufacturers' agents.

Brokers Brokers negotiate transactions for merchandise without having either title to or physical possession of the goods. Brokers usually are retained by sellers to dispose of goods, but occasionally they are employed by buyers to locate goods. They do not, however, under any circumstances, represent both buyer and seller in the same transaction.

The value of the broker lies in his intimate knowledge of a limited and highly specialized market. For example, a broker may deal only in sugar and arrange sales only in the Philadelphia market, which he knows thoroughly. He is retained on a commission basis, receiving compensation only on sales made. Usually the broker's principal (the party retaining his services) carefully specifies the price, terms of sale, and delivery arrangements, leaving the broker with relatively little authority.

Brokers are important in the distribution of food specialties, grain, fresh fruits, cotton, and similar products. They are in a position to give expert advice on market prospects in their own special fields.

Selling agents Selling agents differ from brokers in that they handle the entire output of the principal they represent, have a continuous contractual relationship with the principal, and sell in unlimited territories. Selling agents have fewer restrictions placed on them by their principals in regard to selling price and terms of sale. Often they provide financial assistance to their principals.

Selling agents are important in the distribution of coal, textiles, and food. They sell to wholesalers, industrial consumers, and occasionally retailers. The services of selling agents are advisable when the principal is small or produces merchandise that needs wide distribution. Usually, they are aggressive promoters with many connections among regular wholesalers and industrial consumers, and they take the place of a manufacturer's sales force. One agent often represents several manufacturers.

Manufacturers' agents   Manufacturers' agents are frequently confused with selling agents. Unlike selling agents, however, manufacturers' agents sell only a part of a producer's output, are limited as to the territory they can cover, have less authority over price and terms of sale, and rarely finance their principals. They are used by manufacturers who wish to free themselves from marketing problems but retain close control over distribution. Manufacturers' agents are important in the distribution of machinery, equipment, supplies, steel, and chemicals.

PEOPLE AND THEIR IDEAS
Estée Lauder

The reigning queen of the cosmetics industry

In 1946, Estée Lauder formed a partnership with her husband to market a few preparations developed by her uncle, a cosmetics chemist she had worked for after he arrived in the United States from Vienna in the 1930s. She took over sales and marketing; her husband Joseph, finance and plant operations. Later, when the company was incorporated, she assumed its presidency.

Early in 1973, the founder of Estée Lauder, Inc., the $100-million, 1,000-employee cosmetics company bearing her name, turned the presidency over to her 39-year-old son, Leonard A. Lauder, a Harvard Business School graduate. She assumed the title of chairman formerly held by her husband, who is now executive chairman. Her son, who was interviewed about the change said, "It doesn't mean anybody has retired. It doesn't change the power structure."

Speaking about his mother when he took over the presidency, he said, "When it comes to choice of products, we will defer to Mrs. Lauder's ultimate decision." He uses the impersonal reference when talking about his mother in business. Asked about her qualities, another son said, "She has the ability to keep everyone on their toes." The company projects the image she has cultivated—high fashion and good taste, combined with quality and scientific research (mention is still made of the Viennese uncles who were professors of dermatology).

Born in Vienna, Estée Lauder is America's reigning cosmetics queen since the deaths of Elizabeth Arden and Helena Rubinstein. She is the rival of the king of the cosmetics world, Charles Revson, chairman of Revlon, Inc., whose company, with $400-million a year in sales, is second largest in the $4-billion cosmetics industry. Avon Products, Inc., with its unique door-to-door marketing methods, is the undisputed leader with $900-million. Lauder's marketing is also unique in that its products are sold only through some 2,000 prestige department and specialty stores.

The feud between Charles Revson and Mrs. Lauder is on a social as well as on a business level so it keeps the press busy reporting gossip and social movements. On the business level, the rivals use different approaches in their advertising. Revson promotes the idea of the man telling women how to be desirable. Mrs. Lauder emphasizes that a woman created the scent. On this point her son said, "There's no one who has her nose."

Gift-with-purchase is a give-away sampling technique that the Lauders pioneered. In 1972, they added the technique of purchase-with-purchase, which permits a customer who places a minimum order to buy certain additional merchandise at a discount.

The Lauder family still holds all of the company stock. Although they compensate their executives well and give them responsibility and respect, none has received stock. Energies of the whole family are devoted to the enterprise. Even Lauder daughters-in-law are periodically pressed into service to give makeup demonstrations in stores and interviews on television about new product lines.

The Lauders have a policy of continually adding new products that compete with one another and also broaden the market. New products and new market ventures are expensive to finance. It may take four or five years before red ink turns to black. Leonard Lauder has said, "A private company need not apologize if its ventures progress slowly. If we had been public, we would never have launched some of our products." Undoubtedly Wall Street drools at the prospect of a Lauder stock offering. In answer to the many queries about when this might happen, the son said, "We don't feel we're ready to go public because we have too much investment spending to do."

CONTEMPORARY ISSUES
Situation 17

Are there too many wholesale middlemen?

John and Ray were both surprised to learn how complicated the middleman structure is for most goods and services. "You know, before I took this course," said John, "I thought I knew a fair amount about marketing, but I confess I'm surprised to learn that some products are bought and sold three or four times before we finally buy them in the retail store."

"I was surprised too," agreed Ray, "and as I studied this material I couldn't help but think that all those middlemen are an indication of gross inefficiency in our marketing system. I'd be willing to bet that Sears, Zayres, Penney's, and other big retailers don't buy through wholesalers; they go directly to manufacturers, and that's how they save money and get a big competitive edge. Their formula is the one that works. They benefit and society benefits because it's all more efficient."

"But wait a minute," interjected John. "What about the small retailers —those who can't afford to buy in quantities equal to Penney's? Wholesalers are absolutely indispensable if we're to continue to have independent retailers. Consider, too, our competitive business system. Wouldn't wholesalers automatically be eliminated if they didn't perform a useful economic service?"

"I suppose you are right to a certain extent," admitted Ray. "But I think that a lot of wholesalers hang on simply out of tradition. I predict big manufacturers will soon develop business procedures that will make it economical for them to sell to all retailers, regardless of size. Then the wholesaler will have to go."

SITUATION EVALUATION

1. What economic considerations were overlooked by Ray in proposing that manufacturers would someday sell direct to all retailers?

2. By making the existence of small retailers possible, is the wholesaler supporting something that is really economically unsound?

3. Are wholesalers as inefficient as Ray suggests?

BUSINESS CHRONICLE

Specializing for maximum marketing effectiveness

Maurice Hill, sales manager for the Kingmaker Real Estate Division, was having a discussion with his assistant sales manager, Thor Johnsen. The subject was how to best organize the sales force for maximum sales effectiveness, now that the sales force was large enough that specialization was possible.

Hill: I feel we should have our sales people specialize in a certain kind of property. Selling a home to a family is one thing; selling an apartment building to an investor is quite another. Certainly industrial sites and commercial properties are completely different. Farms and agricultural properties are still another ball game.

Johnsen: The advantages of specialization according to types of property aren't all that important. What is important is to know the area. Specializing in a certain type of property spreads a salesman all over the place. I believe in assigning a salesman to a specific area. He can then know everything about that area. Customers want area knowledge more than they want expertise about a particular kind of property.

Hill: When you specialize in types of property you can assign salespeople according to what they can do best. Females can sell homes better, men sell industrial and commercial properties better, and so on.

Johnsen: You're going to get into trouble with women's lib talking like that. But, anyway, if a salesman has an area that he feels is his very own, he takes an interest in it and learns everything about it. The area specialization system is much better for getting listings. A salesman knows when someone's ready to sell, and he knows the people who live in his area. So much of real estate is on the word-of-mouth level.

QUESTIONS

1. Evaluate the key points in the discussion. What is the pro and con of each point made?

2. Which of the two approaches to specialization is more sound?

3. Consider and discuss the differences between the salesman's two major goals (1) finding and selling to prospects and (2) getting properties for listings. How does the method of specialization affect each of the two goals?

APPLICATION EXERCISES

1. A friend of yours who lives in St. Louis has heard that you are studying business administration and telephones you for advice. He is employed as an assembly-line worker and has saved $7,000, which he wishes to invest in a retail photo-equipment store. He tells you the following story.

"I have been working in a factory for more than ten years. The work is monotonous, and I'm not getting anywhere financially; so I'd like to do something that would be more worthwhile and interesting. I'd like to be my own boss and reap the entire profit of my own labor for myself instead of working for other people and helping them get rich. I'd like to own my own photo-equipment store, because photography has always been my hobby. I like it and know quite a bit about it. I haven't had any business experience, but I believe that I could easily pick up the little there is to learn. Running a retail store can't be too difficult — after all, the customers come to you. How should I go about getting into business? What should I do? I can probably raise more capital, if it's necessary, by borrowing from my father-in-law."

After listening carefully to what he has to say, you tell him that you will write to him after you have had time to consider the matter. Write the letter you would send to him.

2. The following changes in paid attendance for three major sports occurred between 1960 and 1971:

	1960	1971	PERCENTAGE CHANGE
Major League Baseball	20,261,000	29,544,000	45.8
Professional Basketball	1,986,000	6,195,000	311.9
Professional Football	3,195,000	10,560,000	330.5

a. How do you account for the relatively small increase in baseball attendance and the very large increase in basketball and football attendance?

b. Assume you were employed by a major league baseball team and told to "come up with some ideas to increase attendance." Suggest five ideas you think a baseball team could put to good use.

QUESTIONS

1. A department store carries all three of the basic classifications of consumer goods. Give an example of each type. Has the classification of a product anything to do with its location in the store?

2. Differentiate consumer goods from industrial goods. How does the marketing of consumer goods differ from the marketing of industrial goods?

3. What are the marketing functions? Is it possible to eliminate any of these functions in the marketing of a product? Explain your answer.

4. What is meant by a "channel of distribution"? Describe the channels of distribution for fresh milk, shoes, and industrial equipment.

5. How do you account for the fact that the net profit of retail stores is often less than 1 percent of net sales when markups may be as high as 40 percent or more?

6. Why is it that the total annual wholesale business volume is greater than the annual retail volume?

7. Define "brand." What are the different types of brands? What are the advantages of branding?

8. Define each of the principal types of retail store. What are the most important recent developments in retailing?

9. Define wholesaling. What determines whether a given transaction is wholesale or retail?

10. Define and describe the operations of agent middlemen.

marketing and the ultimate consumer 18

CHAPTER 18

THE MARKETING CONCEPT

WHY PEOPLE BUY WHAT THEY DO
Emotional Buying Motives. Rational Buying Motives. Combinations of Buying Motives.

WHY PEOPLE BUY WHERE THEY DO
Reputation of Seller. Services Rendered. Location. Variety of Products Offered.

THE RELATION OF INCOME TO CONSUMPTION
Distribution of Income. How Income Is Spent.

THE RELATION OF POPULATION TO CONSUMPTION
Households. Age. Declining Birth Rate and Constant Death Rate. Population Shifts.

OTHER FACTORS AFFECTING CONSUMPTION
Education. Climate. Sex. Habit.

It is often said, "The consumer is king." The consumer, by deciding what products to buy and where to buy them, determines which products and businesses succeed. This freedom of choice is made even greater with improved mobility (the automobile enables the consumer easily to reach many stores), better communication (television and advertising help the consumer to learn about a greater variety of goods and services), and self-service (direct selection in the store forces the product to stand on its own merits).

In our society, consumers exercise a special freedom: the way they spend their incomes determines how the resources of society will be allocated. An analysis of the way consumers spend their income reveals remarkable variations in spending patterns—not one "typical" pattern. For example, one $15,000-a-year family may spend several times as much for recreation as another family with the same annual income.

Freedom to spend puts pressure on businesses to study the consumer —his wants, buying habits, income, mobility, and other factors influencing consumption. It causes many social questions to be raised.

485

There are thousands of products—appliances, clothing, stationery supplies, cosmetics—that have not been marketed profitably because consumers did not like the color, design, price, durability, or quality. The economic graveyard is studded with the epitaphs of merchants who failed because the location of their stores, their services, or the assortment of goods they provided did not please enough consumers.

The objective of any business is to make sales that are satisfactory to both parties involved. The seller's motive in the sale is to make profit. The buyer's motive is to satisfy a want, need, or desire.

The wants of people are insatiable and varied, but the money they have available to fulfill them is limited. So everyone has the problem of deciding which wants are to be satisfied with the limited amount of money available. Since there are many sellers, there is competition for the limited amount of money buyers have to spend. The intelligent seller knows that "If you want to sell Jane Smith what Jane Smith buys, you must see Jane Smith through Jane Smith's eyes."[1]

THE MARKETING CONCEPT

In recent years, American business has been operating under what is called the "marketing concept." Once mass production could be taken for granted, attention was directed from producing what was generally adequate for most people to producing what was specifically desirable to meet individual needs. Thus the emphasis changed from selling what manufacturers made to making what people wanted to buy. The crux of the marketing concept is to determine market preferences *before* manufacturing starts so that once a product is manufactured it will virtually sell itself. Table 18–1 shows the difference in management thinking when the marketing concept *is* and *is not* applied.

WHY PEOPLE BUY WHAT THEY DO

Consumers' reasons for purchasing are called "buying motives," and can be classified as either emotional or rational. *Emotional motives* are subjective in nature, often impulsive, and not based on logical thinking. Such is the case when a couple buys a sport's car that is uncomfortable to ride in, expensive to insure, and costly to repair.

Rational motives are based on a logical analysis of why a purchase should or should not be made. The same couple deciding to buy a pickup

[1] For a detailed treatment of marketing, see *Marketing Today: A Basic Approach*, by David J. Schwartz (New York: Harcourt Brace Jovanovich), 1973.

Table **18–1**
Marketing Concept Applied and Not Applied

DECISION FACTORS	MARKETING CONCEPT APPLIED	MARKETING CONCEPT NOT APPLIED
Product color	Better do some research to find out which colors most consumers prefer.	We'll give the consumer any color he wants, so long as it's black.
Price	What price will induce the maximum number of consumers to buy and yield us the most profit?	This is the price we'll set. The consumer can take it or leave it.
Product design	Let's show some experimental designs to some prospective buyers and get their view before we go ahead.	Our engineers know how to design products. That's what we pay them for. Turn the whole job over to them.
Choice of retail outlets	Let's reappraise our outlets to see if they are as convenient as possible to the maximum number of consumers.	We'll market this product through the same retail stores we've used for the past ten years.
Number of models	Let's check to determine how many different models the consumers want and then see if we can produce that number profitably.	We'll produce two models. We don't want to complicate production.
Product improvement	We've got to make next year's model even better.	The current model is fine. There's no point in spending money on research.
Results	Firm is aware of changes in consumer preferences. Management knows people's wants vary and is trying to keep abreast. Continued success seems assured.	Firm is committing economic suicide. Consumers will shift to competitive products. Management is ignoring consumer. Continued success is in jeopardy.

truck because it can be used both for family transportation and hauling in connection with the couple's work would be an example of rational buying.

The study of consumer motives is complicated. What may be a rational motive to one person may be emotional to another. The determining factor is what goes on in the consumer's mind at the time of purchase.

Emotional buying motives

These nine emotional motives are discussed in the following section.

1. Superiority 4. Fear   7. Welfare of family
2. Distinction 5. Pleasure   8. The bargain
3. Comfort   6. Imitation 9. Buying for its own sake

Superiority   An inherent drive is the desire to be superior. People enjoy being admired and respected. To earn this admiration, they are often willing to work hard to gain leadership. It is logical to assume, then, that they make purchases for the same reason.

Sellers capitalize on the desire to be superior. A furniture salesman may mention to his prospect that a particular living room will make her the envy of all her friends. A proud mother is told by the clever saleswoman that a certain ensemble will make her daughter the prettiest girl at the party. Directors of correspondence schools admonish young people to enroll in their courses to "become a success." Purchases of expensive automobiles, custom-built homes, perfume, certain tobaccos, and magazines are often based on the desire to be superior.

Distinction   Related to the desire to be superior is the motivation to be different. Those who are wealthy may distinguish themselves by expensive hobbies: raising thoroughbred cattle, owning a stable of race horses, or maintaining a luxurious yacht.

The desire for distinction is evident in fashion goods. Few women like to wear shoes, coats, or dresses that are identical to those worn by other women. To be sure of wearing clothing that is different, women buy exclusive designs or have their clothing tailor-made. A humorist once defined mink as the fur that women wearing ordinary fur coats turn around to look at, and ermine as the fur that women wearing mink turn around to look at.

The craving for some individuality is evidenced in the purchase of many consumer products. Automobiles, even in the lower price ranges, are manufactured in a number of different body styles, as well as in numerous colors, to cater to individual whims. To help the motorist gain even more distinction, a wide assortment of accessories is available. Mass producers of homes often have only one basic design but, by various means, give each home some individuality.

Comfort   Psychologists are in general agreement that human beings are inherently lazy. What ambition we have is acquired. Consumers, therefore, are constantly looking for products that make life easier. This motive can be considered emotional or rational or both. It is listed as an emotional appeal, because people do most often react to the idea of comfort in an emotional manner.

A host of products are sold to satisfy the desire for easy living. Air conditioning is designed to make summertime more comfortable. Dishwashers and garbage disposals free people from unpleasant, time-consuming tasks. Advertisers constantly stress comfort. Such innovations in automobiles as the automatic shift and power brakes and steering were developed to appeal to comfort.

Fear   The buying motive of fear assumes many forms—fear of loss of life or health, fear of losing one's job, fear of social disapproval, fear of accidents. These fears that nearly everyone experiences, coupled with the instinctive urge for self-preservation, make consumers responsive to advertisers who promise freedom from fear. Salespersons show prospects how insurance can eliminate financial fears associated with loss of life or health. Many people are willing to invest in education to assure themselves better job security. Tires are sold in part to relieve fear of accidents. Fear of social disapproval is used extensively by advertisers of deodorants, toothpastes, and personal hygiene items.

Pleasure   An emotional motive that prompts people to make certain purchases is the desire to escape routine. Plays, movies, sports events, and other forms of recreation are "sold" on the basis of this motive. Sellers of swimming pools, television sets, musical instruments, and sporting equipment urge consumers to buy in order to enjoy life. The desire to escape routine is a selling point for travel agencies that arrange vacations. Age, education, occupation, sex, and income are factors in determining what diversion individuals will desire. Motivation for pleasure becomes important as the workweek becomes shorter and as the income is raised.

Imitation   Consciously or subconsciously, people imitate those who have attained prominence. Advertising testimonials appeal to this motive—the implication being that if movie stars, famous athletes, and other leaders endorse a product, then anyone who uses it will be sharing an experience with a famous personage. The picture of a beautiful model applying face cream suggests that anyone who uses the same preparation can be beautiful also.

The compulsion to "keep up with the Joneses" is another manifestation of this motive. Frequently, consumers may not actually want a product but buy it because their neighbors or members of their social set own it. A salesperson selling a new kitchen gadget may subtly remind a couple that every other household in the apartment complex has already purchased one. Sellers of furs, color televisions, sports cars, and swimming pools exploit this motive.

Welfare of family   Sellers capitalize on the fact that most people want to give their families advantages. The encyclopedia salesperson tries to make parents feel that being without his product will jeopardize their children's education. Insurance agents show how, "for just a few pennies a day," a child's college education can be guaranteed. New homes, appliances, vitamins, recreational services, and toys are sold on this basis.

The "bargain"   Mark Twain told us how superior a boy finds the flavor of a watermelon he has stolen. A maturing sense of property rights prevents our carrying this particular boyhood pleasure into adult life, but we continue to experience a special delight out of "getting something for nothing" and, by extension, "getting something for less than it ought to cost." Merchants know this and tempt us continually with markdown sales. We may buy a lamp marked down from $20 to $10, not because we need it (we were probably doing very well without it before the sale came along) or because it is really worth more than we are paying (we seldom stop to analyze a sale, anyway). Instead, we buy it for basically the same reason that made the watermelon taste so good to Mark Twain's boy.

Buying for its own sake   Nobody has estimated how many purchases are made simply because people have money "burning a hole" in their pockets, but the total amount so spent must be enormous. All of us, like the man who drops a coin in the juke box and then walks out before the music begins, respond to the urge to spend just for the sake of spending. Merchants have a way of arranging low-priced items temptingly within reach so that when money drops through the burned holes in our pockets, it falls into their tills.

Rational buying motives

The three major rational buying motives are:

1. Economy
2. Dependability and quality
3. Utility

Economy   People are influenced by appeals to economy. Discount stores owe their existence to this buying motive.

Appeals to economy are used to induce consumers to purchase in larger quantities: "two for the price of one," "save three cents on each package when you buy six," and "buy by the dozen and save." Some economy appeals, such as "compare and save," "down-to-earth prices," "prices you can afford," and "easy on your pocketbook," are more general and may not stand up under scrutiny.

Both the seller and the consumer have a valid interest in selling and buying in larger quantities. For the buyer, a saving may be realized. For the seller, an increase in the amount sold to each customer tends to reduce selling costs and thus to increase profits. It is good marketing policy also, for, in theory, the customer who is sold a larger quantity uses the product over a longer period of time and thus is more likely to develop the habit of using the brand. Economies are sometimes "false economies," since people delude themselves about economy. Also, tests made by a soap manufacturer showed that products purchased in larger quantities are used more freely. We are inclined to put more toothpaste on the brush when we use the large tube than if we have a small one. Such considerations are subtle, but they are points on which business builds sales.

Dependability and quality   A strong rational motive is the desire for dependability and quality—a motive that becomes evident when consumers decide which particular make or model to purchase. For example, after a customer has made the primary decision to buy a television set, he then compares the quality and dependability of the various makes before actually purchasing the set.

Advertisers illustrate quality by showing details of product construction; "built to stand up under the hardest use" and "superior workmanship" are common claims. To satisfy the desire for dependability, sellers frequently offer guarantees. Warranties on appliances, automobiles, and other durable goods are customary. Even toilet preparations, breakfast cereals, and cooking oils are guaranteed to satisfy or the purchase price is refunded. In general, guarantees do cause consumers to place more confidence in the goods and services.

Utility   Intended use of the product frequently plays a major role in buying decisions. This is why the progressive marketer carefully studies the possible uses for his product. For example, if a do-it-yourself home owner has a damp basement wall to cover, his decision about which paint to buy will hinge entirely on solving this problem. He has very little interest in the product per se, so the decision is largely rational. Another home owner listens to a complaint from her daughter that a drawer in her dresser sticks. The mother goes to the store in a rational frame of mind and makes her buying decision on the basis of what can best be used to solve the problem. This important point about use of product as a buying motive once led an official of General Motors to say, "We are not the experts on automobiles. The customer alone is the automobile expert. For only the customer knows whether the product performs to expectations." Thus businesspeople who are most successful develop marketing programs according to what the customer deems to be important rather than on what the manufacturer believes to be important.

Combinations of buying motives

Because both rational and emotional motives are usually involved in a buying decision, advertisers, to influence different types of buyers, appeal to different motives. Although any single advertisement usually highlights only one buying motive, a series of advertisements, run over a period of time, attempts to stimulate several motives that are relevant to what is being promoted.

Personal selling can be directed at the specific motives of a prospect. The following example illustrates how a variety of motives can be used to overcome a customer's price objection:

MRS. SMITH: The price on that studio couch seems awfully high. I think we paid only about $87.50 for a studio couch a few years ago.

SALESPERSON: Yes, Mrs. Smith, that was about the price of a studio couch without an extra cover and innersprings a few years ago. But in this divan-bed you are getting not only a fine piece of furniture that you will use for years, but also an attractive and comfortable bed that you will never need to be ashamed to have company sleep on. You will always be proud of it when you see it in your living room, and the extra years of use will be worth much more than the extra $50 on the initial price. You're actually saving money.

WHY PEOPLE BUY WHERE THEY DO

Two service stations can be on opposite sides of an intersection, yet one may do twice as much business as the other. Why? The answer lies in *patronage motives*—the term applied to reasons people buy *where* they do. The most important patronage motives are:

1. Reputation of seller
2. Service rendered
3. Location
4. Variety of products offered

Reputation of seller

The seller's reputation is an important patronage motive. Merchants who back up claims made in their advertising, give good value, and are ethical become known as reliable businessmen.

The importance of reputation varies with the type of goods being sold. In purchasing jewelry and furs, consumers often inquire about the reputation of various sellers before deciding where to buy. In purchasing staples, such as food, the consumer is usually more concerned with the reputation of the manufacturer than of the retailer.

Many small businesses depend on their reputations for friendly, personalized service to attract customers. The cheery "Good morning" and the "I hope you're feeling better today, Mrs. Baxter" are important. Consumers may pay higher prices because they enjoy personalized attention. Large stores attempt to develop a favorable "store image" by training salespeople to be friendly and courteous and by encouraging executives to participate in community activities.

A large national food chain helps build and maintain its reputation by hammering away continually on what it calls its "Eight magic words for pleasing Mrs. Smith." These words constitute a company policy: *freshness, cleanliness, value, variety, uniformity, convenience, quality,* and *courtesy.*

Services rendered

Cashing checks, extending credit, gift wrapping, and free delivery can be important in building clientele. Although services add to the cost of doing business, they are justified when they attract customers. For example, customers having charge accounts at a store are steadier purchasers and tend to buy more than cash customers.

Location

Convenience of location is an important patronage motive, even though the customer may not be aware of it. A business may be efficient in all respects and yet not succeed if it is not conveniently located. (This subject was discussed in detail in Chapter 16.)

Variety of products offered

Another patronage motive is variety of products. Consumers like to compare an assortment before they buy. Variety of goods takes two forms: breadth of line and number of lines. The term *line* in marketing refers to the number of different sizes, styles, brands, and prices of one type of product. If a store carries shoes in a wide range of prices, styles, colors, and leathers, it has a *broad line* of shoes and can meet the needs of many customers.

Number of lines refers to the different kinds of products that are sold. A shoe store that is strong in a number of lines carries, say, rubbers, slippers, shoetrees, hosiery, and shoe polishes as well as shoes. The desire of consumers to find both a broad line and a large number of different lines is one reason for the development of big department stores, where a customer finds wide assortments of practically everything needed in the home, and supermarkets, where he finds wide ranges of most food items.

Figure **18–1**
Per Capita Income Showing Steady Climb

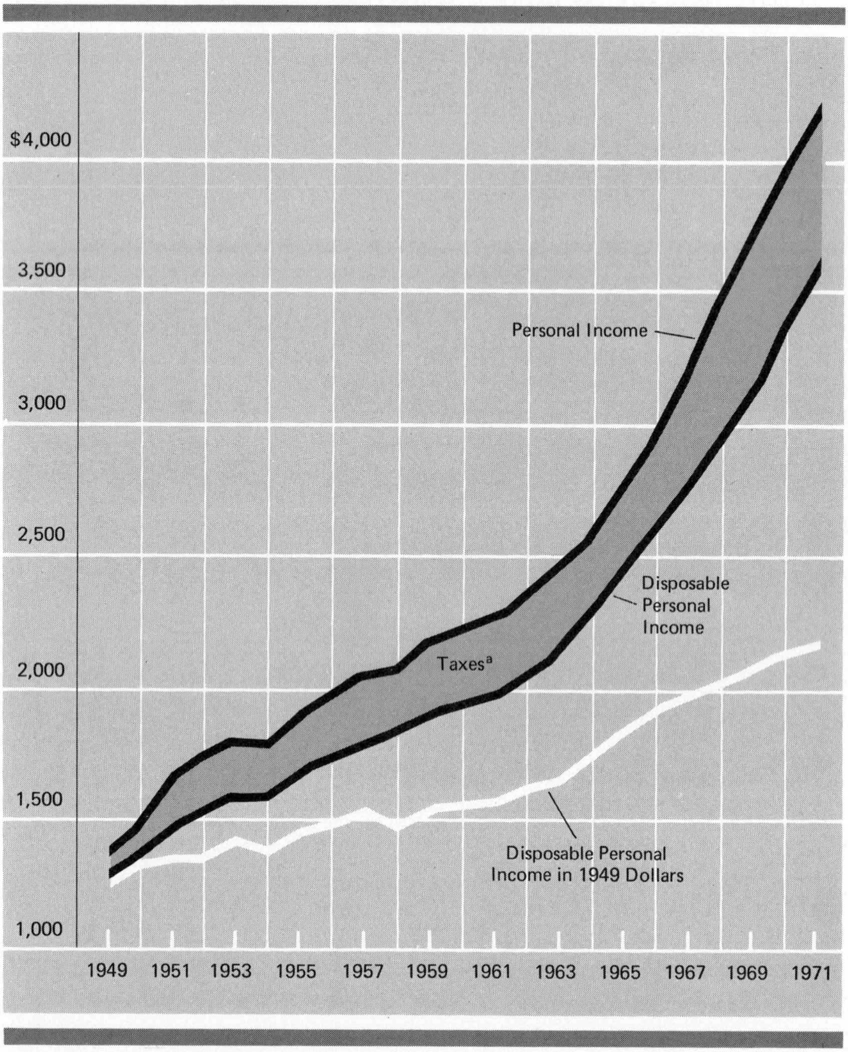

^{a} Mainly income taxes, personal property taxes, and inheritance taxes.

Source: "The Two Way Squeeze," Road Maps of Industry, No. 1687, The Conference Board, April 1, 1972.

Of what significance are these trends to marketing executives?

THE RELATION OF INCOME TO CONSUMPTION

The most important single factor in determining the extent of purchases is personal income. Although a family or an individual can temporarily

Figure **18-2**
The Changing Income Pattern

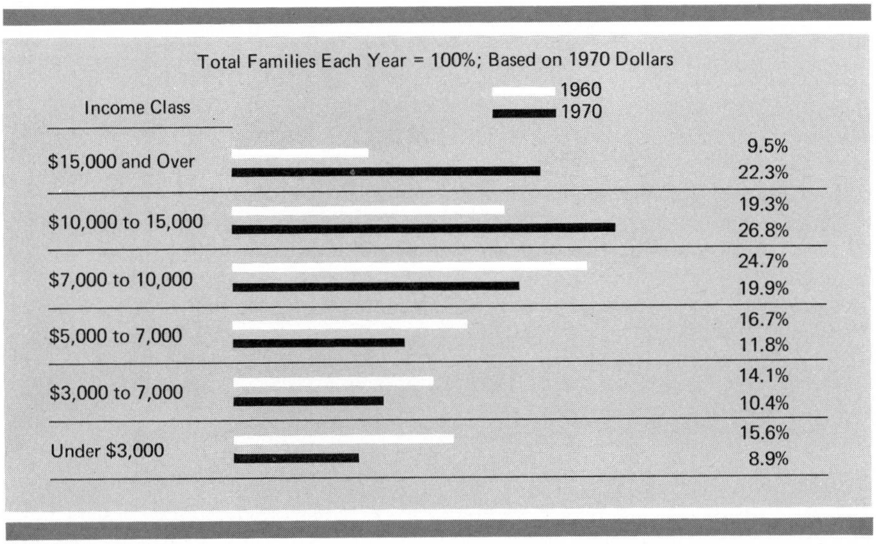

Total Families Each Year = 100%; Based on 1970 Dollars

Income Class	1960	1970
$15,000 and Over	9.5%	22.3%
$10,000 to 15,000	19.3%	26.8%
$7,000 to 10,000	24.7%	19.9%
$5,000 to 7,000	16.7%	11.8%
$3,000 to 7,000	14.1%	10.4%
Under $3,000	15.6%	8.9%

Source: "A Guide to Consumer Markets, 1972/1973," The Conference Board, p. 129.

spend more than its income by drawing on savings or by borrowing, in the long run, total spending is limited by income.

Business people are vitally concerned with fluctuations in income. When total income increases, sales increase; when income decreases, sales drop. So important is income that the U.S. Department of Commerce, trade associations, businesspeople, market-research organizations, and others engage in continuous income analysis as an aid in making decisions. Knowledge of the distribution of income among the population, of regional variations in the relationship of income to sales, and of trends in income is essential to successful marketing.

Income studies are concerned chiefly with *personal disposable income*, which is the income an individual receives after tax and other deductions have been made. (See Figures 18-1 and 18-2.)

Distribution of income

As shown in Figure 18-3, hourly earnings vary considerably by state. For example, the hourly earnings in 1971 for production workers in manufacturing varied widely from the U.S. average of $3.57 per hour. In North Carolina hourly earnings were $2.60 as compared with $5.34 for Alaska. Marketers keep executives informed on income statistics, for consumers have more capacity to buy in some areas than in others.

Figure **18–3**
Market Opportunities Are Not the Same in All States

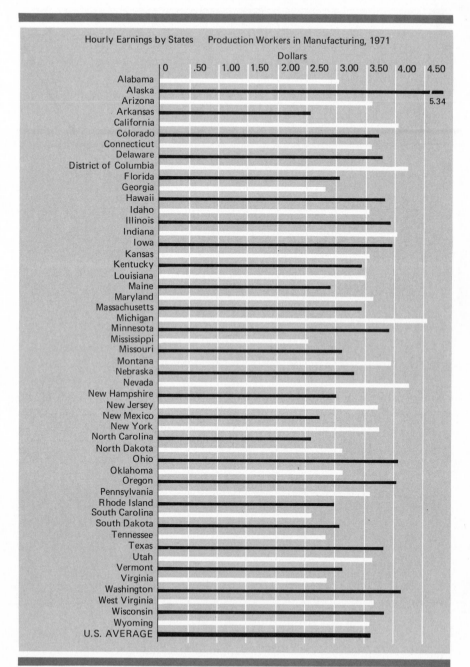

Source: "A Guide to Consumer Markets, 1972/1973," The Conference Board.

Table **18-2**
Personal Consumption Expenditures by Types of Product
in the United States, 1970 ($ Billions)

TYPE OF PRODUCT	PERSONAL CONSUMPTION EXPENDITURES	PERCENTAGE OF TOTAL
Food	$114.0	18.5
Housing	91.2	14.8
Household operations	85.6	13.9
Transportation	77.9	12.7
Clothing accessories, and jewelry	62.3	10.1
Medical care expenses	47.3	7.7
Recreation	39.0	6.3
Personal business	35.5	5.8
Alcoholic beverages	17.7	2.9
Tobacco	11.2	1.8
Private education and research	10.4	1.7
Personal care	10.1	1.6
Religious and welfare activities	8.8	1.4
Foreign travel and other	4.8	.8
	$615.8	100

Source: *Statistical Abstract of the United States, 1972,* p. 315.

Figure 18–2 illustrates income trends. We have, it can be noted, a broad middle- and upper-class that has expanded significantly since 1960.

How income is spent

Table 18–2 shows the percentage of expenditures made for different items in the United States in 1970. Food accounted for the largest share of the consumer's dollar, with household operation, transportation, housing, and clothing each accounting for more than 10 percent. Please note that these are averages. The consumption pattern of any individual household may vary from this standard, depending on size of income, size of household, occupation, age, personal preferences, and other factors.

Breakdowns of consumer expenditures are always revealing, as is demonstrated in Figure 18–4, which shows how the dollar that is spent on the automobile is allocated. Clearly the purchase of an automobile is only the beginning of a broad expenditure pattern. Businesspeople are also aware, however, that once a consumer owns an automobile, his discretionary spending for other products diminishes. Thus, competition is not just Ford versus Chevrolet; it is also Ford and Chevrolet versus a new swimming pool or a European vacation.

Figure **18–4**
The Automobile Dollar

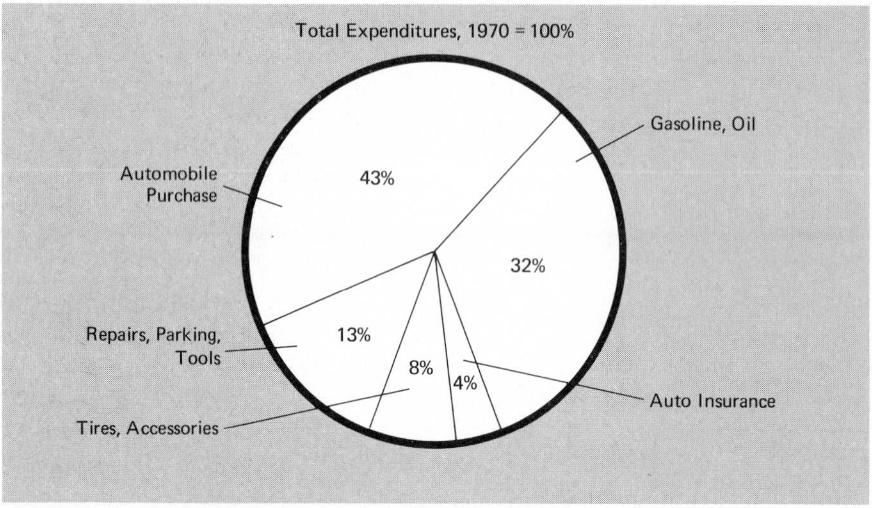

Total Expenditures, 1970 = 100%

Automobile Purchase — 43%

Gasoline, Oil — 32%

Repairs, Parking, Tools — 13%

Tires, Accessories — 8%

4% — Auto Insurance

Source: "A Guide to Consumer Markets, 1972/1973," The Conference Board.

Why does the automobile compete with expenditures
for many other things?

THE RELATION OF POPULATION TO CONSUMPTION

Provided per capita income and other factors remain equal, the larger the population, the larger will be the market. The individual business is interested primarily in changes in population in its trading area—that is, the territory from which it draws most of its customers. Department-store executives are concerned with trends in population of the entire metropolitan area, since their customers come from all parts of the city. The neighborhood hardware dealer, on the other hand, whose store attracts trade from an area of only a few blocks, is interested in whether more or fewer people live in that small area.

Organizations that sell nationwide watch changes in total population. Knowledge of population shifts helps them decide where to open new stores, which existing outlets to close, where additional salespersons are needed, and whether or not to appoint new dealers in an area. (See Figure 18–5.)

The Constitution of the United States provides that a national census of population be taken every ten years. The population statistics prepared by the U.S. Bureau of the Census are of immeasurable value to marketers. Reports are available, not only on states and major cities, but on townships, counties, and even subdivisions of the larger cities. Between the ten-year census periods, the Bureau of the Census makes estimates of population, so data on population changes are available annually.

Households

The number of households is more meaningful for marketers than population figures alone. Until the marketer knows how people in an area are grouped, he doesn't really know what he is dealing with. Households with four or more members are a market that is vastly different from households consisting of three or fewer members. By-and-large, the household, not the individual, is the real buying unit. A 24-year-old woman living alone or with another single person would doubtless spend her money quite differently from a woman of the same age living in a family of five members. The former may be a career woman; the latter, the mother of three young children.

Age

The age composition of the population is important because age influences what people want. One characteristic of our population today is that older persons are increasing in number and as a percentage of the total population. (See Figure 18–5A for expected growth of age groups.) This trend materially affects the demand for certain types of products and services. It means more sales of electric blankets, drugs and medical services, laborsaving conveniences, and a range of products for leisure, such as stamp collector's supplies, garden tools, do-it-yourself equipment, and television sets. Special housing designed for older people includes the marketing of nonskid bathroom floors, low shelves and cabinets, and bathtubs with handles.

Declining birth rate and constant death rate

Our national birth rate (number of live births per thousand per year) has declined significantly in recent years, while our death rate (number of deaths per thousand per year) has remained almost constant. (See Figure 18–6.)

Fewer births occurred in 1970 than in 1960. This means a relatively smaller share of our marketing effort is being directed toward supplying needs of infants and small children. While no one can predict future birth

Figure **18–5**
Population by Age and Sex and Where They Will Live in 1980

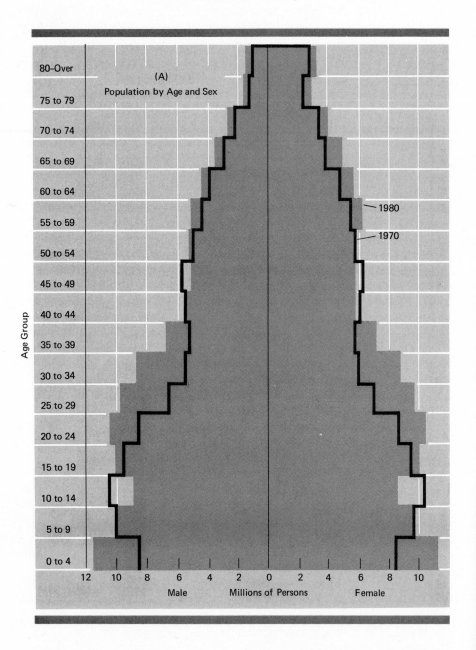

What does this mean to a business planner?

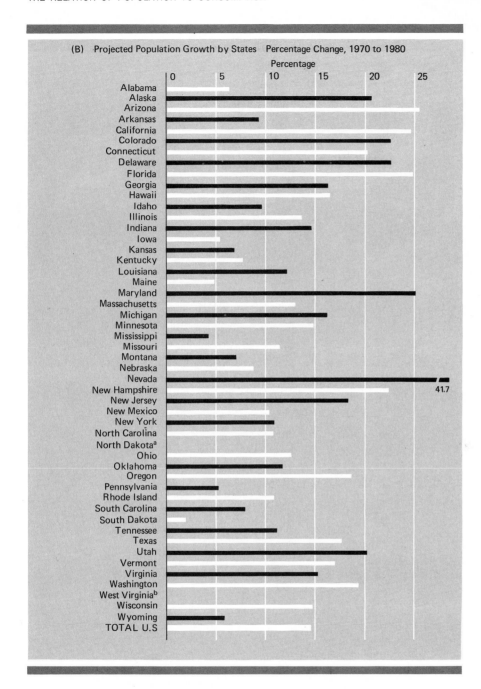

(B)   Projected Population Growth by States   Percentage Change, 1970 to 1980

[a] No change, 1970 to 1980.
[b] Projected decline of −4.1 percent, 1970 to 1980.

Source: "A Guide to Consumer Markets, 1972/1973," The Conference Board, p. 32.

Figure **18–6**
Vital Statistics Rate, 1925–71

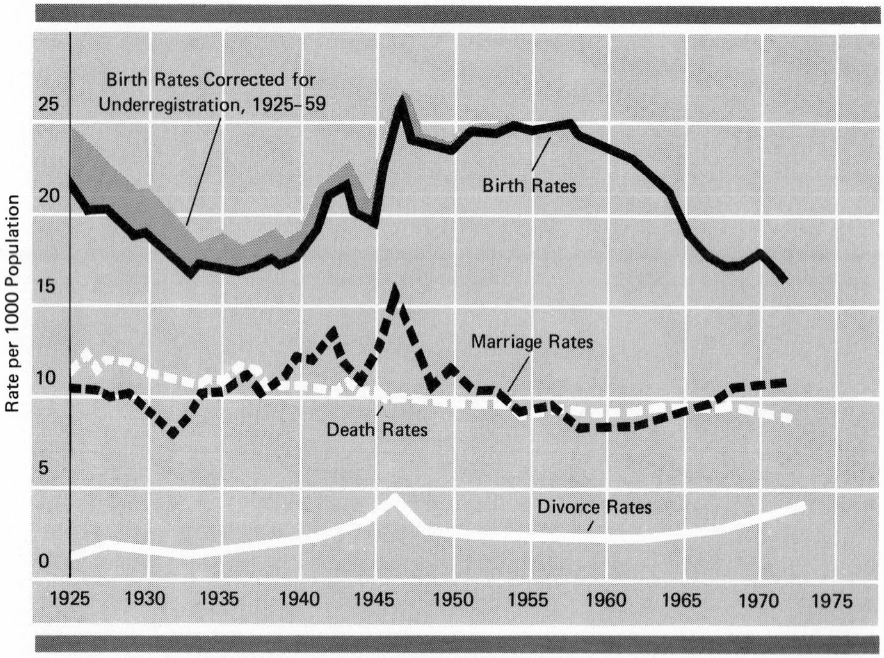

Source: *Statistical Abstract of the United States, 1972*, p. 49.

rates with certainty, it is estimated that a record number of people will marry in the early 1970s, a fact that may help reverse the birth rate decline.

Population shifts

Several population shifts have taken place that directly affect marketing. These include (1) farm-to-city migration, (2) growth of standard metropolitan areas, (3) shift from central cities to suburban areas, and (4) regional changes in population.

Decline in farm population   The movement of population from farm to city has resulted in part from the increasing mechanization of agriculture, which means that fewer people are needed to produce agricultural products. This movement, which has been a population trend of the past 150 years, may reverse with reversed emphasis on farming and rural living.

The farm-to-city migration affects marketing. Small town businesses are affected. City people are more fashion conscious, and they want a wider variety of goods. Urbanites also use more services, such as beauty parlors and commercial amusements.

Growth of standard metropolitan areas[2]   In 1970, 68.6 percent of the U.S. population lived in 243 Standard Metropolitan Statistical Areas, which encompassed about 7 percent of the U.S. land area. This population accounted for nearly two-thirds of the retail and about nine-tenths of the wholesale sales volume.

Shift from central cities to suburban areas   The rush to suburban communities was one of the most important population trends of the 1960s. The rapid formation of new households, congested living conditions in the central cities, racial unrest, and urban decay were the main factors responsible for this trend. Today, the suburbs are the most important single market in the nation — which accounts for the rapid and successful development of shopping centers. What future trends will be is unclear.

Regional changes in population   Population does not increase evenly (see Figure 18–7). California, Florida, Maryland, Arizona, Nevada, and Alaska have experienced phenomenal population growths of 25 percent and more in the last decade, while the North Central states have remained either static or have actually decreased in population.

Study of population trends is of great importance to organizations that distribute nationally. It is said that the chief literary fare of General Robert Wood, who charted the postwar expansion program of Sears, Roebuck and Company, was the *Statistical Abstract of the United States.*** Because Wood learned to anticipate population shifts, he influenced Sears to emphasize department store expansion in those areas where population seemed likely to increase and to reduce its mail-order houses in declining rural areas.

SPECIAL READINGS

Great Sales By Today's Great Salesmen by Lassor Blumenthal. London: Collier Books, 1965 (paperback). This well-written, lively book can provide some balance for this chapter, which dwells on demographics and the wealth of statistical information that is available about markets. The author, who is a veteran business analyst and contributor of articles to *Dun's Review & Modern Industry* and *The American Salesman*, makes this point: In spite of the computer, myriad statistics, buying committees, and business complexity, the fundamental decision to buy or not is still made by a human being. "That someone will have ears and eyes and a brain and a wife and baby and dandruff and crabgrass."

Each chapter in the book examines the personal side of marketing and selling. Each offers a step-by-step analysis of what a successful marketer did to achieve his goal. The chapters are based on the stories of marketers who were interviewed and analyzed by the author. One of the author's main points is that "no exceptional salesman has ever been a pure rationalist."

---

[2] Standard Metropolitan Statistical Areas are used for reporting vital U.S. statistics. A Standard Metropolitan Statistical Area is an integrated economic and social unit with a large population nucleus. Each SMSA contains at least one central city with at least fifty thousand inhabitants.

Figure **18–7**
Percentage of Change in Population by State, 1960–70

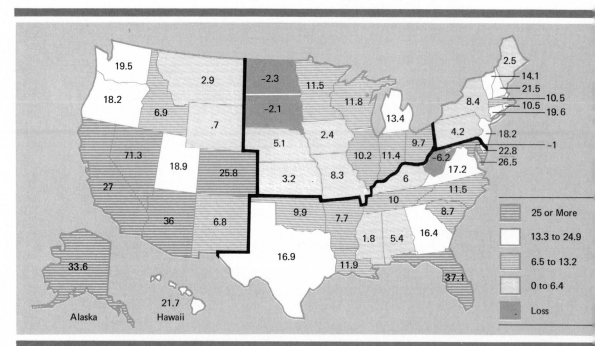

Changes in population by states are indicated by percentage of gain or loss and by tone of color (see key at right). Heavy lines delineate the four regions into which the Bureau of the Census divides the nation: Northeast, South, North Central and West.

Source: *Scientific American,* July 1971, p. 19.

How do you account for this uneven pattern of population expansion?

OTHER FACTORS AFFECTING CONSUMPTION

Education

Education affects consumer demand in two ways. First, it increases the *number of wants.* Education brings one into contact with more customs, products, ideas, and ways of doing things, and these increase one's desire for material, as well as nonmaterial, things. Until one knows that a thing exists, he has no desire for it. It is a truism that it takes less to make a grade school graduate happy than a college graduate.

Second, education changes the character of wants. It tends to make individuals more discriminating, harder to please. Preferences in music, literature, recreation, and style change with increased education. Even color preferences may be affected: It was once found that college graduates tended to prefer pastels and subdued colors, those with less schooling usually liked bright primary colors best.

As is shown in Figure 18–8, rising educational attainment has been impressive. Although the number and proportion of high school and college graduates are expected to increase during the next decade, it is significant that a substantial number still are not expected to complete high school. For example, the number of people with less than twelve years of education in the twenty-five to thirty-four age bracket is expected to rise from 8.4 million in 1965 to 9.2 million in 1985.

Occupation is tied closely to educational attainment. White-collar workers are largely high school and college graduates; most service, agricultural, and blue-collar workers have gone to school less than twelve years. Forecasts indicate that the fastest growing occupational groups will be those requiring the highest educations.

Climate

Those who sell nationally realize that differences in climate materially affect demand. The types of clothing worn in northern states differs in weight, weave, color, and frequently style from that worn in the South. Demand for sporting equipment, heating systems, air conditioners, and, to a certain extent, food, is affected by climate.

Retailers are usually more concerned with weather than with climate, for during extremes in weather, such as heat waves, consumers tend to postpone buying. Retailers in northern cities have learned that snow before Christmas stimulates buying, while warm weather depresses sales. A mild autumn results in fewer sales of winter clothing, and a prolonged winter adversely affects Easter clothing sales.

Sex

Sellers cannot afford to overlook the fact that women occupy the most important place as selector and purchaser of most consumer goods. Even when purchases are made by men, feminine influence is often apparent.

Considerable research is conducted to learn whether buying decisions for specific products are made by men or women. Store layout and decoration, as well as the kind and amount of services, depend in large part on whether the clientele is primarily male or female. The increasing number of women in the labor force is also very significant.

Figure **18–8**
Income and Levels of Education

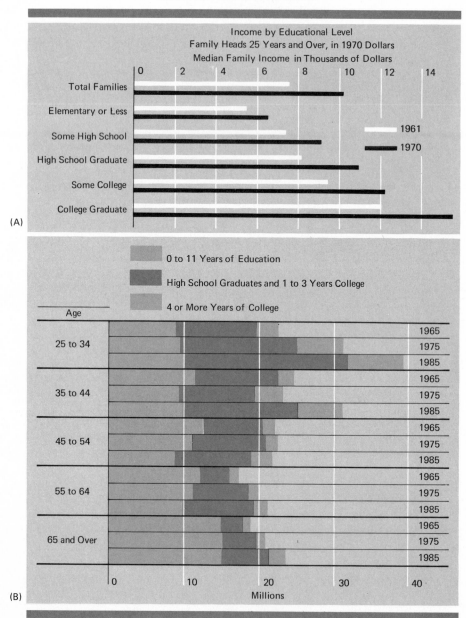

(A)

(B)

Source: A, "A Guide to Consumer Markets, 1972/1973," The Conference Board; B, U.S. Chamber of Commerce.

Human beings are creatures of habit. Consumers tend to develop two types of buying habits that have significance. First, they tend to become habitual patrons of certain stores. A person is inclined to buy most of his gasoline from one service station, his groceries from one or two food stores, and so on. Second, consumers tend to become habitual buyers of specific brands.

Through advertising and other promotional efforts, sellers attempt to influence these habits: to retain the allegiance of those customers already buying their brands or patronizing their stores, and to persuade competitors' customers to change their buying habits.

PEOPLE AND THEIR IDEAS
James Cash Penney

The golden rule in business

James Cash Penney opened his first dry-goods store in the tiny frontier mining town of Kemmerer, Wyoming, in 1902. Today the J. C. Penney Co. is a retail chain of over 1,700 stores, with sales in 1972 of over $5.5 billion. It is the country's foremost merchandiser of soft goods and second only to Sears, Roebuck & Co. in general merchandising. Penney customers, numbered in the millions, have been buying its goods in greater and greater volume. Since 1960, the company has had an increase in sales of 9.6 percent a year, compounded annually.

Penney was born in 1875 in Hamilton, Missouri, the son of a Baptist minister who served without pay and supported himself by farming. After graduating from high school, Penney worked on his father's farm for two years and then in a shoe store in Hamilton. In 1897, in poor health, he followed his doctor's advice, moved to the West, and settled in Longmont, Colorado. There he found employment in the dry-goods store of T. M. Callahan & Co. In 1902 Callahan chose Penney to open a new store in Kemmerer, Wyoming, and gave him the opportunity to buy a one-third interest in it. This store was called the "Golden Rule," reinforcing Penney's firm belief in giving value for value received. Penney bought a similar interest in the company's store in Rock Springs, Wyoming, and later established new stores in partnership with men he trained. By 1911 he had opened twenty-two stores in Wyoming, Colorado, Utah, and the Dakotas. Each of these stores was organized as a partnership, with the operating partner having a one-third share in the business.

The rapidly expanding chain of Penney stores was incorporated in 1913 as the J. C. Penney Co., and its offices were moved to New York City. Under this original incorporation, each managing partner retained a one-third share in his own store. In 1927, however, the company was fully incorporated and reorganized so that the managers of all Penney stores now share in the profits of the entire chain. This feature of profit-sharing is, in J. C. Penney's estimation, the largest single factor in the company's success.

Penney served as president of the company and chairman of the board of directors until 1947, when he retired to become honorary chairman. Until shortly before his death in 1972, Penney was very active and maintained a full-time staff in his New York office to keep up with his correspondence and other activities. Penney's youthful character can be illustrated by his reply when asked about the nation's stress on utilizing youth: "I'm in favor of it. I don't think there is any danger in overdoing it. It's an inspiration to me. Youthful styling is essential if we are to lead and not follow. And we must encourage young people as much as we can to come into retailing."

In 1921 Penney purchased Emmadine Farms in Dutchess County, New York, for the development of agriculture and livestock. In 1936 he turned over the farm, a large herd of pure-bred cattle, and an endowment of $250,000 to the Foremost Guernsey Association with the stipulation that in 1996 they become the property of the University of Missouri. His publications include his autobiography, *Fifty Years' Experience with the Golden Rule* (1950), and *Lines of a Layman* (1956).

CONTEMPORARY ISSUES
Situation 18

Will "the pill" hurt economic growth?

During class the discussion centered on the significant drop in our national birth rate over the past fifteen years. A number of reasons were given: changes in religious attitudes, economic difficulties in supporting and educating large families, and, especially, the ever-widening use of birth control pills.

Ray seemed to be disturbed about the birth rate decline. "This is going to mean slower economic growth, which could have a disastrous effect on our whole economy," he exclaimed. "In just a few years there will be fewer family units, and this will result in cutbacks in everything from new cars to apartment construction."

"Don't panic," reassured John. "The *number* of consumers is important to economic growth, but more important is the *money* people have to spend. Consider India which has three times as many people as we but only a fraction of our consumption."

"I still say I'm right," insisted Ray. "A low birth rate is certain ultimately to have a negative effect on all businesses, whether they produce baby shoes or caskets."

"I admit that the number of units sold may drop," said John, "but the dollar volume will go up because people will buy better quality, and, quite possibly, total economic output may increase because more women will work. Certainly demand for vacations, travel, and time-saving devices should increase. But let us assume, for the sake of argument, that the low birth rate does pose a potentially bad economic problem. How do you propose to solve it?"

"I was hoping you'd ask that," answered Ray. "I have two ideas. First, the federal government could provide a subsidy of, say, $2,000 for each child born after a certain date. Second, the government could change our immigration policy to admit at least a million people a year."

SITUATION EVALUATION

1. What additional points could be made to support each argument advanced?

2. Do you feel a low birth rate is, in fact, apt to slow economic growth? Why or why not?

3. Evaluate Ray's two ideas for stimulating population growth.

BUSINESS CHRONICLE

Catering to consumers

Stella Epstein, the Kingmaker Estates' new advertising manager, was having a sales strategy meeting with Tony DiGrassi, the public relations director, and Maurice Hill, the sales manager. Following are some of the viewpoints expressed.

Epstein: I think we are making a mistake advertising and characterizing our apartment complexes as either attractive for family living or, a good place to retire. I've just moved down here from New York City. There we have complexes that cater to single people — some for younger singles and others for older singles. They're quite successful because people don't live in families as much as they used to. It's more interesting for singles to live with non-family-oriented people.

Hill: The South is still more conservative than New York and the West Coast.

DiGrassi: I think we ought to characterize our apartment complexes according to what people do. Professional people like to live close to one another; blue-collar employees feel more comfortable when they are surrounded by other blue-collar people; and so on.

Epstein: I'm not sure that's a good idea. It fragments society too much. The doctors' and lawyers' kids know only other kids from the same background. If you don't segregate people, they'll understand one another better. We've got too much snobbery based on where you live and whom you associate with now. I don't think a company policy should encourage that!

Hill: We're in business to rent apartments or sell them. A real estate company's policies are not going to make the least bit of difference on how people get along with one another. That's not our job or our worry.

DiGrassi: I'm not sure I agree with you, Maurice. A company has no business encouraging segregation of any kind.

QUESTIONS

1. Evaluate and comment on the various points made in the discussion. Can a real estate company's policies have a social effect? What social matters should a real estate company consider in conducting its business?

2. How are living arrangements changing? Is there a trend away from the family way of living? Just how important is the trend in the real estate business? What should Kingmaker do about it?

3. What appeals are best used in attracting people to a real estate development?

APPLICATION EXERCISES

1. Secure advertisements illustrating an appeal to each of the following emotional motives: superiority, distinction, comfort, fear, pleasure, imitation, and welfare of family. Do the same for these rational motives: economy and dependability and quality. Do some advertisements appeal to more than one emotional or rational motive? Why?

2. The insatiability concept advocated by the economist Adam Smith says in effect that people's wants can never be fully satisfied. Regardless of what and how much people acquire, they still want more. Assuming human wants are insatiable, explain what general changes in consumption would take place in each of these situations. (Consider changes in types of product and service as well as quantity and quality that will be purchased.)

   a. The Wiley family's annual income increased from $10,000 to $20,000 in a five-year period.

   b. The Wilson family's annual income increased from $30,000 to $60,000 in five years.

   c. The Wiliford family's annual income increased from $100,000 to $200,000 in five years.

3. Outline two sales presentations for your favorite make of automobile. Prepare one to influence a young man and the other to influence a young woman to make an automobile purchase. How will these presentations differ?

QUESTIONS

1. What is wrong, from a marketing point of view, with planning in terms of the "typical" consumer?

2. Discuss the following statement: "Probably no individual buys on the basis of either emotional or rational motives alone."

3. Which is more important in appealing to people to buy consumer goods—emotional or rational motives?

4. Can store services be classified as rational and emotional? Illustrate your point by discussing actual examples.

5. Select what you think would be the three most important appeals for selling (a) life insurance, (b) sports cars, (c) spring topcoats, and (d) cake mixes.

6. What are some of the selling techniques that could be used to get customers to buy in larger quantities? To buy better quality? To change to the new styles in clothing?

7. It is said that people are now less constant in where they make their purchases than they used to be. Assuming the statement to be true, can you speculate on what has caused people to be less loyal to any one store?

8. How are the appearance, services, and merchandise of a retail store influenced by the income level of the customers to whom it attempts to appeal?

9. Demonstrate how population factors influence marketing.

10. There are critics who believe it wrong to use emotional appeals such as sex, keeping ahead of the Joneses, and fear of not being accepted, because we are thereby creating a nation of neurotics. "Madison Avenue," these critics say, "sets goals for the nation, and Madison Avenue is sick." (Madison Avenue is where the main offices of many advertising agencies are.) What do you think of this criticism?

11. Which geographic areas do you feel hold the most promise for business expansion in the future? The least? Why?

12. Why do over 65 percent of the people cram themselves into only 7 percent of our land area? Will this situation continue?

19

demand creation functions and pricing

CHAPTER 19

SELLING
Who Sells? Steps in the Selling Process.

SALES MANAGEMENT
Management of the Sales Force. Management of Other Marketing Functions. Evaluation of Sales Performance.

ADVERTISING
Types of Advertising. Advertising Media. The Advertising Agency. The Advertising Department.

THE SOCIOECONOMIC EFFECTS OF ADVERTISING
Values of Advertising. Criticisms of Advertising. Some Conclusions about Advertising.

PUBLIC RELATIONS
Purposes of Public Relations. The "Publics" of Public Relations. Handling Public Relations Situations. Trade Associations and Public Relations.

PRICING

PRICING: THEORETICAL CONSIDERATIONS
Price and the Law of Demand and Supply. Elastic and Inelastic Demand. Pricing under Conditions of Pure Competition. Pricing under Monopolistic Conditions. Profit Maximization.

PRICING: PRACTICAL CONSIDERATIONS
Price Policies. Geographic Factors in Pricing. Other Factors to Consider in Pricing. Pricing and Inflation.

DOES MARKETING COST TOO MUCH?

Every manufacturer, whether he produces computers or pin cushions, faces the task of disposing of his output. Only through the sale of his products does he recover costs of raw materials, machinery, and labor, and earn a profit. But the basics of selling, advertising, and pricing are by no means confined to the manufacturer. Every middleman, from giant wholesalers and retailers to the popcorn vendor, must sell the merchandise that he has purchased. Service businesses—airlines, utilities, banks, insurance companies, and motels also must sell their "products." In a very real sense, success in business depends directly on how well the selling function is performed. It is important, then, for anyone in business to understand the nature of the selling process and the role it plays in our economy. It is frequently said in the business community that "there is nothing wrong with any business that an increase in sales would not cure."

SELLING

Personal selling can be defined as the process of assisting and inducing a prospective customer to buy a commodity or service that has commercial significance to the seller and the buyer.

By this definition, the retail clerk who helps the customers select a pair of shoes is selling. The manufacturer's representative who persuades a wholesaler to stock a certain product and resell it to retailers is selling. The newspaperman who calls on businesses urging them to advertise in his newspaper is also selling.

The basic distinction between selling and advertising is that *selling is personal in nature, whereas advertising is impersonal.* The objective of both is the same — to sell. Advertising and selling are auxiliary to each other. Advertising is used to inform, to lessen buyer resistance, and to pave the way for salesmen. Advertising, in a sense, presells the customer. For instance, a tire company may advertise to make prospective customers aware of the advantages of its tires. Salesmen, however, are still needed to demonstrate the tire and to close the sale.

Who sells?

Over five million people are engaged in selling in the United States. Although they all sell, the nature of their job differs. Retail sales people have the least complicated selling jobs since customers come to the store. This is an excellent place for a student to get initial, "grass roots" experience meeting and observing the public. In most retail sales jobs, minimum selection standards are used and only perfunctory training is provided. Wholesale salesmen and salesmen of brokers and manufacturers' representatives and the like require more extensive qualifications and training, for they call on professional buyers, who want both technical and resale information about what they buy. Manufacturers' salesmen, often highly educated and extensively trained, call on equally well-trained and qualified buyers, who expect them to know not only the technicalities of their product but how to install and use it. Regardless of the level of selling, there are similar basic steps in the selling process. The nature of the selling task determines how complex these steps will be in practice.

Steps in the selling process

The several steps generally followed in making a sale are: (1) locating prospective customers, (2) arranging to see the prospective customer under favorable conditions, (3) demonstrating the value of the product or service, (4) answering the prospective customer's questions and meeting his objections, and (5) closing the sale by convincing the prospect that he should buy. The following illustrates how these steps are taken in an actual selling situation.

John Brown, who sells automobiles, took the license numbers of all cars more than three years old parked in front of neighborhood homes. Then he checked with the license bureau to learn the owners' names and addresses. (Step 1: locating the prospect.) Brown then phoned each owner, asking him if he might show him a new car. One of them, Fred Smith, agreed to talk to him on Saturday afternoon. (Step 2: arranging to see the prospect under favorable conditions.) When they met, Brown explained the new features of the latest model car and gave Smith a ride. (Step 3: demonstrating the product.) Brown answered Smith's questions about upkeep, financing the car, trade-in allowance on his old car, and so forth. (Step 4: answering the prospect's questions and meeting his objections.) In due time, Brown asked Smith to place an order for a new car, giving several reasons why that particular time was a good time to buy. After some deliberation, Smith agreed and signed the contract for purchase of a new car. (Step 5: closing the sale.)[1]

SALES MANAGEMENT

Sales management can be thought of as covering two broad areas within the business organization: management of the personal selling function and management of other marketing functions. So considered, sales management is synonymous with the newer term "marketing management."

The executive in charge of sales management is usually called the marketing manager if his duties are broad or the sales manager if they are relatively narrow. In either case he occupies a position of considerable responsibility in the company, often with the status and title of vice-president.

Management of the sales force

The sales manager is responsible for the recruitment, selection, training, equipping, territorial assignment, quota assignment, supervision, com-

---

[1] For a detailed treatment of selling, see *Salesmanship: A Contemporary Approach,* by Ferdinand F. Mauser (New York: Harcourt Brace Jovanovich), 1973.

pensation, and motivation of salesmen. Frequently he works closely with his company's personnel department on the specialized activities of recruiting and selecting and of setting up compensation plans, but sometimes he may use outside agencies or consultants.

Recruitment of salesmen   Methods of recruitment include advertising in newspapers, visiting colleges and universities, and asking present salesmen and others to suggest likely candidates.

Selection of salesmen   After recruitment, the next step is to select the individuals who show the most promise. Information from completed application forms and statements from previous employers, teachers, and others can give information regarding the fitness of the applicant, though there is a tendency for such statements to be more laudatory than realistic. Many companies rely in part on psychological tests to determine whether the applicant has the aptitude necessary for selling. Since ability to influence other people is necessary in selling, sales managers are interested not only in the courses taken by applicants while in school but in their extracurricular activities.

Training of salesmen   Salesmen must have a knowledge of their company, the products sold, and the wants and buying motives of their customers. They also need skill in selling techniques. A major part of the sales manager's job, then, is to help salesmen acquire the necessary product and service information and selling skill.

Equipping of salesmen   The sales executive provides salesmen with the necessary tools—automobiles, samples and sample cases, portfolios, advertising literature, displays, and the like.

Assignment of territories   The sales manager divides the company's market area into individual sales territories. The purposes of territorial division are:

1. To assign each salesman an optimum number of customers and potential customers. If a salesman's territory is too large, he is inclined to cultivate only the most important accounts and thus fail to get maximum sales volume. If his territory is too small, he may be unable to earn an adequate income.

2. To avoid overlapping of territories. Unless each salesman has a clearly defined territory, there is danger that two or more company salesmen will call on the same customers, a confusion that results in excessive selling costs and creates customer ill will as well.

Figure **19–1**
A Time Analysis for the Average Sales Executive

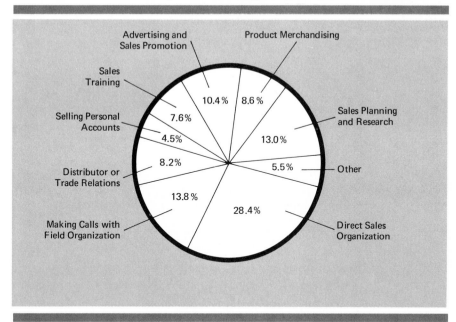

Source: Metropolitan Life Insurance Company.

A number of factors are considered in establishing territories—number of actual or potential buyers, frequency with which calls are made, length of time required to make one call, strength of competition, present acceptance of the company's products, and ability of the salesmen. It is extremely difficult to establish a sales territory that is ideal in size. Sales managers may assign territories on a county, city, or state basis, or they may arbitrarily combine certain geographic areas on the basis of market potential. Many prefer the last, because geographical sales projections for a company's products should be more realistic than economically irrelevant political boundaries.

Assignment of quotas   A *sales quota* is that share of the total marketing task that each salesman is expected to perform. While most sales quotas are expressed in dollar sales volume, salesmen may also be assigned a quota for new accounts, interviews with potential buyers, and units of certain products. A salesman may be given a specific quota for each customer, merchandise line, or section of his territory.

Quotas have two purposes. First, they serve as a control device over sales activity: They designate what the salesman is expected to accomplish. Second, they have psychological value: Most people work harder when they have definite goals. To be of maximum benefit, quotas should be simple, easily understood, fair to all salesmen, and flexible. New quotas are usually assigned for each sales period — often every six months or year. Finally, they should be attainable. Setting unrealistic quotas is damaging to morale.

Supervision of salesmen   Supervising salesmen requires checking their performance. The sales manager may travel with the salesman or review the man's sales records in the office. The degree of supervision varies depending on how experienced the person is, the nature of the selling job, and company policy. In some cases the salesmen's work is checked daily; in others salesmen are largely on their own.

Compensating salesmen   Salesmen are compensated in one of three ways: by straight commission, straight salary, or a combination of the two.

The straight-salary plan speaks for itself. Under the straight-commission plan, the salesman is paid a percentage of his total sales volume. This plan is simple to administer and has a built-in incentive: The more the salesman sells, the more he earns. Some salesmen do not like the commission method, since their income tends to vary.

The compensation plan most often used is a combination of the commission and the straight-salary methods. Combination plans provide both incentive for hard work and reasonable regularity of income. Commissions are usually tied to quotas; for example, frequently sales over quotas pay higher commissions than sales under quotas.

Motivation of salesmen   Selling can often be discouraging. A function of the sales manager, therefore, is to keep the morale of salesmen high. Among the devices used for maintaining good morale are contests, awards, special recognition, and bonuses for outstanding individual performances.

Management of other marketing functions

While company practices differ, there is a trend toward giving the marketing manager responsibility for the performance of all marketing activity within the business, including sales management, credit extension, market research, sales budgeting, advertising, sales promotion, product policies, and, occasionally, transportation. All but two of these — sales promotion and product policies — are treated elsewhere and will not be discussed at this point.

Sales promotion   Sales promotion includes those activities intended to supplement personal selling and advertising. Examples of sales-promotion activities are:

1. Sales bulletins and company publications
2. Point-of-sale material such as counter displays and leaflets
3. Demonstrations and exhibits of company products at trade shows and in retail stores
4. Sampling programs in which consumers are given free products
5. Reports of consumer problems and complaints
6. Company catalogs for use by salesmen and customers

Large companies frequently have a sales-promotion department headed by an executive who reports to the sales manager, marketing manager, or advertising director.

Product policies   Because sales personnel maintain direct contact with consumers, the sales department knows the most about the company's customers. The sales executive has an important voice in decisions about addition or elimination of products from the line, improvement of products, and pricing.

Sales executives are also concerned directly with packaging. While the actual work of package design is performed by specialists, the sales manager usually makes recommendations. The importance of packaging can hardly be overemphasized, as the product's package can have a major effect on sales. This is especially true for consumer goods.

Evaluation of sales performance

A basic responsibility of sales management is the evaluation of sales performance. Sales performance is appraised by comparing present with past accomplishments in the following:

1. Sales volume attained by salesman, by territory, and by each product sold
2. Percentage of total business done in each territory as compared with sales volume achieved by competitors in the same area, if the latter can be ascertained through what is called share-of-market analysis
3. Selling expense as a percentage of sales revenue
4. Number of new accounts gained as compared with established accounts lost in a given period

5. Turnover of salesmen

6. Customer complaints

7. Credit losses

A sales/marketing manager has a complicated and responsible position. While the salesman must be a specialist in selling and providing services to the customer, the sales/marketing manager needs a much broader background. In addition to college training in marketing, a knowledge of management, accounting, research, economics, advertising, and psychology can be very helpful to the sales/marketing executive in his work.

ADVERTISING

Advertising is one of the most conspicuous characteristics of twentieth-century American business. It is an exciting activity. It is loud, lusty, and sometimes ludicrous; and it is colorful, clever, and often creative. As an economic force, advertising is both violently condemned and solidly defended.

Advertising is defined as any form of paid impersonal presentation of goods, services, or ideas for the purpose of inducing people to buy or to act favorably on what is called to their attention.[2]

Advertising is predicated on the basic assumption that consumers must be informed of a product and its specific values before they will purchase it. An inventor may perfect a new device, but unless the public is persuaded to buy, quantity production will not result. Once demand has been created, advertising maintains demand and, if possible, expands it.

Types of advertising

National advertising   This type of advertising is used to sell nationally distributed, branded merchandise, such as soft drinks, automobiles, appliances, and food products. To advertise nationally, a company may buy space in large circulation magazines such as *Newsweek,* or purchase time on television networks.

Retail advertising   Retail, or "local," advertising is used by department stores, chain stores, automobile dealers, and other retailers. It is

---

[2] The word "advertising" is derived from the Latin word meaning "to turn to."

usually much more specific than national advertising in price and terms of sale, and it informs consumers exactly where and when the product or service can be purchased. A retail advertisement often mentions a variety of different items, whereas national advertising is usually restricted to a single product or family of products.

Industrial advertising   Advertising directed to the manufacturer is called industrial advertising. Since there are relatively few industrial consumers compared with ultimate consumers, the volume of industrial advertising is smaller and directed toward specific customers.

Institutional advertising   This type of advertising attempts to enhance the image of the business. Institutional advertising does not mention specific merchandise. Instead, it discusses the stability, reliability, and spirit of a business and its contribution to the public welfare. Banks, utilities, and insurance companies are some of the principal institutional advertisers.

Advertising media

An *advertising medium* is any means used to carry the advertising message to the people it is intended to influence. Sellers have a number of media at their disposal: newspapers, magazines, radio, television, direct mail, billboards, car cards, and many others of less importance. Figure 19–2 shows expenditure trends and relative importance of various media.

The basic problem of the advertiser in selecting media is to find the best one for a desired market. The yardstick for advertising media is both quantitative (how many people will be reached) and qualitative (what type of people will be reached).

For example, an advertiser selling a product bought chiefly by women may have to choose between two newspapers. Newspaper A may be a typical daily newspaper, reaching all types of people, with an advertising rate of, say, $2.25 per page per thousand circulation. Newspaper B may be of the shopping-news variety, reaching housewives largely, and it may have a rate of $5.35 per page per thousand circulation. The choice will depend on a number of factors, but it may well be that the medium with the higher rate per thousand circulation will actually be the more economical, because it may be more effective.

It is apparent that an advertiser has many choices as to how to spend advertising dollars. Standard Rate and Data Service, Inc., of Evanston, Illinois, provides detailed information about rates (costs) and circulation of advertising for specific newspaper, radio, television, and magazine media. This information is available in books that are published periodically and can be secured at some business libraries.

Figure **19–2**
Advertising: By Industry and Medium

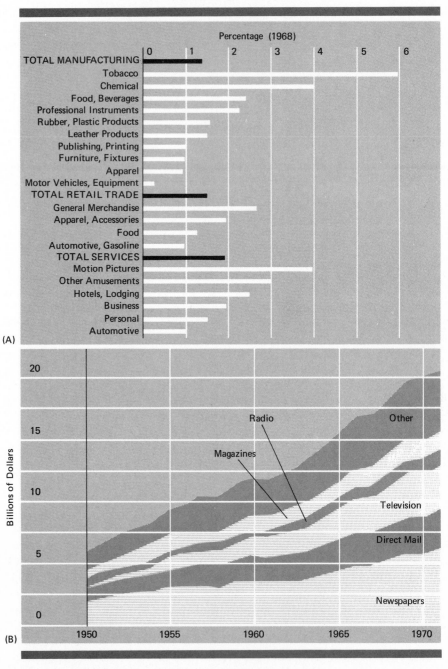

Source: "A Guide to Consumer Markets, 1972/1973." The Conference Board, p. 236.

How do you account for the shift in media emphasis?

Would you consider any of these advertising expenditures excessive?

The advertising agency

An advertising agency** is a service organization composed of specialists who plan, prepare, and place advertising for companies.[3] There are over 15,000 advertising agencies, ranging in size from those employing one or two people to those employing several thousand and maintaining offices in major cities and in foreign countries. Some agencies specialize in preparing specific advertising, such as industrial or financial, while others, known as general agencies, prepare all kinds of advertising for many different clients.

SPECIAL READINGS

**Confessions of an Advertising Man by David Ogilvy. New York: Atheneum, 1963. Advertising leaders, because they are professional communicators who like publicity, are inveterate writers of memoirs. Ogilvy, head of a successful advertising agency, has written a frank ("I made a botch of Oxford"), revealing ("copywriters, work under ferocious pressures, and are apt to be quarrelsome"), colorful ("imitation is the sincerest form of plagiarism") and idea-laden ("make your product the hero of the commercial") biographical account of his life as an advertising man. The book is pitched at the beginner, as indicated by the title of Chapter X, "How to Rise to the Top of the Tree—Advice to the Young." It is also a "how to" book, as indicated by these chapter titles: "Write Potent Copy," "Get Clients," "Manage an Advertising Agency," etc.

When purchasing advertising time or space for its client, an agency receives the wholesale rate from the medium concerned, usually a 15 percent discount from the total cost of the space. The company is charged the retail rate. For example, if a client pays $10,000 for an advertisement in a magazine, $8,500 would go to the publication and $1,500 to the agency. This 15 percent discount (plus a service commission agreed on between client and agency) constitutes the major source of income for the agency.

The work of the advertising agency is usually divided among several specialists. The account executive acts as a liaison man between the agency and the advertiser, usually referred to as the client or account. The account executive is responsible for planning the advertising program and explaining the needs of the client to the agency staff. He should have a broad knowledge of advertising and an intimate understanding of the client's business. He may handle several accounts, but if the advertiser is very large he serves only one. The position of account executive pays well and is a coveted job in advertising.

---

[3] Most, but not all, companies retain outside agencies to perform the highly specialized advertising function. A few larger companies, such as American Home Products Corporation, one of the nation's fifteen leading advertisers, and Shulton, Inc., a large producer of toiletries, as well as a growing number of smaller advertisers have set up their own agencies, called *house agencies*, to handle their own advertising. It is difficult at this point to predict whether a trend toward use of house agencies will gain momentum.

The work of creating advertisements is delegated to copywriters, artists, and designers, or layout experts. Copywriters prepare text material for printed advertising and write commercials for radio and television.

Artists and designers work closely with copywriters to visualize the ideas on which the advertisement is based. Their function is to make sketches, to specify typography and color, and to arrange the elements of the advertisement.

While production of the physical advertisement is the work of engravers and printers, the preliminary work for physical production is performed by the agency production department. This department designates the printers and engravers to be used and sees that they perform their functions.

The media director, or space buyer, is responsible for buying space in magazines and newspapers and time on radio and television. This job is complicated because of the large variety of media from which to choose. To make wise selections, the media director analyzes circulation and audience size and studies the type of people reached by the media.

The advertising department

In retaining an advertising agency, a company does not eliminate the need for its own advertising staff, as is apparent from the following list of functions they perform that cannot be delegated to an agency:

1. Devising a broad advertising plan that can be incorporated into the overall marketing program

2. Determining the size of the advertising budget and ensuring it is properly spent

3. Selecting an advertising agency and acting as liaison with it

4. Supplying information to the agency about the company, its products, and its marketing goals so copy and promotion will reflect these goals

5. Preparing or purchasing various sales-promotion materials

6. Coordinating advertising with selling effort

THE SOCIOECONOMIC EFFECTS OF ADVERTISING

Advertising is a powerful, dynamic force in our economy. By some it is hailed as a great social and economic good that works toward the advancement of society. By others it is criticized severely as an unnecessary economic waste. Following is a brief review of some of the pros and cons of advertising.

Values of advertising

Advertising furthers mass production   Increased demand brought about by advertising makes it profitable for manufacturers to produce in larger quantities. Large-scale production results in a lower unit cost because complicated and expensive machinery cannot be used economically on small lots.

Advertising presells products   Advertising informs consumers of the particular values of competing goods — information that enables them to formulate buying decisions before they enter a retail store. Preselling through advertising becomes increasingly important as more and more merchandise is sold by self-service.

Advertising presses for improvements   To be effective, an advertiser must be able to point out the superiority of a product or service. As a consequence, companies constantly strive to improve products and to develop new ones. It can be said, therefore, that advertising directly encourages innovation and technological advancement.

Advertising is the most economical means for creating demand   In a competitive economy, demand creation is essential. Suppose, as an extreme example, the government passed a law making advertising illegal. What would happen to the company's advertising budget? The company still would have the problem of creating demand; it still would have to tell people about what it sells and let them know about new products and improvements. With advertising outlawed, the result would probably be that money in the old advertising budget would be used for more cumbersome, less effective demand-creation means — larger numbers of salesmen would be hired, old-fashioned trade fairs would be revived, and so on.

Criticisms of advertising

Advertising is too costly   A common criticism of advertising is that it increases the cost of goods and services. The typical layman is astonished to learn that the back cover of a national magazine may cost $70,000, a one-hour network television program $200,000, and a one-page advertisement in a daily newspaper $2,500 or more.

If we look for objective information about a field that is not known for objectivity we find the following: In a study by the Internal Revenue Service, advertising expenditures ranged from highs of 6.0 percent of receipts in tobacco and 4.0 percent in chemicals and motion pictures to lows of 0.1 to 0.2 percent in mining and construction. Advertising expenditures in all media were $22.8 billion in 1972, and, according to Department of Commerce projections, they would rise to $26 billion in 1975 and $36 billion in 1980.

Advertising is purely competitive   This argument states that advertising simply enables one company to attract customers from another and does not bring new customers into the market.

To say advertising is purely competitive and hence wasteful is to suggest that competition as such is wasteful. As we have seen, competition results in efficiencies. Even if the total market for a product were not enlarged, it can be argued that it would still be to the advantage of society to keep competition keen.

A joke common among advertising executives is, "We know 50 percent of our advertising is wasted. The only problem is we don't know which 50 percent." Advertising, it should be remembered, is largely creative, and its effectiveness cannot be evaluated in a purely objective manner.

Advertising makes people want things they cannot afford   There is undoubtedly some truth in this criticism. Human wants are insatiable, and it is perhaps natural to want more than one can afford. Advertising can certainly be credited with whetting the appetite of consumers for more and newer things. But is this necessarily harmful? The urge to own more is a strong incentive to work harder. Production in all societies stems from the people. If they are to produce at the best of their ability, they must want to work hard, to make sacrifices now for later gain, to be willing to educate themselves to their fullest capacities. A want-oriented society creates desire in people to be ambitious; therefore, everyone benefits, for more is produced for everyone.

Closely allied to this attack is the criticism that advertising makes people want the wrong things—that it distorts our sense of values. An enormous amount of advertising, for example, is directed toward improvement of personal hygiene through use of this deodorant or that bathroom tissue. Critics frequently suggest that such promotion makes us overly concerned with relatively unimportant aspects of life.

Advertising is misleading   While most advertising is truthful, there are advertisers who do mislead. Exaggerated, if not erroneous, claims for curing colds, gaining or losing weight, and inducing sleep have worked to the detriment of society. Fortunately, much has been done to correct these malpractices.

The Wheeler-Lea Act, passed by Congress in 1938, makes it unlawful to use false or misleading advertising and empowers the Federal Trade Commission to carry out the provisions of the act. The FTC scrutinizes newspaper and magazine advertisements and monitors radio and television commercials for violations of the law.

It should be noted too that few companies have any desire to deceive or mislead the public. They know that exaggerations and untruths will not build a permanent market for a product; indeed, sales fall off whenever the product does not live up to what the advertising says about it.

Advertising is offensive   Certainly some advertising is not only ineffective but annoying.

"I just can't stand that commercial," "Must they interrupt the program every five minutes to give us *another* message from the sponsor," and "Why don't they sponsor something good for a change," are indeed common complaints. It is an understatement to say that some people are offended by advertising. Charges are made that TV is a vast "wasteland," meaning that many of the programs (the content of which is often determined or at least approved by the advertiser) have little significance and in some cases are damaging to national morality.

Some conclusions about advertising

We must keep in mind two points: First, advertising pays for most of our radio and TV entertainment as well as for our newspapers and magazines. Experiments with pay TV have been mixed and many have failed. While many have tried, few publishers of magazines can stay in business without carrying advertisements. Second, advertisers, being private businesspeople, are inclined to spend their advertising dollars in such a way as to obtain the largest possible audience. That more people will watch a football game than opera or that more people will read a so-called sensational story than an academic article by a social scientist cannot be blamed on advertisers. Perhaps some of this type of criticism more appropriately should be leveled against our family life and educational system. Right or wrong, advertisers are less interested in remaking society than they are in appealing to it as it exists.

A story told about Mark Twain illustrates very well what happens to the businessperson who fails to understand the power of advertising. A "letter to the editor" that reached Twain during his editing days asked if the spider that the reader had found in his newspaper was a sign of good luck or bad. Twain wrote in reply, "[The] spider was merely looking over our paper to see which merchant is not advertising, so that he can go to that store, spin his web across the door, and live a life of undisturbed peace ever afterward."

Many of the criticisms directed at advertising have considerable validity. But this does not mean that we ought to cease advertising; it means we have to improve it. Advertising, in and of itself, is a neutral force; it can be judged good or bad only in the way it is used. It remains the most effective and, for all its extravagance, probably the least expensive way of informing and attracting customers.

PUBLIC RELATIONS

Public relations is the process by which a business attempts to obtain the good will or favorable attitude of the public. All personal and impersonal business contacts with the public are aspects of public relations.

Advertising is a function of sales, or marketing, while public relations can be considered an extension of the executive branch of the company. Advertising is designed to capture a share of the market for the company's products. Public relations is a planned and continuing effort to create good will, public understanding, and trust for the company.

For years, advertising and public relations have been considered separate functions in business. Larger companies had both an advertising department and a public relations department or staff. Within the past few years, there has been a change toward consolidation of the two functions. As one observer put it: "More and more frequently the twin worlds of advertising and PR are becoming the one world of communications." Many of the nation's top five-hundred corporations have created a new executive position, Director of Communications, with jurisdiction over both public relations and advertising.

Purposes of public relations

Public relations is based on two premises: First, the business is dependent on the cooperation of the public for its very existence, and, second, the degree of public cooperation is determined by the attitude of the public toward business.

Specific purposes of public relations are to:

1. Interpret company policies and behavior to the public
2. Counteract distortion of facts caused by rumors
3. "Humanize" the business—give it a personality
4. Win support from the various publics important to the business

The "publics" of public relations

While it is entirely correct to say that business is in contact with the public, from an analytical standpoint the general public must be broken down into specific publics or special-interest groups bound together by some common bond based on their relation to the business. The most important of these publics are:

1. Consumers. This is the largest and most important public of a business, for no business can prosper without customer goodwill.

2. Community. Like an individual, the business will operate in a more supportive environment if it earns the respect of its neighbors.

3. Stockholders. Progressive companies recognize stockholders as a public and therefore maintain programs for stockholder relations.

4. Suppliers. While often a public that is not large in size, suppliers are large in the power they wield. They are prone to be particularly helpful to companies they respect.

5. Dealers. Attitudes and good will of the dealer public who sell company products is very much worth cultivating. A considerable amount of PR effort is wisely expended to "keep the dealers happy."

6. Employees. Usually one of the smaller publics, its importance nevertheless is considerable. A public relations program that overlooks the importance of a company's own employees is shortsighted at best.

Handling public relations situations

Table 19–1 summarizes a number of situations and shows how they might be handled for good or bad public relations. As the table shows, a company has a choice between building good public relations (which will lead to larger sales volume) and creating ill will (which will inevitably lead to a drop in sales).

Trade associations and public relations

A significant development in business during the past fifty years has been the growth of trade-association activity. Trade associations are voluntary,

Table **19–1**
Public Relations Situations

SITUATION	HOW HANDLED UNDER GOOD PUBLIC RELATIONS	HOW HANDLED UNDER BAD PUBLIC RELATIONS
Customer receives defective merchandise that was not guaranteed.	Company offers to make at least a partial adjustment.	Company refuses to make any adjustment, reminding customer that the goods were not guaranteed.
Local university requests financial assistance for research project.	Company promises to consider it and, if possible, make a contribution.	Company refuses, stating that it cannot contribute because it receives too many such requests.
Customer submits an impractical suggestion for improving a company's product.	Company writes thank you letter, with perhaps a brief explanation of why the idea cannot be used.	Company simply ignores the suggestion.
An unusually large number of job applicants wait to be interviewed.	An effort is made to make them all feel comfortable. Extra chairs are brought in, and applicants are told that they will be interviewed as soon as possible.	Insufficient chairs are provided, so that some applicants must stand. Applicants are given no indication as to when they may be interviewed.
Customer is one month behind on payment of bill.	The credit representative writes a courteous letter suggesting that perhaps by oversight the bill has not been paid.	Company threatens suit if payment is not made immediately.
Student contacts local businessman for advice on term project.	Businessman discusses problem with student. Advises him of other sources.	Businessman flatly refuses, saying, "We're too busy. Besides we're here to sell merchandise not give away information."
Company is criticized by local press as being unfair to labor.	Company prepares honest answer explaining its position.	Company refuses to answer the charge, arguing, "How we run our business is our affair alone."
Business leader is asked to address community organization.	Business leader promises to make talk or recommends associate.	Business leader refuses to make talk and does not recommend another person.
Company recalls workers previously laid off but, after workers have returned, realizes a mistake has been made and all returned workers must be sent home.	Company expresses sincere apologies and pays workers wages for the day. Promises to recall them as soon as possible.	Company simply says there was a mistake. Still no work. Does not compensate employees since they did no work.
Small firm solicits business from large company.	Company agrees to consider the vendor's proposition and to keep him informed of their needs.	Company refuses to see vendor, stating that it has more sources of supply now than it needs.

nonprofit organizations of business competitors. There are 2,895 national organizations, with total membership exceeding two million. Examples of leading national trade associations are the National Cotton Council, representing farmers, ginners, merchants, and others who work in the cotton industry; the National Association of Manufacturers, representing 16,000 manufacturers; and the Association of American Railroads, with a membership of 350 railroads.

At least 80 percent of American business is served by trade associations. The bulk of trade association activity consists of gathering and disseminating industry statistics, acting as an industry spokesman in Washington and elsewhere, carrying on public relations programs to build a favorable industrial image, and undertaking product promotion and economic education programs. In appraising the work of these associations it is significant to note their growing awareness of a social responsibility. They are starting to concern themselves with social problems such as environmental research and low-cost housing. On the negative side, many of their members seem to feel that their activities are too general to be of specific company use and that services are inclined to be designed for the dominant section of the membership.

PRICING

Each business, regardless of what it sells, has a pricing function to perform as part of its marketing activity. The prices charged must produce sufficient revenues to cover all direct and indirect costs of doing business and then to yield a profit if the business is to survive and prosper. Pricing technique involves an understanding of accounting, economics, and, to a growing extent, psychology.

Pricing is a phase of business not properly understood by many businesses. Many instances are on record where a firm "priced itself" out of the market by charging too much. Conversely, many firms have underpriced, so they, too, were forced out of business.

To understand pricing it is best to view it first in terms of theoretical considerations and second from a pragmatic standpoint.

PRICING: THEORETICAL CONSIDERATIONS

Price and the law of demand and supply

This economic law holds that the general price level is considerably affected by the relationship of supply to demand. In theory, and often in practice, a shortage causes prices to advance while a surplus causes prices to decline.

The *law of demand* means more goods will be sold at a lower price than at a higher price—for example, we can expect more hamburgers to be sold at 50¢ than at $1.00. Three factors contribute to the law of demand:

1. The principle of diminishing utilities
2. Differences in consumer desire
3. Differences in consumer income

The principle of diminishing utilities   This principle means that the more units we have of something, the less valuable each additional unit is. A second car is less valuable to us than the first, the third is less valuable than the second, and so on.

Differences in consumer desire   The degree to which consumers desire a product helps determine how much they are willing to pay for it.

Differences in consumer income   Consumer income or the ability to pay affects demand. When income goes up demand is strengthened, and, conversely, when income goes down demand is weakened.

Elastic and inelastic demand

While the law of demand generally applies, demand for some goods responds more freely to price changes than demand for other goods. Demand for a given product is said to be *elastic* if a change in price readily produces changes in demand for the product. Demand for automobiles is said to be elastic because more cars will be sold at lower prices and fewer will be sold at higher prices.

Demand for a product is said to be *inelastic* if it is comparatively insensitive to changes in price. Demand for salt and gasoline is considered inelastic since variations in price (within reason) do not change demand significantly.

Pricing under conditions of pure competition

A condition of pure competition is said to exist when no one seller controls enough of the supply of a product to influence price in the market place. Pure competition exists only in the case of some agricultural raw materials such as wheat, corn, and soybeans. No one farmer produces enough of these products to influence price. In industries where there are a number of producers of homogeneous products, one firm might lower its prices to gain a competitive edge. However, in practice, this action would cause producers of similar products to follow suit. And if one producer raises prices above industry levels, consumers are likely to switch to another, cheaper brand.

Pricing under monopolistic conditions

A product that is considered by the consumer as clearly different in some way from all competing products has a market that is characterized by *monopolistic* or *imperfect competition*. A producer in this sense does not have a monopoly like a public utility. It must still compete for its share of the market. But, by making its product distinctive in the eyes of the consumer, the firm does have a *degree* of control over the price.

Bases for non-price competition   Markets for most products are characterized by imperfect competition, which, in effect, means sellers compete mainly on bases other than price. Auto makers for example compete more on style, interior trim, minor mechanical differences, and similar factors than on price.

Profit maximization

Economic theory considers profit a reward for efficient performance of the entrepreneurial function. Profit maximization depends on three interrelated functions: (1) number of units sold, (2) the price at which these units are sold, and (3) the cost of producing and selling this number of units. The best price is one that strikes a reasonable balance between costs and revenue—one low enough to satisfy customers and at the same time high enough for the business to make money.

PRICING: PRACTICAL CONSIDERATIONS

Price policies

Generally, a firm may elect to price its products to meet competition, below competition, or above competition.

Pricing to meet competition   Most businesses intentionally price their products at the "market" or prevailing level. Charging the same as competition is most common when (1) there is little product differentiation, (2) buyers are well aware of the market price, and (3) the seller can do little or nothing to control the market price. Detergents, for example, are usually priced to meet the competition.

Pricing below competition   Some firms deliberately set prices below competition to gain patronage. Discount houses as a matter of policy price below department stores. Many independent service stations intentionally price their gasoline several cents below the "majors." The term *penetration pricing* is applied to the practice of pricing below competition to introduce a new product or expand the market for an old one.

Pricing above competition   If a business markets a product that is unique, distinctive, or prestigious, it may elect to sell above the competitive price. Frequently this policy is followed by "name" restaurants, manufacturers of prestigious apparel, and hotels that have an excellent reputation.

Negotiated pricing   A one-price policy is practical for uniform, standardized products, but, in the case of products that must be made to buyer specifications, negotiated pricing is used. Negotiated pricing is more important in the case of industrial products than for consumer goods. The typical consumer encounters negotiated pricing only in the purchase of real estate, a car, or perhaps a major appliance.

Psychological pricing   Psychological pricing can be defined as using price to suggest either that the product is a bargain or that it is of high quality. Odd pricing ($4.95 instead of $5.00 or $1.98 instead of $2.00) is often used to convey the impression of a bargain. To suggest high quality, dollars only — no pennies — may be used.

Discounts   Several types of discount are used frequently in pricing.

1. Quantity discounts, based either on the dollar value of the transaction or on the number of units involved, are common in selling to both consumers and businesses. *Cumulative discounts* are based on the total amount a customer purchases over a given period, while *noncumulative* discounts are used to encourage large single purchases.

2. Trade discounts are awarded by producers to wholesale and retail

merchants for help in performing marketing functions. To illustrate: A manufacturer might quote its retail price as $100–40 percent–10 percent. The first figure ($100) represents the suggested retail price. The second figure (40 percent) is the trade discount to the retailer, which means he pays $60. The third figure (10 percent) is the wholesaler's discount, and it is calculated on the retailer's price of $60. So, of the $100 retail price the retailer receives $40; the wholesaler, $6 (10 percent of $60); and the manufacturer, $54.

3. <u>Cash discounts</u>. Many firms offer cash discounts as inducements to buyers to pay promptly. A common form is 2/10 net 30, which means that 2 percent of the invoice may be deducted if payment is made within 10 days; otherwise the full amount is due within 30 days.

4. <u>Seasonal discounts</u>. Many businesses market products for which demand is seasonal. To stimulate demand during the off season, some companies offer attractive discounts. Hotels in resort areas such as Miami Beach offer significant discounts during the off season.

Geographic factors in pricing

F.O.B. pricing In F.O.B. (free on board) pricing, all transportation costs are paid by the purchaser from "point x," which may be the producers factory or a warehouse. P.O.E. (point of entry) is a variant form often used by import firms.

Uniform delivery pricing Also known as single-zone pricing, this method regards the entire nation as one zone. All buyers pay the same delivery price.

Zone delivered pricing The nation is divided into two or more zones. All buyers in each zone pay the same transportation costs. Often we hear prices quoted as "slightly higher west of the Rockies," indicating that a firm is using zone pricing.

Basing point pricing One or more cities called "base points" are used to calculate shipping charges. Base points are not necessarily points of production though; a firm's plant may be in Indianapolis, but the base point may be Chicago. Industries that use base points tend to have high freight costs but generally produce highly standardized products, such as cement, chemicals, and sugar.

Other factors to consider in pricing

Manufacturers' suggested prices Manufacturers selling consumer goods to retailers frequently print suggested retail prices on the product. Drug sundries, food staples, and wearing apparel frequently carry the manufacturer's suggested price. The retailer then either sells at the manufacturer's suggested price or in many instances sells below the manufacturer's suggested price, thus creating a bargain impression.

Standard markup percentage Wholesalers and retailers frequently establish selling prices by using a standard markup percentage. A retailer, for example, may have a policy that all merchandise invoiced into the store will be marked up 50 percent on cost. That is, a billfold invoiced into the store at $5 would be marked up 50 percent on cost and sold at $7.50.

Use of the standard markup percentage has many advantages, the most important being simplicity. It is difficult, however, to apply this method to all products since it lacks flexibility. Other factors, such as what the competition charges, usually must be considered also.

Price lining Many retailers follow a price-lining policy. This means that all merchandise offered will be sold at one of a set number of prices. For example, a store may sell dresses at $9.95, $14.95, and $24.95. All merchandise is priced at one of three levels, or lines.

Table 19–2 Forces That Tend to Push Prices Up and Down	
FORCES THAT TEND TO PUSH PRICES UP	**FORCES THAT TEND TO PUSH PRICES DOWN**
A short supply relative to demand	A large supply relative to demand
An increase in wages not matched by an increase in productivity	Stable wages as productivity rises
Lack of efficiency in the use of land, labor, and capital by business	The efficient use of land, labor, and capital by business
Buyers eager to acquire ownership (a bullish attitude)	Buyers resistance to purchasing for any reason (a bearish attitude)
Sellers holding out for higher prices (a bullish attitude)	Sellers eager to sell (a bearish attitude)
Widespread speculation based on the belief that prices will rise	Fear that prices will go down
Government action to increase the supply of money and reduce interest rates	Government action to decrease the supply of money and raise interest rates
Deficit spending by government	A balanced government budget or surplus

Pricing and inflation

Despite a number of severe declines in the general price level in the past 100 years, most of our economic history has been marked by varying degrees of inflation. In the past, periods of economic recession were accompanied by general price declines. However, the recession of 1968–71 was characterized by dangerously high inflation. As a result, in 1971, the president took direct action to control prices and wages—a price commission and pay board were created and given broad authority to approve price and wage increases.

Forces that tend to push the general price level up and down are shown in Table 19–2. As a general rule, forces that push prices up are stronger than forces that push prices down.

DOES MARKETING COST TOO MUCH?

Various studies show marketing costs account for 50 to 60 percent of the selling price of goods purchased by ultimate consumers. People not acquainted with the complexity of the marketing process may conclude that such costs are too high. But the fact that marketing costs generally equal and sometimes exceed production costs does not prove that they are excessive. Judgment can be made only after it is determined whether or not the various marketing functions are performed with maximum efficiency.

Historically, marketing costs relative to costs of production have increased. In 1870, distribution costs amounted to only 25 percent of the consumer's dollar, in contrast with more than 50 percent today. This trend supports the belief that mass production increases the burdens of marketing. However, a percentage comparison of production versus marketing costs can be misleading, because even if marketing costs remain constant, any reduction in production costs will increase the marketing percentage.

There is evidence that marketing costs relative to production costs will be higher in the future. First, an increasing variety of goods is being produced. This means more demand-creation activity, such as advertising, personal selling, and sales promotion, may be necessary. Second, consumers in the aggregate want more, not fewer, services—for example, liberal adjustments on merchandise, parking facilities, and luxurious store surroundings—all of which add to the cost of marketing. Third, as our national income rises, consumers demand more stylish merchandise and product differentiation. They are not willing to wear the same kind of clothing or drive the same kind of automobile as their neighbors. Fourth, while competition tends to eliminate the inefficient, it also is a factor in raising distribution costs. When one department store offers a new service, its competitors will also, and the marketing costs of both increase.

Because of the negative implications of the phrase "the high costs of marketing," it has been advocated that these costs be referred to as "value added." The "value-added" concept is also used in discussions of manufacturing costs — that is, the value added by the production process. There is much to recommend use of the value-added concept when referring to marketing "costs." In sum, marketing creates three of the four economic utilities. Production gives a product form utility, but marketing gives it time, place, and possession utilities.

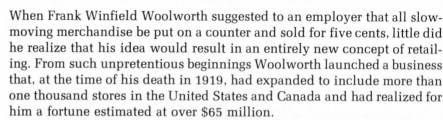

PEOPLE AND THEIR IDEAS
Frank Winfield Woolworth

He mastered nickels and dimes to make millions

When Frank Winfield Woolworth suggested to an employer that all slow-moving merchandise be put on a counter and sold for five cents, little did he realize that his idea would result in an entirely new concept of retailing. From such unpretentious beginnings Woolworth launched a business that, at the time of his death in 1919, had expanded to include more than one thousand stores in the United States and Canada and had realized for him a fortune estimated at over $65 million.

Born in 1852 on a farm near Rodman, New York, Woolworth graduated from the local schools and briefly attended a business college in Watertown, New York. Interested in merchandising from the beginning, he went to work at the age of nineteen in the village store and worked for two years without wages in order to gain experience. It was during this time that he proposed setting up a counter of five-cent goods. The plan was adopted by his employers and was at once successful.

Soon afterward, Woolworth opened a "five-cent" (10-cent merchandise came later, as did still higher prices) store in Utica, New York, with the help of one of his former employers. That venture failed, Woolworth decided, largely because there was an insufficient variety of merchandise. He established his next store in Lancaster, Pennsylvania, which prospered when a line of ten-cent goods was added.

With the success of the Lancaster store demonstrated, Woolworth's brother, C. S. Woolworth, his cousin Seymour H. Knox, his associate W. H. Moore, and several close friends started stores of their own. Branches opened throughout the East. The stores remained independent until 1912, when they merged into the F. W. Woolworth Company which grew into the present $3-billion company. At this point too, as merchandise requirements increased, Woolworth began having goods manufactured especially for the stores, frequently taking the entire output of a factory. The Woolworth company today consists of 1600-plus variety stores in the United States. The English Woolworth company is also prosperous and revolutionized retailing in Great Britain. In addition the company owns the highly profitable Kinney Shoe chain, the Richmond clothing group and Woolworth stores in Canada and Germany.

Woolworth maintained an inflexible policy that store managers should spend most of their time on the sales floor studying customers and their needs. He once wrote in his company general letters circulated to his stores:

> Each manager must study the wants of his customers all the time, not try to please his own taste. . . . To illustrate: In years gone by, there used to be a demand for certain vases, the ugliest ever made, and I was obliged to buy them against my own taste and judgment. And how they did sell! The same thing applies today. Tastes differ and we must have goods for all.

With a rare flair for selecting managers, Woolworth encouraged them to be alert. One of his general letters carried the following:

> "Kick" on every occasion that warrants it. "Kick" intelligently so that your "kick" touches the right spot. If you don't like the goods we buy for you, "kick". . . . "Kick" so that we'll understand your feelings. Don't be satisfied with a simple "kick," but explain why you "kick." We may "kick" back, but you're used to that.[4]

In 1913 the Woolworth Building in New York City was completed; 792 feet high with 57 stories, it was then the tallest structure of its kind in the world. Woolworth resigned as president of the company in 1918 to become chairman of its board of directors, an office he held until his death a year later. The *New York Sun* wrote, "He won a fortune not in showing how little could be sold for much, but much much could be sold for little."

Woolworth was one of the first four merchants elected to the Merchandising Hall of Fame in 1953—the others were Marshall Field, John Wanamaker, and George Huntington Hartford (founder of A & P).

CONTEMPORARY ISSUES
Situation 19

Is too much emphasis placed on emotional appeals in marketing?

One evening Ray and John were watching television in the student lounge. In the middle of a deodorant commercial, John snorted, "I'm getting sick of watching commercials that play on the emotions!"

---

[4] *Skyline Queen and the Merchant Prince, The Woolworth Story*, by John P. Nichols (New York: Trident Press), 1973.

"What do you mean?" asked Ray.

"Well," replied John, "according to commercials, if you wear a certain brand of shirt, the women will love you; if you wear a certain perfume, the men will love you; and if you buy a certain make of car, everybody will love you. Most commercials give us nothing but emotional reasons for buying, not good, solid reasons why we need the product. I think they've gone too far."

"I can't agree with you," Ray said. "People *are* emotional creatures, so it makes sense to use emotional appeals. Besides, don't you believe in love?"

"Nonsense. You know what I mean, Ray. People aren't stupid. An unattractive girl knows that men aren't going to beg for dates just because she uses a certain soap. And sweeter breath has never worked the miracles those ads claim. I think most ads are plain phony—in fact, they're dishonest. I feel a product should stand on its own merits and not have to be merchandised on the basis of emotional appeals that aren't true."

"But, John, look at it this way," Ray countered. "People want to be emotional. If advertisers used only rational reasons in their ads, people wouldn't buy their product. And you know that economic stagnation is no substitute for sustained prosperity."

"Now, Ray," John countered, "don't try to infer that our economy would stop growing if people didn't buy all those products sold emotionally. We could invest our resources in things that did more to advance society—better houses instead of better deodorants, for example."

SITUATION EVALUATION

1. Who has the better viewpoint in your opinion? Explain your answer.

2. Is there any fallacy in Ray's thinking or in John's?

3. Over a period of time, which would tend to be most boring to most people—emotional or rational appeals? Give reasons for your answer.

BUSINESS CHRONICLE

The selling process in real estate

Over coffee, two salesmen for Kingmaker Estates were talking about the buying and selling of real estate. Both were old-timers who had been hired within the past year. They had moved to Florida from cities in northern states. One of them, Fred Potts, had sold an intangible—insurance. The other, Cecil Clark, had sold a tangible—automobiles. They both studied the real estate field sufficiently to pass the real estate agents' examinations and were now both licensed real estate salesmen. Let's tune in on their conversation.

Fred: Do you think it's easier to sell automobiles or houses, Cecil?

Cecil: Well, a house is a much bigger commitment, so I suppose it takes more work to sell one. Also it takes totally different psychology.

Fred: What's the difference?

Cecil: To start with you've always got to start the sales process from the point of view of the buyer. You've got to ask yourself what the buying situation is — what the needs are, who makes the ultimate decision, what they dream about. In selling a house, I find, you've got to learn how to appeal to each member of the family since each is intimately involved in the decision. I find if just one member of the family is really negative about a house, you have a hard time selling it even if other members like it. With a car, if you appeal successfully to the needs and vanity of the person who will do most of the driving, you've made a sale. How do you feel about it?

Fred: You're so right. You've got to start by sizing things up in terms of the buyer. A family that wants a house has certain problems they want to solve. It's up to me to find out what those problems are so I can help solve them. Another thing is that people dream a lot about homes. It's got a romantic side, so I make it a point to sell a dream home instead of a house. Because I used to sell insurance, I was too factual. I began by selling bricks and mortar and talked tax payments and up-keep costs. I soon realized that this information is important, but it doesn't sell. Then I started talking a lot less. People sell themselves on houses — something which seldom happens with insurance.

QUESTIONS

1. What are the major points these men made in their conversation? Are the points sound? Why?

2. Is buying a house more like buying a tangible or an intangible? Explain.

3. What is meant by a problem-solving approach to satisfying a buyer's needs? How does the approach work in the case of real estate?

APPLICATION EXERCISES

1. Clip four articles from your local newspaper that have a public-relations bearing on specific businesses. Write a paragraph about each clipping in which you explain whether the article is good or bad public relations for the company involved. Suggest how the company could encourage such publicity if it is good public relations, or how it could prevent such publicity if it is bad public relations.

2. The Hi Light Printing Company is a large manufacturer of calendars, stationery, and business forms. It employs a sales force of eight salesmen. J. D. Woodruff, president of the company, recently had a heated argument with his sales manager, Dan Sterling. The difficulty arose over the company's star salesman, who several months before had left the company to establish a business of his own in direct competition with the Hi Light Printing Company.

Woodruff was concerned chiefly about the fact that the star salesman had taken with him practically all his former accounts, with an estimated loss to Hi Light of more than 15 percent of its total volume. Woodruff accused his sales manager of allowing the salesman to become too powerful. He maintained that a good sales manager would have been alert to the fact that a salesman was building customer loyalty to himself instead of to the company and the company's products. Sterling's defense was that he had done all he could to avoid this and that a company must be prepared to have such things happen now and then.

Who seems to be right in this matter? What can a sales manager do to prevent this type of situation from happening?

3. Len Barry, a salesman of industrial supplies, had a great deal of difficulty selling a certain large and important account in his territory. The company to which he wished to sell had a fine reputation for ethical business practices. There was a strict policy in the purchasing department that absolutely no gifts or favors of any kind were to be accepted by anyone connected with purchasing. Barry dealt with an assistant purchasing agent, Jan Field – a family man with five children of school age. Barry on several occasions deliberately priced supplies at a figure he knew to be lower than that of the one competitor who always seemed to get the large orders. Quite by accident, Barry discovered that this competitor regularly paid for Field's membership to a very exclusive country club, which a man with Field's salary could not normally afford.

How should Barry handle his problem?

QUESTIONS

1. Through which advertising media would you advertise the following: a self-service laundry, canned soft drinks, typewriter ribbons, farm machinery, cigarettes, coffee? In each case, give reasons for your selection.

2. Does the use of an advertising agency eliminate the need for an advertising department? Why or why not?

3. What do you think might be the bases for friction between an advertising agency and a client company?

4. What are the social values of advertising? What are its social shortcomings?

5. It is said that advertising gives Americans an image of themselves. What does this statement mean?

6. What are the steps in the selling process? Which of these do you believe most difficult to perform? Give reasons for your answer.

7. How does the job of the retail salesman differ from that of the wholesale salesman? The manufacturer's salesman?

8. "Sales quotas have psychological value." Discuss this statement.

9. Why is it desirable that the sales manager have a voice in the design of products, even though he may have no training in design?

10. John Brown has an excellent record as a salesman. Does this qualify him for a job as sales manager? Explain your answer.

11. Define "public relations." How does it differ from advertising?

12. What can a business do to make each employee aware of the fact he is a public-relations representative? Once this awareness is created, how can employees be encouraged to act in the company's interest?

13. What are the different "publics" involved in the public-relations concept? Why is it desirable to study each public separately?

14. How are pricing and a firm's image related? What is the significance of pricing policy?

15. What factors must a manufacturer consider in pricing? A retailer?

16. Does marketing cost too much? Explain why or why not.

20

international business

CHAPTER 20

THE IMPORTANCE OF INTERNATIONAL TRADE

INTERNATIONAL TRADE AND SPECIALIZATION

INTERNATIONAL TRADE AND THE COMPANY
Advantages of Exporting. Advantages of Importing.

PROBLEMS OF INTERNATIONAL TRADE
Differences in Climate. Differences in Language. Differences in Social and Business Customs. Differences in Laws. Trade Barriers. Differences in Currencies and Availability of Dollars.

FACILITATING INTERNATIONAL TRADE
U.S. Department of Commerce Assistance. Foreign Trade Zones. Export-Import Bank. Domestic International Sales Corporations. Foreign Credit Insurance Association.

ORGANIZATION FOR EXPORTING
Indirect Export Channels. Direct Export Channels. Licensing.

ORGANIZATION FOR IMPORTING
Indirect Importing. Direct Importing.

GOVERNMENT CONTROL AND WORLD COMMERCE
The Balance of Payments. Tariffs and Other Controls.

WORLD ECONOMIC COMMUNITIES

MULTINATIONAL CORPORATIONS

World trade, the exchange of goods and services between nations, has long been of tremendous importance to many countries.[1] In fact, history's earliest "big business" crossed international boundaries and passed over the trade routes between nations. The very words "international trade" stimulate the imagination. It is easy to daydream about tramp steamers in colorful harbors like Calcutta, Hong Kong, and Manila; one smells exotic cargoes of spices, coffee, cocoa, and tropical fruits; one feels the hot tropical sun or arctic blasts; one hears foreign tongues and the screeching of sea gulls. Our American tradition is rich with lore of the world trader. The "Yankee trader" was known round the world, and it was Matthew Perry who opened the door for the trader in the Orient.

The era of the Yankee clipper ships is past, but the importance of trade between the United States and other countries continues to grow. The excellence and speed of modern transportation and communications have opened more and more business opportunities for the exporter and importer. A manufacturer of appliances in Ohio can telephone price quota-

[1] Historically, the phrase "foreign trade" was used to describe our trade with other nations. In the early 1960s, when the federal government adopted a policy of vigorous export encouragement, certain influential traders felt that "foreign trade" sounded negative and somewhat suspicious. Thus the tendency arose to give preference to the term "international" or "world trade."

Figure **20–1**
The United States in World Trade

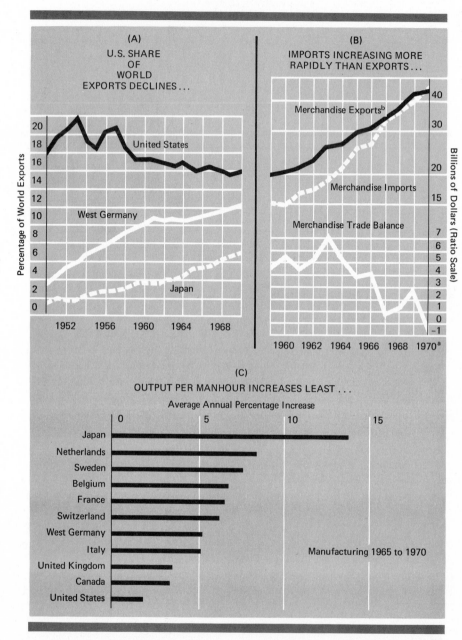

Is the United States losing its ability to compete in world markets?

[a] January-June seasonally adjusted on an annual rate basis.
[b] Exports, excluding military grants.

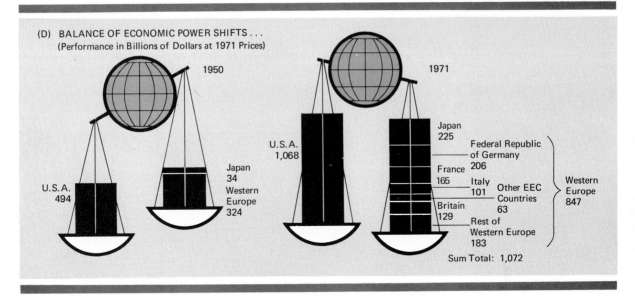

(D) BALANCE OF ECONOMIC POWER SHIFTS...
(Performance in Billions of Dollars at 1971 Prices)

1950

1971

U.S.A.
494

Japan
34
Western
Europe
324

U.S.A.
1,068

Japan
225
Federal Republic
of Germany
France 206
165   Italy
         101   Other EEC
                   Countries
Britain   63
129   Rest of
         Western Europe
         183

Western
Europe
847

Sum Total: 1,072

Source: A, B, The Federal Reserve Bank of Chicago; C, data supplied by the U.S. Department of Labor; D, *German American Trade News*, February 1972.

tions to a customer in Buenos Aires, six thousand miles away. A machinery manufacturer in Birmingham can close a deal with his representative in Stockholm within a few minutes. A department-store buyer in Washington, D.C., can easily visit the principal market cities of Europe several times a year. Opportunity awaits firms and individuals in business willing to learn and understand the intricacies of world trade.

THE IMPORTANCE OF INTERNATIONAL TRADE

World trade is just as important to the nation as domestic trade because it goes beyond the business itself and affects more than just the balance sheet of the individual business. When a business exports or imports it relates to a larger scheme of events. The vital nature of international trade is revealed in this chapter. World trade has economic consequences that relate directly to the value of the dollar, the balance of payments, and the country's international prestige, and the government strongly encourages business to participate in world trade. In this sense, it can be said that world trade is more important to the nation than domestic trade. Business done abroad contributes not only profit which is reflected in a company's financial statements, but also it contributes vitally to the nation's economic health.

A firm engages in international trade when it sells or exports goods or services to a foreign country or when it buys or imports goods or services from another nation. A firm engages in international business when it becomes multinational in its operations, when it operates off-shore plants and facilities, and enters into joint ventures with businessmen of other nations. Thus, export and import is not restricted solely to the movement of merchandise. We export and import capital, technical know-how, patents, trademarks, techniques, and any number of services. Since relatively few people or businesses participate directly in international trade, its importance to the national economy is generally underestimated. One gauge of this importance is that the U.S. exports are a $44.3 billion-a-year business, growing 11 percent each year. More than 3 million American workers owe their jobs to world trade. Every $15,000 of exports, according to the Department of Commerce, equals one job.

The United States is the largest seller of merchandise in the world market. America's share of world exports of manufactures accounted for 19.9 percent in 1971. Figure 20–1 shows the leading trading nations of the world and the extent of U.S. dominance. It is significant, too, that the world's leading traders are also the most prosperous nations.

International trade is especially important to certain segments of the economy. In 1970, for example, we depended on foreign markets to absorb 16 percent of our total agricultural production. For a number of years, American farms have produced great surpluses, which, if not absorbed in part by the foreign market, would create severe domestic economic problems.

Sizable proportions of some of our major products are exported — cotton farm products, 32 percent; leaf tobacco, 43 percent; rice, 62 percent; construction and mining equipment, 29 percent; copper smelting and refining products, 23 percent; and oil-field equipment, 30 percent.

Many U.S. firms are deeply committed on the international scene. In a recent year, the International Business Machines Corporation had total sales of $7.2 billion, with $2.5 billion coming from outside the United States. IBM operated in 108 countries with 99,000 foreign employees, one-third of the company's total payroll. The International Telephone and Telegraph Corporation had worldwide sales of over $5.4 billion, 200 companies and divisions in 67 countries, and a total of 300,000 employees. It derived 40 percent of its sales and a substantial share of its $300 million before-tax income from assets outside the United States.

Imports include commodities that either are not produced in this country or are produced here in insufficient quantity. Some of these, such as coffee, cocoa, and bananas, are so common that we take them for granted. Practically every manufacturer uses some essential raw material

Figure **20–2**
Where the United States Trades ($ Millions)

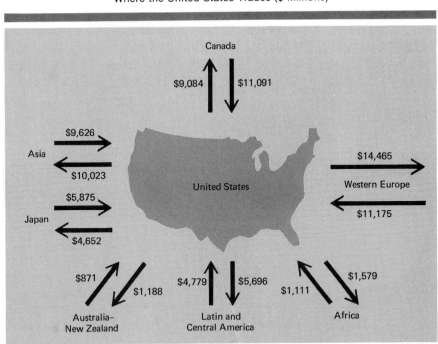

Source: *Statistical Abstract of the United States, 1972,* pp. 768–71.

procured in a foreign market. The steel industry depends on manganese, tin, nickel, zinc, and lead for use in the manufacture of steel alloys. The leather industry imports a large share of the hides needed to manufacture leather products. The rubber industry depends on foreign sources for natural rubber. The American Telephone and Telegraph Company reports that about forty-eight imported materials from at least eighteen countries go into the production of a telephone. Our newspapers buy nearly three-fourths of their newsprint from abroad.

INTERNATIONAL TRADE AND SPECIALIZATION

World trade enables the nations of the world to specialize in commodity production that utilizes each nation's particular economic advantages, such as low-cost labor, mechanized mass-production techniques, and

Figure **20–3**
The Importance of World Trade to the United States

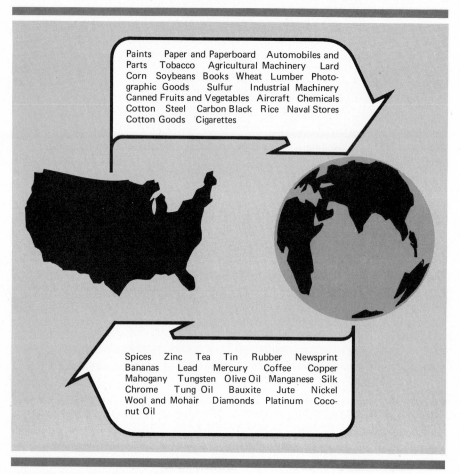

Paints   Paper and Paperboard   Automobiles and Parts   Tobacco   Agricultural Machinery   Lard   Corn   Soybeans   Books   Wheat   Lumber   Photographic Goods   Sulfur   Industrial Machinery   Canned Fruits and Vegetables   Aircraft   Chemicals   Cotton   Steel   Carbon Black   Rice   Naval Stores   Cotton Goods   Cigarettes

Spices   Zinc   Tea   Tin   Rubber   Newsprint   Bananas   Lead   Mercury   Coffee   Copper   Mahogany   Tungsten   Olive Oil   Manganese   Silk   Chrome   Tung Oil   Bauxite   Jute   Nickel   Wool and Mohair   Diamonds   Platinum   Coconut Oil

Source: Adapted from U.S. Department of Commerce data.

favorable climate or deposits of relatively scarce minerals. Essentially, nations export what they do best and import what others do better.

Under ideal conditions, specialization leads to a higher standard of living for all nations participating in world trade. To illustrate, if each nation specializes in the production of goods in which it has an economic advantage and refrains from producing goods in which it has an economic disadvantage, total world production is increased. Then, if each nation trades its surplus production for the surplus production of other nations, all nations will have more of the commodities they need or want.

Potentially, at least, world trade can raise the world standard of living in much the same manner as interstate trade has raised the standard of living in the United States.

INTERNATIONAL TRADE AND THE COMPANY

As a matter of national policy, as a later section of this chapter will show, businesses are called on to increase exports. Exports directly improve our balance of payments (see pages 563–564) and thereby strengthen the soundness of our dollar. They create not only jobs but good will; as former Secretary of Commerce Hodges pointed out, "by incorporating the best of America's technology in a form that people of other countries can see and touch, they [businesspersons doing business abroad] act as friendly ambassadors in a world where we need all the friends we can make."

Advantage of exporting

Exporting, of course, expands the market for a company's products. But behind sales increases are advantages that do not readily meet the eye. Often, profits are greater on foreign than on domestic sales. This is because foreign business represents extra business, and extra business is often more profitable as a result of the working of the rule of incremental profit — profits usually go up faster as volume increases. Suppose a manufacturer has an annual sales volume of $1 million: chances are the profit was greater on the last $100,000 worth of sales than on the first $100,000. Factors such as overhead costs, volume discounts on what the company bought to make its product, and around-the-clock use of plant facilities cause production costs of goods to go down as output increases. That is, profits increase at a faster rate as sales increments are added.

There are further advantages. An office-equipment manufacturer finds that overseas customers in underdeveloped countries actually prefer less complicated and older models because their employees can be retrained to use newer models only at great expense — by sending them to countries that have technical schools they themselves lack. Rebuilt models and trade-ins from the U.S. market also find a more ready market outside our borders. Attractive export sales of trade-ins eases marketing of new models in the United States.

Foreign orders, especially from countries in the southern hemisphere (where it is summer when it is winter here), often follow a sales curve different from the domestic. This can be desirable: Often the peaks and valleys of the domestic sales curve are counterbalanced by the foreign-business sales curve. The general effect of steadier overall output is beneficial for the company as a whole.

Advantages of importing

American companies import goods from foreign countries because they can (1) purchase goods not produced in this country or not produced in sufficient quantity, (2) purchase goods at lower prices than those available domestically, (3) purchase goods that have variety and more prestige or better craftsmanship than domestically produced goods, and (4) create good will among foreign buyers of American products, which in turn leads to a larger volume of export sales—the two-way street idea.

Worldwide trade is advantageous also to businesses not engaged directly in buying from or selling to foreign firms. Thousands of American wholesale and retail firms sell imported goods or goods manufactured from imported raw materials. Shipping, insurance, banking, brokerage, advertising, communications, publishing, and travel businesses all benefit, directly or indirectly, from world trade.

PROBLEMS OF INTERNATIONAL TRADE

International trade is far more complex for American businesses than domestic commerce. One of the favorite indoor sports of foreign traders is to "talk shop" about the difficulties and peculiarities of their field. "Eavesdropping" on such conversations is interesting for it affords a great deal of insight into why foreign trade has complications not found in domestic commerce.

An export agent for an American watch manufacturer, for example, may explain how the price of jewelry in some Asiatic countries is determined by barter rather than by a "one-price-to-everyone" policy. The retailer or wholesaler barters separately with each customer, using a sign-language system in which the customer and dealer hold hands under a black cloth, bid, and close the deal by finger manipulation. The reason for the silent method is that it is considered unethical for one customer to know what another customer pays for goods. In the eyes of the Chinese, disclosure of price might put one of the parties at a disadvantage in another deal for a similar piece of merchandise. An exporter of chinaware will point out that eggcups shipped to the West Indies have to be a smaller size, since eggs produced by hens in that part of the world are smaller than those produced by American hens. A machinery exporter to certain South American countries will explain that the reason for severe treatment from customs officials is often that it may be traditional for the customs officials to receive as pay one-seventh, say, of any penalties levied. A problem once encountered by a Detroit firm was receiving a request for a loan from one of its Far East representatives — the employee wished to purchase a wife.

Trademarks and brand names present special problems when the words occur in more than one language. A trade name that is complimentary in one language may be quite uncomplimentary, even embarrassing, in another.

Differences in climate

A nation's climate influences its commerce. The kinds and amounts of goods produced and consumed and the seasons of production and consumption are determined largely by climate. Because of the heat and moisture in tropical countries, many goods shipped to those regions must be specially packed to prevent spoilage, while many commodities sold to nations with cold climates must be insulated to prevent freezing.

Differences in language

Relatively few Americans are able to converse in more than one of the world's 2,800 languages. Though English is widely accepted as a universal language in commerce, the language barrier persists in many instances. U.S. firms dealing with non-English-speaking nations usually employ nationals of the country in which business is done. Americans as foreigners may not be allowed to work in the country and also, since people prefer dealing with those of their own nationality, the nationals are often more effective.

Differences in social and business customs

Each nation has customs and ways of looking at things that are unique. People of each nation, including our own, can easily be offended and business relationships jeopardized by misunderstandings of traditions or social procedures. For example, Kashmir allows no imports of beef because of the Hindu religion, and Afghanistan allows no pork imports because of the Islamic religion. In order to deal effectively with foreign nations, it is most important to know and understand the customs of each nation.

Differences in laws

Transactions in a foreign country are governed by the laws of that country. Laws pertaining to shipping, taxation, employment, selling, and other phases of business differ widely and can bewilder the American doing business in foreign nations unless he has competent assistance from those who have experience in the country.

Trade barriers

Practically all nations have different regulations pertaining to the kind and quantity of goods that can be imported and exported, tariffs, inspections, and other restrictions on international trade. American firms engaged in foreign trade must be familiar with the regulations of each country with which they do business. Getting goods into another country often involves considerable red tape and even risk of loss.

Differences in currencies and availability of dollars

Currencies differ widely throughout the world. The United States and its possessions use the dollar, but other nations have different currencies that vary in value in relation to the dollar. The currency unit in England is the pound; in Germany, the mark; in France, the franc; in the Philippines, the peso; and so on. A retailer in Paris who buys a shipment of American fountain pens sells them in his store for French francs. The American fountain-pen manufacturer wishes to be paid in American dollars, because he cannot use French francs to defray his business expenses. Converting most foreign currencies into dollars presents a very real problem especially since the dollar has become so unstable. Foreign governments, to protect their limited dollar reserves, usually place restrictions on the amount of currency their businesses can convert into dollars, an action that reduces the amount other countries can buy from us.

To conserve dollars, foreign nations may set import quotas. For example, a South American country may limit the number of American automobiles that may be imported to fifty a year, since unrestricted purchases of autos might soon deplete the dollars it has and perhaps make it impossible for it to buy such necessities as penicillin. (A quota restriction limits the internal supply of sought-after products in countries that have quotas, and the short supply drives up prices in local currency.) The currency restrictions and value of the local currency related to the dollar are different in each country and may even vary from day to day. It is thus necessary for businesspeople to have expert banking advice and assistance in all foreign dealings.

FACILITATING INTERNATIONAL TRADE

Because of a deteriorating balance-of-payments situation, official U.S. policy in recent years has been directed to (1) expanding exports, (2) encouraging American firms to capitalize their foreign operations with off-shore funds, and (3) promoting foreign business investments in the United States.

Foreign investments in the United States are minuscule compared to U.S. investments abroad. However, some of America's most familiar consumer products are marketed by subsidiaries of foreign companies. Pepsodent is made by Lever Brothers, and Good Humor by Thomas J. Lipton, Inc., subsidiaries of Unilever of the Netherlands and the United Kingdom. Shell Oil is also Dutch. Capitol Records is British, and Nestlé is Swiss. American companies in just two years (1967 and 1968) poured over $7 billion each year into European plant-and-equipment investments alone — exclusive of other investments — while by contrast *total* investment of European firms in the United States is under $12 billion (see Figure 20–4).

U.S. Department of Commerce assistance

Because selling in Korea is not the same as selling in Kansas, and doing business in Tokyo varies from doing business in Topeka, the government, through the U.S. Department of Commerce's Bureau of International Commerce (BIC) assists U.S. businesspeople who venture abroad. Business and economic information that is gathered by 468 commercial and economic officers at 152 American embassies and consulates is made available. Such information includes: lists of buyers, distributors, and agents for various products in each country; individual reports on foreign firms; export opportunities; living costs and conditions and advice for living abroad; sources of foreign credit information and financing; directories of foreign advertising agencies and marketing research organizations; and guides to foreign business directories. English translations of relevant business documents and information are on file, and American commercial personnel stand ready to assist and advise through correspondence and by visits to the foreign trade centers where they are stationed. BIC also publishes monthly *Overseas Business Reports* to provide information about foreign markets.

The domestic operations of the Department of Commerce include field offices located in the major cities of the United States. Their international departments assist businesses with day-to-day exporting operations and put them in touch with foreign businesses and facilitating agencies.

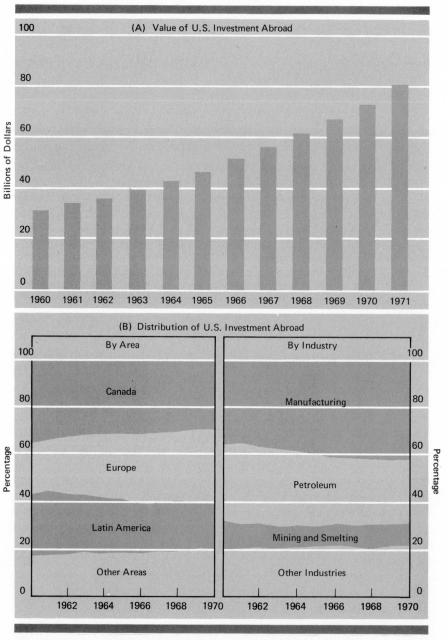

Figure **20-4**
Value and Direction of U.S. Investment Abroad

Source: "Foreign Direct Investment in the Last Decade," Road Maps of Industry, No. 1693, The Conference Board, July 1, 1972.

Should foreign companies be encouraged to make capital investments
in the United States?

Foreign trade zones

U.S. foreign trade zones are operating in New York, San Francisco, Honolulu, Seattle, New Orleans, Toledo, and Mayagüez, Puerto Rico. A *foreign trade zone* is an enclosed area (considered outside U.S. customs territory, but under customs supervision), in or near a port of entry, that is operated as a public utility by a qualified public or private corporation authorized by the Foreign Trade Zone Board.

In these controlled areas foreign and domestic goods may be manufactured, stored, processed, packaged, and displayed without being subject to U.S. customs duties. From these zones, goods may be subsequently imported into the United States or shipped abroad. The zones offer the businessman special advantages, since they allow him to store untaxed inventories of foreign goods, sort out spoiled goods before they go through customs, and display goods and distribute samples without complicated importing paperwork.

Zones provide an alternative for establishing plants abroad, since manufacturers may produce goods in a zone, without paying either U. S. duty on foreign parts shipped to the United States or foreign country duty on U.S. parts shipped abroad. The 33rd Annual Report of Foreign Trade Zone Boards to Congress cited the following examples of activities conducted in their zones.

Caviar: Repack into domestic containers for domestic consumption

Pharmaceuticals: Repack, remark, manufacture into new products

Watch movements: Inventory, examine, assemble using U.S.-made watch cases, repack for export, make cases and movements

Beef: Cut, pack, and forward

There are also over 100 free trade zones and related facilities abroad that can be utilized by U.S. exporters. The Department of Commerce issues a directory of them, which pinpoints locations and explains their proximity to markets and their financial benefits and operating advantages.

Export-Import Bank

The purpose of the government sponsored Export-Import Bank of the United States, referred to as *Eximbank*, is to foster the exports of U.S. products and services. It provides direct loans and financial guarantee programs for foreign purchases of U.S. goods and services.

The reasons for doing this are:

1. To supplement private sources of financing where private sources are unwilling to assume political and commercial risks

2. To extend credit on terms longer than those private lenders care to provide

3. To enable U.S. suppliers to provide terms on major projects competitive with those offered by government-sponsored export financing institutions in other exporting countries.

Eximbank also conducts orientation programs for U.S. business personnel engaged in export trade.

Domestic International Sales Corporations

The Revenue Act of 1971 provides that special export corporations— Domestic International Sales Corporations (DISCs)—be granted special tax treatment. A DISC is a special type of corporation that can be organized under the laws of any state and be owned by any individual, partnership, or corporation. It is somewhat like making a separate corporation out of the international division of a company. Through a domestic corporation qualifying as a DISC, exporters can receive tax treatment for their export income more comparable to that offered by many foreign countries to their exporters. Federal income taxes are deferred on one-half the DISC's export earnings. Deferral continues as long as the earnings of the DISC are used in activities related to exporting. A domestic producer can form a DISC and sell goods it produces to its DISC at cost. In other words, the DISC acts as a trading company and sells abroad the goods it buys from its parent company. Earnings of the DISC are then taxed separately from the parent corporation's, according to the special provisions already described. Small businesses are encouraged to use a DISC, which they can establish with a minimum of difficulty and with a capital of as little as $2,500. The government also encourages groups of producers to set up a DISC.

Foreign Credit Insurance Association

The Foreign Credit Insurance Association is an unincorporated association of over 60 private insurance companies in partnership with the Export-Import Bank. Eximbank underwrites all political risks and 50 percent of commercial risks, with member companies of the FCIA underwriting the remainder.

Review of the types of risks underwritten provides an insight into the complications of exporting.

1. Insolvency of the buyer—failure to pay the insured within six months of the due date of the obligation

2. Transfer risk—inability to convert the buyer's local currency, which was deposited in payment of the obligation, into U.S. dollars

3. Cancellation or nonrenewal of export license prior to shipment

4. War, civil war, rebellion, or civil commotion

5. Expropriation, confiscation, or intervention in the business of the buyer or guarantor by a government authority

6. Additional transport or insurance charges incurred after shipment by diversion of the carrier due to political causes

7. Cancellation of the import license prior to arrival of merchandise

ORGANIZATION FOR EXPORTING

In general, American manufacturers who wish to sell to foreign markets choose one of two methods. One is to sell to foreign markets indirectly through domestic export channels, and the other is to sell directly through the company's own export department.

Indirect export channels

The major indirect export channels are export merchants, buyers for export, and export agents.

Export merchants Export merchants are wholesalers who specialize in buying merchandise from various domestic manufacturers and reselling it in foreign markets. Such businesses handle all details and bear all risks involved in world trade transactions. This channel has two major advantages. The first is simplicity. The American manufacturer need not employ specialized personnel or be concerned with the exacting details of international trade. In fact, selling to export merchants usually is no more complicated than selling to domestic middlemen.

The second advantage is economy. Since the manufacturer incurs no risk, needs no specialized personnel, and need not cultivate foreign demand, his selling costs are low. Because of these advantages, export merchants are used extensively by small American manufacturers who otherwise would not sell to foreign markets.

A principal disadvantage is that no personal contact is made with foreign customers and thus business expansion possibilities are limited. In some instances, the manufacturer does not even know what countries eventually receive his product. The result is that the manufacturer is not always aware of the particular needs of foreign consumers and so has little opportunity to adapt to the market, create demand, or build good will.

Buyers for export   A substantial volume of merchandise is sold to foreign buyers who canvass American markets in search of goods needed by foreign consumers. Foreign buyers generally represent foreign clients, from whom they receive a commission for their purchases. Americans selling to such buyers normally assume responsibility for shipping. The chief advantage of this channel is that it involves no demand-creation expenses. It has two disadvantages: (1) the buyer for export does not provide a stable outlet, for his purchases are generally irregular; and (2) the method is more complicated than marketing through export merchants because the manufacturer marketing goods in this manner must assume shipping responsibilities.

Export agents   Export agents function in world trade much as manufacturer's agents do in domestic trade. They usually represent several noncompeting American manufacturers. Sales are made by the export agent in the name of the manufacturer, who finances and ships the order. Export agents have proved effective when aggressive selling effort is needed to create a demand for American products. There is a feedback of information about the foreign markets, for the export agent usually has overseas customers he has dealt with over a period of years.

Direct export channels

Manufacturers who wish to open their own channels to foreign markets may sell directly to foreign consumers. In such a case the manufacturer establishes his own export department that either sells directly to foreign middlemen or supervises the company's own representatives overseas.

Very large manufacturers usually prefer to be represented more directly by establishing their own sales outlets or even assembly and manufacturing operations in foreign countries. These outlets include foreign branches, foreign subsidiaries, or foreign factories and assembly plants.

Foreign branches   These are actual divisions of the domestic company and function very much like foreign wholesalers, except that they are owned by Americans. Such branches usually employ local personnel insofar as possible. Foreign branches are quite important when a company manufactures technical products that require servicing and parts.

Foreign subsidiaries   Foreign subsidiaries are separate companies owned by parent American corporations but organized under the laws of the foreign country. Frequently, the commodity being sold is shipped in bulk to the foreign subsidiary and then packaged or assembled. This method is often used to obtain favorable tax considerations or to comply manufactures technical products that require servicing and parts.

Foreign factories and assembly plants The closest contact with foreign markets is established when the American manufacturer actually produces in foreign countries. Many foreign countries have laws that make it attractive for companies to build manufacturing facilities. A General Motors plant in Germany will be able to sell its output in all other Common Market countries with no tariff, whereas cars shipped from the United States would have to pay both transportation and tariff. The method has several advantages. First, it avoids most foreign tariff and import restrictions. Second, local labor can be used. Third, transportation of parts to the foreign country is much less costly than transportation of the finished product. Fourth, manufacturing in the country itself helps bring about good will. Automobiles and office machines are examples of products that are very often manufactured in foreign countries by American manufacturers. Products built in foreign countries are then designed specifically for that market.

Large American manufacturers are moving increasingly in the direction of becoming major international producers. So powerful is this trend that in a recent year $4 out of every $5 that the hundred largest U.S. corporations put into new capital equipment investments went into foreign operations. An IBM international spokesman said, "The trend is such a reality that American big business is no longer national, but rather world in character."

Licensing

Agreements are sometimes made between manufacturers in this country and manufacturers abroad on a licensing basis. These agreements encourage the investment of local capital by companies in a given country and bring about a closer relationship between our business and the licensee abroad. For example, in addition to establishing their own assembly plants in several countries, General Motors has licensing agreements for assembling and manufacturing in more than twenty other countries throughout the world.

ORGANIZATION FOR IMPORTING

Importing is in some ways more complex than buying on the home front. Importing channels, like those of exporting, can be either indirect or direct. Indirect importing is purchase from domestic middlemen who specialize in buying goods from foreign firms. Direct importing is buying directly from foreign business organizations.

Indirect importing

Most American businesses prefer buying indirectly through middlemen, who may be import merchants, import commission houses, or import brokers.

Import merchants   The import merchant buys from foreign firms on his own account and assumes all risks. He may specialize in one or a few products, or he may import a wide variety of merchandise. An import merchant maintains a sales force to call on American business firms.

Import commission houses   This type of middleman receives goods on consignment from foreign business firms and sells to American buyers. The import commission house does not take title to goods, but in other respects functions very much like the import merchant.

Import brokers   The import broker brings foreign seller and American buyer together. He does not take title to merchandise and seldom handles it.

The indirect method of importing is popular with American firms for three reasons. First, it makes importing as convenient as buying goods from domestic sources. Also, specialized personnel are not needed, since no direct contact is made with the foreign seller, and the indirect middlemen are usually Americans, a situation that makes for fewer misunderstandings.

Indirect importing has some disadvantages, however. American purchasers can choose only from the import middleman's stock, which usually is not as extensive as that of the foreign producers; moreover, the merchandise may not be exclusive because the middleman will sell to competing firms. Another disadvantage is that no contact is made with the foreign supplier, and it is therefore difficult to exchange information with him. Finally, there is less profit. Some feel that the commission charged by the import middleman can be saved by buying directly.

Direct importing

Most domestic organizations that import directly have an import department and either send buyers to foreign countries or maintain resident buying offices abroad. Resident buying offices may buy for one firm or for a group of noncompeting American firms who share the costs of maintaining the overseas offices.

The effective foreign buyer must have an understanding of the goods being purchased, be able to compare the foreign offerings with domestic goods in price and quality, be familiar with the technicalities involved in foreign trade, and understand methods of doing business abroad.

Importing directly has several advantages. First, it can be more economical since there is no commission paid. Second, it enables the American firm to make purchases that better suit its needs and to find exclusive merchandise more readily. Third, it promotes reciprocal business. A foreign buyer is in an excellent position to make friendly contacts with foreign firms that are prospective customers of the American firm.

The principal disadvantage of direct importing is that it is complicated. In addition, the American importer must handle details and bear all risks. Because of these disadvantages the direct method of importing is used less frequently than the indirect.

GOVERNMENT CONTROL AND WORLD COMMERCE

All countries exert extensive control over international commerce, which is the greatest difference between foreign commerce and domestic. The reason for this regulation lies in the balance of payments.

The balance of payments

All but the smallest countries of the world have balance-of-payments accounts with every other country, just as a business has accounts with those it does business with. The balance of payments is a record of a country's external financial transactions. It includes balances for exports and imports of goods, tourist spending, shipping and transportation services, foreign business investments, and, in the case of the United States, the support of troops overseas and the foreign assistance program.

There is an important difference between balance of payments and balance of trade. The balance of payments includes the balance of trade. The latter has to do solely with the inflow and outflow of goods. The balance of payments includes *all* external financial dealings. If exports of goods exceed imports of goods, we say that there is a favorable balance of trade. If there is an overall financial deficit for a country, there is an unfavorable balance of payments. A country may have a favorable balance of trade and still maintain an unfavorable balance of payments, or vice versa. One year, for example, the United States' favorable balance of trade ($22 billion of exports as compared with $17 billion of imports) helped offset the balance-of-payments deficit caused by the outflow of military and tourist expenditures abroad and by U.S. foreign investments.

When balance-of-payments deficits persist, settlements between countries are made in gold. Thus, chronic deficits are a drain on a country's gold supply, which in the long run can undermine the strength of its currency. Because the United States has had persistent balance-of-payments deficits in recent years, the subject is of paramount concern to the nation.

Between 1950 and 1970, the U.S. gold stock slipped from $25.5 billion to $10.4 billion. Allowed to continue, this development could impair gold convertibility of the dollar.[2] For this reason, the U.S. government has taken steps to reduce the outflow of dollars: Corporations have been asked to restrain their foreign investments, commercial banks to reduce their lending abroad, and Americans to reduce their travel in foreign countries. In addition, the government is actively encouraging foreign tourism in the United States.

Tariffs and other controls

A variety of controls affecting businesses are used by governments to limit imports or increase exports. These include tariffs, import licenses that limit the volume or value of imports permitted, actual quotas on amounts to be imported, licenses for obtaining foreign currencies (called exchange licenses) with which to buy goods abroad, and subsidized exports to increase foreign sales. Tariffs, however, are the major form of control.

A *tariff* is a tax or customs duty levied on imported goods. All authority to establish tariffs is vested in the federal government. Three types of tariff are imposed on imports. Some are *ad valorem* (according to value), as on pickled cucumbers (17½ percent of value); some are specific, as on chestnuts ($.0625 a pound); and others are a combination of the two, as on canned mushrooms ($.04 a pound plus 12½ percent of value).

There are elaborate procedures for the inspection, classification, and valuation of goods. Sometimes it takes months for a final determination of the amount owing on a shipment.

As a result of the Cold War, the United States also exerts export controls. The Department of Commerce, under the Export Administration Act of 1969 (National Security Export Control) administers the issuing of the licenses an exporter must have in order to export to countries that may be a potential military threat. Licenses are used to deprive certain countries of strategic commodities that could increase their military potentialities. Many eastern European countries, the People's Republic of China, and the U.S.S.R. fall under these controls. With the easing of world tensions, perhaps these provisions will be relaxed.

WORLD ECONOMIC COMMUNITIES

The Marshall Plan for the economic recovery of Europe after World War II demonstrated the advantages of economic cooperation among countries. Since the Marshall Plan, the most successful examples of economic cooperation have been the European Common Market, which went into effect

---

[2] The U.S. Government is formally committed to convert into gold only the dollars held by foreign official institutions.

			ESTIMATED POPULATION '000	
COUNTRIES	AREA '000 SQ. KM.	INHABITANTS PER SQ. KM. 1966	1970	1980
Netherlands	33.5	371.7	13 070	15 260
Belgium	30.5	312.3	9 710	9 970
Luxembourg	2.6	128.8	335	345
West Germany	248.5	239.9	60 220	62 390
France	551.2	89.6	50 950	56 305
Italy	301.2	172.4	54 320	58 440
Denmark	43.0	11.4	4 919	5 299
Norway	323.9	11.5	3 864	4 270
Sweden	449.8	17.3	7 999	8 646
Finland	337.0	13.6	4 778	5 035
Iceland	103.0	1.9		
United Kingdom	244.0	224.9	56 410	60 480
Republic of Ireland	70.3	40.9	—	—
Switzerland	41.3	143.9	5 436	6 098
Austria	83.8	87.0	7 365	7 671
Portugal	91.5	100.1	9 590	10 480
Spain	504.7	63.1	32 386	34 491
Greece	130.9	65.7	8 730	9 056
Turkey	780.6	41.2	36 740	
Yugoslavia	255.8	77.2		
ECC	1 167.5	156.1	188 605	202 710
U.S.	9 363.4	21.0	207 480	243 370
Russia	22 402.2	10.5	250 000	280 000

Table **20-1** European Population Projections and Comparisons

Source: European Community Information Service.

in 1965, and the Organization of American States (OAS), which was formed in 1948.

The Common Market and EEC are popular designations for an alliance that is officially titled the European Economic Community. In 1958 representatives of six nations, in one of the most significant events of the century, signed the Treaty of Rome. Thus Belgium, France, Italy, Luxembourg, the Netherlands, and West Germany formed a customs union "to ensure the economic and social progress of their countries by common action in eliminating the barriers which divide Europe." The aim was to form a common market in which not only goods but also men and capital could move freely among nations. A major step in the enlargement of the Common Market was taken January 22, 1972, when representatives from Great Britain, Denmark, Ireland, Norway and the six Common Market countries signed the Treaty of Adhesion to the European Communities.[3] The dream is that this economic union of states will gradually lead to a politically unified Europe, where nations historically torn apart by

[3] At the time of this writing (September 1973), there can be said to be only nine full members, for Norway has not decided yet whether to accept full membership.

internecine wars will dedicate themselves through cooperation to the creation of mutual prosperity.

Now that the Common Market members have eliminated all tariffs among themselves and have established one single tariff for their entire area, it will be more difficult for businesses of outside countries to compete. This is one reason that large American concerns are establishing major manufacturing operations within the Common Market countries, thereby availing themselves of large markets without tariff restrictions.

The removal of internal barriers to trade in agricultural products and the creation of common policies of support and protection for native agriculture will reduce the ability of non-EEC agricultural exporters to compete within the Common Market. Because of this, Washington wants to negotiate tariff reductions with the EEC.

An insight into the efforts of the EEC (and hopefully of common market arrangements of other countries too) is the program established in 1965 for youth exchanges between Common Market countries. Under the program, almost 5,000 young workers annually are able to participate in an international exchange of residences and jobs. The young worker in a Renault plant in France, for example, might switch jobs with a Volkswagen employee in West Germany. Commenting on the purposes of the exchange, the vice-president of the EEC Executive Commission said:

> Everyone knows what great educational benefits young people can derive from a stay in a foreign country. Slowly but surely we are creating conditions under which the young people of the Community, who will be tomorrow's citizens of a United Europe, can be imbued with the European spirit, and we must do all we can to promote the contact. Contact has been far more frequent than some decades ago, but it is still insufficient for our purpose.

It is encouraging to note that since the inception of the European-worker exchange program, various plans for worker-exchanges, including some with the United States, are operating successfully.

MULTINATIONAL CORPORATIONS

U.S. corporations abroad have become formidable powers. How they have exerted themselves has been described vividly by the Frenchman Jean-Jacques Servan-Schreiber,** who noted that Americans have been exporting a technological and managerial revolution. Huge European and Japanese corporations also have been outgrowing their national boundaries. A recent estimate stated that about 300 corporations can be considered multinational. About 200 of these are based in the United States, 100 in other countries.

How important are the multinational corporations? The Conference Board in a recent study reaches these startling conclusions:

Of a gross world product of $3 trillion, approximately one-third is produced in the United States, one-third in the industrial nations of Europe, Canada, Japan, and Australia, and the remaining one-third in Russia, Eastern Europe, China and the developing nations elsewhere.

About 15 percent, or $450 billion, is accounted for by multinational enterprises, $200 billion of this by U.S.-based companies, $100 billion by foreign-based companies which also operate in the United States, and $150 billion by interproduction in other countries.

The proportion contributed by multinational corporations is growing at a rate of 10 percent per year. At this rate the multinational companies will generate one-half or more of the gross world product in less than 30 years.

The basic reason for this phenomenal growth is that the free world has become, in a real sense, one market.

American multinationals overseas employ surprisingly few Americans: Dow Chemical, with 18,000 employees abroad, uses only 200 Americans; General Motors Overseas Operations employs 180,000, with only 300 Americans. The estimated total number of overseas managers for all U.S. corporations runs from 18,000 to 40,000. Overseas experience for executives is definitely considered to be desirable training for those destined to rise in the corporate structure. Most managers going abroad are given specific time periods for their assignments, with promises that if they succeed overseas, there will be chances for advancement when they return home. One interesting result of the use of so many foreign nationals to manage overseas operations is that increasing numbers of them are rising into top management positions of U.S. parent companies. Of the five top executives at Bendix, three are foreign born. A spokesman for Dow Chemical said he believed that more and more foreigners would be competing for and winning top jobs in corporate management in the United States.

SPECIAL READINGS

**The American Challenge by J. J. Servan-Schreiber. New York: Atheneum, 1968 (paperback). This best-selling book has made a noticeable impact on political and economic thinking. It clearly and precisely reveals how American industry and technology have engulfed Europe and the free world. In identifying the power and skill of the American corporation (despite the author's being a European), the book is not anti-U.S. business. His message is primarily that non-Americans should wake up to what is happening under their noses and do something about it. Servan-Schreiber opens his book with an ancient quotation:

> If you give a man a fish,
> he will have a single meal.
> If you teach him how to fish,
> he will eat all his life.
> Tuan-tsu.

The quotation is most appropriate, for the author shows how the American-oriented multinational corporation is organizing the world's resources so the world can feed itself. Indeed, this is a most revealing book!

The burgeoning of multinational business is not universally applauded. While there are many who see the multinational as a positive force ("an economic intrastructure is evolving that can provide the base for a true world political community"), there are others who condemn it as an exporter of jobs and as an exploiter of host countries. There are numerous proposals for bringing multinationals under some form of international control. And there is little question that the implications of this huge topic, which is barely emerging into the public consciousness, will be increasingly debated.

PEOPLE AND THEIR IDEAS
Keiji Kawakami

A small business manager with a social conscience

Americans of Japanese extraction often distinguish themselves in business. Keiji Kawakami is one of them. He is not only successful in making a profit, but his concern for the social ramifications of business has been so noteworthy that he has come to the attention of Washington.

Early in the 1900s, Mr. Kawakami's father came to Hawaii, worked as a laborer in the sugar cane fields and later on the docks as a longshoreman. His son, Keiji Kawakami is now President of Iolani Sportswear and Young Hawaii, clothing manufacturers whose 1972 sales were $3 million. He is also a Director of the Bank of Hawaii and Hawaii Bankcorporation.

Armed with a B.A. degree from the University of Hawaii and an M.S. degree in Marketing from New York University, he started his business in 1953, at the age of 44, with a capital of $5,000. He rented space in an old building for $150 a month and hired four employees. When his firm incorporated in 1955, his work force had increased to fifteen. Today his company is one of Hawaii's foremost clothing manufacturers.

His wife Edith is personnel manager for the corporation, whose personnel policies are exemplary. The company is dedicated to the principle of building on the combined talents of multiracial workers, and employees typically include as many as 16 ethnic groups. One of the personnel goals is "to establish mechanical discipline in production and still respect the fact that each employee is an individual." Unlike most clothing manufacturers, Iolani does not pay its people piecework rates; it pays hourly wages. It has also added what it calls "a vestibule program," which involves women repatriated from mental institutions. Mrs. Kawakami assumes responsibility for training and guiding four such employees now on the payroll.

In the 1960s a profit-sharing program was established, an unusual step for a small company. In 1971 there was over $700,000 in the fund. Employees, of whom there are about 225, become eligible for the profit-sharing plan after three years of service. Many employees have equities of from $10,000 to $14,000. Mr. Kawakami says, "We encourage our people to spend what they earn for the things they need, education for their children, and home facilities and not to try to save for retirement. The profit-sharing plan takes care of that."

Kawakami credits his father with teaching him to value the "enriching experience in which people of various nationalities can feel comfortable in their differences."

CONTEMPORARY ISSUES
Situation 20

Should trade with communist bloc nations receive greater encouragement?

John and Ray were debating the pros and cons of trading more with communist nations.

Ray thinks it is a good idea. "The communist countries can produce some products at lower costs than we can. Meanwhile, we can produce some products at lower costs than they. It just makes good sense to sell those countries products that we produce relatively more efficiently and buy products that they produce relatively more efficiently."

"That makes sense," said John, "but much more is involved. Chances are if we trade more with communist nations, we will have to trade less with nations that have been our political friends for many, many years. I think that would be wrong. Besides," John continued, "when you trade with communist countries, all trade goes through state trading monopolies. Exporting and importing are handled through government agencies. The communist government benefits but the people don't."

"I think your arguments are weak," answered Ray. "Remember, trade permits each country to diversify consumption because the goods it produces in excess of its requirements are exchanged for goods from other countries. This leads to lower costs and greater variety. Then, too," continued Ray, "I think more trade with China and Russia in particular would do a great deal to promote peace throughout the world."

"But," John observed, "you seem to overlook the fact that neither of the two nations you mention are nearly as industrialized as we are. In a pragmatic world it makes sense to trade with the most technologically advanced nations."

"But wouldn't more trade with communist nations help them to gain technology? And wouldn't this help achieve the peace objective I mentioned?" asked Ray.

SITUATION EVALUATION

1. What additional arguments, pro and con, can you advance?

2. Do you agree that trade with communist bloc nations should be increased? Explain.

BUSINESS CHRONICLE

Considering an overseas operation

Allan King had been invited to a conference for southern business leaders held in New Orleans. The purpose of the conference was to encourage American businesses to do more business overseas and to encourage foreign investors to invest in the United States. The U.S. government was conducting such conferences in an attempt to correct the imbalance in the nation's balance of payments.

A representative of the Commercial Division of the Department of Commerce who had a lot of experience in the Far East, especially in Japan, cornered Mr. King at the conference and had a long talk with him. He urged Mr. King to get his company to open an office in Tokyo. He said that the Japanese were more prosperous than ever before, that land prices in Tokyo were among the highest in the world so that by contrast Florida real estate prices would seem cheap to them. Also the Japanese had been witnessing a ten to fifteen percent rise in real estate prices each year for the past ten years and were quite conscious of the profit possibilities in real estate. Furthermore, the U.S. balance-of-payments deficit in favor of Japan was so great that the U.S. government wanted to encourage its businesses to become more active in Japan.

The representative told Mr. King that he should seriously consider an operation in Japan both for patriotic and business reasons. He pointed out that the Japanese government was also concerned about the great balance-of-payments imbalance and therefore was easing restrictions on foreigners doing business in Japan. This would be a good time to get a foothold in Japan—historically a country that rarely encouraged foreign investors.

QUESTIONS

1. Evaluate the proposition. What should Mr. King do?

2. How would Kingmaker Estates go about establishing a Japanese operation?

3. How would operating in Japan differ from operating in Florida? What special problems would be encountered and how could they be overcome? What assistance could Kingmaker get in this venture?

APPLICATION EXERCISES

1. Assume that last summer you had the good fortune to travel in Europe. While in the Austrian Alps you ran across a small village with a toy factory that manufactured dolls in native costumes. The dolls impressed you greatly because of their attractiveness and reasonable price. You realize that there may be business possibilities in importing these to the United States. Before you actually go into negotiations of any kind, you decide to draw up a program of what would be involved in such a venture. Prepare a report on such a program.

2. According to the Statistical Office of the United Nations, per capita gross product for selected countries in 1970 is as follows:

HIGH-OUTPUT COUNTRIES	PER CAPITA OUTPUT	LOW-OUTPUT COUNTRIES	PER CAPITA OUTPUT
United States	$4,734	Ethiopia	$ 65
Canada	3,676	Burma	78
Sweden	4,055	Haiti	91
Denmark	3,141	India	94
Switzerland	3,135	Indonesia	115

    a. Summarize the main reasons for the wide differences in productivity between the high-output and low-output countries.

    b. Explain what the high-output nations have in common. What do the low-output nations have in common?

QUESTIONS

1. Explain how world trade promotes a higher international standard of living.

2. An American manufacturer of typewriters wishes to sell in the Brazilian market. What are some of the difficulties he can expect to encounter?

3. Why is the maintenance of the value of the American dollar important to the United States? To other countries? How does the value of the dollar relate to trade?

4. Why do foreigners invest in the United States? Why do we invest abroad? Is this good?

5. Would tariff reduction be harmful to the American economy in the short run? In the long run? Explain why or why not.

6. Explain balance of payments and balance of trade.

7. Explain the various programs of the government for promoting exports. Why is international trade fostered so much more than domestic trade?

8. What is the EEC? What advantages of this union can you see for American businessmen? What disadvantages?

9. What should the attitude of American students be toward the emerging common markets? Discuss your answer.

10. What is a multinational corporation? Is their development good or bad for the United States? The world?

7

management control and use of

Guesswork—playing it by ear, hunches, and intuition—is a remnant of prescientific times and is now recognized as unsatisfactory for making business decisions. As never before, business management strives to remove the uncertainty surrounding problem-solving by scientific collection, analysis, and interpretation of factual information.

In the following chapters we explore four means of introducing certainty into business—accounting, computers, statistical analysis, and research. These are used extensively in modern business to help find answers to the many variations of two basic questions: How can we cut costs? How can we increase revenue?

information

21
accounting and business management

22
computers and electronic data processing

23
quantitative analysis and the presentation of business information

24
business research and sources of information

21

accounting
and business management

CHAPTER 21

FUNCTIONS OF ACCOUNTING
To Aid Management. To Aid in Borrowing Capital. To Aid Owners. To Meet Government Requirements.

ACCOUNTING AS A PROFESSIONAL FIELD
Specialization by Industry. Public Accountants. Tax Accountants. Government Accountants.

ACCOUNTING PROCEDURES
Recording Transactions. Classifying Transactions. Summarizing Transactions. Interpretation.

COST ACCOUNTING AND STANDARD COSTS

BUDGETING
Purposes of the Budget. Responsibility for Budget Preparation. Parts of the Budget. The Budget Time Period. Flexibility of the Budget.

ACCOUNTING STATEMENTS
The Balance Sheet. The Income Statement.

RATIO ANALYSIS

AUDITING
The Issue of the Auditor's Independence.

ACCOUNTING—MORE THAN FIGURES

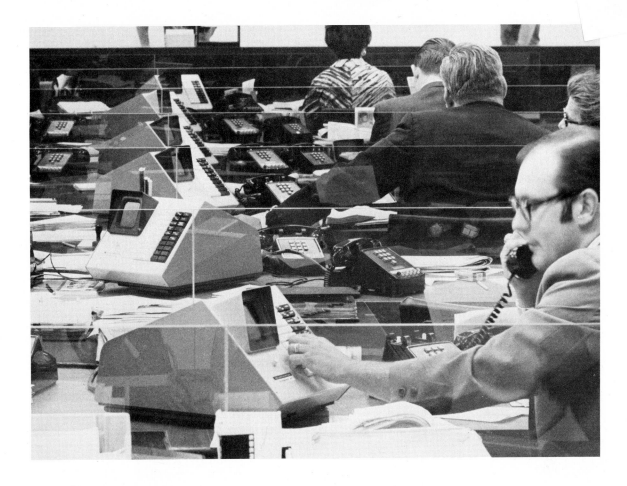

Accounting may be defined as the recording, classifying, summarizing, and interpreting of the financial transactions of a business. Its purpose is to provide an up-to-the-minute picture of the company's financial position and the cost information with which management can make decisions and control the business.

Accounting transactions are highly varied in nature and size. Most transactions are concerned with the shifting or transfer of funds or with the acquisition or giving up of claims to funds. Typical of those transactions that involve expenditures are:

1. Wages, salaries, and commissions paid to employees

2. Payments for goods and services

3. Payments for equipment, land, and buildings; and for interest on borrowed capital

4. Outlays for taxes

Examples of common receipt transactions are:

1. Proceeds from the sale of goods
2. Income from rented property and proceeds from land and buildings sold
3. Income from investments in other businesses and interest from loans
4. Tax refunds

Many other transactions and adjustments in business are also recorded, such as *depreciation* (the stated loss in value of a fixed asset as it gradually wears out), the return of goods to suppliers by the business, loss or damage of merchandise and other property, and the evaluation of inventories. *Inventory* is all of a business' goods that are in storage, in process, or ready for sale.

It is the responsibility of the accountant to provide meaningful information about the business for those who manage it as well as for shareholders, government agencies, investors, and creditors. The accountant provides data to answer questions such as: "What is the value of the owners' share of the business?" "How much profit or loss resulted from last year's operations?" "How much does it cost to make a given product?" "What is the indebtedness of the company?" "What taxes must the business pay?"

The terms "accounting" and "bookkeeping" are frequently used interchangeably and synonymously. Accounting is the much broader term. Bookkeeping is the routine and more or less clerical phase of accounting. Bookkeepers are concerned mainly with the systematic recording of financial transactions, providing the data the accountant uses.

Accountants, on the other hand, generally devise systems and forms for recording transactions, determine how these transactions should be classified, establish the procedures for making summaries of transactions, and consolidate and interpret the company statements.

Accountants often participate in making company policy, whereas bookkeepers, because of their limited training and the routine nature of their work, do not. The distinction between accounting and bookkeeping is important; to regard them as one and the same is to overlook the strategic role accounting plays in business management.

FUNCTIONS OF ACCOUNTING

To aid management

The most important functions of accounting are to supply and interpret figures essential to sound business decisions and to show the financial status and operating results of a business. Accounting can reveal, for example, whether (1) the costs of doing business are excessive, (2) money is being invested properly, (3) company property is correctly valued, (4) the various operations of the business are contributing their fair share to company profits, (5) additional funds should be borrowed, or (6) earnings of the business are satisfactory.

Accounting serves management further by providing a continuous record of all financial transactions. Every dollar received, spent, invested, or otherwise handled is accounted for. Since records are kept over a period of years, management can compare current performance with past, and current financial status with that of previous years. In short, accounting gives management objective measures of progress and efficiency.

Table 21–4 on pages 591–593 shows accounting figures that have been gathered from many companies and then summarized by industries. The comparisons such figures make possible are of considerable value to management.

Accounting aids management also by establishing checks and balances on all financial activities of the business. Opportunities for the embezzlement and theft of company assets are greatly reduced through careful accounting procedures.

Two specialized accounting techniques that serve management particularly well are cost accounting and budgeting. These are discussed in detail on pages 582–585.

To aid in borrowing capital

When a business wishes to borrow funds, the bank or other lender inquires into its financial status. The balance sheet and the income statement (discussed later) are the best evidences the creditor can obtain as to whether the business is a good financial risk. A business that keeps inadequate or confusing records has less chance of having its credit requests approved than does the firm with carefully kept records.

To aid owners

Most large corporations are owned by stockholders who take no active part in the management of the business. These investors are concerned mainly with the profitability of their company. Financial records of a company's activities prepared by accountants are consulted by people interested in the company's stocks.

To meet government requirements

Government has more interest in the individual business than most people realize. There are laws, regulations, and taxes that make severe demands on a business' record-keeping and financial reporting. Laws that regulate employee wages and hours, the Federal Old-Age and Survivors Insurance Program, federal and state income and withholding taxes, sales taxes, and a host of other special taxes make it mandatory that accurate and complete records be kept. Such records also help in tax planning, which assures that sufficient funds are set aside to pay taxes when they fall due.

ACCOUNTING AS A PROFESSIONAL FIELD**

Of all the specialized positions in business, few are more professional in nature than accounting. Achieving a high degree of proficiency in accounting requires years of study and experience. Since accountants in essence verify the honesty and correctness of the company's basic records, all states provide an opportunity for persons engaged in accounting to earn the coveted designation of certified public accountant, commonly abbreviated CPA. While the exact requirements vary among the states, the CPA designation means that the individual has completed a prescribed educational program in accounting, has had several years' experience in accounting work, and has passed a comprehensive examination in accounting and in subjects related to it. In addition to these rigid requirements, the individual interested in becoming a CPA must possess a good character. (See Table 21–1 for Michigan CPA requirements.)

The CPA is qualified to perform difficult and complex accounting work. Many certified public accountants are engaged in public accounting (see page 580); others are employed by private organizations.

Specialization by industry

It is desirable that the chief accountant in a business have an intimate knowledge of the problems peculiar to that type of business. For ex-

SPECIAL READINGS

** An Accounting Primer by Elwin M. Midgett. New York and Toronto: New American Library, 1968 (paperback). This is a layman's book that teaches how to apply the practices and principles of accounting to business and personal finance. It includes a dictionary of definitions, which explores in detail the various subdivisions in the field of accounting.

Written in nontechnical language, it simplifies accounting in order to provide "The ABC's of accounting for the non-accountant." It is a practical approach to accounting, focusing on "how to do it" and "what will help you in business right now." Examples are: When, where, and how do you take best advantage of discounts? How are payroll taxes computed—where are there savings for the employers? Can a business buy on credit and still be worth what the balance sheet indicates?

Whereas the book is a popularization of a complicated subject, it is academically sound for it is written by the chairman of the Department of Business Education at Middle Tennessee State University.

Table **21–1**
Requirements for the CPA Certificate in Michigan, 1973

SIGNIFICANCE OF THE CERTIFICATE

The CPA Certificate is granted to those who have met the requirements for practicing Public Accounting as enacted by the State of Michigan for the benefit and protection of its citizens. In summary, these requirements deal with general qualifications, education, examinations and experience.

GENERAL QUALIFICATIONS

Applicant must be:

1. A citizen of the United States, or a person having declared an intention of becoming a citizen.

2. A resident of Michigan, or a person having an office or employed in Michigan.

3. Of good moral character.

EDUCATION

Prior to the examination, the applicant must satisfy one of the following requirements:

1. Completion of a curriculum required for a baccalaureate degree from an educational institution recognized by the Board with a minimum of 21 semester hours or 33 quarter hours in accounting subjects, including the subject of auditing.

2. (Prior to January 1, 1975), a high school graduate may substitute, for a qualifying baccalaureate degree, four years full-time, continuous practical experience with a CPA firm, immediately preceding the date of application. The Board may accept evidence of sufficient technical education in accountancy in lieu of one year of CPA firm experience in meeting the educational requirements, but this substitute does not reduce the length of qualifying experience needed for the CPA certificate.

3. (Subsequent to January 1, 1975), every applicant shall have completed a curriculum required for a baccalaureate degree from an educational institution recognized by the Board with a minimum of 21 semester hours or 33 quarter hours in accounting subjects including the subject of auditing.

The Board prescribes standards for recognition of educational institutions. The North Central Association of Colleges and Secondary Schools and the five other affiliated regional accreditation associations are recognized, among others.

THE CERTIFICATE OF EXAMINATION

The applicant must pass written examinations on the following subjects:

Theory of Accounts	Commercial Law
Practical Accounting	Auditing
Economics and Finance	

A Certificate of Examination will be issued upon the passing of all five subjects. An applicant will be given credit for each subject with a passing grade of 75%. An applicant shall be expected to receive a passing grade in all subjects within the period covered by six successive examinations. Failure shall be prima facie evidence that the applicant is not qualified and that his credit should be cancelled.

Examinations are given in May and November. Applications must be filed with the Michigan State Board of Accountancy at least 60 days in advance of each examination accompanied by a fee of $50.00.

EXPERIENCE FOR THE CPA CERTIFICATE

Qualifying practical experience shall have been obtained within a period of six years immediately prior to the filing of an application with the Board for the Certificate as a Certified Public Accountant, and shall have included work of a type normally directed toward the expression of an independent opinion on financial statements. The experience shall have been obtained in a responsible audit position, either under the direction and supervision of a practicing Certified Public Accountant of this or any other state, or, under certain conditions, in a governmental agency.

Applicants with a qualifying baccalaureate degree shall have a minimum of two years of qualifying experience.

Applicants who qualified for examination without a qualifying baccalaureate degree shall have a minimum of four years of qualifying experience.

The Board is the judge of the quality of the experience.

GRANTING THE CPA CERTIFICATE

The Michigan State Board of Accountancy shall grant a Certificate of Certified Public Accountant to a person who:

1. Meets the general qualifications established by the Board,

2. Passes the examination and receives the Certificate of Examination,

3. Satisfies the experience requirements, and

4. Files an application for the CPA Certificate, acceptable to the Board, and pays an additional fee of $25.00.

Source: The Michigan State Board of Accountancy.

Note: Requirements vary from state to state. The requirements for Michigan are reasonably typical of those for most states.

ample, accounting touches on many legal problems. Unless the accountant is familiar with regulations that pertain to the specific industry,
he will be unable to render the best possible service. Consequently, if a
steel company planned to employ a chief accountant, it would give preference to the individual who had obtained accounting experience in
steel or a related industry. Likewise, a department store would prefer to
employ an accountant with substantial experience in retail accounting.

Public accountants

Businesses of all sizes commonly retain the services of public accountants
to help with the more difficult phases of accounting, especially with the
preparation of tax statements and company audits (see pages 595–596).
Public accountants are independent organizations or individuals that
specialize in selling their services to businesses. Their principal services
are to

1. Review the accounting needs of the business and advise as to
   proper records and methods of record-keeping

2. Audit and testify to the fairness of the financial records

3. Install accounting systems or modernize those in use and train personnel to use them effectively

4. Prepare periodic financial statements and assist management in
   their interpretation

5. Aid in the preparation and use of budgets and inventory controls

6. Assist in establishing sound credit procedures

7. Prepare tax returns and plan tax programs

8. Give general advice as to the soundness of the proposed business
   policies

Public accounting firms are increasingly broadening their services in
management consulting, installation of computer systems, personnel
testing, market research, and other areas. Expansion seems to extend into
all areas where the systematic gathering of facts and scientific methods
can be used in business decision-making.

Tax accountants

Because of the numerous exacting and complex tax regulations with
which businesses must comply, many accountants become expert in tax

accounting and are able, because of their intimate understanding of tax law, to save a business money as well as legal difficulties.

Government accountants

Many accountants specialize in government accounting. The federal, state, and local governments collect large sums in the form of taxes and spend large sums to carry on the work of the government. These transactions must be recorded, classified, summarized, and interpreted in much the same manner as business transactions. The Internal Revenue Service, for instance, employs accountants in the handling of the millions of income tax returns.

ACCOUNTING PROCEDURES

Large companies have a centralized accounting department, headed by a controller or chief accountant, that is responsible for keeping all financial records. In the small business, the owner or manager uses the services of an outside accounting firm to keep his books or perhaps does the work himself with the assistance of a clerical employee.

Recording transactions

The first step in the accounting procedure is to record each transaction. The original recording of financial transactions is made in the books of original entry, or journals. A business may have, for example, a cash receipts journal, a cash disbursements journal, a sales journal, a purchases journal, and a general journal. In large businesses, thousands of transactions must be recorded. Various mechanical devices, therefore, are used to make possible rapid recording of transactions. For example, in mechanized banking, when a customer makes a deposit at a branch bank, the teller who uses a machine to record the new balance in the customer's bankbook is recording the deposit simultaneously on the customer's account ledger at the branch bank and at the bank's central office. Thus, at the close of each day, a bank with thirty-seven branches will have a summary of deposits and withdrawals for each branch bank, as well as for the bank as a whole.

Even in the small business, memory alone cannot be relied on as a record of all transactions that take place. Unless accurate records are kept, numerous unanswerable questions regarding income and expenditures will arise. In many respects, the journal in which the record of transactions is kept is like the airline pilot's flight diary.

Classifying transactions

It is not sufficient that financial transactions merely be recorded in journals. The transactions must be taken from the books of original entry and placed in books of final entry, called ledgers. The process is called posting. All transactions involving money owed the business by customers are kept in one set of ledgers, and transactions showing money the business owes to creditors are kept in another set.

Summarizing transactions

Once financial transactions have been recorded and classified by accounts, the third step can take place: summarizing the information. This involves the preparation of financial statements, the two most common of which are the balance sheet and the income statement. (See pages 585–588 and 588–590.)

Interpretation

The last step in the accounting procedure is drawing conclusions from the summary statements. Skill and knowledge of accounting are needed to perform this step satisfactorily. The trained accountant can study financial statements and determine whether funds are being used properly, whether the company's debt is excessive, and whether sufficient cash is on hand to operate the business successfully. Interpretation is the most significant of all accounting procedures.

COST ACCOUNTING AND STANDARD COSTS

The ever-increasing emphasis placed on business efficiency has led to the development and wide use of cost accounting, or cost analysis. Cost accounting is an extension of general accounting that is used to determine in detail the costs incurred in performing a specific business activity.

Through cost accounting it is possible to determine the costs of handling the average order, producing a single unit of a product, selling a single unit, or even writing a business letter. The general cost-accounting procedure is to prorate all fixed and variable expenses of the business to the single activity being studied.[1] Thus, if a shoe manufacturer wants to determine how much it costs to produce a pair of shoes of a given type, the costs incurred for labor, materials, supplies, wear and tear on machinery, tools, rent, interest on borrowed money, and other expenses are allocated to the type of shoe produced. The total amount for a type, divided by the number of shoes of that type produced, gives the cost of a single pair of shoes.

Cost accounting is also used in computing a selling price for goods, for only after a manufacturer knows his production costs can he know whether his selling price is high enough to cover costs and provide a profit.

To make cost accounting particularly valuable, accountants compute standard costs for activities being studied. Standard costs indicate what the cost of an activity *should be*; cost accounting reveals what it *actually* costs to perform the operation. If actual costs exceed the standard costs, an investigation is in order. Such an investigation may reveal that the workers are inefficient, that materials are wasted, and so on. In standard costing, management has a yardstick for controlling expenses.

BUDGETING

A *budget* is a financial forecast or plan that shows expected income and expenditures for a business over a given period of time. Expressed in other terms, the budget is the quantification of plans. Ideally, it is prepared one year in advance and shows a detailed breakdown of both anticipated income and anticipated expenditures. If income equals expenditures, the budget is said to be balanced. If receipts are more than expenditures, there is a surplus; if receipts are less than expenditures, there is a deficit.

Purposes of the budget

A carefully constructed budget aids business management in several ways. First, it serves as a guide in planning business operations. When it is known how much revenue is expected in a given period of time, it is possible to plan the expenditures necessary for producing the income.

---

[1] Fixed expenses are those that do not vary with business volume, such as interest on a long-term loan. Variable costs are those that do vary with volume, such as raw materials used and labor.

Second, a budget sets business goals and establishes limits for the purchase of raw materials, advertising, labor, and other business costs. When a sales manager understands that his department has a fixed amount for traveling and entertainment expenses during a period of time, he plans those expenditures carefully and tries to stay within the limits. Without such limitations, planning is difficult, and operations are hampered by uncertainty. Thus the budget serves to control specific business operations. When payroll expense exceeds the amount appropriated, corrective action can be taken. Without the budget, management would never know whether the departments within the business were overspending or underspending. Proper budgeting helps business avoid exhausting funds prematurely.

Third, the very act of preparing a budget causes company executives to review their operations critically and to eliminate waste and inefficiency. When they present their case for a new budget, executives are asked to justify their requests, a procedure that is often a soul-searching experience.

Responsibility for budget preparation

Since the overall business budget affects every department within a business, key people from each department usually participate in its preparation. In many organizations, a formal budget committee is established. Ultimately, the budget is the full responsibility of the chief executive, who must approve it.

As the financial nerve center of the business, the accounting department plays an important part in development of the budget by supplying management with financial facts and cost studies as needed.

Parts of the budget

The overall business budget is actually a group of budgets, one for each department or functional activity within the business. The sales budget shows the total expected sales volume, which may be broken down by commodities sold, territories covered, or other similar factors. This budget is generally considered the most important of the "sub-budgets," for all other plans are related to the revenue received from sales. A selling expense budget shows the amount that will be needed to pay salesmen, deliver merchandise, and perform other marketing functions.

Closely allied to this budget is the advertising budget, which specifies the amount to be spent for advertising. The production budget shows the number of units expected to be produced; on the basis of this budget, a materials budget for necessary supplies, raw materials, and parts is prepared. Similarly, labor and manufacturing expense budgets are prepared. When the overall budget is completed, each department in the business is given a definite performance goal, sometimes called a quota. Then a money appropriation to cover the expected costs for accomplishing the task is allocated.

The budget time period

Budgets are usually established on an annual basis but may then be further broken down by quarter and by month. The shorter budgetary time periods permit management to exercise closer control over business activities.

The budget period depends on the nature of the business. Manufacturers often plan budgets for time periods of several years, since many activities, such as new plant construction, are long range. In many retail businesses, budgets cover relatively short time periods of several weeks or months.

Flexibility of the budget

A budget is a plan or guide, not a hard and fast rule. Business is dynamic, and frequently conditions change before the budget period expires. A rise in the price of raw materials, for example, will necessitate a budgetary adjustment. New competition may make it desirable to spend additional funds for advertising. Wisdom dictates that the budget be reconsidered as conditions change.

ACCOUNTING STATEMENTS

Accounting facts are presented in the form of accounting statements. The most important of these are the balance sheet and the income statement, which provide the overall financial picture of the business.

The balance sheet

Since the balance sheet shows the financial status of a business at a specific time, it changes with each day's business activity. It is therefore prepared as of a specific date, usually the last day of the year. It indicates the assets, liabilities, and equity of the owners of the business — what the business owns and what it owes. A sample balance sheet appears in Table 21–2.

Table **21–2**
Sample Balance Sheet

DEXTER WHOLESALE COMPANY
Balance Sheet
December 31, 19—

ASSETS

Currents assets

Cash		$ 15,000	
Accounts receivable	$21,000		
Less allowance for doubtful accounts	800	20,200	
Notes receivable		3,000	
Merchandise inventory		76,200	
Prepaid insurance		1,700	
Prepaid rent		3,200	
Total current assets			$119,300

Fixed assets

Equipment	$18,600		
Less accumulated depreciation	3,400	$ 15,200	
Buildings	$88,000		
Less accumulated depreciation	21,000	67,000	
Land		12,000	
Total fixed assets			94,200

Investments (permanent)

Stock in American Supply Company		13,000
Total assets		$226,500

LIABILITIES AND STOCKHOLDERS' EQUITY

Liabilities

Current liabilities

Accounts payable	$ 27,000	
Notes payable	3,100	
Accrued wages payable	2,600	
Accrued taxes payable	1,700	
Accrued interest payable	820	
Other expenses now payable	1,100	
Total current liabilities		$ 36,320

Long-term liabilities

Mortgage payable	40,000
Total liabilities	$ 76,320

Stockholders' equity

Common stock (1,000 shares at $100 par value each)	$100,000	
Retained income	50,180	150,180
Total liabilities and stockholders' equity		$226,500

Assets   Assets are the various items of value — property or resources — the business has: cash, merchandise, land, equipment, patent rights, and so on. On the balance sheet, assets are ordinarily classified into current, fixed, and investment assets.

Current assets.   Current assets include cash and other items that will normally be converted into cash in a relatively short period of time — usually less than one year. Specific examples of current assets are money on hand, money in checking accounts, checks not yet deposited, and postal money orders. Inventories and merchandise on hand, but not sold, are current assets, since they will probably be turned into cash in a few months' time. Money owed to the company by customers and others (called *accounts receivable*), less allowances for doubtful accounts, is also a current asset.

Fixed assets.   Fixed assets are items that are usually not for sale by the business but used for long periods of time — usually more than one year. Examples are land, buildings, equipment, and machinery. While fixed assets are permanent in nature, they ordinarily decrease in value (depreciate) each year. A machine that was valued at $1,000 when new may depreciate at a rate of 10 percent, or $100, each year. When three years old, the machine would be shown on the balance sheet as a fixed asset worth $700.

Investment assets.   Sometimes a company invests some of its funds in the securities of other corporations. Such investments may be to secure extra income or to control the management of the second company. Investment assets are usually indicated separately on the balance sheet.

Intangible assets.   Assets that do not have tangible form but are of value to the business are called intangible assets. An important intangible asset is good will. Good will refers to the valuation the company puts on its public acceptance, which is determined by length of time the business has been in operation, established brand names, and similar factors.

If a business is sold, the purchaser may be expected to pay for these intangible factors, which causes the business to earn profits. It is impossible, of course, to determine the precise value of a company's good will, and wide variations occur in companies' evaluations of such assets. Some companies omit good will entirely from accounting statements, others give it a token value of a dollar, while still others value it in thousands or even millions of dollars. Under accepted accounting practices, good will is never shown unless it has been purchased. Other examples of intangible assets include patents, franchises, copyrights, and trademarks.

Liabilities   Liabilities are the money a company owes to bankers, employees, suppliers of goods and raw materials, holders of bonds, and others who have advanced money or sold goods or services on credit to the business. Liabilities are usually classified as either current or long term.

Current liabilities.   Current liabilities are short-term debts that must be paid in less than one year. Short-term bank loans, wages earned by employees but not yet paid, interest on long-term debts, and taxes are examples of current liabilities. Money owed to suppliers of goods and services, usually *accounts payable* on the balance sheet, is another very common current liability.

Long-term liabilities.   Long-term liabilities, such as mortgages, bonds, and long-term notes, are debts that extend over a period of more than one year.

Equity and the meaning of "balance"   The equity section of the balance sheet shows the owners' equity (right to share) in the assets of the business. Undistributed company earnings are shown in the proprietorship (share-of-ownership) section.

Basic to an understanding of accounting is an understanding of the equation

$$\text{assets} - \text{liabilities} = \text{owners' equity}$$

or, stated differently,

$$\text{assets} = \text{liabilities} + \text{owners' equity}$$

In conventional accounting, assets are listed on the left-hand side of the balance sheet, and liabilities and equity on the right. The totals of each column are always equal. Any change in an asset is always reflected in a corresponding change in either a liability account or in the equity section —hence the term *balance*.

The income statement

The income statement, also called the revenue-and-expense statement or the profit-and-loss statement, is a second essential summary of financial activity. It is a detailed summary of business operations over a specific period of time. Such statements are often prepared monthly and quarterly, in contrast to the yearly preparation of the balance sheet.

Preparation of the income statement precedes the construction of the balance sheet, since equity cannot be known until the operating results are summarized. The income statement is very important to the business, since it tells, for example, what specific expenses were incurred in operating the business and what the reason was for a profit or loss.

A sample income statement is shown in Table 21–3. While the accounting principles involved in the preparation of such a statement are basically the same in all types of industry, the terminology used varies widely. Ordinarily, however, an income statement has four component

Table **21-3**
Sample Income Statement

BROWN WHOLESALE HARDWARE COMPANY
Income Statement
December 31, 19—

Income from sales			
Gross sales		$384,600	
Less returns and allowances		3,800	
Net sales			$380,800
Cost of goods sold			
Merchandise inventory, January 1, 19—		$138,000	
Purchases	$192,820		
Less purchase returns and allowances	2,600		
Net purchases		190,220	
Cost of merchandise available for sale		$328,220	
Merchandise inventory, December 31, 19—		96,200	
Cost of goods sold			232,020
Gross profit on sales			$148,780
Operating expenses			
Selling expenses			
Salaries and commissions	$ 52,610		
Advertising	4,500		
Delivery expense	9,200		
Total selling expenses		$ 66,310	
Administrative expenses			
Salaries and wages	$ 21,000		
Bad debts	1,100		
Depreciation on building	2,800		
Depreciation on equipment	790		
Supplies used	1,900		
Utilities	2,100		
Total administrative expenses		29,690	
Total operating expenses			96,000
Net profit from operations			$ 52,780
Financial income			
Income on stock owned			1,900
Gross income			$ 54,680
Financial expense			
Interest			4,500
Net profit or loss			$ 50,180

parts, or sections: (1) operating income, (2) cost of goods purchased and sold, or cost of goods manufactured and sold, (3) operating expenses, and (4) profit or loss for the period.

Operating income The income section shows the amount received by the company for goods sold minus returns and allowances and discounts given to purchasers. The result is called net sales.

Cost of goods sold   The cost of goods sold is computed by adding the cost of inventory at the beginning of the period and the net cost of goods manufactured or purchased during the period, then subtracting from this the total cost of inventory at the end of the period. The cost of goods sold is then subtracted from the net sales figure. The result is the gross profit on sales.

If the company is a manufacturer, a detailed breakdown of cost of goods manufactured will be included in the cost-of-goods-sold section. Such a breakdown shows raw materials consumed, labor used, and manufacturing expenses.

Operating expenses   The third section of the income statement includes all expenses incurred in the operation of a business. Operating expenses usually are classified as selling expenses and administrative, or general, expenses. Selling expenses include advertising, salesmen's salaries and commissions, delivery and transportation expenses, and depreciation of selling equipment. Administrative expense consists of rent, taxes, depreciation, heat, light, power, office supplies, and administrative salaries.

The advantage of a detailed breakdown of operating expenses is that a comparison can be made between specific expense items from time to time. The purpose is to measure the efficiency of the various business functions. Results of one business can thus be compared with operating results of similar businesses.

Net profit or loss   When computed, all operating expenses are subtracted from the gross profit on sales. The result is called net profit or loss from operations.

Finally, all income from sources other than sales is added to the net profit or loss from operations, and from this total are subtracted any miscellaneous expenses not included in the operating-expense classification. The result is then the net profit or loss for the stated period of time.

This process may be expressed in the following simplified formula:

net profit or loss = net sales − cost of goods sold − all other expenses

RATIO ANALYSIS

The accounting analyst usually makes a detailed study of the financial status of a business through the use of ratios. Numerous ratios have been developed for the purpose of illuminating various features of the company's financial position. When computed, the ratios of one company can be compared with those that have been established as standards for companies of similar size in the same line of business. (See Table 21-4.)

Table 21-4
Cost of Doing Business Ratios—Corporations

The following operating ratios provide a guide to the average amount spent by corporations for these items. They represent a percentage of business receipts as reported by a representative sample of the total of all federal income tax returns* filed for 1967–68.

INDUSTRY	TOTAL NUMBER OF RETURNS FILED	COST OF GOODS SOLD %	GROSS MARGIN %	COMPEN-SATION OF OFFICERS %	RENT PAID ON BUSINESS PROPERTY %	REPAIRS %	BAD DEBTS %	INTEREST PAID %	TAXES PAID %	AMORTIZATION DEPRECIATION DEPLETION %	ADVERTISING %	PENSION & OTHER EMPLOYEE BENEFIT PLANS %
ALL INDUSTRIAL GROUPS	1,534,360	70.71	29.29	1.91	1.31	.86	.34	2.75	2.88	3.62	1.17	1.07
CONTRACT CONSTRUCTION	123,180	83.24	16.76	3.41	.54	.51	.21	.67	1.81	1.83	.19	.61
General building contractors	44,341	88.86	11.14	2.49	.40	.22	.16	.84	1.21	1.00	.18	.33
Highway, street & heavy construction	12,435	82.21	17.79	2.26	.53	1.15	.21	.72	1.91	3.74	.10	.54
Special trade contractors	40,189	76.16	23.84	5.44	.85	.64	.22	.56	2.62	1.95	.28	.92
Plumbing, Heating & Air Conditioning	15,117	79.93	20.07	4.97	.58	.19	.28	.31	2.01	.91	.25	.98
Electrical work	9,101	78.05	21.95	4.95	.55	.18	.35	.34	2.43	1.06	.19	1.19
WHOLESALERS & RETAILERS	465,841	78.07	21.93	1.85	1.42	.28	.22	.58	1.31	.90	1.03	.31
RETAILERS	315,581	72.92	27.08	1.91	2.11	.35	.25	.64	1.50	1.11	1.50	.33
Food stores	22,249	78.88	21.12	.63	1.57	.33	.04	.19	1.04	.99	1.23	.43
General merchandise	20,814	64.03	35.97	.73	2.55	.38	.43	1.21	1.98	1.42	2.55	.47
Apparel & accessories	32,701	64.24	35.76	3.01	5.05	.29	.23	.44	1.65	.86	2.00	.28
Furniture, home furnishings & equipment	27,687	66.44	33.56	4.33	2.73	.32	.59	.73	1.67	.89	2.74	.31
Automotive dealers & gasoline service stations	50,644	84.25	15.75	1.63	.92	.19	.18	.62	.97	.57	.86	.14
Eating & drinking places	57,492	46.62	53.38	4.33	5.09	1.12	.11	.76	3.42	3.01	1.30	.34
Building materials dealers	16,776	75.45	24.55	3.36	.88	.37	.47	.66	1.57	1.13	.73	.34
Hardware stores	7,360	70.38	29.62	4.81	2.16	.24	.34	.64	2.02	1.01	1.28	.27
Farm equipment dealers	5,919	84.07	15.93	2.68	.56	.25	.37	.60	1.02	.77	.50	.18
Drug & proprietary stores	18,783	69.90	30.10	3.38	2.89	.33	.08	.35	1.56	.97	1.20	.36
Liquor stores	7,662	79.57	20.43	4.20	1.82	.25	.06	.34	1.75	.84	.39	.15
Jewelry stores	6,727	55.51	44.49	5.11	4.07	.43	1.25	.66	2.00	.77	3.37	.45
WHOLESALERS	142,531	84.20	15.80	1.75	.59	.20	.19	.51	1.08	.65	.49	.29
Groceries & related products	16,052	89.44	10.56	.94	.47	.18	.10	.25	.56	.45	.27	.21

INDUSTRY	TOTAL NUMBER OF RETURNS FILED	COST OF GOODS SOLD %	GROSS MARGIN %	SELECTED OPERATING EXPENSES								
				COMPENSATION OF OFFICERS %	RENT PAID ON BUSINESS PROPERTY %	REPAIRS %	BAD DEBTS %	INTEREST PAID %	TAXES PAID %	AMORTIZATION DEPRECIATION DEPLETION %	ADVERTISING %	PENSION & OTHER EMPLOYEE BENEFIT PLANS %
WHOLESALERS, Continued												
Electrical goods, hardware, plumbing & heating equipment & supplies	15,752	79.58	20.42	2.39	.66	.19	.29	.47	.96	.57	.80	.41
Petroleum bulk stations	6,105	85.17	14.83	1.45	1.01	.46	.23	.64	2.11	1.44	.29	.18
Alcoholic beverages	3,876	82.94	17.06	1.01	.38	.13	.08	.21	4.22	.35	.93	.28
Dry goods & apparel	6,111	80.59	19.41	2.22	.75	.06	.18	.83	1.06	.39	.58	.29
Drugs, chemicals & paints	5,847	82.07	17.93	1.40	.54	.15	.15	.49	.69	.84	.71	.33
Lumber & construction materials	7,284	83.84	16.16	2.21	.61	.24	.29	.59	.98	.83	.28	.32
Machinery, equipment & supplies	20,888	77.47	22.53	3.09	.72	.21	.31	.81	1.05	1.02	.58	.42
Motor vehicles & automotive equipment	11,336	76.65	23.35	2.31	.98	.17	.29	.53	.97	.60	.86	.32
Farm products — raw materials	5,628	93.25	6.75	.58	.24	.26	.06	.75	.40	.70	.15	.08
MANUFACTURING	197,023	70.05	29.95	1.16	.85	1.37	.17	.97	3.06	3.79	1.44	1.45
Beverage industries	3,105	59.18	40.82	.81	.55	.89	.10	.89	12.24	1.67	5.06	.81
Food and kindred products	17,592	76.17	23.83	.69	.54	.80	.12	.64	3.21	1.92	2.52	.70
Tobacco manufacturers	107	57.67	42.33	.26	.18	.47	.02	.90	17.25	1.08	6.04	1.01
Textile mill products	6,571	79.23	20.77	1.33	.68	.86	.13	1.11	1.93	2.78	.58	.72
Apparel & other fabricated textile products	17,682	76.96	23.04	2.33	1.07	.23	.15	.79	2.05	.83	.82	.69
Lumber & wood products, except furniture	9,672	76.59	23.41	1.98	.72	.83	.22	1.27	2.65	6.17	.41	.58
Furniture & fixtures	6,636	71.57	28.43	2.82	.96	.54	.25	.63	2.29	1.67	1.07	.92
Paper & allied products	3,934	68.38	31.62	1.06	.85	2.35	.13	1.24	2.37	5.32	.82	1.09
Printing, publishing & allied industries	24,402	65.58	34.42	2.98	1.32	.58	.42	.83	2.36	2.63	1.13	1.29
Chemicals & allied products	10,597	60.30	39.70	.87	.78	1.45	.16	1.05	1.87	4.69	4.23	1.52
Petroleum refining	410	66.13	33.87	.15	1.47	1.62	.22	.88	5.64	9.11	.55	.88
Miscellaneous petroleum & coal products	968	70.55	29.45	2.30	.92	2.32	.40	.74	2.01	3.23	.68	.88
Rubber & miscellaneous plastics products	6,290	67.38	32.62	1.50	1.19	1.31	.21	.95	3.32	3.20	1.72	1.71
Leather & leather products	2,747	74.39	25.61	1.88	1.26	.56	.18	1.05	2.22	1.27	1.43	.92
Stone, clay & glass products	9,060	66.50	33.50	1.81	.80	2.65	.35	1.20	2.94	5.84	.73	1.49
Primary metal industries	4,691	70.09	29.91	.70	.56	4.97	.07	1.22	2.65	6.09	.35	2.23

Fabricated metal products, except machinery & transportation equipment	24,353	70.71	29.29	2.62	.84	1.27	.20	.76	2.33	2.48	.85	1.36
Machinery, except electrical	21,200	65.12	34.88	1.77	.84	1.13	.18	1.06	2.53	3.59	.89	1.85
Electrical machinery, equipment & supplies	10,737	69.27	30.73	1.05	.86	.73	.18	1.08	2.32	2.58	1.37	1.46
Transportation equipment, except motor vehicles	2,867	77.79	22.21	.47	.96	1.20	.06	.94	2.38	2.41	.28	2.48
Transportation equipment (not elsewhere classified)	716	80.10	19.90	1.34	.59	.35	.26	.65	1.58	1.06	.78	.46
Motor vehicles, & motor vehicle equipment	2,523	74.23	25.77	.30	.47	.91	.18	1.21	3.47	2.82	1.07	2.79
Motor vehicles	986	74.38	25.62	.16	.45	.78	.19	1.30	3.70	2.73	1.14	2.96
Motor vehicle parts & accessories	1,537	73.41	26.59	1.04	.58	1.59	.10	.70	2.23	3.31	.72	1.85
Jewelry & silverware	1,127	69.42	30.58	3.03	.72	.54	.15	.94	2.09	.96	1.81	.84
Costume jewelry	690	71.19	28.81	5.80	1.36	.30	.06	.70	2.24	.64	1.09	.42
Toys & sporting goods	1,508	69.04	30.96	1.91	1.43	.62	.94	1.73	2.53	1.98	3.90	.92
SERVICE, TRANSPORTATION & COMMUNICATION												
Security & commodity brokers, dealers, exchanges & services	4,281	—	—	10.71	2.55	.20	.21	7.31	2.88	.72	1.07	2.64
Insurance agents, brokers & service	24,197	—	—	16.27	2.77	.19	.66	1.09	2.23	1.64	1.04	1.64
Hotels, rooming houses, camps & other lodging places	18,067	48.97	51.03	2.38	6.34	2.98	.38	5.78	6.37	8.74	2.37	.51
Laundries, laundry services & cleaning & dyeing plants	16,844	59.34	40.66	5.15	3.21	1.56	.16	.86	3.48	4.90	1.09	.70
Advertising	9,704	75.09	24.91	4.85	1.62	.18	.13	.30	1.19	1.15	2.60	.95
Automobile parking, repair & services	22,335	47.02	52.98	5.06	5.96	1.94	.46	3.77	3.62	21.50	.91	.38
Electric companies & systems	217	40.61	59.39	.36	.34	.03	.18	7.36	10.05	15.00	.41	1.66
AGRICULTURE & MINING												
Agriculture forestry & fisheries	32,448	73.67	26.33	2.91	2.16	1.80	.17	2.11	2.27	4.31	.48	.29
Mining	14,441	48.09	41.91	1.54	.86	1.74	.15	1.65	2.72	15.70	.14	1.18

Note: Figures given are selected from a D&B report that lists many more specific business categories. For those interested in comparable statistics for partnerships and proprietorships, these are also available from Dun & Bradstreet, Inc.

Source: Dun & Bradstreet, Inc.: New York; Copyright © 1971 by Dun & Bradstreet, Inc. Data based on U.S. Treasury Department, Internal Revenue Service, Statistics Division, *Sourcebook of Statistics of Income.*

How do you account for the wide differences in gross margin for different types of businesses such as retailers and wholesalers? Why is there such a wide difference in taxes paid by business classification? What accounts for differences in depreciation rates?

Of what value is this type information to a businessperson or to a banker evaluating a loan request?

Following are the seven most important ratios used by company management, as selected and explained by the New York Stock Exchange in its booklet *Understanding Financial Statements*, prepared for investors.

1. Pre-tax profit margin.   This is the ratio of profit, before interest and taxes, to sales. It is expressed as a percentage of sales and is found by dividing the operating profit by sales.

2. Current (or working capital) ratio.   Probably the most generally used for industrial companies, this is the ratio of current assets to current liabilities. A two-for-one ratio is the standard. A gradual increase in the current ratio usually is a healthy sign of improved financial strength. Ordinarily, a ratio of more than four or five to one is regarded as unhealthy, and may in fact be the result of an insufficient volume of business to produce a desirable level of earnings.

3. Liquidity ratio.   This is the ratio of cash and equivalent (marketable securities) to total current liabilities. It is also expressed as a percentage figure and results from dividing cash and equivalent by total current liabilities.

    This ratio is important as a supplement to the current ratio because the immediate ability of a company to meet current obligations or pay larger dividends may be impaired despite a higher current ratio.

4. Capitalization ratios.   These are the ratios of each type of investment in the company to the total investment, such as long-term debt, preferred stock, common stock, and surplus.

5. Sales to fixed assets.   The ratio is computed by dividing the annual sales by the value before depreciation and amortization of plant, equipment, and land at the end of the year. The ratio is important because it helps point up whether or not the funds used to enlarge productive facilities are being spent wisely.

    In most cases a sizable expansion in facilities should lead to larger sales volume; if it doesn't, the added money tied up in the plant, equipment, and land is not producing properly or is not being utilized fully. There is also the possibility that sales policies should be altered. It often takes time to build up a demand that is equal to increased production capacity, and, in the meantime, the ratio of sales to fixed assets will naturally suffer.

6. Sales to inventories.   This ratio is computed by dividing the year's sales by the year-end inventories. The so-called inventory turnover is important as a guide to whether or not the enterprise is investing too heavily in inventories. In this event a setback in sales or a drop

in commodity prices would be particularly unfavorable. A more accurate comparison would result from the use of an average of inventories at the beginning and at the end of the year.

Because inventories are a larger part of the assets of a merchandising enterprise than of most manufacturing companies, this ratio is especially important in the analysis of a retail business. A high ratio indicates a good quality of merchandise and correct pricing policies; a definite downtrend may be a warning signal of poor merchandising policy, poor location, or "stale" merchandise on the shelves.

7. <u>Net income to net worth</u>. This ratio, one of the most significant of all financial ratios, is derived by dividing net income by the total of the preferred stock, common stock, and surplus accounts. It supplies the answer to the vital question: "How much is the company earning on the stockholders' investment?" Naturally, a large or increasing ratio is favorable.

AUDITING

Proper accounting makes possible many management efficiencies and assures protection of the interests of government, owners, and creditors. In addition, accounting is an aid in preventing fraud, which in a recent year was responsible for 1.4 percent of business failures. So important is accounting to the business that it must be checked periodically for accuracy.

The specialized branch of accounting concerned with verifying accounting records and practices is called *auditing*. Auditing also is used to review the validity of accounting decisions. For example, if the auditor, on examining depreciation procedures, feels that certain assets are not being depreciated at the proper rate he refuses to certify the accuracy of the company accounts.

Audits may be made by any of three groups: internal auditors, who are regularly employed by the company; public accountants, who are retained to audit the firm's accounts; and government auditors. The public accountant is frequently called on to verify business records. His audit involves the actual counting of cash, determination of the value of assets, and verification of inventories. Since auditors not only check accounts for accuracy but are on the alert for fraud, public accountants, licensed by the state and occupying a disinterested position, are generally retained for such work. When a public accountant has completed his work, he certifies that in his opinion the accounting records and statements present fairly the financial position of the company as of a certain date. While the auditor's certification does not absolve management of the responsibility, it does assure everyone concerned that the financial status of the company is as the accounting records indicate.

Government auditors include bank examiners, who audit the accounts of banks; auditors of the Interstate Commerce Commission, who examine the books of public transportation agencies; and auditors of the Internal Revenue Service, who audit business records to verify tax reports.

The issue of the auditor's independence

Instead of being responsible primarily to his client, the CPA as auditor is now held by the SEC to be accountable in the courts for any misrepresentation from which investors suffer financial damage. The CPA is in a difficult situation because to do an impartial audit he should be completely independent; yet it is the management that retains him. The SEC in an attempt to resolve this intolerable situation has recently strengthened the position of the CPA by requiring companies to notify them of a change in auditors and to detail any accounting disagreements that may have arisen between management and the outside accountants. Pressure seems to be mounting to devise means, legislative or otherwise, to make CPA auditors truly independent from the business client who retains him. Evidence of such pressures was reported in the *New York Times* on February 13, 1972, "The recent Continental Vending case has drawn further attention to the deplorable readiness of accountants to assist in the construction of financial statements that are concealing rather than revealing, albeit technically adhering to generally accepted accounting principles and auditing standards."

ACCOUNTING—MORE THAN FIGURES

A profound change has occurred at the executive levels of accounting with the coming of the computer. The company controller, the man whose job formerly was keeping the books and saying "no" to spending has become a key executive who is now showing management what it *can* do and how to do it. *Dun's* magazine editorializes that "as time goes on, executives are going to be feeling the weight of his presence even more forcefully."

The catalyst that changed the role of the controller was the computer. As companies computerized, top management found that the person who knew what to put into the computer and who could understand and analyze the results was the company controller. As a result, in many large companies, powerful controller departments grew. As one observer put it, "The computer freed the controller from the numbers game. He is now the navigator. He tells the company where it has been, where it is, and where it is going."

Freed by the computer from endless manipulation of numbers, the controller now has time to relate the numbers to the actual business. As a full-fledged member of the management team, the new controller finds that he spends as much time dealing with people as he does in analyzing numbers. When a successful controller was asked what he felt his most important function was, he answered, "I'm the guy who asks the embarrassing questions." At a conference, a panel of controllers was asked why so many ambitious business graduates wanted to start their business careers in the controller's office. Two of the replies were: "You're not trapped in the hierarchy of a production or a marketing department. You gain a lot of visibility. You sail faster." The controller gets to know marketing, production, and a smattering of engineering. It's a tremendous cross-discipline—for one who wants to get to the top."

PEOPLE AND THEIR IDEAS
Clarence C. Finley

"Finley's position is the highest and most important that a black man has reached in a major white firm."

The above quotation appeared in *Ebony* magazine when the 49-year-old Finley was named executive vice-president of Burlington House Products Group of Burlington Industries, Inc., in 1972. He reached his eminence via the accounting route.

He graduated from high school in Chicago, where he was a straight-A student, and started work as a file clerk at Charm Tred Mills, which was taken over 18 years later by the nation's largest textile producer, Burlington Industries. Extremely curious by nature, from the position of file clerk he rotated into many jobs and thus attracted the attention of Charm Tred's president, Ben Greenberg. When he was drafted into the Air Force in 1943 to serve as a fighter pilot, Mr. Greenberg encouraged him to come back to the company after the war, promising him that he would progress as he qualified himself.

His innate curiosity and intense interest persisted. Given the position of assistant office manager when he returned from the service, he managed to handle everything he could induce others to allow him to try, which included bookkeeping, credit, payroll, customer and mill contact work, and many other administrative functions. He felt accounting was the key to a business, so decided to study it in depth.

He is an advocate of the work-during-the-day and go-to-school-at-night philosophy for those who have the necessary physical stamina and can take the mental and emotional pressures of the double load. He went to school at night for a period of eight years while he continued to be promoted at work, and he eventually earned himself a degree in accounting at Northwestern University. After that he studied law at John Marshall Law School in Chicago.

Asked about whether being black presented problems, he said, "From the outset, Mr. Greenberg's commitment eliminated the job as a racial one. My race worked neither for me nor against me." He continued on to pun—"You might say my rise was colorless!"

Interestingly, when asked which step in his career was the most important, he said, "the extra step," which he recommends as the formula for success for young people interested in achieving in business." He defines the "extra step" as "that extra effort, that seeking something beyond the requirement of the job that takes you out of a minimal framework and gives you a scope that might carry you anywhere."

He is very much an advocate of learning by being curious while on the job. As company controller he involved himself in operations, merchandising, and factory planning. "This is the way I learned, which meant developing expertise of the total concept—administration, operations, marketing—which can be summed up by relating all your assets to the market place."

His style is soft-spoken and mild-mannered. When asked what motivated him, big money, ambition, or what? he answered, "It probably was some of both, but mainly I think it was an innate competitive spirit that impels one to excel."

Mr. Finley reads widely and likes to play bridge. He finds time to assume civic responsibilities and serves on the board of the Interracial Council of Business Organizations, which helps prospective entrepreneurs get started.

CONTEMPORARY ISSUES
Situation 21

Should business accounting practices be carried into the home?

As he was studying the material for the current assignment, John commented to Ray, "It occurs to me that managing the family budget offers a real opportunity for the application of accounting principles."

"What do you mean?" asked Ray.

"Well," replied John, "the typical family always faces the problem of trying to make ends meet—regardless of how much income they have. This is because they don't budget. The average person can tell you the amount of his house payment and his car note, but he has only a hazy notion of where the rest of his money goes."

"But what's so bad about that?" asked Ray. "I disagree with what you're trying to say. Business is different from personal living. I agree that very close control must be exercised over income and expenditures *in business*, but people should enjoy their money as much as possible. Besides," continued Ray, "trying to account for every penny of income and every expense item might take several hours each week—time that could be spent enjoying life not simply trying to account for it in a monetary sense. Consulting the budget every time you want to go out to dinner or have a big weekend or buy a present for someone is just not my idea of the good life."

"The good life indeed!" exclaimed John. "Do you realize that more than 200,000 people went bankrupt last year largely because of mismanagement of their money? Do you think they are enjoying the good life? Ignoring accounting principles in management of family finances constitutes a serious national problem."

SITUATION EVALUATION

1. Who has the better argument? Give reasons for your answer.

2. Based on your personal observation, do you feel most families have only a hazy idea of how they spend their money?

3. Would reasonable application of accounting principles to family management help or hinder happiness? Explain your response.

BUSINESS CHRONICLE

Bookkeeping and tax services

The management group planning the new subsidiary company, Service All, Inc. (see the chronicle for Chapter 4), was discussing the possibility of offering accounting as one of its services.

It was felt that when leases were signed or property was transferred, many of the principals involved in such transactions were in need of accounting service and tax advice. Such matters as tax rates and the handling of profits or losses incurred were topmost in the minds of the people involved. If Service All would offer accounting services, they would probably be welcomed. The idea was to offer bookkeeping and tax advisory services on a yearly basis. For example, if an investor purchased an income-producing property such as an apartment house, Service All would undertake to collect rents, pay taxes, mortgages, and other bills, and fill out necessary tax reports for a fixed monthly charge. Individuals living in Kingmaker developments could get their income tax forms prepared for an annual fee.

The management of Service All, Inc. felt that tax matters and book-keeping were growing problems for most people and that servicing these needs would be a welcomed and good source of business. Service All management agreed that much of the tax work could be standardized, which would result in modest and attractive fees. The feeling was that when individuals do their own tax work and bookkeeping they unnecessarily waste a great deal of time. The expert who sets up a standardized system can do the same work in a fraction of the time it would take someone who is inexperienced.

QUESTIONS

1. What kinds of bookkeeping and tax services would individuals dealing with a real estate development company like Kingmaker Estates require?

2. Evaluate the business possibilities of the proposal. Do you recommend that Service All provide the service? Why?

3. What is the future of bookkeeping and tax services as described?

APPLICATION EXERCISES

1. Joseph C. Wilson, president of Xerox Corp., said: "To set goals, to have almost unattainable aspirations, to imbue people with the belief that they can be achieved—these are as important as the balance sheet, perhaps more so."

   Michael Rothman, Financial Vice-president of the Harwood Companies, Inc., said: "Two businesses earn exactly the same profits and have the same net worth. One works exclusively with subcontractors, while the other subcontracts no production and produces all goods and services with its own employees. How do you record the inherently greater value that the second company possesses, in terms of the skilled labor it has? How should this inherently greater value be expressed on the balance sheet? Wouldn't this be significant to an investor or potential acquirer?"

   The above statements, made by men well-informed about accounting matters, indicate there is much that accounting statements do not reveal. Make a list of items that are important in judging the true worth of a business but are not reflected in accounting statements. Indicate how each of the points you list could be reported or evaluated by someone trying to size up a company accurately.

2. Lydia Grey, an elderly neighbor of yours, has recently opened a small florist shop. The business is doing surprisingly well because of Miss Grey's knowledge of flowers and because of her friendly disposition. Miss Grey's only major trouble is that she has absolutely no talent for record-keeping. She asks you if you would be willing to come in for a few hours a week, set up a bookkeeping system, and keep a set of books

for her. You agree to do this. Describe in detail the bookkeeping system you would use.

3. Secure a corporation financial statement. Give recommendations as to how it could be made more understandable to the layman.

QUESTIONS

1. Define accounting. What is the difference between accounting and bookkeeping?

2. Why is it essential to the public interest that the requirements for the CPA certificate be rigid?

3. What are the steps in the accounting procedure? Which of these is most important? Explain your answer.

4. What is cost accounting? Show how cost accounting can lead to greater efficiency in each of the following: a retail store, a manufacturing establishment, a wholesale establishment.

5. What are standard costs? What purpose do they serve?

6. What is a budget? What are the major purposes of a budget? Why should the budget be considered flexible?

7. What is an asset? What are the different kinds of asset?

8. The New York Stock Exchange requires that all companies with listed stocks periodically issue balance sheets and income statements that have been certified by a public accountant. Why is such a policy a good one?

9. Why does an audit involve taking inventories? Some businesses have large stocks of goods that may be difficult to evaluate, such as stocks of coal owned by a utility. What methods for taking inventory can be used to simplify inventory-taking in such cases?

10. The manager of a gas station spends an average of six hours a week on an impressive set of books. How can one determine whether this is too much or too little time? Is there such a thing as being too enthusiastic about accounting?

11. "I'm the guy who asks the embarrassing questions" is a quote from this chapter. What kinds of question would these be?

CHAPTER 22

THE DEVELOPMENT OF ELECTRONIC COMPUTERS
The Paperwork Explosion. History of Data Processing.

BACKGROUND INFORMATION FOR UNDERSTANDING COMPUTERS
Advantages of Computers. Limitations of Computers. Types of Computers. The Binary Code.

HOW THE COMPUTER WORKS
The Computer System. Computer Hardware. Computer Software. How to "Converse" with a Computer. Programming. Computer Language. Systems Analyst—Liaison between Programmer and User.

APPLYING THE COMPUTER IN BUSINESS
Specific Uses. The Systems Concept. Batch and Real-Time Processing. Time Sharing. Process-Control, or "Blue-Collar," Computers. Computer—Plans and Operations.

THE COMPUTER AND TOMORROW

22

computers and electronic data processing

The electronic computer is an amazingly efficient tool that increases man's capacity to do intelligent work and to handle masses of data. Computers have become the world's fastest growth industry (see Figure 22–1). Many feel that it will become the world's largest industry before the turn of the century, surpassing the automobile and petroleum industries.

Its development in the 1940s ushered in what can be called the "second industrial revolution." The first, which started in England in the 1760s, replaced man with machines as a source of muscle power; the second, to quote the late Norbert Wiener, a key individual in the development of electronic computers, "added [mental] power to the brains and minds of men."

Data processing—the classifying, sorting, calculating, summarizing, recording, and reporting of factual information—is not a new function, but until the advent of the computer, it was performed mentally and manually. When electronic computers are used to convert data into useful information, the process is called *electronic data processing*, or EDP.

Figure **22-1**
The World's Largest Growth Industry May Soon Surpass the
Automobile and Petroleum Industries

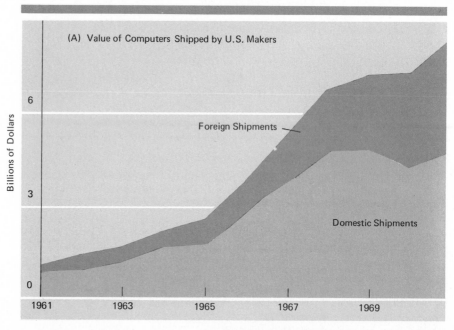

(A) Value of Computers Shipped by U.S. Makers

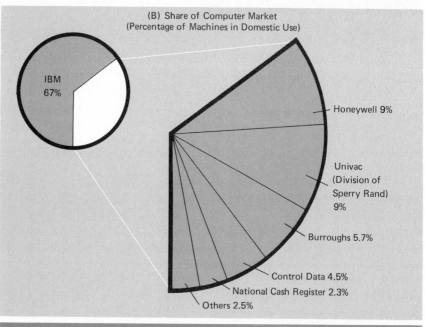

(B) Share of Computer Market
(Percentage of Machines in Domestic Use)

Source: Data from the International Data Corporation.

THE DEVELOPMENT OF ELECTRONIC COMPUTERS

The paperwork explosion

In a very real sense, the computer was invented out of necessity. Our uses of data had expanded so greatly in recent years that without the computer most large enterprises and communications systems — the space program, modern airport development and passenger seat reservation facilities, long distance telephone dialing, and other major undertakings — would now be drowning in paperwork or simply would not exist.

A few examples will show how paperwork has proliferated in modern society. In 1940, approximately 96 million local and 2.3 million long distance telephone calls were placed daily. By 1971, total local calls were 487 million (up 550 percent), while long distance calls were 29 million (up 1300 percent). It is estimated that half the women in the nation would have to be telephone operators to handle today's calls if the 1940 methods were still being used.

Stock-market transactions climbed from 372 million shares traded on organized exchanges in 1940 to 5,916 billion in 1971. The paperwork involved in this mammoth increase was so overwhelming that even with the rapid installation of computers, the New York and American Stock Exchanges remained closed on Wednesdays in 1968 to give the brokerage houses extra time to cope with the backlog of orders. There was a similar gigantic growth in the insurance business, a significant proliferator of paperwork — from approximately $115.5 billion worth of life insurance policies in force in 1940, the total increased to $1,504.7 billion in 1971.

In 1971, Americans carried over 275 million credit cards of all types: 35 million bank cards, 90 million oil company cards, 120 million retail store cards, 5 million rent-a-car cards, 1.8 million air travel cards, and 5 million "travel and entertainment" cards. Some 9,300 banks offer credit cards.[1]

In sharp contrast, the credit card business in 1940 was limited largely to localized charge accounts that could be used only at the store that issued them. Localization was necessary because accounts had to be checked manually to determine balances. Now the computer makes rapid account determinations possible regardless of where in the nation the card is issued. As a result, one can project that ours will soon be a cashless, and even a checkless, society.

The foregoing examples, just a few of the more obvious ones that could be cited, demonstrate the effectiveness of computers in helping man cope

---

[1] From "The Credit Card's Painful Coming of Age," Irwin Ross, *Fortune*, October 1971, p. 108.

with massive amounts of detail. Since the businessperson of tomorrow will be confronted with ever-increasing amounts of paperwork, it is imperative that he understand what the computer can do for him, as well as what it cannot do.

History of data processing

For hundreds of years mathematicians had recognized a need for a mechanical device to expedite the data processing functions. At first progress was very slow. In 1642, Blaise Pascal, a French inventor, built a simple, manually-operated calculating machine. An English mathematician, Charles Babbage (1791–1871), pioneered in the development of the forerunner of the modern computer; however, because he received little financial support and encountered engineering problems, his plan for a differential calculator was not finished.

In the latter part of the nineteenth century, definite strides were made toward the development of the modern computer. Around 1880, W. H. Odhner invented the pinset calculator, which performed arithmetical operations by mechanical devices.

In 1885, William Burroughs produced the first adding machine, and in the same year Herman Hollerith introduced the first punch-card calculating system.

It was not until the early 1940s that the major step of programming was introduced, made possible by a calculator that could perform sequenced arithmetical operations. However, although it was possible to tell the calculator to perform automatically a sequence of operations, the machine nonetheless was a mechanical device that had moving parts, and it performed at a speed of only one operation per second.

The first truly electronic computer, called ENIAC (Electronic Numerical Integrator and Calculator), was developed in 1946 at the University of Pennsylvania. This achievement, combined with the pressing need for developing faster ways to process data, provided the impetus for greater research in this field, and the first computer designed for commercial purposes, UNIVAC I, was delivered in 1951 to the U.S. Department of Commerce for use by the Bureau of the Census.

Since then, progress in computer engineering has been phenomenal and has resulted in three "generations" of computers. The first generation, which appeared in the early 1950s, used vacuum tubes for circuitry. These computers were bulky and generated so much heat that massive amounts of air conditioning had to be installed for people to be able to work with them; also, by today's standards they were slow, doing fewer than one thousand additions per minute. The second computer generation, introduced about 1960, used transistors instead of vacuum tubes, an

Figure **22–2**
The Four Generations of Computer Circuitry

First generation, center; second generation, upper left; third generation, upper right. Below, fourth generation, called large-scale integrated circuits, are appearing in the very latest computers, such as Burroughs B1700.

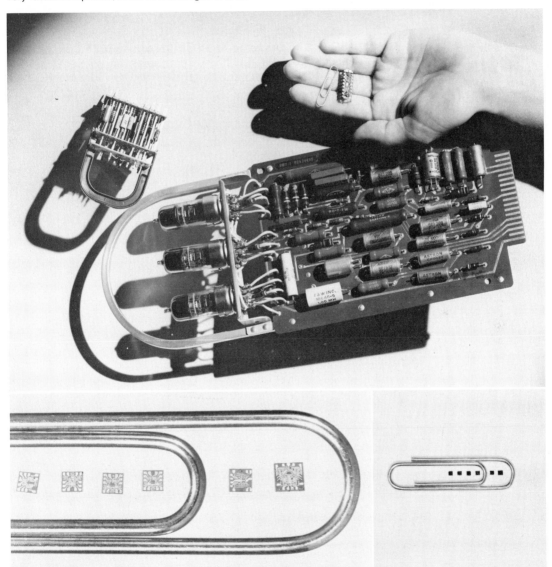

Source: Burroughs Corporation.

innovation that reduced the size of the computer and speeded up its operations by ten times.

In the mid-1960s the third generation of computers appeared, marked by increased speed and data-storage capacity. An example is the IBM system 360, model 65, which can multiply two ten-digit numbers at a rate of more than two million complete calculations per second—a task that would take a person using just a pencil and paper thirty-eight years of non-stop work. The third-generation computers use particles of silicon the size of a pinhead as electronic circuits (see Figure 22–2). The fourth generation, even more advanced, is on its way.

So rapid is progress in the computer field that the differences between today's most advanced model and UNIVAC I are more pronounced than those between the modern jet airliner and the Wright Brothers first aircraft. When we consider that the first computer weighed thirty tons, it seems incredible that computers can now be made light enough and compact enough to ride in jet liners and space vehicles.

BACKGROUND INFORMATION
FOR UNDERSTANDING COMPUTERS

Advantages of computers

Computers owe their already established and rapidly expanding popularity to their ability to increase business efficiency. Specifically the computer:

1. Performs data processing functions faster than human beings—data that once required days or weeks to process are now completed in seconds or minutes

2. Processes data much more accurately than human beings, thereby reducing costly mistakes both in time and money

3. Handles data processing work too complicated for human beings, since it can "think" about many variables so fast that it appears to consider them simultaneously

4. Stores information compactly, thereby reducing the physical space required for record-keeping

5. Makes tremendous volumes of data readily available—a function called "information retrieval"

6. Reduces the cost of data management—while computers represent a substantial initial investment, the savings that result from speed

and accuracy, as well as reductions in labor and storage, tend to lower overall costs

7. Frees human beings for more creative and challenging assignments

Limitations of computers

Despite their great advantages, computers present a number of problems, including:

1. High initial cost of equipment and installation

2. Complications arising from conversion from manual to computer techniques

3. Shortage of personnel trained in computer technology

4. Resistance by tradition-oriented managers, who feel threatened and overwhelmed and fear they will be replaced by the computer

The computer industry has been overcoming these problems successfully, and, as a result, cost reductions and design changes now even make it economical for small businesses to use computers or to share them.

Types of computers

There are three principal types of computers in operation today: digital, analog, and hybrid.

A *digital computer* deals with distinct or separate numbers; every operation performed is basically arithmetical. The input (data) given to the digital computer consists of numbers, along with instructions on what to do with these numbers.

While digital computers count, analog computers measure. An *analog computer* deals with physical measurements, such as latitude, longitude, height, wind, temperature, and air pressure. The automobile speedometer and weather barometer are very simple, though nonelectronic, types of analog computers. The analog machine is especially important in engineering, scientific, and technical research. This computer performs its operations by simulation—in effect, it acts out the operation it is asked to perform. The input is an actual model of the system to be analyzed.

A statistical analysis of the results obtained from an opinion poll would require a digital computer, the input being numbers. How much power a nuclear plant can generate once the initial starting conditions are known is a problem best solved by the analog computer, whose components would be set up to represent the nuclear power plant or system.

A *hybrid computer*, which is used for complex engineering problems,

Figure **22–3**
Two-Valued, or Bi-Stable, Devices

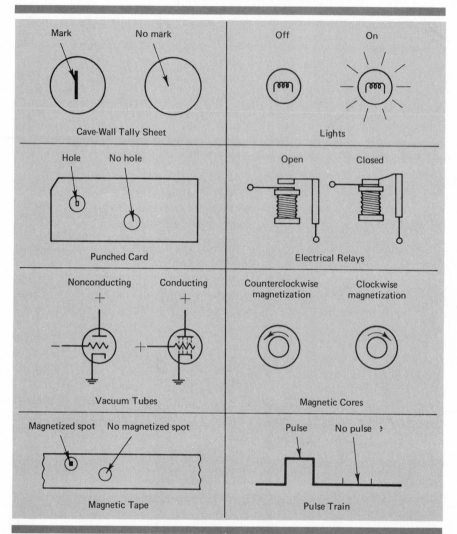

These devices are frequently used in computers to remember numbers. One condition is arbitrarily chosen as zero, the other as one.

combines design elements of both the digital and analog computers.

Since the digital computer is the one most widely used for business applications, the remainder of this chapter will be devoted to it.

The binary code

The language used by the computer is the *binary code*. Today many children learn the binary system in the third and fourth grades as part of the "new math."

One could think of the computer as having only two fingers on which to count. (Since man has ten fingers, the decimal, or base-ten, system is the natural one for him to use.) The term *binary* pertains to, is characterized by, or is made up of two elements. The phrase *binary code* refers to a base-two system; that is, any number can be expressed as a combination of two distinct characters, zero and one.

The memory and arithmetic elements of an electronic digital computer are made so that they are either open or closed, on or off, magnetized clockwise or counterclockwise, or lit or unlit (see Figure 22–3). In spite of references to it as a "super brain," the computer is basically a simple machine. Almost every part in a computer has only one job to do: to say, when asked, either "yes" or "no."

In the early days of the computer, programmers had to cope with the task—not difficult, but laborious—of converting input information from the base-ten system (the one we are all used to working with) to the base-two system (the number language of the computer). With advances in computer design, however, the problem no longer exists. Today, both input and output are in decimal form. While a computer's internal manipulations are still binary, a computer can now be programmed to work out the standard conversion routines.

HOW THE COMPUTER WORKS

The computer works much like the mind. In solving any problem, the mind performs five basic functions: input, storage, calculation, control of information, and output. Computer operation also involves these same five basic functions.

The computer system

Input Just as the human mind needs certain information to solve a given problem, so does the computer's brain. The process of feeding such data to the computer is called "input." The different ways this can be done will be discussed in a later section in this chapter.

Central processing unit (CPU) The core of any computer setup is the Central Processing Unit (CPU) (see Figure 22–4). This core unit which is the most complex and powerful part of the computer includes the storage, calculation, and control units.

Storage. Data put into the computer must be stored until needed. The computer must hold, or memorize, information. Each storage location has an "address" so the computer knows where to find the information it wants. In addition to the data needed to solve a problem, the computer also stores instructions on how to use data that it is fed.

Figure **22–4**
Anatomy of a Computer (Central Processing Unit = CPU)

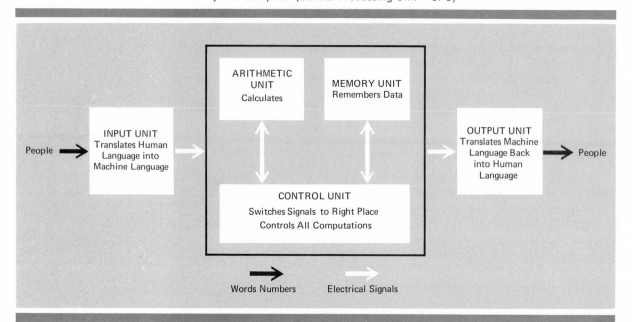

Calculation. Just as the trained human mind can do arithmetic, the calculation section of the computer adds, subtracts, multiplies, divides, and compares numbers. The computer's calculating or arithmetic-logic unit operates on the same principle as an adding machine. The computer system up to this point takes inputs of data that are fed into it, stores them, and makes them available as needed by the calculation unit.

Control. The control unit is the central nervous system for the whole computer installation. It guides the computer along each step of the operation to see that everything is done in proper sequence. By selecting, interpreting, and executing the instructions programmed into it, the control unit directs and coordinates the entire operation of the computer complex.

Output Output is the act of reporting answers after the problem has been worked out — or, we can say, it is the end result of the data processing operation. Because the computer works with numbers and formulas, machine output has to be converted into a printed report that can be read by human beings. Sometimes an output is fed into another machine, often by means of magnetic tape. The output unit thus provides communication between machine and man or between machine and machine.

Computer hardware

Hardware refers to the physical components that make up the computer installation. There are two categories of hardware: first, the Central Processing Unit (CPU) and, second, a variety of supporting devices called peripheral equipment.

What is needed for a basic computer system is a CPU unit, a device for getting information in, and another to get information out. As every camera buff knows, the more peripheral gadgetry one has for a camera, the more things he can do with it. The same applies to computers. A basic installation will contain the following hardware:

1. CPU, the core computer, which contains a memory core, a calculating unit, and control center—all of which operate at nearly the speed of light.

2. Console, or instruction center, which is comparable to an airplane cockpit in that it has the controls that enable the specialist to operate the computer system. It has switches, lights, and a typewriter keyboard. Through the typewriter unit, the operator feeds data into the computer and receives data out of it.

3. Card reader (if cards are used) that scans standard eighty-column punched cards column by column, simultaneously translating the holes in the card into the binary language of the computer.

4. Card punch, an operation that punches and verifies punching accuracy of eighty-column cards at one hundred cards per minute.

5. High-speed printer that prints out up to one thousand two hundred lines per minute. It prints an entire line of 120 or more characters at once, unlike a typewriter, which prints only one character at a time.

6. External storage unit, a component on many computers, which feeds data into the internal memory of the CPU as it is needed.

Computer software

Software refers to the programs and programming preparation aids used by computer personnel to give the computer its instructions. These must be prepared by experts possessing sophisticated skills.

One could easily assume, incorrectly, that the hardware elements of the computer are the most costly, since they are tangible, complicated machinery. Actually, the cost of software may represent 50 percent or more of the price paid for the total computer installation. Software receives an increasing share of computer costs as hardware becomes more standardized and the software programs more complex as the computer is given assignments of greater difficulty. (See Figure 22–5 for a projection of the two expenditures.)

Programming costs can be greatly reduced when problems fit into a scheme that can be standardized. Generalized software packages ("pack-

Figure **22–5**
Estimated Billions of Dollars Spent
by Computer Users — Software Far Exceeding Hardware

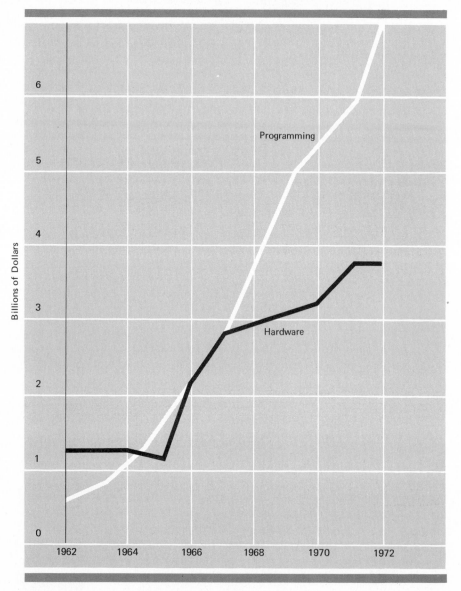

aged programs'') are used when many businesses have similar problems.
For example, most insurance companies have similar operations. Thus,
programmed packages that perform similar billing and accounting tasks
can be used by many insurance companies with little modification. As

more software standardization economies are realized, computer use by smaller firms becomes more feasible.

Computer users currently are spending an estimated $2 billion annually on software programs. Since many highly skilled manhours go into the design of programs, there has been a search to find a legal means for protecting investments in programs from exploitation by others. The Patent Office has held that, in general, programs are not patentable. In 1968, however, the Court of Customs and Patent Appeals ruled that programs can be patented if they meet normal tests of patentability (that is, where the program is new and would not have been apparent to others skilled in computer programming). The decision means that users of a patented program would have to pay royalties to the patent holders. The decision may not be final, since the Patent Office is asking the court to reconsider. The question of whether programs are patentable may go as high as the Supreme Court.

How to "converse" with a computer

Just as different means are available for people to communicate with one another (telegram, telephone, television), options also exist for them to communicate with the computer.

Punched cards   This computer communication device is most familiar to the layman, since he comes in contact with punched card pay checks, highway toll cards, utility bills, or school registration forms.

The standardized punched card ($7^3/8$ inches by $3^1/4$ inches) is made of special paper that resists contraction or expansion caused by temperature or humidity changes. It is called the Hollerith card, named after its inventor, Dr. Herman Hollerith, and was first used in tabulating machines for the 1890 census.

The card is divided into eighty consecutively numbered vertical columns, each with twelve horizontal positions or rows. With holes punched according to rows and columns, combinations of letters, numbers, or punctuation can be communicated to the computer. A hole or lack of a hole in a column indicates that an electronic signal can or cannot pass through the card. Thus the computer is triggered in terms of binary one or zero so it can translate the punched card information into the binary system to instruct its CPU.

Punched paper tape   Information can be punched on paper tape instead of on cards. The uses of paper tape are somewhat limited in business, because making corrections or inserting additional items can be difficult; for the most part, though, paper tape is inexpensive and easy to handle. Punched tape from cash registers or other kinds of business machines can easily be fed into computers for further processing.

Magnetic tape   Magnetic tape is the most widely used method for recording computer data. It has three important advantages, the first of which is speed. Some computers read up to 300,000 characters per second from magnetic tape, compared with about 1,200 characters per second from punched cards. Next, it is very compact—one 10½ inch reel of tape can hold the equivalent of 250,000 punched cards. Third, magnetic tape can be reused indefinitely, for old data can be erased when new data is recorded.

A single computer can be used to process data from one or several types of input. For example, in figuring a payroll, both new and stored data may be required. Fresh data from an employee's weekly payroll record may be fed into the computer from punched cards. Rates of pay, social security deductions, and sick day accumulations probably will come from stored information on the magnetic tapes that serve as the computer's external memory. Magnetic tape is most often used for storage of information that might be needed later.

Random access devices   Magnetic-disk units, which look something like phonograph records, are used in cases requiring immediate accessibility to large-volume master-data records. As the disks that store the data spin around, the computer has immediate random access to what is needed; the data need not be approached in sequence as is necessary for information stored on tapes. A magnetic-drum unit is another random access device that stores enormous amounts of data. Magnetic disks and drums make information available to the computer more quickly than tape.

Magnetic ink and optical scanners   Many documents, such as checks, are printed with magnetic ink characters that can be read by both people and computers. An optical scanner has a set of electronic patterns stored in its memory. A photoelectric cell scans the material to be read and then converts characters into electric impulses. The scanner reads any character that matches the patterns stored in its memory.

Typewriter   A computer information counter, or console, has a typewriter as a part of its control unit. An operator, using the typewriter keyboard, can thus enter information directly into the computer. The typewriter is also activated by the computer. It can feed out certain types of data, such as short answers to problems and information that alerts the operator to programming errors that should be corrected.

Video terminal   One of the more spectacular and newer devices now gaining wide acceptance, a video terminal looks like a small television set on top of a typewriter keyboard. In a personnel department, for example, it can be used to great advantage. An employee's code is punched on the keyboard and his records are immediately flashed on the screen. The examiner can thus obtain desired information at a glance. Alteration of records and additions to and deletions from the file can be made by typing in the change, a procedure that cuts down on file-searching and paper-shuffling.

It is also worth noting that some terminals may "read" from a light pen, so that drawings can be constructed in a "conversation" between the artist or draftsman and the computer.

Programming

A *program* is a set of instructions developed by computer specialists to tell the computer what to do, how to do it, and in what sequence it should be done. The computer must follow slavishly the step-by-step directions prescribed by the programmer.

Some of the most successful programmers are blind or physically handicapped people who, because of their infirmity, can perhaps better concentrate on the field. Demand for programmers far exceeds supply, which is also a reason the handicapped find opportunity here.

To write a program, the programmer must first understand the problem to be solved. Usually a flow chart of the problem is made—a line sketch that shows the breakdown of the problem into its component parts and their relation to one another. The flow chart is similar to a marked road map, supplied to a motorist by an automobile club, that traces the sequence of routes, towns, cities, and stopover places suggested in making a trip.

Because the computer only makes simple yes-no decisions, a programmer must exercise great judgment and ingenuity in preparing very detailed instructions. A clever programmer can save many hours of computer machine time by deciding which yes-no decisions are needed for the computer to arrive at the desired answer. If human errors are made in the program and transmitted to the computer, it issues wrong answers. The computer can be no more accurate than the person who prepares the program. It is commonplace to hear that a computer can perform in seconds what takes a person hours to do. The opposite is also true. A mistake that a person makes in a second can take a computer hours to find!

Computer language

Programmers must be able to communicate with the computer system. Since the computer does not understand English, communications must be translated or programmed into a machine language that relates to a binary base. Several programming languages are used. The most commonly used computer oriented languages are FORTRAN (FORmula TRANslation), which was developed for scientific applications. COBOL

(COmmon *Business* Oriented *Language*), which closely resembles English, is the major language used in business data processing. There are a number of other computer languages, one of which — PL1 (Programming Language 1) — is attaining some prominence. Developed by IBM, it attempts to bridge the gap between scientific and business languages and can be used for both types of programming. The language used depends upon the requirements of the company, training of the personnel, equipment available, and the nature of the problem to be solved.

Systems analyst — liaison between programmer and user[2]

A major problem in the effective application of electronic data processing is that of communication between the user and the computer center. To overcome this problem, a liaison person, called a *systems analyst*, is employed to bridge the communications gap between the programmer and the user or requisitioner of that data. Interestingly enough, the systems analyst is first an expert in the user's area of concern and second a computer expert.

For example, before a programmer writes a program for the registrar's office at a university, a systems analyst, who thoroughly understands university registration procedures, course-crediting methods, and grading systems, would be employed to tell the programmer what is required.

A dialog between an analyst and a programmer might run as follows:

PROGRAMMER: "Do you want your print-out arranged by colleges within the university and by student ID number to show the number of hours carried?"

ANALYST: "No, our user wants the information to be reported alphabetically by student name, not by college, so he can spot students who are carrying less than a full class load."

PROGRAMMER: "We could use student ID numbers as the basis for getting information rapidly from the computer."

ANALYST: "That won't do. Students frequently ask for information after graduation, and in all probability they would have forgotten their student ID number. It would be better to use their social security numbers."

PROGRAMMER: "This print-out will be a list on standard 17x11 paper."

ANALYST: "That's really not what the user wants. He needs the information on punched cards that can be correlated with other records, consolidated and certified, so there is only one record, kept in one place, on each individual student. The information we supply must be flexible in form so that it can be tied in with other records."

---

[2] A Census Bureau report on the American job and skills market revealed that in 1970 the computer field had 161,337 computer programmers and 79,949 computer systems analysts.

From the foregoing dialog, one can easily see why the services of a systems analyst are required.

APPLYING THE COMPUTER IN BUSINESS

Applications of the computer in business increase each year. Banks, brokerage houses, insurance companies, utilities, large retailing organizations, transportation agencies, and large manufacturing concerns all make extensive use of computers.

Specific uses

Payroll accounting   This repetitive, highly detailed chore, common to all businesses, readily lends itself to efficient handling by a computer. Often it is the first business function to be computerized.

In recent years, payroll processing has become increasingly complex. Business not only has the obligation to see that employee paychecks are accurate and are released on time but is responsible for making appropriate deductions for federal, state, and local income taxes; social security; bond purchases; pension contributions; and the like.

Billing   Utilities, telephone companies, department stores, and other organizations with large numbers of customers are extensive users of EDP.

A group of doctors in San Francisco are linked by telephone to the Bank of America's new professional billing service. During the day, billing information on each patient is transmitted to the bank over regular telephone lines by inserting pre-punched account cards into a card reader. Twenty-five seconds per patient is all the time required for the doctor's staff to record charges. The next day the doctors receive detailed statements of the transactions. At the end of the month, they receive a consolidated statement of the month's activity. The bank bills patients, receives payments, and credits doctors' accounts.

Warehousing and inventory control   Use of computers for inventory control and warehousing ties in with many other operations of a business. For example, the Sara Lee Company, a leading producer of frozen baked goods, is highly automated and computer controlled. Mixing and blending of ingredients are tied to inventory control, as are time cycles for production, oven temperatures, billing and shipping, and stock conditions in the retail outlets.

Graphics Peripheral equipment involved in graphic designs and plotting can be tied to computers to prepare maps, chart diagrams for traffic flow, and density graphs of populations; the equipment can even help engineers and architects draw up a design. Several cities have complete population figures on computer. When asked, the computer will, for example, draw a density map of all families with incomes over $10,000 or of families with children under sixteen (see Figure 22–6).

The systems concept

Most businesses perform a variety of complex and interrelated functions —sales, credit checking, production, inventory control, shipping, and billing. When an item is sold, all functions are affected.

Using computers, large businesses are developing what are called "integrated total information systems." These systems collect and coordinate information about all facets of a business.

To illustrate, General Electric has developed such a system, which links 65 sales offices located in 49 states, 18 distribution warehouses in 11 states, and 40 product departments with 53 manufacturing plants in 21 states. When a customer telephones a local sales office to place an order, the salesman enters the required data into the computer system while the customer is still on the phone. Then the computer makes a credit check to see if GE wants to sell to him and also determines if the item is in stock at a convenient location. If the computer answers "yes" to both questions, the system then issues an order slip, bills the customer, updates the inventory records, checks the updated inventory to see if an order to factories to replenish inventory at the various distribution points is needed, and then relays the message back to the GE salesman that the customer's order is on its way. This whole operation takes less than fifteen seconds!

But even more amazing and significant than the factor of speed is the *integration* of the system. Notice that the following business functions were handled by the computer: credit checking, order entry, billing, inventory control, production scheduling, shipping, time and sequence control, and all the bookkeeping that once required many clerks. Departmental boundaries were in a sense dissolved—hence the phrase "integrated information."

Large retailers are also moving rapidly toward integrated total information systems.

Cash registers are being replaced by a machine—a point-of-sale terminal, or POS—that not only takes money like a cash register but reads and verifies credit cards, tells a computer what was bought, and checks credit ratings. For retailers the greatest advantage in addition to checking credit comes from quick reports of what people are buying and how much of which goods are left in stock. Furthermore, the POS system saves time of

Figure **22–6**
Examples of Computer Graphics

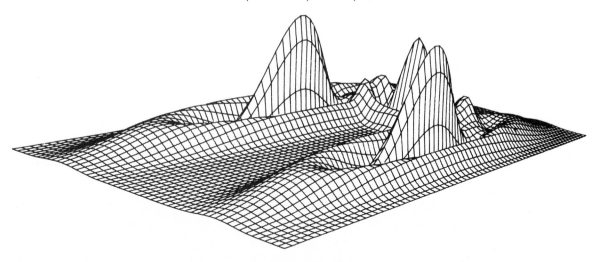

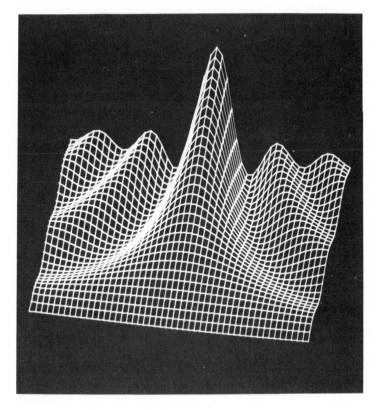

Source: California Computer Products, Inc., and Adage, Inc.

clerks and customers and handles the huge billing problem with infinitely more efficiency. According to industry forecasts, POS terminals will replace at least one-half of the large store cash registers by 1976. Sears, Roebuck is reported to be leading the way in the switch-over with Montgomery Ward and J. C. Penney following suit.

Batch and real-time processing

There are two ways in which the computer is used to relate to time: one is called *batch* processing and the other *real-time* processing. Most data processing in the past has been of the batch variety — transactions saved for a period of time and then processed as a batch. Batch processing is sequential and cumulative in nature. The time required to accumulate data into batches in many instances deteriorates the value of the data, making the information historical rather than current. The information may be useful for business control and planning purposes but is of limited value in current operations. Hence there has been the recent tendency to push development of what is called real-time processing.

The real-time method insures that the output is available quickly enough to be useful in controlling a current operating activity. Real-time processing requires immediate (not periodic) transaction input from all input originating stations. Records are updated as transactions occur, rather than at the end of a day, a week, or a month.

A widely known real-time operational system is the ticket and scheduling system used by most airlines. These systems accept inquiries from widely dispersed points, examine the stored file of accumulated information, and respond directly to the inquirer. Real-time processing involves updating the master file or description of the current situation with every transaction, regardless of the frequency. Banks, for instance, are rapidly developing real-time processing. Tellers at many window stations in many bank branches key-punch customer transactions, as they occur, into a consolidated computing center. Thus a current record of each customer's account is ready at any time for credit inquiries. Future developments in real-time processing show great promise.

Time sharing

One of the more recent innovations in computer usage is *time sharing*, a plan whereby many people simultaneously use a computer through input/output devices located at remote points. This has come about because a computer should not be allowed to stand idle — the expense is prohibitive.

The advantages of such multiprocessing systems are considerable, yet they have not been explored too deeply because of the newness of the systems. One really remarkable aspect is the fact that from one to three hundred users can have simultaneous access to the computer while each feels he alone is using it. At the same time, the system is multiprocessing batch jobs, such as payroll or inventory-control functions. Relatively small businesses thus have ready access to full-service computers that ordinarily only large companies could afford.

The time-sharing computer installation contains its own executive-type monitoring program to handle its own usage. The control program schedules all jobs, handles all input and output routing, gives priorities to what is done, and assures job and data secrecy while at the same time allowing common data and programs to be accessible to various jobs.

The subscriber to the time-sharing service pays for this data processing in much the same way as telephone services are paid for. There are charges for initial installation as well as basic monthly fees; what is probably most expensive are the per transaction charges, which, like long-distance calls, vary according to the nature of the transaction. While time-sharing services are still not used extensively, one can reasonably assume, in view of the many advantages, that time sharing will be greatly expanded in the future. Regional and even national networks of data processing services are likely to emerge.

Process-control, or "blue-collar," computers

Although their objectives and functions differ, the process-control and data computers are basically the same mechanism. The process-control computer, or robot, senses, lifts, measures, and reacts; it does the "blue-collar work" of the assembly-line worker, tool-and-die maker, and plant crew, and makes mechanical processes more economical. The data computer, on the other hand, does the "white-collar work" of the clerk, accountant, and mathematician.

Robots generally duplicate work previously done by humans, work that is not suitable for humans, or work people are not capable of doing. Robots differ from specialized machines because they can be made to do many tasks. Two robot systems that are commonly used today are (1) point-to-point, program-controlled robots for simple put-and-take tasks and (2) continuous path program-controlled robots for more complex tasks. Both types can be reprogrammed by the user to do a variety of jobs but need be programmed only once for each job.

Between 1960 and 1969, sales of process-control computers increased on an average of 30 percent each year. In 1969 more than 4,000 process-control computers were in operation, compared to only four hundred in 1964. A spokesman for the industry predicts that by 1975, between two-thirds and three-fourths of all installed computers will be connected to some sensing or measuring device. Data and process-control computers are now being interconnected in order to serve total management purposes better.

Continuous flow industries, such as petroleum, chemicals, utilities, metals, aerospace, and transportation, are the largest users of process-control computers, for here the functions of regulating, sensing, and reacting are important. There is also increased growth in operations separated in time such as monitoring hospitals, organizing traffic, and assembling car parts.

Computer—plans and operations

The California Aqueduct System (Figure 22–7) of the California Department of Water Resources is the largest single hydro project in the world. The 450-mile system, along which the country's longest bicycle path is being completed (see Figure 22–7B), moves water from the northern half to the southern half of the state. The system includes 27 pumping and power plants, 66 check structures with 213 separate gates, and a minimum of 49 major turnout structures where water is delivered to customers.

Probably the first question that occurs to anyone considering the system is: "Why is such an elaborate system needed merely to let water flow through an aqueduct?" The answer lies in what the system must accomplish. Normally it would take a particle of water eight to ten days to travel 450 miles. Without special controls, water input at the beginning of the system would have to be forecast at least eight to ten days in advance to provide service to the terminal end. Under controlled volume arrangements that regulate speed of flow at many points, the system can respond quickly to changes in demand.

Area control centers monitor and/or control events at the check structures, pumping plants, flow measurement stations, and turnouts. Each area control center contains a digital computer, which operates through a console that is the primary man/machine interface for the system (see Figure 22–7C). The peripheral equipment included at an area control center includes high speed paper tape equipment, mass information storage devices, an input/output teletypewriter, and other essential peripherals. The area control center makes a complete scan of all remote sites under its surveillance every minute.

Computers, in addition to playing an important role in operating the aqueduct system, also played a crucial role in building the facilities. A total enumeration of all possible operations of the project were programmed ahead of time. Thus, in November 1971, for example, nine studies of 44 years each (528 months of hypothetical operations) were made. One of the big computer problems was to provide construction specifications for an optimal system at each installation (see Figure 22–7A). One aspect of the studies required calculating the proper balance between water reservoir storage capacity and pumping capacity. At the A. D. Edmonston pumping plant, the aqueduct passes over the Tehachap Mountains. In full operation, the plant's fourteen pumps require a power capacity of 896,000 kilowatts. In one year of full operation this plant alone consumes 6.4 billion kilowatt hours of energy. Because of billing rules of electric utility companies, power must be paid for evenly over twelve months of a year, based on one peak value (since power companies must build capacity to handle peaks). The objective sought by the computer was to find a total system operating over a five year period that would reduce peaks and produce a uniformly low set of monthly power requirements. It is hard to determine exactly how much money the computer saved by providing an optimal system. However, "a conservative estimate of the savings is that the method saves each month . . . at the A. D. Edmonston plant . . . about 100,000 kilowatts per month, or about $1.7 million a year."[3] This is a dramatic example of how the computer serves in planning plant capacities.

THE COMPUTER AND TOMORROW**

A perceptive observer, well acquainted with the computer and its development, when asked what the computer can do and will do for the business executive, said, "It can all be summarized in one word — SCOPE!" In other words, the computer broadens the executive's capabilities. EDP frees him from routine chores, enabling him to devote more time to analysis, planning, and creative effort; it provides him with consolidations of information so he can see the past and current records of the business and thereby be in a better position to guide its future. Moreover the computer can show him the whole operation on a broad scale; as a consequence, he can quickly test many alternatives through use of

SPECIAL READINGS

** Man and the Computer by John Diebold. New York: Avon Books, 1970 (paperback). A successful business executive and computer pioneer examines the social impact of the computer. He considers the long-term questions that the computer poses, along with such matters as the training of managers, educational technology, international disparities and business responsibility. The book concludes with an excellent bibliography of selected readings about computer-related subjects.

[3] Don't Reject Dynamic Programming for Complex Systems," John Matucha, *Computer Decisions*, April 1972, pp. 18–23.

Figure **22–7**
California Aqueduct System

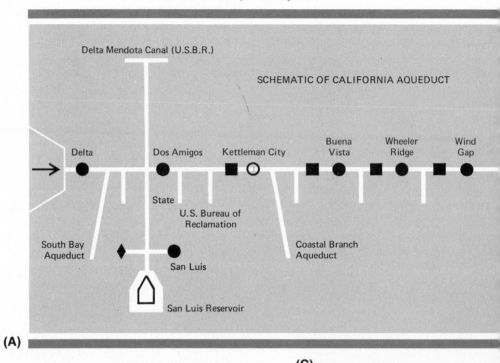

(A)

(B)

(C)

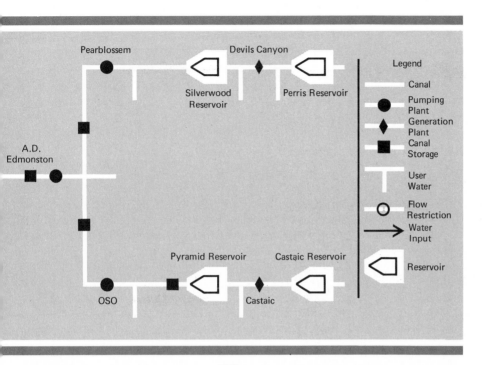

(D)

Source: California Department of Water Resources; F & M Systems Company, a Division of Fischbach and Moore, inc.,

Dallas, Texas; C, "Don't Reject Dynamic Programming for Complex Systems," John Matucha, *Computer Decisions*, April 1972, pp. 18–19.

models and simulations, trying them out theoretically before putting them into practice. Perhaps, ironically, the computer can also give him time to combat the impersonal effects of computerized management. As one airline manager put it, "Freeing employees of routine work means that more courteous employees are out front dealing with the public and personalizing their service." An interesting concept related to computerization was expressed by a member of management of a highly automated European mail order house:

> We view paper as being an obsolete medium and try to eliminate it wherever possible. Modern business has actually been moving away from using paper for a long time. In the early days letters were written in longhand and entries were made in ledgers with pen and ink. This was really a most extravagant use of paper because so little was fitted onto a page.
>
> Then came the typewriter. One typed page held what, if the same job were done in longhand, would take three or four pages and more. The typed page eventually gave way to the punched card. Information from many typed pages could be held on a small card.
>
> And now even cards are being eliminated. Indeed the magnetic drum has eliminated paper entirely. A proper goal for management.

As the executive finished his explanation he turned to his desk to prove his point. He punched a code on the keys of a video terminal device and immediately the extensive inventory record he had called for appeared on the screen—no paper!

The amount of information being gathered is growing rapidly. Detailed records on every individual in the United States are becoming increasingly available. Now, more than ever before, credit checking agencies, banks, the government, and employers have personal information about the people with whom they deal. There is and should be a deep concern about how far society and its institutions can go in delving into and accumulating data on the private lives of individuals. The record-keeping efficiency of a computerized society will certainly find managers of tomorrow confronted with very serious questions about the right of privacy. For a number of reasons, many people either feel hostile toward computers or are afraid of them. First, computers are mysterious, and man has a natural fear of the unknown. Second, man seems to be threatened by computers in two respects: They tend both to dehumanize him because they are so impersonal and powerful, and they threaten him by taking away his job. The dehumanizing feelings people develop about computers were colorfully expressed by a harassed student who said, "The only time I get any attention around here is when someone bends my IBM card!"

What we all have to remember is that the computer is only a tool: It can do nothing until a human being first tells it what to do. Another wag made the point another way: "Man is still the lowest-cost, nonlinear, all-purpose computing system that is capable of being mass-produced by unskilled labor."

PEOPLE AND THEIR IDEAS
Thomas J. Watson

THINK and the man who made it IBM's corporate byword

IBM's phenomenal growth from a small business-machine manufacturer to one of the largest industries in the world is attributable primarily to the imagination, energy, and foresight of Thomas J. Watson. Over the years, by means of an elaborate program of sales instruction and technical training, he broadened the company's scope to include, in addition to business machines of all types, the extremely complex electronic calculators and giant computers that are widely used today in government, industry, defense, and scientific research. By the mid 1950s, IBM circled the globe with offices and plants in eighty-three countries, employed some sixty thousand people, and had sales of over $563 million.

Thomas J. Watson was born in Campbell, New York, in 1874. He was educated at Addison Academy, New York, and at the Elmira School of Commerce. In 1898 he joined the National Cash Register Company and worked for fifteen years as a salesman and sales executive. In 1914 he became president of the Computing-Tabulating-Recording Company, which in 1924 was renamed the International Business Machines Corporation. He remained president until 1949, when he retired to become chairman of the board. That same year he created the subsidiary IBM World Trade Corporation to direct the company's extensive overseas operations.

A large part of Watson's success can be ascribed to his extraordinary ability to promote his products and to the intensely personal way in which he ran his expanding company. He established country clubs, bands, choirs, and instructional classes of all types for the benefit of his employees. He paid high wages and refused to dismiss his workers during the Depression. In return, he demanded loyalty, perseverance, and dedication. The now famous watchword "THINK" was initiated by Watson and displayed at IBM locations everywhere. He was perhaps one of the few businessmen able to mold a great corporation to his own image.

Watson supported numerous philanthropies and gave generously to medical research, religious groups, young people's organizations, and educational institutions. A confirmed internationalist, he actively promoted world trade and was a dedicated believer in the United Nations and other international groups. He received the U.S. Medal of Merit as well as other national and international honors.

Thomas J. Watson, Jr., IBM's former board chairman, had this to say about his father:

An industry becomes a growth industry because it meets the needs of its times. Some companies do this better than others. The reason, I've always felt, why some move ahead faster is that their managers develop a sensitivity to historical trends. They are able to see long-term needs. And they believe in their own vision. My father was such a man.

I remember very well an evening in 1923 when my father told us at dinner that he was changing the name of Computing-Tabulating-Recording Company to International Business Machines. I was nine at the time, and thought this a pretty big name for something that didn't impress me very much. But he, like most business leaders, could perceive trends where others could see only events. When my father died in 1956, IBM was doing business in eighty-three nations abroad.[4]

CONTEMPORARY ISSUES
Situation 22

Will we be robots in the year 2000?

One evening John and Ray were discussing one of their favorite topics — what the future would be like. "Do you realize," observed John, "that we'll just be reaching our peak when the year 2000 rolls around? If the experts are even half right in their predictions, this will really be a fantastic world."

"Chances are it will," agreed Ray, "but will it be worth living in?"

"Why do you say that?" asked John. "Don't you look forward to new inventions to do just about anything, weekend trips to any place in the world, disease control, and, as *Time* magazine predicts, an average annual income of $21,000 per family? Aren't you excited by what the future holds?"

"Well, to be very frank, I have mixed feelings," confessed Ray. "The way things are going there will be much less personal freedom. The computer will know everything about you, there will no longer be any personal privacy, and, as I see it, we'll be living in an electronic police state."

"But if you're honest about your income tax and don't break any laws, what do you care if the computer does know everything about you? If electronic devices manage to keep everybody honest, the world will be safer and better all the way around," said John.

"You may be right, but there are other aspects of the future I think I don't like," continued Ray. "The future as projected seems so artificial, so efficient, so homogenous — everything will be controlled, and we'll have a push-button society. I ask myself, 'Will there be any room for individual creativity and self-expression in the year 2000?'"

[4] Albert Love and J. S. Childers, eds., *Listen to Leaders in Business* (New York: Holt, Rinehart and Winston, 1962), p. 263.

"You worry too much," answered John. "First, changes in our living patterns, though seemingly rapid, will actually be gradual—you'll have time to get used to them. Second, the things that worry people so much today—jobs, money, health, accidents, and so on—will hardly seem like problems anymore. And third, people have always feared technology, and, as history shows, their fears proved to be groundless."

SITUATION EVALUATION

1. Do you feel Ray is justified in being concerned over the possible loss of individuality and privacy by the year 2000?

2. What additional points can you offer to support each viewpoint regarding the quality of life in the year 2000?

3. What can today's college student do to remain flexible and receptive to ever-accelerating change in the decades just ahead?

BUSINESS CHRONICLE

Computer applications for home and office

It was Allan King's policy to urge all his employees to participate in developing ideas for the company. They were stimulated to cooperate in two ways. There was a formal suggestion system and a committee screened and evaluated all suggestions. Payments were made for suggestions that were used. Employees also participated in "Planning for the Future" meetings that most of the company's departments held periodically. Significant results of these meetings were reported to Mr. King who presented the best ideas to the corporation's executive planning committee.

The Accounting Department was very interested in computers and made three suggestions:

1. The company should install an on-line computer system that connected each of its six sales offices. Since they were dispersed over a 120-mile area, the offices had trouble communicating. The idea was that each salesman would make a summary of what kind of property each prospect interviewed wanted. These summaries would then be flashed to each branch real estate sales office and property listings in each office would be compared with what was wanted. In this way prospects would be made aware of properties they might be interested in over a larger area.

2. The company should establish a coaxial computer-TV network to connect all properties in Kingmaker developments. Films for TV could be ordered and scheduled from Kingmaker offices via computer. It was felt that each home and business would eventually have its own computer system and that Kingmaker ought to take the lead since the applications of computers were easier to establish in planned communities such as those

Kingmaker sponsored. It was felt that computer/communications/TV companies would be interested in cooperating with various test installations. As a result Kingmaker would get much desirable publicity and thus build an image as a progressive company.

3. The company should develop a computer program to facilitate the planned tax and bookkeeping service of its subsidiary Service All (see the chronicle for Chapter 21). The cost of the computer could then be amortized in part by rental payments from Service All.

QUESTIONS

1. Evaluate the three ideas. What are the advantages and disadvantages for on-line prospect need summaries? What does the future hold for computer applications in the home?

2. What should Kingmaker do in these three areas?

3. What do you think of King's two methods for encouraging employees to submit creative ideas? What can you suggest to encourage Kingmaker employees to become more creative?

APPLICATION EXERCISES

1. Interview five students and ask them how they feel about computers. Ask the following questions (you may add to this list): Are computers dehumanizing? What benefits are derived from them? Are they to be feared? What will they do to the future? Write a paper summarizing your findings.

2. Select an extensive user of computers in your community, such as a large utility, bank, insurance company, distributor, or transportation company. Get in touch with the person in charge of computer operations and ask him how the computer has affected total employment of personnel in data processing before and after computer installation. In addition, ask him to explain not only how the computer has affected this particular department, but how it serves the entire company. Prepare a paper on your findings.

QUESTIONS

1. Define data processing. Is all data processing electronic? Explain your answer.

2. How do you account for the exceptionally rapid development of computers since 1946? Explain the statement: "Computers are still in their infancy."

3. What are the principal advantages and limitations of computers?

4. Differentiate between analog and digital computers. Which is more widely used in business and why?

5. What is the binary code? Why is it used instead of the decimal system in computer operations?

6. Explain briefly the five basic functions performed by the computer.

7. A basic computer installation consists of what types of hardware? What is computer software?

8. What is an analyst? A programmer? What does each do?

9. Define programming and explain why it is critically important. What computer oriented languages have been developed?

10. What are the major applications of the computer to business? Explain the systems concept. Why is its popularity almost certain to increase?

11. Explain the advantages and limitations of batch processing, real-time processing, and time-sharing.

12. "Magnificent as it is, the computer can do nothing that a man cannot do with pencil and paper." Do you agree with this statement? Will the computer diminish the importance of the human mind? Explain your answer.

13. The Honeywell Corporation, manufacturer of computers, has the following slogan: "Computers are people." What is the significance of the statement?

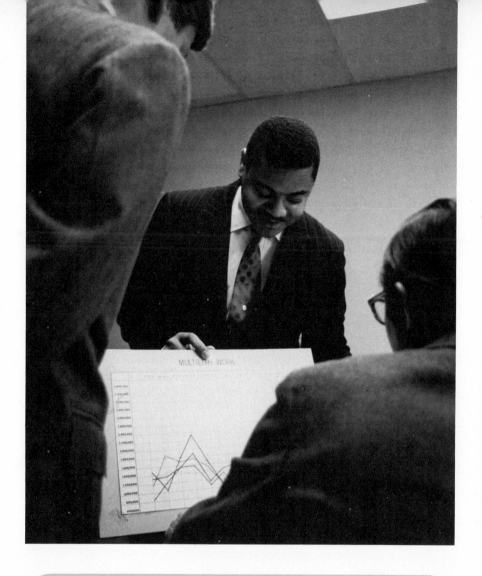

CHAPTER 23

HOW STATISTICS SERVE MANAGEMENT

STATISTICAL DEVICES AND TECHNIQUES
    Averages, or Measures of Location. Index Numbers. Correlation Analysis.
    Sampling. Time-Series Analysis.

STATISTICS, ELECTRONIC DATA PROCESSING, AND SYSTEMS ANALYSIS

PRESENTATION OF STATISTICAL DATA
    Tables. Graphs.

THE BUSINESS REPORT
    Basic Principles of Report-Writing. Organization of Reports.

CAUTION IN THE USE OF STATISTICAL ANALYSIS
    Forecasting.

23

quantitative analysis and the presentation of business information

The saying "Figures don't lie, but beware of fools who use figures" suggests a point of view for this chapter. So much statistical information crosses an executive's desk that it can be overwhelming. Used correctly, quantitative information is helpful; used indiscriminately, it can lead to faulty conclusions.** Examples of statistics we see daily are:

85 percent of national population watched moon-landing telecast

GNP tops last year's level by 3½ percent

Cost of living up 0.6 point

Per capita income now $4,400

Cost of doing business increased 7 percent last year

81 percent of customers prefer new package

SPECIAL READINGS
**How to Lie with Statistics by Darrell Huff. New York: W. W. Norton, 1954 (paperback). This short, lively book has long been a top seller on the subject of how statistics can deceive. It shows the reader how to judge statistics to avoid being misled by them. It covers such subjects as the sample with the built-in bias and how to talk back to statistics. Completely nontechnical in nature, cleverly illustrated by Irving Geis, it enables the reader to develop judgment in presenting statistics and in appraising them.

In popular usage, *statistics* means numerical data. The field of statistics, however, has a much broader scope than the mere compilation of numbers; it embraces the collection, analysis, interpretation, and presentation of numerical data.

Those who specialize in statistics are called statisticians. Statisticians are trained in mathematics and, increasingly, in the use of computers. Business statisticians, in addition, are usually trained in business administration and economics.

The statistical method is not to be considered synonymous with research, although statistics are a very important tool in many phases of research activity. Research personnel have the responsibility for defining the research problem and planning the research activity; they determine what data are needed, why they are needed, and the general method for collecting them.

HOW STATISTICS SERVE MANAGEMENT

The broad function of statistical analysis is to supply information helpful in making management decisions. The more important ways statistics benefit management are given below.

1. Statistics give meaning to masses of data.   Numerical data have no value until they are organized and interpreted. But when this is done well a picture emerges in which essentials stand out from the mass of detail.

2. Statistics save time.   When data are presented so they can be grasped and interpreted quickly, less time is required to understand its significance than when the data are available only in raw form. A manufacturer using thousands of rivets a month may have a contract with a supplier that gives him the right to reject any shipment containing more than 3 percent defectives. On a random sampling basis of each incoming shipment (a statistical technique to be discussed later), the manufacturer decides whether to accept or reject shipments without inspecting the whole lot. This is an example of the use of a statistical tool that saves time.

3. Statistics help eliminate guesswork.   Statistics substitute facts for guesses and hunches.

4. Statistics facilitate measurement of business efficiency.   Through the orderly collection, analysis, and interpretation of numerical data, it is possible to develop yardsticks for measuring how well a

business is doing in comparison with similar businesses, with previous time periods, and with other operations. For example, a trade association's annual report on the results of departmental merchandising and operating makes it possible for a department-store management to compare its operations with the composite experience of other stores—on such matters as cash discounts earned on purchases, average payroll cost per transaction, and sales per square foot of selling floor space.

Through the use of statistics it is also possible to develop yardsticks for measuring the efficiency of departments within a business. If one production department wastes more material than others, something is wrong. Comparisons such as these are not possible unless statistical data are collected. In essence, statistics serve a "bird-dog" function by pointing to matters that need examination.

5. Statistics make forecasting possible. Forecasting, which involves projection of the demand for a product, is a prime necessity for long-range business planning. Accurate forecasting is not possible without statistics, for in the forecasting procedure, consideration must be given to changes in population, income, competition, and other factors. Proper statistical trend analysis indicates what plans should be made to meet future conditions.

However, with regard to the fifth benefit, a word of caution is in order. It should *not* be inferred that forecasting is as precise or as accurate as the other statistical techniques with which it is usually associated. A discussion of the shortcomings of forecasting appears at the conclusion of this chapter.

STATISTICAL DEVICES AND TECHNIQUES

A detailed description of statistical techniques is beyond the scope of this book, but a general description of the chief statistical devices, beginning with averages, or "measures of location" (the term statisticians prefer to use), is useful as an introduction.

Averages, or measures of location

A function of statistics is to reduce complicated masses of data to simple, concise facts. The statistical device for this purpose is the *average*, defined as a *single numerical value descriptive of a group of values*.

The word average is one of the most common in the business vocabulary. Executives think in averages—average incomes; average sales per day, week, month, or year; average profits; average costs; average daily output; and average markup. Laymen also are interested in averages—average rainfall, average temperature, average weight, and average height. Students are interested in grade averages, and sports fans in individual player and team averages.

Types of average   While statisticians have developed a number of different types of measures of location, or averages, for most purposes only three are used—the arithmetic mean, the median, and the mode.

The arithmetic mean.   The arithmetic mean—or, as it is often called, the arithmetic average—is the simplest and most frequently used average. When the layman uses the word "average" in everyday conversation, he means the arithmetic average. When no mention is made of the specific type, it is assumed that the average meant is the arithmetic mean.

The arithmetic mean is computed easily—just add all the items in a series and divide by the total number of items. The arithmetic mean of examination scores is found in the following manner:

STUDENT	GRADE
A	91
B	90
C	85
D	82
E	79
F	76 ← MEDIAN
G	74
H	73
I	73 ← MODE
J	73
K	62

$$11\overline{)858} = 78 = \text{ARITHMETIC MEAN}$$

The median.   The median is frequently called the "position average," because it is computed by arranging items in order from smallest to largest. The midpoint number is the median. In the example of student grades shown above, the median is seventy-six, there being five numbers above and five below that number.

The mode.   The modal average, which is not widely used, is the number that occurs most frequently in a series of data. Thus, in the example of student grades, seventy-three is the mode. A modal average is most easily found by arranging all numbers in sequence from highest to lowest. On occasion there may be two or three modes. When this occurs, reference is made to bimodal, trimodal, or even multimodal averages.

Obviously, the average for a large series of numbers differs, depending on which averaging method is used. For example, annual per family income in a major city in a recent year was as follows, averaged by the three methods.

ARITHMETIC MEAN	$9,850 per family
MEDIAN	$7,800 per family
MODE	$6,670 per family

Notice that the thinking of a sales executive evaluating the size of his market on the basis of average income per family is conditioned by which average is used. The arithmetic mean is larger in this example because extremely high incomes, some over $100,000, are included in the averaging process. Insofar as income analysis is concerned, the modal average is the most meaningful, since it represents the income received by more people than any other. An interesting example of how averages can be used is seen in Figure 23–1; the averages on which this comparison is based are arithmetic means.

Index numbers

Another common statistical device is the index number, used to compare business activity during one time period with similar activity during another time period. Through the use of index numbers, one can answer the questions: "How do wholesale egg prices today compare with last year?" "How does the cost of living now compare with five years ago?" While the construction of an index number can be quite complicated, the theory behind it is simple.

1. A certain figure of one time period is selected as a base and is given a weight of 100 percent. This "certain figure" can represent any type of statistical data—carloadings, miles traveled, number of persons employed, prices paid, tons produced, dollar sales volume.

2. Corresponding data for a later time are then expressed as a percentage of the base period.

Study this simple illustration. Assume you wish to construct an index number for automobile sales. You select a certain year, say 1961, as the base period. Passenger automobile sales in that year were 5.5 million. Therefore, since this is the base period, 5.5 million = 100 percent. In 1972, sales were 10.2 million. Expressed in percentage form, the index for 1972 is 185.5. Comparing data in percentage form like this is usually much simpler and more understandable than comparing numerical data.

Correlation analysis

Correlation analysis is a statistical procedure used to compare relationships between two or more variable sets of data. If one finds that a close

Figure **23–1**
Intercity Differences in Living Costs

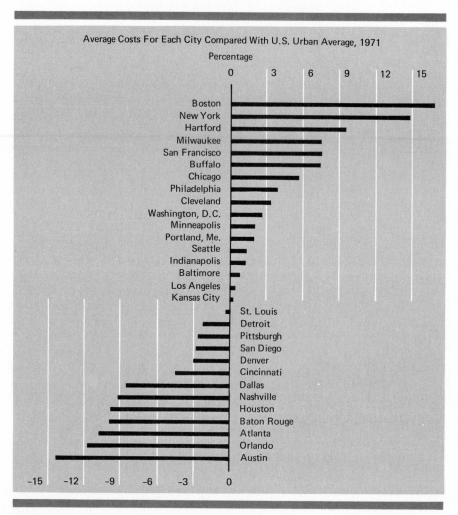

Source: "A Guide to Consumer Markets, 1972/1973," The Conference Board.

How does your area compare?

relationship exists between company sales and national income, the two sets of data are said to be correlated. The closer this relationship, the higher the degree of correlation.

Numerous correlations or relationships may be found. Burglaries tend to correlate with unemployment—the more unemployment, the greater the number of burglaries. Retail sales are usually found to correlate with personal income—as income goes up, so do retail sales, and vice versa.

The major objective of correlation analysis is to find one series of data that can be used to predict sales. A chemical company, for example, found a close correlation between sales of sulfuric acid and steel production. The steel industry in turn finds its sales closely correlated to auto sales. Sales of detergents and soaps vary according to the water hardness in a city, and retail sales relate to the payroll schedules of local industries.

Sampling

A basic statistical technique is the construction of *samples* for use in research. A sample is a relatively small number of items or individuals that, taken collectively, have the same essential characteristics as the much larger group from which the sample is taken. The larger group, called the <u>universe,</u> or <u>population</u>, includes all things or entities that might have been selected.

Examples of samples and universes   There are limitless varieties of universes. All Cincinnati homeowners combined constitute a universe, as do all poultry producers in the United States. A jar of wheat taken from an entire carload is a sample; the carload is the universe. In a study made of attitudes toward a new breakfast cereal, the sample consists of the housewives interviewed, and the universe includes all housewives in the market area who had a chance of being selected for interview.

Use of samples   Samples are used widely in business research for several reasons. To study all things or individuals in almost any universe would be not only too time consuming and expensive but often impossible. For example, to obtain the attitudes of present Dodge owners regarding the current model, one would question only a small fraction of 1 percent of owners. To survey the many thousands of Dodge owners would involve a huge expenditure. If the sample is properly constructed, interviews with only a few hundred Dodge owners ought to yield results just as valid as if every Dodge owner were surveyed.

Construction of samples   While construction of a sample looks easy, in practice it is complex. How large the sample should be, what characteristics it must possess, when the sample should be taken, and similar decisions can be made best by qualified statisticians. If the sample is not constructed properly, results are likely to be misleading. The important point is that the sample should reflect the characteristics of the total universe.

A sample can be either controlled or random. A *controlled* sample is chosen deliberately—for example, a particular number of housewives with two or more children under 15 years of age will be interviewed. Of course, statisticians attempt to make the controlled group representative of the particular group under study. A random sample is chosen in such a manner that the selection of any member of the universe does not affect the selection of any other member. That is, each unit has the same chance of being included in the sample. The word _random_ suggests that it is simply a matter of chance that a particular member is selected. Random number tables are found in many statistics books and can be used to obtain a random sample. For example, first the names in the Chicago telephone directory are numbered. Then names are picked according to a random number table. These names constitute a random sample, which may then be used for, say, a telephone survey of some sort.

Time-series analysis

Much statistical work is concerned with making time-series analyses, or studies of the factors underlying changes in economic activity. Their purpose is to help answer questions such as, "How much raw material will we need in the third quarter?" "Is our inventory large enough for the Christmas season?" "Should we expand business operations this year or wait until a more favorable time?" "What are the very long-run prospects for our business?"

Three important types of time-series analyses are seasonal variations, cyclical fluctuations, and secular trends.

Seasonal variations   Practically all businesses experience variations in sales volume. Department stores, for example, have peaks during the Christmas season. Paint stores do a major portion of their business during the spring and summer months. If variation is great, the business is called "highly seasonal." In this category are drive-in movies, textbook publishers, some resort hotels and motels, and, to a lesser extent, bottlers of soft drinks.

It is essential for several reasons that management know and understand the seasonal sales pattern of the business.

1. Retailers can plan purchase of inventories to avoid being overstocked or understocked.

2. Manufacturers can plan the purchase of raw materials and supplies, as well as determine labor requirements.

3. More meaningful business comparisons can be made. Since sales volume in most businesses varies from month to month, a compari-

son of one month's sales with those of a previous month is not particularly meaningful. It is much wiser to compare, for example, June sales this year with June sales last year than it is to compare this June's sales with this March's sales.

For easy, rapid comprehension and for emphasis, information about seasonal sales variations is often put in the form of charts or graphs.

Cyclical fluctuations   Cyclical fluctuations — or business cycles, as they are usually called — are variations in business activity that occur over a period of several years. Generally the pattern is as follows: A period of prosperity marked by high employment, business expansion, high incomes, construction of new factories and buildings, and other favorable economic activities, is followed by a period of recession. The recession represents a curtailment of production, increasing unemployment, decreasing income, and other unfavorable economic characteristics. Unless checked, the recession develops into a third and severe phase, a "depression," characterized by very large unemployment, many business failures, and a very definite slowdown of economic activity. Gradually, however, business conditions begin to improve, and "recovery" sets in. Recovery, marked by increases in production, employment and other economic activities, leads into prosperity, and the cycle is complete.

Since the business cycle affects most businesses and individuals in the economy, it is a matter of national concern. Accordingly, government agencies study business cycles and stand ready to implement various programs intended to restrict economic downturns and, if possible, prevent depression.

Individual businesspersons, while unable to influence the direction of cyclical fluctuations, attempt to tailor their own business plans to coincide with the cycle. For example, from the standpoint of the individual business, it would be desirable to expand during the depression phase, when costs are low, rather than during a period of prosperity, when costs are much higher. It is extremely difficult, if not impossible, however, to know when one phase ends and another begins.

An understanding of business cycles requires thorough training in business statistics and economics. Business-cycle forecasts are usually made, therefore, only by large business organizations that can afford the services of a highly trained economic forecaster. Most businesspersons attempt to keep abreast of economic changes by reading business indicator pages of business newspapers and magazines and by studying reports of government agencies and trade associations.

Secular trends   Secular, or long-term, trends are the general movement of a series of data over a relatively long period of time. No precise number of years is required for a secular trend; most experts treat it as covering twenty to thirty or more years. Secular trends will cut across a large number of seasonal fluctuations and several business cycles.

The businessperson is interested in two types of secular trends: the trend of national business activity and that of his particular industry.

The secular trend for individual business organizations does not necessarily follow the national secular trend. In the 1890s, for example, the wagon and harness industries were large and important. However, the advent of the automobile practically eliminated both. New inventions, improved processes, changes in consumer preferences, and similar factors can affect the secular trend of any particular business either favorably or unfavorably.

STATISTICS, ELECTRONIC DATA PROCESSING, AND SYSTEMS ANALYSIS

As was discussed in Chapter 22, statistics are the major part of any computer's input, programming, and output.

A method of applying statistical methods and advanced technologies to the solution of complex problems is called *systems analysis*. The identifying characteristic of systems analysis is that it deals with problems as a whole, not just with their separate parts. The following example provided by the du Pont Company illustrates use of systems analysis, the computer, and statistics.

The Fabrics & Finishes Department (of du Pont) had a problem with paints. It was making about 20,000 varieties (different kinds, colors, and container sizes) at nine plants, and the problem was to schedule production so that (1) each product would be available in the right amount, when and where it was needed; (2) manufacturing costs would be reduced by making each product in the optimum batch size; (3) plant facilities would be better utilized; and (4) warehouse inventories would be adequate but not excessive.

The answer: an inventory system that keeps daily records of sales; prepares invoices; keeps tabs on all stocks and calculates when to reorder each product; and figures how much of each product to make, considering demand rates, batch limitations and other factors. Scheduling of men, equipment and materials is still the job of plant management, but the system gives them more information to work with than they ever had before.

The system is supervised by the Accounting and Analysis Section of F & F's Data Processing Center and uses computer facilities of the Treasurer's Department's Nemours Data Center. Information for the system comes in from plants and warehouses daily (by mail and telephone) and is processed by the computer at night.

Some results of the system: (1) better production scheduling; (2) lower manufacturing costs; (3) reduced warehousing costs through reduced inventories (a reduction of more than a million dollars in stocks of consumer paints alone); (4) help in evaluating and eliminating slow-moving items (the number of products has dropped from 20,000 to about 15,000); and (5) information never before available on products, manufacturing and handling costs, [and] sales and customer orders.

PRESENTATION OF STATISTICAL DATA

Presentation of statistical data means more than just passing along numerical facts to executives; it implies preparation of the data in such a way that executives can grasp quickly the significance of the information. Thus, those responsible for the collection and analysis of data must be concerned also with putting facts together in a manner that is clear and concise. Data presented in either tabular or graphic form are called *descriptive statistics*.

Tables

Much statistical data are presented in tabular form. A title at the top of each table describes what the table is intended to show. Data within the table are arranged vertically in columns and horizontally in rows. At the top of each vertical column is a caption that tells briefly what the data in the column represent. At the left of horizontal rows of data is information, called the "stub," which tells what the horizontal rows represent. Variations, of course, can be made to suit different requirements.

Tables are used when it is important to show actual figures. Their chief disadvantage is that they are difficult to interpret. Tables take more time to read and understand than do the graphic presentations discussed below.

Graphs

Again, it is important to emphasize that the chief purpose of statistical analysis is to present information to management in the clearest, most concise, and most easily understood manner possible. If the presentation of information is too complex, it may be misunderstood or not understood at all.

Graphic methods of presenting data are often superior to tabular arrangements in several important respects.

Figure **23–2**
Examples of Statistical Illustrations

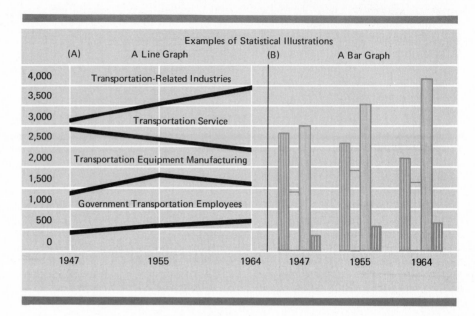

1. Information is less complicated. Graphic devices are easier to understand, because they make it possible for the viewer to bring the areas of significance quickly into focus without a careful study of columns and rows of data.

2. Comparisons are easier to make. In tables, the reader makes his own comparisons of data; in graphic presentations, comparisons are already made for him.

3. Time is saved. Graphic devices are a form of "statistical shorthand." Since data are more simply presented, time is saved in interpreting it.

4. Interest is greater. Tables often appear cold and formal. Graphic devices can be constructed in interesting ways. Graphic devices recognize that most people would rather look at pictures than read.

5. Group presentation is easier. For presenting information to several people simultaneously, graphic devices are much better than tables.

On the negative side, graphic devices are more difficult to prepare than tables, and the amount of training needed for construction of graphs is greater. Some artistic talent and imagination are needed to prepare graphs.

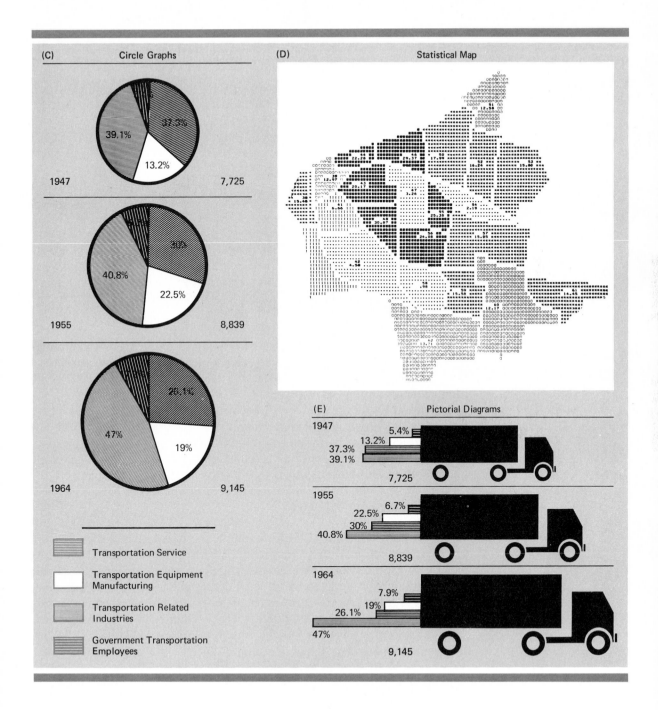

(C) Circle Graphs

1947   7,725

1955   8,839

1964   9,145

Transportation Service

Transportation Equipment
Manufacturing

Transportation Related
Industries

Government Transportation
Employees

(D) Statistical Map

(E) Pictorial Diagrams

1947   5.4%   13.2%   37.3%   39.1%   7,725

1955   6.7%   22.5%   30%   40.8%   8,839

1964   7.9%   19%   26.1%   47%   9,145

As might be expected, the expense is greater. Furthermore, graphs ordinarily cannot show exact figures as can tables.

The most popular method for presenting data is graphic presentation, which includes line or curve graphs, bar graphs, circle graphs, statistical maps, pictorial diagrams, and similar devices.

Line or curve graphs   The line or curve graph, sometimes called the line diagram, is probably the most widely used of all graphic devices. It is ideally suited to the representation of time-series data, such as is shown in Figure 23–2A. The time factor is plotted along the horizontal scale, with the data series plotted on the vertical scale. Points are then plotted in the chart and connected with lines.

Line or curve graphs are widely used to show economic and business trends. Industrial production, retail sales, and employment during certain periods of time are usually shown by this device.

Bar graphs   Bar graphs are used when statistics are to be compared. They are of two major types: vertical and horizontal. An example of a vertical bar graph, sometimes called a column graph, is shown in Figure 23–2B. The vertical bar graph ordinarily is used for comparing data of various time intervals. It is ideal, for example, in comparing the average temperatures for each month during a year.

Horizontal bar graphs are used to compare data of the same time period. A horizontal graph might be used, for example, to show customers by size of family, with a separate bar for two-person families, another for three-person families, and so on.

Construction of bar graphs is relatively simple. In the horizontal bar graph, the data being compared are shown to the left of the graph and the unit of measurement is shown at the top or bottom. In vertical bar graphs, the factors being compared are described at the bottom of the graph and the unit of measurement appears at either or both sides of the graph.

Because the length of the bar represents the quantity, bar graphs are especially easy to understand.

Circle graphs   The circle graphs—sometimes called section diagrams or pie diagrams because they are shaped like a pie and statistically segmented as a pie is cut—are another common graphic device. The circle equals 100 percent and the items being compared are given a "piece," or percentage, of the graph in proportion to their size. Circle graphs are used widely to show how the sales dollar is divided among cost of production, profit, expenses, and other factors. The distribution of the tax dollar is also shown frequently in circle graphs. Circle graphs are not desirable, however, if highly accurate comparisons are to be made. Circle graphs are shown in Figure 23–2C.

Statistical maps   Statistical maps are used when it is desirable to relate data of different geographical regions—cities, counties, trading areas, states, countries, or the world. Most statistical maps are either shaded or in dot form. Generally, the darker the shading or the heavier the concentration of dots, the greater the quantity represented. An example of a statistical map is Figure 23-2D.

Pictorial diagrams   In pictorial diagrams, sometimes called pictographs or pictograms, pictorial symbols are used to show quantities of data. Samples are shown in Figure 23–2E. Because of their novelty, cleverly constructed pictorial diagrams have important attention-getting value. They are not used, however, to present time-series information or to show data when a high degree of accuracy is needed.

THE BUSINESS REPORT

When the research, or investigation, is finished and the statistical data are analyzed, interpreted, and put in tabular or graphic form, the remaining step is to prepare a report for management. The report should be clear, impersonal, and accurate. It should be a complete presentation of information based on the research and statistical analysis.

Basic principles of report-writing

Any well-written report requires hours of hard work and careful thought. The technique of report-writing, though it is a complicated skill, can be mastered—and it is an especially valuable tool for the junior business executive. There is no more effective way than the well-written report to demonstrate one's grasp of a business problem, organizational ability, intelligence, and capacity for analysis. Often, members of higher echelons of management will make it a point to inquire about the writer of a report that impresses them and will consider such a person for more important positions.

Action taken on the information contained in a report depends in part on how well the report is written. Poorly prepared reports are likely to be confusing, misunderstood, and passed over lightly. Certain rules, if followed, are certain to improve the effectiveness of the report. Rudyard Kipling, in his poem "The Elephant's Child," most handily spelled out the basic points the business report should cover in order to be complete.

It would be worthwhile to memorize the following four lines from that poem.

> I keep six honest serving men,
> They taught me all I knew.
> Their names are what and where,
> And when, and how and why and who.[1]

Here are some additional report-writing suggestions:

1. The report should be prepared with the reader in mind. If the reader has little technical background, technical words and phrases should be kept to a minimum. Many successful report-writers feel they can be most effective if they assume that the reader knows nothing about the subject.

2. The report should be developed so that it can be read rapidly and easily. This can be accomplished through clear subtitles for all sections, topic sentences at the beginning of each paragraph, clear, crisp paragraphs, and short sentences.

3. The report should use proper English and avoid vague, unintelligible statements. It should be not only clear enough to be understood but clear enough to assure that it will not be misunderstood.

4. The report should be objective. The writer should refrain from allowing his personal feelings to intrude. Reports should refrain from exaggeration.

5. The report should be neat and attractive. It should always reflect good taste and be a credit to the writer.

6. The report should be developed to answer all of the reader's questions. The job is not to include all the writer knows, but to include all the reader needs to know.

7. The report should be well organized. This point is discussed below.

Organization of reports

Reports should be organized so that all necessary information is presented in a logical sequence. Most reports can be divided into five major sections. In the outline, commonly referred to as the *business report form*, the sections are arranged in a sequence that is desirable from the viewpoint of the busy executive.

---

[1] From Rudyard Kipling *Just So Stories*, "The Elephant's Child." Reprinted by permission of Mrs. George Bambridge, Doubleday & Company, Inc., Macmillan & Co. Ltd., and the Macmillan Company of Canada Ltd.

Introduction. The introduction answers the first question in the mind of the busy executive who finds a report on his desk. This question is "What is this report about?" The first section introduces the reader to the report by telling him concisely of its purpose, background leading up to its preparation, and methods employed in making the study. Included in this section are a title page, statement of the problem, name of the person preparing the report, and its date.

Conclusions. At first glance, it may seem odd to have the conclusions immediately after the introduction, since a conclusion is usually a summation or final statement. Here again, however, one considers the interest of the person for whom the report is prepared. The first question in the busy executive's mind after he reads the introduction is "What was found out in the investigation?" It is logical, then, that a concise listing of the major findings or conclusions should appear at this point.

Recommendations. The next step after a summary of the findings is designed to answer the executive's next question, "What should we do about the findings?" Here a recommended course of action is presented in condensed form.

Discussion or body of the report. This section, as might be expected, contains the bulk of the report, because the first three sections—the introduction, conclusions, and recommendations—to be most effective, should be concise and directly to the point. The discussion thus provides detailed information concerning the findings, the evidence and factual information on which conclusions and recommendations are based, and in general the answers to questions that might be raised. Headings and subheadings are used to make the discussion easier to read.

Appendix. The appendix, if one is necessary, contains long tables, charts, bibliographies, and any other detailed data that would materially hinder easy reading of the report itself but is needed to give substance to findings and to preserve valuable reference materials.

The popular business report form just described is highly usable for presenting business information. The order of the sections can be shifted about to suit the needs of the problems at hand, but for most purposes the form as presented above is very effective. A top executive in one of America's largest industrial concerns said of it:

> This type of report form suits people in various positions in the company interested in the work from various points of view. The busy executive, interested only in the highlights of the investigation, may read only the introduction, conclusions, and recommendations. The engineer, on the other hand, may be interested in the details supplied by the discussion, and the young fellow assigned the task of carrying out some of the recommendations will probably have to wade through the appendix.

CAUTION IN THE USE OF STATISTICAL ANALYSIS

Perhaps you have heard such statements as "Anything can be proved with statistics" or, to quote a humorous definition, "A statistician is a person who draws a mathematically precise line from an unwarranted assumption to a foregone conclusion." Unfortunately, there is a basis for these gibes of which it is prudent to be aware.

Several examples will help illustrate. Does cigarette smoking cause lung cancer? Using identical statistical information, different groups of experts have drawn different conclusions. Does fluoride added to a city's water supply reduce tooth decay? Again, on this controversial issue, opposite conclusions are drawn from identical data. Does the profit position of an industry, such as steel, justify a wage increase for employees? Quite frequently, using identical facts, labor leaders "prove" that profits are excessive and that workers are being exploited, while management "proves" that profits are so low that future plant modernization is impossible.

Frequently, the statistical "proof" that is offered, when analyzed, actually proves nothing. For example, an advertisement for cough medicine may say, "Found more effective in three out of four cases." More effective than *what* is a logical but often unanswered question.

Students are urged to be exceptionally careful in the analysis of statistical information. They should consider three key questions:

1. Did the persons collecting the information have a point to "prove" or were they objective?

2. Were reliable statistical techniques employed throughout the research procedure?

3. Is all the pertinent information included, or is some factual information withheld?

Above all, it should be remembered that statistics can be dangerous in the hands of people who lack proper qualifications to collect and analyze them or have a vested interest in proving a predetermined conclusion.

Forecasting

Forecasting is an especially precarious field. Whereas forecasters are armed these days with increasingly sophisticated tools and methods and are growing in public visibility, their output is not always soundly conceived and is often inaccurate. *Business Week*, in an article that was critical, declared, "In a sense, almost all of them [forecasters] owe their success to luck rather than 20/20 foresight." In 1972, reviewing forecasts that were made for 1971, the *New York Times* stated, "The predictions made by the business community . . . fared better than those of the Federal Government, which had an exceptionally poor year." The article went on to say, "Forecasters long have had an unsavory reputation in some quarters and those who take them seriously should be aware that they operate with total disregard of the possible legal consequences of their exercises." Among the many forecasts that were cited as being wrong, the biggest and most influential was one in the 1971 President's Economic Report on GNP, which missed the mark by some $18 billion. It was reported at a conference on forecasting techniques that of four major forecasts studied over the 1964–69 period, three were found to have made worse predictions than a "naive" model in which growth in the future would be the same as it was in the past.

It is wise, then, to develop a healthy skepticism about all statistics, forecasts, and generalizations. "Scrutinize the obvious" is excellent advice. For example, in business circles and elsewhere we often hear talk about the increasing youthfulness of the "average American." Actually, the opposite is true. Both birth and death rates have declined, so of course, the "average American" is getting older.

PEOPLE AND THEIR IDEAS
Louis I. Dublin

A statistical innovator

Louis I. Dublin achieved world-wide recognition as one of the outstanding authorities on the applications of vital statistics to public health. Throughout his long and distinguished career with the Metropolitan Life Insurance Company, Dr. Dublin demonstrated the many important uses to which statistics could be put in combating disease and assessing public health.

Born in 1882 in Lithuania, Dr. Dublin trained as a biologist and statistician at the College of the City of New York and Columbia University and received a Ph.D. from Columbia in 1904. He joined the Metropolitan Life Insurance Company in 1909 and two years later was chosen to organize the company's Statistical Bureau. He remained director of its operations until his retirement in 1952, during which time he amassed data from the health records of 30 million policy-holders. Under his leadership, the Bureau won international acclaim for the outstanding manner in which it obtained and disseminated significant information about mortality, causes of death and illness, population characteristics, and the changing patterns of American family life.

Dr. Dublin accurately foresaw, twenty years in advance, the great decline in the incidence of tuberculosis in the United States. He was among the first to focus on the growing menace of diabetes and the role of obesity in shortening life. He spent a full year researching the facts on fluoridation before giving the program his overwhelming endorsement. His report *Water Fluoridation: Facts, No Myths*, was published by the Manhattan Public Affairs Committee.

Concerned with all aspects of public health, Dr. Dublin served as president of the American Statistical Association (1924), the American Public Health Association (1931–32), and the Population Association of America (1935–36). His advice was frequently sought by both voluntary health groups and the government; he served, at various times, as Director of the American Cancer Society, the National Tuberculosis Association, and the National Health Council, and as consultant to the Bureau of the Census, the Public Health Service, the National Research Council, and the Veterans Administration. During World Wars I and II, he was closely involved with the activities of the Red Cross.

In 1959 Dr. Dublin received the Sedgwick Memorial Award of the American Public Health Association, and in 1961 he was elected to the Insurance Hall of Fame—one of the highest honors awarded in the life insurance field. He was the author of numerous books and articles, among them, *Twenty-Five Years of Health Progress, Suicide: A Sociological and Statistical Study, Factbook on Man from Birth to Death*, and his autobiography, *After Eighty Years*. Dr. Dublin died in March 1969 at the age of eighty-six.

CONTEMPORARY ISSUES
Situation 23

What is the rightful place of statistical analysis?

On the subject of statistics, John and Ray were, as usual, on opposite sides: John was very statistically oriented; Ray was not. In fact, Ray seemed to be unduly afraid of the subject and attacked it wherever possible. After the class period, the two continued their argument.

"To me statisticians, as a class, grossly overestimate their capabilities. Besides that they can't communicate. If you ask them to explain what they are talking about, they only make things even more confusing. I get lost after the first sentence of the so-called explanation. I've never yet met a statistician who could communicate to nonstatisticians about his area."

"The trouble with you, Ray, is that you have a mental block about statistics," John replied. "You don't really want to understand—otherwise, you would make the effort and realize the importance of statistics."

"Why don't the statisticians you admire so much do a better job of forecasting, if what they do is so objective and scientific?" Ray asked. "I read an article that reviewed the annual forecasts of the leading economists—supposedly expert statisticians—for the past ten years. I could have done a better job reading tea leaves. In fact, when some U.S. senators were investigating the outrageous fees charged by mutual funds, they proved that they could use a dart board and do as well selecting stock as the statistical experts did."

"You can't condemn the whole field of statistics because it falls down occasionally in the area of forecasting," John said.

"But," Ray persisted, "they fall down in more than forecasting. What about planning? Why are our new airports inadequate on the day they are dedicated? Open a new expressway and congestion occurs at points that were never anticipated. Planners could use a little common sense, in addition to statistics."

SITUATION EVALUATION

1. Why are some people repelled by or afraid of statistics? What can be done to make statistics more understandable to average people?

2. How would you answer Ray's charges?

3. Do statisticians have the sole responsibility for forecasting and planning?

4. What are some advantages of statistics—advantages John failed to point out in his argument?

BUSINESS CHRONICLE

Using statistics to make business decisions

One of Mr. King's dreams is to build a small city for approximately 50,000 people to be located near an existing major metropolitan area. The new city will include residences of all types—schools, churches, hospitals, shopping areas, office buildings, municipal services, and some manufacturing facilities. It is expected that at least ten years will be needed to complete the project. Mr. King wants to develop this project outside Florida for two reasons: (1) He doesn't want all his eggs in one carton if the Florida economy slumps and (2) he wants the challenge of working in a new environment. Mr. King asked his marketing research director to make a preliminary investigation and select what he feels are the top ten metropolitan centers for the new project. Mr. King is interested in such factors as population growth rates, climate, and employment stability. King plans to cater to families with incomes in excess of $15,000.

The marketing director assembles the following information about the ten metropolitan centers he feels are the best candidates for the project.

METRO-POLITAN CENTER	POPULATION CHANGE IN PERCENT 1960–70	PERCENTAGE OF FAMILY HOUSEHOLDS WITH INCOME OVER $15,000 IN 1970	AVERAGE TEMPERATURE JANUARY (AVERAGE FOR THIRTY-YR. PERIOD 1930–60)	AVERAGE TEMPERATURE JULY	PERCENTAGE UNEMPLOYED 1971	MEDIAN AGE 1971
Atlanta	36.7	26.1	44.7	78.9	3.6	27.5
Denver	24.8	24.8	28.5	72.9	3.0	29.2
Houston	40.0	22.6	53.6	83.0	3.1	26.1
Indianapolis	17.5	23.9	29.1	75.2	4.9	27.3
Memphis	14.2	16.2	41.5	81.3	4.2	26.2
Minneapolis	22.4	28.6	12.4	72.3	4.5	29.5
Phoenix	45.8	21.3	49.7	89.8	4.5	27.7
Pittsburgh	−0.2	18.8	28.9	72.1	5.3	33.6
San Diego	31.4	23.2	56.2	71.1	6.2	25.8
St. Louis	12.3	22.9	31.9	78.1	6.2	31.8

Source: *Statistical Abstract of the United States, 1972*, pp. 179, 838–897.

QUESTIONS

1. Do you agree with Mr. King's reasons for not wanting to build his new project in Florida? Do you think satellite cities have a good future? Why?

2. Based on the information presented for the ten cities selected as candidates for "The Kingdom" (the name King has tentatively selected), which do you feel is the most promising? Why?

3. What additional kinds of information, economic, legislative, competitive, etc., would be required to make a final decision?

APPLICATION EXERCISES

1. Assume you are commissioned to determine which of the states named below has, on the average, the most reckless drivers. You are given the following information about death rates per 10,000 caused by automobile accidents for selected states for a recent year.

STATE	DEATH RATE PER 1,000	STATE	DEATH RATE PER 10,000
Alabama	3.73	Michigan	2.69
California	2.52	Nebraska	3.04
Florida	3.12	New York	1.70
Idaho	4.02	Ohio	2.39
Massachusetts	1.59	West Virginia	3.01

a. Why are death rates alone not enough to determine which state has the most reckless drivers?

b. What additional information do you need to determine which state has the most reckless drivers?

c. How do you account for the apparent safe driving of people in Massachusetts and New York?

d. "Statisticians should be careful not to jump to conclusions." Explain.

2. According to the *Statistical Abstract,* the birth and death rates per 1,000 for recent years are as follows:

	BIRTHS	DEATHS
1960	23.7	9.5
1965	19.4	9.4
1968	17.5	9.7
1969	17.7	9.5
1970	18.2	9.4

In a brief report explain
a. Why birth rates vary significantly more than death rates.
b. Why, despite continuing improvements in medical science, the death rate changed very little between 1960 and 1970.

QUESTIONS

1. What is meant by the statement, "Statistics are management tools"? How do statistics serve as tools of management?

2. What are the different kinds of average? What are the uses of each? Which average is most useful? Explain your answers.

3. What are index numbers? Of what value are they?

4. Define and give examples of a sample and a universe. Explain the use of samples in research.

5. Define and explain the purpose of time-series analysis. Define seasonal fluctuation, cyclical fluctuation, and secular trend. Why is a knowledge of each important to a business?

6. Devise three specific business situations in which you would make use of graphical presentation of statistical data. In each case, what would be the advantages and disadvantages of using such a presentation?

7. What are the purposes of a business report? What are the rules for writing an effective business report?

8. "While we see many figures, we still have to communicate in language" is a statement made by a key executive who was complaining about the inability of many college-trained people to write effectively. What was the significance of his remark?

9. What are some of the dangers of placing too much reliance on statistics?

24

business research

CHAPTER 24

WHAT IS RESEARCH?
Business Research Defined. Reasons for Increased Interest in Research.

TYPES OF RESEARCH
Basic Research. Background Research. Applied Research.

RESEARCH METHODOLOGY: THE SCIENTIFIC METHOD

STEPS IN THE RESEARCH PROCEDURE
Recognition of the Problem. Informal Investigation. Formal Investigation.

SOURCES OF BUSINESS INFORMATION
Journals. Directories. Government Publications. How to Locate Specific Secondary Information. The Balance between Information, Research, and Experience.

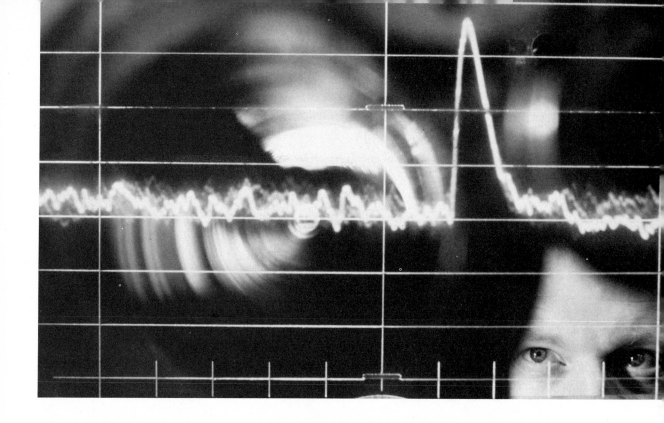

and sources of information

As a businessman, Norton Simon parlayed a $7,000 investment in a bankrupt orange juice plant into a $1 billion conglomerate with 10 divisions that produces everything from catsup to matches to magazines to television programs. As an art collector, he has assembled one of the world's greatest private art collections. In 1965, he paid $2,234,000 for a Rembrandt painting, the second highest price ever paid for a single picture. People close to Simon claim that the worst you can say to him is, "We have always done it this way." Reporters who interview him say they find themselves answering more questions than they ask. It is also said that Simon can hardly be imagined doing anything halfway. *"He gets absolutely all the facts possible before making a move."* Research, the subject of this chapter, is the fact-finding arm of business.

WHAT IS RESEARCH?

Money expenditures are an indication of the tremendous efforts that have gone into research and development in recent years. Total expenditures on R&D (as it is commonly abbreviated) for all sectors (private and public) skyrocketed from $6 billion in 1955 to an estimated $28 billion in 1971 (see Figure 24–1). Yet, it is somewhat startling to note that in 1969 Stanford Research Institute stated that "60 percent of the products of the seventies have not been invented yet."

The basic key to progress in any field is research, the chief function of which is to solve problems. Earlier, you read about many of the problems of business management. A few random examples are:

Should the package or design of a product be changed?

How can turnover of employees be reduced?

Should a new store be located in or near a shopping center?

Should advertising for a particular product be directed at women or men, at middle- or low-income groups, at farmers or urban residents?

How can bad debts be reduced?

How can a more equitable wage and salary scale be established?

How much should plant capacity be increased in the next five years?

Should prices be increased?

What new products should be developed to stay ahead of competition?

Research in business methods, practices, forecasting, and markets is now firmly established. Most large and medium-sized firms have created research departments. Despite its nearly universal acceptance, the research function is seriously misunderstood by some who still regard it as a mysterious, somewhat impractical "academic" function. Actually, research activities are as practical as they are interesting.

Business research defined

Business research can be defined as the orderly gathering of facts and the interpretation of information about business problems. It can be thought of also as a planned procedure for making improvements in business practices.

Research in engineering, chemistry, and physics aids business through the development of new and improved products and production techniques. Because of the specialized technical background required for such research, however, it is usually conducted only by those trained in

Figure **24–1**
Research and Development Funds by Performance Sector and by Source, 1956–71

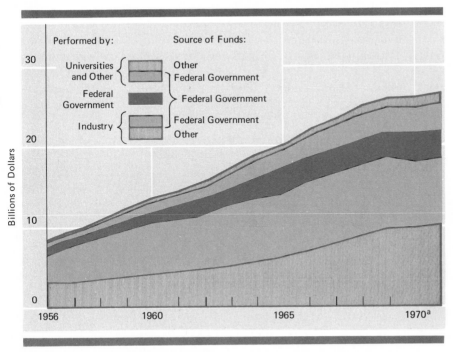

ª 1970 and 1971 estimated.
Source: *Statistical Abstract of the United States*, 1972, p. 518.

the physical sciences. Here we shall consider mainly those forms of research performed by persons trained in business and economics and in related social sciences.

Research can be conducted in an unplanned, informal manner, as a sideline activity of some individual who has other major duties, or as a planned, full-time activity of an individual or department. The small merchant who makes an effort to listen carefully to comments of his customers about the quality, price, and variety of goods and then bases his merchandising decisions on such facts is carrying on research informally. Such gathering of information, while helpful, is inclined to be haphazard. In the remaining part of this chapter, the word "research" refers only to the orderly or planned gathering and analysis of facts.

Reasons for increased interest in research

Two basic factors underlie management's increased emphasis on research. First, business is becoming more complex. Rule-of-thumb pro-

Figure **24–2**
Typical Research Findings for TV Viewing Hours per Day by Household Members

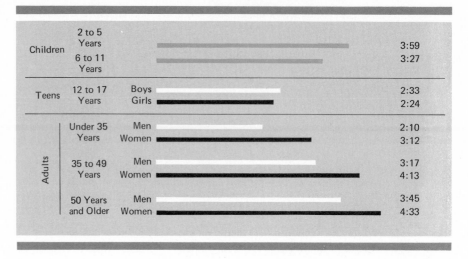

How would this information affect advertising expenditures?

cedures and guesswork can no longer be relied on for business decisions. To guess at how many units can be sold, what the selling price should be, how the product should be transported, and how it should be advertised is asking for failure. An automobile manufacturer will spend enormous amounts to bring out a new model. Ford, for example, spent $71 million on just the development costs of the Maverick. Surely a maximum effort should be made to reduce the risk of failure. Research provides information that narrows the margin of risk in decision-making.

Second, business is highly competitive. If an error is made in product design (so that people find the design less attractive than that of the competition), the sale of the product will suffer. Advertising, to be effective, also requires various kinds of research. Each business must try to invest its advertising budget, for example, to reach the greatest number of potential customers at the lowest possible cost. Figure 24–2 is an example of research related to advertising.

The overriding reason for the growth in R&D is that business leaders know that effective research leads to profits. Studies of corporations show that companies that are leaders in research and the consequent marketing of successful new products are also more profitable. For example, the tiny transistor, invented in 1947 at the American Telephone and Telegraph Company's Bell Laboratories, gave birth to the solid-state electronics industry, which in 1972 had sales of about $2.7 billion and employed some 800,000 people.

TYPES OF RESEARCH

Basic research

The term "basic," or "pure," research refers to investigation whose chief function is to add to human knowledge, practical or theoretical, rather than to solve a problem. It is investigation for investigation's sake. A college professor interested in the effects of color on children's sleeping habits may find that children surrounded by certain shades of gray at bedtime go to sleep more quickly than those surrounded by shades of red. Such findings are the result of pure research.

At a later date, however, a manufacturer may take the professor's findings and apply them in producing wallpaper colors for children's bedrooms. Thus, basic research often provides the basis for later business application. Most basic research is conducted by foundations and universities and through sponsorship of the federal government. It is understandable that mainly the largest businesses in fields such as chemicals, medicine, and electronics, conduct basic research.

Background research

Background research provides data needed for other types of research. A good example is most of the work done by the Bureau of the Census. Census findings concerning backgrounds of populations as to educational attainments, occupational classifications, and condition of housing provide a wealth of statistical data that are used later in both pure and applied research. Insurance industry statistics of life expectancy, disease rates, and incidence of accidents are further examples of background research.

Applied research

Applied research is concerned with solving specific business problems. From the standpoint of volume, money invested, and people employed, applied research receives a great deal more attention than either pure or background research. Applied research can be discussed according to the areas in which it takes place: product development, personnel, economic analysis, finance, and marketing.

Product and technological research   The greatest share of a company's R&D expenditure goes into new product and technological development. Significantly, these expenditures grow each year, because they are directly tied to business profits. Management has been deeply impressed with studies showing that companies that expand the fastest and are the most profitable are also the ones that introduce the newest and most improved products. Stepped-up innovation continues to shorten product life; hence companies that do not wish to fall behind must invest increasingly in R&D.

Personnel research   The field of personnel management uses research to determine how best to select, train, compensate, and motivate employees. One of the basic tools used in personnel research is the job analysis. This procedure, which was discussed in Chapter 11, determines what qualifications and training an individual needs to perform the job, what safety measures should be taken to protect the worker, and how much he should be paid.

Another type of personnel research is the motion-and-time study. This involves careful observation of the work performed by individuals, the object being to eliminate wasted motion and time.

The employee-attitude survey is another research technique. Employees are asked questions that will reveal the state of their morale, and management can use the results to take appropriate action to improve it.

Economic research   Economic research is concerned with economic trends likely to affect a business in a general rather than a specific way. Such research is generally conducted by large corporations or trade associations for the purpose of planning for the years ahead. It may include studies pertaining to

1. Long-term growth possibilities of the firm

2. Forecasts of economic conditions, such as changes in national wealth and income, and how these changes will affect the business

3. Industry trends and developments

4. Long-run strength of competitors

Financial research   Financial research is concerned with financial planning. Research may be conducted to determine how best to secure additional capital, invest company reserves, refinance maturing issues, reduce company indebtedness, and reduce fixed financial charges on borrowed funds. The objectives of financial research are to place the company in the most advantageous financial position and to help maximize profits.

Marketing research   Probably more applied business research is conducted in marketing than in all other business areas combined, the reason being that the market is so unpredictable. Because of its dynamic nature, it must continually be reexamined and evaluated in order to keep abreast of changes.

The scope of marketing research is extensive. A petroleum company making traffic counts to determine location desirability, a newspaper securing education and income data to develop profiles of its subscribers, a taste test by a beverage concern to produce popular flavors, a tractor manufacturer interviewing farmers to discover why its tractors are not selling, and a study by an automobile firm on trade-in values of used cars — these are all examples of marketing research. The field is especially interesting and educational to work in because of the range of projects undertaken.

RESEARCH METHODOLOGY: THE SCIENTIFIC METHOD

As a general principle, the quality of research is determined by how closely the scientific method is — or can be — followed.

Employment of the scientific method in business has lagged behind its use in the physical sciences, where exact measurements, experimentation, and testing are accepted practices. More and more business researchers, however, are applying the scientific method to business problems. Briefly stated, its chief characteristics are given below.

1. The scientific method requires rational, as contrasted with emotional, thinking. Logic, the method of accurate, systematic reasoning, must be employed throughout. It requires that the researcher be free from personal prejudice or bias. Past experiences, intuition, or opinionated views of persons in authority should not be permitted to sway the researchers, for permitting personal habits, feelings, or beliefs to affect attitudes toward the study of a problem is unscientific.

2. Ideally, the scientific method requires that the findings in any investigation be reproducible. In the physical sciences, this requirement is axiomatic — that is, all scientists using the methodology described in a research report will reproduce identical findings. Unfortunately, the ideal of reproducibility is seldom achieved in the social sciences; and because a large portion of business research is in the social sciences, much of it is *not* reproducible. In one instance, a large soap company commissioned three established marketing research companies to do research on an identical project. Each company produced a different set of findings; they did not agree with one another.

Much of the research in the social sciences and in business deals with people and their behavior. Since behavior is largely unpredictable, the ideal of reproducibility in research is seldom possible to attain. Because of this social science and business research findings can seldom be used without combining them with past experience, sound judgment, and, indeed, intuition. The most that can be claimed for social science/business research is that it can increase the odds for making right decisions. This point was once capsulized in a Sherlock Holmes story in this manner: "People as individuals are unpredictable enigmas. In the aggregate, they tend to become mathematical certainties."

3. The scientific method requires complete independence for the researcher. Far too much research is conducted to "prove a point" rather than to discover a solution. Individuals not thoroughly disciplined in the scientific method unwittingly uncover "evidence" that supports an incorrect conclusion.

A cartoon once very perceptively used this point as its basis for humor. It showed a harassed assistant entering a door marked "research." His comment to the researcher was, "Quick, my boss just thought of a fact, now he wants you to prove it."

4. The scientific method requires thoroughness. All possible solutions to a problem must be explored, for what sometimes seems to be the least likely answer may turn out to be the best.

5. The scientific method requires that the researcher be completely honest in the interpretation of research findings. While deliberate dishonesty in research is rare, too frequently otherwise high-quality research loses its value because the researcher hedges in his findings. The following is an example of faulty "research."

Mr. Smith was director of marketing research for the manufacturer of a food item. Company sales volume was declining, and there was some evidence, from consumer complaints, that the product flavor had deteriorated. The company president held a very definite opinion that the product flavor was perfectly all right. He finally authorized the research director to undertake a product taste study. The resulting study clearly showed that deteriorated product flavor was the cause of the sales decline. The market research director remembered the company president's attitude and, rather than risk offending him, reported that the product was "apparently satisfactory." Because of this nonscientific, nonprofessional approach, no corrective action was taken to improve the product until much later.

STEPS IN THE RESEARCH PROCEDURE

Recognition of the problem

The first step in the research procedure is recognition that a problem exists. The personnel director may observe an increased turnover of employees and undertake research to determine why. Or, if the sales manager notes that sales to drug outlets are on the decline, this too is a problem that may require research.

Management becomes aware of problems in many ways. One research project very often leads to discovery of other problem areas. For example, a study to determine the effectiveness of salesmen may suggest that a study be conducted of the procedure used to select salesmen or of the actual sales potential in different territories. It is the responsibility of researchers to discover and recognize problems, as well as to encourage others within the company to do so.

Problems in business are not always easily recognized. Much thinking and preliminary exploration is often necessary to detect areas in which research is needed, as the following quotation suggests:

> . . . the ability to perceive . . . the occasion for a problem, and especially a problem *whose solution has a bearing on the solution of other problems*, is not a common talent among men. For no rule can be given by means of which men learn to ask significant questions. It is a mark of scientific genius to be sensitive to difficulties where less gifted people pass by untroubled with doubt.[1]

Informal investigation

After a problem has been recognized, it must be defined as clearly as possible. This involves gathering all available information. The researcher will discuss the problem with company executives, employees, wholesalers, retailers, consumers, or anyone else who may be able to throw light on the subject. During the informal investigation, a special effort should be made to check all company records and published information. The informal investigation should result in a very concise definition of the problem and the determination of the most logical method for collecting the data needed to solve it. The decision as to whether or not to undertake the project is often not made until after the informal investiga-

---

[1] Morris Cohen and Ernest Nagel, *An Introduction to Logic and Scientific Method*, Harcourt Brace Jovanovich, 1934, p. 200.

tion, which may reveal, for example, that costs for the project would be too high or that meaningful results would not be forthcoming.

Formal investigation

Step three in the research procedure is the actual collection of data in an orderly, systematic manner. Three basic methods are used to collect data: survey, observation, and experiment.

Survey   The survey is a procedure for collecting data by asking questions and is the most common business research method. Sometimes referred to as the "questionnaire technique," since the information is usually recorded on questionnaires, the survey is used for a variety of purposes. Consumers may be questioned about their taste preferences, buying habits, living standards, and personal interests and opinions. Businesspeople may be queried about their production and sales plans, expansion programs, attitudes toward new and improved products, opinions about probable economic trends, employment practices, credit and other business policies, and similar topics.

Two basic kinds of question are asked in the survey method: factual questions (What kind of car do you drive? What brand of soup did you last purchase?) and opinion questions (What do you like most about your present brand of breakfast food?)

Survey information can be collected in several ways, some of which are described below.

Mail questionnaires.   The mail questionnaire is a set of questions sent to a selected group of people. This technique is often used when information from a wide area is needed. When the number of people who return questionnaires is large, it is a low-cost way to collect information. The chief disadvantage is that often only a small percentage of people return the questionnaires. Also, the people who respond may not be typical of the universe from which the sample was selected.

Personal interviews.   In the personal interview, which is used in an endless variety of research studies, trained interviewers ask questions of selected people. While interviews generally are held in homes, offices, or stores, researchers occasionally interview people at athletic events, on streets, in buses, outside theaters, and so on. The personal-interview technique usually results in a high percentage of interviews in relation to people approached, thus overcoming a disadvantage of the mail questionnaire. On the negative side, personal interviews are expensive. The "human element" is also present, which can cause bias in the answers given by the respondent.

Telephone interviews.   The telephone is used extensively for collecting information, especially about radio and television listening habits.

One organization specializes in calling a certain number of people daily and asking, "Is your radio or television set turned on? If so, to what program are you listening?" Telephone interviewing is the quickest way to obtain data, and the cost per interview is low. Interviews, however, must be brief, and questions ordinarily cannot be of a personal nature because of the reluctance of people to talk about personal matters to someone they have not met.

Panel, or consumer-jury, interviews. A fourth means for securing consumer response is the panel, or consumer jury, in which the people who form the panel are selected carefully to represent a group typical of those to whom the business wants its product to appeal. Panels range in size from a dozen people to several hundred or more. Members of the panel may be questioned about anything from their shoe-buying habits to their favorite household pets. The main advantage of the panel is that information on many topics is readily available. Members of consumer panels may or may not be compensated for their cooperation.

The panel method has its limitations. Its members may answer questions as "experts" rather than as ordinary shoppers. Moreover, panels are hard to maintain; people drop out, fail to cooperate, or otherwise make it difficult to keep the group a representative one.

Observation   The observation method is a procedure for collecting data by actually watching certain events take place. Unlike the survey method, no questions are asked. The observation method can be used for a variety of studies—for example:

Workers and their jobs. A trained observer can watch workers perform their tasks and record the exact movements made and the time taken to complete each movement. Motion picture cameras and video tape machines are used to make studies of this kind. Results lead to work simplification and time savings.

Locations for business establishments. The observation method is used to find suitable locations for stores and other businesses. The number of cars passing a location, for example, is of value in site selection for service stations. Much observation takes the form of what are called "traffic counts," which may be of either foot or vehicle traffic.

The chief advantage of the observation technique is that it is objective and can be quite accurate. It reveals what actually takes place rather than what people say takes place. The major disadvantage is expense. One researcher can observe relatively little at any one time. Moreover, if the problem under study relates to consumer attitudes, observation is not likely to make clear why the given consumer behaves as he does.

Experiment   This method is used to collect facts through controlled experiments or tests. It is often the most reliable and scientific research method. Examples include experiments that test:

The effectiveness of advertising. Firms selling goods by mail frequently test the strength, or "pull," of sales letters by the experimental method. One sales letter is sent to a mailing list of, say, ten thousand people, while a second letter describing the same product in a different manner is sent to a second group of ten thousand. The letter resulting in the larger number of orders is used for later sales campaigns.

The effectiveness of training. In this research experiment, training is given to one group of employees but not to a second, comparable group. The production records of the two groups are compared to determine whether training increased production and, if so, by how much. By keeping a record of performance of the two groups over an extended period of time, management can determine both the long- and short-run significance of training.

The effects of working conditions on employee output. Various experiments have been conducted to determine desirable room temperature, the effect of music on employee production, whether employees produce more if they work individually or in groups, and so on.

Future products and techniques. A manufacturer who wishes to introduce a new product will want to be sure, before producing in volume, that the product will receive customer acceptance. He may, therefore, conduct a number of experiments to determine the best merchandising methods. For example, he may test the price by selecting several comparable cities and selling the product at different prices in each. In this way, the manufacturer is helped in determining the ideal price. In similar fashion, the manufacturer may test advertising appeals and sales campaigns to learn how best to market a product.

The experimental method, while often desirable, is not used extensively because, first, controlled experiments are difficult to construct; second, experiments take a good deal of time and money; and, third, they may reveal company areas of interest to competitors because they are often carried on in public.

SOURCES OF BUSINESS INFORMATION**

Information useful in solving business problems comes from both primary and secondary sources. Primary sources of information are those that supply original data. The researcher collects such information by going directly to people who have first-hand knowledge. A primary source to determine consumer reaction to a new product would be the people who use or could use the product. The methods described in the preceding section are all used to collect primary information. Secondary sources are those based on information already collected from primary sources.

It is almost impossible for students to appreciate how much secondary data is available. Often, primary research projects are undertaken when the needed information is already available in published form. *A primary objective for all who study business administration should be to learn where to find information that already exists.*

Briefly discussed below are some of the major sources of business information. This description is only representative; to list all of the thousands of secondary sources is, naturally, impractical.[2]

Journals

Personnel management.   Leading periodicals in personnel management include *Personnel and Guidance Journal*, *Personnel*, and *Personnel Administrator*. These magazines contain articles and reports on the performance of the various personnel functions, such as hiring, compensating, and training workers. Other articles concern such matters as fringe benefits, methods for measuring worker productivity, and personnel research.

Marketing.   The field of marketing has several important journals and magazines, including *Journal of Marketing*, *Journal of Marketing Research*, *Purchasing*, *Sales Management*, and *Industrial Marketing*. These publications present a wide variety of information about recent govern-

[2] Other general references are listed at the beginning of the glossary in the appendix.

ment legislation, research projects completed, and specific company practices.

Advertising. Advertising is one of the most highly specialized areas of business, and, accordingly, a number of periodicals are devoted exclusively to it. The most important are *Advertising Age, Broadcasting,* and *Advertising and Sales Promotion.* Emphasis is on research, news about advertising agencies and personnel, and methods and techniques in advertising.

Insurance. Excellent information about current practices and problems in the field of insurance can be found in *Best's Review, Statistical Bulletin of the Metropolitan Life Insurance Company,* and *National Underwriter.*

Retailing. *Women's Wear Daily, Journal of Retailing, Chain Store Age, Vending Times,* and *Department Store Management* are some of the leading publications in this field. Trends in fashion, reports on consumer research, retail sales, store-management activities, and sources of merchandise are major areas covered.

Transportation. Ideas for solving transportation problems can be found in *Railway Age, Airlift, Distribution World Wide,* and *Traffic Management.* Among the topics discussed are rate structures, improvements in equipment, operational problems, and news of competitive practices.

Finance. The field of finance is very well covered in business publications, among which are *Barron's, Financial World, Wall Street Journal,* and *Banking.* Data on credit policies, the financial condition of industry, economic trends, and information about specific financial practices are included.

Office management. Individuals interested in learning more about latest office-management practices will find *Office, Executive,* and *Office Products and Secretary* helpful.

Labor relations. Leading publications in this area are *American Labor News, Industrial and Labor Relations Review,* and *Labor.*

General industry. Current information concerning production processes and techniques, such as maintenance of equipment, automation, and new products, is available in several publications, including *Factory, Survey of Current Business,* and *Steel.*

Management. There are several magazines that stress the importance and application of sound management. *Nation's Business, Harvard Business Review, Dun's Review, Business Week, Industrial Management,* and *Fortune* are leading magazines in this area.

Directories

A business directory contains detailed information about specific companies or industries. Dozens of directories are available to the businessman. Most of them fall into one of three categories: directories of sources of supply, directories of periodicals, and directories of corporations.

Directories of sources of supply.　A leading directory of this type is *Thomas' Register of American Manufacturers*, which is a purchasing guide supplying the names and addresses of manufacturers of thousands of different products. All manufacturers are listed under product headings. Thus, under "brushes," all brush manufacturers are listed. Such a directory is very helpful to purchasing agents, who need to know sources of supply. Companies selling to specific industries also find the *Thomas' Register* helpful.

Specialized one-industry directories are available for food, janitor's supplies, metal products, eating places, and other specific industries.

Directories of periodicals.　Directories of this kind are intended to help advertisers select media in which to advertise. Periodical directories give key information about magazines, newspapers, radio, and television. Specific facts about publication dates, circulation figures, production techniques, and advertising rates are included.

The most widely used media directory is *Standard Rate and Data Service*. This publication comes in several sections, the most important being: newspapers; radio and television; consumer magazines, farm publications, transportation advertising; and business papers. Another directory of this type is *Ayer's Directory of Publications*.

Directories of corporations.　These directories supply detailed information about corporations. Information about a specific company usually covers location of the business, date of organization, history and growth, methods of financing, extent and kind of indebtedness, names of key executives, real estate owned, and similar topics. Widely known corporation directories are *Moody's Investors Service* and *Standard and Poor's Corporation Services*.

Government publications

The largest single source of published business information is the federal government. Research reports and statistics on almost every conceivable business problem are published by various federal agencies. Chief of these agencies are the Department of Agriculture, the Department of Commerce, and the Department of Labor.

Department of Agriculture.　This department issues publications helpful to the farmer and to the thousands of firms that process, manufacture, and sell farm products. Some of these are *Agricultural Situation*, issued monthly, which gives reports on farm prices, production, and economic problems in agriculture; *Agricultural Marketing*, issued monthly, which includes a wide variety of agricultural information and statistics on marketing, size of harvests, prices, and similar matters; and

Agricultural Statistics, issued annually, which includes analytical statistics for agriculture and related fields.

Department of Commerce.   The Department of Commerce publishes
more information of value to the businesspeople than any other government agency. The Census Bureau, a division of the Department of Commerce, collects huge quantities of statistics. Every ten years a census of
population is taken that, besides counting the people, reveals where they
live, their race, birthplace, national origin, education, marital status,
age, employment, and other characteristics. Such statistics are very
helpful in determining the size and composition of markets.

Other censuses include the Census of Agriculture, Housing Census,
Census of Manufacturers, Census of Transportation, and Census of Business. Each of these contains a wealth of information valuable to business.

The Department of Commerce also publishes *Survey of Current Business,* a monthly periodical with articles and statistics on business activity
and economic conditions.

Patent Commission.   Few people are aware that patents and the
names and addresses of their holders are readily available.[3]

How to locate specific secondary information

A certain amount of skill is needed to consult secondary sources efficiently. To search through thousands of publications in a hit-or-miss
fashion would be tedious, expensive, and a waste of time. Correct procedure requires that the researcher learn how to use library services.

Many large companies maintain well-equipped technical and business
libraries. Municipal and university libraries are open to almost anyone
conducting research. While libraries have trained personnel to assist in
finding information, the researcher should be able to help himself. Of
primary importance is a knowledge of how to use these source indices,
a few of which are listed below.

1. Business Periodicals Index.   Articles from several hundred publications are listed.

2. Ulrick's International Periodical Directory.   Periodicals from various countries in business related fields are given.

3. The Public Affairs Information Service.   Important articles on public affairs and economics are classified in this index.

---

[3] To get a copy of a patent, send the patent number and 50¢ to the Commissioner of Patents,
Washington, D.C. 20231. (Patents on designs are 20 cents each.) To reach an inventor or
assignee, write to the individual in care of the Commissioner of Patents and be sure to
cite the patent number.

4. Readers' Guide to Periodical Literature.   This index classifies the articles published in hundreds of magazines under subject headings.

The balance between information, research, and experience

We have now considered the use of primary sources of information (research) and secondary sources of information (publications and reports). In doing so we are impressed with how much effort one must expend to keep informed. The successful manager makes information absorption a way of life. Why do businesspeople so relentlessly seek knowledge? The answer has been provided by the sages: knowledge is power.

Keeping abreast of knowledge, never easy, grows even more complex. Paradoxically, as the world becomes smaller and more affluent, business and markets become larger and more sophisticated. This growing complexity caused one astute person to remark that the computer *had* to be invented—and, fortunately, it *was* invented. Today, men are able to extend their minds through use of the computer at the very point in space and time when it becomes most essential for them to do so.

However, even with computers, a wealth of secondary information to draw upon, and the ability to undertake research, many, if not most, business decisions are nevertheless still made on the basis of personal experience. Experience is relied upon so widely because business is fast-moving and there is, in most instances, not enough time to gather sufficient information each time a decision has to be made. As a result, most business decisions are made with insufficient and inaccurate knowledge.

Because experience is used most extensively, let us consider the matter of experience before we close this chapter. Experience is indeed a good school for knowledge; however the tuition is high. In fact, it is so high that Bismarck was led to observe: "Fools say they learn by experience. I prefer to profit by other's experience." From this statement we can profit from two points about experience: *we should learn to rely on the experience of others as well as our own.* Business people who are most effective are those who know how to use and draw upon experience of others. The second point is: *Experience becomes obsolete; we must guard against making decisions on the basis of experience that is no longer valid.*

In summary, then, the individual interested in becoming an effective decision-maker will (1) devise ways to keep his experience current, (2) learn to gather and draw on the experience of others, (3) observe carefully what goes on in the business environment, and, importantly, (4) will strive to learn from his mistakes. There is wisdom in the old saying: "Fool me once, shame on you. Fool me twice, shame on me."

PEOPLE AND THEIR IDEAS
David Sarnoff

RCA's old man of the future

For more than half a century David Sarnoff had been fascinated by the possibilities of transforming scientific theory and laboratory technology in electronics and communications into goods and services for the betterment of mankind. At the age of seventy-eight, he was active chairman of the board of the Radio Corporation of America (RCA), the largest communications organization in the world.

David Sarnoff was born in 1891 in a tiny village in Minsk, Russia. In 1900 he emigrated to America, where his father had come a few years earlier. He attended New York City schools but took a job selling newspapers to help support his family. By the time he was fifteen, he had become the principal support of his ill father, his mother, three brothers, and a sister. He began working as a messenger boy for the Commercial Cable Company, learned the Morse Code, and soon became a wireless operator for the Marconi Wireless Telegraph Company. In 1912 he picked up the message that the *Titanic* was sinking and stayed at his station seventy-two hours relaying messages to aid rescue operations.

He was appointed commercial manager of Marconi in 1917, a position he retained when RCA absorbed the company in 1919. Ten years later Sarnoff became president of RCA, pulling it through the depression and separating it finally from its former controllers—General Electric and Westinghouse. In 1947 he became chairman of the board of RCA, its subsidiary, NBC, and other associated companies. In 1966 he relinquished his position as chief executive officer, whereon his son became president. He stayed on as chairman of the board until 1970 when he died.

David Sarnoff's particular gift had been his ability to understand the nature of scientific development in the fields of electronics and communications, to foresee the areas of progress, and to visualize how such technology could be converted into marketable products. During his long association with RCA, Sarnoff played a significant part in the development of electronic communications, beginning with the wireless and continuing to the shortwave radio, the home radio receiver, network radio broadcasting, black-and-white television, and color television. Virtually all these accomplishments were achieved over fierce competition and opposition from within the business, from without, and at times from the government.

Recognized as an expert in communications, Sarnoff was frequently called on for advice by all branches of the Armed Services. During World War II, he served as a colonel in the Signal Corps and made an important contribution to communications in the European theatre. He was later promoted to the rank of Brigadier General and was decorated with the Army's Legion of Merit and the Presidential Medal of Merit.

CONTEMPORARY ISSUES
Situation 24

Hunch versus the scientific method

"One thing bothers me as we study business, Ray. We talk so much about using the scientific method to make business decisions, yet many business decisions are made on the basis of hunch. I think a lot can be said for using research to solve problems and to answer questions, but sometimes a hunch results in a bigger profit."

"I'm surprised to hear you say that," said Ray. "Anyone who plays hunches today is foolish. He can't succeed over the long run in business."

"Now it's my turn to be surprised," countered John. "What about that manufacturer who played a hunch on the hula-hoop? He didn't do a lot of research, and consider the money he made. Meanwhile, I understand that Ford spent millions researching the Edsel model, and it turned out to be the flop of the decade."

"Obviously, there are exceptions to every rule," continued Ray, "but you're making a big mistake if you don't apply the scientific method whenever possible."

"You're probably right to some extent," agreed John, "but there are so many situations in business when you have to play it by hunch—making investments, for example. There's no research method in the world that can guarantee you what the stock market will do tomorrow or next week. And I don't see how the scientific method can tell a business what its competitor is going to do or how well the public will accept a new breakfast cereal. I still think a businessperson has to have a sixth sense—call it intuition—to succeed."

"You know, John," observed Ray, "we both are ignoring experience in this discussion. Most of what we know is related to experience. Maybe decision-making is a combination of all three: the scientific method, experience, *and* intuition."

SITUATION EVALUATION

1. Is there any validity in John's point of view? What is he overlooking?

2. Is it possible that both the scientific method and intuition are used in making business decisions? Explain your answer.

BUSINESS CHRONICLE

How does business adjust to change in trends?

Executives in the sales division of Kingmaker Estates observed how trends relate to their real estate business.

1. Condominiums. Retirees from northern states, a large market in Florida, once bought a considerable number of single dwellings but now appeared more interested in buying condominiums. There seemed to be no clear preference for either large high-rise apartment complexes or small garden-type multiple dwellings.

2. Trailer parks. Trailer park facilities were decreasing in popularity. Parks that once had high occupancy rates were tapering off in popularity. The reasons for this change were unclear.

3. School facilities. The continued decline in the birth rate seemed to indicate less need for school and recreational facilities in planning communities. The question remained, will the birth rate continue to decline, stabilize, or increase?

4. Household size. Household sizes were shifting. What size apartments and condominiums should be offered in future high-rise developments? What should the ratio between efficiency size apartments and four, five, six, and more rooms be?

5. Employment of women. Studies indicate that a higher percentage of all women in various age categories are employed today than in the past. How does this relate to the construction costs and designs of new residential units?

QUESTIONS

1. What kind of research should be undertaken to provide information to assist in making decisions related to the above problems? How can necessary information be secured?

2. Would it be better for Kingmaker to do its own research or to obtain an outside research company? What are the pros and cons of each approach?

3. What on-going research projects should Kingmaker be conducting?

APPLICATION EXERCISES

1. It is impossible for a manager to read and digest all the information available in magazines, newspapers, and reports (such as the *Wall Street Journal*) that pertain directly or indirectly to business. It is important, therefore, that a manager be selective in his reading material. Based on an examination of publications in your library, make a list of four magazines, two newspapers, and two reports you feel would well serve the general informational needs of a manager. Justify your selections.

2. In the library, examine two leading publications in each of the following fields: personnel management, marketing, advertising, insurance,

retailing, transportation, finance, and office management. Would you recommend any of these as general guides to career selection? Why or why not?

3. The Allen-Harvey Dairy Company of Chicago has the opportunity to invest in bottling and distributing a line of fresh-fruit beverages that was developed in Los Angeles, where it is being sold successfully. The dairy company management believes the product has good possibilities for the Chicago market. The investment would be large, however, and the product is one with which the company has had no experience. Consequently, management would like to undertake thorough research before deciding whether or not to go into the venture. Outline a research program that you believe would assist management in making this decision.

QUESTIONS

1. What is the fundamental purpose of business research? What specific values does it have for a business firm?

2. What is the trend in R&D expenditures likely to be in the future? What factors press for increases or decreases in expenditures?

3. Differentiate among pure, background, and applied research.

4. Mention two examples each of specific problems that could be solved through product, personnel, economic, financial, and marketing research.

5. Compared to research in the physical sciences, is business research really scientific? Discuss your answer.

6. Explain the five characteristics of the scientific method.

7. "The first step in the research procedure is recognition of a problem." Is this always easy? Discuss your answer.

8. In making a survey, when would you use personal interviews? The telephone? The mail? Explain your answer.

9. What types of research study can best be made by the observation method? The experimental method?

10. The executive who has a good awareness of information sources possesses a valuable business asset. What can you do to start a continuing and systematic program for learning how to put your hands on information?

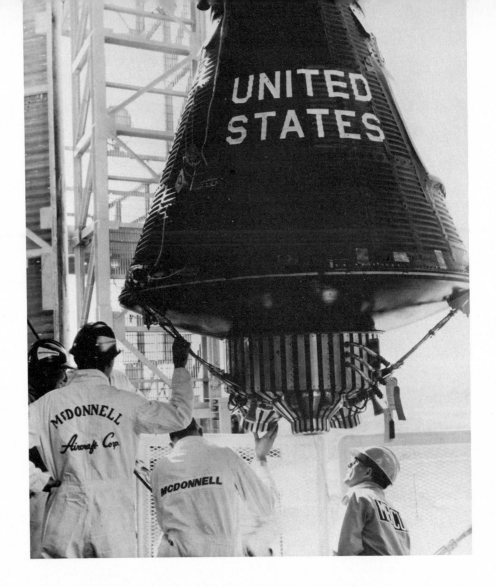

In preceding chapters we have been concerned primarily with the specific business environment, examining in detail the nature of a business establishment and its internal functions.

We turn now to the last major aspect of business: how the business world relates to government. This is a wide-ranging topic, one that assumes ever-increasing importance. In these concluding chapters we shall consider the legal aspects of business and its growing involvement with government. In conclusion we will consider what the future holds for business and for you, the student, as tomorrow's managers.

8

business, government, and the future

25
legal consideration in business

26
business and government

27
the future and business

25

CHAPTER 25

WHY BE FAMILIAR WITH BUSINESS LAW?

BUSINESS LAW DEFINED

CONTRACTS
Essentials of Contracts. Formality of Contracts. Assignment of Contracts. Performance and Discharge of Contracts. Breach of Contract.

LAW OF AGENCY / LAW OF EMPLOYER AND EMPLOYEE

BANKRUPTCY
Bankruptcy Act. Types of Bankruptcy. Bankruptcy Procedure.

SALES OF PERSONAL PROPERTY
Transfer of Title. Rights of Sellers. Rights of Buyers. Warranties.

LAW OF REAL ESTATE

LAW OF NEGOTIABLE INSTRUMENTS
You be the Judge. Requirements for Negotiability. Endorsement.

TRADEMARKS, PATENTS, AND COPYRIGHTS
Trademarks. Patents. Copyrights.

COMBINING A BUSINESS DEGREE WITH A LAW DEGREE

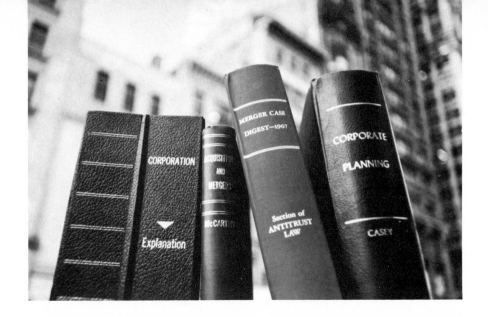

legal considerations in business

There is an old and not entirely facetious saying that "A man who serves as his own lawyer has a fool for a client." Law is a highly specialized field, requiring years of study and experience. Yet a basic knowledge of certain legal terms, processes, and procedures is valuable to anyone planning a business career. The overall problem of compliance is summed up well by Earl W. Kinter, former chairman and general counsel of the Federal Trade Commission, in the dedication of his book, *An Antitrust Primer*: "To the perplexed businessman—who must always obey the law without always knowing what the law is."

WHY BE FAMILIAR WITH BUSINESS LAW?

There are several reasons why familiarity with business law is desirable. First, such knowledge helps one to avoid common legal blunders. It is similar to taking a course in hygiene. Certainly that course does not qualify a student to be a physician, but it should help him avoid certain health hazards. For example, the wording of a partnership agreement can determine how payment to a retiring partner will be taxed. A payment for "good will"—stated as such—will be taxed as a capital gain. If, instead,

683

the same amount is paid as a "guarantee payment," it will be taxed as ordinary income—a tax rate that would usually be considerably higher than the capital gains rate.

Second, an acquaintance with business law helps one to recognize when professional legal service is needed. If a businessman is completely ignorant of business law, he does not readily recognize when he needs legal aid.

Third, a knowledge of business law helps one to appreciate his rights as an individual and as a business person. Unfortunately, some people prey on those who, not knowing their rights and privileges, do not adequately protect themselves. Recently an important patent was granted to the Marks Polarized Corporation, Whitestone, N. Y., for a device that transforms glass panels from clear to opaque and back. The invention grew out of a Navy and Air Force contract for development of a protective shutter for nuclear flashes. Had the contract the company drew up not specified that it would retain all commercial rights to military research, it would not now own this important patent.

BUSINESS LAW DEFINED

Business law refers to the rules, statutes, codes, precepts, and regulations, enforceable by court action, that have been established to provide a legal framework within which business may be conducted. Business law is of three types: mandatory law, permissive law, and prohibitive law. Mandatory laws are laws that force the businesses to do something. Examples are pollution control laws and building safety codes. Permissive laws are laws that businesses may take advantage of to protect themselves—patents, trademarks, and copyrights. Examples of prohibitive laws are licensing laws, which allow only a licensed business to operate as a taxi company, liquor store, or beauty salon.

Business law is indeed complex. Our objective here is to provide basic terminology and concepts that are useful in the practice of business administration.

CONTRACTS

Basic to practically every business transaction is the contract—an agreement between two or more persons or businesses that is enforceable by court action. No businessperson can escape making contracts.

Essentials of contracts

While all contracts are agreements, not all agreements are contracts. For an agreement between two or more parties to constitute a contract and therefore be enforceable, the following six conditions must be met.

There must be an offer An offer is simply a proposal by one party, called the offeror, to enter into a contract with a second party, called the offeree. The offer may be communicated in conversation (either in person or over the telephone) or in writing (by letter or telegram). Sometimes offers take the form of an act. For example, the presence of a public transit vehicle on a city street is an offer to carry passengers.

The offer must be sufficiently specific so that a court of law could reasonably determine the intention of the parties. In this connection, we must differentiate between *offers* and *invitations* for offers. An advertisement or store window display that states prices and qualities of merchandise is not an offer. Rather, it is an invitation to customers to come into the store and offer to buy the merchandise.

Ordinarily, the party making an offer can revoke it at any time before it is accepted.

There must be an acceptance A second essential element of the contract is acceptance of the offer by the party to whom it is made. If, for example, Jones made an offer to sell a house to Brown, someone else, say, Smith, could not accept.

Acceptance must conform to the terms of the offer to be legally enforceable. If a party receiving an offer modifies its terms, he is in effect rejecting the offer by making a counteroffer. Acceptance of the modified contract must then come from the party who made the original offer.

There must be genuineness of assent There are many types of mistakes that invalidate assent: mistakes as to fact, such as whether a house has gas or electric heat; mistakes as to the existence of the subject matter, as when two farmers meet in town and one sells a cow to another only to find later that the cow had died prior to the sale; and mistakes as to the identity of parties, as when a young man named Smith gets goods on credit when he says he is Mr. Smith's son. The storekeeper thinks he is the rich John Smith's son, when actually he is the son of Thomas Smith, a poor man. The law does not treat all mistakes in the same way. Some mistakes do not influence the contract at all; others may make the agreement unenforceable or nonbinding.

There must be consideration In general, consideration is an essential element of the enforceable contract. A promise is binding on a person only when he has received something in exchange for his promise. Consideration may take the form of money, goods, services, or forebearance of a right. In the contract to purchase an automobile for $2,500, the $2,500 is the consideration. The grandfather who agrees to pay his grandson $500 if he will not smoke until he is twenty-one receives the grandson's forebearance of a right as consideration. The amount of the consideration is generally immaterial to the validity of the contract.

Parties to the agreement must be competent   Certain classes of persons have only limited contractual capacity. Minors (in most states, persons under eighteen years of age), intoxicated people, and insane persons have contractual capacity only for necessities—clothing, food, shelter, medical care. In all other contracts made with such persons, the minor or insane persons can disaffirm the contract, though it is enforceable on the sane adult. Under contracts made for necessities, the minor or insane person can be held responsible for a reasonable price for necessities furnished. The minor who receives emergency treatment at a hospital is liable for the costs. Intoxicated persons, convicts, aliens, and corporations limited by their charters also have limited contractual capacity. Minority, for purpose of contracting, should not be confused with other laws that provide for a minimum voting age, drinking age, driving age, draft age, or age to hold public office.

Contracts must be for lawful purposes   Any contract whose performance involves an act in violation of a governing law is illegal. In states where gambling is illegal, for example, promises to pay gambling debts are not enforceable. A lender of money who attempts to collect interest on his loan in excess of the state's legal limit may lose all right to interest or the illegal part thereof—though not, usually, to the principal. Contracts which restrain trade unduly or which are detrimental to the public welfare are illegal.

Formality of contracts

Contracts may be either oral or written. The major disadvantage of an oral contract is that providing proof of the agreement is difficult. Certain classes of contract are required by statute to be in writing. These include contracts that cannot be fulfilled in less than one year, contracts for the transfer of real estate, and contracts for the sale of personal property in excess of sums ranging from $50 to $2,500, depending on the state. One example of a common type of written contract is the lease form. In many cases a written contract may be altered verbally by mutual agreement, provided there is proof that a mutually acceptable alteration has been made.

Assignment of contracts

An assignment is the means whereby one party transfers his rights or obligations in a contract to another who was not a party to the original contract. The party transferring the rights is called the *assignor*, and the party receiving them is called the *assignee*.

A party who has payments due or to become due under a contract can assign the right to these payments to another. The right to receive property also can be assigned. A merchant who has contracted to purchase a shipment of goods may transfer the right to these goods to some other party.

An important exception to the right of assignment concerns those contracts involving personal services. An employer who has made a contract with an employee cannot assign his rights in that contract to another. A building contractor cannot assign his right to erect a structure to another, because the party hiring relies on the skill of the contractor selected. Nor can a legal firm under contract to represent a company transfer this right to another legal firm, since, it must be assumed, the firm selected was chosen because of its special abilities.

Performance and discharge of contracts

Performance of a contract involves fulfillment of its terms. Sometimes, however, the terms may not be carried out. For example, both parties may agree to terminate the agreement, which discharges the contract and releases both parties from their obligations. Under certain conditions, performance by one or both parties may be excused and the contract terminated. Examples are the death or illness of a party who was to perform personal services, changes in laws that would make performance of the contract terms illegal, and destruction of the subject matter of the contract — death of identified animals under contract for sale, for instance.

Breach of contract

Breach of contract is the failure to perform an obligation or duty called for in a contract, except in situations such as those indicated above. A party that fails to perform according to the contract, cannot so perform, or will not perform is guilty of breach of contract.

The party that is injured by the breach of contract is entitled to a remedy. He has the right to rescind the contract — that is, to act as though no contract had ever been made. Or he may obtain a court order requiring that the other party pay damages or carry out the terms of the contract.

When a court orders damages paid, it issues a judgment against the defendant—the person breaking the contract. Property of the defendant may be sold to satisfy this judgment. If the defendant does not have sufficient property to satisfy the judgment and if he is a wage earner, most states permit *garnishment* of his wages. Under garnishment, the employer of the defendant is ordered to withhold a certain amount of the wage earner's usual wage each payday until the judgment is satisfied. The wages are then said to be *garnisheed*.

LAW OF AGENCY

Agency is a relationship whereby one person is authorized to act for another in transactions with a third party. The *principal* is the party granting the authority to act, and the *agent* is the party given authority to act. The agent may be a person, a partnership, or a corporation.

Practically any legal transaction can be negotiated by an agent. Exceptions are voting, making a will, and executing an affidavit. Any person legally competent to act for himself may appoint an agent.

An agent is distinguished from an employee in that the agent has power to negotiate contracts, whereas the employee does not. Agents are used in a very wide variety of circumstances. The stockbroker acts as agent for his client, the realtor for a property owner, and so on. A typical sales agency contract is shown in Figure 25–1.

Obligation of principal to agent   The principal is under obligation to compensate the agent for services rendered according to their contract; reimburse the agent for necessary expenses incurred in behalf of the principal, unless it is otherwise agreed; and indemnify the agent for losses suffered in transacting the principal's business.

Obligation of principal to third party   The principal is liable to third parties for damage or injury caused by the agent's acting within the scope of duties he owes the principal.

Obligation of agent to principal   An agent is obligated (under penalty of possible personal liability) to follow the instructions of his principal and to act within the scope of the powers vested in him. He owes his principal undivided loyalty—that is, he should not use his agency powers to further either his own interest or that of a third party. He is obligated also to exercise the skill and care ordinarily expected from such agents, to account for all property or money belonging to his principal, and to keep the principal informed of all pertinent facts so that the principal can protect his business interests.

Figure **25-1**
Sales Agency Contract

EXCLUSIVE SALES AGENCY CONTRACT

AGREEMENT made this the . . . . day of . . . ., 19 . . ., by and between the Yum Yum Candy Company, a New Jersey corporation having its principal place of business at East 32nd Street, Jersey City, New Jersey, hereinafter called the Manufacturer, and Fred Tallent, 34 West Colorado Street, Birmingham, Alabama, hereinafter called the Sales Agent.

WITNESSETH:

WHEREAS, the Manufacturer is engaged in the business of manufacturing and selling Yum Yum Candy products; and

WHEREAS, the Manufacturer desires to appoint the Sales Agent and the Sales Agent desires to become the sales representative of the Manufacturer's aforesaid products.

NOW, THEREFORE, in consideration of the mutual covenants and agreements herein contained, the parties do hereby agree as follows:

(1) Exclusive Agency: The Manufacturer hereby appoints Fred Tallent as exclusive Sales Agent in Florida, Alabama, Mississippi, and South Carolina to sell the confectionery products manufactured by the Manufacturer.

(2) Compensation to Be Paid: The Manufacturer shall pay to the Sales Agent as compensation for his services a commission of eight and one half percent ($8\frac{1}{2}\%$) of the net invoice price of all shipments of its products to any part of his territory for which payment shall have been received. Net invoice price as used here shall mean the price which is actually collected after all applicable discounts are deducted. The compensation shall be paid on the twentieth day of each month for all shipments paid for during the preceding calendar months.

(3) Term of Agency: The term of the sales agency shall be five years from the date hereof.

(4) Soliciting Sales; Quoting Prices; Forwarding Orders: The Sales Agent shall not solicit or accept any orders outside the states of Florida, Alabama, Mississippi, and South Carolina. In obtaining sales of the Manufacturer's products, the Sales Agent shall quote only the prices and terms set forth in the annexed schedule or such prices and terms as may be fixed hereafter by the Manufacturer. The Sales Agent shall forward all orders promptly to the Manufacturer, and each order shall be subject to the Manufacturer's acceptance. The Manufacturer shall forward to the Sales Agent two copies of invoices covering shipments of its products to any part of his territory.

(5) Agent May Employ Salesmen: The Sales Agent shall have full authority to employ such salesmen at such compensation and on such other conditions as he deems proper to sell in the territory herein set forth the goods of the Manufacturer. The contract to be made by the Sales Agent with such salesmen shall contain a provision that such salesmen are the employees of the Sales Agent and are to be paid by him alone, and that in employing such salesmen, he is acting individually and not as agent or attorney for the Manufacturer.

(6) Furnishing of Samples and Advertising Matter: The Manufacturer shall furnish its Sales Agent at its own expense a reasonable supply of samples and advertising matter to be used by him in connection with his agency hereunder. Sample cases are the exclusive property of the Manufacturer and the Sales Agent shall return them to the Manufacturer at the Manufacturer's expense, upon the termination of this agreement.

(7) Payment of Expenses: The Sales Agent shall assume and pay all the costs of conducting the sales agency hereunder. This shall include the aforementioned commissions or other compensation to salesmen in his employ.

(8) Termination of Agreement: If the Sales Agent violates any provision of the agreement, or becomes insolvent or bankrupt, the Manufacturer may, on ten days' written notice to the Sales Agent terminate this agreement, but the Manufacturer shall be obligated to pay the Sales Agent the commissions earned by him up to the date of termination.

IN WITNESS WHEREOF, etc.

From: *Forms of Business Agreements with Tax Ideas,* William J. Casey, 1965, Institute for Business Planning

LAW OF EMPLOYER AND EMPLOYEE

The law of employer and employee (or of master and servant, as it was once called) is very important in business.

The relationship between employers and employees is contractual even when no written agreement is used. An employer is obligated to his employees to provide

1. Reasonably safe machines and other equipment

2. A reasonably suitable workplace

3. Competent work companions (an employee is not expected to work with reckless, intoxicated, or careless associates)

4. Necessary instruction in the use of dangerous equipment

In recent years many statutes have been enacted that greatly restrict the power of an employer to discharge an employee arbitrarily. In certain situations covered by some regulatory legislation, for example, an employee may be discharged for

1. Deliberate disobedience of any reasonable order, disloyalty, or insubordination

2. Gross moral misconduct, such as defrauding the employer, or theft

3. Unquestionable incompetence, prolonged illness, or permanent disability

Completion of the job, as in seasonal fruit canning, is, of course, justification for discharge, as is a cutback in production.

BANKRUPTCY**

Bankruptcy Act

The Constitution of the United States provides that Congress shall have the power to establish uniform laws on bankruptcy throughout the nation. The Chandler Act, an amendment of the original federal Bankruptcy Act of the 1890s, was passed in 1938. It is the legislation under which bankruptcy cases are administered. Under this act, provision is made for the sound, orderly discharge of financial obligations of debtors who are insolvent.

The fundamental intent of the bankruptcy law is to enable honest debtors unable to pay their debts to be relieved of their financial obligations by a fair distribution of their assets among their creditors. This action, in effect, "wipes the slate clean" and permits the individual or business to begin anew.

SPECIAL READINGS

** In the Name of Profit, *Profiles in Corporate Irresponsibility*, by Robert L. Heilbroner, and others. Garden City, N. Y.: Doubleday, 1972. This book was conceived by a Pulitzer Prize-winner, David Obst. Its best known contributor, Robert L. Heilbroner, is one of the country's most readable economists and social critics.

It consists of a series of true stories about executives whose desire for profit led them into making immoral decisions. These stories are not about men who were criminals who got into business to further their ambitions. They are about well educated and respected corporation career executives who, in the course of their careers in the corporate culture, were carried away by greed.

This is not a book about scandal and dramatic misdeeds. The foreword states: "This book however deals not with the baneful results of corporate irresponsibility but with its roots in human behavior. It tries to show what sort of men run the super corporations, what their values are, and why they act as they do."

In terms of personalities, it thoughtfully examines what happens to some men when they come into corporate power structures and are left entirely free to maximize profits. Questions such as the following are raised and answered through character profiles: What kind of men run some corporations? How can "good men" behave so badly? Does working for a corporation mean violating one's conscience?

In a concluding chapter of the book, "Controlling the Corporation," Heilbroner considers the matter of controlling corporations so the executive abuses described can be prevented.

At one time there were debtors' prisons for those who could not meet their financial obligations. A person or firm that went bankrupt in earlier days had almost no chance to go into business again. Today, however, it is recognized that even under good management occasional bankruptcies cannot be avoided. They are part of the price that must be paid for the privilege of doing business in a highly competitive private enterprise economy.

Types of bankruptcy

There are two types of bankruptcy—voluntary and involuntary. Voluntary bankruptcy is a process initiated by the person or organization wishing to be adjudged bankrupt. Involuntary bankruptcy proceedings are initiated by the creditors of a person or business. Railroads, banks, insurance companies, building and loan associations, and incorporated cities do not come under the Bankruptcy Act. Involuntary bankruptcy cannot be

Figure **25–2**
Failure Trends

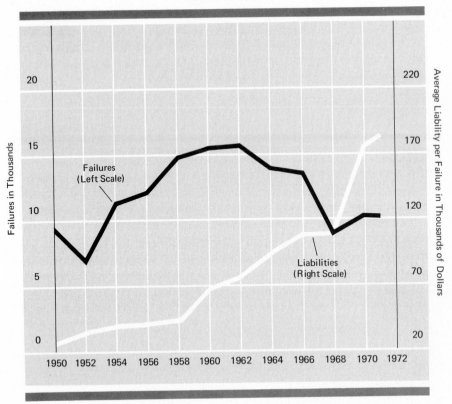

1971 ended the year-to-year failure upsurge that had persisted since the fourth quarter of 1969. Business failures eased 4 percent to 10,326 from the three-year high of 10,748 reached in 1970. Dollar liabilities involved in the casualties, however, continued to rise and set a new record of $1,926,929,000.

Million dollar bankruptcies climbed to an unprecedented 292 and were largely responsible for boosting the dollar total. Casualties involving losses in the $25,000 to $1 million range held within a fraction of their number in the previous year. Virtually all of the slowing in 1971 was concentrated in failures with liabilities under $25,000.

Source: The Failure Record through 1971, compiled by the Business Economics Department, Dun & Bradstreet, Inc.

forced on wage earners with an annual income of less than $1,500 or on farmers. All other persons and businesses can come under the terms of the Bankruptcy Act by either a voluntary or an involuntary proceeding if debts of $1,000 or more are outstanding.

To institute involuntary proceedings, creditors must prove that the debtor has committed one or more acts of bankruptcy, as set forth in the Bankruptcy Act.

Experience in recent years shows there is little relationship between the level of personal income and the rate of bankruptcy.[1] In 1970, 169,427 personal (nonbusiness) bankruptcies were filed in the United States.

Bankruptcy procedure

After a petition for adjudication is filed and a party is adjudicated bankrupt by the federal district judge, the bankrupt's estate is referred to the bankruptcy court, a division of the federal district court. A "referee in bankruptcy" is appointed, and he calls a meeting of creditors, who elect a "trustee" to manage the bankrupt's estate. The claims of creditors are determined, and the assets are distributed according to the priorities of various creditors, as set forth in the Bankruptcy Act.

The order of priority in claims is as follows: (1) expenses of the court in preserving the estate after filing of the petition, (2) wages of employees of the bankrupt earned within the months before commencement of bankruptcy proceedings, (3) reasonable expenses of creditors in proposing a plan for the discharge of bankruptcy, (4) taxes due any governmental unit, and (5) debts having priority established by state and federal laws.

Funds remaining are then divided among creditors on a pro-rata basis. To illustrate, if the amount of indebtedness (after payment of the above) totaled $10,000 and assets were only $2,500, each creditor would receive 25 percent of the amount owed him.

After completion of the administration of the estate the referee in bankruptcy reports the case back to the federal district judge, who hears the petition of the bankrupt for his discharge and either grants or denies the discharge, according to the circumstances of the case.

SALES OF PERSONAL PROPERTY

For legal purposes, personal property includes all property other than real estate—motor vehicles, clothing, securities, furniture, food, cattle, and so on. Each sale of such property is a contractual relationship governed by certain legal provisions.

Transfer of title

It is important to know *when* title or legal ownership passes. Should goods be lost, damaged, or destroyed, loss is suffered by the party holding

[1] *Finance Facts Yearbook* (Washington, D.C.: National Consumer Finance Association, 1970), p. 53.

title. There are many situations involving future delivery, condition of goods, or some other contingency, which make it difficult to determine exactly when title passes.

Certain rules have been formulated concerning transfer of title where the parties have not made any agreement to the contrary. Following are the most important.

1. Under a contract to sell specific goods in which the seller is duty bound to do something to the goods to put them in a deliverable condition, title does not pass until that thing is done. To illustrate, the Brown Automobile Company sold Smith a used automobile, promising to replace all the tires with new ones. Prior to replacing the tires, however, the car was destroyed through no fault of either party. The Brown Automobile Company had to bear the loss, because it had failed to put the car in a deliverable condition.

2. When goods are sold on a trial or approval basis, title passes when the buyer commits any act that signifies acceptance, or when he has kept the goods for longer than a reasonable length of time.

3. If the contract to sell states that the seller is to deliver the goods to a designated place, title does not pass until goods are so delivered.

4. If the contract to sell states that goods are to be shipped F.O.B. (free on board) point of origin, title passes when the goods in a deliverable condition are delivered to the point of shipment. Thus, if a manufacturer in Chicago sells a piano to a buyer in St. Louis F.O.B. Chicago, title and the accompanying risk pass to the buyer when the piano is put on the train in Chicago.

5. Title to goods does not pass until the seller puts the goods beyond his own control and identifies them as for a specific buyer. Suppose, for example, that a poultry producer agreed to sell one thousand chickens from his flock of ten thousand. Prior to the actual selection of the one thousand chickens, the entire flock was destroyed. Title had not passed because the chickens had not been identified.

6. In C.O.D. (cash on delivery) shipments, title passes to the buyer when the goods are delivered by the seller to the carrier.

Rights of sellers

Unpaid seller's lien. So long as an unpaid seller has possession of goods, even though title has passed to the buyer, he has a lien for the purchase price until the goods are either delivered or paid for. However, when the seller extends credit, the buyer has right to possession of the goods without first paying for them.

Stoppage in transit.   When a buyer of goods is or becomes insolvent, an unpaid seller has, under certain conditions, the right to resume possession of goods while they are in transit—that is, before delivery to the buyer.

Rights of buyers

The buyer has the right to refuse goods over and above the quantity agreed on. If more than the agreed amount is tendered, the buyer may reject them all, keep that portion contracted for, or accept all. If fewer goods are delivered than ordered, the buyer can either reject them all or accept them and pay the contract price. The buyer also has the right to inspect goods prior to acceptance.

Warranties

A warranty is a legal promise by a seller that property is or will be as represented. Warranties usually are made as a means of inducing the buyer to make a purchase. An *express warranty* is one that contains a specific statement of fact regarding the characteristics of the property sold. For example, statements such as "This suit is 100 percent wool," "This house is four years old," and "This automobile has a new motor" are all express warranties. Should the purchaser later learn that the statements were untrue, he is entitled to an appropriate remedy.

An *implied warranty* differs from an express warranty in that it is not stated in specific terms but is implied by operation of law. For example, the consumer has an implied warranty that the retailer has the right to sell the goods offered in his store. Other implied warranties are that the goods will be fit for the purpose indicated by the seller and that the goods sold by description or sample will correspond to the description or sample. In mail-order purchases from a catalog, it is implied that the goods will be as portrayed and described.

The buyer has certain remedies if the seller is guilty of a breach of warranty. In such a case he may

1. Keep the goods but subtract from the price paid an amount that equals the difference between the warranted value and the value of the goods received

2. Keep the goods and sue for damages

3. Refuse the goods

LAW OF REAL ESTATE

"Real estate," or "real property," refers to land and anything permanently attached to it. Unless otherwise restricted, ownership of land carries with it ownership of everything beneath and above the earth's surface.

Certain broad regulations apply to the use of property, whether real or personal. The most important of these are the following.

1. Property may be sold, through legal action, to pay taxes or debts.

2. Property may be taken, with fair compensation, for public use. Exercise of this government right, called *eminent domain*, occurs when property is acquired for such purposes as public parks, highways, and municipal buildings.

3. Property cannot be used for any purpose contrary to law. For example, property cannot be used for manufacturing purposes if the property is in an area zoned for purposes other than manufacturing.

4. Property cannot be used in such a way as to infringe on the rights of others.

Considerable formality is involved in the transfer of real property. Land and all that pertains to it (fixtures) can be disposed of outright by the owner, in which case he will execute a deed to the purchaser; or he can enter into a contract to sell his land on an extended payment basis, commonly called a "land contract," under the terms of which he agrees to give the purchaser a deed to it on payment in full therefore. On the death of the owner, land goes to the person or persons whom he designates by his will, or, if he dies without leaving a will, land descends to his heirs in the manner designated by the statutes of the state wherein it is located.

Deeds are of two major types, the *quitclaim deed* and the *warranty deed*. In the quitclaim deed, the grantor conveys merely the interest he holds and says nothing else about the quality of the title. In the warranty deed, the grantor conveys his interest and in addition contracts to the effect that he has good title, except as to liens or other encumbrances noted in the deed, and is personally liable for any defects in the title that are not noted.

LAW OF NEGOTIABLE INSTRUMENTS

Negotiable instruments are a special form of written contractual obligation used extensively in business transactions. Common examples include checks, promissory notes, and bills of exchange.

Negotiable instruments serve chiefly as substitutes for money—in other words, as credit instruments. Thus they are very convenient and are regarded, indeed, as indispensable in modern business.

Following is an example of legal involvement arising out of negotiable instruments. This extract is from a publication that illustrates how executives can develop legal awareness.

You be the judge

Does a prompt stop payment order on a check you issued always protect you?

What happened: More than one hasty businessman has drawn comfort from the fact that he has paid his bills by check. His ace-in-the-hole for rectifying a mistake is the stop payment order to his bank. If he moves promptly —let us say, the day after issuing the check—he can still save the bacon. At least, that is the widespread impression.

Norm Weston, of the Cattle Traders Company, knew Sig Malter casually, as he had bought cattle from him on infrequent occasions. Malter called on Tuesday and spoke to Weston. "I have 20 heifers I want to sell," he told Weston.

"Okay, I'll send a man around to look them over," Weston answered.

Inspection on Wednesday led to approval. On Thursday, Weston mailed Malter a check for $5,000. Early Friday morning the trading company had a visitor.

"That cattle you bought from Malter is not his. We have a lien on it," the visitor said. Weston's feet, comfortably stretched on the desk, hit the floor with a bang. "Call the bank!" he told his secretary. "Stop payment on that $5,000 check!"

Next he telephoned Malter. "We deny the lien," Malter answered. "It's not valid. Sorry about the check, but I've already deposited it."

Weston shrugged. "We don't intend getting in the middle of this argument. Take back the cattle—the check won't be paid."

Bad news came to Weston the next week in a telephone call from Malter's bank. "About that check to Malter that you stopped—he already drew on it for $3,500. It's up to you to make good on it."

"You paid on it?" Weston was astonished. "Didn't you even wait until it cleared?"

"Not with an old depositor like Malter," the bank answered. "He has privileges. We assumed your check was perfectly valid."

LEGAL CONSIDERATIONS IN BUSINESS

"I won't pay a cent," Weston retorted: "I gave my bank a stop payment notice in time. If you choose to pay on a check before it clears, that's your baby, not mine."

The bank officer answered, "On the contrary, we have the law on our side. We do not have to anticipate a stop payment order we know nothing about."

The bank sued for the $3,500.

Did Weston have to pay?

The decision

For the bank: It had paid out on the check on Friday prior to the time it could have been advised by Weston's bank of the stop payment order. It is, in parlance of the law, a "holder in due course" — which means the bank has a right to protection so long as the check was validly issued and the bank had no way of knowing it had been stopped.

A bank has the privilege of allowing a depositor to withdraw money on an uncleared check, a Federal District Court said. The fact that it may take a risk with a depositor is its own concern, and no argument can be raised by a man who issues a valid check. (254 F. Supp. 265)

Second thoughts: Fortunately for those who issue checks one day and seek to stop them the next, most banks do not permit a depositor to draw on it before it clears. However, this is not an invariable rule by any means, and oldtime depositors can have special privileges.

When you issue a stop payment order, remember it goes to *your* bank and not the payee's. *Your* bank knows about it — but *his* does not.[2]

Requirements for negotiability

For an instrument to be fully negotiable, it must meet certain legal requirements.

1. The negotiable instrument must be in writing and must be signed by the maker or drawer. The form of writing is generally immaterial. Pen and ink, pencil, a typewriter, or printing constitute "writing" in the legal sense.

2. The negotiable instrument must contain an unconditional promise or order to pay a certain sum in money. A promise or order that reads "on condition that" obviously would be conditional, and the instrument would be nonnegotiable.

---

[2] *The Businessman & the Law.* Published twice monthly by Man & Manager, Inc., 799 Broadway, New York, N.Y. 10003. Used with permission.

3. The negotiable instrument must be payable on demand or at a fixed or determinable future time.

4. The negotiable instrument must be payable to order or to bearer.

Endorsement

The usual method of transferring or negotiating a negotiable instrument is by endorsement—writing one's name on the back of the instrument. Technically there are five forms of endorsement.

Blank endorsement This form of endorsement is the most common. The payee or holder of the instrument writes his name on the reverse of the instrument without making any designation of the endorsee. A blank endorsement is not recommended unless the instrument is delivered immediately to another party. To illustrate, a payroll check endorsed in blank and lost can be cashed by any finder who presents it at a bank.

Special endorsement This form of endorsement specifies the endorsee. The person endorsing the instrument endorses it, for example, "pay to the order of Wilbur Wright" and then signs his name. In this case, Wright may thereafter endorse the instrument in blank if he so chooses.

Restrictive endorsement This endorsement restricts the negotiability of the instrument to a specific purpose. Common forms of restrictive endorsement are "for deposit only" (signed), "for collection only" (signed), and "pay to First National Bank only" (signed).

Conditional endorsement This form of endorsement makes it possible to transfer the instrument, although the person to whom it is transferred will hold the same, or the proceeds thereof, subject to the rights of the endorser. The person paying the instrument may, however, ignore the condition and make payment to the holder, whether the condition has been fulfilled or not. Examples are "Pay to Wilbur Wright on the arrival of shipment 606" (signed), or, "Pay to Mary Wright when she becomes twenty-one" (signed).

Qualified endorsement A person who endorses a negotiable instrument becomes liable to the subsequent holder should the maker fail to pay it. To illustrate, a retail merchant receives a check from a customer. The merchant endorses the check and delivers it to a wholesaler. The wholesaler endorses it and presents it to a bank for collection. The bank, however, finds that the check is worthless. The bank now has recourse against the wholesaler, who in turn has recourse against the retailer; and the retailer has recourse against the customer who wrote the check. Such endorsements are called "unqualified."

A holder of a check or other negotiable instrument who wishes to be exempt from liability for the default of the party primarily responsible for the payment of the instrument can endorse the check by writing "without recourse" before his name. This is called "qualified endorsement." This notation is important when a person, whether he is in business or not, cashes a check for someone else.

TRADEMARKS, PATENTS, AND COPYRIGHTS

There is an important area of law that provides businesspeople protection for intangible assets such as brand names or trademarks (which, as in the case of Coca Cola, might well be that company's single most valuable asset), patents, and copyrights. Businesses often spend large amounts of time and money assuring that everything possible is done to provide necessary legal protection in this complicated field.

Trademarks

A trademark or brand name, *if used properly* remains the exclusive property of its owner forever. Trademarks can be registered under the Lanham Act of 1946. This act defines a trademark as any word, name, symbol, or device, or any combination of those adopted and used by a manufacturer or merchant to identify his goods and distinguish them from those manufactured or sold by others. The purpose of a trademark according to federal statute is "to identify goods, and distinguish them from those manufactured and sold by others." However, trademarks and brand names must be handled with utmost caution, for careless treatment of them can literally destroy their protection. Federal law states that the right to a registered trademark is forfeited "when any course of conduct of the registrant, including acts of omission or commission, causes the mark to lose its significance as an indication of origin."

Business history is studded with examples of trademarks that have been lost because they have become generic terms—cellophane, escalator, aspirin, linoleum, kerosene, and celluloid are well-known examples.

Once it can be proved that the meaning for a trademark has been changed in the mind of the public, there is danger that the trademark can fall into public domain, unless it can be proved that the company that owned it regularly took steps to identify its trademark. A key principle is that the trademark must always be identified *as* a trademark when a company uses it. One rule must always be followed. A trademark should *never* be used as a noun. It is always an adjective. In the courts it was shown that the Otis Elevator Co. used "Escalator" as a noun in its own advertising. The trademark should have been used as "An Escalator moving staircase" instead of merely "escalator." Because of such careless usage, which is deemed to confuse the public, the word is now generic and can be found in the dictionary and be used by anyone.

The cost of willful trademark infringement can run high, as illustrated by the following case. The makers of a brand called Dutch Paint were ordered to pay more than $339,000 to the makers of Dutch Boy paints. The sum was for the profit they had made on the sale of paint under that name plus legal fees. The Dutch Paint makers were not allowed to deduct the losses or their unprofitable years from the total earnings of the profitable ones. They were not even permitted to deduct income taxes paid during the years for which they had to give the profits back.

Patents

Patents run for 17 years and are not renewable. Businesses watch the expiration dates of their patents and of those owned by their competitors. If licenses to use patents have been granted, the payment of royalties stops. In 1972, for example, more than 30,000 patents expired, which meant that they went into the public domain for anyone to use.

Large libraries have the weekly *Official Gazette* of the Patent Office, which features abstracts of all patents. There is also an annual index of patents published in two parts: an alphabetical index of patentees and a subject matter index.

Copyrights

Copyrights are granted without prior search to see whether anything similar has been copyrighted and may be used to register artistic designs of packages and labels as well as anything else that is printed or illustrated. Registration applications are available free of charge from the Registrar of Copyrights, Library of Congress. Copyrights run for a period of twenty-eight years and may be renewed once.

COMBINING A BUSINESS DEGREE WITH A LAW DEGREE

Often students who are interested in both law and business opt to take a degree in both fields. The combination is highly desirable. Surely many

Figure **25–3**
Requirements for Admission to the Bar, New York State

ADMISSION BY EXAMINATION

Applicant must be a citizen of the United States, 21 years of age, of good moral character, and an actual resident of New York for six months immediately preceding date of
examination for which application is made, or he must declare that he intends in good faith
to establish actual residence in New York before the date fixed for the examination and to
maintain such actual residence for at least six months prior to applying for admission to the
bar. Though this petition must be entitled in the department in which applicant resides,
he may apply for examination in any department, providing he secures written permission of
the Board so to do. To establish the requirements for pre-legal education, applicant must
show: (1) graduation with an approved degree from an accredited college; or (2) completion
of at least three years pre-legal college work at an accredited college. If applicant is not a
college graduate before he begins the study of law, he must obtain from the State Department of Education a law student's qualifying certificate, and he must file this certificate
with the Clerk of the Court of Appeals at any time prior to taking the bar examination. To
commence study of law in New York, a student must be at least 18 years of age. He can
qualify to take the examination as follows: (1) by presenting a degree from an approved law
school showing his graduation therefrom; or (2) by law study for four years in the office of
an attorney admitted to practice in the Supreme Court of New York; or (3) partly by law
study and partly by attendance at a duly approved law school. Time for filing is at least
thirty days and not more than sixty days prior to the examination. Applicant, wishing to
qualify for admission by law office study, must file before commencing such study a certificate of his supervising attorney with the Clerk of the Court of Appeals, which certificate
shall state the date of commencement of the period of law office study. Examinations are
given in March and July. Every applicant for examination shall pay a fee as required by section 465 of the Judiciary Law ($25).

After passing the bar, he must appear personally before the Committee on Character
and Fitness of the department or judicial district of his residence, presenting at that time
affidavits of two responsible persons of said judicial district, attesting to applicant's good
moral character; one of these affidavits must be executed by a practicing attorney of the
Supreme Court residing in that district.

ADMISSION WITHOUT EXAMINATION

An attorney applicant may be admitted without examination if he is at least 26 years of
age, a citizen of the United States, is and for not less than six months immediately preceding the application has been an actual resident of this state, and has been actively engaged
in the practice of law for at least five years, or has served as a full-time law school teacher
for five years immediately preceding the application.

Note: Regulations for the practice of law vary from state to state. The requirements for New York State
shown below are reasonably typical of those for most states.

Source: *Rules for Admission to the Bar*, West Publishing Co., 1972.

executives have risen to the top by the law route. Business schools and
law schools at larger universities often cooperate to offer programs of
study that make it possible for students to obtain degrees in both fields.
Credits for some courses are interchangeable, so the total number of
courses normally required if each degree is taken separately is reduced.
Figure 25–3 provides the typical requirements for admission to the bar.

PEOPLE AND THEIR IDEAS
William Randolph Hearst

America's most fabulous newspaper baron

William Randolph Hearst thrived on controversy. In spite of constant outcries against his use of techniques of mass journalistic appeal, he was, throughout a newspaper career of over sixty years, one of the dominant figures in American journalism and builder of a vast publishing empire. He raised sensationalistic journalism to unprecedented heights and his methods have had a profound influence on journalism in this country.

Hearst was born in 1863 in San Francisco, the only child of a wealthy mineowner, rancher, U.S. senator from California, and publisher of the San Francisco *Daily Examiner*. He attended Harvard University, but after two years returned to San Francisco and persuaded his father to let him take charge of the failing *Examiner*. Adapting the methods of Joseph Pulitzer's New York *World*, Hearst made the *Examiner* the most enterprising, brilliant, and sensational newspaper San Francisco had ever seen—and doubled its circulation within a year.

Moving to New York in 1895, Hearst bought the unsuccessful New York *Morning Journal*, which he remade in the format of the *World* and sold for one cent a copy. To the *Journal* he brought new editors and reporters, respected authors, and talented men he obtained from other newspapers by paying them higher salaries. By the use of numerous illustrations, glaring headlines, and sensational articles on crime, scandal, and disaster, he waged a dramatic circulation war with Pulitzer's *World* and ushered in the era of "yellow journalism."

With successful operations in San Francisco and New York, Hearst was now ready to launch the Hearst newspaper chain. In Chicago, he established the evening *American* in 1900 and the morning *Examiner* in 1902. He started the Boston *American* and the Los Angeles *Examiner* in 1904. By 1927, the Hearst chain published twenty-five dailies in seventeen cities from coast to coast, as well as seventeen Sunday papers.

Meanwhile, Hearst had entered the magazine field and had acquired twenty-four periodicals in the United States and England, including *Good Housekeeping, Harper's Bazaar, Cosmopolitan, House Beautiful*, and *Town and Country*. He also came to control the International News Service facilities, several syndicates, the Sunday supplements *American Weekly* and *Puck*, the Hearst Metrotone News, a dozen radio stations, and Cosmopolitan motion pictures.

Politically, as well as editorially, Hearst was a controversial figure and was often criticized for his conflicting views. A Progressive in his youth, he fought for the eight-hour working day, women's suffrage, and antitrust legislation. In the 1930s he zealously opposed New Deal reforms.

He frequently turned on political leaders he had once supported. He fought hard for Woodrow Wilson's election to the Presidency in 1912 and 1916 and then turned violently against him on the issues of American entry into World War I and sponsorship of the League of Nations. Politically ambitious himself, he served two terms as representative of the Eleventh New York District in Congress but failed in two attempts to become mayor of New York City and one attempt for the governorship of New York State.

One of the world's richest men in the 1920s and early 1930s, Hearst lived sumptuously, filling his several estates with antiques and art treasures collected from all parts of the globe. During the long depression of the 1930s, however, he was forced to liquidate or consolidate some of his properties and to sell much of his fabulous art collection.

Hearst died in California in 1951. After his death, his magnificent estate, San Simeon, was turned over to the state of California and has become a popular tourist attraction.

CONTEMPORARY ISSUES
Situation 25

Should crime and violence on TV be outlawed?

One evening John, Ray, and several of their friends were heatedly discussing a recent report that advocated government restrictions for television networks and stations in order to stop shows with crime and violence.

It was John's position that television should be "free" to show whatever programs people want to watch. "Study after study indicate that a large segment of our population prefers a murder mystery to a cultural program. Now, you can't blame television for this. Television doesn't make taste — it simply gives people what they want to see. Moreover," he explained, "if the government could dictate what television stations can show, then soon it will be telling preachers what they can preach, teachers what they can teach, and so on. Before long, our basic freedoms will be destroyed."

"Wait a minute, John," Ray insisted, "You're way off base. Don't you have a social conscience? I suspect there's a direct correlation between the increasing number of crime shows produced by TV and our rising crime rate. With so much robbery, drug addiction, gang fighting, police defiance, and the like being shown in TV, people begin to tolerate violence, and some misguided ones think it's the popular thing to do."

"Well, even if you are right, I still don't accept government control over TV programing," replied John. "TV must be kept free of censor-

ship. I'd rather suffer some of the consequences of bad television programing than lose freedom of speech."

"But I don't equate outlawing violence on TV with losing freedom of
speech," responded Ray. "We didn't exactly lose our right not to be
searched when the FAA required every passenger boarding an airliner to
have his carry-on luggage inspected."

SITUATION EVALUATION

1. Who has the better argument and why?

2. Would regulation of television programing interfere with freedom of
   speech?

3. Is there some other way television programing could be modified without the intervention of the federal government?

BUSINESS CHRONICLE

Real estate operations and law suits

The law is intimately involved in real estate operations because there are
legal implications and requirements in real estate transactions. In fact,
real estate firms are especially susceptible to law suits. Following are
four cases where Kingmaker was taken to court and sued.

1. Juan Sanchez, a salesman working for Kingmaker, left to start his
own real estate business. After he left, Kingmaker sold a factory site for
$660,000 which Sanchez had obtained as a listing. Sanchez claimed that
half of the commission belonged to him, even if he was no longer an
employee.

2. Bill Clements, a salesman for Kingmaker, secured a listing for a
piece of farm land. The price for the land was so attractive, that another
Kingmaker salesman, George Catleft, bought the property for himself. Six
months later he sold it for $20,000. The original owner who got $7,000
less Kingmaker's commission for the property heard about this. He sued
Kingmaker for $13,000 plus damages charging that Kingmaker had not, as
his agent, served his best interests.

3. Katherine Fisher put a $1,000 down payment on a house. The offer
was accepted by the house owner. Kingmaker contracts clearly state that
once down payments were accepted by property owners, they would be
forfeited if purchase was not completed within the specified time period.
Ms. Fisher claimed that the Kingmaker salesman had misrepresented the
property. She sued to get her deposit back.

4. Kingmaker sold a house for $60,000. The owner said at the time he

listed it with Kingmaker that he had had it listed with another broker who wasn't doing anything about selling it. Within two weeks, Kingmaker had sold the house. The other broker sued Kingmaker for the commission and damages stating that he had an exclusive listing on the house.

QUESTIONS

1. Evaluate each case and explain whether or not the law suit could have been avoided.

2. How can Kingmaker reduce its number of law suits?

3. Is legal work of a large real estate company best handled by outside law firms or, if there is enough to keep a lawyer busy, should the company hire its own lawyer?

APPLICATION EXERCISES

1. A recent survey indicates that less than 5 percent of all air travelers have ever read the contractual "fine print" on their ticket. Obtain a used ticket and summarize the air carrier's legal responsibility to the passenger.

2. Joel Bradley rented a building, hired some employees, borrowed some money from a bank, and stored an inventory of frozen foods in a public warehouse. In a brief paragraph describe a legal document that might be required for each of Bradley's actions.

3. Secure three advertisements that demonstrate how a company is seeking to keep control of its trademarks.

QUESTIONS

1. What specific conditions must be met for an agreement to constitute a contract?

2. What is a minor? Do you agree with the widely accepted practice that minors should not have full contractual capacity?

3. What is garnishment? Many employers look on garnishment orders with extreme disfavor. Explain this attitude.

4. What specific legal transactions cannot be negotiated by an agent?

5. Under the law of employer and employee, how is the employer obligated to the employee?

6. What is the essential difference between voluntary and involuntary bankruptcy? Under what circumstances do they come about? Explain your answer.

7. What is the basic difference between personal property and real property?

8. What is the main function served by negotiable instruments? What are the requirements an instrument must meet to be negotiable?

9. "A little knowledge of law can be a dangerous thing." Is this a misleading statement? Discuss your answer.

10. What are the advantages of combining a business with a law degree? What other combination degrees are possible with a business degree?

11. What must a company do to keep its trademarks valid?

CHAPTER 26

GOVERNMENT REGULATION OF BUSINESS
History of Government Influence over Business.

BUSINESS LEGISLATION
The Sherman Antitrust Act. The Clayton Act. The Federal Trade Commission Act. The Robinson-Patman Act. The Wheeler-Lea Act. Consumer Product Safety Commission.

THE PRESENT STATUS OF GOVERNMENT REGULATION
The Attack on Current Problems. What Is Too Big? The Revitalized FTC.

GOVERNMENT REGULATION OF PUBLIC UTILITIES
Why Utilities Are Regulated.

TAXATION AND BUSINESS
The Power to Tax. Purpose of Taxation. Expenditure Trends. VAT, the Value Added Tax. The Negative-Income Tax. Sources and Uses of Tax Collections. Federal Revenue Sharing.

THE GOVERNMENTAL ROLE IN PERSPECTIVE

A LOOK AT NATIONAL PRIORITIES

26

business and government

All business is influenced in a host of ways by federal, state, and local governments. There are laws, codes, ordinances, and other forms of restrictions that stipulate the procedure for organizing a business; determine in part the location of a business; dictate various construction specifications for reasons of safety, community zoning, and employee working environment; specify minimum ages, wages, and hours, and standard working conditions of employees; influence advertising and selling practices; regulate the sale of corporate securities; attempt to maintain free competition; and specify procedures for dissolving a business.

The vice-president of marketing for the Theo. Hamm Brewing Co. mentioned that differing laws and regulations in the 22 states where his company operates pose major problems. As an example, he stated that in some states sales promotion is more closely regulated than in others. "We may be able to use illuminated point-of-sale signs in one state, but not in another."

Governmental action is not all restrictive; governmental units also perform a variety of services for business. These include police and fire protection, postal service, scientific aids, business information, and subsidies and other financial aid.

In some cases, the government can be regarded as a direct competitor of business. Two examples are the sale of life insurance to veterans and the generating of electric power under the Tennessee Valley Authority. In other cases, government and private corporations work closely together on projects neither could undertake nor manage alone. COMSAT, the communications satellite corporation, and NASA, the National Aeronautics Space Administration, are examples of such cooperative efforts.

GOVERNMENT REGULATION OF BUSINESS

History of government influence over business

Until late in the nineteenth century, business was largely unregulated, but since that time government influence in and regulation of business have increased steadily. Rugged individualism prevailed in the early development of the country. The fact that government was weak made it possible for strong, dedicated, and sometimes ruthless personalities, like the railroad builder Cornelius Vanderbilt, the merchant Marshall Field, the steel magnate Andrew Carnegie, and the oil baron John D. Rockefeller to exploit, organize, and make available to the people the resources of the country. Eventually, these people amassed such power that it became necessary for the government to establish curbs.

One of the first moves to regulate business was the establishment of the Interstate Commerce Commission in 1887. The original purpose of the the commission was to prevent rate discrimination by railroads.[1] Shortly thereafter, in 1890, the Sherman Antitrust Act was passed to curb the growth of trusts and monopolies, which threatened free competition.

In 1913 another step toward government regulation was taken in the passage of the Federal Reserve Bank Act, which resulted in a variety of controls over the banking system.

It was with the Great Depression, however, that government regulation of business took its greatest leap forward. The election of Franklin Delano Roosevelt as President in 1932 marked the introduction of the New Deal — a sweeping program of government-directed economic action designed to lift the country out of the Depression. Extensive controls were placed on the economy: Agricultural production was regulated, rigid restrictions were placed on banking and finance, public works were instituted on a gigantic scale, and extensive labor legislation was enacted. Although many of the controls did not survive the Depression, the government

---

[1] The ICC has jurisdiction also over buses, trucks, express companies, pipelines, and inland waterways.

changed from a passive force in the economy to the active promoter and controller of economic welfare that it is today.

World War II resulted in the most stringent economic controls this nation has seen. In its all-out effort to win the war, the government regulated raw materials, production, distribution of consumer goods, prices, rents, interest, and many other business activities.

The conclusion of World War II saw an end to most emergency controls. The government did not, however, revert to its passive status of the pre-depression era. Instead, peacetime government influence over business continues to increase. Today no one challenges the statement that "the government is in business to stay." David Lilienthal, the man who directed the building of the huge TVA power project for the government and later switched to private business, made the following comparison concerning working for the government versus private business.

> I found a great appeal in the idea of taking a small and quite crippled company and trying to make something out of it. Building. That kind of building, I thought, is the central thing in American free enterprise, and something I'd missed in all my government work. I wanted to try my hand at it. Now, about how I felt. Well, it felt pretty exciting. It was full of intellectual stimulation, and a lot of my old ideas changed.[2]

During World War II, business learned to cooperate closely with government. Since then, businesses seem to accept (though seldom admit) the need for government regulation and action. While business leaders often cry hard and loud about the evils of "too much government," it is doubtful that many of them would care to revert to the past, for they recognize that:

1. Considerable government regulation of economic activity is essential in today's complex world.

2. The government, as an instrument of the people, can guide and assist business in many useful ways.

Business leaders now take a much more active role in helping to formulate economic policy, rather than simply objecting, as they once did, to proposed regulation on the grounds that government intervention is bad.

Steps have been taken to give more than lip service to improved business and government liaison and understanding. In the summer of 1970, a plan was activated by the President's Commission of Personnel Interchange whereby 40 promising, young company executives in the "$18,000 and over" salary brackets are exchanged for 12 to 18 months with an equal

---

[2] John Brooks, *Business Adventure* (New York: Weybright & Talley, 1969), p. 260.

number of similar civil service employees. The chairman of the Commission said, "It will improve individual understanding for more effective working relationships between government and business, and encourage a continuing interchange of management practices. As the program continues to grow, it should imbue fresh thinking into inbred organizations and demonstrate the benefits of cross-fertilization."[3]

BUSINESS LEGISLATION

There are many laws influencing wages, prices, labor relations, housing, agriculture, defense spending, and other areas. Those discussed here constitute the principal legislation designed to maintain a competitive business climate.

The Sherman Antitrust Act

A monopoly may be defined as a firm that controls such a large part of the total business done in an industry that it can dictate or control the market prices for the output of that industry. During the 1880s powerful monopolies developed in the sugar, oil, whiskey, tobacco, shoe machinery, harvesting machines, and cash register industries—monopolies that were working against the public interest.

Accordingly, Congress passed the Sherman Antitrust Act in 1890. This act provided that "every contract, combination . . . or conspiracy in restraint of trade or commerce among the several states . . . is hereby declared to be illegal" and that "every person who shall monopolize or . . . combine or conspire to monopolize . . . shall be deemed guilty of a misdemeanor." Violators of this law can be fined $5,000 or sent to prison for one year, or both.

The framers of the Sherman Act regarded bigness per se as bad. Through the years, however, the philosophy has developed that mere size does not make a business undesirable from the standpoint of public well-being. In fact, businesses today are encouraged to grow, so long as they do not use their size and power to unfair advantage.

The Clayton Act

The Clayton Act, passed in 1914, supplemented and strengthened the Sherman Antitrust Act, which proved to be too indefinite. The Clayton

---

[3] David J. Mahoney, President, Norton Simon, Inc., *Nation's Business*, March, 1970, p. 44.

Act is much more specific, stating that where the effect will be to lessen competition substantially or tend to create a monopoly, certain practices are unlawful. Practices that are specifically condemned in the Clayton Act and its later amendments are:

1. Discrimination in price between purchasers of like grade, quality, or quantity of a commodity "where the effect of such discrimination may be substantially to lessen competition or tend to create a monopoly in any line of commerce"

2. Contracts or agreements that require the buyer to purchase additional merchandise in order to secure the items desired

3. Interlocking directorates in directly competing corporations

4. Acquisition by a corporation of more than a limited amount of stock in a directly competing corporation

The last two items were intended to prevent monopolies. Authority to enforce the provisions of the Clayton Act was vested in the Federal Trade Commission, which was created shortly after the act was passed.

The Federal Trade Commission Act**

While the Sherman Antitrust Act prevents combinations and restraint of trade and the Clayton Act deals with specific unfair trade practices, the Federal Trade Commission Act was passed to control unfair trade practices generally. Passed in 1914, this act provides that "unfair methods of competition in commerce are hereby declared unlawful." A five-member commission was established to define and detect unfair trade practices. Examples of practices that the commission has found to be unfair are:

SPECIAL READINGS

**The Closed Enterprise System, Ralph Nader's Study Group Report on Antitrust Enforcement, by Mark J. Green, with Beverly C. Moore and Bruce Wasserstein. New York: Grossman Publishers, 1972. Nader opens his introduction to the book with a direct attack on corporations by stating: "This is a report on crime in the [executive] suites. It is a report on the closed enterprise system and its human, political, and economic costs to Americans."

The authors examine critically the government's antitrust apparatus—the Department of Justice and the Federal Trade Commission. The book states that its primary purpose is to bring into the open the state of affairs in corporations suspected of being in violation of antitrust laws. Similarly, the government's antitrust activities are brought under scrutiny. To justify this goal, Louis D. Brandeis is quoted, "Sunlight is said to be the best of disinfectants." Provocative and controversial, the book, by means of case studies, examines mergers, the automobile industry, the professions, and the oil industry. As a result of these investigations, Nader predicts that antitrust enforcement "will make a comeback to show the modern relevance of this traditional wisdom." Here he contradicts Richard Hofstadter, who commented that the antitrust movement was "one of the faded passions of American reform."

1. Use of false or misleading advertising to deceive the public
2. Misbranding of goods as to quality, durability, composition, ingredients, origin, and so on
3. Bribery of customers' employees to obtain orders
4. Bribery of competitors' employees to learn trade secrets
5. Making false statements to the disadvantage of a competitor's products, services, financial status, and similar matters
6. Advertising and selling rebuilt, reconditioned, or old merchandise as new
7. Advertising free goods or gifts but then requiring that the customer buy something else to obtain them
8. Using business schemes based on chance or lot
9. Coercion by a group of retailers to force suppliers to sell goods to them at a certain price
10. Using containers that convey a false impression of the contents

The Federal Trade Commission may act on complaints received from businesses or consumers, or it may undertake action on its own accord. After a complaint is received that the commission believes is justified, it gives the suspected violator thirty days to answer the charge. If the commission is not satisfied with the answer, it will make a further investigation. If the suspected violator is still believed guilty, the commission issues a "cease and desist order" to stop the basis for the complaint. If this order is ignored, the case goes to court, a step that is seldom necessary, since few businesses are willing to face such unfavorable publicity or spend the money required to defend their position.

The Robinson-Patman Act

The Robinson-Patman Act, passed in 1936, regulates marketing activity. The Sherman Antitrust Act was intended primarily to curb monopolistic practices of manufacturers. But with the appearance of giant marketing establishments, mainly chain-store systems and mail-order houses, it became apparent that unfair competition existed also in marketing. Some marketing organizations had become so powerful that they could induce their suppliers to grant them major price concessions, free services, advertising allowances, and other advantages not enjoyed by small retailers and wholesalers.

The most important provision of the Robinson-Patman Act prohibits "discrimination in price between different purchasers of commodities of like grade and quality, where any of the purchases involved are in interstate commerce, and where the effect may be substantially to lessen competition or tend to create a monopoly in any line of commerce, or to injure, destroy, or prevent competition with any person who either grants or knowingly receives the benefit of such discrimination or with customers of either item." Price differentials that result from quantity purchases are permitted if they are based on actual differences in cost of manufacturing, selling, and delivering.

The Robinson-Patman Act, administered by the Federal Trade Commission, is generally regarded as successful in making competition in marketing reasonably equitable.

The Wheeler-Lea Act

In 1938, the Wheeler-Lea Act was passed to amend the Federal Trade Commission Act of 1914. Basically, the Wheeler-Lea Act is intended to strengthen the previous legislation. Three changes were made.

1. Jurisdiction of the Federal Trade Commission was broadened to include practices that injure the public but that do not necessarily injure a competitor. Prior to the Wheeler-Lea Act, only action harming competitors was considered unlawful.

2. The commission's authority was given teeth. Cease and desist orders become final sixty days after being served. For failure to obey there is a fine that increases daily until paid.

3. False advertising of food, drugs, cosmetics, and therapeutic devices was declared illegal.

Consumer Product Safety Commission

For the first time in the country's history, the Federal Government is empowered to set safety standards for all products found "in or around" a household or school, except motor vehicles,[4] boats, tobacco, insecticides, food, drugs, and cosmetics, which are covered by other legislation. When he signed it, the President called the Consumer Products Safety Act, passed on October 28, 1972, "the most significant consumer-protection legislation passed by the 92nd Congress." Enactment of the law was a major goal of consumer groups. It contains a novel provision, new in control legislation—it allows consumers to initiate court action to force

---

[4] Resetting the mileage recorded on the odometer in an automobile dashboard, an old trick of unscrupulous used-car dealers, is now illegal under federal legislation. The law enables the purchaser of a vehicle with false odometer mileage to sue the seller for three times the amount of any damage he incurs or for $1,500, whichever is greater. But to collect, the buyer must prove fraudulent intent by the seller.

the government to take action, if it seems to be dragging its feet. The law created the Consumer Product Safety Commission, which is independent of any other federal agency. Since the Commission communicates directly with Congress and the White House, it can wield enormous powers. Five commissioners, serving staggered seven-year terms, have power to:

1. Set mandatory safety standards on product performance, design, construction, labeling, warnings, and information for use

2. Ban products violating the Commission's standards

3. Direct that products found deficient be recalled, replaced, repaired, or have the purchase price refunded

THE PRESENT STATUS OF GOVERNMENT REGULATION

The attack on current problems

Antitrust policy in the United States seems to run hot and cold, depending upon the prevailing mood. Whenever scandals involving big business occur or the concentration of power is brought to public attention, antitrust enforcement agencies flare into action. Three books that appeared recently—Ralph Nader's The Closed Enterprise System, Mintz and Cohen's America, Inc., and John Blair's Economic Concentration— aroused public concern by arguing that the immense power of large corporations enables the corporations to charge excessive prices, engage in collusion, ignore product safety, and shirk environmental responsibility. These critics pointed out that the 200 largest U.S. corporations control about two-thirds of all manufacturing assets. The Chairman of the House-Senate Subcommittee on Economy in Government, Senator William Proxmire, has been making a stir about the military-industrial complex. Military spending now totals more than $80 billion a year, which is 8 percent of the GNP. Proxmire has charged that the big companies get most of this business. He states, "The Pentagon increasingly resorts to practices that reduce competition and relies more and more heavily on negotiated procurement. Formally advertised competitive military contract dollar awards dropped from 13.4 percent in fiscal year 1967 to 11 percent in fiscal year 1969. Single source procurement increased to 57.9 percent."[5]

At the same time, with balance of payments deterioration, it is argued that antitrust enforcement should be relaxed because our competitive position in foreign markets is hurt by gigantic corporations of other nations that are not hampered by antitrust restrictions.

[5] "The Pentagon vs. Free Enterprise," Senator William Proxmire, Saturday Review, January 31, 1970, p. 14.

What is too big?

The debate brings up one recurring question—What is too big? The government seems to be putting on the brakes. In a 1969 speech, the Attorney General set guidelines for corporate giants by suggesting that the government would act to prohibit acquisitions by any of the country's largest corporations. Much convincing evidence is cited about the contribution of small versus large firms. One of the most telling charges is that huge business is reluctant to change because it does not want to take losses on old installations. There is also much evidence that the significant innovations come from the smaller firms. The glaring example of the U.S. steel industry, which has fallen disgracefully behind foreign competitors in modernizing plants, is widely cited. The fast, low-cost oxygen steel-making process that is widely used abroad was first installed in the United States by the comparatively small McLouth Steel Corporation. More than ten years passed before the giants, U.S. Steel and Bethlehem, moved to the superior process to any degree.

Limits to size, however, would be difficult to establish. Nader's group advocates a flat $2 billion in annual sales as maximum size. To this a Federal Trade Commission spokesman replies, "Do you apply the same limits to an aerospace company and a candy manufacturer?"

The revitalized FTC

There is no question that the FTC has been revitalized and has made some bold moves. It has set up consumer advisory boards in 11 cities and promises more in other cities. It has taken a strong position in getting advertisers to document their claims and promises to investigate each industry, having started with the automobile industry because that industry takes one of the biggest bites out of the consumer dollar. It issued a new precedent-setting rule when it required corrective advertising for the first time. ITT Continental Baking Company was ordered to devote one-fourth of a year's advertising budget to counteract the effects of misleading statements previously made about the dieting qualities of its Profile bread. The renewed vigor of enforcement agencies promises a lot of rethinking of business practices and new policy formulation.

GOVERNMENT REGULATION OF PUBLIC UTILITIES

The discussion so far shows that the government stimulates competition. An exception is found in the case of public utilities—those businesses that possess special franchises issued by government. Such utilities—usually gas, water, electric, telephone, telegraph, and sewage disposal companies — operate as monopolies.

Why utilities are regulated

Public utilities are regulated because they are monopolies. The reasons they are monopolies are several:

Everyone in a community makes use of several public utilities. Since the utilities are absolute necessities, the public expects them to operate in the public interest. Because of the nature of the services they provide, it would be economically and often physically infeasible to have competing utilities. Two electric utilities or telephone companies serving the same community would be chaotic. Public utilities require a very large initial investment. Investment per dollar of gross revenue received is approximately six times as great as the investment needed in manufacturing industries. Capital would be difficult to attract if investors were not assured that their utility would be the only one of its kind in the community. Since the original investment is so great, it follows that large-scale operations are necessary to make service available at low cost.

To grant monopolist privilege without controls would invite severe problems. The utility could give poor service and charge exorbitant prices. To prevent this, government closely regulates the services offered and rates charged by the utility. Responsibility for this regulation is centered in state agencies called "public service commissions."

TAXATION AND BUSINESS

The subject of taxation is of exceptional concern to practically everyone. While most people agree that taxes are essential, the average person is inclined to feel his burden is too heavy. In the pages that follow, taxation and its influence on the business organization are discussed briefly.

The power to tax

The power to tax is granted the federal government by Article I, Section 8, of the Constitution, which reads in part, "The Congress shall have power to levy and collect taxes, duties, imports, and excises to pay the debts and provide for the common defense and general welfare of the United States." Federal tax laws can be enacted only by the Congress. Since the states may exercise any powers not delegated to the federal government or

Figure **26–1**
Total Government Expenditures
and Gross National Product Compared

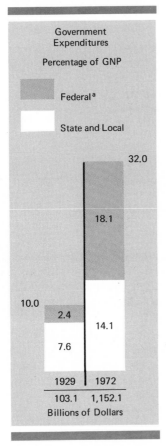

ᵃ Grants-in-aid included in state and local expenditures only to avoid double counting.

Source: Federal Reserve Bank of Chicago, *Business Conditions*, February 1973, p. 7.

reserved for the people themselves, the various state governments can also levy taxes. The power of local government units to tax is determined by the state constitutions. Federal taxes must be equal throughout the United States, but state and local taxes vary widely in kind and amount.

Purpose of taxation

The purpose of taxation is to provide funds for government and public services. Taxation is also used as a regulatory device. For example, income taxes as presently constituted tend to make for greater equality in

Figure **26-2**
Sharp Increase in Total Federal
Expenditures, 1940–72

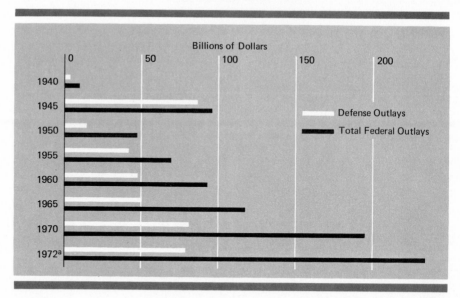

ᵃ Estimated.
Source: *Statistical Abstract of the United States, 1972*, p. 249.

the distribution of wealth. Adjustments in income tax rates are sometimes made to stimulate consumer spending and capital investment by business. Tariffs are levied to restrict the amount of foreign goods sold in the country.

Expenditure trends

Expenditures of the local, state, and national governments individually and collectively have shown a decided upward trend both in absolute amount and as percentages of the GNP. The rise in federal expenditures, and their share of the GNP, are shown in Figure 26–2.

Business leaders tend to feel that taxes reduce profits that would otherwise be used to expand and improve plant facilities and to pay dividends that would stimulate the economy. Furthermore, because a large share of the tax burden is added to the selling price of goods and services, consumption is reduced.

Most businesses, however, appreciate the fact that large tax reductions are impossible so long as the public requests more government assistance and the nation requires a strong defense posture. As a result, businesses are interested in the effective use of each tax dollar.

VAT, the value added tax

It is very possible that the United States will eventually follow the example of the Common Market countries and introduce a value added tax, or VAT. Many governments are finding it desirable to reduce the burden of direct taxation and to mask taxation as far as possible, for as the ancient tax collectors of Rome put it, "The ideal tax is the one that gets the most feathers out of the goose with the least squawk."

VAT collects its tax throughout a product's commercial life. It is imposed at each stage of production from raw material through retail sale. Lower rates of tax are imposed on such goods and services that are considered essential. VAT also makes sense when coping with balance-of-payments problems because VAT can be rebated on exports and imposed on imports. VAT has an ecological benefit—it would extend the use of manufactured goods because secondhand goods would not be required to bear the tax.

It is clear that increasing revenues will be needed to finance the growing social requirements citizens expect from their government. This raises a clear-cut question: What kind of tax? VAT is considered to be one of the most attractive alternatives. It is politically risky to try to collect growing revenue needs from direct taxes on real estate, income, cigarettes, gasoline, and liquor.

When first conceived in 1941 by W. W. Mount of Warren, New Jersey, it was suggested to replace all federal taxes on business and personal income. The tax base for VAT is not total sales but the difference between the amount received from customers and the amount paid for outside goods and services. These figures are kept routinely by every business so it would require little extra accounting, according to its proponents. The following might be a tax calculation for a typical business:

Sales to customers	$100,000
Less cost of purchases	40,000
Value added (tax base)	$ 60,000

Payment of the tax would be at the prescribed rate on the $60,000 value added base. It should not be thought that the $40,000 of outside expense goes untaxed. Obviously, since it was purchased from others it becomes someone else's "Sales to customers," and the process described above is repeated.

VAT, as with any suggested new form of taxation, is quite controversial. Critics say it is complicated and regressive (that is, it hits the poor harder than it does the wealthy). It is also considered the most neutral of all taxes. As Professor Dan Smith of Harvard puts it, "It is neutral as between labor-intensive and capital-intensive forms of production, and between vertically integrated companies and those active at only one level. It is neutral in its impact on the choice between debt-financing and equity-financing in business. It is neutral as between all types of consumer goods and services, except insofar as some are specifically exempted. And it is neutral as between efficient and inefficient producers."

The negative income tax

Another new form of taxation that has been receiving attention is the negative income tax. This system is intended to equalize incomes with a downward extension of the income tax structure, which now extends only upward—that is, people get taxed more as their income increases. Under the proposed system, people with incomes below the minimum level would receive income payments just as people above poverty levels pay income taxes. The idea was advanced by Professor Milton Friedman of the University of Chicago in 1962. The advantages he cited were that it would strengthen the economy and be a spur to individual initiative because it would enable low income people to make their own decisions on spendings and savings. An essential feature of the plan is that as an individual's income rises above the poverty level, the tax payments he receives are reduced. The individual is always better off when his own earnings are higher.

The present large and growing social welfare programs are succeeding only in perpetuating the vicious cycle of poverty. With the negative income tax, everyone would be assured a minimum income without being dependent upon a dehumanizing social-welfare apparatus. An important question that is raised is: Would payments to those who earned less than a certain amount reduce their incentive to work? The results of an unusual test of 1,300 families indicates that payments would have no such effect.**

Sources and uses of tax collections

Personal income tax   The Sixteenth Amendment to the Constitution, enacted in 1913, enables the federal government to levy a tax on personal incomes. The personal income tax is the government's largest single source of revenue. Employers who pay wages or salaries to employees are required by law to withhold a certain portion of such wages and remit it directly to the Internal Revenue Service. Personal income taxes, with similar withholding requirements, are also levied by many states and cities.

Corporation income tax   The federal corporate income tax applies to all corporations engaged in business for a profit. Profits made by sole

SPECIAL READINGS

** "A Negative Income Tax Experiment" by David N. Kerslaw. *Scientific American*, October 1972. There is every indication that businessmen and business students will be required to broaden their outlooks in the future. Scientists also feel that they have been too narrow. Attempts to overcome deficiencies of narrowness, much formerly specialized literature now deals with wider subjects. In order that scientific and nonscientifically trained people understand each other better, they should begin reading each other's literature. For example, businessmen should familiarize themselves with what scientists are thinking about.

Scientific American, a monthly magazine, carries many articles such as the one that describes and discusses the negative income tax experiment. A student who wishes to equip himself to cope with the future challenges of society, would do well to familiarize himself with this significant and interesting magazine.

proprietorships and partnerships must be reported by the individuals owning these businesses on their personal income tax reports.

Most state governments also levy a tax on corporate profits. The rates applied are generally much lower than those levied by the federal government.

Sales tax   Most states and some cities now levy a sales tax on goods sold at retail. Usually these taxes, which range from 1 to 7 percent of the selling price (see Table 26–1), are levied on all goods purchased, although exceptions are sometimes made for necessities, such as food or drugs.

General property tax   City, county, and other local governments obtain the largest part of their revenue from a general property tax levied

Table **26–1**
1972 State Sales Taxes[a]

Alabama	4%	Louisiana	3	Ohio	4
Alaska	None	Maine	5	Oklahoma	2
Arizona	3	Maryland	4	Oregon	None
Arkansas	3	Massachusetts	3	Pennsylvania	6
California	3.75	Michigan	4	Rhode Island	5
Colorado	3	Minnesota	4	South Carolina	4
Connecticut	7	Mississippi	5	South Dakota	4
Delaware	None	Missouri	3	Tennessee	3.5
Florida	4	Montana	None	Texas	4
Georgia	3	Nebraska	2.5	Utah	4
Hawaii	4	Nevada	3	Vermont	3
Idaho	3	New Hampshire	None	Virginia	3
Illinois	4	New Jersey	5	Washington	4.5
Indiana	2	New Mexico	4	West Virginia	3
Iowa	3	New York	4[a]	Wisconsin	4
Kansas	3	North Carolina	3	Wyoming	3
Kentucky	5	North Dakota	4	District of Columbia	5

[a] Many states authorize local communities to impose their own additional sales tax. For example, New York City adds 3 percent to make effective rate of 7 percent.
Source: Tax Foundation, Inc.

against privately owned property in the community. Both personal property and real estate are taxed after valuation is determined by a tax assessor.

Excise tax   In the main, excise taxes are not levied on commodities or services that are regarded as absolute necessities. Most often, the tax is levied on the manufacturer, who adds it to the cost of the product. Such a tax is often called a "manufacturers' excise tax." The consumer is often unaware that the price for tires, radios, automobiles, electric appliances, and guns, might include one or more excise taxes.

Some excise taxes are collected by the retailer and for that reason are called "retailers' excise taxes." Commodities taxed in this fashion have included so-called luxuries, such as certain types of luggage, purses, jewelry, clocks, silverware, and cosmetics. The customer is usually aware of the retail excise tax, since it is added to the retail selling price of the product.

The federal excise tax on liquor deserves separate mention because of its importance as a source of revenue. In an average year, approximately 6 percent of federal tax revenue stems from the liquor tax; as much as one-half of the retail price of liquor may be tax. All state and many local governments also levy taxes on liquor, as well as gasoline and tobacco.

Custom duties   An exclusive right of the federal government is to levy a tax on goods imported into this country. This tax serves two purposes: to raise revenue and to protect producers from the competition of lower-priced foreign goods. Goods that cannot be produced domestically, such as coffee and bananas, usually are permitted to enter the United States duty free. Federal receipts by taxation and expenditures by category are shown in Figure 26–3.

Federal revenue sharing

When Congress enacted the State and Local Fiscal Assistance Act of 1972, a new concept in taxation called "revenue sharing" emerged. The law requires the federal government to return to the states a share of federal income taxes collected during the preceding year. In 1973, the first year of revenue sharing, $5.3 billion were returned to the states. The states are authorized to keep a certain percentage of the shared formula for state projects and are required to distribute (pass through) the remainder to local governments. It is anticipated that $25 billion will be shared over the next four years.[6]

[6] "Revenue-Sharing Bonanza—Latest Plans of Cities, States," *U.S. News and World Report,* March 5, 1973, p. 21.

Figure **26–3**
The Budget Dollar

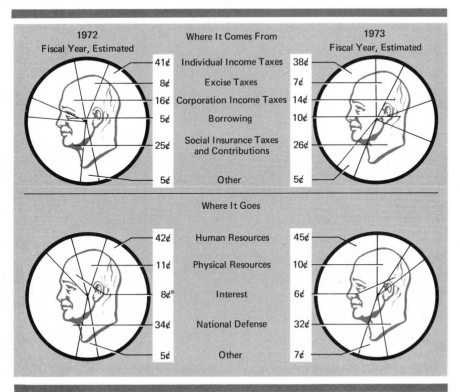

ᵃ Excludes interest paid to trust funds.
Source: Office of Management and the Budget.

The percentage of federal income taxes to be shared with local governments is set by law. The money is apportioned under a complex formula that involves population, income, and local taxes. States and communities in which people have relatively low incomes get proportionately more, as do localities that generate more taxes of their own.

Local communities are permitted considerable latitude in the way they spend shared revenue. Local projects involving social, transportation, sanitation, and educational needs appear to benefit most.

The idea behind revenue sharing is that states and municipal governments are more aware of local needs and can spend money more efficiently than the federal government which is more distantly removed from local problems. While most members of Congress, governors, and mayors endorse revenue sharing, the concept is criticized by some on the grounds that (1) a better alternative would be to reduce federal income taxes, (2) wealthier states and communities receive proportionately less than poorer areas, (3) cutbacks must be made on existing federal programs, and (4) the federal government cannot afford to share revenue because, in most years, the federal budget operates at a deficit.

THE GOVERNMENTAL ROLE IN PERSPECTIVE

By whatever yardstick is used, the government's role in the economy has expanded significantly since 1960. Federal spending amounted to $92.2 billion in 1960 and rose to $211.4 billion in 1971. Federal government expenditures for 1972 are the equivalent of 18.1 percent of the gross national product. If state and local government spending is added, the proportion rises to 32.0 percent of the GNP.

In 1971 defense spending was more than double 1960. In 1971 nondefense spending was 108 percent over 1960. There are many reasons for the great rise between 1960 and 1971:

1. An 11 percent increase in the population and a corresponding increase in services needed

2. Social security and welfare programs, the major sector of nondefense expenditures, which more than doubled, rising from $18 billion to about $41 billion, partly because of Medicare and the larger population of those over 65

3. New programs of federal aid to education, which rose from $700 million to over $4 billion

4. The National Aeronautics and Space Administration expenditures, which shot up from $370 million to $4.4 billion annually

5. Expanded governmental payrolls, which increased more than 50 percent—more than three times the 14 percent increase in total civilian employment over the same period

The consequence of such expenditure expansion has been a budget deficit. In spite of record business prosperity in recent years and the resulting increases in tax revenues (for when business prospers, the tax take goes up), there just is not enough money to pay for ambitious domestic programs and to fight wars too. Should there be cessation of wars, the economy, which is more vigorous than ever before, could produce budget surpluses or finance further programs. Built-in increases required to meet fixed obligations under current federal programs are

Figure **26–4**
How Much Is a Billion Dollars?

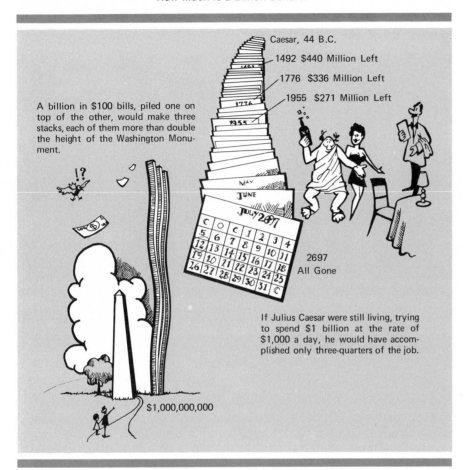

A billion in $100 bills, piled one on top of the other, would make three stacks, each of them more than double the height of the Washington Monument.

Caesar, 44 B.C.
1492 $440 Million Left
1776 $336 Million Left
1955 $271 Million Left

2697
All Gone

$1,000,000,000

If Julius Caesar were still living, trying to spend $1 billion at the rate of $1,000 a day, he would have accomplished only three-quarters of the job.

In 1972, the federal debt was $455.8 billion.   Source: Adapted from the *New York Times.*

rising at a rate of $7–$10 billion per year. At the same time, revenues under conditions of normal economic growth are rising at a rate of at least $12 billion per year. Figure 26–5 shows post-Vietnam budget projections.

For the past thirty years our formerly laissez-faire capitalistic society has been shifting to a welfare state. Today, $32 out of every $100 of the GNP are spent by federal, state, or local governments, and as recently as 1950 that ratio was only thirteen out of every hundred. GNP can be spent either (1) by individuals as they choose, or (2) by society as a whole

Figure **26–5**
The Shifting Emphasis in Federal Budget Expenditures

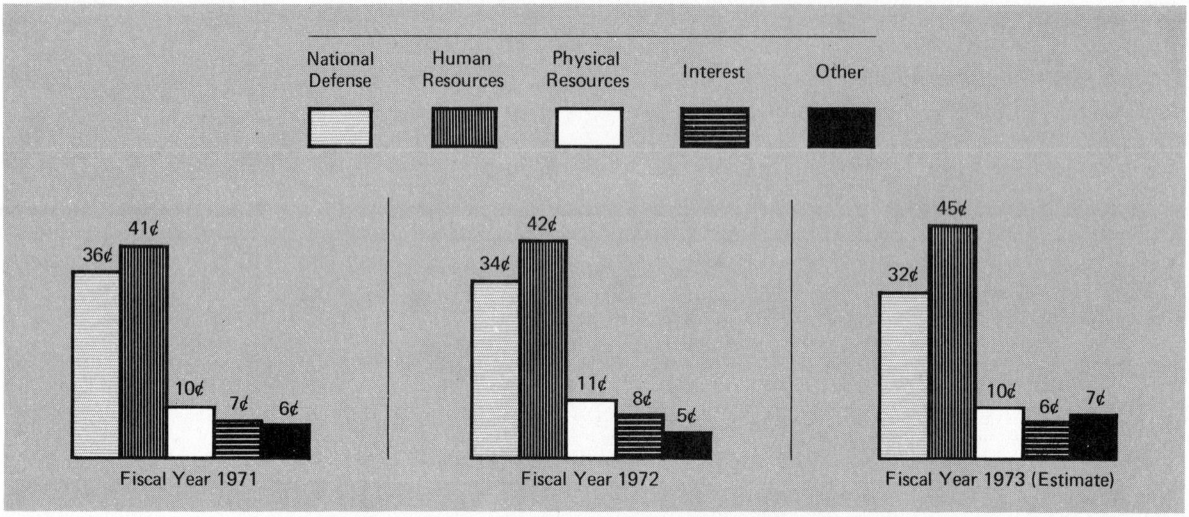

National Defense | Human Resources | Physical Resources | Interest | Other

Fiscal Year 1971: 36¢, 41¢, 10¢, 7¢, 6¢
Fiscal Year 1972: 34¢, 42¢, 11¢, 8¢, 5¢
Fiscal Year 1973 (Estimate): 32¢, 45¢, 10¢, 6¢, 7¢

Note: *Human resources* include: education and manpower, health, income security, and veterans benefits and services. *Physical resources* include: agriculture and rural development, natural resources and environment, commerce and transportation, and community development and housing. *Other* includes: general government, international affairs and finance, space research and technology, and the federal government share of federal employees' retirement and allowances. *Interest* is net of interest paid to the trust funds.

Source: Office of Management and Budget, "The U.S. Budget in Brief," U.S. Government Printing Office.

through taxation. The pendulum has definitely swung to the choice-by-society tendency through government expenditures. There is every reason to believe that the trend toward social rather than individual spending will continue.

In the later part of the twentieth century big government is as much a part of our society as is big business. About thirteen million people are now employed by the government—federal, state, and local. Some of the nation's largest companies do fifty to seventy-five percent of their business with the government. *Fortune* estimates that three hundred companies have permanent liaison offices in Washington.

Many of today's projects are beyond the scope of even the biggest of American businesses. Urban redevelopment, pollution control, space programs, and mass transportation can only be effected by business and government working together more closely.

An area of growing concern is the matter of coping with bigness—Big Business and Big Government. As bureaucracy grows, often the individual's frustrations in attempting to deal with it grow too. Bigness proliferates red tape. One solution to this problem, which originated in the

Scandinavian countries and is now being extended in the United States, is the idea of ombudsmanship. An *ombudsman* is a government official who is appointed to receive and get action on grievances against government (and perhaps business). He, or his office, is where the business-person or individual can turn when he feels his hands are tied in trying to deal with the government. There is reason to believe that an ombuds-man-like function will become more important in the future.

A LOOK AT NATIONAL PRIORITIES

Over a decade ago, President Eisenhower's Commission on National Goals placed high priority on social objectives. It recommended that increased attention and money be allotted to education, health, urban renewal, agricultural policy, and economic growth. Since that report was issued, expenditures for social and environmental programs tripled, advancing from about $8 billion in 1960 to $30 billion in 1970. (Refer back to Figure 26–5.)

There is increasing skepticism about whether public expenditures are solving socioeconomic problems. Rising welfare rolls in periods of increasing prosperity suggest that the country is still a long way from breaking the vicious grip of welfare dependency.

The national housing goals for the decade ahead as stated in the 1968 Housing Act will greatly concern business – 26 million new or rehabili-tated housing units are called for in the next ten years. Meeting this goal will be difficult and will require extensive government and business cooperation. Part of the housing goal is to lower the cost of housing by improving technology in the building industry. Pressures are being brought to bear to make largely outmoded building codes more rational, to make zoning in cities and suburbs more flexible, and to urge states-manlike leadership on the part of the union officials to change work rules so they encourage rather than hamper the use of mass-production tech-niques in housing.

The pollution control measures discussed in Chapter 16 will also bring business and government closer together. Reducing pollution to accept-able levels will lead to higher prices in many areas, which means that prices people pay will represent more closely true costs to society. During the change-over process to control pollution, it may be necessary to ex-tend government loans or give tax credits to those companies that cannot finance pollution-control devices themselves.

Increasing numbers of people feel that the problems of crime, pollu-tion, poverty, and the general instability of society should be given significantly higher priorities in the value scales of both government and business. Today's business student will be able to make tremendous contributions to tomorrow's society by assisting in the continuing co-operation of business and government.

PEOPLE AND THEIR IDEAS
Ralph Nader

The twentieth century's biggest impact on business

Ralph Nader's biographer, Charles McCarry,[7] states that Ralph Nader has convinced "a very large segment of the population, that General Motors is symbolic of almost everything that is wrong with life in the United States." Nader first came to the attention of General Motors in 1965 when he published *Unsafe at Any Speed*, which helped make Nader's name a household word in many parts of the world. The book told the world that, in its lust for profits, the automobile industry knowingly was routinely marketing unsafe cars.

How the book came to be published is a fascinating story that illustrates how, in an age characterized by multinational corporate giants, the smallest of businesses can make an impact that upsets the titans. Oddly, the idea for Nader's book was not his. A small publisher, Richard Grossman of Grossman Publishers in New York, commissioned the book, which Mr. Grossman titled. Grossman had never heard of Nader. He went to a man who had written an article on automobile safety. However, the man was too busy to do the book, so he referred Grossman to Nader, who had supplied him with background data on automobile safety. Nader agreed to write the book and dedicated it to Frederick H. Condon, a classmate at Harvard Law School who had been crippled in an automobile accident. Grossman's company was so small (he was half of a two-man company) that when the book came out he peddled it to book stores by driving loads of it around in his station wagon. Eventually the book sold 70,000 copies in hard cover and a quarter-million in paperback.

Nader is a true crusader. He is eminently well qualified by virtue of brains and education to take the lead as a reformer. He graduated *magna cum laude* from Princeton University in 1955. In 1958, he graduated from the Harvard Law School. An early friend said, "He had the eyes of a re-former." He lived in a rooming house alone, had few worldly possessions, and seemed to own only one necktie. It is said that Nader's great gift is not to be bored by the obvious. Nader claims that looking at everything as if

[7] *Citizen Nader*, Charles McCarry (New York: Saturday Review Press, 1972).

he were nineteen years old makes this possible. He has an additional gift — his ability to free others of their indifference.

Nader's father was an intensely patriotic immigrant from Lebanon who taught his son not to trust power. What subsequently happened to Nader proved his father right. While Nader was working with the Senate Investigating Committee on the automobile industry, General Motors hired detectives to follow him and to dig up whatever they could to discredit him. The result was that later, James Roche, president of General Motors (which in terms of wealth would be the sixth largest country in the world), had this to say when summoned to the Senate subcommittee: "I deplore the kind of harassment to which Mr. Nader has apparently been subjected . . . to the extent that General Motors bears responsibility, I want to apologize here and now to the subcommittee and to Mr. Nader."

In 1966, President Johnson signed the National Traffic and Motor Vehicle Safety and Highway Safety acts, which Nader advocated, bringing the design of motor vehicles under federal regulation. In 1967–68 Congress passed the Wholesale Meat Act, the Natural Gas Pipeline Safety Act, Radiation Control for Health and Safety Act, and the Wholesale Poultry Act, all advocated by Nader.

Nader cannot be characterized as the nemesis of big business alone, for he is actively investigating the government and pollution sources. He established various groups of "Nader's Raiders," one of which investigated the Federal Trade Commission, and in 1971 he announced plans to investigate Congress itself. Senator Ribicoff said, "I've never known anyone like Ralph Nader—one man who believes he's a majority." Unionist Joseph Yablonski, talking about things he accomplished, said, "Ralph was the magical unknown variable that could grab victory from the jaws of defeat."

As the world's leading reformer, Nader probably has faith in the future for he has written: "Indians in the woods saw things that the white man never saw because the Indians were trained to see them. We can do the same in our technological society."

CONTEMPORARY ISSUES
Situation 26

Should tax rates be increased for the wealthy and reduced for the middle-class and poor?

John came across an item in the newspaper about a prominent politician who promised, if reelected, to work for the enactment of a new tax plan that would significantly raise taxes for the wealthy, moderately reduce them for the middle class, and greatly reduce taxes for the poor people. "What do you think of that plan?" John asked.

"Well," Ray responded, "I'm sure it's a good vote-getter because there are a lot more poor and middle-class people than wealthy folks. But in terms of economic soundness, I'm not impressed. As I see it, increasing taxes to the wealthy works to the disadvantage of both the middle and poor classes."

"Why do you say that?" asked John.

"Well, as I see it," Ray answered, "I think we spend too much time worrying about how the tax burden should be levied. We should be more concerned about increasing productivity. The wealthy people are more inclined to invest money in speculative type investments such as oil drilling explorations and real estate developments. If we taxed this population segment more, we would lose a source of capital so necessary for economic development."

"OK," injected John, "but if we cut taxes for the middle and poor classes, it would mean more take-home pay for them. This means they would spend more for a wide variety of products which would cause economic expansion."

"I think there is merit in what you say," responded Ray, "but the wealthy class is more likely to spend money where it will do the most good over the long run."

"Well, how to apportion taxes in a way that will do the most economic good is a tough assignment," admitted John, "but I have one idea that might make everyone happy and produce economic growth."

"What's that?" asked Ray.

"Cut taxes for everybody, rich, middle class and poor," John answered.

SITUATION EVALUATION

1. Who has the better argument, John or Ray?

2. What additional arguments, pro and con, could be advanced in support of each position?

3. Does it really make any difference in terms of economic growth how the tax burden is allocated? Explain.

BUSINESS CHRONICLE

Dealing with the government

Receiving approval for property development plans is a complicated business. Properties must be carefully surveyed, engineering layouts must be drawn up, and all details must be filed for approval with the various state and local agencies involved. These may include Planning Boards, Environmental Control Boards and Building Permit Offices, the State Department of Health (for drainage approval), School Boards (for educational services approvals), Department of Highways (for road construction and road access approvals), the Utility Commission (for utility lead-in approvals), and so on.

Requests for approvals are often time consuming; months and even years go by before projects can be officially started. Often large amounts of capital are tied up in properties while they await approval.

To facilitate getting project approvals, the management of Kingmaker Estates decided to set up a Department of Environmental Management. In the past, plans were sometimes rejected after being held up for long periods of time, simply because the company did not know what was required from an ecological point of view. Since the ecological approach to planning was so new, Dr. Elwood Mair, a biologist from the University of Florida, was employed as Director of Environmental Management. The assistant to the chief engineering draftsman from the State of Florida's Department of Highways was hired and put in charge of preparing technical proposals. It was felt that getting employees with non-business backgrounds would make it easier to deal with government agencies. It was felt that former government employees would better understand bureaucratic procedures and thus be able to deal with it more effectively.

Another move to improve government relations was to sponsor (i.e. pay for) a documentary film for the State Department of Conservation.

All Kingmaker employees dealing with government agencies were instructed to consult with the agencies during the time plans were drawn up. It was believed this procedure would expedite matters and would reduce the number of plans that were either rejected or requested to be altered.

QUESTIONS

1. Evaluate the various moves that were made to improve government relations. What are their advantages and drawbacks?

2. What other steps can be taken to get approvals more quickly?

3. Are government agencies anti-business? Why is it that many businessmen think that government is anti-business?

APPLICATION EXERCISES

1. The U.S. Department of Commerce makes available a large number of publications as aids to small business. Refer to the governmental publications section of your library and compile a list of government publications that would be useful for someone planning to start a retail store.

2. Assume the newspapers have just announced that Congress is about to reopen the issue of anti-trust. John Laski, who works for IBM as a sales-

man, feels that large corporations are being overly harrassed by government. He decides to write a letter to his Congressman urging him to take a stand against more anti-trust legislation. Loretta Slade, a housewife, is concerned about rising prices. She decides to write a letter to her Congresswoman to take a stand for more anti-trust legislation because she feels that bigness and reduced competition raises prices. Write the two letters that you think these people might send.

3. The primary function of taxation is to raise revenue for public needs. Taxes can also be used to give direction to human behavior.
   a. What are the pros and cons of increasing the taxes on cigarettes by at least 50 cents a package in an effort to induce more people to quit. As part of the legislation authorizing the tax, revenue collected would be earmarked for (1) research and treatment of lung diseases and (2) an educational campaign designed to induce people to not smoke.
   b. Next, develop at least three other types of tax that directly or indirectly might help to improve the environment (a tax on no deposit–no return bottles is one example).
   c. In principle, do you favor using taxes for directing human behavior? Why or why not?

QUESTIONS

1. Review the most important causes for increased government control of and influence in business.

2. Trace government legislation concerning monopolies and restraint of business from the Sherman Antitrust Act through the Wheeler-Lea Act and explain the purposes of each act.

3. What are the provisions of the Federal Trade Commission Act? In reviewing the provisions, what additions or changes can you suggest to improve the act?

4. Is "big business" bad? Give reasons for your answer.

5. Define "public utilities." What are the characteristics of public utilities?

6. A widely read author feels that as the country grows wealthier the government should receive, through higher taxes, more of our wealth. It is his contention that the government, for example, will build housing projects, maintain national parks, provide for better education, and so forth, whereas individuals are inclined to spend only for personal indulgences. How do you feel about this?

7. From your own experience, do you think businessmen are for or against government controls? On what evidence is your conclusion based?

8. What are VAT and the negative income tax? What are their pros and cons? Explain your stand on these taxation possibilities.

9. What is the revenue-sharing issue? What will future trends be in the matter of revenue sharing?

10. What are the national expenditure categories? What would your spending priorities be?

11. What is an ombudsman? What do you feel the future of this idea will be?

12. Which is worse, big business or big government? How can the evils of each be reduced?

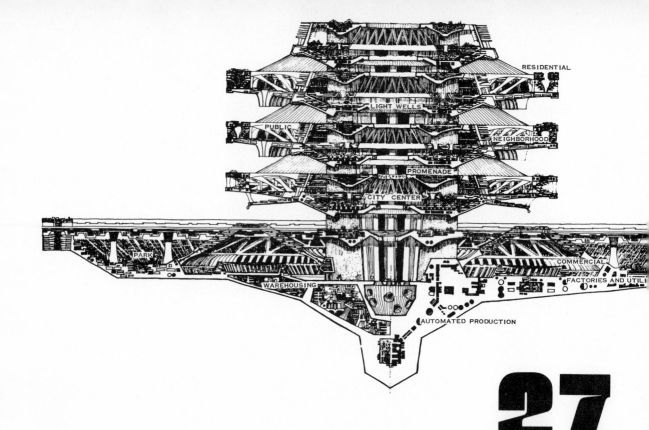

27

CHAPTER 27

IS BUSINESS QUALIFIED TO DEAL WITH SOCIAL CHANGE?

THE SPECTRUM OF CORPORATE SOCIAL ACTIVITIES

DYNAMIC CHARACTERISTICS AND THE CHALLENGE OF CHANGE
Entrepreneurship. Emphasis on Innovation. Changing Methods and Techniques. Scientific Discovery.

CHANGES RELATED TO BUSINESS
Business Looks Further Ahead. Is Growth Progress? Urbanization Trends. Increasing Education. Growing Leisure Time and Boredom.

CHANGING ATTITUDES OF BUSINESS MANAGEMENT
Growing Public-Mindedness. Growing Employee-Mindedness.

THE OPPORTUNITY

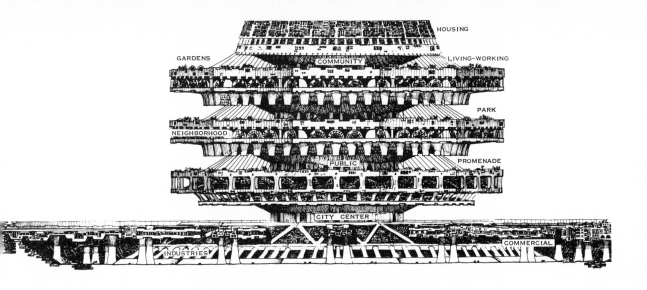

the future and business

A story is told about a young man who volunteered for the Peace Corps after he got a degree in Business Administration. His mission was to help a so-called underdeveloped country raise its standard of living by improving its commerce. When he arrived in his host country, he was distressed that the people did not want to work.

"What," he asked a local resident who was lounging about, "do you think you will accomplish for yourself and your country, just sitting there idly? Why don't you help develop your trade, build factories, and exploit your resources?"

"Why?" asked the man.

"To industrialize," replied the Peace Corps business expert.

"Why industrialize?"

"So you can make lots of money."

"What's the good of money?"

"Money will give you leisure."

"What will I do with leisure?"

"Then you can take it easy."

"But that's what I'm doing now!"

737

The question raised is simply whether industrialization and emphasizing efficiency, productivity, and ownership of material possessions at the exclusion of human considerations is a proper social goal. Many people in our society doubt it. You have had an overview of American business. You have studied how it effectively harnesses resources of materials, money, machines, manpower, and management to produce an impressively high standard of living. Therefore as a thoughtful person, it is proper for you to ask, as does the local resident in our anecdote: Does it make sense? There is a pervasive feeling in the country that overemphasis on economic productivity has gotten our social order out of balance and that growing affluence amid a deteriorating environment and community life does *not* make much sense.

It is now widely debated whether business, as one of society's most powerful institutions, should continue to focus solely on economic pursuits. Society is caught up in change as never before.** The resulting problems must be solved. As thoughtful persons, we must ask ourselves which institutions in society—government, schools, the military, churches, or business—can best solve the social problems that change brings.

In this chapter we make the assumption that business, or probably a combination of business and government, shows the most promise for solving future problems. Business is a technological society's tool for putting its resources to use. Because business is the best institution we have for maniputating resources to achieve goals, the social renaissance that we must have if we are to survive is the prime responsibility of business. There is little doubt of public insistence that the corporate structure be broadly committed to improvement of the social environment.

IS BUSINESS QUALIFIED TO DEAL WITH SOCIAL CHANGE?

Corporate management is far from agreeing that corporations should assume more social responsibility. Where they have tried, results have been mixed; the record has not been impressive.

There are problems when management does turn its attention to social problems.

1. Stockholders of corporations often discourage management from doing anything other than "sticking to business." L. L. L. Golden[1] comments, "It is a serious matter for management, as it is for the nation, that as many as 16.9 percent of stockholders of major corporations are opposed to easing the tensions in the country."

[1] *Saturday Review*, December 12, 1970, p. 60.

Some years ago a stockholder sued a corporation for making a contribution to Princeton University. Management was upheld, as the following excerpt from the unanimous opinion of the Supreme Court of New Jersey indicates:

> When the wealth of the nation was primarily in the hands of individuals, they discharged their responsibilities as citizens by donating freely for charitable purposes. With the transfer of most of the wealth to corporate hands and the imposition of heavy burdens of individual taxation, they have been unable to keep pace with increased philanthropic needs. They have, therefore, with justification turned to corporations to assume the modern obligations of good citizenship in the same manner as humans do.

2. Business has had little or no experience in dealing with social problems. As one commentator points out, if you bring six physicists together, or six chemists, they wouldn't disagree too much on the basics of tackling a problem in their field. But if you bring six business experts or economists together you would probably end up with six very different views on how to tackle a social problem.

3. Many business-related social problems are ambiguous. For example, business is asked to reduce prices while increasing expenditures for pollution control. It is asked to hire submarginal workers who will do submarginal work while at the same time to improve product quality. W. S. Rukeyser evaluates this predicament as follows: "The challenge to think systematically about large, ambiguous questions is inherently daunting, and is one that many businessperson — activists by nature — may be reluctant to take up. But if businesspersons are to manage events, rather than be managed by them, there is no alternative."

4. A feeling of pessimism prevails. H. Ross Perot, President of Electronic Data Systems, Inc., spells out the reason why corporation executives are inclined to back away from social problems. "There is a feeling now among all of our people that the problems are so large that nothing can be done about them. There is a human mechanism that switches us off the unpleasant things."

5. Present business leaders are not qualified to undertake to solve social problems. The question is raised as to whether the types of people who select to go to business schools and who rise in management positions are not too narrow in their outlooks and training and too competitive by nature to succeed where human values are more important than monetary values.

THE SPECTRUM OF CORPORATE SOCIAL ACTIVITIES

Regardless of the difficulties that may be encountered, business has been assigned a leading role in social change. Business education and recruitment efforts must be redirected in order to supply the new kinds of leaders that will be required. The Committee for Economic Development (CED), a prestigious organization of businessmen and educators, issued a report in 1971 on the *Social Responsibilities of Business Corporations*. It compiled a comprehensive checklist that the individual company can review and relate to its own aims and capabilities. The report is expected to exert considerable influence on corporations in the future. The list, reproduced below, was published in the report with the advice that "each company must select those activities which it can pursue most effectively."

ECONOMIC GROWTH AND EFFICIENCY

Increasing productivity in the private sector of the economy

Improving the innovativeness and performance of business management

Enhancing competition

Cooperating with the government in developing more effective measures to control inflation and achieve high levels of employment

Supporting fiscal and monetary policies for steady economic growth

Helping with the post-Vietnam conversion of the economy

EDUCATION

Direct financial aid to schools, including scholarships, grants, and tuition refunds

Support for increases in school budgets

Donation of equipment and skilled personnel

Assistance in curriculum development

Aid in counseling and remedial education

Establishment of new schools, running schools and school systems

Assistance in the management and financing of colleges

EMPLOYMENT AND TRAINING

Active recruitment of the disadvantaged

Special functional training, remedial education, and counseling

Provision of day-care centers for children of working mothers

Improvement of work/career opportunities

Retraining of workers affected by automation or other causes of joblessness

Establishment of company programs to remove the hazards of old age and sickness

Supporting where needed and appropriate the extension of government accident, unemployment, health and retirement systems

CIVIL RIGHTS AND EQUAL OPPORTUNITY

Ensuring employment and advancement opportunities for minorities

Facilitating equality of results by continued training and other special programs

Supporting and aiding the improvement of black educational facilities, and special programs for blacks and other minorities in integrated institutions

Encouraging adoption of open-housing ordinances

Building plants and sales offices in the ghettos

Providing financing and managerial assistance to minority enterprises, and participating with minorities in joint ventures

URBAN RENEWAL AND DEVELOPMENT

Leadership and financial support for city and regional planning and development

Building or improving low-income housing

Building shopping centers, new communities, new cities

Improving transportation systems

POLLUTION ABATEMENT

Installation of modern equipment

Engineering new facilities for minimum environmental effects

Research and technological development

Cooperating with municipalities in joint treatment facilities

Cooperating with local, state, regional and federal agencies in developing improved systems of environmental management

Developing more effective programs for recycling and reusing disposable materials

CONSERVATION AND RECREATION

Augmenting the supply of replenishable resources, such as trees, with more productive species

Preserving animal life and the ecology of forests and comparable areas

Providing recreational and aesthetic facilities for public use

Restoring aesthetically depleted properties such as strip mines

Improving the yield of scarce materials and recycling to conserve the supply

CULTURE AND THE ARTS

Direct financial support to art institutions and the performing arts

Development of indirect support as a business expense through gifts in kind, sponsoring artistic talent, and advertising

Participation on boards to give advice on legal, labor, and financial management problems

Helping secure government financial support for local or state arts councils and the National Endowment for the Arts

MEDICAL CARE

Helping plan community health activities

Designing and operating low-cost medical-care programs

Designing and running new hospitals, clinics, and extended-care facilities

Improving the administration and effectiveness of medical care

Developing better systems for medical education, nurses' training

Developing and supporting a better national system of health care

GOVERNMENT

Helping improve management performance at all levels of government

Supporting adequate compensation and development programs for government executives and employees

Working for the modernization of the nation's governmental structure

Facilitating the reorganization of government to improve its responsiveness and performance

Advocating and supporting reforms in the election system and the legislative process

Designing programs to enhance the effectiveness of the civil services

Promoting reforms in the public welfare system, law enforcement, and other major governmental operations[2]

There were extensive press reactions to the CED report and the spectrum of social activities that it spelled out. Most of them were favorable; a few were negative. The following samples are instructive.

Milwaukee Journal (July 10, 1971)   Business no longer can afford to measure success solely in terms of profit and loss statements.

Wall Street Journal (August 26, 1971)   The often raised question . . . is whether high ethical standards are compatible with the profit motive, which surely must remain the driving force of the economy. Another driving force, however, is the businessman's traditional optimism, and any optimistic view of the world would hold that virtue is not only its own reward but that it brings rewards.

St. Louis Post-Dispatch (July 9, 1971)   The CED committee concluded, quite correctly . . . that greater corporate involvement in efforts to solve the nation's problems serves enlightened self interest in both the long and short range. . . . Surely the time is long past when corporation responsibility ends with an annual contribution to the United Fund. In their day-to-day operations, most large businesses profoundly influence a whole community of people, and it is simply good business to see that the influence is a worthwhile one.

Time Magazine (July 1, 1971)   That business has a responsibility to society beyond the making of profits is by now a commonplace, though still far from universally granted idea. Businessmen have often been confused, however, by the exact nature of their responsibility to improve society and how to carry it out. . . .

Minneapolis Tribune (July 7, 1971)   The CED committee calls for both voluntary involvement and partnership with government on social problems. Up to now, voluntary involvement has suffered whenever profits are down. . . . Meanwhile, even without major additional expenditures, business could vastly improve its social performance by weighing more heavily the impact of its decisions on the social and physical environment.

Hartford Times (September 12, 1971)   Two months ago, spokesmen for the Committee for Economic Development warned American industrialists that unless they diluted their preoccupation with favorable quarterly earn-

[2] *Social Responsibilities of Business Corporations*, Committee for Economic Development, 1971, pp. 37–40.

ings reports, and tackled the dragons of social programs, they were going to face a loss of public faith. . . .

Journal of Accountancy (August 1971)   The conclusions of the CED policy committee present a challenge both to business and to the accounting profession. If the definition of accounting as "A discipline which provides financial and other information essential to the efficient conduct and evaluation of the activities of any organization" is to remain valid, the profession must respond to this challenge.

The methods for measuring social as well as economic performance must be developed. If the accounting profession does not assume the initiative, others will.

Washington Post (August 4, 1971)   If [the CED Trustees] did it as cynical flimflam, as a propaganda concoction that they would inject into schools, offices and communications systems of the country, you can really object; and, if we believe it and get other people to believe it, we deserve the future they're preparing for us.

Christian Science Monitor (July 1, 1971)   The CED document is a useful benchmark as to where some of the Fortune 500 are in their thinking about corporate responsibility today. But the demurrers to the report suggest that business is by no means agreed among itself on the degree of its problem-solving role for society at large.

Chicago Tribune (July 24, 1971)   The report contains a vigorous dissent from Philip Sporn, a former president of the American Electric Power Co. His thesis is that there would be less demand for business to sponsor and finance social projects if it did its own job properly.

Instead of directing business along an ambitious course of social activism, Sporn thinks the committee should concentrate on improving the manner in which it discharges its existing responsibilities. In the long run, we think, his advice is in the interest of the public as well as of business.

Business and Society (July 15, 1971)   Some of the most trenchant comments of this cliche-ridden statement were made by two CED trustees who dissented vigorously from the main conclusions.

DYNAMIC CHARACTERISTICS AND THE CHALLENGE OF CHANGE

Before we consider using the powerful institution of business to cope with the problems of social change, let us review the dynamics of business so we can understand fully what this powerful tool is. Then we will examine briefly some of the problems of change. We will conclude by putting the dynamics of business on one side of the scale and emerging change on the other. The book and your course of study closes by asking you to decide whether business will and can meet its challenge. We hope you will ask yourself two personal questions. Should you assume part of the responsibility for facing the challenge of the future? What role should you claim for shaping the future? Consider the words of John W. Gardener, former Secretary of HEW: "The cynic says, 'One man can't do anything.' I say, 'Only one man can do anything.' "

Entrepreneurship

The starting point for a discussion about business dynamics must be about the essential ingredient of entrepreneurialism. The word "dynamics" comes from Greek words that mean "Have strength to do and then perform it" and "I am able." *Entrepreneur* is defined as one who undertakes to start and conduct an enterprise, usually assuming full control and risk. Obviously we cannot have dynamics without entrepreneurs. They provide the spark in society that sets ideas into motion. In any society more good ideas are lost than are put into action mainly because the willingness to venture is lacking. America consists of people who ventured to its shores in search of opportunity. Entrepreneurship is described as spirit, especially found in the young. The tendency as people age is for them to become less and less willing to risk failure. The opposite of the entrepreneur is well described by J. D. Williams who wrote ". . . any critic can establish a wonderful batting average by just rejecting every new idea." Without the fortunate heritage of entrepreneurialism, American business would not be dynamic. Fears are being expressed that affluence and overdependence on government may be causing this trait to disappear from the American scene.

Emphasis on innovation

Americans traditionally welcome innovation, which includes development of new products, improvements in existing products, introduction of new machines, and development of automation. Innovation emphasizes improvement not only in products, but in methods. For example, the idea of "flow" greatly increased labor's productivity and efficiency by allowing the worker to stand still while the work to be done flows to him at the best height for work. Proper use of equipment and scientific factory layout can be just as important as the production machine used.

American firms also are making increasing use of the systems concept. This concept is based on the idea that one must not lose sight of the forest for the trees—that a business is not a group of individual and isolated operations to be studied separately, but a system of interrelated parts functioning together. Systems innovations that eventually make the worker's job easier and permit the business to turn out more products per

746   THE FUTURE AND BUSINESS

man-hour include improvements in environmental factors in his work area, such as the use of music, color, and light; improvements in materials, such as the replacement of heavy metals with lightweight plastics, which are easier to cut, mold, and handle; and such psychological factors as incentive pay plans and proper job placement. While spectacular inventions and revolutionary industrial methods sometimes occur, systems improvements usually come about gradually and are the product of many minds. Change builds change, each of which may be minor in itself, though the long-run achievement may be dramatic.

New products   A very significant characteristic of American business is the intensive search for new products, thousands of which appear each year.

Consider for a moment innovations in the food and textile industries since 1935. Prepared baby food, precut packaged meat, quick-frozen foods, canned soft drinks, semibaked bakery goods, instant coffee and tea, and packaged baking mixes are only a few of many new foods products. In the textile industry a number of synthetic fibers such as nylon, dacron, polyester, and Acrilan have gained wide acceptance.

A major innovation has many important effects on business as well as on society. The invention of television is a notable example. Here are a few of the thousands of ways television, now taken for granted, affected business.

1. New factories and new equipment were needed to produce television sets.

2. New industries arose to produce parts needed by television manufacturers.

3. Manufacturers of projection equipment, sound equipment, and film benefited from greater sales.

4. A system for distributing and servicing sets had to be established.

5. Retailers had a new, popular product to sell to the public.

6. Listing of programs caused the growth of special newspaper sections and magazines.

7. Advertisers were given a new medium to use to carry their message to consumers.

8. Demand was created for television engineers and repairmen; numerous courses of study and specialized schools came into being to supply necessary training.

9. A demand arose for numerous creative people — actors, script writers, directors, and camera technicians.

Table **27–1**
Changes in Product Sales Indicate Dynamic Nature of Business

PRODUCT	SALES IN THOUSANDS	
	1960	1971
Clothes dryers	1,260,000	3,377,000
Automatic washing machines	2,601,000	4,270,000
Wringer and spinner washing machines	763,000	339,000
Dishwashers	555,000	2,477,000
Food disposals	760,000	2,294,000
Blenders	455	4,200
Can openers	1,200	4,800
Corn poppers	780	2,750
Vacuum cleaners	3,313	7,973
Radios	10,695	8,224
Television (black and white)	5,708	4,848
Television (color)	120	6,349
Tape recorders	295	8,747
Effervescent wine (million gallons)	1.7	23.6
Cotton consumption per capita (pounds)	23.2	19.1
Wool consumption per capita (pounds)	2.3	0.9
Noncellulosic per capita (pounds)	4.4	24.3

Source: U.S. Department of Commerce.

What reasons account for the significant changes in demand? What products do you feel will increase and decrease in popularity during the next ten years?

10. The radio manufacturing and broadcasting industries faced new competition. Improvements both in the construction of radios and in radio programing followed.

11. The movie industry found new competition. To retain a large movie-going audience, motion picture companies and theaters sought ways to make movies "better than ever."

12. To make home viewing more pleasant, rooms were often added or remodeled, benefiting the construction industry, and new products such as TV dinners and TV tables were developed.

13. Satellites for instantaneous transmission have made worldwide and outer space television communication possible. They have been instrumental in many areas, particularly in the space program, in international affairs, and in business and government cooperation.

Thus far, the innovation that has had the greatest effect has been the automobile. In the early 1900s there was only an infant automobile industry; some seventy years later, the automobile industry had become the nation's giant business. In personal expenditures for services it is exceeded in costs only by medical and health services; in retail sales automobiles are exceeded only by expenditures for foods. But innovations in space research, chemicals, computers, and nuclear power may turn the world into something stranger than our wildest science-fiction portrayals.

Improved products and planned obsolescence   A truism in business is that no product is ever regarded as perfect. Each year designers, engineers, chemists, physicists, stylists, and other creative people work to improve products that are already widely accepted. The refrigerator, for example, has gone through a series of changes over the years, and in the next decade it is certain to be improved still further. Innovations are made regularly in thousands of other products, from clothing to light bulbs.

Many consumer-goods manufacturers follow a policy of *planned obsolescence:* Products are changed deliberately—often annually. Changes may be actual improvements or merely change for change's sake. People are becoming more and more critical of planned obsolescence because it is wasteful. Emphasis on ecology, which stresses the conservation of resources, and attitudes of the past that stem from periods of scarcity cause people to question whether it is best for society to throw away clothing that would still serve to keep the body warm or to junk a refrigerator because it doesn't defrost itself.

However, there is an argument in favor of planned obsolescence. There is doubt that a continually expanding economy could be maintained without it, and new model changes keep wide sections of industry modern and change-oriented.

Changing methods and techniques

The dynamic nature of American business is illustrated by the rapid changes taking place in methods and techniques of business operations. In each phase of business, great emphasis is placed on increasing efficiency, which means getting a greater yield from a given input of effort or resources. Thus, an attempt is made to obtain greater production per manhour, incur fewer bad debts in credit extension, increase sales per salesman, obtain greater results per dollar of advertising, operate offices with fewer employees, reduce scrap and waste in production, and so on. An effort is made to obtain greater efficiency through the careful training and utilization of employees and the application of scientific methods to business.

Efficiency in production   The rate of advance in American productivity has averaged about 2 percent a year for the past hundred years; in recent

Figure **27–1**
Growth for Close of the Twentieth Century

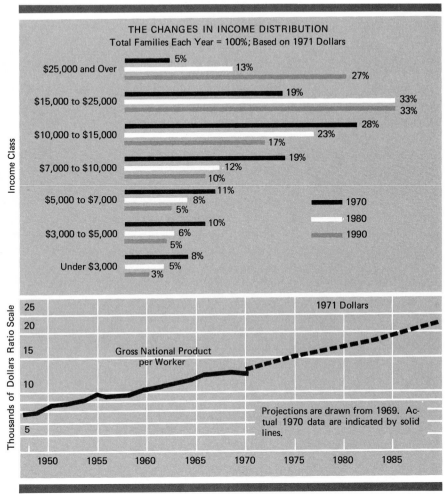

Source: *A Look at Business in 1990*, U.S. Department of Commerce, pp. 47 and 55.

years, though, the average annual increase has ranged from 3.4 percent to 6 percent. If this advance continues, the possibilities for our future material welfare stagger the imagination (see Figure 27–1). Since a basic ingredient of continued progress is the American frame of mind, it seems reasonable to assume that, barring a nuclear war, progress in productivity will continue.

It is distressing to find that most people do not realize how productivity relates to the dynamics of our economy. Surveys disclose that only a fraction of the population understand that productivity is the key to living standards. Productivity is to industry what work is to the individual. Stephen Leacock wrote: "I am a great believer in luck, and I find the harder I work the more I have of it." The same applies to society, the more productive it is, the luckier it becomes.

Efficiency in marketing   Marketing trends that promise greater efficiency include (1) development of better liaison between manufacturers and retailers, (2) rise of new marketing institutions, such as discount houses, which cut costs and distribute goods more economically, and (3) leasing of industrial equipment, such as trucks and machinery, to extend markets. Leasing is a form of specialization that places problems of the usage and maintenance of equipment in the hands of experts who can realize efficiencies not possible for individual owners.

Other major marketing innovations are self-service, vending machines, and shopping centers. The continued trend toward self-service eliminates the use of salespeople in selling merchandise. Self-service first became important in food stores, but now it is used extensively by other retailers. Savings that result from lower labor costs and larger merchandise turnover cut retail distribution costs greatly.

In 1971, over $6 billion worth of goods were sold through vending machines as compared with $2 billion in 1958 (see Table 27–2). The trend toward more vending-machine selling will continue, for vending machines reduce labor expense and provide consumers with products at the time and place desired.

Efficiency in management   Efficiencies result from management knowhow. Improvements in production, marketing, and finance suggest that management is being better understood and more effectively practiced.

Because it is accepted that the success of any organization can be traced directly to its management, more and more effort is being made to improve management techniques. This effort takes many forms—university-sponsored conferences and short session training schools for executives; professional management clubs such as the Society for the Advancement of Management and the Academy of Management; and a growing body of authoritative literature in the field of management.

Scientific discovery

Scientific discoveries ultimately have applications in business. Information retrieval, for example—the application of computers to searching for information—greatly increases both the availability of information and the rate at which industries apply scientific developments. The discovery of the homogenizing process quickly led to many new and improved products. Homogenized milk, paints, and shortening rapidly

Table 27–2 Vended Volume, 1958 and 1971[a]		
	1958	1971
Packaged confections	$244,575,000 **543,500**	$ 664,326,000 **844,683**
Bulk confections	$ 58,500,000 **1,125,000**	$ 233,818,000 **1,232,242**
Cigarettes	$820,703,000 **717,400**	$2,239,534,000 **948,232**
Cigars	$ 7,952,000 **45,500**	$ 22,308,000 **53,417**
Soft drinks (cups)	$103,588,000 **105,300**	$ 455,550,000 **213,753**
Soft drinks (bottles)	$267,588,000 **764,500**	$ 644,193,000 **844,068**
Soft drinks[b] (cans)		$ 561,673,000 **333,733**
Coffee—hot drinks	$ 99,518,000 **113,900**	$ 451,959,000 **246,132**
Ice cream	$ 23,299,000 **31,700**	$ 41,102,000 **49,504**
Milk	$ 45,925,000 **41,750**	$ 170,668,000 **84,720**
Hot canned food	$ 14,928,000 **17,100**	$ 77,559,000 **48,628**
Prepared food		$ 265,327,000 **69,823**
Pastries[c]		$ 88,311,000 **85,935**
All others	$446,000,000	$ 593,367,000

[a] Boldface figures denote number of machines on location.
[b] Before 1967 soft drinks (cans) was combined under soft drinks (bottles).
[c] Before 1970, pastries was combined under prepared food.
Source: *Vend* Magazine.

became commonplace. The splitting of the atom has already led to atomic propulsion of ships and atomic generating plants. The mix of factors that contribute to modern productivity increases is dramatically illustrated in Figure 27–2.

CHANGES RELATED TO BUSINESS

Business looks further ahead

The time lag between capital outlay decisions and first resulting sales widens steadily as technological advances are made. It is common in business to make expenditures that cannot produce income for a number

Figure **27-2**
Factors Influencing Increased Productivity

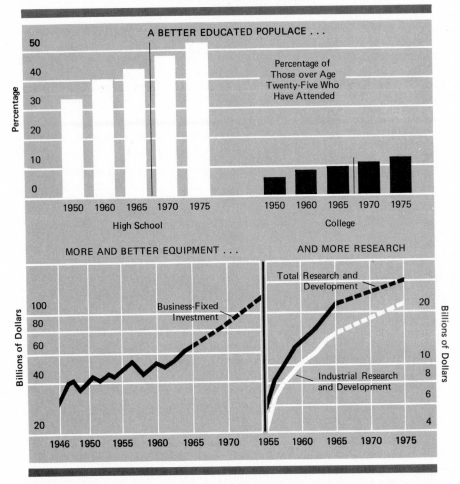

Source: U.S. Department of Commerce, U.S. Bureau of the Census, National Science Foundation, *CMB*.

How does this relate to planning your personal future?

of years. Such situations require very complicated planning. Often, for instance, expenditures are made at one price level, and, because of time lag, sales are made at another price level. It takes a large utility company two years to plan a modern generating plant and another three to five years to complete it. The Union Carbide Corporation reports that the time lag between test tube and chemical tank car can be as great as seventeen years.

As the trend toward greater complexity continues, policy decisions become more and more difficult. Those who have overall responsibility for decision-making must rely increasingly on quantitative analysis, reports, and forecasts, and less and less on personal observation, experience, and guesswork. Obviously, week-to-week and month-to-month plans provide too limited a basis for sound business policy. It is easy to see why there is a tendency in business to make long-range economic projections to aid management in planning capital budgets, long-range financing programs, goals for long-range sales programs, new products, and territory development. Detailed projections for most businesses are not made beyond a period of from one to three years. Forecasts for the future naturally vary greatly, depending on the industry and the outlook of the management. But it can be called characteristic of American business to look far into the future—and to view that future with optimism.

Is growth progress?

This new question, which must indeed sound strange to businesspersons and politicians, is increasingly creeping into discussions about the future. Growth, especially in business and political circles, has always been considered synonymous with progress. It is now evident that growth creates problems. Using growth as a measure of progress without evaluating the social disutilities created by it is short-sighted. It is hard to imagine business switching to a status quo philosophy after such a long history of dedication to growth. Yet growth does accelerate depletion of resources, steps up pollution, and intensifies quality of life problems.

Highly developed industrial nations with smaller land areas and larger population concentrations than the United States are already actively concerned with placing limitations on growth. Since the United States, too, may have to place constraints on growth, it is of interest to review the major points in Sicco L. Mansholt's statement on growth restriction. Mansholt is President of the European Economic Community (EEC). He calls for:

1. A reduction in per capita income to economize energy and raw materials

2. A substantial cut in the number of private cars in a decade's time

3. Reurbanization, using less raw materials for building, and bringing workplaces and residences closer together

4. Top priority for energy research, especially solar power

5. New tax laws to encourage and protect non-polluting and recycling industries, vehicles, and appliances

Proposing car rationing, Mansholt said fossil fuels will be exhausted in twenty or thirty years. Thermonuclear fuel might be available by about 2010, but there is need for an earlier solution and for more adequate safeguards against the radioactive contamination and effect on the world's heat balance of nuclear fuel manufacture. "Speaking more generally, how much energy can we afford to consume, since all energy production creates heat, 70 percent of which is lost?" Mansholt asks. Solar power adds no unnatural pollution or heat and is "an issue we should go into urgently." Tax exemption for recycled products, which are cleaner but more expensive, would go with a "CR" (clean and recycled) certificate, which the EEC could issue. Mr. Mansholt considers advertising "more and more antisocial" as it "stimulates (purely) material growth." He said he did not, however, favor banning all advertising.[3]

The debate on acceptable limits of growth should include providing employment and the need to improve living conditions for the underprivileged. The quality of life is affected, not only by pollution and overcrowding, but by material things such as transportation, housing, and working conditions. It is not a question simply of limiting growth; it is a question of controlling it so social as well as economic benefits are provided.

Urbanization trends

In Chapter 18, we discussed populations as markets and the continued trend toward urbanization. Cities in the conventional sense, have become obsolete. They no longer have, as they once had, an easily identifiable central core called "downtown" around which the life of the city revolves. The metropolis (the concentrated urban center) has become the megalopolis (the multicentered urban complex). Figure 27–3 shows where one study estimates that most of the country's population will be in the year 2000 — in three major urban areas. The same study also projects that factories and businesses will be strategically located so they will relate efficiently to these areas in terms of the source of manpower and communications and markets. Populations in these areas will be highly mobile as living conveniences become readily available all through the area. Already, approximately one out of every five Americans moves each year. Over 400,000 mobile homes are sold each year. This greatly affects business. It means a work force that may be less loyal to the company, the deterioration and development of communities at rapid rates, the breakdown of barriers between cities, and consequent changes in how populations are serviced by newspapers, retail outlets, and recreational facilities.

It is doubtful whether the ideal pattern for how large concentrations

[3] *European Community*, August/September, 1972, pp. 17–18.

Figure **27-3**
The Three Major U.S. Urban Centers in the Year 2000

The United States is becoming increasingly urbanized and by the year 2000, according to a study made by the Urban Land Institute, there will be three gigantic urban regions (shown on the map) in which 60 percent of the population will live on only about 7 percent of the land. (Alaska and Hawaii are not included in the study.) The projections were made from a computer study of population trends under the direction of Dr. Jerome P. Pickard, the director of the institute which is a nonprofit research organization. This concentrated character of urban regional development places a great strain upon resources such as water supply, air and the land itself, Dr. Pickard warned, and will raise major planning problems. Dr. Pickard points out, other areas of the country will experience only slow growth. Thus, he says, "Large areas of the nation will be preserved as open country — regions of mountains, plains, hills and valleys."

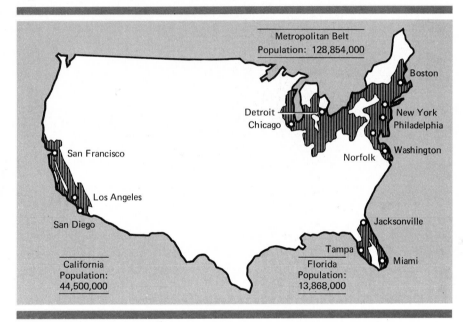

Source: Adapted from the *New York Times*, April 9, 1967.

of people can live contentedly together has yet been found. Major emphasis in the future will have to be devoted to arrangements for living and for servicing populations. As Jay Forrester of MIT says, "Some forms of growth are no longer possible, others pointless — we need a new folklore, one that emphasizes quality of life rather than quantity."

Increasing education

Much value has always been placed on education in the United States. Even so, most people have not received an advanced education. We are,

Figure **27–4**
Increasing Education

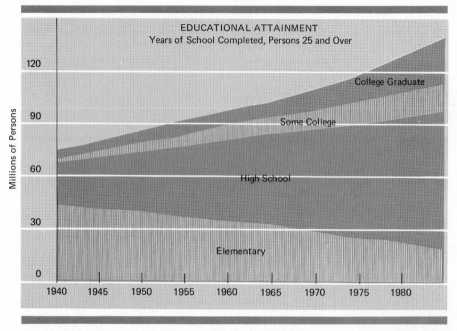

Source: "A Guide to Consumer Markets, 1972/1973," The Conference Board.

however, making progress. In 1900, only 4 percent of those reaching college age enrolled in college. By 1950, this percentage had increased to 30 percent, and it is probable that by 1978, 40 percent of all persons reaching college age will obtain at least some higher education (see Figure 27–4).

This trend will affect business in many ways. A better-educated population will want more facts about the goods and services it buys. With more education, the character of wants changes. People with more education usually want better goods. And, business will benefit from having available a larger supply of well-trained employees.

Growing leisure time and boredom

During the past century, a gradual reduction in the length of the work-week has taken place, with a corresponding increase in the amount of leisure time for most people. Leisure time is important to business, since it affects both the kind and amount of goods and services that people buy. As leisure time increases, so does demand for recreation, travel, books, and similar products and services.

Table **27-3**
U.S. Farm Productivity

		1935-39	1966-70
CORN	Man-hours per acre	28.1	5.6
	Yield bushels per acre	26.1	77.0
WHEAT	Man-hours per acre	8.8	2.9
	Yield bushels per acre	13.2	28.3
MILK	Man-hours per cow	148	74
	Milk per cow (pounds)	440	900
EGGS	Man-hours per 100 eggs	1.7	0.4
Eggs per chicken per year		129	219
FERTILIZER	Expenditures in millions of dollars	306	2249

Source: *Statistical Abstract of the United States, 1972*, pp. 596 and 604.

Does education relate to farm productivity?

Leisure seems to be a mixed social blessing now that we have acquired it in quantity. The price we had to pay for it was mechanization, which is dehumanizing because it brings with it (1) the often deadly routine factory work, (2) bigness of factories, machines, and corporations, which makes people feel small, (3) the requirement to work away from the vicinity of the home and neighbors, which makes for loneliness, and (4) the need to commute over traffic clogged highways or rush-hour transit systems, which is cheerless and drab.

And what have we got for this price? We have been delivered into the arms of *boredom*, which *The National Observer* and others call "The Illness of the Age." It is called the root of violence and drug addiction. Bertrand Russell claimed that "half the sins of mankind are caused by fear of it." "Monotony permeates America today. Our superhighways are monotonous. Our supercities are monotonous. Our supercorporations are dull places to work, for white and blue collars alike. Our leisure time activities are often boring too."[4]

Whereas boredom is probably something men have always had to cope with to some degree, behavioral scientists point out that in our industrial society boredom is *chronic*. One of them wrote (out of boredom?), that ours is "the land of the free and the home of the bored." Psychologists have found that a monotonous environment causes people to deteriorate—their thinking is impaired, they show childish emotions, their visual perception becomes disturbed, and their brain wave patterns

[4] *The National Observer*, May 13, 1972, p. 1.

change. However, boredom itself is not the actual difficulty. The difficulty lies in not knowing how to cope or live with it. As Bertrand Russell wrote further, "Accomplishing worthwhile ends requires a capacity for enduring boredom and monotony." Since boredom is of such grave social concern, it certainly will receive more attention from business in the future.

CHANGING ATTITUDES OF BUSINESS MANAGEMENT

Another evidence of the dynamic character of American business is the changing attitude of business management toward the public, employees, and competition.

Growing public-mindedness

Since the Great Depression, much public criticism is directed at business. Before that time business leaders had taken relatively little interest in community welfare. Since the Depression, however, business in general — especially large corporations — has increasingly recognized a definite obligation to take an active interest in community affairs. Today, businesses support a variety of public service programs, such as Community Chest drives, library and museum building programs, and scholarships for promising young people.

As business shows a greater interest in the community, the community hopefully gains a greater respect for business. People will perhaps realize that their welfare is affected by the well-being of business. A company forced to shut down its plant or reduce its labor force is usually quick to offer a public explanation, for it knows that not only the workers immediately concerned but the smaller businesses and the community at large will be affected. Public understanding of the place of business in society is still far from adequate.

Growing employee-mindedness

The labor union movement has been a major factor causing management to give more consideration to the rights, feelings, and privileges of employees. But business has learned that merely reaching mutually satisfactory agreements with employees does not result in the most efficient use of labor. It is now accepted that a program of "human relations" is helpful in attaining maximum productivity.

Business is increasingly aware of the social and moral overtones of its decisions. The industrial paternalism of the past, in which the owner-managers tried to control the lives of their employees, is dead. It is the wage earner and his acceptance or rejection of our economic and political system that, in the long run, dictate the course the nation takes.

THE OPPORTUNITY

Future economic progress depends on the collective efforts of individuals. The national welfare is really a combination of many individual welfares. Because of the vast possibilities for future economic development, persons who have high ethical principles and strive to perform business functions efficiently face an unparalleled opportunity to serve society and, in so doing, to reap large rewards and personal satisfaction for themselves.

The theme of this final chapter—dynamics—spells opportunity. Opportunity, because innovation must originate in the mind of some imaginative person. No one has a monopoly on ideas. The top executive is by no means necessarily in the best position to innovate; in fact, persons most acquainted with an operation are often too close to it for the objectivity that innovation requires. Also, those steeped in tradition may be least willing to experiment.

Perhaps, now, as never before in history, American business offers to the person of intelligence, integrity, and initiative both substantial material rewards and the satisfaction that comes only from service to one's fellow men. On a thousand fronts, the gauntlet is down. If history shows anything, it shows that on those thousand fronts there will be millions of Americans eager to accept the challenge. Whatever the future may be, those who elect to become part of the business world will play a major role in shaping a better America and a better world.

PEOPLE AND THEIR IDEAS
John H. Dessauer

The billions nobody wanted—the story of Xerox

The story of the Xerox Corporation is probably the most dramatic in contemporary business history. It fits the pattern of American folklore:

(1) nice guys will win out in the end, (2) build a better mousetrap and you will be rewarded, (3) imagination, hard work, and belief in ideals can move mountains, and (4) America is the land of opportunity for those from other shores.

A leading character in this epic story was John Hans Dessauer. One of Dessauer's colleagues said, "He is the man, alone in industry, who recognized the potential of infant technology [xerography, Greek for 'dry copying'] and created within his tiny company the technical team which transformed that company and revolutionized business practices throughout the world."

In 1935, a political refugee from Germany, Dessauer got a job as a young engineer in a Rochester, New York, firm—Haloid, which later became Xerox. As head of research, Dessauer prevailed upon his associates at Haloid to share his faith in an obscure, unperfected process called electrophotography. It was invented by Chester Carlson, who spent seven futile years trying to sell his brain child to business (Kodak, IBM, and A. B. Dick were among those who turned it down), research foundations, and governments. The little Haloid company, with the urging of Dessauer, gambled its existence on converting Carlson's unwanted invention into its first commercial copier in 1950. The 1950s spawned many instant successes. Xerox was not one of them. It was an instant flop. It wasn't until 1959, under Dessauer's developmental genius, that the company produced the 914 copier, quite possibly the most successful commercial product in history. In fact, the 100 shares of Haloid that a Rochester cab driver bought for $1,000 in 1942 are worth around $1,500,000 some thirty years later. The stock has split 180 times, and earnings have multiplied 4,300 percent.

Hundreds of business decisions were involved before success was assured. In his book, *My Years With Xerox*, Dessauer tells, for example, of one problem: The need to attach a fire extinguisher to the 914 (because it sometimes burst into flames) was thought to be disastrous to sales. The problem was solved by attaching the extinguisher but labeling it "scorch eliminator." This is a joke, but a serious joke, for commercial success or failure often hinges on such seemingly minor matters. Asked whether he would risk the fate of a company today as he did in the 1950s, Dessauer replied, "I would have to be psychoanalyzed to say if I would take the same risk again. It's when you're very young and naive that you have the courage to make the right decisions!" Dessauer, in talking about his background said, "My professional experience and training have been primarily technical, plus a good sprinkling of business knowledge."

Xerox today is a $1½ billion company, selling its products in more than 90 countries and manufacturing them in the United States, Great Britain, the Netherlands, and Japan. Xerox usually appears when "Best Managed" companies are selected; *Dun's Review* in 1972 picked it as being among the nation's top five best managed companies. The reason was given as executive motivation.

CONTEMPORARY ISSUES
Situation 27

Is American business too hectic?

"You know, John," commented Ray, "as this course begins to wind down, I confess I'm increasingly reluctant to make business a career. It seems business is too demanding, too hectic. I've read reports that the rapid pace in today's business is probably the single greatest cause of high blood pressure, ulcers, obesity, and heart attacks. On top of that, business executives often neglect their families and cause other people to be unhappy."

"Ray, I don't think you're approaching it objectively," responded John. "The rapid pace of today's business world is what makes it exciting and challenging. Besides, industrial psychologists say every person has a different achievement level. The tempo of today's business offers each individual the opportunity to reach the achievement level that is best for him."

"Well," Ray observed, "I still think American business has gotten to be too hectic. It may sound exciting now to hear about executives who travel 250,000 miles a year and who must transfer to another city every three or five years. But that sort of life would soon get old to me. I want to spend more time with my family and enjoy the simple pleasures of life. Also, it's said a man cannot serve two masters. It's impossible to serve one master, the job, and another master, the home. The intensity and pressure of business today is a contributing factor to the increasingly high divorce rate."

"I still don't believe American business is too hectic," answered John. "There are many management theories founded on the premise that work is as natural and necessary as play or rest. I once had a professor who told us, 'Hard work makes happy people.' He also said that there has never been a death certificate signed, 'he died of overwork.' I think the same point can be made for an exciting career in business. Happy people are busy people."

"I still don't agree," commented Ray. "I prefer to see our society slow down. The three-martini lunch, the intense competition, the preoccupation with profit don't sound like the good life to me."

"Well, thank goodness, to each his own," observed John. "In the words of Harry Truman, 'If you can't stand the heat, then get out of the kitchen.'"

SITUATION EVALUATION

1. What additional points, pro and con, could be made?

2. Is there any real evidence that business executives are more happy or less happy than non-business executives?

3. Are you more or less inclined to make business a career than you were when this course began?

BUSINESS CHRONICLE

Kingmaker estates and confrontation about the future

Allan King as president of his influential company and as an enlightened business person, was invited to appear on a closed-circuit television program that linked eight cities—New York, Los Angeles, San Francisco, Washington, Chicago, Dallas, Atlanta, and Miami. Two-way audio intercommunication between all cities and the panelists made it possible for a viewer, say in Chicago, to ask a panelist, say Mr. King, why the shore line where he went fishing in Florida was being built in such a way that the marsh lands that once attracted bass were disappearing.

Besides Mr. King, other panelists were the consumer activist, Mr. Ralph Nader; former secretary of HUD, George Romney; former administrator of the U. S. Environmental Protection Agency, William Ruckelshaus; the president of the Sierra Club, Phillip Berry; the chairman of the board of U. S. Home Corporation, Robert Sinnerman; and the chairman of the Environmental Systems International, Barry Berkus.

Two comments that were called in and caused Mr. King to reflect considerably were:

1. Land development companies are too dedicated to what they believe is growth thinking when it isn't growth that they are fostering; rather, it is a society of disposables that they are pushing. Land development companies are just like the beverage companies that put their product in no-refund bottles that litter up the streets and the drive-in restaurant that is responsible for paper and cartons being strewn all along our highways. The developers do things the easy way—they build on virgin farm lands, and urge people to move out of the city, and thus cause slums to develop in the cities. This is America's way of discarding its housing. Why don't you tackle the slums and keep the cities viable?

2. Why don't developers take responsibility for properties after they develop them? They build, sell, and move on, assuming no continuing responsibility.

1. From a business point of view, what do you think of Mr. King's appearance on the television program?

2. What future does this kind of communication hold for our communities?

3. What do you think of the two comments that are cited? How should Mr. King have answered them?

APPLICATION EXERCISES

1. The moon exploration program through the last of the Apollo flights cost an estimated $25 billion over a ten-year period.
   a. Assuming the average population during this period was 200 million, compute the per capita cost of the project. What was the per capita *monthly* cost?
   b. Despite the low per capita cost of the project, why were many people opposed to it?
   c. In your opinion, could the $25 billion have been better spent? Explain.

2. Statistics indicate that money spent for basic and applied research by government, universities, and industry increased dramatically during the 1950s and the 1960s. For the first few years of the 1970s however, expenditures for this purpose showed signs of leveling out. Prepare a brief report in which you
   a. Relate the importance of basic and applied research to economic development, and
   b. Explain what some of the long-run results will be if relatively less emphasis is placed on research.

3. Even the most casual survey of rush-hour automobile traffic streaming in or out of U.S. cities will reveal that the majority of cars carry only the driver. Certainly very rarely can an automobile be observed with all passenger seats occupied. An obvious step to pollution reduction and fuel conservation is to increase seat occupancy ratios. Following are two examples designed to increase seat occupancy.
   a. Some U.S. universities designate the most desirably located parking structures on campus as "ecology parking." Only cars coming to campus carrying more than two passengers have access to this parking that is located most conveniently.
   b. The following article which appeared in the International Edition of the *Herald Tribune* May 24, 1973, describes a Polish plan for increasing passenger ratios.

UNDER POLISH SYSTEM, DRIVERS
WANT TO PICK UP HITCHHIKERS

WARSAW, May 23 (UPI).—To anyone familiar with highway scenes in the West, it sounds too good to be true: well-scrubbed, courteous hitchhikers, both men and women, and drivers eager to pick them up, with practically no fear of being mugged.

That's how it works under Poland's unique hitchhiking system, which offers rewards to motorists who give lifts and in return assures them of decent riders. The scheme went into its sixteenth season May 1.

Anyone 16 or older can participate. He pays 45 zlotys ($2.25) and fills out a detailed application form. He receives a blue passbook readily identified by drivers because of a large red and yellow dot on its cover.

The passbook contains an insurance certificate to cover costs relating to injuries suffered while hitchhiking. It also contains a series of numbered coupons.

Payment With Coupons

When the hitchhiker gets a ride, he gives the driver a number of coupons depending on how far he travels. At the end of the hitchhiking season, which runs to September, drivers turn in the coupons, and those with the most get prizes. This year one man won a new car.

"But it works the other way, too," an official said. "The coupons are numbered, as are the application forms. If a hitchhiker is discourteous or causes any trouble to the driver, he can be traced. And if he is reported, that fellow won't be hitchhiking through our organization any more."

The official said that in the last three years not a single case of theft or hooliganism has been reported in connection with a card-carrying hitch-hiker.

Devise and present your plan for increasing passenger ratios. Work out details for administering your plan in a business-like fashion. Be sure to consider all aspects including costs, rewards, publicity, administration, etc.

QUESTIONS

1. Is business qualified to deal with social change? What should the extent of its social involvement be?

2. Evaluate the controversial CED report. What would a similar report of your own consist of?

3. Why is it wise for someone considering business as a career to understand the dynamic concept of American business? What trends discussed in this chapter will affect careers in the future?

4. It is said that entrepreneurship is one of the free enterprise system's greatest strengths. How does it contribute to our economic system? What disadvantages accrue from the uncontrolled use of the entrepreneurship factor?

5. What is the difference between change and progress? Discuss three business changes that are not necessarily progressive.

6. Are there more opportunities in business now than there were twenty-five years ago? Give reasons for your answer.

7. Is a policy whereby businesses deliberately try to make products obsolete by yearly model or style changes good or bad for society? Discuss both sides of the question.

8. Does nature allow unlimited growth? Assuming that containment is a healthy policy, how can society curb undesirable growth?

9. What is the energy crisis, and what can be done about it?

10. Boredom is considered a serious and mounting problem. What can be done to alleviate this problem?

11. A foreign visitor said, "In the United States productivity is a state of mind." Describe this state of mind and its advantages and short-comings.

Appendix

career selection

A primary reason for going to college is to prepare for a useful and satisfying career. Yet surprisingly few students actually plan their life work, and most fail to realize that career decisions made in college affect their entire lives. Indeed, many people never discover the work for which they are best suited.

This appendix is intended to help students face realistically the challenge of career planning. The following pages discuss present and future opportunities, the importance of choosing a career carefully and thinking about it early, steps to follow in choosing a career and a company, and personal qualities needed to get a desired job. Sources of information on career opportunities in various areas of business also are presented.

Most people make final career decisions by the time they reach age twenty-five. Since retirement is customarily at age sixty-five, your career decision is one you will live with and suffer or enjoy for forty years. Unfortunately, the career decision must be made early in life, before the person making it has acquired experience and maturity. The young person must therefore give much attention to studying his abilities and matching them with opportunities. While this book deals with business, there is no intention on the part of the authors to "sell" a career in business. If, after studying the text, the student does not feel drawn to some area of business, a useful purpose has nevertheless been served, and he would do well to seek out occupational areas that he will find more attractive.

A final word on career preparation is in order. College placement authorities recommend vigorously that students prepare themselves for a career during all the years they are attending college. To delay preparation until the time of graduation seriously handicaps the graduate.

BROAD TRENDS IN EMPLOYMENT FOR THE 1970S

Industries may be viewed as either *service producing* or *goods producing* (see Table A–1). In 1970 most of the nation's workers — 47.3 million, or 63.7 percent of the total — were employed in service producing industries, while 26.9 million, or 36.3 percent, were active in goods producing industries.

Employment prospects for college educated people are much better in service producing industries than in those that produce goods. In 1970, 16 percent of service workers were college graduates, while only 7 percent of workers in goods industries were college educated. Moreover, with the exception of contract construction, most of the anticipated gains in employment are in service producing industries (services, government, trade and finance, insurance, and real estate).

It is interesting that the percentage increase in employment of women in business management in recent years has outpaced the percentage increase for men. In the past, young women have shied away from business administration as an area of study. This was probably because many of them felt, with certain justification, that business was a man's world and that women worked mostly in supporting rather than directing roles. This view has changed to a point where increasing numbers of women college graduates in business are readily placed in responsible jobs.

Opportunity unlimited, but . . .

There are clear indications that the demand for qualified junior and senior college graduates in the areas of business administration will continue to be brisk. College graduates continue to form an ever increasing part of the American labor force. From a level of 8.1 percent in 1952, the proportion of college graduates in the work force rose to 11.1 percent in 1962, and to 13.7 percent by 1971. It is anticipated that by 1980 college graduates will make up one out of every six workers in the labor force.[1]

However, in commenting on employment opportunities for the next several years, editors of the 1973 edition of *College Placement Annual* said, "While most everyone is more optimistic, few people believe that college recruitment will be back to the "boom" proportions of four or five years ago. There should be more jobs, but there may be more competition, too — not only from your own classmates but from returning service men and women."[2]

Table A–2 covering recruitment activities of well-known large and

---

[1] The *New York Times*, January 8, 1973, p. 53.
[2] *College Placement Annual* 1973, P.O. Box 2263, Bethlehem, Pennsylvania 18001, p. 11.

Table **A–1**
College Graduates as a Percentage of Employees,
by Industry, 1970

	COLLEGE GRADUATES AS A PERCENTAGE OF TOTAL EMPLOYMENT
SERVICE INDUSTRIES	
Trade	6
Government	30
Services and miscellaneous industries	19
Transportation and public utilities	5
Finance, insurance, and real estate	16
GOODS INDUSTRIES	
Manufacturing	2
Agriculture	3
Contract construction	4
Mining	12

Source: United States Department of Labor, *Manpower Report of the President*, transmitted to Congress on March 1972, pp. 106–7.

medium-sized companies, which represent a wide variety of business interests, shows comparative starting salaries and salary trends for graduates according to their majors.

A paradox confronts the college graduate in the 1970s. The demand for college graduates is expected to continue to grow rapidly in this decade, as it has in recent decades. No lessening of demand is anticipated, since, in a knowledge-intensive society pressures continue to build up for educated people. Yet, beginning in the late 1960s, evidence started to appear that the road to job hunting success was becoming bumpy. In the early 1970s, it worsened. The winding down of the Vietnam War resulted in a decline in jobs in the highly technical war industries. Furthermore, larger numbers of young people went on to complete their college education. So, while there are more jobs, there is also a growing number of available applicants (see Figure A–1). Since the job outlook is always a matter of supply and demand, candidates most likely to be selected are those who are best suited for the available jobs.

In this type of job market, it may well be that the college graduate whose academic studies have been most relevant to labor market needs and requirements will experience least difficulty in job adjustment in his immediate post-college years. To assure relevancy, the student should relate his program of study to job outlook predictions. Table A–3 presents the Bureau of Labor Statistics forecast for business administration and related professions. The *Occupational Outlook Handbook*, published regularly, is available in libraries or from the Superintendent of Documents, Washington, D.C. 20225, for details on any vocational field.

Table A-2
Salaries, by Subject and by Type of Work

MALE, BACHELOR'S-DEGREE CANDIDATES
NATIONAL AVERAGE MONTHLY SALARY OFFERS BY CURRICULUM

BY CURRICULUM FOR ALL TYPES OF EMPLOYERS	NO. OFFERS 1972-73 1-2 PERIOD CUMULATIVE	AVERAGE $ OFFERS			CHANGE FROM 1972-73 1-2 PERIOD CUM. OFFERS		1972-73 1-2 PERIOD CUM. 80 PERCENT	
		1972-73 1-2 PERIOD CUMULATIVE	1972-73 1ST PERIOD	1971-72 YEAR'S TOTAL	1972-73 1ST PERIOD (= 100)	1971-72 TOTAL (= 100)	HIGH	LOW
BUSINESS AND HUMANITIES								
Accounting	1,364	$886	$874	$854	101.4	103.7	$990	$782
Business—General (inc. Mgmt.)	595	745	733	726	101.6	102.6	900	590
Humanities and Social Sciences	138	705	694	702	101.6	100.4	869	541
Marketing and Distribution	242	734	727	706	101.0	104.0	877	591
ENGINEERING								
Aeronautical	32	897	891	884	100.7	101.5	966	828
Chemical	443	954	949	928	100.5	102.8	1,009	899
Civil	359	902	891	869	101.2	103.8	966	838
Electrical	946	918	913	888	100.5	103.4	991	845
Industrial	219	886	892	871	99.3	101.7	992	780
Mechanical	1,000	916	909	894	100.8	102.5	986	846
Metallurgical (inc. Metallurgy and Engrg.-Ceramics)	77	917	932	881	98.4	104.1	999	835
Technology and Industrial	115	841	791	824[b]	106.3	102.1[b]	997	685
SCIENCES								
Agricultural Science	47	744	779	694	95.5	107.2	873	615
Chemistry, Mathematics, and Physics	100	828	791	795	104.7	104.2	957	699
Chemistry	37	824	763	783	108.0	105.2	921	727
Mathematics	51	827	791	795	104.6	104.0	974	680
Physics	12	845	875	818	96.6	103.3	[a]	[a]
Computer Science	57	864	867	812[b]	99.7	106.4[b]	977	751
	5,734							

[a] Not computed; fewer than 20 offers.   [b] Data taken from 1971-72 pilot study.

NATIONAL AVERAGE MONTHLY SALARY OFFERS BY TYPE OF EMPLOYER

BY TYPE OF EMPLOYER	NON-TECHNICAL CURRICULA				TECHNICAL CURRICULA			
	NO. OFFERS 1972-73 1-2 PERIOD CUMULATIVE	AVERAGE $ OFFERS			NO. OFFERS 1972-73 1-2 PERIOD CUMULATIVE	AVERAGE $ OFFERS		
		1972-73 1-2 PERIOD CUMULATIVE	1972-73 1ST PERIOD	1971-72 YEAR'S TOTAL		1972-73 1-2 PERIOD CUMULATIVE	1972-73 1ST PERIOD	1971-72 YEAR'S TOTAL
Accounting—Public	1,128	$904	$895	$877	5	$976	$950	$892
Aerospace and Components	22	811	796	777	325	891	875	880
Automotive and Mechanical Equipment	74	802	776	811	168	907	911	901
Banking, Finance, and Insurance	221	698	697	685	33	742	704	746
Building Materials Mfrs. and Construction	69	776	777	754	286	907	907	873
Chemicals, Drugs, and Allied Products	93	805	820	788	505	947	940	904
Electrical Machinery and Equipment	57	774	762	775	337	908	902	877
Electronics and Instruments	62	795	821	771	437	912	909	890
Food and Beverage Processing	52	753	703	739	32	858	862	767
Glass, Paper, Packaging, and Products	39	802	824	782	102	928	928	892
Merchandising and Related Services	305	688	676	674	26	781	770	742
Metals and Metal Products	35	818	823	786	270	905	896	874
Petroleum and Products (inc. Nat. Gas)	62	808	808	800	204	944	920	931
Research/Consulting Organizations	11	691	689	729	183	888	894	853
Tire and Rubber	37	786	717	744	99	901	891	889
Utilities—Public (inc. Transportation)	72	804	806	760	383	898	896	875
	2,339				3,395			

Source: U.S. Bureau of Labor Statistics.

OCCUPATION	ESTIMATED EMPLOY-MENT, 1970	AVERAGE ANNUAL OPENINGS TO 1980	EMPLOYMENT PROSPECTS
Table **A–3** Job Outlook for College Graduates in the 1970s			
BUSINESS ADMINISTRATION AND RELATED PROFESSIONS			
Accountants	491,000	31,200	Excellent opportunities. Strong demand for college trained applicants. Graduates of business and other schools offering accounting should have good prospects.
Actuaries	5,200	300	Excellent opportunities. Strong demand for recent college graduates who have backgrounds in mathematics and have passed actuarial examinations.
Advertising workers	141,000	8,400	Slow growth. Opportunities will be good, however, for highly qualified applicants, especially in advertising agencies.
Bank officers	174,000	11,000	Employment is expected to grow rapidly as the increased use of computers enables banks to expand their services.
City managers	2,600	200	Excellent opportunities especially for persons with master's degrees in public or municipal administrations.
Economists	33,000	2,300	Excellent opportunities for those who have graduate degrees in teaching, government and business. Young people with bachelor's degrees will find employment in Government and as management trainees in industry and business.
Employment counselors	8,000	1,100	Excellent opportunities for those who have master's degrees or experience in the field. Graduates with bachelor's degrees and 15 hours of counseling-related courses will find favorable opportunities in state and local employment.
Managers and assistants (hotel)	195,000	14,400	Favorable outlook, especially for those who have college degrees in hotel administration.
Manufacturers salesmen	510,000	25,000	Favorable opportunities for well-trained workers, but competition will be keen. Best prospects for those trained to handle technical products.
Marketing research workers	23,000	2,600	Excellent opportunities, especially for those who have graduate degrees. Existing marketing research organizations are expected to expand and new research departments and independent firms set up.
Personnel workers	160,000	9,100	Favorable outlook, especially for college graduates with training in personnel administration. More workers will be needed for recruiting, interviewing, and psychological testing.

Public relations workers	78,000	4,400	Rapid increase due to population growth and rise in level of business activity. An increasing amount of funds will be allocated to public relations work.
Securities salesmen	200,000	11,800	Good opportunities.
Statisticians	24,000	1,400	Very good opportunities for new graduates and experienced statisticians in industry and government.
Systems analysts	100,000	22,700	Excellent opportunities due to rapid expansion of electronic data processing systems in business and government.
Technical writers	20,000	1,000	Good prospects for those having college courses in writing and technical subjects plus writing ability.
Underwriters	55,000	2,740	Favorable opportunities especially in metropolitan areas.
Urban planners	88,000	750	Very good prospects for those who have training in city and regional planning. Construction of new cities and towns, urban renewal projects, and beautification and open space land improvement projects will spur demand for these workers.

Source: U.S. Bureau of Labor Statistics.

What are the best prospects from your point of view?

There is considerable evidence that many students are not careful enough in relating their study programs to the realities of the job marketplace. An interesting and revealing study made by the Bureau of Labor Statistics in 1972 indicated that of one million employed persons who had received bachelors or advanced degrees in 1970 and 1971, less than 60 percent said their jobs were directly related to their major study field, and about 20 percent said their jobs were somewhat related (see Table A–4). This means that over 40 percent were either far from the bull's eye or altogether off target in matching their educational preparation with the job they ended up in.

The proportion of people of employable age will be smaller in the future. People now go to school longer, retire earlier, and live longer than they once did. There is reason to believe this trend will continue, with the result that there will be a larger proportion of our population in the pre-work and post-work age brackets. Thus, the economic burden on the working group will become heavier, for this is the group responsible for producing for the needs of society. Viewed in a positive manner, such a situation certainly holds opportunity for those entering the labor force.

Bright as the overall future employment picture appears, a word of caution is needed.

Figure **A–1**
New Graduates Versus New Jobs

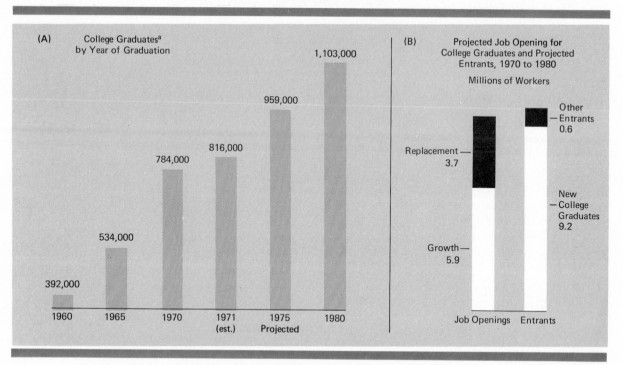

(A) College Graduates[a] by Year of Graduation

1,103,000
959,000
816,000
784,000
534,000
392,000

1960   1965   1970   1971 (est.)   1975 Projected   1980

(B) Projected Job Opening for College Graduates and Projected Entrants, 1970 to 1980

Millions of Workers

Other Entrants 0.6
Replacement 3.7
New College Graduates 9.2
Growth 5.9

Job Openings   Entrants

[a] Bachelor's first professional degree. Data cover graduates of both public and private institutions.
[b] Includes reentrants, delayed entrants, and immigrants.

Source: A, Office of Education; B, U.S. Bureau of Labor Statistics.

The editors of the *College Placement Annual* make seven specific recommendations for finding the right job in the 1970s:[3]

1. Don't press the panic button and become alarmed. Despite what you may have heard or read, most graduates are able to get a job.

2. Utilize your career planning and placement office early, the earlier the better. Here you will find information about career fields and employment opportunities, personal counsel if you want it, as well as advice on how best to mount your job-finding campaign.

3. Don't wait for a job to come knocking on your door. The days of five job offers for every graduate are gone, at least for the foreseeable future.

[3] Ibid., p. 11.

Table **A–4**

Relationship of Work of Degree Recipients
to Their Major Field of Study, October 1971 (Percentage Distribution)

RELATIONSHIP AND REASON	TOTAL	TYPE OF DEGREE		MAJOR FIELD OF STUDY				
		BACHELORS	ALL OTHER	BUSINESS OR COMMERCE	EDUCA- TION	HUMANI- TIES	SOCIAL SCIENCES	ALL OTHER
RELATIONSHIP OF WORK TO FIELD								
Total employed:								
Number (thousands)	1,024	766	186	178	258	140	198	250
Percentage	100.0	100.0	100.0	100.0	100.0	100.0	100.0	100.0
Directly related	58.1	52.0	77.4	51.2	77.9	44.4	35.1	67.6
Not directly related	41.9	48.0	22.6	48.8	22.1	55.6	64.9	32.4
Somewhat related	19.0	19.7	16.5	35.9	8.3	24.4	20.2	13.8
Not related	22.9	28.3	6.2	12.9	13.8	31.1	44.7	18.6
MAIN REASON FOR WORK NOT DIRECTLY RELATED								
Number (thousands)	429	368	42	87	57	78	128	81
Percent	100.0	100.0	a	100.0	a	100.0	100.0	100.0
Only job could find	44.0	44.5	—	37.7	—	36.8	43.4	39.7
Better opportunities for advancement than in major field	12.0	12.1	—	18.2	—	10.3	11.5	8.2
To see if liked kind of work	12.0	11.5	—	15.6	—	11.8	14.2	11.0
Did not want to work in field	5.7	4.8	—	—	—	11.8	8.8	5.5
All other	26.0	27.0	—	28.6	—	29.4	22.1	35.6

Note: Persons under age 35 in the civilian noninstitutional population in October 1971 who received baccalaureate or advanced degrees in 1970 or 1971 and who were not enrolled in school full time in October 1971.
a Percent not shown where base is less than 75,000.
Source: U.S. Bureau of Labor Statistics.

4. Set your sights on your primary target but also explore alternatives that may not be related directly to your major or goals. Utilize all available sources—Chambers of Commerce, state employment services, classified advertising sections. Don't overlook opportunities that may exist in your own backyard; you may want to contact small, local employers who do not recruit on campus because of limited needs but who occasionally hire college graduates.

5. Launch a mail campaign.

6. Keep a number of irons in the fire and keep them hot. Face up to the fact that you can't be as selective as you might wish, and don't risk concentrating all your efforts in a single place.

7. Don't become discouraged, even if you choose an "interim" job until you find what you really want, or if you decide to work your way around the world. Indeed, some day, looking back, you may decide that the first few years out of college were the most enriching of your life.[4]

The special situation concerning female managers

To conform with the law, industry must develop female managers. Consequently, employment and promotion opportunities for females will be exceedingly attractive in the years ahead. However, the weaving of women into the management fabric of business is not without its problems. Young women intent on succeeding would do well to concern themselves with these special problems, for understanding them provides clues for how to get ahead.

A study made in 1972,[5] was based on 114 interviews made with 78 women who were successful in management for over two years and with 36 who had failed in their management assignments. Age, experience, and type of education were found to be the greatest plus factors in assuring success. Nearly half of the successful women were over 36 years old. Young employees frequently admit that they do not like working for women, especially those under twenty-five. Employees tend to fear ridicule if they must admit they work for a younger woman. One young man's remarks on this point sum up feelings that generally are expressed: "If you explain that your female boss is as old as your mother and has been working forever, your buddies and girl seem to understand and don't bug you about cooperating and doing a good job for her." Of course, this attitude may begin to change as women managers become more commonplace.

Not surprisingly, failure rates for nonbusiness degree college graduates were higher than for those who had degrees in business administration. The study concluded that "workers generally resented [those without degrees in business] for not having the background, language and skills of the business or industry they entered."

THE BENEFITS OF A WISE CAREER CHOICE

Greater satisfaction

A person's job helps determine his degree of happiness. People whose work is rewarding are inclined to be happy in their off-hours. The reverse is equally true.

[4] A relevant government publication that covers such subjects as self-appraisal, preparing a résumé and letters of application, sources of job information, and job interviewing is: U. S. Department of Labor, "Merchandising Your Job Talents." Available for 40 cents from the Superintendent of Documents, U.S. Government Printing Office, Washington, D.C. 20225.

[5] *Training in Business and Industry*, February 1973, pp. 54–55.

For some, the word "work" has an unpleasant connotation. To many, it means something people have to do, rather than something they enjoy doing. Work in our emerging new society should be enjoyable, not drudgery. It should offer psychological rewards, not loss of individuality. Joseph Conrad captured the essence of the meaning of work when he wrote:

> No, I don't like work. I had rather laze about and think of all the fine things that can be done. I don't like work—no man does—but I like what is in the work—the chance to find yourself. Your own reality—for yourself, not for others—what no other man can ever know. They can only see the mere show, and never can tell what it really means.[6]

Greater financial and other rewards

It is a truism that people who enjoy their work and are engaged in some activity for which they are well qualified are more productive than people who are dissatisfied in and poorly qualified for their jobs. In the former case, the individual is almost certain to warrant promotions with greater opportunities; in the latter, he is likely to make little or no progress. Wise career selection is a step in the direction of larger income, increased responsibility, and greater prestige.

Greater contribution to society

Every citizen in our nation has an obligation to contribute to the social welfare. As we noted earlier, if a person is engaged in work for which he is best suited, he is also making his greatest contributions to the nation. In one very real sense, what is best for the individual is best for society. Without question, if each individual in our society made a perfect career choice, the prosperity of the nation would be increased.[7]

WHAT IS THE RIGHT CAREER?

The choice of a career must be made by the individual, although others should be asked for advice. In order to evaluate possible careers, the individual should consider several factors. The career should:

---

[6] Joseph Conrad, *Heart of Darkness*, Robert Kimbrough, ed., (New York: W. W. Norton, 1963).

[7] It should be noted that our society suffers from a great deal of underemployment. People who work in jobs that are below their maximum level of capability are said to be underemployed. Much underemployment can be traced directly to poor career choice.

1. Be one for which the person has a marked aptitude. Success is much more certain if genuine interest in and natural ability for the work exist.

2. Offer opportunity for growth. It should enable a person ultimately to make full use of his abilities.

3. Offer long-term financial rewards consistent with the individual's personal goals and with his ability to achieve those goals.

4. Give a person a feeling of usefulness. If he is to achieve success, he must take pride in his work. For most of us, prestige and dignity are necessary.

Begin thinking early

College and university placement directors note that students seldom give serious consideration to the choice of a career or employer until they are about to graduate. The main reasons for this are: (1) the natural inclination to postpone making decisions, (2) preoccupation with other matters, (3) the widespread belief that "there is still plenty of time before I have to make up my mind, (4) the feeling that luck or fate will finally determine what they will do, and (5) the lack of knowledge on which to base a decision.

As a result, jobs are all too often selected on the basis of mere chance — "My uncle works there and got me the job." Such casualness is frequently the full extent of the student's endeavor to place himself properly for his forty-five or more years of work-life.

Know yourself

Essential to intelligent career selection is a knowledge of self — of one's own interests and aptitudes. Many colleges and universities have established vocational testing programs (often free) intended to help the student discover those careers for which his intelligence and talents best equip him.

While a great variety of tests are available as part of any vocational testing procedure, the customary ones are interest determination, aptitude, intelligence, and personality tests. For some types of work, such as accounting and selling, special skill and aptitude tests have been devised.

Aptitude should not be confused with interest. Tests may reveal that a person has considerable aptitude for a field in which he has no interest. It is inadvisable to force interest in an area for which there is little natural inclination.

Obtain summer and part-time employment

An excellent way to get to know the nature of specific careers is through summer and part-time employment. If, for example, a student is thinking of banking as a possible career, a summer or part-time job in a bank will help him reach a decision. In a number of colleges and universities, "co-op" or "work-study" plans are in operation. Under these arrangements, business organizations accept a certain number of students for limited employment while the students complete their formal education. After graduation, those with such experience may join the business for which they have worked.

Care should be taken to evaluate work experience perceptively. It is incorrect to judge most careers on the basis of a specific job given to an inexperienced, temporary employee. Such jobs are necessarily elementary and routine, and they carry little responsibility. It is important to note that executives in the food industry do not place stock on shelves or take inventories themselves, and managers in the oil industry do not fill gasoline tanks or clean windshields. While the student does the menial tasks, however, he can study their implications for management.

The intelligent student will use the temporary job to "get behind the scenes" for observation and study purposes. Persons and jobs at higher responsibility levels should be observed. While on the job, the student should ask such questions as: "For the persons with responsibility, what lies behind the activities being carried on?" "Would I like to be doing what people with responsibility are doing?" "Would I be stimulated over a period of years by doing what people with authority are doing?" Answers to such questions will provide insights and enable the student to match his qualifications and interests with what goes on at the heart of the business or occupation.

Talk with persons who can help you

In colleges and universities that have a vocational guidance service, advice should be sought from someone on the guidance staff. Such conferences can be particularly valuable if the student has already taken a vocational guidance examination.

Many schools hold special events, known as "career days" or "job clinics," that bring employment directors and other company representatives to the college to discuss career opportunities with students. Fraternities and professional societies often invite executives to meet with their groups for similar discussions. And, of course, instructors can give excellent counsel on careers in many fields.

The student should keep his mind open to all ideas for careers. Whenever a job area sounds interesting, it is wise to talk with someone actually working in the field. While executives are busy and should not be disturbed unnecessarily, most are happy to assist sincerely interested young people by discussing job possibilities in a realistic and practical way.

Read career guidance literature

A variety of books, pamphlets, and brochures are available that deal with the characteristics of almost every occupation. A section at the end of this appendix lists publications that are helpful in the selection of a business career. Since it is to everyone's advantage to encourage young people to secure proper jobs, materials pertaining to the subject are generally easy to secure. If a career publication is not to be found in available libraries, usually the organization that publishes it will be glad to furnish a copy at little or no cost.

It is advisable to inform oneself thoroughly about a job field prior to making personal inquiries. People consulted about jobs are always impressed by evidence that the person to whom they are talking has had the foresight to find out about their particular field before the interview.

WHAT IS THE RIGHT COMPANY?

After one has decided on a particular career, the next logical step is to secure employment with a company that offers a good opportunity for practical learning. Key factors to consider are discussed below.

Training offered

The important thing for the ambitious young person is that he place himself in a position where he can learn. Many companies invest thousands of dollars in training an employee before he can make any substantial contribution to the firm. The value of such training should not be underestimated. It makes for progress within the company, and, if the employee should terminate employment at a later date, it will be useful in securing another position. The first two or three years in a career should be regarded as a kind of internship.

Formal training may not necessarily be most desirable; the company with no formal training program at all may be best under certain circumstances. Learning comes with responsibility; generally, then, the job that provides responsibility (under intelligent supervision) as quickly as the learner can assume it is the best training ground.

Promotional possibilities and financial remuneration

A person with initiative quite naturally wants to advance as rapidly as his ability to master the work permits. In considering a company, therefore, an applicant is wise to obtain answers to such questions as: "What are the long-range promotional possibilities?" "What are the professional backgrounds of the company's present top executives?" "Does the company promote from within?"

All too often a job is selected entirely on the basis of the starting salary, which can be a poor indicator of long-range opportunity. Actually, starting salary, while it is important, should not be given primary consideration. Other factors—promotion possibilities, exposure to responsibility, and long-run earning possibilities—should be given proper weight. A question the applicant should attempt to have answered is, "If I take a job with this company, what will my income and position be five, ten, and twenty years from now?"

YOUR FIRST JOB—AND THE PART MONEY PLAYS

Advice on how to evaluate job offers is likely to begin with the obvious "All other things being equal. . . ." The recipient of a specific offer has difficulty, however, making anything equal, even when he considers a factor like salary. Salary, the quantitative measure among factors influencing the graduate's selection of a specific position, requires more than casual inspection. Dollars represented by the salary offer may vary in importance when questions like these are applied to a specific offer:

Is this offer within the usual range for a beginning employee for the location and type of position? If the answer is no, are the reasons for the variation sound?

What is the salary picture for the future?

What are the other incentives, such as a stock option plan, worth in hard cash?

Are there dollar advantages available, for example, through programs of financial assistance for employees pursuing further education—either advanced degrees or refresher courses?

What will these dollars buy, not according to an abstract index, but for an employee with his known individual needs and wants?

Sometimes, salary comparisons become only a statistical exercise and provide no valid basis for decision-making. However, examination of the circumstances surrounding a salary offer should provide more light on a confusing subject.

Source: *College Placement Annual* 1973, P.O. Box 2263, Bethlehem, Pennsylvania 18001, p. 22.

Working environment

Another important consideration involves the physical surroundings in which the individual will work, the location of the company, and the personnel already employed. It may be difficult to get the "feel" of a company before accepting a job, but since it is important, an attempt to do so is in order. Most employers would not object to an applicant's request to tour their company and to meet some of the company employees. Discussions

Figure **A-2**
Employee Benefits

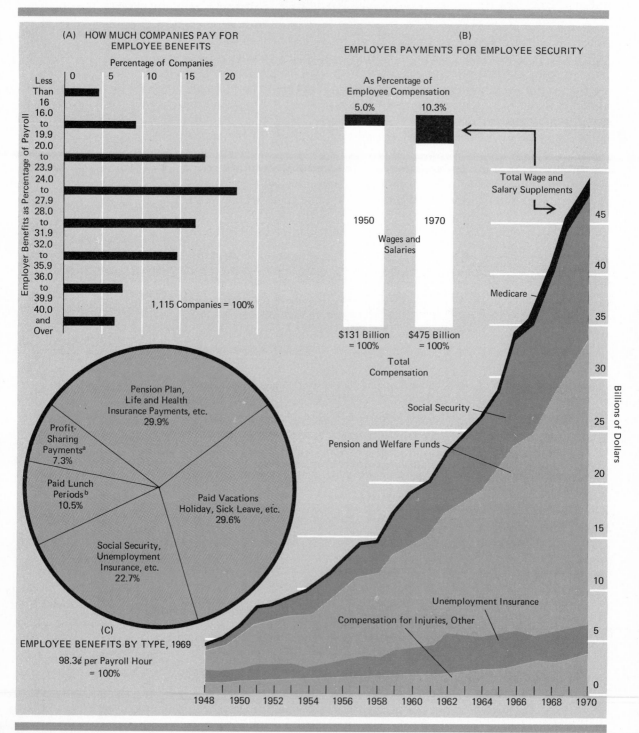

(A) HOW MUCH COMPANIES PAY FOR EMPLOYEE BENEFITS

Percentage of Companies

Employer Benefits as Percentage of Payroll

Less Than 16
16.0 to 19.9
20.0 to 23.9
24.0 to 27.9
28.0 to 31.9
32.0 to 35.9
36.0 to 39.9
40.0 and Over

1,115 Companies = 100%

(B) EMPLOYER PAYMENTS FOR EMPLOYEE SECURITY

As Percentage of Employee Compensation

5.0% 1950
10.3% 1970

Wages and Salaries

$131 Billion = 100%
$475 Billion = 100%

Total Compensation

Total Wage and Salary Supplements

Medicare

Social Security

Pension and Welfare Funds

Unemployment Insurance

Compensation for Injuries, Other

Billions of Dollars

45
40
35
30
25
20
15
10
5
0

1948 1950 1952 1954 1956 1958 1960 1962 1964 1966 1968 1970

(C)

Pension Plan, Life and Health Insurance Payments, etc. 29.9%

Profit-Sharing Payments[a] 7.3%

Paid Lunch Periods[b] 10.5%

Social Security, Unemployment Insurance, etc. 22.7%

Paid Vacations Holiday, Sick Leave, etc. 29.6%

EMPLOYEE BENEFITS BY TYPE, 1969

98.3¢ per Payroll Hour = 100%

[a] And other bonuses. [b] Also includes rest-periods wash-up time, etc.

Source: "Employee Benefits in Private Industry," Road Maps of Industry, No. 1674, The Conference Board, September 15, 1971.

and careful observation can do much to tell the applicant whether he will fit in.

Prospects for company growth

Companies that are expanding or planning to expand usually have greater opportunities for advancement than firms that have reached full growth. But jobs and job openings depend, of course, on particular circumstances, and a fully developed company with many older executives may offer a great opportunity for younger replacements.

Employee benefits

Another factor to consider is employee benefits, including profit-sharing plans, bonus arrangements, retirement and group life insurance plans, paid vacations, and recreational facilities. However, the applicant should remember that although it is perfectly in order for him to inquire about fringe benefits and to have them explained, undue interest in them may be construed by an employer as an indication that the applicant is more concerned with what he can get out of a job than with what he can put into it.

Since 1960, annual employer contributions for Social Security have soared to a point where in 1970 they cost 10.3 percent of total employee compensation as is indicated in Figure A–2B. In addition, employee benefits in 1969 accounted for 98.3¢ per payroll hour as indicated in Figure A–2C. Awareness of information such as this will enable a job seeker to be less naive when it comes to understanding the compensation problem. And he will understand that labor costs to the employer are considerably greater than the amount indicated on the employee's pay check.

Choice of a career and choice of a company in which to pursue that career are two separate considerations. While each decision is important, selection of a career is, all things considered, the more important. Changing companies is much easier than changing careers. Changing companies is a common practice; sometimes it is advisable. Changing careers, on the other hand, usually means that a person must start over to acquire new education and experience.

GETTING THE DESIRED JOB

After one chooses a career and selects a company that offers him a promising future, the next step is to get the job. The ability to write a good letter of application and to prepare a personal résumé of past work experience, education, extracurricular activities, and military service is important.[8] Also helpful are a pleasing personality and good character. The following lists indicate what employers regard as favorable and unfavorable personal characteristics.

FAVORABLE	UNFAVORABLE
Strong motivation toward success	Lackadaisical approach to life
Ability to speak clearly and correctly	Poor voice, grammar, and diction
Humility — the realization that there is much to be learned	A "know-it-all" attitude
Poise	Nervousness, uneasiness, apprehension
Willingness to start at the bottom	Too much concern about initial salary and employee benefits
Better-than-average academic record	Poor academic record
Evidence of constructive extra-curricular activities	No record of active participation in campus life
Experience of having earned at least part of expenses while in school	Complete financial support from others while in school
Definite career plans	No real consideration given to career plans
Good personal appearance	Poor personal appearance

CAREER VERSUS JOB ORIENTATION

The college graduate seeking a position with a company or the student preparing himself for the job market should avoid thinking in terms of "getting a job." One could say that "getting-a-job" thinking is "hourly-

---

[8] It is difficult to prepare skillfully a letter of application and a résumé (also called a personal data sheet). Before undertaking the preparation of either document, an applicant should consult books that discuss the psychology involved, proper business English, and suitable formats. An excellent source is the *College Placement Annual,* which is found in most college and university placement offices.

wage" oriented, implying a fixed trade or specific skill to offer an employer, such as that of a carpenter, waitress, or automobile mechanic. A college graduate should not view himself as having a fixed skill that he will sell to a company for x amount of dollars per week. In reality, a college graduate is hired for his potential as a planner, director, and controller of the resources of a business. Thus, it is accurate to say that a college graduate hired by a company enters into a career tract rather than into a fixed job. A career tract, or avenue, leads to various levels of responsibility and into a variety of work activities that are limited only by the size of the company and the capabilities of the job holder.

Thus, the graduate's first position should be thought of as a negotiation for entry into a position and what it can lead to. This is an important concept: It means that the individual will properly place emphasis on the question "Where will I be going in the company?" rather than on "What will I be doing when I start work?" Employers are impressed by job candidates who are future-oriented in terms of a career tract, because such job applicants will talk refreshingly of long-range contributions to the company and of personal ambitions and goals that extend beyond the first job assignment.

Someone once said, "You'll make a living between 9 and 5; you'll make a success between 7 and midnight." Willingness to work and a reflection of this attitude in seeking jobs or promotions do more than anything else to pave the way to success.

GOING INTO BUSINESS FOR ONESELF

As we have seen, there are advantages in owning and operating one's own business. The records show, however, that the chances for limited success or even failure outnumber the chances of great success. Nevertheless, as a general principle, going into business for oneself is to be encouraged.

It is usually wise for a person who contemplates having his own business to obtain experience as an employee in a business of the type he wants to start. Many of the most successful retail stores, advertising agencies, manufacturing plants, and real estate firms were founded by people who, after completing their formal education, served as employees until they had obtained a sound grasp of the intricacies of business management.

Success in one's own business relates closely to one's psychological makeup. The Department of Commerce developed the following self-analysis test to help individuals determine whether they have the psychological makeup to become successful entrepreneurs.

Can You Succeed in Your Own Business?

Under each question, check the answer that says what you feel or comes closest to it. Be honest with yourself.

Are you a self-starter?
- ☐ I do things on my own. Nobody has to tell me to get going.
- ☐ If someone gets me started, I keep going all right.
- ☐ Easy does it, man. I don't put myself out until I have to.

How do you feel about other people?
- ☐ I like people. I can get along with just about anybody.
- ☐ I have plenty of friends—I don't need anyone else.
- ☐ Most people bug me.

Can you lead others?
- ☐ I can get most people to go along when I start something.
- ☐ I can give the orders if someone tells me what we should do.
- ☐ I let someone else get things moving. Then I go along if I feel like it.

Can you take responsibility?
- ☐ I like to take charge of things and see them through.
- ☐ I'll take over if I have to, but I'd rather let someone else be responsible.
- ☐ There's always some eager beaver around wanting to show how smart he is. I say let him.

How good an organizer are you?
- ☐ I like to have a plan before I start. I'm usually the one to get things lined up when the gang wants to do something.
- ☐ I do all right unless things get too goofed up. Then I cop out.
- ☐ You get all set and then something comes along and blows the whole bag. So I just take things as they come.

How good a worker are you?
- ☐ I can keep going as long as I need to. I don't mind working hard for something I want.
- ☐ I'll work hard for a while, but when I've had enough, that's it, man!
- ☐ I can't see that hard work gets you anywhere.

Can you make decisions?
- ☐ I can make up my mind in a hurry if I have to. It usually turns out O.K., too.
- ☐ I can if I have plenty of time. If I have to make up my mind fast, I think later I should have decided the other way.
- ☐ I don't like to be the one who has to decide things. I'd probably blow it.

Can people trust what you say?
- ☐ You bet they can. I don't say things I don't mean.
- ☐ I try to be on the level most of the time, but sometimes I just say what's easiest.
- ☐ What's the sweat if the other fellow doesn't know the difference?

Can you stick with it?
- ☐   If I make up my mind to do something, I don't let *anything* stop me.
- ☐   I usually finish what I start — if it doesn't get fouled up.
- ☐   If it doesn't go right away, I turn off. Why beat your brains out?

How good is your health?
- ☐   Man, I *never* run down!
- ☐   I have enough energy for most things I want to do.
- ☐   I run out of juice sooner than most of my friends seem to.

Now count the checks you made.

How many checks are there beside the *first* answer to each question?   ____

How many checks are there beside the *second* answer to each question?   ____

How many checks are there beside the *third* answer to each question?   ____

If most of your checks are beside the first answers, you probably have what it takes to run a business. If not, you're likely to have more trouble than you can handle by yourself. Better find a partner who is strong on the points you're weak on. If many checks are beside the third answer, not even a good partner will be able to shore you up.

Source: *Small Marketers Aid*, No. 71, Small Business Administration, Washington, D.C., 1972.

SUGGESTED REFERENCES FOR CAREER INFORMATION

General references

Business and Blacks, Efforts to Increase Minority Employees and Entrepreneurs, by the editors of *The Wall Street Journal.* Princeton, N. J.: Dow Jones Books, 1970 (paperback).

The preface of this collection of twenty-one articles from *The Wall Street Journal* states that the editors have kept an eye on the assimilation by business of blacks, Puerto Ricans, and other minority groups. The result is this collection of articles, which provides valuable insights. Significantly, the editors state: "No matter how great the improvement in a racial group's education, housing, medical care or social acceptance, it cannot hope to be absorbed into the national life until it can move freely in the commercial life — holding its share of jobs, advancing to positions of responsibility and prestige, owning its proportion of companies."

Careers . . . for the Seventies, by the editors of *The National Observer.* Princeton, N. J.: Dow Jones Books, 1969 (paperback).

The articles in this book discuss careers by describing the people in them — their backgrounds, their education, their family life, the money they make, their dreams and aspirations. The individuals who were chosen to write about have one thing in common — dedication to and satisfaction in their jobs. Not all of the careers relate to business. Nonetheless, all of the jobs are interesting to read about because they provide an understanding of what it is that is required for an individual to find fulfillment through work. The articles on an advertising creator, a banker, a foreign service officer, a government official, a stock broker, and a traveling salesman are especially related to business.

Here Comes Tomorrow, Living and Working in the Year 2000, by the editors of *The Wall Street Journal.* Princeton, N. J.: Dow Jones Books, 1967 (paperback).

This series of articles from *The Wall Street Journal* was published in a more permanent and readily accessible form "for the benefit of students and others concerned with the not-so-distant future." The student intent upon planning for a career will do well to consider the implications of these forward-looking pieces. The editor states that to gather the information for the articles, scores of scientists and authorities in various fields were interviewed. The not-so-surprising conclusion is that the future holds a mixture of promise and peril. The editor states: "The hope is that the more we know about the possibilities (of the future), the better our chances for avoiding the peril and realizing the promise."

The Road to the Top, by the editors of *The Wall Street Journal,* edited by Michael Gartner. Princeton, N. J.: Dow Jones Books, 1972 (paperback).

The articles, written by various staffers of the *Wall Street Journal,* point out that in the 1970s there are many roads to the top. The articles trace careers of men who have taken different paths, describe how these people operated along the way, and discuss their policies and philosophies. The stories are fascinating to read. While they do dwell mostly on success, there is one article "about the disenchantment some men feel after arriving in the executive suite — and about how they simply quit to start all over again." The editor concludes, somewhat whimsically, that "the battle, it seems, is sometimes more fun than the victory."

A Survey of Federal Government Publications of Interest to Small Business, Third Edition. Washington, D.C.: Small Business Administration, 1969 (45¢).

This highly useful, 85-page booklet lists, briefly describes, and indicates availability of booklets, pamphlets, and leaflets published by various government agencies that "are most likely to be of assistance to the small business community." The references outline the help available from federal agencies and in nontechnical language describe the laws related to small business that the agencies enforce. The preface states, "Small business operators interested in obtaining a government contract, improving their management, or extending their marketing operations abroad, will find publications listed in this survey which will provide them with useful information." Inside the back cover is a list of the Small Business Administration field offices with their addresses.

SPECIFIC BUSINESS CAREER REFERENCES
The trade associations named below are excellent sources of information about careers.

ACCOUNTANTS
American Institute of Certified Public Accountants
666 Fifth Avenue
New York, N. Y. 10019

Financial Executives Institute
50 W. 44 Street
New York, N. Y. 10036

Institute of Internal Auditors, Inc.
170 Broadway
New York, N. Y. 10038

National Association of Accounting
505 Park Avenue
New York, N. Y. 10022

National Society of Public Accountants
1717 Pennsylvania Avenue, N. W.
Washington, D. C. 20006

ACTUARIES
Casualty Actuarial Society
200 E. 42 Street
New York, N. Y. 10017

Society of Actuaries
208 S. LaSalle Street
Chicago, Ill. 60604

ADVERTISING
American Advertising Federation
1225 Connecticut Avenue, N. W.
Washington, D. C. 20036

American Association of Advertising Agencies
200 Park Avenue
New York, N. Y. 10017

Association of Industrial Advertisers
41 E. 42 Street
New York, N. Y. 10017

BANKING
American Bankers Association
Personnel Administration and Management Development Committee
1120 Connecticut Avenue, N. W.
Washington, D. C. 20036

Federal Deposit Insurance Corporation
Director of Personnel
550 17 Street, N. W.
Washington, D. C. 20429

National Association of Bank Women, Inc.
National Office
111 E. Wacker Drive
Chicago, Ill. 60601

National Consumer Finance Association
1000 16 St., N. W.
Washington, D. C. 20036

CITY MANAGERS
International City Management
1140 Connecticut Avenue, N. W.
Washington, D. C. 20036

HOSPITAL ADMINISTRATION
American College of Hospital Administrators
840 North Lake Shore Drive
Chicago, Ill. 60611

Association of University Programs in Hospital Administration
1 DuPont Circle, N. W.
Washington, D. C. 20036

Bureau of Health Professions Education and Manpower Training
National Institute of Health
Bethesda, Md. 20014

HOTEL MANAGERS AND ASSISTANTS
American Hotel and Motel Association
888 Seventh Avenue
New York, N. Y. 10019

Council on Hotel, Restaurant, and Institutional Education
1522 K Street, N. W.
Washington, D. C. 20005

INDUSTRIAL TRAFFIC MANAGERS
American Society of Traffic and Transportation, Inc.
22 W. Madison St.
Chicago, Ill. 60602

INSURANCE
American Mutual Insurance Alliance
20 N. Wacker Drive
Chicago, Ill. 60606

Institute of Life Insurance
277 Park Avenue
New York, N. Y. 10017

Insurance Information Institute
110 William Street
New York, N. Y. 10038

Life Insurance Agency Management Association
170 Sigourney St.
Hartford, Conn. 06105

Life Underwriter Training Council
1922 F Street, N. W.
Washington, D. C. 20006

National Association of Insurance Agents
96 Fulton Street
New York, N. Y. 10038

National Association of Life Underwriters
1922 F Street, N. W.
Washington, D. C. 20006

National Association of Public Insurance Adjusters
1613 Munsey Building
Baltimore, Md. 21202

MARKETING RESEARCH
American Marketing Association
230 N. Michigan Avenue
Chicago, Illinois 60601

PERSONNEL WORKERS
American Society for Personnel Administration
19 Church Street
Berea, Ohio 44017

Public Personnel Association
1313 E. 60 Street
Chicago, Ill. 60637

PLANNING AND PLACEMENT COUNSELORS
College Placement Council
P. O. Box 2263
Bethlehem, Pa. 18001

PROGRAMMERS
American Federation of Information Processing Societies
210 Summit Avenue
Montvale, N. J. 07645

Association for Computing Machinery
1133 Avenue of the Americas
New York, N. Y. 10036

Data Processing Management Association
505 Busse Highway
Park Ridge, Ill. 60068

PUBLIC RELATIONS
The Information Center
Public Relations Society of America, Inc.
845 Third Avenue
New York, N. Y. 10022

Service Department
Public Relations News
127 E. 80 Street
New York, N. Y. 10021

RECREATION WORKERS
National Industrial Recreation Association
20 N. Wacker Drive
Chicago, Ill. 60606

National Recreation and Park Association
1700 Pennsylvania Avenue, N. W.
Washington, D. C. 20006

SALESMEN
Sales and Marketing Executives International
Student Education Division
630 Third Avenue
New York, N. Y. 10017

STATISTICIANS
American Statistical Association
810 18 Street, N. W.
Washington, D. C. 20006

Interagency Board of U. S. Civil Service Examiners
for Washington D. C.
1900 E Street, N. W.
Washington, D. C. 20414

Society for Industrial and Applied Mathematics
33 S. 17 Street
Philadelphia, Pa. 19103

SYSTEMS ANALYSTS
American Federation of Information Processing Societies
210 Summit Avenue
Montvale, N. J. 07645

Data Processing Management Association
505 Busse Highway
Park Ridge, Ill. 60068

OCCUPATIONAL OUTLOOK REPRINT SERIES

The Federal Government has prepared an extensive variety of bulletins
which objectively describe various occupations. Below are listed those
which relate directly or indirectly to business. The bulletins are available
from the Superintendent of Documents, Washington, D. C. 20402.

BULLETIN NO.	TITLE	PRICE (CENTS)
1650–2	Accountants	10
1650–3	Advertising Workers, Marketing Research Workers, Public Relations Workers	15

BULLETIN NO.	TITLE	PRICE (CENTS)
1650–4	Personnel Workers	10
1650–5	Industrial Traffic Managers, Purchasing Agents	10
1650–31	Counseling and Placement Occupations: School Counselors, Rehabilitation Counselors, Employment Counselors, College Placement Officers	15
1650–35	Lawyers	10
1650–36	Librarians, Library Technicians	15
1650–40	Photographers, Photographic Laboratory Occupations	15
1650–41	Programmers, Systems Analysts, Electronic Computer Operating Personnel	15
1650–42	Psychologists	10
1650–43	Recreation Workers	10
1650–45	Social Workers	10
1650–48	Urban Planners	10
1650–50	Bookkeeping Workers, Office Machine Operators	10
1650–51	Cashiers	10
1650–56	Automobile Salesmen	10
1650–57	Insurance Agents and Brokers	10
1650–58	Retail Trade Salesworkers, Wholesale Trade Salesworkers, Manufacturers' Salesmen	15
1650–59	Real Estate Salesmen and Brokers	10
1650–60	Securities Salesmen	10
1650–96	Foremen	10
1650–124	Banking: Bank Clerks, Tellers, Bank Officers	15
1650–125	Insurance Business	10
1650–127	Government (except Post Office) Federal Civilian Employment, State and Local Governments, Armed Forces	15

APPLICATION EXERCISES

1. A wise procedure, when thinking about getting a job upon graduation, is to investigate the backgrounds of various companies you may be interested in working for. It is prudent to start following the affairs of companies you are interested in while you are in school. Thus by the time you are ready to graduate, you will already be knowledgeable about company affairs. Select a company you are interested in. At the library and from other sources (literature is often available at a school's placement office), gather all the information you can about a company.

Write a report about the company. The report should include a forecast both for the company's future and for the future of the industry that the company is in.

2. Prepare a personal résumé for use in obtaining the kind of employment which interests you. Consider including information about your education, work experience, type position desired, personal interests, references, employment goals, activities and other facts which will help a prospective employer evaluate you.

3. Would you hire yourself? Why or why not? Prepare a plan for making yourself a more desirable job candidate.

QUESTIONS

1. Why, when career selection decisions are so important, are young people often so casual about making them?

2. What is the future outlook for jobs in business? Which areas are most promising?

3. It is true that the "best suited" candidates are selected for jobs. How can one prepare to become the "best suited"?

4. How does it happen that only 60 percent of college graduates end up in jobs in fields for which they are trained?

5. What can a woman do to improve her chances for promotion into jobs with responsibility?

6. What are the benefits of a wise career choice? What are the consequences of failing to choose the right field?

7. Why is "knowing yourself" even more important in selecting a career area than "knowing the company" or "knowing the job area"?

8. Why are part-time and summer jobs considered important by employers even when they may not relate to their company or to the job they have in mind for the applicant?

9. What are the factors to consider in determining the "right company" to work for?

10. What are employee security benefits, and how much do they cost a company? What are employee benefits, and how much do they cost a company?

11. From the company point of view, what are considered favorable job applicant characteristics? Unfavorable characteristics?

glossary of business terms

The specialized vocabulary in business is extensive. Consequently, this glossary has had to be a selective one. Words adequately defined in dictionaries and often defined with a business slant in the chapters of this book are not given here. For example, such terms as "strike," "brand," and "personnel" do not appear. Words from specialized disciplines, such as law and statistics, though related to business and defined in the pertinent text chapters, also are not given here.

There are several excellent references available for students interested in acquiring a broader knowledge of business terms and sources of business information. The following are among these references.

REFERENCES

A Dictionary for Accountants, Fourth Edition, Eric Louis Kohler. Englewood Cliffs, N.J.: Prentice-Hall, 1970.

The Dictionary of Administration and Supervision, Ivan S. Banki. Los Angeles, Calif.: Systems Research, 1971.

A Dictionary of Arbitration and Its Terms, Katherine Seide, American Arbitration Association. Dobbs Ferry, N.Y.: Oceana Publications, 1970.

Dictionary of Business and Scientific Terms, David F. Tver. Houston, Tex.: Gulf Publishing Co., 1968.

Dictionary of Computers, Anthony Chandor. Baltimore, Md.: Penguin Books, 1970.

Dictionary of Data Processing, Claude Camille. London: Harrap, 1970.

Dictionary of Data Processing Terms, Harold A. Rodgers. New York: Funk and Wagnalls, 1970.

Dictionary of Economic and Statistical Terms, James M. Howell. Washington, D.C.: U.S. Government Printing Office, Department of Commerce, 1969.

Dictionary of Economics and Business, Erwin E. Nemmers. Totowa, N.J.: Littlefield, Adams, 1970.

Dictionary of Economic Terms, Alan Gilpin. London: Butterworths, 1970.

Glossary of Economics (including Soviet terminology in English/American, French, German, and Russian), compiled by Floyd Lamar Vaughn. United Kingdom: Elsevier Publishing Co., 1966.

Instant Business Dictionary, Lewis E. Davids. Mundelein, Ill.: Career Institute, no date.

Roberts' Dictionary of Industrial Relations, Revised Edition, Harold S. Roberts. Washington, D.C.: Bureau of National Affairs, 1971.

BUSINESS TERMS

absorption Acquisition of one business by another.

accelerated depreciation When the government tax laws allow certain types of assets to be depreciated faster than the standard legal rate.

accommodation endorser A second signer to a promissory note who also guarantees it.

account executive An executive who acts as a liaison between an advertising agency and a client.

accounting Recording, classifying, summarizing, and interpreting the financial transactions of a business.

accounts payable Money owed by a business to those who have supplied it with goods and services.

accounts receivable Money owed to a company by its customers.

accretion Growth by addition, generally by acquiring other companies.

accrued dividends Dividends due but not paid.

ad valorem Duty based on the value of the article.

advertising Any form of paid, impersonal presentation of goods, services, or ideas for the purpose of inducing people to buy or to act favorably on what is called to their attention.

advertising agency A company that prepares and places advertising and promotes distribution of products and services for others.

advertising, industrial Advertising directed to producers or manufacturers.

advertising, institutional Advertising that attempts to enhance the image of the business that makes or sells a given product or service.

advertising, local See advertising, retail.

advertising medium Any means used to carry an advertising message to the people it is intended to influence.

advertising mix The proportions of various media used to make a total advertising campaign.

advertising, national Advertising used to sell nationally distributed and branded merchandise.

advertising, retail Advertising by retailers in local media (sometimes called local advertising).

advertising, trade Advertising directed toward retailers and distributors, urging them to buy manufacturers' merchandise to resell.

affiliation The relationship between two companies when one partially or wholly owns the other or both are subsidiaries of a third.

amortization Discharge of a debt by payment of scheduled installments.

analog computer A computer that uses physical quantities, usually voltages, to represent values and that performs its operations by simulation.

appraisal An official valuation, as for sale or taxation.

arbitration An attempt to settle labor disputes whereby both parties agree in advance to abide by the decision of a third party (the arbitrator).

assets The various forms of property owned by a business.

auditing A specialized branch of accounting concerned with verifying accounting records and practices.

authority The right to make decisions and the power to direct subordinates.

authorized stock   The maximum number of shares that a company may issue according to its articles of incorporation.

automation   The application of fully automatic procedures in efficient performance and control of a sequence of standardized and repetitive processes.

bad debt   Uncollectable receivable.

balance of payments   The total record of a country's external financial transactions, including commodity and service transactions, capital transactions, and gold movements.

balance of trade   The record of a country's exports and imports (not to be confused with balance of payments).

balance sheet   A statement of the financial condition of a business at a given date showing total assets, total liabilities, plus net worth or deficit.

bank acceptance   A bank draft or trade acceptance drawn on a bank rather than an individual company.

bar graph   A graph in which quantities are represented by vertical or horizontal bars of length.

bear   A securities purchaser who sells short anticipating that the market will drop. *See also* short sale.

Big Board   Term applied to the New York Stock Exchange.

bill of lading   A receipt issued by a transportation company for merchandise.

binary   Referring to the mathematical base of two.

biodegradable   Substance, such as packaging material, that decomposes naturally.

blacklist   An illegal tabulation of the names of union "troublemakers" and organizers, sometimes circulated among employers.

blue chip   Company that is exceptionally strong financially (in reference to stocks).

blue-collar workers   Those who engage in manual activity, such as factory workers, truck drivers, tool-and-die makers, and farm operators.

board of directors   A group of persons elected by the stockholders to direct the affairs of a corporation.

bond   A certificate of indebtedness sold to raise long-term capital.

bond indenture   A detailed statement that describes the rights and privileges of bondholders and the rights and privileges of the issuing company.

bookkeeping   The routine, relatively clerical phase of accounting.

books of original entry   *See* journal.

book value   Actual money value of all corporate assets.

boycott   A concerted effort by workers to stop the purchase of goods or services from an employer.

brand, distributor's   *See* brand, private.

brand, manufacturer's   A brand sponsored by a manufacturer.

brand, national   A brand distributed nationally.

brand, private   A brand sponsored by a wholesaler, a group of wholesalers, or a retailer (also called distributor's brand).

breakeven point   The point at which a company shows neither profit nor loss.

brokers   Businessmen who negotiate transactions for buying or selling merchandise without having title to or physical possession of goods.

budget   A financial forecast or plan that shows expected income and expenditures for a business over a given period of time.

bull   A securities purchaser who buys in anticipation of a rise in price.

business   (1) Commercial activity in general; (2) Any establishment that serves the public by manufacturing or distributing goods or services.

business cycle   The phases of good and poor business through which the economy of a country passes.

business research   The orderly procurement of facts and the interpretation of information about business problems.

buying motives   Customers' reasons for purchasing specific goods or services.

call option   The right to retire bonds at the convenience of the issuing company before the maturity date.

capital   Wealth used to produce more wealth.

capital gain or capital loss   The profit or loss realized from sale of a capital asset.

card punch   A device for punching data onto cards to be fed into a computer.

card reader   A device for reading punched cards into a computer memory.

carrier   A company that engages in the transportation business.

cash flow   A corporation's earnings plus its depreciation.

central processing unit (CPU)   The "core" of a computer which stores, calculates, and controls the data.

charge-account credit   A system under which the consumer buys goods on account and pays at a later date (used in consumer credit).

chattel mortgage   A legal device used in short-term financing when the collateral is movable property.

check off   Collection of union dues by the employer.

C.I.F.   Cost of article plus insurance and freight.

class rate   The freight rate that applies when all commodities being shipped are in the same class.

clearings   Volume of checks processed for collection by banks.

clearinghouse   Association where banks exchange checks drawn on one another.

closed-mortgage bond   A bond that places a limit on the number of bonds that can be sold on the property used as backing.

COBOL (Common Business Oriented Language)   A computer language widely used in coding scientific applications.

collateral   An asset used as security against the repayment of a loan.

collective bargaining   The procedure by which representatives of management and labor meet to discuss and resolve their differences.

commercial paper   Promissory notes, trade acceptances, or other similar negotiable short-term obligations issued by finance companies and other corporations.

commodity   Anything that is movable, of value, and therefore salable.

common carrier   A company that offers transportation to the public and operates on regular schedules between two fixed terminals over a definite route. (Taxis are also considered common carriers.)

common stock   Equity shares in a corporation that partake in dividends after preferred stock is paid.

compiler A computer program that converts procedure- or problem-oriented language into a code suitable for programming.

conglomerate A corporation made up of companies in unrelated lines of business.

consumer goods Goods purchased by ultimate consumers for personal and household consumption—primarily divided into convenience, shopping, and specialty goods.

containerization A transportation service in which goods are packed in a sealed container at the point of origin. The seal is not broken until the container reaches the point of destination.

contingent liability A recorded item that may or may not become a liability.

contract An agreement between two or more persons, enforceable by law.

contract carriers Companies engaged in "for hire" transportation business (with the exception of taxis).

convenience goods Products that consumers purchase frequently, in small quantities, and with a minimum of effort.

convertible bonds A security that can be exchanged for other securities, usually common stock, at a set rate of exchange.

cooperative A socialistic form of business ownership rendering a service to its owner-members on a nonprofit basis.

cooperative advertising Advertising placed by retailers and paid for at least in part by the manufacturers whose products are advertised.

copywriter A person who prepares text material for printed advertising or who writes commercials for radio or television.

corporation "An artifical being, invisible, intangible, and existing only in the contemplation of the law. Being a mere creature of law, it possesses only those properties which the charter of its creation confers upon it, either expressly or as incidental to its existence." Chief Justice John Marshall

cost accounting An extension of general accounting used to determine the detailed costs involved in performing a specific business activity.

coupon bond A bond with interest coupons attached to it that can be cashed in for the amount of interest stated on them on the date specified.

CPA Certified public accountant.

credit The amount of indebtedness that may be incurred. A credit entry in accounting is an entry posted on the right-hand side of the ledger.

credit unions Employee organizations that provide savings and loan services for members.

creditor A person or organization to whom a debt is owed.

current assets Cash and those items that will be converted into cash within a relatively short period of time—normally less than one year.

current liabilities Short-term debts that must be paid in less than one year.

cybernetics Comparative studies of computers and the human nervous system.

debenture bonds A company's direct obligations not secured by any specific property.

debug To search for and correct errors in computer programs or hardware.

deficit The net loss that occurs when a business's expenditures exceed its income.

demand deposit A bank deposit that can be withdrawn at any time, with no advance notice, by the depositor.

demand draft *See* sight draft.

demurrage Railroad charges on cars not unloaded within forty-eight hours.

depreciation The stated loss of value of a fixed asset as it gradually wears out.

digital computer A computer in which each value is expressed by one of a set of finite states (distinct or separate numbers); every operation it performs is basically arithmetical.

discount In banking, a charge similar to interest, deducted from notes in advance.

disk memory A random-access memory in which bits of information are stored magnetically on a set of parallel disks.

diversification A program of acquiring subsidiaries in industries other than that in which the present company is engaged.

dividends The portion of a corporation's earnings paid to its stockholders.

division of labor *See* specialization.

draft An unconditional order in writing made by one party (the drawer) and addressed to a second party (the drawee) ordering him to pay a specified sum to a third party (the payee).

drum memory A random-access memory in which bits of information are stored magnetically on a cylindrical surface.

ecology Study of human populations in terms of their environment.

entrepreneur An individual who initiates a business enterprise, securing the necessary capital and assuming the risks involved.

equity The owner's share in the assets of the business.

factoring Short-term financing through the sale of accounts receivable to a financing agency.

featherbedding A labor union requirement of employing more personnel for a task than management considers necessary.

fidelity bond A purchased pledge of assurity that protects employers against such things as theft, forgery, and embezzlement by employees.

field warehousing A method of facilitating financing whereby a warehouseman assumes control of merchandise on a company's premises so that a warehouse receipt may be issued for use as collateral.

first-mortgage bond A bond secured by a first mortgage on property.

fiscal year Accounting year instead of calendar year.

fixed assets Things of value owned by a business but usually not for sale.

fixed expenses Costs that do not vary with business volume.

F.O.B. Free on board freight cars or other transportation means.

FORTRAN (FORmula TRANslator) A widely used computer language.

founders' and management stock Stock given to promoters and managers who have been instrumental in organizing the corporation.

franchise An exclusive arrangement binding parties, usually a manufacturer or operating company and a private distributor, to do business together in a certain way.

freight forwarders Transportation specialists who provide a comprehensive shipping service to the public.

fringe benefit Compensation for labor in a form other than wages — for example, pensions or insurance.

futures Contracts whereby sellers agree to deliver at some (usually specified) future date.

general mortgage bond A bond secured by all property owned by a company.

goods *See* consumer goods; convenience goods; industrial goods; shopping goods; specialty goods.

good will An intangible asset representing a company's public acceptance. It is often given an estimated monetary value.

gross national product (GNP) The total market value of a nation's goods and services before any deductions or allowances are made (such as depreciation).

group insurance An employee benefit that provides low-cost insurance based on group rates.

hardware The physical components that make up the computer installation, consisting of the central processing unit and other supporting devices, as contrasted with software and systems.

high flyer A stock issue characterized by widely fluctuating prices.

holding company A company engaged principally in owning equities in other companies and in controlling them but not in operating them.

income statement A detailed summary of business operations over a specific period of time (also called profit-and-loss statement or revenue-and-expense statement).

incorporate To form a corporation.

index numbers Numbers used to measure relative price levels.

industrial goods Goods used in the production of consumer goods or other operations.

inflation A rising price level.

injunction A court order directing a person or persons to refrain from a certain act or acts.

input Information in a form in which it can be put into a computer.

insurance A process by which one party (the insurer) agrees, for a sum of money (the premium) that is paid by a second party (the insured), to pay the second party a certain sum if he should suffer a specified loss.

installment credit Consumer credit where the customer pays for the item he has bought in fractional amounts.

intangible assets Assets that do not have tangible form but are of value to the business, such as a brand name and good will.

interest Payment for the use of money that has been borrowed, usually expressed as a percentage per year of the amount owed.

inventory All the goods of a business — in storage, in process, or ready for sale.

investment trust *See* mutual fund.

invoice An itemized list of goods, stating their price, reference number, and quantity, sent by the seller to the buyer.

issued stock That portion of authorized stock that has been sold.

job analysis A detailed study of a job to learn what duties are performed, what equipment and tools are used, what physical and mental attributes are needed by the worker, the nature of working conditions, the responsibilities of the worker, and the relationship of the job to other jobs in the company.

job analyst The person who makes a job analysis.

job description A record of the important facts about a job, used in personnel administration.

job specification A statement, based on the job description, of the physical, mental, educational, and other qualifications a worker must have to perform a particular job.

journal An accounting term that designates books of original entry or original recording of the financial transactions of a business.

keypunch machine In data processing, the machine used for recording information on punch cards by punching holes in them on impulses from a manually operated keyboard similar to that of a typewriter.

labor force All people over sixteen years of age who are willing and able to work and who are either employed or seeking employment.

labor production The amount of work of an acceptable quality produced by an individual or group of individuals in a given period of time.

laissez faire An economic theory that advocates a policy of noninterference by the government in the conduct of business.

L.C.L. Less-than-carload lot, used in transportation.

ledger Books of final entry in accounting.

lessee One who leases property from another.

lessor One who leases property to another.

letters of credit Credit documents whereby a bank substitutes its own credit for its customers'.

liabilities The money a company owes.

limited partnership A form of business ownership based on an agreement between one or more general partners whose liability is unlimited and one or more special, or limited, partners whose liability is limited to the amount of capital they have contributed to the firm.

line In marketing, a vendor's classification of merchandise according to style, price, or brand.

line and staff A form of organization that combines line executives and staff executives. The line executives make all major decisions and issue orders, but they make use of advice from staff specialists.

line of credit A predetermined limit on the amount a bank will lend a customer without additional investigation or demands for collateral.

line organization A form of organization in which orders and authority flow in a straight line from the chief executive to lower management levels.

lockout The closing of a factory or other place of business by an employer in order to make the employees agree to terms.

long-term capital Capital used to finance relatively permanant investments.

long-term liabilities A company's debts of more than one year.

loss leader An item on which little or no profit is made, offered for sale in the hope that it will attract customers who will also buy other merchandise.

management (1) The activity of determining the objectives or goals of the business; planning what to do, when to do it, and how and by whom it will be done; establishing work procedures; and fixing controls to make certain that the work is done correctly; (2) The people who perform this activity.

markdown A reduction from the original selling price of an item.

market value The price commanded by stocks, bonds, or other assets at any given time.

marketing (1) The economist's definition: The phenomenon that gives a product time, place, and possession utility; (2) A modern business definition: All nonmanufacturing business activities and communication efforts concerning the value of a product, from its planning through its ultimate consumption.

marketing research Studies pertaining to the marketing of a product or service.

markup The difference between what the retailer pays for goods and his selling price.

mass production The large-scale production of goods using standardized and interchangeable parts.

maturity date Date on a bond indicating when the money borrowed by means of the bond will be repaid.

mechanical design That phase of product design that gives the product its physical characteristics.

media See advertising medium.

media director The advertising man responsible for selecting and buying magazine, newspaper, and billboard space and radio and television time (also called space buyer).

mediation An attempt to settle labor disputes with the assistance of a disinterested third party (the mediator).

memory In data processing, equipment used to store computer programs and data.

merchandising Those activities that pertain to selecting and buying merchandise for resale—marking, pricing, and promoting its sale.

merger A combination of two businesses, usually through purchase of one by the other.

middle management The second level of management in an organization. Middle management is responsible for developing operational plans and procedures to implement the broader plans and procedures conceived by top management.

money income The amount of money earned by a worker in a given period (in contrast to real income).

mortgage bonds Bonds secured by a mortgage on the assets owned by the issuing corporation. Mortgage bond issues may be either closed or open-end.

motion-and-time study A detailed analysis of the separate parts of a labor operation, used to increase efficiency and to improve work habits.

municipal (tax-exempt) bonds Bonds issued by state and local governments on which interest is exempt from federal income tax and usually from state and city tax.

mutual fund   A company that uses its capital to invest in other companies (also called investment trust).

negotiable obligation   An obligation that can be transferred from one person to another by endorsement.

nonprofit corporation   A variation of the corporate form of ownership allowed in some states to facilitate operation of nonprofit organizations, such as universities, hospitals, and cooperatives.

non par value stock   Stock that does not have a printed value on the stock certificate.

note   A written promise to pay a debt.

open-account credit   A form of short-term credit under which goods are sold with payment expected at a later date.

open-end mortgage   A mortgage that does not specify the dollar value of bonds that may be issued on the property used for backing.

open to buy   The unspent portion of a retail buyer's budget allocated to a particular class of products.

operating management   The lowest rung on the managerial ladder. Operating management includes foremen and supervisors immediately responsible for directing the work of employees.

order bill   A bill of lading that is negotiable.

organization   The process of logically grouping activities, delineating authority and responsibility, and establishing working relationships so that both the company as a whole and its individual employees can perform their work with maximum efficiency and effectiveness.

over-the-counter market   The trading of unlisted securities outside the organized stock exchanges.

overhead   Nonspecific expenses, such as telephone, rent, and taxes, that cannot be related directly to any particular business operation.

par value stock   The fixed dollar value of a stock, printed on the stock certification.

partnership   An association of two or more persons who co-own a business for profit.

pension plan   A plan that provides retirement income for employees.

personnel management   The selection and training of employees and the development of their abilities and attributes so that they will be productive, contented, and loyal to the company.

piggyback service   A railroad service by which loaded trucks are shipped on rail flatcars.

planning   The management function of determining what should be done and how, when, and by whom.

posting   The process of transferring financial information from one record to another.

preemptive right   The right that protects a stockholder from losing his proportionate interest in the corporation.

preferred stock　Capital stock that has priorty in any of several ways over the corporation's common stock.

premium　The price paid an insurance company for assuming a particular risk.

primary boycott　The refusal of workers to patronize their own employer.

prime rate　The interest rate charged by commercial banks to their large customers who enjoy the highest credit rating.

product design　The first step in the manufacturing process, during which the physical aspects and appearance of a product are determined.

product mix　The total variety of products offered by a middleman or a manufacturer.

product planning　Deciding where and how to manufacture a product.

production　The process by which raw materials or industrial goods are converted into useful goods capable of directly or indirectly satisfying wants.

production control　Management of the production program.

profit　The income realized by a business after costs and expenses have been deducted from sales.

profit-and-loss statement　See income statement.

profit-sharing　A plan under which employees share some of the company's profits after the owners have received their return.

programming　In data processing, converting a problem into a series of steps for a computer.

promissory note　An unconditional promise in writing made by one individual or firm (the maker) to another (the bearer); it is signed by the maker, who agrees to pay the bearer a specified sum of money on demand or at a stated future date.

proxy　A legal statement by which a stockholder transfers to someone else the right to cast his votes.

public accountant　An independent organization or individual specializing in selling accounting services to others.

public relations　The process by which a business attempts to obtain good will or a favorable attitude from the public by acting in the best interests of those with whom it comes in contact.

punch card　A 3 x 7 inch card for punching and printing in a keypunch machine for use as a unit of computer input.

quality control　The manufacturing function that makes certain that designated standards are met throughout the manufacturing process.

quota　See sales quota.

real income　Purchasing power measured by the quality of goods and services that money will buy rather than by the amount of money received (money income).

registered bond　A bond that has the name of the owner registered with the issuing company. Interest payments for such bonds are mailed directly to the bond owners when they fall due.

research and development (R&D)　An organized effort by business to discover and develop new products and processes.

reserve　In banking, that portion of deposits withheld from loanable funds.

revenue-and-expense statement　See income statement.

sales budget A budget that shows the total expected sales volume, broken down by commodities sold, territories covered, or other similar factors.

sales promotion Advertising, displays of various kinds, store services, special sales, and other activities used to attract customers to a store, create good will, and sell merchandise.

sales quota That share of total sales that should come from each salesman or sales territory.

secondary boycott The refusal of employees to handle goods of an employer other than the one for whom they work.

selling The process of inducing and assisting a prospective customer to buy a commodity or service or to act favorably on an idea that has commercial significance to the seller.

selling expense budget A budget that shows the amount needed to pay salesmen, deliver merchandise, and perform other selling functions.

serial plan A plan for repayment of a bond issue that stipulates that a certain number of bonds will be retired each year.

shopping goods Products of relatively high unit value, normally purchased only after the customer has compared the price, style, quality, and general suitability of several offerings.

short sale Sale of securities or commodities that are not owned, in anticipation of being able to buy them later at a lower price.

short-term capital Capital usually borrowed for from thirty days to a year (also called working capital).

short-term financing Capital obtained for a short period of time either by borrowing cash or buying on credit.

sight draft A draft that is payable on demand (also called demand draft).

simulation An imitation of a real business situation for learning.

sinking fund A plan that calls for the periodic deposit of money with a trustee to provide for eventual repayment of a bond issue.

small business An independently owned and operated concern that is not dominant in its field of operation.

software The programs and programming aids used by computer personnel to give the computer its instructions (for example, punched cards or magnetic tapes).

sole proprietorship A business owned by a single person who receives all profits and takes all risks.

specialization The process by which each individual within a business is responsible for one or a relatively few particular tasks or business functions (often called division of labor).

specialty goods Products to which the consumer is particularly attracted and for which he is willing to make a special purchasing effort.

specification A statement from the purchasing department that indicates what is wanted on an order. It may be a blueprint, description, etc.

standard costs A standard determined by accountants against which costs can be measured.

standardization The act of establishing and maintaining specific production criteria as to materials, weights, and dimensions.

standard metropolitan statistical area A county or group of adjacent counties that contains at least one city of fifty thousand or more people.

stock certificate   A certificate of ownership, issued by a corporation, that is evidence of shares of stock.

stock-subscription warrant   A right given to present stockholders so that they can buy issues of new stock.

straight bill   A bill of lading that is nonnegotiable.

style design   The phase of product design that adds attractiveness, distinctiveness, and aesthetic value to the product.

surety bond   A bond that protects against the failure of a third party to fulfill a contractual obligation.

surplus   The money left on hand when receipts exceed expenses.

surtax   A tax of level or increasing proportion levied on the tax paid on incomes.

tariff   A tax or customs duty levied on goods imported from other nations.

time-and-motion study   See motion-and-time study.

time draft   A draft payable at a future date.

ton-mile   The movement of one ton of freight over a distance of one mile.

top management   The highest level of management in an organization. Top management determines the broad objectives, policies, and procedures of the company.

trade association   An association of business firms or people in similar areas formed on the basis of mutual interest for the exchange of information.

trade discount   A discount extended to those only within a particular industry.

treasury stock   Stock that was originally issued to the investing public but has since been reacquired by the issuing corporation.

trust indenture   See bond indenture.

trustee   An individual or (most often) a bank or other financial institution appointed by a company issuing bonds to represent the bondholders.

turnover   The number of times during a given period in which the average amount of stock (merchandise) on hand is sold.

underwriter   (1) One who purchases securities for public distribution; (2) An insurance specialist who examines insurance applicants.

union-management contract   A contract that spells out the terms of and procedures for the relationship between an employer and a union.

unissued stock   Authorized stock that has not been sold.

variable costs   Costs that vary with the volume of business.

warehouse receipt   A receipt from a warehouseman for merchandise stored in his warehouse.

warrant   Right to buy securities at a specific price.

white-collar workers   Office workers, managers, and those self-employed persons who do not perform manual tasks.

wholesaler   A business that sells to, or negotiates sales with, customers who buy for resale or for industrial or institutional use.

working capital   See short-term capital.

zone   An area for real estate designation as residential, commercial, or industrial.

Credits for chapter opening and part opening photos:

PART 1	John Murello	2
Chapter 1	Charles Harbutt, Magnum	4-5
Chapter 2	Chuck Abbott, Rapho Guillumette	34-35
Chapter 3	Bob Rieb	60
PART 2	Bruce Davidson, Magnum	86-87
Chapter 4	Lynda Gordon, Carla Hirst Wiltenburg	88-89
Chapter 5	Yvonne Steiner	113
Chapter 6	David Attie	139
PART 3	Harbrace Photo	164-165
Chapter 7	Ormond Gigli, DPI	167
Chapter 8	Lynda Gordon	195
Chapter 9	Syd Greenberg, DPI	231
Chapter 10	Allyn Baum, Rapho Guillumette	253
PART 4	American Telephone and Telegraph Co.	284
Chapter 11	Zenith Radio Corp.	287
Chapter 12	Harbrace Photo, Bethlehem Steel Corp., U.S. Navy Photo, Aluminum Co. of America	318-319
Chapter 13	Merrim from Monkmeyer Press Photo Service	347
PART 5	Matson Navigation Co.	373
Chapter 14	Harbrace Photo	375
Chapter 16	Standard Oil Co., N.J.	432
PART 6	Abernathy Photo Co.	459
Chapter 17	Francis Laping, DPI	461
Chapter 18	Bruce Davidson, Magnum	485
Chapter 19	Photos courtesy of Doyle Dane Bernbach Inc.	513
Chapter 20	Harbrace Photo	545
PART 7	Western Electric Co.	573
Chapter 21	Bunker Ramo Co.	575
Chapter 22	California Computer Products, Inc.	602
Chapter 23	Harbrace Photo	634
Chapter 24	Radio Corporation of America	659
PART 8	NASA Photo	680
Chapter 25	Joseph Gianetti	683
Chapter 26	Harbrace Photo	708
Chapter 27	Paolo Soleri	737

Credits for historical sketches:

1 Wide World Photos 29 2 Photo courtesy of Johnson Publishing Co., Inc. 54 3 Brown Brothers 80 4 Wide World Photos 107 5 Culver Pictures 133 6 Photo courtesy of General Motors Corp. 158 7 Photo courtesy of Getty Oil Co. 188 8 Photo courtesy of Bank of America 225 9 Photo courtesy of Dow Jones & Co., Inc. 248 10 Herald Sun Photo, Durham, North Carolina 279 11 Library of Congress 311 12 ILGWU-Justice Photo 340 13 Photo courtesy of Ford Motor Co. 366 14 Photo courtesy of General Motors Corp. 398 15 The Bettmann Archive 426 16 Wide World Photos 453 17 UPI 478 18 Pach Bros., New York. Photo courtesy of J.C. Penney Co., Inc. 507 19 Culver Pictures 538 20 Photo courtesy of Bank of Hawaii 568 21 Photo courtesy of Burlington Industries, Inc. 597 22 Culver Pictures 629 23 Harris & Ewing. Photo courtesy of Metropolitan Life Insurance Co. 653 24 Karsh, Ottawa. Photo courtesy of RCA 676 25 Culver Pictures 703 26 Wide World Photos 730 27 Photo courtesy of Xerox Corp. 759

Index

A

Academy of Management, 752
Accommodation endorser, 184
Account executive, 523
Accountants:
  government, 581; public, 580;
  tax, 580–581
Accounting:
  auditing in, 595–596; budgeting
  and, 583–585; classifying transactions in, 582; computers and,
  596–597, 619; cost, 582–583; defined, 575; functions of, 576–578;
  interpretation of, 582; procedures,
  581–582; as professional field,
  578–581; ratio analysis in, 590–
  595; recording transactions in,
  581–582; summarizing transactions
  in, 582; transactions, 575–576
Accounting statements:
  balance sheet, 585–588; income
  statement, 588–590
Accounts receivable, 186
Administration. See Management
Advertising:
  account executive, 523; agency,
  523–524; cost of, 525–526; criticisms of, 525–527; defined, 520;
  department, 524; institutional, 521;
  media, 521–522; socioeconomic ef-
  fects of, 521–528; types of, 520–
  521; values of, 525
Affluent Society, The (Galbraith), 13
Agency, law of, 688–689
Agent middlemen, 477–478
Agriculture, Department of, 673–674
Air pollution, 450
Air transportation, 418–419
America, Inc. (Mintz and Cohen), 716
American Federation of Labor (AFL),
  333
American Institute of Certified Public
  Accountants, 12
American Stock Exchange, 237
Antitrust policy, 716
Apply, Lawrence A., 139
Arbitration, 357
Argyris, Chris, 157
Arithmetic mean, 638–639
Assets, 587
Auditing, 595–596
Automation, 376, 378–379

Automobile industry, 747–748
Automobile insurance, 262–266
Averages, 637–638, 640

B

Babbage, Charles, 605
Baily, Nathan A., 72–73
Balance of payments, 563–564
Balance sheet, 585–588
Bank acceptance, 185
Bankruptcy, 690–693
Bankruptcy Act, 690–693
Banks:
  commercial. See Commercial
  banks; Federal Reserve System,
  209–210; investment, 211–212;
  mutual savings, 212–213
Bar graphs, 648
Batch processing, 622
Bell, Alexander Graham, 23
Billing, 619
Bills of exchange, 697–700
Bills of lading, 186–187
Binary code, 609–611
Birth rates, 499, 502
Blacklists, 351
Blair, John, 716
Blake, Robert, 157
Bonds:
  averages, 241; convertible, 175;
  corporation, 170–171, 173; coupon,
  173; debenture, 175; denomina-
  tions of, 173; fidelity, 268; fi-
  nancing through, 169–176; in-
  dentures, 172; interest rate on, 171–
  172, 173; maturity dates, 173–174;
  methods of retiring, 176; mortgage,
  174–175; municipal (tax-exempt),
  176; price fluctuations of, 174;
  quotations, 240–241; surety, 268;
  trustees for, 172–173; types of,
  174–176; with warrants, 175–176
Boredom, on the job, 757–758
Borrowing. See Credit; Loans
Boycotts, 354
Brand name products, 471–472
Brokerage houses, 219–222; information service, 247–248
Brokers, wholesaling, 477
Budgeting, 583–585
Burroughs, William, 606

Business:
  complexity of, 125; computers
  used in, 619–627; creativity and,
  16–18; criticisms of, 63–66; defined, 15; dynamics of, 744–752;
  education. See Business education;
  efficiency, 9–13; ethics of, 71–80;
  failures, 120; government regulation of, 43–45, 709–712, 716–717;
  innovation of, 745–748; location of.
  See Location; objectives of, 5–9,
  147–149; pressures on, 65–66;
  problems facing, 15–16; research.
  See Research; service. See Service
  businesses; small. See Small
  businesses; social change and,
  738–744; social responsibilities of,
  61–80; society and, 752–759;
  standard of living and, 9–13; taxes
  and, 718–726; technology and, 10,
  13–15
Business cycles, 643
Business education:
  advantages of, 18–21; career choice
  and, 23–24; financial news for,
  234–235; importance of, 22–26;
  liberal approach to, 21–22; for sole
  proprietors, 24; supplements to,
  26–28
Business Ethics Advisory Council,
  78–80
Business information sources, 670–
  675; directories of, 672–673;
  government publications, 673–674;
  journals, 671–672; primary, 670–
  671; secondary, 671, 674–675
Business law:
  of agency, 688–689; bankruptcy,
  690–693; contracts, 684–688; copyrights, 701; defined, 684; of employer and employee, 690; need
  for familiarity with, 683–684;
  of negotiable instruments, 697–700;
  patents, 701; personal property
  sales, 693–696; of real estate, 696;
  trademarks, 700–701
Business legislation, 712–716
Business news. See Business information sources; Financial news
Business ownership. See Corporations; Partnerships; Sole proprietorships
Business Periodicals Index, 674

Business report, 649–651
Business research. *See* Research
Business risk. *See* Risk
Buyers, rights of, 695
Buying, 386–387; as marketing function, 467; for resale, 393–395;
Buying motives:
  combinations of, 491–492; defined, 486–487; emotional, 487–490; rational, 490–491

C

Call option, 176
Capital:
  accounting as aid to borrowing, 577; for cooperatives, 106; for corporations, 100–101; defined, 45; effect of leasing on, 188; for small businesses, 116, 120, 121; for sole proprietorships, 92; *See also* Long-term capital; Short-term capital
Capitalism:
  challenge of, 52–54; compared to socialism and communism, 48–52; defined, 46; nature of, 45–48; *See also* Private enterprise
Capitalization ratios, 594
Career selection, 23–24, 28–29, 767–795
Carload rates, 411
Carnegie, Andrew, 80–82, 141, 710
Carriers. *See* Transportation
Central Processing Unit (CPU). 611–613
Certificates of deposit, 205–206
Certified checks, 208
Chain stores, 474
Chandler Act, 690–693
Channel of distribution, 468–471, 473
Charge-account credit, 200–201
Charts, organizational, 143
Chattel mortgages, 187
Checking accounts, 206–207
Checks, 697–700
Circle graphs, 648
Civil Rights Act of 1964, 293
Class rates, 410–411
Clayton Act, 712–713
Climate:
  consumption affected by, 505; international trade and, 553
Closed Enterprise System, The (Nader), 716
Cohen, Jerry S., 716
Collateral, 186–187
Collection procedures, 199–200
Collective-bargaining procedure, 354–355; arbitration, 357; mechanics of, 356; mediation, 356–357; preliminaries, 355; union contract, 357–359

Commerce, Department of, 674
Commercial banks:
  checking accounts and, 206–207; loans made by, 202, 207–208; services of, 208–209
Committee for Economic Development (CED), 740–744
Commodity information, 243
Commodity rates, 411
Common Business Oriented Language (COBOL), 617–618
Common carriers, 408
Common Market. *See* European Economic Community (EEC)
Common stock, 180–181
Communication:
  with computers, 615–617; internal, 153–155; management and, 152–155; types of, 154
Communications satellite corporation (COMSAT), 710
Communism, compared to capitalism, 49, 51–52
Compensation, 296–299
Competition:
  benefits of, 37–39; foreign, 15
Competitive bidding, 396
Computers:
  accounting and, 596–597, 619; advantages of, 608; batch processing for, 622; binary code used for, 609–611; business applications, 619–627; card punch in, 613; card reader in, 613; Central Processing Unit (CPU) of, 611–613; communication with, 615–617; development of, 604–607; external storage unit in, 613; future of, 627–629; hardware, 612–613; input in, 611; languages, 617–618; limitations of, 608–609; operation of, 611–619; output in, 612; plans and operations, 626–627; process-control, 623, 626; programming, 617, 618–619; real-time processing for, 622; software, 613–615; systems analysts for, 618–619; systems concept, 620, 622; time sharing of, 622–623; types of, 609
Conceptualization, 16, 18
Conglomerates, 246
Congress of Industrial Organizations (CIO), 334
Consumer credit, 200–204
Consumer Credit Protection Act, 204
Consumer goods:
  classifications of, 464–466; marketing of, 464–467, 468–471
Consumer Product Safety Commission, 716
Consumer Products Safety Act, 715–716
Consumer-jury interviews, 669

Consumers:
  brand names and, 472; buying motives of, 486–492; laws protecting, 203–204; patronage motives of, 492–493; public relations and, 529
Consumption:
  climate and, 505; education and, 504–505, 506; habit and, 507; income related to, 494–498; news and indices, 245; personal per capita expenditures, 124; population related to, 498–504; of services, 127; sex and, 505
Containerization, 423, 424
Contract carriers, 408
Contracts:
  assignment of, 687; breach of, 687–688; enforceability of, 684–685; essentials of, 685–686; formality of, 686; fulfillment of, 687
Contributory pension plans, 279
Control function, 151
Convertible bonds, 175
Cooperatives, 106–107
Co-partnership. *See* Partnerships
Copeland, Lammot du Pont, 439–440
Copyrights, 701
Corporations:
  accounting and, 577; advantages of, 98, 100; board of directors of, 103–104; bonds issued by, 170–171, 173; charter for, 103; close, 98; control of, 105–106; defined, 97; disadvantages of, 101–102; environmental control departments of, 69–70; financial ratings of, 99; multinational, 566–568; news coverage of, 245–246; nonprofit, 97; officers of, 104; open, 98; organization of, 102–103; profit, 97; taxes on, 101–102, 722–723
Correlation analysis, 639–641
Cost:
  of advertising, 525–526; of marketing, 537–538; standard, 582–583; of storage, 389; of transportation, 406–407
Cost accounting, 582–583
Coupon bonds, 173
Creativity, 16–18
Credit:
  charge-account, 200–201; consumer, 200–204; installment, 201–202; limits, 199; line of, 199; open-account, 182; retail, 200–203; *See also* Credit management
Credit bureaus, 203
Credit Exchange, Inc., 197, 199
Credit investigation, 196–199
Credit management:
  commercial, 196–200; consumers, 200–204; objectives of, 196
Credit policy, 150

Credit terms, 182–183
Credit unions, 202–203
Creditors, 170
Custom duties, 724
Customer. *See* Consumers
Cyclical fluctuations. *See* Business cycles

D

Data processing. *See* Electronic data processing (EDP)
Death rates, 499, 502
Debenture bonds, 175
Decision-making, 752–754
Demand, law of, 531–532
Demand deposits, 206–207
Depreciation, 576
Depression, 231, 360, 710, 758
Dessauer, John H., 759–760
Development. *See* Research
Dickerson, O. D., 123
Diesel, Rudolph, 115
Directories, business information sources, 672–673
Discount rate, 210
Discount retailing, 474
Discounts, 534–535; quantity, 390
Distribution. *See* Channels of distribution
Diversion-in-transit privilege, 412–413
Domestic International Sales Corporations (DISCs), 558
Dow-Jones averages, 241
Drafts, 184–185
Dubinsky, David, 340–341
Dublin, Louis I., 653–654
Dun & Bradstreet, Inc., 197, 198

E

Earl, Harley J., 398–399
Ecology, land use and, 446–452
Economic Concentration (Blair), 716
Economic research, 664
Education, 16; business. *See* Business education; consumption effected by, 504–505, 506; trends in, 755–756, 757
Electronic data processing (EDP), 627, 644–645; defined, 603; history of, 605–607; *See also* Computers
Electronic Numerical Integrator and Calculator (ENIAC), 606
Emergency Employment Act of 1971, 331
Employees:
and changing work ethic, 287–288; compensation plans, 296–299; discharge of, 301; discipline of, 304–

Employees: (continued)
305; discontent of, 288–290; motivation of, 302–311; promotion of, 301; public relations and, 529; selection of, 293–295; services and fringe benefits for, 299–300; sources of, 291; training of, 295–296; transfer of, 301
Employer and employee, law of, 690
Employers' associations, 350–351
Employment policy, 150
Endorsement, 699–700
Endowment insurance, 276
Entrepreneurs, 39, 114–115, 745
Environmental programs, 69–71
Ethics, 71–80
European Economic Community (EEC), 564–566, 754
Excise tax, 724
Executives:
job and leisure profile of, 145; line, 142–143; staff, 142–143; *See also* Management
Experience, 675
Experimental method, in research procedure, 669–670
Export agents, 560
Export-Import Bank (Eximbank), 557–558
Exporting:
advantage of, 551–552; direct channels, 560; foreign factories and assembly plants, 561; indirect channels, 559–560; licensing, 561

F

Factory location. *See* Location
Fair Credit Reporting Act, 203–204
Federal Deposit Insurance Corporation (FDIC), 211
Federal Reserve Act, 209, 710
Federal Reserve System, 209–210
Federal Trade Commission (FTC), 527, 714, 715, 717
Federal Trade Commission Act, 713–714, 715
Fidelity bonds, 268
Field, Marshall, 710
Financial news, 27; interest in, 231–232; nonstatistical, 235, 236, 245–248; reasons for reading, 232–235; statistical, 235, 237–245; types of, 235–236
Financial research, 664
Financial reporting services, 247
Financing:
internal versus external, 167–168; as marketing function, 468; stock sold for, 177–181; through bonds, 169–176; *See also* Long-term capital; Short-term capital

Finley, Clarence C., 597–598
Fire insurance, 260–261
Firing policy, 301
F.O.B. pricing, 535
Ford, Henry, 366–367
Ford, Henry, II, 74
Forecasting, 652–653
Foreign competition, 15
Foreign Credit Insurance Association (FCIA), 558–559
Foreign trade. *See* International trade
FORmula TRANslation (FORTRAN), 617
Forrester, Jay, 755
Franchising, 128–131
Francis, Clarence, 302–303
Free enterprise. *See* Private enterprise
Freight forwarders, 413
Fringe benefits, 299–300
Functional design, 381–382

G

Galbraith, John Kenneth, 13
Gardener, John W., 745
Garnishment, 688
General property tax, 723
Getty, J. Paul, 188–189
Giannini, Amadeo Peter, 225–226
Golden, L. L. L., 738
Gompers, Samuel, 333
Goods:
acquisition of, 386–387; consumer. *See* Consumer goods; industrial, 466–467; purchase of. *See* Purchasing
Goodyear, Charles, 115
Government:
accounting and, 577–578, 581; crime insurance and, 268; economic role, 726–728; environmental agencies of, 69; expenditures, 720, 726–729; factory location and, 438–439; international trade and, 555–559; 563–564; news coverage of, 246–247; procurement, 387, 395–398; regulation of business, 43–45, 709–712, 716–717; regulation of public utilities, 717–718; regulation of transportation, 411–412, 421; taxation and, 718–726
Government publications, 673–674
Graphics, computers and, 620, 621
Graphs, 645–646, 648
Gross national produce (GNP), 42, 128, 720, 726; allocation of, 13; defined, 10; increased standard of living and, 10–11
Gross national welfare (GNW), 11
Growth restriction, 753–754

Guaranteed annual wage (GAW), 363–365

H

Habit, consumption affected by, 507
Hardware, computer, 612–613
Health, Education and Welfare, Department of (HEW), 289
Health insurance, 269–270
Hearst, William Randolph, 703
Hess, Leon, 114
Hiring techniques, 291–295
Hollerith, Herman, 606
Housing and Urban Development, Department of (HUD), 268
Human Organization, The (Likert), 157
Human Side of Enterprise, The (McGregor), 157

I

Importing:
    advantages of, 532; direct, 562–563; indirect, 562; organization for, 561–563
Incentive, 90, 96, 117
Income:
    consumption related to, 494–498; distribution of, 495–497; retailing affected by, 444–445; taxes on, 722
Income statement, 588–590
Indentures, 172
Index numbers, 639
Individual proprietorship. *See* Sole proprietorships
Industrial advertising, 521
Industrial goods, 466–467; marketing, 472–473
Industrial parks, 440–441
Industrial purchasing, 386–387; compared to buying for resale, 393–395; conceptual change in, 392–393; organization for, 387–388; price and, 390–391; quality determination, 388–389; quantity determination, 389–390; service as consideration in, 391–392
Industry. *See* Business; Corporations; Manufacturers
Inflation, 15, 537
Injunctions, 352
Inland marine insurance, 261–262
Innovation, 745–748
Installment credit, 201–202
Institutional advertising, 521
Insurance:
    automobile, 262–266; companies, 213, 258–259; criminal loss, 267–268; defined, 256; fire, 260–261;

Insurance: (continued)
    health, 269–270; law of large numbers and, 256–257; liability, 267; life. *See* Life insurance; limited-payment, 275–276; marine, 261–262; moral hazards and, 258; purchase of, 277–278; qualifications for, 257–258; self-insurance, 255–256; types of, 259–277; workmen's compensation, 269
Interest rates, 171
Internal Revenue Service, 722
International markets, 247
International trade:
    businesses and, 551–552; climate and, 553; currency differences and, 554; Domestic International Sales Corporations and, 558; economic aspects of, 549–551; economic commodities, 564–566; Export-Import Bank and, 557–558; exporting organization, 559–561; facilitating, 555–559; Foreign Credit Insurance Association and, 558–559; foreign trade zones and, 557; government and, 555–559, 563–564; importance of, 547–549; importing organization, 561–563; language and, 553; laws governing, 554; multinational corporations and, 566–568; problems of, 552–554; social customs affecting, 553; specialization and, 549–551
Interpersonal Competence and Organizational Effectiveness (Argyris), 157
Interstate Commerce Commission (ICC), 710
In-transit privilege, 412
Inventory, 576; computers and, 619
Investment:
    guidelines for, 223–225; information on, 233–234
Investment banks, 211–212

J

Job analysis, 664
Johnson, John Harold, 54–55
Journals, 671–672
Junior executive, 145

K

Kawaja, Michael, 123
Kawakami, Keiji, 568–569
Kennedy, John F., 77–78
Kennedy, Joseph P., 29–31
Kilgore, Bernard, 248–249
Kinter, Earl W., 683
Kipling, Rudyard, 649–650

L

Labor:
    attitude towards unions, 338–340; collective bargaining and, 354–359; current objectives of, 363–365; defined, 319–320; earnings of, 326–327; environmental control and, 70; factory location and, 435–436; legislation. *See* Labor legislation; management, relations with, 348–354; organized. *See* Unions; production and productivity, 320–325; in service businesses, 123, 124–125, 126–127; specialization. *See* Specialization; unrest. *See* Strikes; *See also* Unemployment
Labor force, 319–320; women in, 327–328
Labor legislation:
    state "right-to-work" laws, 362–363; Taft-Hartley Act, 361–362; Wagner Act, 360
Labor-Management Relations Act. *See* Taft-Hartley Act
Land, Edwin C., 113
Land use, ecology and, 446–452
Language:
    computers, 617–618; international trade and, 553
Lanham Act, 700
Larry, R. Heath, 362
Lauder, Estée, 478–479
Law. *See* Business law; Business legislation; Labor legislation
Law of large numbers, 256–257, 273
Leacock, Stephen, 750
Leadership, 306–310
Leasing, 188, 750
Legislation. *See* Business legislation; Labor legislation
Leisure time, 756–757
Less-than-carload (l.c.l.) rates, 411
Less-than-truckload (l.t.l.) rates, 413
Liabilities, 587–588
Liability insurance, 267
Life insurance:
    business uses of, 270–271; endowment, 276; level-premium plan, 274–275; mortality table for, 271–274; natural premium plan, 274; policies, 275–277; premiums, 274–275; term, 276
Likert, Rensis, 157
Lilienthal, David, 711
Line graphs, 648
Line organization, 141–142
Line-and-staff organization, 142–143
Liquidity ratios, 594
Livingston, J. A., 246
Loans:
    commercial, 207–208; consumer, 202–203; short-term, 182–187; term, 187

Lobbies, 351, 353
Location:
    community selection, 435–439, 443–445; importance of, 434–435; industrial park concept, 440–441; land use and ecology, 446–452; for manufacturing facilities, 435–443; of retail store, 443–446; sources of aid, 441–443; specific site selection, 440, 445–446
Lockouts, 351–352
Long-term capital:
    obtaining, 169; *See also* Bonds; Stocks

M

Mail questionnaires, 668
Management:
    accounting as aid to, 576–577; business objectives of, 147–149; changing attitudes of, 758–759; collective bargaining and, 354–359; communication and, 152–155; control function of, 151; defined, 139–140; efficiency in, 752; functions of, 147–152; labor, relations with, 348–354; levels of, 144–147; line organization, 141–142; line-and-staff organization, 142–143; middle, 145; need for, 140–141; operating, 146; of personnel, 287–288; planning for career in, 28–29; planning as function of, 149; policy-making of, 149–151; research and, 660–661, 664; sales, 515–520; social change and, 738–739; statistics as aid for, 635–636; theories of, 157–158; top, 144–145; union policies disliked by, 350
Management of credit, 196–204
Managerial Grid, The (Blake and Mouton), 157
Manpower Development and Training Act (MDTA), 330–331
Mansholt, Sicco L., 753–754
Manuals, organizational, 143–144
Manufacturers:
    locations for, 435–443; marketing and, 468–471; prices suggested by, 536
Manufacturers' agents, 478
Marine insurance, 261–262
Marketing:
    brands and, 471–472; channels of distribution, 468–471, 473; concept, 486; costs of, 537–538; defined, 462; efficiency in, 750–752; functions of, 467–468; history of, 462; *See also* Consumption
Marketing management, 139
Marketing research, 664–665

Marketing system, 10
Maslow, Abraham, 157
Mass production, 10
McGregor, Douglas, 157
Meany, George, 362
Measures of location, 637–640
Mechanization, 376
Median, 638–639
Mediation, 356–357
Mercantile agencies, 197–199
Merchants, export, 559–560
Metric system, 385
Middle management, 145
Miller, Charles S., 114–115
Mintz, Morton, 716
Modal average, 638–639
Monopolies, 712, 718
Morale, 303–311
Morality. See Ethics
Mortgage bonds, 174–175
Mortgages, chattel, 187
Motion-and-time study, 664
Motivation, 302–311
Motivation and Personality (Maslow), 157
Motor truck transportation, 414–415
Mount, W. W., 721
Mouton, Jane S., 157
Municipal (tax-exempt) bonds, 176
Mutual companies, 259
Mutual funds, 213–214, 242–243
Mutual savings banks, 212–213

N

Nader, Ralph, 716, 730–731
National Aeronautics and Space Administration (NASA), 710, 726, 727
National Committee on Household Employment, 127
National defense, 15
National Labor Relations Act. See Wagner Act
National Labor Relations Board (NLRB), 360, 361
Negative income tax, 722
Negotiable instruments, law of, 697–700
New Deal, 710
New Patterns of Management (Likert), 157
New York Stock Exchange (NYSE), 214, 237; brokerage houses and, 219–222; buying and selling on, 221; functions of, 216–217; listing of securities on, 217–219; membership of, 216
New York Times indices, 241
No-fault auto insurance, 266
Noise pollution, 450, 453
No-par-value stock, 177

O

Observation method, in research procedures, 669
Occupation. *See* Career selection
Occupational Safety and Health Act (OSHA), 300–301
Ocean marine insurance, 261–262
Odhner, W. H., 606
Office management, 140
Officers, corporate, 104
Ombudsmanship, 729
Open-account credit, 182
Operating management, 146
Order bill, 187
Organization:
    charts and manuals, 143–144; defined, 140; forms of, 141–143; need for, 140–141
Organization of American States (OAS), 565
Over-the-counter markets, 222
Over-the-counter quotations, 241

P

Package design, 382
Packer Produce Mercantile Agency, 199
Panel interviews, 669
Par value stock, 177
Partnerships:
    agreement, 95–96; general, 94–96; limited, 96–97
Pascal, Blaise, 605
Patents, 701
Pemberton, John S., 114
Penney, James Cash, 507–508
Pension funds, 214
Pension plans, 276–279
Perot, H. Ross, 739
Personal interviews, 668
Personal property sales, 693–696
Personnel department:
    compensation plans and, 296–299; functions of, 290–301; hiring by, 293–295; services and fringe benefits, 299–300; training programs and, 295–296
Personnel management, 139, 290
Personnel research, 664
Pictorial diagrams, 649
Piggyback service, 415
Pipeline transportation, 417–418
Planned obsolescence, 748
Planning, 752–753; *See also* Organization
Plough, Abe, 114
Pollution, 450, 452, 453, 729
Pool-car service, 413
Population:
    age composition of, 499; birth and

Population: (continued)
death rates, 499–502; consumption related to, 498–504; growth, 16; mobility of, 754; retailing affected by, 433–444; shifts in, 502–504
Power, factory location and, 436, 438
Preferred stock, 178–180
President's Commission on National Goals, 729
President's Commission of Personnel Interchange, 711–712
President's Economic Report on GNP, 653
Price-lining policy, 536
Pricing, 531; competition and, 38, 532–534; demand elasticity and, 532; geographic factors in, 535; inflation and, 537; law of demand and, 531–532; as marketing function, 468; markup, 536; under monopolistic conditions, 533; negotiated, 534; policies, 150, 533–535; practical considerations, 533–537; price-lining policy, 536; profit maximization and, 532; psychological, 534; under pure competition, 532–533; theoretical considerations, 531–533
Prime contractors, 398
Private carriers, 408
Private enterprise:
characteristics of, 36–42; competition in, 37–39; government and, 43–45; growth and, 42–43; property ownership and, 36–37; See also Capitalism
Process-control computers, 623, 626
Product design, 381–382
Product policy, 149–150
Product research, 663–664
Production:
automation and, 376, 378–379; characteristics of, 376–381; competition and, 38; control, 384–385; defined, 375; efficiency in, 748–750; importance of, 375–376; labor, 320–325; labor as cost of, 324–325; mechanization and, 376; news and indices, 243–245; planning, 383–384; specialization and, 380–381; standardization and, 380; transportation as cost of, 406–407
Production management, 139–140
Productivity, 748–751, 752; of labor, 320–325; trends in, 323–324, 377
Profit, as objective of business, 5–9
Profit maximization, 533
Profit sharing, 298–299
Profit system. See Private enterprise
Programming, computer, 617, 618–619
Promissory notes, 183–184, 697–700
Promotion, sales, 518–519

Property:
ownership, 36–37; personal, 693–696; taxes on, 723–724
Proxy, 106
Public Affairs Information Service, 674
Public relations:
community and, 529; consumers and, 529; dealers and, 529; defined, 528; employees and, 529; purposes of, 528; situations, 529, 530; stockholders and, 529; suppliers and, 529; trade associations and, 529, 531
Public utilities, government regulation of, 717–718
Punched cards, 615
Punched paper tape, 615
Purchasing:
by government, 395–398; industrial. See Industrial purchasing; See also Buying; Buying motives

Q

Qualitative analysis. See Statistics
Quitclaim deeds, 696
Quotas, for salesman, 517–518

R

Racial discrimination, 15
Railroads:
advantages of, 409–410; auxiliaries to, 413; disadvantages of, 410; importance of, 408–409; rates, 410–412; services, 412–413
Randall, Clarence B., 21–22
Random access devices, 616
Ratio analysis, 590–595
REA Express Agency, 413
Readers' Guide to Periodical Literature, 675
Real estate, law of, 696
Real-time processing, 622
Report-writing, 649–650
Resale buying, 393–395
Research:
applied, 663; background, 663; basic, 663; defined, 660–661; economic, 664; experimentation and, 669–670; financial, 664; growth of, 661–662; marketing, 664–665; method used in, 665–666; observation and, 669; personnel, 664; problem definition and recognition, 667; procedure, 667–670; product, 663–664; surveys and, 668–669; technological, 663–664; types of, 663–665
Résumé, 293

Retailing:
advertising for, 520–521; chain store operation, 474; dynamic developments and trends in, 474–475; location of store, 443–446; marketing and, 468–471, 473–475
Returned-goods policy, 150
Revenue sharing, 724–726
Rickenbacker, Edward Vernon, 426–427
Risk, 41–42; examples of, 253–254; methods of meeting, 254–258
Risk rating, 171
Risk-bearing, as marketing function, 468
Robinson, F. M., 114
Robinson-Patman Act, 714–715
Rockefeller, John D., 23, 311–312, 710
Rockwell, W. F., 393
Rollins, O. J., 114
Roosevelt, Franklin Delano, 710
Ruckelshaus, William D., 453–454
Rukeyser, W. S., 739
Russell, Bertrand, 757, 758

S

Salary, 299–300; See also Income
Sales management, 515–520
Sales promotion, 518–519
Sales quota, 517–518
Sales tax, 723
Salesmen:
compensating, 518; equipping of, 516; motivation, 518; quotas and, 517–518; recruitment of, 516; selection of, 516; supervision of, 518; territories of, 516–517; training of, 516
Sampling, 641–642
Sanders, Colonel Harland, 133
Sarnoff, David, 676
Savings accounts, 208
Savings and loan associations, 213
Science, 42–43
Scientific method, 665–666
Seasonal sales variations, 642–643
Secular trends, 643–644
Securities:
listing of, 217–219; See also Bonds; Stocks
Securities Exchange Act, 222–223
Security. See Collateral
Security exchanges, 214–222
Self-evaluation, 29
Self-insurance, 255–256
Self-service, 750–751
Sellers, rights of, 694–695
Selling:
defined, 514; as marketing function, 467; steps in process of, 514–515; See also Retailing; Salesmen

Selling agents, 477–478
Service:
acquisition of, 386–387; competition and, 38; as objective of business, 5–9
Service businesses:
characteristics of, 124–125; development of, 125; future in economy, 126–128; types of, 122–124
Sex, consumption affected by, 505
Shareholders. See Stockholders
Sherman Antitrust Act, 710, 712, 713, 714
Shopping centers, 750
Shopping goods, 465
Short-term capital:
types of, 182–187; uses for, 181–182
Simon, Norton, 113
Sinking-fund, 176
Sloan, Alfred Pritchard, Jr., 158
Small Business Administration (SBA), 131–132
Small Business Administration (SBA) Act, 116, 131–132
Small businesses, 115–116; aid for, 131–132; capital for, 116, 120, 121; characteristics of, 116–117; conditions conducive to, 117–118; creativity and, 117; failure of, 121–122; franchises as, 128–131; operating advantages of, 118–119; operating disadvantages of, 119–121; opportunity and, 117
Smith, Dan, 721
Socialism, compared to capitalism, 48–51
Society:
change and, 738–744, 752–758; management's attitude towards, 758–759; relation to business, 61–63, 66–68
Society for the Advancement of Management, 752
Software, computer, 613–615
Sole proprietorships, 39, 90–93; business education for, 24; capital for, 92
Spaulding, Asa T., 279–280
Specialization, 16, 380–381; international trade and, 549–551; transportation and, 407
Specialty goods, 465
Spot trading, 243
Standard of living:
business efficiency and, 9–13; service businesses and, 125
Standardization, 380, 468
State and Local Fiscal Assistance Act, 724
Statistical maps, 649
Statistical news, 235, 237–245
Statistics, 635–636; application of, 644–645; descriptive, 645; devices

Statistics: (continued)
as management aids, 635–636; presentation of, 645–649; and techniques, 637–644; truth and, 652
Stock:
authorized, 177; averages, 241; common, 180–181; cumulative and noncumulative preferred, 179; financing through, 177–181; market value, 177–178; participating and nonparticipating preferred, 179–180; pre-emptive rights, 178; preferred, 178–180; quotations, 237–241; sale of, 178
Stock companies, 258–259
Stock exchanges. See American Stock Exchange; New York Stock Exchange
Stockbrokers. See Brokerage houses
Stockholders, 98, 144; powers of, 105–106; pre-emptive rights of, 178
Storage, as marketing function, 467–468
Storage facilities, 389
Straight bill, 186–187
Strikebreakers, 352
Strikes:
cost of, 347–348; issues and duration of, 348, 349; prevention of. See Collective bargaining; types of, 353–354
Style design, 382
Subcontractors, 398
Surety bonds, 268
Surveys, 668–669
Swift, Gustavus F., 23
Systems analysis, 644–645
Systems concept, 745
Szent-Györgyi, Albert, 17

T

Tables, use of, 645, 646
Taft-Hartley Act, 361–362
Tariffs, defined, 564
Tax accountants, 580–581
Tax exempt bonds, 176
Taxes, 718–726; corporation income, 101–102, 722–723; customs duties, 724; excise, 724; negative income tax, 722; personal income, 722; property, 723–724; purpose of, 719–720; revenue sharing, 724–726; sales, 723; value added tax, 721–722
Team effort, 16
Technological research, 663–664
Technology, 10, 16
Telephone interviews, 669
Tennessee Valley Authority, 710
Term insurance, 276
Term loan, 187

Through rate, 411
Time sharing, 622–623
Time-series analysis, 642–644
Title, transfer of, 693–694
Top management, 144–145
Townsend, Robert Chase, 107–108
Trade. See International trade
Trade acceptance, 185
Trade associations, 529, 531
Trademarks, 700–701
Traffic management, 140, 420–421
Transportation:
air, 418–419; carrier classification, 408; carrier selection, 419; containerization, 423, 424; as cost of production, 406–407; economic significance, 405–407; factory location and, 436; future of, 425–426; government regulation of, 411–412, 421; intermodal, 421–423; as marketing function, 467; for natural resources, 407; pipeline, 417–418; rail. See Railroads; specialization and, 407; traffic management and, 140, 420–421; truck, 414–415; water, 415–417
Transportation (DOT), Department of, 423, 425
Transportation Act, 411
Truck transportation, 414–415
Trust fund pension plans, 278
Trust indentures, 172
Trustee, 172–173
Typewriter, computer, 616

U

Ugliness pollution, 450, 452
Ulrick's International Periodical Directory, 674
Unemployment, 15, 328–329; causes of, 329–330; hard-core, 330; measurement of, 331–332; remedies for, 330–331
Union contracts, 357–359
Unions:
American Federation of Labor (AFL), 333; collective bargaining and, 354–359; Congress of Industrial Organizations (CIO), 334; current trends, 337; general structural arrangements of, 335; history of, 333; independent, 334; legislation concerning. See Labor legislation; objectives of, 337–338, 363–365; policies disliked by management, 350; reasons for, 332; strikes by. See Strikes; transportation integration and, 423; white-collar, 335–337; workers' attitudes toward, 338–340
UNIVAC I, 606

Urban decay, 15
Urbanization, 754–755
Utilities. *See* Public utilities

V

Vail, Theodore N., 23
Value added tax (VAT), 721–722
Vanderbilt, Cornelius, 710
Vending machines, 475, 750–752
Video terminal, computer, 616–617

W

Wage garnishment, 688
Wages. *See* Income

Wagner Act, 360
Warehouse receipts, 187
Warehousing, computers and, 619
Warranties, 695–696
Warrants, 175–176
Warranty deeds, 696
Water pollution, 450
Water transportation, 415–417
Watson, Thomas J., 629–630
Welfare, 15, 729
Wheeler-Lea Act, 527, 715
White-collar unions, 335–337
Wholesaling, 468–471, 475–478
Wilde, Oscar, 73
Williams, J. D., 745
Wilson, Kemmons, 114

Women, 15; business owners, 121; in labor force, 327–328; statistical profile of, 292
Woolworth, Frank Winfield, 538–539
Work ethic, changing nature of, 287–288
Work experience, 27–28
Work force. *See* Labor
Workmen's compensation insurance, 269
World Economic Communities, 564–566
World Health Organization (WHO), 450
World trade. *See* International trade